Philosophy of Film and Motion Pictures

BLACKWELL PHILOSOPHY ANTHOLOGIES

Each volume in this outstanding series provides an authoritative and comprehensive collection of the essential primary readings from philosophy's main fields of study. Designed to complement the *Blackwell Companions to Philosophy* series, each volume represents an unparalleled resource in its own right, and will provide the ideal platform for course use.

Philosophy of Film and Motion Pictures
An Anthology

Edited by

Noël Carroll and Jinhee Choi

Blackwell
Publishing

© 2006 by Blackwell Publishing Ltd

BLACKWELL PUBLISHING
350 Main Street, Malden, MA 02148–5020, USA
9600 Garsington Road, Oxford OX4 2DQ , UK
550 Swanston Street, Carlton, Victoria 3053, Australia

The right of Noël Carroll and Jinhee Choi to be identified as the Authors of the Editorial Material in this Work has been asserted in accordance with the UK Copyright, Designs, and Patents Act 1988.

First published 2006 by Blackwell Publishing Ltd

2   2006

Library of Congress Cataloging-in-Publication Data

Philosophy of film and motion pictures: an anthology / edited by Noël Carroll and Jinhee Choi.
    p. cm. — (Blackwell philosophy anthologies)
  Includes bibliographical references and index.
  ISBN-13: 978-1-4051-2026-5 (hard cover: alk. paper)
  ISBN-10: 1-4051-2026-6 (hard cover: alk. paper)
  ISBN-13: 978-1-4051-2027-2 (pbk.: alk. paper)
  ISBN-10: 1-4051-2027-4 (pbk.: alk. paper)
  1. Motion pictures. I. Carroll, Noël (Noël E.) II. Choi, Jinhee. III. Series.

PN1994.P575 2006
791.43'01 — dc22
                                        2004030884

A catalogue record for this title is available from the British Library.

Set in 9 on 11pt Ehrhardt
by SPI Publisher Services, Pondicherry, India

The publisher's policy is to use permanent paper from mills that operate a sustainable forestry policy, and which has been manufactured from pulp processed using acid-free and elementary chlorine-free practices. Furthermore, the publisher ensures that the text paper and cover board used have met acceptable environmental accreditation standards.

For further information on
Blackwell Publishing, visit our website:
www.blackwellpublishing.com

Contents

Contents

Acknowledgments

The editor and publisher gratefully acknowledge the permission granted to reproduce the copyright material in this book:

1   Roger Scruton, "Photography and Representation," *The Aesthetic Understanding* (London: Methuen, 1983, reprinted 1998 by St Augustine's Press, South Ben, IN): 119–48 (from reprint). © 1983 by Roger Scruton. Reprinted with permission of Curtis Brown Ltd, London on behalf of Roger Scruton.

2   Dominic McIver Lopes, "The Aesthetics of Photographic Transparency," *Mind*, 112, July 2003: 1–16. Reprinted by permission of Oxford University Press Journals.

3   Terrence Rafferty, "Everybody Gets a Cut," *The New York Times Magazine*, May 4, 2003: 58, 60–1.

4   Stanley Cavell, excerpts from *The World Viewed: Reflections on the Ontology of Film* (New York: Viking Press, 1971): 16–41. Reprinted by permission of Stanley Cavell.

5   Susanne K. Langer, "A Note on the Film," *Feeling and Form: A Theory of Art Developed from Philosophy in a New Key* (New York: Charles Scribner's Sons, 1953), 411–15.

6   F. E. Sparshott, "Vision and Dream in the Cinema," *Philosophical Exchange*, Summer 1971: 111–22. Reprinted by permission of F. E. Sparshott.

7   Gregory Currie, "The Long Goodbye: The Imaginary Language of Film," *British Journal of Aesthetics* 33(3), July 1993: 207–19.

Reprinted by permission of Oxford University Press Journals.

8   Arthur C. Danto, "Moving Pictures," *Quarterly Review of Film Studies* 4(1), Winter 1979: 1–21.

9   Noël Carroll, "Defining the Moving Image," *Theorizing The Moving Image* (New York: Cambridge University Press, 1996): 49–74. Reprinted by permission of Cambridge University Press.

10 Gregory Currie, "Visible Traces: Documentary and the Contents of Photographs," *The Journal of Aesthetics and Art Criticism* 57(3), Summer 1999: 285–97. Reprinted by permission of Blackwell Publishing.

11 Noël Carroll, "Fiction, Non-Fiction, and the Film of Presumptive Assertion: A Conceptual Analysis," *Film Theory and Philosophy*, eds. Richard Allen and Murray Smith (New York: Oxford University Press, 1997): 173–202. Reprinted by permission of Oxford University Press.

12 George M. Wilson, "*Le Grand Imagier* Steps Out: The Primitive Basis of Film Narration," *Philosophical Topics* 25(1), 1997: 295–318. Reprinted by permission of George M. Wilson.

13 Gregory Currie, "Unreliability Refigured: Narrative in Literature and Film," *The Journal of Aesthetics and Art Criticism* 53(1), 1995: 19–29. Reprinted by permission of Blackwell Publishing.

14 Noël Carroll, "Film, Emotion, and Genre," *Passionate Views*, eds. Carl Plantinga and

Greg M. Smith (Baltimore: Johns Hopkins University Press, 1999): 21–47, 260–2 (notes). Reprinted by permission of The Johns Hopkins University Press.

15 Kendall Walton, "Fearing Fictions," *Journal of Philosophy* 75(1), January 1978: 5–27. Reprinted by permission of the Journal of Philosophy, Columbia University.

16 Alex Neill, "Empathy and (Film) Fiction," *Post Theory*, eds. Noël Carroll and David Bordwell (Madison: University of Wisconsin Press, 1996): 175–94.

17 Berys Gaut, "Identification and Emotion in Narrative Film," *Passionate Views*, eds. Carl Plantinga and Greg M. Smith (Baltimore: Johns Hopkins University Press, 1999): 200–16. Reprinted by permission of The Johns Hopkins University Press.

18 Deborah Knight, "In Fictional Shoes: Mental Simulation and Fiction," first published in this volume. © 2006 by Blackwell Publishing Ltd.

19 George M. Wilson, "Morals for Method," *Philosophy and Film*, eds. Cynthia A. Freeland, and Thomas E. Wartenberg (New York: Routledge, 1995): 49–67. This is a revised version of Chapter 10 in Wilson's *Narration in Light: Studies in Cinematic Point of View* (Baltimore: Johns Hopkins University Press, 1986): 191–207. Reprinted by permission of The Johns Hopkins University Press.

20 Paisley Livingston, "Cinematic Authorship," *Film Theory and Philosophy*, eds. Richard Allen and Murray Smith (New York: Oxford University Press, 1997): 132–48. Reprinted by permission of Oxford University Press.

21 Jinhee Choi, "National Cinema, the Very Idea," first published in this volume. © 2006 by Blackwell Publishing Ltd.

22 Joseph H. Kupfer, "Film Criticism and Virtue Theory," *Visions of Virtue in Popular Film* (Boulder: Westview, 1999): 13–34.

23 Mary Devereaux, "Beauty and Evil: The Case of Leni Riefenstahl's *Triumph of the Will*," *Aesthetics and Ethics: Essays at the Intersection*, ed. Jerrold Levinson (Cambridge: Cambridge University Press, 1998): 227–56.

24 Melinda Vadas, "A First Look at the Pornography/Civil Rights Ordinance: Could Pornography Be the Subordination of Women?" *The Journal of Philosophy* 84(9), 1987: 487–511.

25 Bruce Russell, "The Philosophical Limits of Film," *Film and Philosophy* (Special Edition, 2000): 163–7. Reprinted by permission of the Society for the Philosophic Study of the Contemporary Visual Arts.

26 Karen Hanson, "Minerva in the Movies: Relations Between Philosophy and Film," *Persistence of Vision* 5, 1987: 5–11. Reprinted by permission of Karen Hanson.

27 Lester H. Hunt, "Motion Pictures as a Philosophical Resource," first published in this volume. © 2006 by Blackwell Publishing Ltd.

General Introduction

In the eighteenth century, only the wealthiest and most privileged persons could have had a theater in their own homes. But today in virtue of television, video cassette recorders, and DVD players, most citizens of the industrialized world have something very like a theater – and often two or more – in their households. These "theaters," of course, do not feature live dramas, but rather motion pictures – pictures stored on some sort of template like film and shown in a way that imparts the impression of movement. And from that impression, moving images are born, vistas are opened, and stories are told.

Though many of us today might yearn for the delicate and quaintly imaginative stagecraft of an antique era, surely Vattel – the creator of spectacles for the Bourbon court – would envy the magic-making capacities of the contemporary motion picture artist. The display of fireworks and explosions, and the armies of clones and whatever on view nightly in our living rooms and dens would have staggered Vattel's comprehension. Perhaps his master would have given his kingdom for one of our TVs. The development of the motion picture has been an awesome step in the democratization of culture, providing the many with access to spectacles of the type that heretofore were the normal fare of the exceptionally few or of the many only on special occasions.

Motion pictures have become a fixture of everyday life in the modern world. They have been integrated into a wide variety of cultural processes involving education and the communication of information, and they have spawned their own practices – of art-making, entertainment, and documentary recording – with their own tradi-

tions. It would be surprising if a social enterprise as substantial as the motion picture did not attract philosophical attention. Thus predictably, the philosophical literature pertaining to it, especially in recent years, has grown exponentially. This anthology, in part, is an acknowledgment of that trend.

But what does philosophical attention to the motion picture comprise? In contrast to empirical research, philosophy is the discipline that is primarily preoccupied with the "logic" or conceptual frameworks of our practices.[1] So a philosophical perspective on the motion picture involves attending to the conceptual frameworks of our motion picture practices. This includes: (1) the analysis of the concepts and categories that organize our practices (for example, asking what is film or what is a documentary?); (2) the clarification of the relations between those organizing concepts and categories (for example, can what falls under the category of *film* also fall under the category of *art*, or is there some reason that precludes the former from being an instance of the latter?); (3) the resolution of the conceptual paradoxes, tensions, and contradictions that the relevant practices appear to provoke (for example, how is it possible for us to fear fiction films?); (4) the elucidation of the forms of reasoning – the modes of connecting concepts – appropriate to our practices (for example, what techniques of interpretation are suitable or valid with respect to classic Hollywood movies?); and (5) the discovery of the metaphysical presuppositions and entailments of the conceptual frameworks of the relevant practices (for example, what kind of narrators, ontologically speaking, do fiction films presuppose?)

1

Pursuing these lines of inquiry composes the largest part of the philosophy of the moving picture. However, as the articles in this anthology frequently attest, there is also a part of the enterprise that, like the philosophy of mind, segues with cognitive science and evolutionary psychology. For the philosophy of motion pictures involves thinking about things like attention, emotion, recognition, inference, and so forth and, therefore, needs to be at least informed by scientific psychology, a feature of the philosophy of the motion pictures evinced amply in many of the essays in this volume.

Given the ever-growing importance of motion pictures to our culture, such questions about the logic and/or conceptual frameworks of our motion picture practices have come increasingly to the fore. The purpose of this anthology is to air a selection of some of the most pertinent recent writing on these philosophical topics.

With the exception of S. K. Langer's "A Note on the Film," the writing in this volume has all been published since 1970 by philosophers who have grown up in the epoch of the motion picture. That is, they were born after the invention and popularization of the motion picture, and, as a result, movies have been an unexceptional feature of their cultural landscape. For the philosophers born before World War II, a visit to the movie theater was an ordinary pleasure, while for those born after World War II, in addition to a trip to the cinema, the repertoire of film history has also been continuously available on TV and then video cassettes and DVDs. Because of their ever-expanding familiarity with motion pictures, more philosophers are asking more questions about moving pictures than ever before, and they are posing their inquiries with heightened sophistication, precision, and refinement. Thus, the last three and a half decades have benefited from an unparalleled philosophical scrutiny of a diversity showcased in this collection.

But though the philosophy of the motion picture is flourishing, particularly at present, it would be an error to think that it is only a concern of recent vintage. For the philosophy of the motion picture arrived on the scene very soon after those inaugural moving pictures – namely, films – became ensconced as a significant cultural force. Early on, film was enmeshed in an intense philosophical debate. Because of its photographic provenance, many argued that film could not be an artform. For, it was assumed, photography was

nothing but the mechanical reproduction of whatever stood before the camera lens. Just as a mirror reflection of a table full of decoratively arranged viands is not an artwork, no matter how much it might resemble some still life, so it was argued, neither is a photograph – whether still or moving – an artwork. It is merely a slavish recording with no art to it. As mechanical processes, photography and cinematography allegedly afford no space for expression, imaginative elaboration, and/or creativity and, therefore, are artless.

Though early film theorists, like Rudolf Arnheim, vigorously disputed the case against film art, the prejudice has lingered into the present and been advanced in a philosophically adept fashion by Roger Scruton. Since the issue of whether film can be art was historically the first philosophical challenge leveled at the motion picture, we begin this anthology in honor of it – leading off the first section with Scruton's brief against the possibility of film art and then following that with Dominic McIver Lopes's case in favor of an art of motion pictures.

The debate over whether films or motion pictures can be art hinges on certain presuppositions about what kind of thing a film is. Those who deny it art status presume that it is essentially photographic, and, furthermore, presuppose that photography, by definition, is mechanical in a way that is categorically inhospitable to art making. But is this true? What is film? To what category does it belong? In Part II, a gamut of answers to this question is interrogated by various philosophers. Suggestions canvassed include not only that film is essentially a photographic instrument, but also that it is a language, that it is a form of dream, and finally that it is a moving picture or image.

As indicated, the first moving pictures were the products of photographic film. Many of these images were documentary in nature, such as the famous *actualités* of the Lumière Brothers. Moreover, inasmuch as the film camera was designed to be – first and foremost – a recording device, there has long been an association between film and documentation to the extent that one of the most enduring genres of the moving image has been the documentary or nonfiction film. Part III of this anthology takes up the question of the nature of such filmmaking, with two philosophers setting out contrasting conceptions of the nonfiction film.

Though the nonfiction film represents one of the oldest traditions of motion picture making, it is probably not the sort of endeavor that first comes to mind when people think of cinema. In all likelihood, at the mention of movies the majority of us start thinking about narrative fictions, surely the most popular type of motion pictures to date. So in Part IV of this volume, we turn to the issue of the narration of fiction films and the special problems and complexities that contemporary philosophers imagine it to involve.

Motion pictures are intimately bound up with the emotions. When it comes to fiction films, one might be tempted to call them E-motion pictures. Films not only move; they move us (emotionally). Many film genres take their very labels from the emotions they are typically designed to engender, such as horror films, suspense films and tearjerkers. Part V of this text is focused on the relation of motion pictures to the emotions. It opens with a discussion of the way in which movies engage the garden-variety emotions and then goes on to grapple with certain apparent anomalies pertaining to our emotional responses to fiction – namely, how is it possible to be moved by cinematic fictions, since we know the events they depict do not exist? How can we, for example, recoil in fear at the onset of the Green Slime when we know that there is no such thing?

Much of our affective engagement with filmed fictions centers upon our relations with characters. But what is the nature of that emotional relation? In the fifth section, several philosophers explore different conceptions of it, including identification, empathy, and simulation.

We not only respond to films emotionally in the moment. We also talk about them afterwards with each other and analyze and assess them. Film criticism – pursued by professional critics and ordinary viewers alike – is a part of the practice of cinema along with filmmaking and film viewing. Just as philosophers reflect upon the conceptual frameworks that organize the latter activities, they also examine the concepts and modes of thinking – the categories and procedures – that facilitate the practice of film criticism. Sometimes called metacriticism, the philosophy of film criticism epistemically weighs the appropriateness of alternative interpretive protocols and attempts to reconstruct rationally the categories that inform the conduct of criticism. In Part VI, George M. Wilson rejects a dominant style of contemporary academic film interpretation and offers a series of more nuanced critical concepts in its stead. Then in subsequent essays, different philosophers attempt to distill the saving remnant of and to defend for critical discourse respectively the organizing concept of cinematic authorship and the very idea of a national cinema.

If only because of the connection between motion pictures and the emotions, movies inevitably come in contact with morality. How do films stand in relation to right and wrong? Are some motion pictures morally salutary, and, if so, how? Can some films contribute to the cultivation of virtue? But aren't other films morally pernicious and even harmful – such as pornographic films? Yet how is it possible for a film to be harmful and what should we do about it? Can we censor such films? And how are we to respond to motion pictures that appear to be artistically accomplished but also evil? In what way do moral factors and artistic ones come into play in an all-things-considered judgment of a film? These are the sorts of issues that vex Part VII of this anthology.

The final section, Part VIII, is preoccupied with the relation of motion pictures to knowledge in general and to philosophical knowledge in particular. Obviously not all films add to our fund of knowledge and perhaps even fewer can lay claim to the title of philosophy. But might it be the case that at least some motion pictures can satisfy the criteria required to count as genuine knowledge, philosophical or otherwise? Skeptics argue "no," for genuine knowledge claims, they assert, demand to be backed by evidence and, especially in the case of philosophy, by argument. Yet fiction films are bereft of evidence and argument; so even if they convey truths, those truths do not amount to knowledge, since they have not been justified by means of evidence and argument.

Nevertheless, this species of skepticism is liable to attack from at least two different directions. On the one hand, it may be countered that the view of knowledge, and particularly the view of philosophical knowledge, countenanced by the skeptic is too narrow. Or, alternatively, it may be demonstrated that narrative fictions possess structural resources that enable them to mount what may be reasonably described as arguments. Both strategies are deployed against the skeptic in the closing section of this volume.

Perhaps needless to say, the topics selected for discussion herein are but a sampling of the issues that intrigue and engage contemporary philosophers of the moving image. Another anthology might propose an entirely different agenda, emphasizing, for example, the relation of motion pictures to the preoccupations of political philosophy.

We would never suggest that the itinerary through the field offered between these covers is the only way of introducing beginning students to the philosophy of the motion picture. It is a fairly representative overview of the kind of work produced by so-called analytic philosophers of film. But one might enter the conversation by a different route. What is important is simply to begin somewhere. So we invite you to start here and now.

N.C.

Note

1 For a fuller account of this view of philosophy, see the introduction to Noël Carroll, *Philosophy of Art: A Contemporary Introduction* (London: Routledge, 2000).

PART I

Film as Art

Introduction

Film and philosophy first encounter each other over the issue of whether or not film can be an artform. This is the question of whether or not *some* films can be artworks, since it is obviously not the case that all films are artworks. Ballistics tests, for example, are not.

This is a philosophical question because it concerns the concept of art. Specifically, can the concept of art be applied to some films? That is, can certain films, at least, meet the criterion or criteria requisite for the concept of *art* to be applicable?

This question became pressing by the end of the first decade of the twentieth century, if not earlier. At that time, the film medium was in the process of acquiring greater visibility and influence in society. Though it had started as a technological novelty, its practitioners and proponents had higher ambitions for it. They aspired for recognition; they clamored for legitimacy. They no longer wished to be regarded as the poor step-sister of theater.[1] They wanted film to be acknowledged as an artform in its own right.

However, not everyone was willing to accord this status to the fledgling medium, not even after it had produced arguable masterpieces, such as *Intolerance* and the works of Charlie Chaplin. The source of this resistance, moreover, had consolidated decisively *before* the invention of cinema, taking its inspiration from the reservations voiced against the possibility that photographs could be artworks.

Allegedly, photographs cannot be art. Film, it was said, merely added movement to photography. Film is *just* moving photography. Film is essentially no more than a photographic instrument. Therefore, since photographs cannot be art, neither can films be.

Because we are so accustomed to accept photographs and films as artworks – because we believe that we have already come across many artistic masterpieces in these media – the preceding argument sounds strange to us. But its motivation may not be as bizarre as it seems at first blush.

Those who are skeptical about the possibility of an art of photography took special notice of the fact that photographs are mechanical productions. They are the result of sheer causal processes – sequences of physical and chemical reactions. Because of this, they suspected that photography precluded the creative, expressive, and/or interpretive contribution of the photographer. Photographic images, on this construal, are nought but the slavish product of a machine – an automatic mechanical process – not a mind. Press a button and voilà!

The skeptics presupposed that, by definition, art required the creative, expressive, and/or interpretive input of an artist. But, they contended, photography is a mechanism. It affords no space for creative, expressive, and/or interpretive invention. Therefore, it fails to meet the criteria requisite for art status; it cannot be art. And since film is essentially photography, films cannot be artworks either.

Furthermore, the skeptics took note of the kind of mechanism photography is. It is a machine for reproducing the appearance of whatever stands before the lens of the camera. It is a recording mechanism. Consequently, they argued that photography could not be an artform in its own right. A photograph of an artwork of the sort one can purchase in a museum bookstore is not an artwork itself; it is merely a reproduction of an artwork. Similarly, the CD of Bach's *Brandenburg Concertos* is not a musical masterwork, but only the record of one. The photograph and the CD give us access to antecedently existing artworks, but they are not artworks themselves. They are recording media, not artistic media.

Photographs and, by extension, films are something like time capsules – temporal containers – that preserve past artistic achievements. They are temporal conveyances. But just as the ice cream truck is not the ice cream, so these recording devices are not the artworks they make available to us, nor are they artworks in their own right. Moreover, applying this reasoning to dramatic films, it was deduced that films are not artworks on their own steam but merely slavish recordings – moving photographs, if you will – of theatrical artworks.

Much of what is referred to as classical film theory was dedicated to rebutting these arguments against the possibility of film art.[2] Film theorists, like Rudolf Arnheim, maintained that despite their mechanical dimension both photography and film had the capacity to be expressive. Arnheim emphasized especially the ways in which the film image fell short of the perfect reproduction of its subjects and he claimed that this lacuna granted the filmmaker the opportunity to treat those subjects creatively.

Film theorists, notably the Soviet montagists, also stressed that film is not reducible to photography; film editing is at least as fundamental an element of the medium, if not a more important element than the photographic constituent. And since editing can rearrange the spatio-temporal continuum, including the order of events in a play, film need *not* be a mere or slavish recording of anything – of any naturally occurring sequence of events or, either, of any theatrical ones. Thus, film, via editing, had the resources to support authorial intervention, interpretation, and expression. The filmmaker was not confined to the slavish reproduction of the world. The filmmaker could also "create" worlds – worlds of works of art.

It is against the background of this longstanding debate about the possibility of photography and film to produce art, properly so-called, that Roger Scruton's "Photography and Representation," and Dominic McIver Lopes's response – "The Aesthetics of Photographic Transparency" – need to be read. For Scruton's article is an extremely sophisticated, philosophical variant of the traditional suspicion that photography and film cannot be art; while Lopes's article is an equally sophisticated rejoinder which also has the advantage of clarifying, in part, what is at stake in aesthetically appreciating photographic images, whether still or moving.

It is important not to dismiss Scruton's arguments against the possibility of film art out of hand. It is true that it appears to fly in the face of common sense. But common sense can be mistaken; for centuries it held females to be necessarily inferior to males. Moreover, it is not clear that Scruton cannot assimilate to his own viewpoint much of the evidence that common sense might attempt to marshal against him. For instance, if you observe that there are artistic masterpieces on film, like Chaplin's *The Gold Rush*, that appear to be counterexamples to Scruton's conclusions, Scruton may respond that if the movie *The Gold Rush* is a masterpiece, then it is not a cinematic masterpiece – not itself a case of *film* art – but a case of a theatrical artwork which has been photographically recorded on film. That is, it is a dramatic (or comedic) masterpiece preserved on film, but the film itself is no more an artwork than the postcard of *School of Athens* is an instance of Raphael's genius.

Scruton's master argument has three major movements:

1 Photography is not a representational art.
2 A film is at best a photograph of a dramatic representation.
3 Therefore, film itself is not a representational art.

This master argument, in turn, is bolstered by three other arguments, each designed to substantiate the first premise of the master argument. These three supporting arguments may be called: (1) the causation argument, (2) the control argument, and (3) the aesthetic-interest argument. Scruton does not appear to have additional argumentation to reinforce the second premise of his master argument. He seems to presume that this premise is completely uncontroversial. This a shortcoming to which we must return. However, first let us look at Scruton's reasons for advancing the first premise.

The causation argument. Scruton holds that a representation is necessarily an expression of thought. If snow falling on a mountainside distributed itself so as to cast shadows in such a way that the result resembles the face of Jackie Chan, it would not, according to Scruton, constitute a representation of Jackie Chan. Why not? Because a representation, properly so-called, requires the expression of thought and there is no thinking behind our imagined snow storm. It is a natural event, a bald series of causes and effects, the sheer product of physical laws rather than human agency. So: no thinker – no thinking – no portrait.

Similarly, a photograph is putatively a sheer causal process. Photographs can occur without human agency. A malfunctioning camera with a hair trigger can click off a perfectly focused snapshot. Bank surveillance cameras do not require human operators. And even more fancifully, one can imagine a cave containing a puddle of naturally occurring photographic salts with a tiny crack overhead that allows light to flow in the manner of a pin-hole camera; that package of light rays, we may further speculate, could fix the image of a nearby tree on the floor of the cavern.[3] A randomly occurring, "natural" photograph of this sort would not require a human photographer. And for that reason, someone like Scruton would not wish to count it as a representation, no matter how closely it captured the look of the neighboring tree.

What the preceding examples imply is that photography does not necessarily require a camera operator. At minimum, a photograph may be the result of an utterly physical process of causation. Scruton calls such a photograph an ideal photography – a photograph stripped down to its essence in such a way that it gives us a glimpse of what a photograph minimally is.

Since such a photo does not require human agency, it will not express a thought. Therefore photography, conceived minimally, essentially, and ideally, need not express thoughts. But since representation, according to Scruton, requires the expression of thought, what the case of the ideal photograph reveals is that photography, considered essentially, is not representational.

This argument is likely to provoke the objection that Scruton wrongly presupposes that representation demands the expression of thought. But in a perfectly respectable way of speaking, barometers *represent* atmospheric pressure and yet they express no thoughts.

This is a fair observation. However, it is not conclusive. Recall that what is at issue for Scruton is whether photography can be a representational

art. And it does appear that anything that lays claim to the title of *art* should be in the business of expressing thought.[4]

In pointing to the sheer causal dimension of photography, Scruton means to draw a distinction between photography – or photography as it is revealed essentially to be in its idealized form – and painting. A painting has the property of intentionality by which Scruton appears to signal that it (1) be about something because (2) its author intends it to be. That is, for Scruton, a painting is intentional both in the sense that it is directed and that it is a vehicle for an authorial thought (such as an interpretation of what it is about).

Ideal photographs, on the other hand, are not intentional in these senses. They are supposedly sheer causal processes. The appearance of the tree fixed photographically on the floor of the cave is not *about* the tree. How could it be? It expresses no thought about the tree as a painting that pictured it majestically might. The photograph is simply the result of a natural process, indicating the presence of no more thought than a river overflowing its banks would.

Moreover, whereas the painting can portray imaginary things, a photograph allegedly always renders the appearance of something that literally existed before the lens of a camera. Photographs, that is, present the spectator with a referentially transparent context – that is, in the standard case, the photo P is the effect of cause C (say, a tree) in such a way that the existence of P permits one to infer the existence of C (a tree or some tree-like visible configuration). Paintings, on the other hand, are referentially opaque. From a painting of an angel, you are not entitled to infer the existence of an angel. Paintings can be about what painters imagine; their subject need not exist. This too is a feature of intentionality, sometimes called intentional inexistence.

Painting is a representational art because it involves intentionality – which is intimately related to the capacity to express (authorial) thoughts about its subjects.[5] Photography, conceived of in terms of its ideal or essential form, produces its images causally rather than intentionally, and, therefore, does not express thoughts. Consequently, photography is not a representational art, and, neither is film, since film is basically photography.

The control argument. This argument, which Lopes calls the style argument, presupposes that a genuine representational artform is such that, in principle, an artist working in that medium has complete control over it. A representational artform is a vehicle for the expression of thought. Ideally, every element in a representational artform serves or should be capable of serving the articulation of thoughts.

In addition, for the purpose of clarifying her ideas and/or emotions, the artist may imagine whatsoever she needs; she is not restrained by what is. Painting as a vehicle of intentionality can meet these demands. However, the photographer lacks comparable levels of control.

The camera is like a mirror; it captures whatever is before the lens, whether or not the photographer is aware of the details and/or intends to photograph it. For example, some of the "Roman" soldiers in Stanley Kubrick's *Spartacus* can be seen wearing wristwatches – a detail in the image that the cinematographer missed and never intended to record. But photography is a causal process; if something was in front of the lens, the procedure guarantees, all things being equal, that it will be in the image, no matter what the camera operator desires.[6]

If wristwatches appear on ancient Roman soldiers in a painting, we would infer that the painter put them there intentionally and we would ask what she intended by them. On the other hand, when details like this erupt in historical films, as they so often do, we surmise that things have gotten out of control, since we understand that the photographic process is an automatic, causal affair, abiding blindly according to the laws of chemistry and optics.

Moreover, there are so many things in front of the camera lens that may make an inadvertent appearance in the final print. Typically there are far too many details – large and small – for the photographer to notice. Too many surprises arrive uninvited in the finished photograph. With a painting, everything that is on the canvas is there because the painter intended it to be there. There are no surprises, no unintended wristwatches. Not so the photograph. A detail will appear in a photo because it was on the camera's turf whether or not the photographer took heed of it. Furthermore, there are an indefinitely large number of such potential details lying in wait for the photographer. So in this sense, the painter may be said to have more control than the photographer.

Because paintings are intentionally produced, the artist has a level of control such that there is nothing whose presence in the representation

shocks her. But photographers are frequently taken aback by what they *find* in their photos, because the causal process that they set in motion evolves ignorantly, irrespective of what the photographer believes, desires, or intends.

As well, the photographer not only lacks sufficient control over the details that may crop up in her work; she also lacks the kind of imaginative freedom the painter possesses, inasmuch as she can only literally present what can be placed before the camera. The ingredients of a photographic image are limited to reality, in contrast to the painter who can picture whatever she fancies. Magritte, for example, can represent a stone suspended in mid-air, defying the laws of gravity. A photographer could never actually photograph such a rock, because it does not exist in nature to be dragooned as a camera subject. So, once again, the painter can exercise a degree of control over his image that the photographer cannot hope to match.

Because representational art involves the expression of thought, only media that afford a high level of control suit it. For the clarification of thought requires a certain malleability. Photography, however, is recalcitrant in this respect: it is tethered to what is *and* it incorporates details beyond the photographer's ken. Unlike painting, it is not a representational art, because it provides insufficient control. Ditto film, for the same reasons. Remember those wristwatches.

The aesthetic-interest argument. This argument, which Lopes calls the object argument, maintains that if something is a representational art, it must be capable of sustaining aesthetic interest. An aesthetic interest is an interest we take in something *for its own sake*, i.e., because of the kind of thing it is. We take an aesthetic interest in a novel when we are preoccupied by the kind of thing it is – essentially an expression of thought – rather than, say, as an object heavy enough to prop open a door.

According to Scruton, photography cannot command our aesthetic interest. Why not? Because a photo is strictly analogous to a mirror. If we are interested in what shows on the surface of a mirror that is because we are interested in the object so reflected there and not in the reflection itself. When I brush my hair in front of the mirror, I am interested in my hair and not the mirror reflection as such. That is, I do not take an interest in the mirror reflection for its own sake; my interest is not directed at the mirror *qua* mirror. It's my dwindling patch of grey that concerns me.

Scruton claims that the same is true of photographs; we are interested in them for what they show – long-departed relatives, for example – and not for their own sake. It is the object in the photograph and not the photograph as an object that commands our attention.

Contrarily, we are interested in paintings because they are expressions of thought. Mirrors are not expressions of thought, but optical phenomena thoroughly beholden to the lawlike operation of natural, causal processes. They deliver appearances to us mechanically. So there is no point in taking an interest in them in the way we care about paintings. In fact, the only way to take an interest in the images in mirrors, if we are not physicists, is to be interested in what they show us – for instance, the parking space into which we are trying to back our car.

Similarly, photos record appearances; they do not convey thoughts. We are interested in the photo of x – maybe one of Emma Goldman – because we are interested in learning how Emma Goldman looked. We are not interested in the photo for itself, by only as a mechanical transmitter of appearances. Thus, we take no aesthetic interest in photos.

Another way to see what Scruton is getting at is to recall a key word in the title of Lopes's article – namely, "transparency." We have already noted that photographs are referentially transparent in contrast to the opacity characteristic of the products of intentionality; there is a causal connection between the photo and the object that gives rise to it such that the photo supplies grounds for inferring the existence of the object in the photo. But in addition, both Scruton and Lopes hold that the photograph gives us indirect perceptual access to the object. The photograph is a special way of seeing an object – just as seeing an object through a mirror is a special, indirect way of seeing my receding hairline.

Specifically: we see objects *through* photographs. That is the way in which they are perceptually transparent. But for people like Scruton, if photographs are perceptually transparent, then it is not the photograph in its own right that occupies us. It is the object to which the photograph gives us perceptual access that interests us, either for its own sake, or otherwise.

Suppose the object is something very beautiful – like a budding flower – of the sort whose appearance folks are typically said to value for its own sake. Scruton argues that the putative aes-

thetic interest here is in the beautiful flower. Our attention is not directed at the photograph itself, but at the appearance of the flower which the photograph delivers transparently, mechanically, as through a glass brightly. It is not, in a manner of speaking, a beautiful photograph, but a photograph of a beautiful thing. And it is the beautiful thing that is the object of our aesthetic interest, properly speaking.

The director Dziga Vertov called cinema "the microscope and telescope of time." Just as perceptual prosthetic devices like microscopes and telescopes enable us visually to penetrate both infinitesimal and vast spaces, photographic processes enable us to "see into" the past "to bridge temporal distances" at a glance. But, equally, just as in the normal run of affairs, neither the microscope nor the telescope is the object of our interest, neither is the photograph. With respect to all three, we see "through" them; they are transaparent.

Thus, we are not interested in the photo for the sake of the object it is. The photo, therefore, does not sustain our aesthetic interest. So photography is not a representational art. Consequently, if film is basically, essentially photographic in nature, then it is not a representational artform either. If a film appears to encourage aesthetic interest – as Kurosawa's *Throne of Blood* certainly does – that is because it is a photograph of a dramatic representation. It is the dramatic representation itself – as enacted before the camera – that holds our interest and not the photographing of it, just as it would be Bill Irwin's pantomime and not the looking glass that would be the object of our aesthetic interest if Irwin's performance were relayed to us though a mirror.

These three sub-arguments are the basis for Scruton's contention that photography is not a representational art, the first premise of his master argument against the possibility that some films are (representational) artworks. These arguments are undeniably formidable, even if they strike contemporaries as a bit cranky. But are they also decisive? Let us see why they may not be.

Against the causation argument. Scruton correctly points out that the production of a photograph does not *necessarily* require the intentional contribution of a human agent. It can result from a process of sheer physical causation with no intentional input. This shows us that intentionality is not an essential feature of a photograph. There *can* be idealized photos – photos minus intentionality – which are photographs nonetheless. But if there is no intentionality, they cannot be said to be expressions of thought for they lack thought content (something they are about). Thus, ideal photographs are not representational artworks in the sense advocated by Scruton.

However, even were this the case, what about actual photographs, not ideal ones? When we revere the photos of Weston, Atget, and Adams as works of (representational) art, we are thinking of real, "live" photographs, not ideal ones. And when it comes to actual photos like these, we believe, on eminently defensible grounds, that the intentions of these photographers are expressed in their images. These photos do convey thoughts, attitudes, and emotions; these photos do offer interpretations about the content toward which they direct our attention; they are unquestionably intended to do just that by their authors.

The pertinent photographs possess intentionality in the ways Scruton requires and should count as works of (representational) art on his terms. Who cares whether or not ideal photographs (in Scruton's sense) can be representational artworks if actual photographs can be representational artworks? For if some actual photographs *are* artworks, then some photographs *can* be art. *Pace* Scruton, then, the photographic medium is capable of supporting representational art.

That what Scruton calls ideal photos – which might also be labeled "minimal" photos – are not representational artworks does not imply that actual photos are not artworks of the relevant sort. Scruton appears to think that if intentions are not necessarily involved in producing a photo, then intentions are necessarily not involved in the production of photos. But this is fallacious modal reasoning. The fact that a bank surveillance camera records the presence of an intruder automatically – *sans* the intervention of any intention – does not entail that intentionality and intentions are not productively engaged when I select my subject, choose the lens, film stock, and aperture setting I desire, and adjust the lighting for my purposes as I prepare to execute my photograph.

From the fact that photographic status does not necessarily mandate intentionality, it does not follow that anything legitimately considered to be a foursquare specimen of photography must lack intentionality. This is simply a *non sequitur*. And it is upon such a logical gaff that the causation argument founders.

Rather, we can argue that even if ideal photos lack intentionality and are not (representational)

artworks for that reason, that does not entail that actual photos are equally compromised. For actual photos can have intentional content and be intentionally produced and thus they can satisfy the criteria Scruton expects for representation. And if photography can be representational on these grounds, so can film.

Of course, Scruton may assert that anything short of his ideal photography is not the genuine article. But when contemplating whether some photos *are* artworks, why would we give greater significance to how they *might* have been made as opposed to how they *were actually* made? In calling the former *ideal*, Scruton seems to be exploiting the ambiguity between something that is paradigmatic versus something that does not exist. But Scruton's ideals are hardly paradigmatic of photographs as they do exist, since, by his own admission, his ideal photos are few and far between – that is, if they exist at all.

Furthermore, Scruton cannot argue that if causation is involved in the production of a work, then that precludes the kind of intentionality requisite for art status. For were that so, virtually no medium could be said to produce art, since almost all of them have an ineliminable causal dimension. After all, a paintbrush is a tool; when an artist applies paint to her canvas, she sets a causal process in motion. But that scarcely forecloses the expression of thought.

Against the control argument. The expression of one's thought requires control. If there is no control over the medium in question, then one is simply not expressing one's own thought. Indeed, if there is no control whatsoever, then it is doubtful that any thought is being expressed at all. Furthermore, if you believe that there is an essential connection between the expression of a thought and the possession of a style, then if one lacks control over one's medium, what one produces lacks style. No control – no style; no style – no (representational) art.

A first response to the control argument is that it is utopian. If what is required for art status is *total* control of a medium, then we will be compelled to discount as artforms most of the practices we now esteem as such. Most artists have to make compromises with their medium – to adjust what they envision to the materials at hand. A theater director will have to set her drama on certain actors who may bring to the role qualities – of voice, of temperament, etc. – she never imagined; she will have to make do with what she has to work with. Similarly, a choreographer will have to exhibit his work on a specific stage that may imbue a performance with unexpected aesthetic properties; if the stage is smaller than anticipated, it may impart an impression of constraint that may or may not enhance the dance. Every musician will have to negotiate the peculiarities of each individual instrument. Architects and sculptors are perhaps even more obviously limited in the degree to which they can exert their will on their media. But even the imagination of the painter will have to live with the resources – such as varieties of paint – and their attendant qualities that are available to her.

Few artforms, if any, confirm the fantasy of total control. Are we to say then that no medium is capable of producing art? Rather, it is more advisable to lower our sights – to require only that artistic media afford to their practitioners sufficient control, instead of total control. And this recognition transforms the issue: does the film medium permit sufficient control for a film-maker to project intentional content – i.e., to express thoughts and feelings?

We can begin to assemble a positive answer to this question by recalling some of the observations noted in the course of the rebuttal of the causation argument. There we noted that a photographer has a range of variables at her fingertips to enable her to articulate and convey her thinking and feeling. First she can select her subject matter; surely it is not random happenstance that accounts for the consistency of the oeuvres of Diane Arbus and Nan Goldin. And then, of course, the photographer may also choose the kind of camera, lens, film stock, aperture, and level of lighting that she judges to be appropriate to whatever it is she intends to express. Moreover, she may set up the shot – posing it, deciding the camera-to-subject distance, electing the costumes, props, and make-up, not to mention her choice of the very models who disport themselves with this regalia.

Furthermore, the photographer frequently takes a series of photos of any given subject, settling finally on the one from various alternatives that best matches her vision. And once the picture is executed, the photographer can go on to clarify more precisely her expression by exploiting laboratory processes, such as printing, cropping, air-brushing, and so forth.

At each stage in the creation of a photograph there are choices that can be made, and opting for one alternative rather than another – a wide-angle lens rather than a long lens – may make a difference that expresses with sharper specificity the content and/or qualities of the thoughts and/or feelings the photographer aspires to convey. Doesn't this constitute sufficient control of the medium – at least enough to count photography as a (representational) artform?

There are two kinds of reasons to think so. First, there seems to be an arresting catalogue of analogies between many of the controllable variables for modifying the photographic image and many of the expressive variables in painting – for example, the choice of subject, lighting, scale, framing, and so on. Second, we already know that variations along these dimensions have proven to be adequate enough for us to differentiate the thoughts and feelings Robert Mapplethorpe intends to express from those of Julia Margaret Cameron.

Ex hypothesi, whether a medium possesses sufficient control to warrant classification as a representational artform can be tested by asking whether there exist enough alternative variables of articulation available in the medium to facilitate the determination of distinctive stylistic profiles. That we can detect stylistic contrasts between a photo by Cindy Sherman and one by Lucas Samaras and go on to associate them with the expressions of different thoughts, then, indicates that photography possesses the wherewithal sufficient to effectuate representational artworks.

The style or form of an artwork is the ensemble of choices that function to realize its point or purpose – for example, the expression of thought and/or emotion.[7] Control is required in order to possess a style and to express thoughts. The level of control is a function of having a range of articulatory variables at one's disposal such that the choice of one rather than the other makes a stylistic and/or expressive difference. Choice from a field of alternative options with contrasting qualities clarifies expression and specifies style. Photography has multiple dimensions that permit a wealth of strategic decisions in order to implement the photographer's intentions. This has proven to be a sufficient amount of control for artistic purposes, since it is evident that we are able to discern and isolate the different "authorial intentionalities" of a Richard Avedon, an Annie Liebowitz, and an Henri Cartier-Bresson.

Film, if anything, provides even more levers of stylistic control and choice than photography. Neither medium allows for absolute control. But arguably, no artform does. The real issue is whether a medium abets sufficient control. And on these grounds, contra Scruton, photography and film appear to satisfy what we can expect of a (representational) artform.

Against the aesthetic-interest argument. Just as Plato disparaged the credentials of painting and poetry by analogizing them to mirrors, so Scruton demotes photography and film. For if photos and films are like mirrors, then they no more express thoughts than the glass in front of you on your bathroom cabinet. Its currency is minted in the form of mere appearances rather than intentionality. Moreover, if photography and film are strictly analogous to mirrors, then we do not care about them for their own sake; we care about or take an interest in them for the sake of the objects they show us. I do not care about the snapshot of my father as a photograph but as a reminder of Dad.

Lopes refers to the capacity of film to function as a window onto past objects, events, persons, and actions as "photographic transparency." Moreover, some such notion as transparency underwrites Scruton's claim that film is not a representational art because it is not capable of commanding our attention to the kind of object it is. Therefore, photography and film cannot sustain aesthetic interest. For if they are transparent, we see through them and our interest lands on the appearance of whatever they present images of. If it is a photo of the Battle of the Somme, then my interest lies in the Battle of the Somme. It makes no sense for me to be interested in the photo as such. For it is transparent – which Scruton seems to believe is rather like being effectively invisible.

It is this aspect of Scruton's brief against photography that primarily draws Lopes's fire. Lopes points out that even if a photograph is transparent, that does not entail that seeing an object through a photograph is the same as seeing the same object "face-to-face." For example, according to the theory of photographic transparency, I can see my brother through a black-and-white photo. But this is different than meeting him for a drink, since he will arrive at the bar in living color. That is, just as the artillery officer sees the target through infra-red binoculars, we have indirect perceptual access to the past through the agency of photography. But just as directly seeing the target with the naked eye will not reveal the target to be all red, so seeing the object of a black-and-white photograph directly shows it to be multi-colored.

Thus, there are differences between seeing an object indirectly in a photo and having a close encounter of the third kind with it. Some of these differences include not only coloration, but also: that objects in photographs are decontextualized in ways that may be revelatory; that photos are frozen moments, disclosing aspects otherwise occluded; that the object depicted in the photo is absent, inviting an opportunity for scrutiny that might in "real life" be dangerous, callous, insensitive, impolite, or confusing; and that that absence can make nostalgia an appropriate response to someone or something, whereas this would be an absurd reaction were they "in our face."

In short, because of the difference between photographic seeing and face-to-face seeing, photographs, in virtue of features of the photographic medium, can defamiliarize the objects whose appearances they convey. Defamiliarization, in turn, may serve as an artistic strategy for expressing thoughts about the relevant objects. Thus, even if photographs are said to be transparent, their divergence from face-to-face or direct seeing leaves open the possibility of artistic defamiliarization and, thence, the expression of thought and feeling. Consequently, if a photograph, by dint of its medium, expresses a thought and/or emotion about its object, then we may take an interest in the photograph *qua* photograph – that is, we may take an aesthetic interest in the way in which the photograph deploys the characteristic features of its medium to express thought.

Our concern, in other words, need not be confined to the appearance of the object as relayed to us by the photograph. The defamiliarizing potential of photography can be mobilized to express thoughts about the objects portrayed and this process, in consequence, can give rise to ruminating about the way in which the kind of object a photograph is has given birth to a thought. Our interest is aesthetic in this case in the way that Scruton and Lopes understand that concept – it is an interest in the photograph-as-object for its own sake – for what it achieves, in lieu of the sort of medium it inhabits.

So far we have been wrestling at length with Scruton's defense of the first premise of his master-argument. This has been a somewhat complicated exercise because Scruton himself advances the case for his first premise in a very elaborate and nuanced fashion. But his argument also hinges upon a second premise – that film is, at best, a photograph of a dramatic representation. Without this premise, Scruton cannot extrapolate what he conceives to be the limitations of photography against film's candidacy for standing as a representational artform. So now we must interrogate the second movement in Scruton's argument.

Luckily, sketching reservations about Scruton's second premise need not be as intricate as working through the objections to Scruton's first premise, since Scruton himself offers little by way of justification to substantiate his assertion that films are nothing more than photographs of dramatic representations. He seems to regard this to be self-evident, which is remarkable – since it is patently false.

Films are not merely *photographs* of dramatic representations for the obvious reason that films are not merely photographs. Photography is not the only constituent element that comprises film. In addition, for example, there is also editing. So even if Scruton's arguments against photography were persuasive, they could not be carried over to film, since the edited dimension of film can express thoughts, can facilitate a sufficient level of control, and can afford a locus of aesthetic interest.[8] Nor can the rich repertoire of techniques available to the filmmaker for coordinating the audio with the visual components of the film be reduced to the photographic aspect of the medium. Film, in sum, has many more dimensions than the photographic one. So were photography/cinematography disabled in the way that Scruton alleges, it still would not follow that film is comparably incapacitated.[9]

Another problem with Scruton's second premise is that it presumes that the image track of a film is exclusively photographic. Undoubtedly, for the most part, this has been true of most films. But it is not *necessarily* true of motion picture images, as one realizes when one contemplates the development of new movie technologies, such as computer-generated mattes. As recent installments of *Star Wars* and *Lord of the Rings* establish, whole cities and whole armies can be created without primary recourse to the mediation of traditional photography. They can be concocted out of thin air, digitally fabricated, if you will. Indeed, in the future, entire feature films are likely to be constructed in the computer.

Though it might be more accurate to call these optical inventions moving images,[10] we continue to call them films in honor of the first medium that gave us motion pictures. But photographic film is not the only delivery system for what we call films

(a.k.a. motion pictures) in the broader sense. And since some of these delivery systems need not employ photographic film in any way,[11] it is false that a dramatic film is a photograph of a dramatic representation. It could be a computer-generated representation in its own right.

Moreover, it should be clear that computer-generated imagery faces none of the challenges previously leveled at photography. Such imagery does not mirror anything nor can it be said to be transparent because it creates its own object. What appears on screen is as under the control of the CGI specialist as what appears on the canvas is under the control of the painter. Nor can there be any question of whether CGI imagery can express thoughts. It can do so exactly in the way that a painting does.

Thus, the second premise of Scruton's master argument is as troubled as the first. Consequently, at this point in the dialectic it seems fair to say that skeptics, like Scruton, have failed to make their case. We may continue to cleave to the common-sense belief that (some) films are art.[12] The burden of proof has been shifted back to the skeptic.

If the debate between Scruton and Lopes looks back to the earliest stages of the evolution of the film medium, what worries Terrence Rafferty in his "Everybody Gets a Cut" is a recent technological development, notably the ascendancy of DVDs (Digital Video Disks) as a leading channel for the dissemination of cinema. Scruton charges that the oldest component of the motion picture medium precludes its attainment of art status. Rafferty has no problems with photography, but he admonishes us that the distribution of films on DVDs will cancel the artistic status of film, precipitating a fall from aesthetic grace.

What is the basis of Rafferty's anxiety? He feels that the DVD gives too much discretion to the viewer, thereby undermining the authorial control of the filmmaker to such a degree that the result is no longer worthy of the title *art*. The DVD provides opportunities for interactivity that Rafferty thinks were scarcely feasible under previous regimes of film viewing, such as watching movies at the local theater or on broadcast TV.

This interactivity, first and foremost, involves the ability of the viewer to skip over parts of the film and thus to view scenes in a different order than the author mandated in the original cut of the film. This, Rafferty fears, will make the viewer the de facto editor of the film – the person who determines the cadence, the emphasis, and, thereby, many of the most significant aesthetic properties of the film. For Rafferty, this is tantamount to the utter capitulation of artistic authority on the part of filmmaker.

Furthermore, recent DVDs have included alternative endings of the films they showcase. This troubles Rafferty because he suspects that it will tempt filmmakers to relinquish their authorial responsibility – to leave it to the viewer (a.k.a. consumer) to choose his own ending. And this, Rafferty insinuates, will lead inevitably to a lowering of rigor. Like the interactive potential of DVDs to permit the viewer to indulge in only those sequences that are to his taste, so the inclusion of optional endings will seduce audiences to take the least line of resistance.

In any event, Rafferty predicts that the augmentation of the interactive prowess of viewers will lure the filmmaker into shirking his duty (which is the creation of a unified, complete, self-sufficient artifact – where these terms are supposed to be at least partially definitory of art). Thus, Rafferty warns, the DVD may herald nothing short of the self-deconstruction (the auto-dismantlement) of the art of film.

Technological innovations are often taken as harbingers of artistic doom. The arrival of the sound film occasioned prophecies of the end of the art. Now, with the advent of the DVD, Rafferty sees perdition in view. But, as an initial response to Rafferty's horror of interactivity, one may point out that, with a painting, the viewer usually has a great deal of autonomy regarding the itinerary of her eye, but no one thinks that the interactivity involved in looking at paintings endangers their art status. Moreover, many artists in the twentieth century – such as John Cage and Merce Cunningham – cultivated the use of open structures that enticed audiences to find interactively their own significance in the relevant works. Interactivity and audience autonomy are not, in other words, incompatible with art in principle.

Undoubtedly, Rafferty will cry "foul!" here. The works of Cage and Cunningham were intended to be open. Films, however, are supposed to be closed. DVDs make them something they are not meant to be, something, in fact, at odds with the kind of art, film art, movies are intended as. But let us suppose that films are mandated to be closed; that there should be no skipping of the scenes that bore us and no repeating those we like. What do we make of what happens when the audience violates this contract?

Certainly not that the film has lost its mandated unity. The mandated authorial intention to watch all the scenes in the order presented is still in sway. If viewers choose to disrespect it, that shows that it is the viewer, not the artist, who is not holding up his end of the bargain. Many readers are said to pass over the chapters portraying the battles in *War and Peace*. That hardly counts against Tolstoy's status as an artist or against *War and Peace*'s pedigree.

Likewise, in the 1950s many films were shown on television in formats like "Million Dollar Movie" or "The Movie of the Week." These programs repeated the same movie every day of the week, often several times a day. If there was a scene in a film that one particularly enjoyed – say the rescue of the child from the burning orphanage in *Mighty Joe Young* – it was easy to time your viewing so that you could tune in and see that and nothing else. However, that no more compromised the unity of *Mighty Joe Young* than sneaking from one theater to another in a multiplex to catch one's favorite moments does. The DVD makes such "connoisseurship" easier, but it does not impugn the integrity of the works so sampled. The author's mandate is still in evidence. The author cannot stop the viewer from flaunting it. The filmmaker is only an artist, not a policeman.

Many artforms allow a degree of audience autonomy in the pace with which one absorbs the pertinent work. You can read a novel as quickly as you choose and there are no obstacles and no rules against returning to earlier sections and re-reading them. Artforms can tolerate certain amounts of interactivity without losing artistic credentials.

Rafferty, however, appears to deny film the sort of interactivity one might find in regard to a painting, a novel, a sculpture, a poem, and a cathedral. For Rafferty, it is an essential feature of the art of film that the filmmaker be in complete control over the viewer's experience – that is, in control of precisely what she sees, when and for how long.[13] This is especially strange, since, as Rafferty himself points out, a latitude of audience freedom has been the aim of at least some of the most ambitious filmmakers, including Jean Renoir. This is not mentioned to maintain that audience autonomy is an essential condition of film, but only to propose that no discussion of the nature of film can be convincing unless it countenances at least the possibility of fairly liberal amounts of interactivity.

Moreover, if some of the kinds of interactivity promoted by the DVD format are inadmissable because they sunder the unity of the work, that is surely the fault of the misuse of the DVD by the viewer and not of the filmmaker, who in the first instance created a coherent whole. Nor does it compromise the unity of that work if after viewing the film in its entirety, one uses the scene selection function of the DVD to deepen one's appreciation of some portions of the film by replaying them.

Likewise, there is no reason to suppose that if the filmmaker has provided more than one ending for his story, he has neglected his artistry. For if each ending works, each version is unified. Furthermore, if the film is designed to engage the viewer in the comparative contemplation of the variations incited by the alternative endings, then the work is not only highly unified, but complexly and contrastively diversified as well. This is not to say that most DVDs with alternative endings are structured like this. Nevertheless, some may be, such as, arguably, the DVD edition of *28 Days Later*.

That is, the possibility of multiple endings in the same film can be a source of stimulating artistic invention, as it is in the case of Tom Tykwer's film *Run Lola Run*. Thus, the DVD format could inspire the sophistication of an art of theme and variation in film narration. Admittedly, this art

has not burst onto the scene yet. But as technical innovations like the DVD arrive, it is far more profitable to think about the way in which they enable new artistic possibilities, rather than brooding over the way they might inhibit past ones. For in truth, DVDs in no way threaten the creation of unified films by artists, even if they slacken the hold the filmmaker can assuredly exert on the viewer. The choice to neglect the mandate of the film has always been open to viewers. Many have chosen to make out, while most of the rest of us watch (the screen).

This section concerns the relation between the medium and the status of film as art. Perennially, commentators have charged that this or that aspect of the medium would somehow deny film access to the kingdom of art. These alarms began in the beginning with apprehension about the photographic component of cinema and nowadays continue, shuddering at the proclivities of the DVD. These dire forebodings have consistently come a cropper. The problem with such aesthetic jeremiads is that the theorists who propound them fail to attempt to imagine the ways in which new developments in technology may bring in their train new possibilities. We need to be thankful that we have artists to do that.

N.C.

Notes

1 In her selection in Part II of this volume (see chapter 5), Susanne K. Langer writes: "For a few decades it [film] seemed like nothing more than a new technical device in the sphere of drama, a new way of preserving and retailing dramatic performances." See S.K. Langer, "A Note on the Film," in this volume.

2 For a discussion of classical film theory, see Noël Carroll, *Philosophical Problems of Classical Film Theory* (Princeton, New Jersey: Princeton University Press, 1988).

3 This example is adapted from Berys Gaut's excellent article "Cinematic Art," *The Journal of Aesthetics and Art Criticism* 60, no. 4 (Fall, 2002), pp. 199–212. If you are interested in this topic, this essay is highly recommended.

4 Of course, even this may be too stringent a requirement. Perhaps all that can be asked of a medium is that it be capable of expressing thought. But then, contra Scruton, certainly photography can do that. It is too demanding to require of a medium that, in order to be accorded the status of representational art, every instance in that medium convey thoughts.

And, in this context, aren't the photographs of Walker Evans sufficient to show that some photographs can – because they have – communicated thoughts?

5 Franz Brentano argued that intentionality was the mark of the mental.

6 The "ceteris paribus" clause here is meant to cover, among other things, that the camera is being operated competently and conventionally and that the results are not being touched up in the lab.

7 This view of artistic form is defended in Noël Carroll, *Philosophy of Art: A Contemporary Introduction* (London: Routledge, 1999).

8 Editing allows the filmmaker the opportunity to rearrange for expressive purposes the scenes of a preexisting drama and to juxtapose rapidly – at a velocity rarely viable on stage – details from different parts of the performance for interpretive effect. So even when the film is derived from an already existing theatrical work, it need not be a mere photographic documentation thereof. For example, see Guy Maddin's film *Dracula: Pages from a Virgin's Diary*.

9 One could, of course, go on at far greater length in demonstrating that the cinematographic image is not analyzable down to the photographic image without remainder. Such exercises were the mainstay of classical film theory, their sensitivity to the possibilities of film technique being one of the reasons why it is still profitable to read them today.

For example, it was often pointed out that the film camera may move around the dramatic scene, thereby giving the film director a device for interpreting the action that the theatrical director cannot approximate readily. Thus, once again, we see that the film image is not just a photographic recording of a pro-filmic dramatic event with movement added.

Furthermore, there is a feature of photography/cinematography that enables the filmmaker to achieve something no theatrical director can rival – the ability to turn the natural environment into an expressive character. By putting the action in an actual setting – as, for example, Kim Ki-Duk does in *Spring, Summer, Fall, Winter ... and Spring* – the film director can imbue the drama with the expressive qualities of real landscapes with a degree of control and variety difficult, if not practically impossible, for a theater director to equal, even a theater director who is staging his spectacle outdoors. Thus, photography can make a creative contribution to a dramatic representation – that is, be an indispensable part of one – and not merely the slavish reproduction of a dramatic enactment that could exist independently of the camera.

More could be said on these matters, but we leave it to readers to work out further these differences on their own.

10 In the next section of this anthology, Noël Carroll argues in his "Defining the Moving Image" that we should re-christen and reconceptualize the area of inquiry now called film or cinema studies as moving-image studies. Indeed, he would prefer to call this very volume *The Philosophy of the Moving Image*.

11 Imagine a motion picture narrative constructed digitally from end to end and then delivered to a reception site by a satellite feed. I doubt that ordinary users of everyday English would hesitate to call it a film (or, more likely, a movie).

12 It should be pointed out that even if Scruton had proven that films could not be representational artworks, he still would not have shown that they could not be some other sort of art. Perhaps films could achieve a para-musical art status, as was the aim of the makers of City Symphonies like Ruttman and Cavalcanti.

13 It is interesting to note that it is exactly this potential of film, which is exploited in most mass movies, that leads T. W. Adorno to argue that they are not art but ersatz art.

1

Photography and Representation

Roger Scruton

Critics and philosophers have occasionally been troubled by the question whether the cinema is an independent art form – independent, that is, of the theatre, from which it borrows so many conventions.[1] This question can be traced back to a more basic one, the question whether photography is capable of representing anything. I shall argue that it is not and that, insofar as there is representation in film, its origin is not photographic. A film is a photograph of a dramatic representation; it is not, because it cannot be, a photographic representation. It follows that if there is such a thing as a cinematic masterpiece it will be so because – like *Wild Strawberries* and *La règle du jeu* – it is in the first place a dramatic masterpiece.

It seems odd to say that photography is not a mode of representation. For a photograph has in common with a painting the property by which the painting represents the world, the property of sharing, in some sense, the appearance of its subject. Indeed, it is sometimes thought that since a photograph more effectively shares the appearance of its subject than a typical painting, photography is a better mode of representation. Photography might even be thought to have *replaced* painting as a mode of visual representation. Painters have felt that if the aim of painting is really to reproduce the appearances of things, then painting must give way to whatever means are available to reproduce an appearance more accurately. It has therefore been

said that painting aims to record the appearances of things only so as to capture the experience of observing them (the *impression*) and that the accurate copying of appearances will normally be at variance with this aim. Here we have the seeds of expressionism and the origin of the view (a view which not only is mistaken but which has also proved disastrous for the history of modern art) that painting is somehow purer when it is abstract and closer to its essence as an art.

Let us first dismiss the word 'representation'. Of course this word can be applied to photography. We wish to know whether there is some feature, suitably called representation, common to painting and photography. And we wish to know whether that feature has in each case a comparable aesthetic value, so that we can speak not only of representation but also of representational art. (There is an important feature – sound – in common to music and to fountains, but only the first of these is properly described as an *art* of sound.)

1

In order to understand what I mean by saying that photography is not a representational art, it is important to separate painting and photography as much as possible, so as to discuss not actual

Roger Scruton, "Photography and Representation," *The Aesthetic Understanding* (London: Methuen, 1983, reprinted 1998 by St Augustine's Press, South Ben, IN): 119–48 (from reprint). © 1983 by Roger Scruton. Reprinted with permission of Curtis Brown Ltd, London on behalf of Roger Scruton.

Roger Scruton

painting and actual photography but an ideal form of each, an ideal which represents the essential differences between them. Ideal photography differs from actual photography as indeed ideal painting differs from actual painting. Actual photography is the result of the attempt by photographers to pollute the ideal of their craft with the aims and methods of painting.

By an 'ideal' I mean a logical ideal. The ideal of photography is not an ideal at which photography aims or ought to aim. On the contrary, it is a logical fiction, designed merely to capture what is distinctive in the photographic relation and in our interest in it. It will be clear from this discussion that there need be no such thing as an ideal photograph in my sense, and the reader should not be deterred if I begin by describing photography in terms that seem to be exaggerated or false.

The ideal painting stands in a certain 'intentional' relation to a subject.[2] In other words, if a painting represents a subject, it does not follow that the subject exists nor, if it does exist, that the painting represents the subject as it is. Moreover, if x is a painting of a man, it does not follow that there is some *particular* man of which x is the painting. Furthermore, the painting stands in this intentional relation to its subject because of a representational act, the artist's act, and in characterizing the relation between a painting and its subject we are also describing the artist's intention. The successful realization of that intention lies in the creation of an appearance, an appearance which in some way leads the spectator to recognize the subject.

The ideal photograph also stands in a certain relation to a subject. A photograph is a photograph *of* something. But the relation is here causal and not intentional.[3] In other words, if a photograph is a photograph of a subject, it follows that the subject exists, and if x is a photograph of a man, there is a particular man of whom x is the photograph. It also follows, though for different reasons, that the subject is, roughly, as it appears in the photograph. In characterizing the relation between the ideal photograph and its subject, one is characterizing not an intention but a causal process, and while there is, as a rule, an intentional act involved, this is not an essential part of the photographic relation. The ideal photograph also yields an appearance, but the appearance is not interesting as the realization of an intention but rather as a record of how an actual object looked.

Since the end point of the two processes is, or can be, so similar, it is tempting to think that the

intentionality of the one relation and the causality of the other are quite irrelevant to the standing of the finished product. In both cases, it seems, the important part of representation lies in the fact that the spectator can see the subject *in* the picture. The appreciation of photographs and the appreciation of paintings both involve the exercise of the capacity to 'see as', in the quite special sense in which one may see x as y without believing or being tempted to believe that x *is* y.

2

Now, it would be a simple matter to define 'representation' so that 'x represents y' is true only if x expresses a thought about y, or if x is designed to remind one of y, or whatever, in which case a relation that was *merely* causal (a relation that was not characterized in terms of any thought, intention, or other mental act) would never be sufficient for representation. We need to be clear, however, why we should wish to define representation in one way rather than in another. What hangs on the decision? In particular, why should it matter that the relation between a painting and its subject is an intentional relation while the photographic relation is merely causal? I shall therefore begin by considering our experience of painting and the effect on that experience of the intentionality of the relation between a painting and its subject.

When I appreciate a painting as a representation, I see it as what it represents, but I do not take it for what it represents. Nor do I necessarily believe that what is represented in the painting exists nor, if it does exist, that it has the appearance of the object that I see *in* the painting. Suppose that a certain painting represents a warrior. I may in fact see it not as a warrior but as a god. Here three 'objects' of interest may be distinguished:

1 The intentional object of sight: a god (defined by my experience).
2 The represented object: a warrior (defined, to put it rather crudely, by the painter's intention).[4]
3 The material object of sight: the painting.[5]

The distinction between 1 and 2 is not as clear-cut as it might seem: it would become so only if we could separate the 'pure appearance' of the painting from the sense of intention with which it is endowed. We cannot do this, not only because we can never separate our experience of human activity from our understanding of intention but also because in the case of a picture we are dealing with an object that is manifestly the expression of thought. Hence we will look for clues as to how the painting is intended to be seen and – such being the nature of 'seeing as' – our sense of what is intended will determine our experience of what is there.

The 'inference' view of perception, the view that there are certain things that we *basically* see (sense-data, etc) from which we then *infer* the existence of other things, is wrong both as a matter of philosophical psychology, since there is no criterion for distinguishing datum and inference, and as a matter of epistemology, since it is only if we sometimes have knowledge of the 'inferred' entities that we can have knowledge of the experience.[6] The point applies also to intention: we do not see the gestures and movements of another person and then infer from them the existence of intentions; rather, we see the gestures as intentional, and that is the correct description of what we see. But of course we cannot choose to see just what we will as a manifestation of intention. Our ability to see intention depends on our ability to interpret an activity as characteristically human, and here, in the case of representational art, it involves our understanding the dimensions and conventions of the medium. Art manifests the 'common knowledge' of a culture;[7] as E. H. Gombrich has made clear, to understand art is to be familiar with the constraints imposed by the medium and to be able to separate that which is due to the medium from that which is due to the man. Such facts lead us to speak of understanding or misunderstanding representational painting.

Although there is not space to discuss fully the concept of 'understanding' that is involved here, it is worth mentioning the following point: to understand a painting involves understanding thoughts. These thoughts are, in a sense, communicated by the painting. They underlie the painter's intention, and at the same time they inform our way of seeing the canvas. Such thoughts determine the perception of the one who sees with understanding, and it is at least partly in terms of our apprehension of thoughts that we must describe what we see in the picture. We see not only a man on a horse but a man of a certain character and bearing. And *what* we see is determined not by independent properties of the subject but by our understanding of the painting. It is the way the eyes are painted that gives that sense of authority, the particular lie of the arm that reveals the arrogant character, and so on. In other words, properties of the medium influence not only what is seen in the picture but also the way it is seen. Moreover, they present to us a vision that we attribute not to ourselves but to another person; we think of ourselves as sharing in the vision of the artist, and the omnipresence of intention changes our experience from something private into something shared. The picture presents us not merely with the perception of a man but with a thought about him, a thought embodied in perceptual form.[8] And here, just as in the case of language, thought has that character of objectivity and publicity upon which Frege commented.[9] It is precisely when we have the communication of thoughts about a subject that the concept of representation becomes applicable; and therefore literature and painting are representational in the same sense.

3

The ideal painting has no particular need for an identity of appearance with its subject. In order to present a visual account of the Duke of Wellington, it is not necessary for an artist to strive to present an exact copy of the Duke's appearance.[10] Indeed, it is tempting here to dispense with the notion of appearance altogether, to construe the painting as a conventional or even quasi-linguistic act which stands in a semantic relation – a relation of reference – to its subject, and which presents a visual appearance only as a means of fulfilling a referential function. Such a view would explain, perhaps better than all rival theories of representation, the role of intention in our understanding of art.[11]

I do not know how far those philosophers influenced by Gombrich's arguments – arguments emphasizing the place of convention in our understanding of visual art – would wish to take the analogy with language. I do not know, for example, whether a convention according to which colours were to be represented by their complements – a red object by a patch of green, a yellow object by a patch of blue – would be conceivable for such philosophers, conceivable, that is, as a mode of pictorial representation. It is undeniable, however, that such a painting would convey to someone who understood the convention as much information

Roger Scruton

about its subject as another painting in which the colours copy the original. More bizarre conventions could also be imagined: a painting could be constructed entirely out of dashes and circles, arranged according to the grammar of a visual code. Given the right conventions, such a painting would count, according to the reference theory, as an extremely faithful representation of its subject. It would be read as a kind of scrambled message which had to be decoded in order to permit an understanding of what it says.

However, we cannot treat the visual connection between a painting and its subject as an entirely accidental matter, accidental, that is, to any process of representation that the painting may display. For we cannot deny that representational painting interests us primarily because of the visual connection with its subject. We are interested in the visual relation between painting and subject because it is by means of this relation that the painting represents. The artist presents us with a way of seeing (and not just any way of thinking of) his subject. (Hence the revolutionary character of such painters as Caravaggio and de la Tour.) It is this visual relation which seems to require elucidation. We cannot explain pictorial representation independently of the visual aspect of paintings and still expect our explanation to cast light upon the problem of the visual relation between a picture and its subject-matter. And yet it is that relation which is understood by the appreciative spectator.

That objection is of course not conclusive. It also seems to assume that a semantic theory of art (a theory which sees representation in terms of reference) must necessarily also be a linguistic theory. Surely there could be relations of reference that do not reflect the conventions of language, even relations that need to be understood in essentially visual terms. Let us, then, consider what such a conception of reference might be like.

It is no accident that language has a grammar. The existence of grammar is a necessary part of language and part of the all-important connection between language and truth. But there is a further significance in grammar, at least as grammar is now conceived. For the contemporary logician, grammar is primarily a 'generative' function, a means of building complex sentences from the finite number of linguistic parts. Taken in conjunction with a theory of interpretation, a proper grammar will explain how speakers of a language understand an

indefinite number of sentences on the basis of understanding only a finite number of words.[12] In this way we can show how the truth or falsehood of a sentence depends upon the reference of its parts, and the concept of reference in language becomes inextricably bound up with the idea that from the references of words we may derive the truth conditions of sentences. This 'generative connection' between reference and truth is part of the intuitive understanding of reference which is common to all speakers of a language.

It is here, I think, that we find a striking difference between language and painting. While there may be repertoires and conventions in painting, there is nothing approaching grammar as we understand it. For one thing, the requirement of finitude is not obviously met. It is clearly true that we understand the representational meaning of, say, a Carpaccio through understanding the representational meaning of its parts. But the parts themselves are understood in *precisely the same way*; that is, they too have parts, each of which is potentially divisible into significant components, and so on ad infinitum. Moreover, there seems to be no way in which we can divide the painting into grammatically significant parts – no way in which we can provide a syntax which isolates those parts of the painting that have a particular semantic role. For in advance of seeing the painting, we have no rule which will decide the point, and thus the idea of syntactic or semantic rules becomes inapplicable. The means whereby we understand the total representation are identical with the means whereby we understand the parts. Understanding is not secured either by rules or by conventions but seems to be, on the contrary, a natural function of the normal eye. As we see the meaning of the painting, so do we see the meaning of its parts. This contrasts sharply with the case of reference in language, where we *construct* the meaning of the sentence from the reference of its parts, and where the parts themselves have reference in a way that is ultimately conventional.

There seems to be no justification, then, for thinking of representation in terms of reference. We could, however, insist that the relation of a painting to its subject is one of reference only by removing from 'reference' that feature which leads us to think that an account of reference is also an account of understanding. To speak of the connection between a word and a thing as one of reference is to show how we understand the word, for it is to show how the truth conditions of sentences containing the word are determined. If we speak of reference in describing paintings, therefore, we should not think that we thereby cast any light on the *understanding* of representation. What representation is, how we understand it, and how it affects us – those questions seem to remain as obscure as ever. The only thing that remains to support the invocation of reference is the fact that paintings may be true or false. It is that fact which we must now consider.

4

The fact that a painting may be true or false plays a vital role in visual appreciation. We could not explain realism, for example, either in painting or in literature, unless we invoked the concept of truth. Again we must emphasize information (and therefore the concept of reference) in our understanding of the painter's art; or at least we are obliged to find some feature of the painting that can be substituted for reference and which will show how the connection with truth is established.

Such a feature, as a matter of fact, has already been described: we may describe realism in terms of what we see *in* the painting. We therefore analyse truth not in terms of a relation between painting and the world but in terms of a relation between what we see in the painting and the world. Goya's portrait of the Duke of Wellington is realistic because the figure we see in the painting resembles the Duke of Wellington.[13] The truth of the painting amounts to the truth of the viewer's perception; in other words, the 'intentional object of sight' corresponds to the nature of the subject. Those thoughts which animate our perception when we see the realistic painting with understanding are true thoughts.[14] Truth is not a property of the painting in the direct way in which it is the property of a sentence, and the possibility of predicating the truth of a painting does not open the way to a semantic theory of art any more than it opens the way to a semantic theory of, for example, clouds, or of any other phenomenon in which aspects may be seen.

Although distinctions may be made between true and false pictures, an aesthetic appreciation remains in one sense indifferent to the truth of its object. A person who has an aesthetic interest in the *Odyssey* is not concerned with the literal truth of the narrative. Certainly it is important to him that the *Odyssey* be lifelike, but the existence of Odysseus and the reality of the scenes described are matters of aesthetic indifference. Indeed, it is characteristic of aesthetic interest that most of its objects in representation are imaginary. For unless it were possible to represent imaginary things, representation could hardly be very important to us. It is important because it enables the presentation of scenes and characters toward which we have only contemplative attitudes: scenes and characters which, being unreal, allow our practical natures to remain unengaged.

If the concept of representation is to be of aesthetic importance, it must be possible to describe an aesthetic interest in representation. Only if there is such a thing as aesthetic interest which has representation as its object can there be representational art (as opposed to art that happens to be representational). It is commonly said that an aesthetic interest in something is an interest in it for its own sake: the object is not treated as a surrogate for another; it is *itself* the principal object of attention. It follows that an aesthetic interest in the representational properties of a picture must also involve a kind of interest in the picture and not merely in the thing represented.[15]

Now, *one* difference between an aesthetic interest in a picture, and an interest in the picture as a surrogate for its subject, lies in the kind of reason that might be given for the interest. (And to give the reasons for an interest is to give an account of its intentional object and therefore of the interest itself.) If I ask someone why he is looking at a picture, there are several kinds of reply that he might give. In one case his reasons will be reasons for an interest only in the things depicted: they will describe properties of the subject which make it interesting. Here the interest in the picture is derivative: it lies in the fact that the picture reveals properties of its subject. The picture is being treated as a means of access to the subject, and it is therefore dispensable to the extent that there is a better means to hand (say, the subject itself). With that case one may contrast two others. First, there is the case where the person's reasons refer only to properties of the picture – to pictorial properties, such as colour, shape, and line – and do not mention the subject. For such a person the picture has interest as an abstract composition, and its representational nature is wholly irrelevant to him. Second, there is the case where the reasons for the interest are reasons for an interest in the *picture* (in the way it looks) even though they make essential reference to the subject and can be understood as reasons only by someone who understands the reference to the subject. For example, the observer may refer to a particular gesture of a certain figure, and a particular way of painting that gesture, as revelatory of the subject's character (for example, the barmaid's hands on the counter in Manet's *Bar aux Folies-Bergères*). Clearly, that is a reason not only for an interest in the subject but also (and primarily) for an interest in the picture, since it gives a reason for an interest in something which can be understood only by looking at the picture. Such an interest leads naturally to another, to an interest in the use of the medium – in the way the painting presents its subject and therefore in the way in which the subject is seen by the painter. Here it could not be said that the painting is being treated as a surrogate for its subject: it is *itself* the object of interest and irreplaceable by the thing depicted. The interest is not in representation for the sake of its subject but in representation for its own sake. And it is such an interest that forms the core of the aesthetic experience of pictorial art, and which – if analysed more fully – would explain not only the value of that experience but also the nature and value of the art which is its object. We see at once that such an interest is not, and cannot be, an interest in the literal truth of the picture.

5

If I were to describe, then, *what I see* in a picture, I would be bound not merely to describe the visual properties of the subject but also to provide an interpretation of the subject, a way of seeing it. The description under which the subject is seen is given by the total thought in terms of which I understand the picture. In the case of portraiture, this interpretive thought need not be a thought about the momentary appearance of the subject: it need not be the thought 'He looked like that'. The thought may relate to the subject not as he appeared at any one moment but as he was or, rather, as the artist saw him to be. The appearance may be presented only because it embodies the reality, in which case it will be the reality that is understood (or misunderstood) by the spectator.

One of the most important differences between photography and portraiture as traditionally practised lies in the relation of each to time. It is characteristic of photography that, being under-

stood in terms of a causal relation to its subject, it is thought of as revealing something momentary about its subject – how the subject looked at a particular moment. And that sense of the moment is seldom lost in photography, for reasons that will shortly be apparent. Portrait painting, however, aims to capture the sense of time and to represent its subject as extended in time, even in the process of displaying a particular moment of its existence. Portraiture is not an art of the momentary, and its aim is not merely to capture fleeting appearances. The aim of painting is to give insight, and the creation of an appearance is important mainly as the expression of thought. While a causal relation is a relation between events, there is no such narrow restriction on the subject-matter of a thought. This perhaps partially explains the frequently made comment that the true art of portraiture died with the advent of photography and that representational art, insofar as it still pursues an ideal of realism, is unable to capture, as the realist ought to capture, the sense of the passage of time.[16]

Of course a photographer can aim to capture that fleeting appearance which gives the most reliable indication of his subject's character. He may attempt to find in the momentary some *sign* of what is permanent. But there is a great difference between an image which is a sign of something permanent and an image which is an expression of it. To express the permanent is to give voice to a thought about its nature. To give a sign of the permanent is to create something from which its properties may be inferred. Someone may remain silent when asked to defend his friend, and from that silence I infer his friend's guilt. Yet the person has certainly not expressed the thought that his friend is guilty. Similarly a photograph may give signs of what is permanent despite the fact that it is incapable of expressing it.

6

The ideal photograph, as I mentioned earlier, stands in a causal relation to its subject and 'represents' its subject by reproducing its appearance. In understanding something as an ideal photograph, we understand it as exemplifying this causal process, a process which originates in the subject 'represented' and which has as its end point the production of a copy of an appearance. By a 'copy' of an appearance I mean an object such that what is seen in it by someone with normal eyes and understanding (the intentional object of sight) resembles as nearly as possible what is seen when such a person observes the subject itself from a certain angle at a certain point in its history. A person studying an ideal photograph is given a very good idea of *how something looked*. The result is that, from studying a photograph he may come to know how something looked in the way that he might know it if he had actually seen it.

With an ideal photograph it is neither necessary nor even possible that the photographer's intention should enter as a serious factor in determining how the picture is seen. It is recognized at once for what it is – not as an interpretation of reality but as a presentation of how something looked. In some sense, looking at a photograph is a substitute for looking at the thing itself. Consider, for example, the most 'realistic' of all photographic media, the television. It seems scarcely more contentious to say that I saw someone on the television – that is, that in watching the television I saw *him* – than to say that I saw him in a mirror. Television is like a mirror: it does not so much destroy as embellish that elaborate causal chain which is the natural process of visual perception.

Of course it is not necessary to define the subject of a photograph in terms of this causal process, for the subject could be identified in some other way. But the fact remains that when we say that *x* is a photograph of *y* we *are* referring to this causal relation, and it is in terms of the causal relation that the subject of a photograph is normally understood. Let us at least say that the subject is so defined for my logical ideal of photography: that premise is all that my argument requires.

It follows, first, that the subject of the ideal photograph must exist; secondly, that it must appear roughly as it appears in the photograph; and thirdly, that its appearance in the photograph is its appearance at a particular moment of its existence.

The first of those features is an immediate consequence of the fact that the relation between a photograph and its subject is a causal relation. If *a* is the cause of *b*, then the existence of *b* is sufficient for the existence of *a*. The photograph lacks that quality of 'intentional inexistence' which is characteristic of painting. The ideal photograph, therefore, is incapable of representing anything unreal; if a photograph is a photograph of a man, then there is some particular man of whom it is a photograph.

Of course I may take a photograph of a draped nude and call it *Venus*, but insofar as this can be understood as an exercise in fiction, it should not be thought of as a photographic representation of Venus but rather as the photograph of a representation of Venus. In other words, the process of fictional representation occurs not in the photograph but in the subject: it is the *subject* which represents Venus; the photograph does no more than disseminate its visual character to other eyes. This is not to say that the model is (unknown to herself) acting Venus. It is not she who is representing Venus but the photographer, who uses her in his representation. But the representational act, the act which embodies the representational thought, is completed before the photograph is ever taken. As we shall see, this fictional incompetence of photography is of great importance in our understanding of the cinema; but it also severely limits the aesthetic significance of 'representation' in photography. As we saw earlier, representation in art has a special significance precisely because of the possibility that we can understand it – in the sense of understanding its content – while being indifferent to, or unconcerned with, its literal truth. That is why fictional representation is not merely an important form of representational art but in fact the primary form of it, the form through which the aesthetic understanding finds its principal mode of expression.

One may wish to argue that my example is a special one, that there are other ways of creating fictional representations which are essentially photographic. In other words, it is not necessary for the photographer to create an independent representation in order for his photograph to be fictional. Suppose he were to take a photograph of a drunken tramp and label it *Silenus*. Would that not be a fictional photograph, comparable, indeed, to a painting of Silenus in which a drunken tramp was used as a model?

This example, which I owe to Richard Wollheim, is an interesting one, but it does not, I think, establish what it claims. Consider a parallel case: finding a drunken tramp in the street I point to him and say 'Silenus'. It is arguable that my gesture makes the tramp into a representation; but if it does, it is because I am inviting you to think of him in that way. I have expressed a representational thought: imagine this person as Silenus. And I have completed the thought by an act of ostension toward its dozing subject. The act of ostension might on some other occasion be accomplished by a camera (or a frame, or a mirror, or any other device which isolates what it shows).

The camera, then, is being used not to represent something but to point to it. The subject, once located, plays its own special part in an independent process of representation. The camera is not essential to that process: a gesturing finger would have served just as well. If the example shows that photographs can be representations, then it shows the same of fingers. To accept that conclusion is to fail to distinguish between what is accidental and what is essential in the expression of a representational thought. It is to open the way toward the theory that everything which plays a part in the expression of thought is itself a representation. Such a view does not account for the aesthetic significance of representations. It also, however, and far more seriously, implies that there is no distinction between representational and nonrepresentational art. The concept of representation that I am assuming makes such a distinction, and it makes it for very good reasons. I am not tempted by such dubious examples to abandon it. One might put the point by saying that a painting, like a sentence, is a *complete* expression of the thought which it contains. Painting is a sufficient vehicle of representational thought, and there may be no better way of expressing what a painting says. That is why representation can be thought of as an intrinsic property of a painting and not just as a property of some process of which the painting forms a part.

Consider also the second feature mentioned above: the subject of an ideal photograph must appear roughly as it appears in the photograph. By its very nature, photography can 'represent' only through resemblance. It is only because the photograph acts as a visual reminder of its subject that we are tempted to say that it represents its subject. If it were not for this resemblance, it would be impossible to see from the photograph how the subject appeared, except by means of scientific knowledge that would be irrelevant to any interest in the visual aspect of the photograph. Contrast here the case of an electron microscope, which punches out on a ticker tape a codified indication of a crystal's atomic structure. Is that a representation of the atomic structure? If it is, then why not say that any causal relation which enables us to infer the nature of the cause from the properties of its effect provides us with a representation of the cause in the effect? Such a concept of representation would be uninteresting indeed. It is impossible, therefore, that the ideal photograph should represent an object except by showing how it appeared at a certain

moment in its history and still *represent* it in the way ideal photography represents anything. How indeed could we make sense of an ideal photograph representing its subject *as* other than it appeared? We could do so only if we could also say that a photograph sometimes represents its subject as it appears; that is, if we could say that representation here is 'representation as'. But consider this sentence: x is an ideal photograph of y as z. It seems that we have no means of filling out the description 'z', no means, that is, of filling it out by reference only to the photographic process and not, say, to some independent act of representation that precedes or follows it. One might say that the medium in photography has lost all importance: it can present us with what we see, but it cannot tell us how to see it.

We *must* be aware of the three features mentioned above if we are to appreciate the characteristic effects of photography. In looking at an ideal photograph, we know that we are seeing something which actually occurred and seeing it as it appeared. Typically, therefore, our attitude toward photography will be one of curiosity, not curiosity about the photograph but rather about its subject. The photograph addresses itself to our desire for knowledge of the world, knowledge of how things look or seem. The photograph is a means to the end of seeing its subject; in painting, on the other hand, the subject is the means to the end of its own representation. The photograph is transparent to its subject, and if it holds our interest it does so because it acts as a surrogate for the thing which it shows. Thus if one finds a photograph beautiful, it is because one finds something beautiful in its subject. A painting may be beautiful, on the other hand, even when it represents an ugly thing.

7

Someone might accept the general difference I have indicated between an aesthetic interest and an attitude of curiosity, and accept too the implication that something is a representation only if it is capable of carrying a reference to its subject without merely standing as a surrogate for it. He still might argue, however, that it is possible to be interested in a photograph *as* a photograph and find it, and not just its subject, beautiful.

But what is it to be interested in a photograph as a photograph? Of course one might have a purely abstract aesthetic interest in a photograph as a construction of lines and shapes (as one is intended to appreciate Man Ray's Rayogrammes, for example). One can have a purely abstract aesthetic interest in anything; photography is only a representational art if our interest in a photograph as a photographic 'representation' is a type of aesthetic interest.

Let us return to the previous discussion of representation in painting. It appears that there is a prima facie contradiction between saying that I am interested in a thing for its own sake and saying that I am interested in it as a representation of something else. In attempting to reconcile these two interests, it is necessary first to restrict the place of truth in aesthetic interest. Truth is aesthetically relevant only insofar as it may be construed as truth to the situation presented rather than 'truth to the facts'. From the point of view of aesthetic interest, it is always irrelevant that there should be a particular object which is the object represented or, if there is such an object, that it should exist as portrayed. That is not to say, of course, that an aesthetic interest does not require things to be in general roughly as they are shown; but that is another matter.

As I have already said, this conflicts with the typical way in which we are interested in photographs. Knowing what we know about photographs, it is at least natural that we should be interested in them both because they are true to the facts and because they tell us useful things about their subject-matter. It seems, therefore, that the emotional or 'aesthetic' qualities of a photograph tend to derive directly from the qualities of what it 'represents'; if the photograph is sad, it is usually because its subject is sad; if the photograph is touching, it is because its subject is touching, and so on. It is worth reflecting on why there could not be a photograph of a martyrdom that was other than horrifying. One's curiosity here would be no different from one's curiosity in the act itself. Hence it would be as difficult (and perhaps also as corrupt) to have an aesthetic interest in the photograph as it would be in the real situation. By contrast, a painting of a martyrdom may be serene, as is Mantegna's great *Crucifixion* in the Louvre. The painting has emotional qualities in defiance of the qualities of its subject. In the case of a photograph – say of the victim of some accident – one's attitude is determined by the knowledge that this is how things are. One's attitude is made practical by the knowledge of the causal relation between photograph and object. This is not to deny that one might be interested in a photograph for its own sake and at the same time maintain a proper distance from its subject, even when it depicts a scene of agony or death. But the real question is, Can we have such an interest in a photograph without having the same interest in its subject? Can I have an aesthetic interest in the photograph of a dying soldier which is not also an aesthetic interest in the soldier's death? Or, rather, can I maintain that separation of interests and still be interested in the 'representational' aspect of the photograph? If we are distanced from the photograph only because we are distanced from its subject, then the important distinction that I wish to emphasize, between interest in the representation and interest in the subject, has still not been made. It seems necessary to show that photography *can* – by itself – create that sharp separation of interests which is everywhere apparent in serious painting. Consider too the photographs of old London. How is it possible to detach one's interest in their beauty from an interest in the beauty of London as it was? Regret is here the appropriate reaction to the photograph (as it is not – or at least not normally – an appropriate reaction to a Canaletto). 'That is how it looked!' is the central index of one's emotion.

Consider, then, the reasons that may be given in answer to the question, 'Why are you looking at that?' With a photograph, one mentions the features of the subject; with a painting, one mentions only the observable aspect captured in the picture. This essentially is what distinguishes an interest in a representation as a surrogate from an interest in a representation for its own sake. Suppose now that someone wishes to argue that it is *not* inevitable that we treat photographs, even ideal photographs, as I have described. Let us see what the consequences of such a position might be.

8

Imagine that we treat photographs as representations in just the same way that we treat paintings, so that their representational natures are themselves the objects of an aesthetic interest. What are the consequences if we study photography in such a way that it does not matter whether its subject actually existed or actually looked like the thing we see in the picture? Here we are interested not in the subject but in its manner of presentation. If there *can* be such an interest in a photograph, it suggests that a photograph may sometimes be the expression of a representational thought and not merely a simulacrum of its subject.

An interest in an object for its own sake, in the object as a whole, must encompass an interest in detail. For if there is nothing *for* which one contemplates an object, as has frequently been argued, there is no way of determining in advance of looking at it which features are, and which are not, relevant to one's interest.[17] It is for this reason that we cannot rest satisfied with nature but must have works of art as the objects of aesthetic judgment. Art provides a medium transparent to human intention, a medium for which the question, Why? can be asked of every observable feature, even if it may sometimes prove impossible to answer. Art is an expression of precisely the same rational impulses that find an outlet in aesthetic interest; it is therefore the only object which satisfies that interest completely.

The photographer, then, who aims for an aesthetically significant representation must also aim to control detail: 'detail' being here understood in the wide sense of 'any observable fact or feature'. But here lies a fresh difficulty. The causal process of which the photographer is a victim puts almost every detail outside of his control. Even if he does, say, intentionally arrange each fold of his subject's dress and meticulously construct, as studio photographers once used to do, the appropriate scenario, that would still hardly be relevant, since there seem to be few ways in which such intentions can be revealed in the photograph. For one thing, we lack all except the grossest features of style in photography; and yet it is style that persuades us that the question, Why this and not that? admits such fruitful exploration in the case of painting. Style enables us to answer that question by referring solely to aspects of the painting rather than to features which are aesthetically irrelevant, or in no way *manifest* in what is seen.[18] The search for meaning in a photograph is therefore curtailed or thwarted: there is no point in an interest in detail since there is nothing that detail can show. Detail, like the photograph itself, is transparent to its subject. If the photograph is interesting, it is only because what it portrays is interesting, and not because of the manner in which the portrayal is effected.

Let us assume, however, that the photographer could intentionally exert over his image just the kind of control that is exercised in the other representational arts. The question is, How far can this control be extended? Certainly there will

be an infinite number of things that lie outside his control. Dust on a sleeve, freckles on a face, wrinkles on a hand: such minutiae will always depend initially upon the prior situation of the subject. When the photographer sees the photographic plate, he may still wish to assert his control, choosing just this colour here, just that number of wrinkles or that texture of skin. He can proceed to paint things out or in, to touch up, alter, or *pasticher* as he pleases. But of course he has now become a painter, precisely through taking representation seriously. The photograph has been reduced to a kind of frame around which he paints, a frame that imposes upon him largely unnecessary constraints.[19]

In other words, when the photographer strives towards representational art, he inevitably seems to move away from that ideal of photography which I have been describing toward the ideal of painting. This can be seen most clearly if we consider exactly what has to be the case if photography is to be a wholly representational art – if it is to manifest all those aspects of representation that distinguish it from mere copying and which endow it with its unique aesthetic appeal. No one could deny that from its origins photography has set itself artistic ideals and attempted to establish itself as a representational art. The culmination of that process – which can be seen in such photographs as Henry Peach Robinson's 'Autumn' – is to be found in the techniques of photo-montage used by the surrealists and futurists (and in particular, by such artists as László Moholy-Nagy and Hannah Höch). Here our interest in the result can be entirely indifferent to the existence and nature of the original subject. But that is precisely because the photographic figures have been so cut up and rearranged in the final product that it could not be said in any normal sense to be a *photograph* of its subject. Suppose that I were to take figures from a photograph of, say, Jane, Philip, and Paul, and, having cut them out, I were to arrange them in a montage, touching them up and adjusting them until the final result is to my mind satisfactory. It could very well be said that the final result represents, say, a lovers' quarrel; but it is not a photograph of one. It represents a quarrel because it stands in precisely the same intentional relation to a quarrel that a painting might have exhibited. Indeed, it is, to all intents and purposes, a painting, except that it happens to have employed photographic techniques in the derivation of its figures. Insofar as the figures can still be considered to be photographs, they are photographs of Jane, Philip, and Paul and not photographs of a lovers' quarrel. (Of course the fact of their *being* photographs might be aesthetically important. Some ironical comment, for example, may be intended in using figures cut from a medium of mass production.)

The history of the art of photography is the history of successive attempts to break the causal chain by which the photographer is imprisoned, to impose a human intention between subject and appearance, so that the subject can be both defined by that intention and seen in terms of it.[20] It is the history of an attempt to turn a mere simulacrum into the expression of a representational thought, an attempt to discover through techniques (from the combination print to the soft-focus lens) what was in fact already known.[21] Occasionally, it is true, photographers have attempted to create entirely fictional scenes through photography and have arranged their models and surroundings as one might on the stage, in order to produce a narrative scene with a representational meaning. But, as I have argued, the resulting photograph would not be a representation. The process of representation was effected even before the photograph was taken. A photograph of a representation is no more a representation than a picture of a man is a man.

9

It might be felt that I have begged the question in allowing only one way in which photography may acquire representational meaning, a way which inevitably leads photography to subject itself to the aims of painting. One may argue that a photographer does not choose his subject at random, nor is he indifferent to the point of view from which he photographs it or to the composition in which it is set. The act of photography may be just as circumscribed by aesthetic intentions as the act of painting. A photograph will be designed to show its subject in a particular light and from a particular point of view, and by so doing it may reveal things about it that we do not normally observe and, perhaps, that we might not have observed but for the photograph. Such an enterprise leads to effects which are wholly proper to the art of photography, which therefore has its own peculiar way of showing the world. Why is that not enough to give to photography the status of a representational art?

I do not think that such an objection need cause me to revise my argument. For exactly the same might be said of a mirror. When I see someone in a mirror I see *him*, not his representation. This remains so even if the mirror is a distorting mirror and even if the mirror is placed where it is intentionally. The intention might even be similar to the intention in photography: to give a unique and remarkable view of an object, a view which reveals a 'truth' about it that might otherwise have gone unobserved. One could even imagine an art of mirrors, an art which involves holding a mirror aloft in such a way that what is seen in the mirror is rendered by that process interesting or beautiful.

This art of mirrors may, like the art of photography, sometimes involve representation. It may, for example, involve a representation of Venus or of Silenus in the manner of the two types of 'fictional' photographs considered earlier. But representation will not be a property of the *mirror*. It is impossible that I could, simply by holding a mirror before someone, make him into a representation of himself. For after all, whether I look at him or at the mirror, in either case it is *him* that I see. If the mirror is to become the expression of a representational thought, it too must be denatured; like the photomontage, it must be freed from the causal chain which links it to its subject. One can perhaps begin to see the truth in Oliver Wendell Holmes's description of the daguerreotype as a 'mirror with a memory'.[22] It was just such a mirror that led to the downfall of Lord Lambton.

It does not matter, therefore, how many aesthetic intentions underlie the act of photography. It does not matter that the subject, its environment, activity, or light are all consciously arranged. The real question is, What has to be done to make the resulting image into a representation? There are images which are representations (paintings) and images which are not (mirrors). To which class does the photograph belong? I have argued that it naturally belongs to the latter class. Photography can be *made* to belong to the former class by being made into the principal vehicle of the representational thought. But one must then so interfere with the relation between the photograph and its subject that it ceases to be a *photograph* of its subject. Is that not enough to show that it is not just my ideal of photography which fails to be a mode of representation, but also that representation can never be achieved through photography alone?

A final comparison: I mark out a certain spot from which a particular view of a street may be obtained. I then place a frame before that spot. I move the frame so that, from the chosen spot, only certain parts of the street are visible, others are cut off. I do this with all the skill available to me, so that what is seen in the frame is as pleasing as it might be: the buildings within the frame seem to harmonize, the ugly tower that dominates the street is cut off from view, the centre of the composition is the little lane between two classical façades which might otherwise have gone unnoticed, and so on. There I have described an activity which is as circumscribed by aesthetic intentions as anything within the experience of the normal photographer. But how could it be argued that what I see in the frame is not the street itself but a representation of it? The very suggestion is absurd.

10

Here one might object that representation is not, after all, an intrinsic property either of a painting or of a description. Representation is a relation; an object can be described as a representation only if one person uses it to represent something to another. On this view, there is no such thing as 'being a representation'; there is only 'having a representational use.' And if this were the case, my arguments would be in vain. Photographs are as much, and as little, representations as paintings, as gestures, as mirrors, as labels, and as anything else that can play its part in the process of communication.

The objection is more serious, and reflects a well-known dispute in the theory of meaning. Meaning, some say, is a property of a sentence; others, for instance, H. Paul Grice, argue that meaning is primarily a relation between utterance and speaker.[23] Now, even for Grice, there remains a distinction between utterances which are articulate and utterances which are not. Sentences are to be distinguished from nods of the head in that they participate in and exemplify a grammar, and through that grammar they can be understood independently of the context of their use. By being articulate, the sentence can stand alone as the principal expression of a thought. There arises a kind of interest in the sentence (and in its content) which is independent of any direct involvement in the act of communication. Meaning can be read *in* the sentence and need not be inferred from surrounding circumstances.

Similarly, painting, being fully articulate, can attract attention as the principal expression of a process of thought. It can be understood in isolation from the special circumstances of its creation, because each and every feature of a painting can be both the upshot of an intentional act and at the same time the creation of an intentional object. The interest in the intentional object becomes an interest in the thought which it conveys. A painter can fill his canvas with meaning in just the way that a writer may fill his prose. This is what makes painting and literature into representational arts: they are arts which can be appreciated as they are in themselves and at the same time understood in terms of a descriptive thought which they articulate.

In photography we may have the deliberate creation of an image. Moreover, I may use a photograph as a representation: I may use a photograph of Lenin as a representation of him, in the way that I might have used a clenched fist or a potato or a photograph of Hitler. The question is, What makes the image *itself* into the principal vehicle of representational thought? I wish to argue that an image can be deliberate without being properly articulate. The image becomes articulate when (a) the maker of the image can seriously address himself to the task of communicating thought through the image alone, and (b) when the spectator can see and understand the image in terms of the process of thought which it expresses. To satisfy (a) we require a painterly approach to detail; to satisfy (b) we must distract the spectator's attention from the causal relation which is the distinguishing feature of photography. Either way, the persistence of that relation – in other words, the persistence of the *photographic* image – can only hinder representation. It can contribute nothing to its achievement. This is perhaps what James Joyce meant when he wrote the following in his Paris notebooks of 1904:

> Question: Can a photograph be a work of art? Answer: A photograph is a disposition of sensible matter and may be so disposed for an aesthetic end, but it is not a human disposition of sensible matter. Therefore it is not a work of art.

If Joyce meant by 'work of art' what I mean by 'representation', then he was clearly getting at the same point. The property of representation, as I have characterized it, is the upshot of a complex pattern of intentional activity and the object of highly specialized responses. How can a photograph acquire that property? My answer is that it can do so only by changing in precisely those respects which distinguish photography from painting. For it is only if photography changes in those respects that the photographer can seriously address himself to the thoughts and responses of his spectators. It is only then, therefore, that the photograph becomes a proper *vehicle* of representational thought.

11

Photography is not representation; nor is it representation when used in the cinema. A film is a photograph of a dramatic representation, and whatever representational properties belong to it belong by virtue of the representation that is effected in the dramatic action, that is, by virtue of the words and activities of the actors in the film. *Ivan the Terrible* represents the life of Ivan, not because the camera was directed at *him*, but because it was directed at an actor who *played the part of* Ivan. Certainly the camera has its role in presenting the action, much as the apparatus of production has its role on the stage. It directs the audience's attention to this or that feature and creates, too, its own peculiar effects of atmosphere. Proper use of the camera may create an interest in situations that could not be portrayed on the stage. Hence photography permits the extension of dramatic representation into areas where previously it would not have been possible, just as music, which is not a representational art, enabled Wagner to create for the first time a theatrical representation of a cosmic theme.[24] (Consider, for example, the camera in Bergman's *Persona*, where it is used to create a dramatic situation between two characters, one of whom never speaks. Such mastery is perhaps rare, but it has existed as an ideal since the earliest days of cinema.) Nonetheless, the process of photography does not, because it cannot, *create* the representation. Thus documentary films are in no sense representations of their subject-matter. (Which is not to say that they cannot involve the realization of elaborate aesthetic ideas: it is hardly necessary to mention Leni Riefenstahl's film of the Berlin Olympics.) A cinematic record of an occurrence is not a representation of it, any more than a recording of a concert is a representation of its sound. As all must agree, representation in the cinema involves an *action*, in just the way that a

play involves an action. The action is understood when the audience realizes that the figure photographed is attempting to portray adventures, actions, and feelings which are not his own, and yet which are nevertheless the proper subject-matter of aesthetic interest. It follows that the fundamental constraints which the cinema must obey as an art form – those constraints which are integral to its very nature as a representational art – are dramatic ones, involving the representation of character and action. ('Dramatic' here does not mean 'theatrical', but is applied in the sense which Henry James gave to it when he spoke of the novel as a form of dramatic art.) To succeed as cinema, a film must have true characters, and it must be true to them; the director can no more sentimentalize with impunity than can the novelist or the playwright. The true source of the badness of most cinema lies, of course, in the fact that the gorgeous irrelevancies of photography obscure the sentimentality of the dramatic aim.

Photography, far from making dramatic representation more easy, in fact makes it more difficult. Indeed, the possibility of dramatic success in the cinema is a remote one, for which there are two reasons. The first, and somewhat shallow, reason is that the film director is photographing something which either is or purports to be a part of the actual world. It follows that he can only with the greatest difficulty convey to his audience an appropriate sense of detail. Typically the audience is given no criterion of relevance, no criterion which settles what must be attended to. Was the audience meant to notice the man on the street corner, the movement of the eyebrow, the colour of the macintosh, the make of the car? In every cinematographic image, countless such questions remain unanswered. There are various reasons for this. For one thing, a film is fixed with respect to all its details; although it is a dramatic representation, it cannot exist in more than one performance. Therefore features of interpretation cannot be separated from features of the action: there is no such distinction. It is only in understanding the representation as a whole that I come to see what I should be attending to. Furthermore, the cameraman operates under a permanent difficulty in making any visual comment on the action. The difficulty can be solved, but its solution is perforce crude in comparison with the simpler devices of the stage; crude because it must both create irrelevancies and at the same time persuade us to ignore them. (Consider, for example, the ritualized expressionism of *Der blaue Engel* or *The Cabinet of Doctor Caligari*. Even Fritz Lang's *Siegfried* contains reminiscences of this *commedia dell'arte* mannerism, whereby the actor attempts to divert the audience's attention from the infinite irrelevance of detail, toward the dramatic meaning of the whole. Of course more recent directors have emancipated themselves from the theatrical constraints of expressionism; as a result they have at least felt happy to ignore the problem, even if they could not solve it.)

In the theatre the situation is different. The necessary limitations of the stage and the conventions of stage performance, which derive from the fact that the play exists independently of its performance, provide a strong representational medium through which the dramatic action is filtered. Someone with a knowledge of the conventions will see at once what is relevant and what is not. Symbolism in the theatre is therefore clear and immediate, whereas on the screen it is too often vague, portentous, and psychologically remote. Consider, for example, *L'Eclisse*, where the camera, striving again and again to make a comment, succeeds only in inflating the importance of the material surroundings out of all proportion to the sentiments of the characters. The effect is to render the image all-engrossing, while at the same time impoverishing the psychology.

It is for this reason that what often passes for photographic comment in the cinema ought more properly to be described as photographic *effect*. The camera may create an atmosphere – it may be an instrument of expression – but it is unable to make any precise or cogent analysis of what it shows. Consider the techniques of montage, used to such effect by the Russians. Eisenstein argues that there is a precise parallel between the technique of montage and the sequential structure of verse.[25] For example, each image that Milton presents in the following passage corresponds to a precise and unambiguous shot:

> ... at last
> Farr in th'Horizon to the North appear'd
> From skirt to skirt a fierie Region, stretcht
> In battailous aspect, and neerer view
> Bristl'd with upright beams innumerable
> Of rigid Spears, and Helmets throng'd, and
>   Shields
> Various, with boastful Argument portraid,
> The banded Powers of *Satan* hasting on
> With furious expedition ...

(One may note the cinematographic device 'and neerer view' and the very Eisensteinian quality of the image that follows it.) The contention is that for each of Milton's images one may find a cinematic shot that somehow 'says the same thing'; the total montage would form a dramatic unity in precisely the same sense, and for the same reason, as Milton's lines. The director will be doing something analogous to the poet: he will be focusing attention on carefully chosen details with a view to creating a unified expression of the prevailing mood.

It should be noted, however, that each shot in the montage will also present infinitely many details that are *not* designed as objects of attention. The shot corresponding to 'Helmets throng'd' will capture that idea among others, but it will also say much more that is irrelevant. It will not be able to avoid showing the kind of helmet, for example, the material, size, and shape of it. By so concretizing the thought, the camera leaves nothing to the imagination. As a result the detail that really matters – the thronging of Satanic helmets – is in danger of being lost. It was for this reason that Eisenstein developed techniques of contrast and composition in order to control more effectively the attention of his audience. It is a testimony to his genius that the poetry of *Ivan the Terrible* has rarely been rediscovered by subsequent directors. Even in Eisenstein, however, comment comes primarily through drama rather than through image. The whole effort of photography lies in expression and effect. And interestingly enough the clearest examples of photographic comment in the cinema come when once again the causal relation between image and subject is replaced by an intentional one. Consider the following sequence from *The Battleship Potemkin*:

1 Title: 'And the rebel battleship answered the brutality of the tyrant with a shell upon the town.'
2 A slowly and deliberately turning gun-turret.
3 Title: 'Objective – the Odessa Theatre.'
4 Marble group at the top of the theatre building.
5 Title: 'On the general's headquarters.'
6 Shot from the gun.
7 Two very short shots of a marble figure of Cupid above the gates of the building.
8 A mighty explosion; the gates totter.
9 Three short shots: a stone lion asleep;
    a stone lion with open eyes;
    a rampant stone lion.
10 New explosion, shattering the gates.[26]

Here we have one of Eisenstein's most striking visual metaphors. A stone lion rises to its feet and roars. This amazing image (impossible, incidentally, outside the limitations of the silent screen) acts as a powerful comment on the impotence of imperial splendour precisely because it startles us into a recognition of the underlying thought. But we know that this cannot be a photograph of a stone lion roaring. It is, rather, the intentional juxtaposition of unconnected images; it is the intention that we see and which determines our understanding of the sequence. It is of course lamentable that such art should have subjected itself to the inane mythmaking revealed in the titles to this script; that does not alter the fact that, if there is art here, it is an art which is essentially photographic.

The second and deeper point I wish to mention is extremely difficult to express in terms that would be acceptable to the contemporary analytical philosopher. I shall try not to be too deterred by that. Photography, precisely because it does not represent but at best can only distort, remains inescapably wedded to the creation of illusions, to the creation of lifelike *semblances* of things in the world. Such an art, like the art of the waxworks, is an art that provides a ready gratification for fantasy, and in so doing defeats the aims of artistic expression. A dramatic art can be significant only if it is, at some level, realistic; but to be realistic it must first forbid expression to those habits of unseriousness and wish fulfilment that play such an important part in our lives. Unless it can do that, the greatest effects of drama – such as we observe in the tragedies of the Greeks, of Racine, and of Shakespeare – will be denied to it. Art is fundamentally serious; it cannot rest content with the gratification of fantasy, nor can it dwell on what fascinates us while avoiding altogether the question of its meaning. As Freud put it in another

context, art provides the path from fantasy back to reality. By creating a representation of something unreal, it persuades us to consider again those aspects of reality which, in the urgency of everyday existence, we have such strong motives for avoiding.[27] Convention in art, as Freud saw, is the great destroyer of fantasies. It prevents the ready *realization* of scenes that fascinate us, and substitutes for the creation of mere semblance the elaboration of reflective thought.

The cinema has been devoted from its outset to the creation of fantasies. It has created worlds so utterly like our own in their smallest details that we are lulled into an acceptance of their reality, and persuaded to overlook all that is banal, grotesque, or vulgar in the situations which they represent. The cinema has proved too persuasive at the level of mere realization and so has had little motive to explore the significance of its subject. It is entirely beguiling in its immediacy, so that even serious critics of literature can be duped into thinking that a film like *Sunset Boulevard* expresses an aesthetic idea, instead of simply preying on the stereotyped fantasies of its audience.

Moreover, the cinema, like the waxworks, provides us with a ready means of realizing situations which fascinate us. It can address itself to our fantasy directly, without depending upon any intermediate process of thought. This is surely what distinguishes the scenes of violence which are so popular in the cinema from the conventionalized death throes of the theatre. And surely it is this too which makes photography incapable of being an erotic art, in that it presents us with the object of lust rather than a symbol of it: it therefore gratifies the fantasy of desire long before it has succeeded in understanding or expressing the fact of it. The medium of photography, one might say, is inherently pornographic.

Notes

I have benefited greatly from discussions with Richard Wollheim, Mark Platts, John Casey, Peter Suschitzky, and Ruby Meager, as well as from the criticisms of Robert A. Sharpe and Rickie Dammann, my fellow symposiasts at a conference organized in Bristol by Stephan Körner, to whom I am grateful for the opportunity to reflect on the nature of photography.

1 See for example, the discussion in Allardyce Nicoll, *Film and Theatre* (London, 1936; New York, 1972).

2 See Franz Clemens Brentano, *Psychology from an Empirical Standpoint*, ed. Linda McAlister (London and New York, 1973); Roderick M. Chisholm, *Perceiving* (London and Ithaca, NY, 1957), chapter 11; and G. E. M. Anscombe, 'The Intentionality of Sensation', in R. J. Butler (ed.), *Analytical Philosophy*, Second Series (Oxford, 1965).

3 I think that in this area nonextensionality (intensionality) and intentionality should be sharply distinguished, so that the claim is not affected by any

argument to the effect that casual relations are non-extensional.

4 I pass over the problem here of selecting and describing the appropriate intention.

5 For the material/intentional distinction, I rely on Anscombe.

6 The most famous arguments for this conclusion occur in Kant's *Critique of Pure Reason* (in particular in the 'Transcendental Deduction') and in Wittgenstein's *Philosophical Investigations*, part I.

7 The importance of 'common knowledge', its complexity as a phenomenon and its natural co-existence with conventions has been recognized in the philosophy of language; see especially the interesting discussion in David K. Lewis, *Convention: A Philosophical Study* (Cambridge, Mass., 1969; Oxford, 1972).

8 I have discussed elsewhere what I mean by the 'embodiment' of thought in perception; see my *Art and Imagination*, chapters 7 and 8.

9 G. Frege, *Translation from the Philosophical Writings*, p. 79.

10 There is a problem here about 'identity of appearance' on which I touch again elsewhere.

11 Nelson Goodman, the most important exponent of a semantic theory of art, manages to reconcile his approach with a view of photographs as representational; see his *Languages of Art: An Approach to a Theory of Symbols* (Indianapolis, 1976), p. 9n.

12 I draw here on the now familiar arguments given by Donald Davidson in 'Truth and Meaning' (*Synthèse*, S.67; 17: 304–23), which originate with Frege and which were given full mathematical elaboration in Alfred Tarski's theory of truth.

13 That is, provided the painting is independently *of* the Duke of Wellington.

14 See n. 8, above.

15 Hence the tradition in philosophy, which begins with Kant, according to which representation constitutes a threat to the autonomy of art.

16 I am thinking of recent exercises in 'photographic' realism by such painters as Ken Danby and Alex Colville. More traditional styles of realism have also emerged in open opposition to both the clinical lines of the photographic school and the contentless images of abstract expressionism. Witness here the paintings of David Inshaw and Robert Lowe.

17 See for example, Stuart Hampshire, 'Logic and Appreciation', in William Elton (ed.), *Aesthetics and Language* (Oxford, 1954; New Jersey, 1970).

18 See Richard Wollheim's interesting discussion 'Style now', in Bernard William Smith (ed.), *Concerning Contemporary Art* (Oxford and New York, 1975).

19 This argument is hinted at in B. Croce, *Estetica*, 10th edn (Bari, 1958), p. 20.

20 See for example, Aaron Scharf, *Creative Photography* (London, 1975) and Rudolf Arnheim, *Film as Art* (California, 1957; London, 1958).

21 See especially Henry Peach Robinson, *The Elements of a Pictorial Photograph* (London, 1896).

22 Holmes, quoted in Beaumont Newhall, *History of Photography* (New York, 1964; London, 1972), p. 22.

23 'Meaning', *Philosophical Review*, LXVI (1957), pp. 377–88.

24 See my 'Representation in Music' *Philosophy JL 76*; 51: 273–82.

25 See Sergei Eisenstein, 'Word and Image', *The Film Sense* (London, 1943; New York, 1969).

26 Discussed by V. I. Pudovkin, *Writing*, trans. I. Montagu (London, 1954), p. 88.

27 See *The Standard Edition of the Complete Psychological Works of Sigmund Freud*, ed. James Strachey, 24 vols. (London, 1953–74; New York, 1976), IX, p. 153; XI, p. 50; XII, p. 224; XIII, pp. 187–8; XIV, pp. 375–7; XX, p. 64.

The Aesthetics of Photographic Transparency

Dominic McIver Lopes

When we look at photographs we literally see the objects that they are of. But seeing photographs as photographs engages aesthetic interests that are not engaged by seeing the objects that they are of. These claims appear incompatible. Sceptics about photography as an art form have endorsed the first claim in order to show that there is no photographic aesthetic. Proponents of photography as an art form have insisted that seeing things in photographs is quite unlike seeing things face-to-face. This paper argues that the claims are compatible. While seeing things in photographs is quite unlike seeing things face-to-face, nevertheless seeing things in photographs is one way of seeing things. The differences between seeing things by means of photographs and by means of the naked eye provide the elements of an account of the aesthetic interests photographs engage.

Anybody interested in the aesthetic value of art must now wonder how an encounter with a work of art (for example, Andy Warhol's *Brillo Boxes*) can engage any aesthetic interest not also engaged by a very similar non-art object (for example, *Brillo* boxes). Thoughtful persons may go on to ask what has changed in our thinking about art so as to provoke this puzzle, given that mimesis was for many philosophers down the centuries a reason to value art. Much has been said about such matters in relation to *Brillo Boxes, Fountain*, and *4'33"*, but the puzzle and the question about its origins also arise

in relation to photography. Tacit recognition of this fact evidently motivates a widespread strategy in theorizing about photographs. It is thought that to find the aesthetic value of photographs, one should identify the differences between experiences of objects in the flesh and experiences of photographs of those objects. I hold the following two claims: (1) when looking at photographs, we literally see the objects they are of, and (2) seeing photographs as photographs engages aesthetic interests that are not engaged by seeing the objects they are of. I assume the truth of (1) and argue for (2). In addition, since they appear incompatible, I also argue that (1) and (2) are consistent. The argument for this depends on the argument for (2) together with a correct interpretation of (1).

1 The Sceptic's Challenge

Roger Scruton (1983) has famously mounted a sceptical challenge to (2). The challenge comprises arguments for an equivalence thesis which asserts that any interest we take in photographs, when we view them as photographs, is wholly an interest in the actual objects that were photographed and not an interest in the photographs themselves. Scruton offers two arguments for the equivalence thesis. The arguments share a common core, an argument for the claim that there is no photographic representation.

Dominic McIver Lopes, "The Aesthetics of Photographic Transparency," *Mind*, 112, July 2003: 1–16. Reprinted by permission of Oxford University Press Journals.

Representations, according to Scruton, stand in an intentional relation to what they represent. That a drawing, for instance, represents an object does not entail that the object exists – drawings are fictionally competent. The explanation of this is that representations are essentially tokens in communicative action; they bear Gricean non-natural meaning. It follows that understanding a successful representation *as a representation* – taking into account that it is a representation – requires recognizing a thought that is embodied in the representation. (This account of representation is obviously heterodox. States of thermometers, speedometers, RAM chips, perception, and belief are usually counted as representations, yet none of them bear Gricean non-natural meaning and some of them do entail the existence of their objects. However, we should concede Scruton's narrow usage of 'representation'. A charge of heterodoxy is not an argument. Moreover, it is possible that Scruton's arguments may be refitted so as to allow that photographs are representations in a broader sense of the notion.)

Scruton also holds that since photographs stand in a causal relation to objects photographed, understanding a photograph *as a photograph* involves knowing, first, that it is a copy of the appearance of some object and, second, that it is a causal trace of that object. Its being a causal trace of an object means that the object exists and appears as it does in the photograph. A representation can misrepresent its object, but there is a sense in which a photograph is necessarily accurate. Cases in which we might be inclined to say that a photograph is inaccurate – as when we say that a wide angle lens exaggerates the size of the sitter's nose – are cases in which we have misread a perfectly accurate photograph by misunderstanding the working of the photographic mechanism. In understanding a photograph as a photograph, we know that we are seeing the transmitted appearance of something that actually occurred.

Thus Scruton arrives at a contrast between representations and photographs. Understanding a representation involves grasping a thought because representations figure in the communication of thoughts. Understanding a photograph involves knowledge of the appearance of the photograph's cause because photography is a mechanism for capturing appearances. Scruton concludes that photographs are not representations.

This argument does not show that photography has nothing whatever to do with representation. One may photograph a representation, including a fiction. A photograph of Ariadne's epiphany is a photograph of a staged representation: the objects of the photograph are actors who represent Ariadne and Dionysius. That some photographs of representations generate the illusion that they are representations may explain why we erroneously believe that photographs are representations. But no photograph can derive fictional competence or the power to misrepresent from having a representation as its object; it remains a photograph of actors and props. Representations *shown by means of photographs* are not photographic representations.

Scruton gives two arguments intended to build upon the core argument and establish the equivalence thesis. Both assume that an aesthetic interest in an image is an interest in seeing the image as the kind of thing it is.

This assumption when taken in conjunction with the core argument demonstrates that aesthetic interest in a representation is an interest in the thought it embodies, as that thought is communicated in the medium, by way of composition, brush strokes, and the like. Scruton writes that 'the creation of an appearance is important mainly as the expression of a thought' (1983, pp. 109–10). Photographs, however, do not represent but record objects' appearances. Therefore any interest we take in a photograph that is grounded in an understanding of it as a photograph must be an interest in the photographed object and its appearance. When this interest involves the exercise of aesthetic concepts, the concepts apply to features of the object photographed, not to features of the photograph itself. Scruton writes that 'if one finds a photograph beautiful it is because one finds something beautiful in its subject' (1983, p. 114). Photographs may serve as conduits for aesthetic interest, but they cannot be objects of aesthetic interest in their own right, as long as they are seen as photographs. Call this the 'object argument'.

The object argument does not show that a photograph cannot attract aesthetic interest of any kind whatsoever. It may have formal properties that are worth attending to, comprising a very pretty shade of green or ingeniously balanced masses. Nevertheless, to esteem a photograph's formal virtues or to revile its formal vices is not to engage with the photograph as a photograph. Such engagement involves seeing the photograph as transmitting the appearance of the photographed object, not as a mere arrangement of lines, shapes, and colours. One might, of course, appreciate the formal properties of the *photographed object*, but that, again, is to use the photograph as a conduit for aesthetic interest, not to make it an object of aesthetic interest *qua* photograph.

There are two kinds of mistake we can make about candidate art forms. On the one hand, we may believe that a medium is not an art form when it is. This is an easy mistake to make, since it is caused by a failure to notice what is worth attention and it is frequently rather difficult to tell what is worth attention. On the other hand, we may believe that a medium is an art form when it is not. This should be a difficult mistake to make, since our finding anything to be worthwhile is a good reason to think that it is worthwhile. Of course, there is the possibility that we are subject to an illusion and perceive value where none exists, but in that case we are obliged to provide an error theory which diagnoses the source of the illusion. The object argument does precisely this: it locates the source of our misapprehension that photographs excite genuine aesthetic interest to our confusion of properties of photographs with properties of objects photographed. It is in the nature of photography to solicit this confusion.

Scruton's second argument, the 'style argument', assumes that an aesthetic interest in a representation, *qua* representation, is an interest in a thought as it is expressed in a representational medium in a way that is subject to the artist's control. An interest in a photograph, viewed as a photograph – and so as a mechanically caused copy of an object's appearance – can only be an interest in the photographed object's appearance. But this is something over which the photographer can exercise scant control. So no photograph can capture the appearance of the photographed object in a way that betrays the photographer's style. But aesthetic interest is always an interest in an object viewed as an artefact.[1] Therefore, photographs cannot be objects of aesthetic interest, *qua* photographs.

A walk around any group photography exhibition provides ample evidence that photographs have perceptible stylistic properties that tie them to their makers; aficionados of photography can readily recognize an Arbus, a Weston, or a Levine. The style argument is surely unsound and Scruton's critics have made it their primary target.[2] They rightly emphasize that the argument requires us to underestimate badly the degree of control photographers exercise over the appearance of their photographs. This control is not limited to the appearance of the photograph's surface and formal properties; it extends to the properties the photographed object is seen to have. A photograph records a moment in time and the photographer selects which moment is recorded. Emulsion, focal length, depth of field, exposure, grain, filtering, and contrast fall within the photographer's control and determine what features of a scene come through in a photograph and with what degree of visual salience. The photographer also controls how the photographed object is seen simply by selecting which image to print and display of the many that were taken. Image-selection is an important photographic technique, one at which some photographers are better than others, and one the exercise of which can result in the expression of an individual style.

Whatever doubt these points cast on the style argument, they do not by themselves impeach the sceptic's total case for the equivalence thesis. The object argument is independent of the style argument and must be addressed independently. Scruton's critics frequently miss this fact and thus fail to respond adequately to his challenge.

Having argued that 'attention to detail in a photograph isn't necessarily attention to the subject as such. On the contrary, it may be attention to a manner of representing the subject', William King (1992, p. 264) concludes that the equivalence thesis is false. This does not follow. The failure of the style argument shows that what properties the photographed object is shown as having are partially subject to the photographer's control – sufficiently so for individual style to be discernible. But this provides no reason to deny that the photographed object, with the properties it is shown as having, is the object of our attention when we see a photograph and understand it as a photograph, even when we notice features of the photographed object, as it is photographed, that betray the photographer's style. Were Mapplethorpe the only person to photograph calla lilies, a photograph of a calla lily would be readily recognized as a Mapplethorpe by any suitably informed viewer, even when this viewer's aesthetic interest is entirely consumed with the calla lily.

Nigel Warburton acknowledges the independence of the style and object arguments but then adds that since photographs express individual styles, 'photography's alleged lack of representational potential appears simply beside the point' (1996, pp. 395–6). This is also a mistake. Supposing that some photographs engage aesthetic interest because they express individual style, it does not follow that the interest lies in the photographs rather than their objects. The equivalence thesis is consistent with the possibility that we perceive photographic styles and that our perception of them evokes aesthetic interest, provided that the interest so evoked is not an interest in photographs seen as photographs. Stylistic properties of photographs may be appreciated in the way that their formal properties are appreciated. To show that aesthetic interest in photographic styles is an interest in photographs as photographs, it is necessary to address the object argument for the equivalence thesis.

2 Photographic Transparency

It is hard to see how to answer the sceptic's challenge head-on. Photographs stand, by definition, in a causal relation to objects photographed. Moreover, it seems plausible to suppose that understanding a photograph as a photograph necessarily involves knowing that it is the product of a causal process originating in the photographed object. Perhaps we should interrogate the assumption that is common to the object and style arguments – namely, that an aesthetic interest in an object is an interest in the object understood as the kind of thing it is? After all, we may have as much motivation to reject the common assumption as we have to accept the equivalence thesis. Anyone who is convinced that the equivalence thesis is false may dismiss arguments for it as a *reductio* of the common assumption. They may assert that we can take an aesthetic interest in a photograph *qua* photograph without understanding it to be the product of a causal process originating in the photographed object. This is not the only available strategy, however. An alternative strategy concedes that photographs are not representations in Scruton's sense by assuming, as Kendall Walton has argued, that photographs are transparent.[3]

To say that photographs are transparent is to say that we see through them. A person seeing a photograph of a lily, literally sees a lily. She does not see a lily face-to-face, for there is no lily in front of her; nor is the photograph a lily – it is an image of a lily. Rather, her seeing a lily through a photograph of a lily is like her seeing a lily in a mirror, through binoculars, or on a closed-circuit television system. As in all these cases, seeing a lily through a photograph is indirect seeing in the sense that the lily is seen by seeing the image; even so, indirect seeing is seeing. Walton remarks that 'the invention of the camera gave us not just a new method of making pictures and not just pictures of a new kind: it gave us a new way of seeing' (1984, p. 251).

Seeing through photographs is one species of generic seeing, where to see something is to have an experience that is caused, in the right way, by the thing seen. There is ample disagreement about how to characterize the experience and the causal relation required for seeing. Walton replaces causation with belief-independent counterfactual dependence, such that seeing requires an experience whose content is counterfactually dependent on visible properties of what is seen and independent of the perceiver's beliefs. One sees a tomato, for example, only if a difference in the visible properties of the tomato would have made a difference in the content of the perceiver's experience of it. (This account requires some qualifications but they are not germane to the question whether we see through photographs.) Photographs preserve the belief-independent counterfactual dependence required for seeing. Above a threshold of acuity, any visible difference in a tomato would have made a difference in the visible properties of a photograph of the tomato and thereby in the content of the experience of seeing the photograph. Meeting this condition is not, however, sufficient for seeing through. A visual experience of the text of a description of a tomato generated by a computerized tomato-surveillance system may be counterfactually dependent in the required way on the tomato's visible properties and yet we do not see the tomato through the text. Walton proposes that there must be a relation of similarity between the scene and an image when we see through the image to the scene and he offers an account of the similarity relation that he has in mind. While alternative proposals have been made, nothing hinges for present purposes on which proposal is correct – their purpose is to rule out seeing through some representations (for example, computer-generated texts), not to rule in seeing through photographs.

Transparency is sometimes confused with illusion. There are two main conceptions of perceptual illusion. According to one, illusion entails delusion – the illusion of seeing a pool of water makes for the belief that there is a pool of water before one's eyes. According to the second, when one is subject to an illusion, one has an experience whose content is not veridical although one may not be led to believe falsely that the world is as the experience represents it. The experience is illusory not because it engenders a false belief but because there are possible circumstances in which it would engender a false belief. In the Müller-Lyer illusion the lines appear to differ in length and there are possible circumstances in which one would thereby come to believe that they do differ in length, but one might believe otherwise, having measured the lines. At any rate, that photographs are transparent does not mean that they delude. One may see a lily through a photograph without thereby coming to believe that there is a lily before one's eyes, just as one may see a lily in a mirror without coming to believe that there is a lily there, in the direction of gaze. Moreover, seeing a lily through a photograph does not engender a false belief that one is seeing a lily; the transparency thesis entails that this belief is true. Neither does the transparency of photographs entail that photographs issue in non-delusive illusions. For some photographs, there are no circumstances in which seeing through them could engender the false belief that what one sees is before one's eyes. In normal circumstances, seeing through a photograph happens simultaneously with seeing the photographic surface itself and is consistent with the belief that what is before one's eyes is a photograph, not the photographed object. Photographic transparency is not photographic invisibility.

Nor should the claim that photographs are transparent be confused with a claim about their accuracy. A photograph is necessarily accurate in the sense that it carries information by means of a causal process. In another sense, a photograph is inaccurate, since it may cause or dispose one to have false beliefs about the objects photographed. A colour photograph of a red apple carries information about the apple's redness, though it may carry the information by having a colour indistinguishable from that of an orange seen in ordinary light, with the result that we are liable to believe falsely that the apple is orange in colour.

A final mistake is to think that photographic transparency rules out either intervention on the part of the photographer or the role of photographic conventions in the photographic process. That photographs are transparent is perfectly consistent with their being a human accomplishment. As Walton notes, 'people often *show* me things and in other ways induce me to look this way or that. They affect what I can see or how I see it – by turning the lights on or off, by blowing smoke in my eyes, by constructing and making available eyeglasses, mirrors, and telescopes' (1984, p. 261). If seeing survives human interventions of these types, as it surely must, so does seeing through photographs. A similar point can be made with regard to conventions. Conventions governing seeing, such as the convention that convex mirrors be used on cars, do not blind us. Photographic conventions, such as the convention to 'correct' the convergence of vertical parallels (for example, in photographs of tall buildings), need not render photographs opaque.

When one sees a photograph as a photograph one literally sees the photographed object. It is worth considering the logical relationship between this claim and Scruton's claim that photographs do not represent. Some think, wrongly, that non-representation entails transparency. Thus Gregory Currie holds that photographs represent since they are not transparent. It is, he argues, a condition upon seeing that it provide information about the location of objects in egocentric space and photographs fail to provide this kind of information, so we do not see through photographs (1995, pp. 72–5). Granting that this argument is sound, it does not follow that photographs represent. According to the sceptic, photographs fail to represent because understanding a photograph involves knowing that its appearance is the result of a causal process. The sceptic may concede that photographs are opaque for the reason Currie gives and yet insist that they are not representations because they are caused appearances. The truth, contrary to Currie, is that if photographs are transparent, then they do not represent in Scruton's sense. (They do represent in the wider sense that is now current.)

3 The Value of Seeing Through

The claim that photographs are transparent looks to be consistent with the equivalence thesis. Indeed, it seems to provide a stronger substitute for the core, no-representation argument for the equivalence thesis. Denying the conclusion of the core argument, that photographs do not represent, means denying that photographs are transparent. Moreover, if seeing a photograph just is one way of seeing the photographed object, any interest in seeing the former is merely an interest in seeing the latter. The transparency claim appears to abet

Dominic McIver Lopes

scepticism about the aesthetic interest of photographs as photographs! In this case, however, appearances are misleading. When properly construed, the transparency claim shows what is wrong with the object argument and also provides the materials for an account of the aesthetic interest of photographs that confutes the equivalence thesis.

Seeing an object through a photograph is not identical to seeing it face-to-face. The transparency claim shows only that the interest one may properly take in seeing a photograph as a photograph is necessarily identical to the interest one may properly take in *seeing the photographed object through the photograph*. It does not show that interest to be necessarily identical to any interest one may have in seeing the object face-to-face. The sceptical challenge may be stated thus: if seeing a photograph is seeing the object photographed then any aesthetic interest taken in seeing the photograph as a photograph is an interest in seeing the photographed object, but if there is a photographic aesthetics then aesthetic interest in seeing the photograph as a photograph cannot be identical to interest in seeing the photographed object, so photographs cannot attract aesthetic interest *qua* photographs. Encouraged by acknowledgement of the transparency of photographs, this argument equivocates on 'seeing the photographed object'. Removing the equivocation, the argument is invalid: if seeing a photograph is seeing the object photographed then any aesthetic interest taken in seeing the photograph as a photograph is an interest in seeing the photographed object *through the photograph*, but if there is a photographic aesthetics then aesthetic interest in seeing a photograph as a photograph cannot be identical to interest in seeing the photographed object *face-to-face*, so photographs cannot attract aesthetic interest *qua* photographs.

The interest to be taken in seeing a photograph as a photograph is necessarily identical to the interest one may properly take in seeing the photographed object through the photograph. This is consistent with taking an aesthetic interest in seeing the photographic surface and its formal properties. Seeing through the surface does not block seeing the surface itself: photographic transparency is not photographic invisibility. But to take an interest merely in the photographic surface, without thereby taking an interest in seeing the photographed object through the surface, is not to see the photograph as a photograph. The assumption, shared with the Scrutonian sceptic, is that

proper appreciation of a photograph is appreciation of the photograph for what it is. The transparency thesis divulges what photographs are, namely instruments for seeing through.

A photographic aesthetics grounded in transparency is viable if seeing something through a photograph may arouse an interest not satisfied by seeing the same object face-to-face. Photographs animate objects that we would barely notice when we see them face-to-face. The puzzle is how the claim that we see things through photographs can illuminate this phenomenon. In solving this puzzle two questions to ask are: do we ever have any interest in seeing a photograph specifically because it is transparent? and is this interest an aesthetic interest?

Several factors mark seeing an object through a photograph apart from seeing the object face-to-face. To make a start, here are five (the list is by no means exhaustive).

First, it is often remarked that photographs capture their objects fixed at a moment in time. This means we see photographed objects as having properties that are not normally revealed when we see the same objects in the flesh. Rudolf Arnheim writes that in photographs 'the rapid course of events is found to contain hidden moments which, when isolated and fixed, reveal new and different meanings' (1986, p. 118).

Second, photographic seeing through normally obtains in the absence of the object seen, whereas face-to-face seeing obtains only when the object seen lies before the eyes. Put another way, photographic seeing through bridges distances, either spatial or temporal. This fact about photographs explains many of the uses to which they are put. Walton notes, for instance, that through photographs 'we can see our loved ones again, and that is important to us' (1984, p. 253). Obviously, nostalgia for an object cannot be evoked by seeing it face-to-face.

A third, connected, feature of photographic seeing through is that it isolates the photographed object from the context it would normally be seen to inhabit. With change of context comes a change in the properties the object itself may be seen to have. A corollary of the injunction to place things in context so as to see them more fully is that decontextualizing can be revelatory. Seeing through photographs decontextualizes.

At the same time, however, the presence of a camera is an essential part of the context in which we see an object photographically – what we see through a photograph is always before a camera. Moreover, the camera sometimes intrudes upon or disturbs what it photographs, especially when it is a person, thereby showing it in a way inaccessible to the naked eye. This is a fourth feature distinctive of photographic seeing through.

Finally, seeing photographs is typically twofold in the sense that it melds seeing the photographed object and its properties with seeing the photograph itself and its properties. This does not mean that the photographed object is seen to have all the properties of the photograph or vice versa: we do not see the Eiffel Tower as a few centimetres in height when we see it through a postcard, nor do we see the postcard as a Parisian tourist attraction. Photographic seeing through is always simultaneous with plain vanilla seeing of a photograph. In this respect seeing an object through a photograph differs from seeing it in the flesh.

If this list contains no surprises, that is what we should expect. All five features undoubtedly form the core of our ordinary, theoretically innocent experiences of photographs as photographs – that is, our seeing them in the context of knowledge of what they are. Since the sceptic contends that photographs can excite no aesthetic interest when we see them as photographs, a rebuttal of his argument best sneaks nothing exotic or unfamiliar into what counts as seeing a photograph as a photograph. It is a virtue of this list that it contains nothing of which ordinary spectators of photographs are unaware.

Granting that an interest in seeing things through photographs may not be satisfied by seeing the same objects face-to-face, the case has not yet been made for a photographic aesthetics: it remains to be shown that the interest is an aesthetic interest. Assume that an interest is aesthetic only if its satisfaction requires possession of an aesthetic concept (perhaps the interest is satisfied by having a certain representational mental state that includes an aesthetic concept as a component). This is a relatively strong conception of aesthetic interest and assuming it sets the bar high. Nevertheless, the challenge can be met. (Clearing the bar still leaves room for tolerating a great deal of scepticism about photographs. That some interest satisfied in seeing things through photographs is an aesthetic interest is consistent with the complaint that *many* other interests we have in seeing through photographs are just the same interests we have in seeing objects face-to-face. We may find a photograph worth seeing

just because it shows us a beautiful face, where this is equally a reason to see the face without photographic aids. Clearing the bar is difficult yet commits us to little.)

How we see an object, where this is cashed out by listing the properties we see the object as having, is sometimes aesthetically significant. We may therefore have an aesthetic interest in seeing things through photographs. At least two clusters of aesthetic concepts modify photographic seeing through and apply in virtue of its five distinctive features.

Photographs can promote clear seeing, foregrounding features of objects that are difficult to discern face-to-face. In some cases they are able to do this because they show objects removed from their temporal and environmental contexts, when these contexts make some properties of objects difficult to discern. In other cases, the absence of the object is crucial: for example, we might notice features of a very dangerous or disturbing object that we could not notice in the presence of danger or disturbance. Finally, features of the photographic surface can be used to highlight features of the photographed object. The luminosity gradients of a black and white photograph can bring out surface texture in the object photographed. Clarity of seeing belongs to a network of related concepts, most notably authenticity, accuracy, and truthfulness, all of which are regularly deployed in giving reasons to look at some photographs – and not to look at others.

In addition, photographs afford revelatory, transformative, defamiliarizing, or confessional seeing when they show us objects as having properties that they could not be seen to have face-to-face. Here the capacity of the photographic process to record its own disturbing effect on objects in a scene, especially persons, comes first to mind. But there are photographs whose transformative vision capitalize upon other features of seeing through.[4] We not uncommonly defend the value of seeing photographs by referring to their power to reveal otherwise invisible facets of the world and this justification entails no false views about the nature of photography.

What may be called a documentary aesthetics has two dimensions. One measures the authenticity, accuracy, or truthfulness of a photograph; the other measures its promotion of revelatory, transformative, or defamiliarizing seeing. Throughout this space the interest of photography is tied to its nature.

Dominic McIver Lopes

The language of documentary aesthetics clearly figures in actual photographic criticism, but the sceptic may retort that the expressions of the language name not aesthetic concepts but rather concepts of cognitive evaluation. While there is reason to think that some concepts of cognitive evaluation are also concepts of aesthetic evaluation, it suffices to note that the sceptic's retort far outruns his plan to deflate the aesthetic aspirations of photography. That is, the sceptic never denies that aesthetic evaluation encompasses cognitive evaluation. He never denies that seeing photographs is sometimes revelatory and therefore worthwhile. All he denies is that photographs are revelatory *as photographs*, and this challenge only has purchase because it seems that when seeing a photograph is revelatory, the source and object of the revelation is the object photographed, not the photograph itself. We have seen that the source and object of the revelation is sometimes the object *as it is seen through the photograph* and it is in cases such as this that some of photography's aesthetic aspirations are realized.

An aesthetic interest in a photograph is properly an interest in the photograph itself, not some other object. Since photographs are transparent, an interest in a photograph as a photograph is an interest in it as a vehicle for seeing through it to the photographed scene. This is not an interest limited to the scene itself; it is an interest in the scene as it is seen through the photograph. Thus our aesthetic interest in a photograph, on the present account, is an interest in the photograph as it enables seeing through. It is an interest that photographs can foster and satisfy and face-to-face seeing cannot. As in the case of all artworks, we are engaged by what may be described as the way the artistic materials are handled in order to evoke and sustain an experience. The materials of photography are the world itself. They are handled by determining the content of seeing through.

The failure of the object argument invites us to revisit the style argument and provides an additional reply to those who doubt that any interest satisfied by seeing through photographs is an aesthetic interest, for if style concepts are aesthetic concepts, the perception of photographic style satisfies an aesthetic interest. It is not enough to reply to the style argument by observing that photographs are reliably classified by aficionados according to their authorship – after all, perceptible stylistic features may not be features of the photograph seen as a photograph. But when a photograph's style is expressed in exactly what we see

through it, seeing its style is part of seeing it as a photograph. A photograph can embody style in two ways, then. The photographer may employ effects that control the appearance of the photograph without controlling what we see through it. The sceptic is right to complain that noticing these effects is not part of seeing a photograph as a photograph. Alternatively, the photographer may control what we see through her photograph in a way that betrays its style. Noticing these symptoms of style is part of seeing a photograph as a photograph. Thus many of the variables photographers control so as to make their photographs identifiably theirs determine what we see through their photographs (for example, staging, timing of shots, selection of negatives, choice of emulsion, focal length, depth of field, exposure, grain, filtering, and contrast). The original objections to the style argument are vindicated when placed within a conception of the aesthetics of photographic transparency.

Photographic seeing through may foster and satisfy aesthetic interests that face-to-face seeing cannot foster or satisfy. The equivalence thesis is false. It is fair to conclude, modestly, that photographs engage genuine aesthetic interest when seen as photographs.

More ambitiously, one might seek a distinctive aesthetics of photographs, as against hand-made pictures. If photography is the only transparent art medium, this ambition has also been realized: what is achieved by seeing an object through a photograph is only achieved by seeing it through the photograph. However, some authors hold that we see through at least some paintings, prints, and drawings as well as through photographs (for example, Lopes 1996). If these authors are right, we have only made a start towards the realization of the ambitious enterprise. The next step would be to show that photographic seeing through satisfies some aesthetic interests not satisfied by seeing through any other kind of picture. Yet nothing encourages us to discount the possibility that the ambitious enterprise is doomed to failure because seeing through some hand-made picture will do as well as seeing through any photograph.

That photographs are transparent has been assumed here without argument. But the bare outlines of a new argument for the transparency of photographs now come into view. Unless Scrutonesque scepticism is well-founded, an explanation is needed of how photographs, seen as photographs, can be objects of some aesthetic interest. If the hypothesis that photographs are transparent delivers the best explanation of their value, even redeeming the available replies to the sceptic, then we have good reason to conclude that photographs are transparent. The challenge is to show that any other replies to the sceptic are inferior because they do not fully explain the aesthetic interest photographs rightly generate.

A correct conception of the value of photography as an art form depends on accepting that photographs are transparent. Since few accept this, it follows that many – including many of those who believe it to be an art form of profound

value – misapprehend the value of photography. Is this an objection to the account on offer? Perhaps it is. But then again, the account explains a curious fact about discussions of photography, namely that more than a century after its invention there continue disagreements about its status as an art form. Even among those who agree that some photographs belong in the art galleries, there is remarkably little consensus about why they do. That we should disagree for so long about the value of photography suggests that we have failed to comprehend its nature.[5]

Notes

1 Scruton accepts the implication that natural scenes cannot be proper objects of aesthetic appreciation.
2 The principal critics are Wicks 1989, King 1992, Warburton 1996, and Gaut 2002.
3 The original arguments are in Walton 1984. For criticisms see Warburton 1988, Currie 1995, and Friday 1996; Walton replies in Walton 1997.
4 Several examples are given extended discussion in Savedoff 2000.

5 For helpful comments and criticisms, I am grateful to Jonathan Cohen, David Davies, Sherri Irvin, Mohan Matthen, Bradley Murray, Patrick Rysiew, James Shelley, Scott Walden, and Kendall Walton, as well as to audiences at Simon Fraser University, the University of British Columbia, the 2002 meeting of the Canadian Philosophical Association, and the Light Symposium.

References

Arnheim, R. 1986: 'Splendor and Misery of the Photographer'. In *New Essays in the Psychology of Art*. Berkeley: University of California Press.

Currie, G. 1995: *Image and Mind: Film, Philosophy and Cognitive Science*. Cambridge: Cambridge University Press.

Friday, J. 1996: 'Transparency and the Photographic Image'. *British Journal of Aesthetics*, 36, pp. 30–42.

Gaut, B. 2002: 'Cinematic Art'. *Journal of Aesthetics and Art Criticism*, 60, pp. 299–312.

King, W. K. 1992: 'Scruton and Reasons for Looking at Photographs'. *British Journal of Aesthetics*, 32, pp. 258–65.

Lopes, D. M. 1996: *Understanding Pictures*. Oxford: Oxford University Press.

Savedoff, B. E. 2000: *Transforming Images*. Ithaca: Cornell University Press.

Scruton, R. 1983: 'Photography and Representation'. In *Aesthetic Understanding*. London: Methuen. [Repr. in this volume: see chapter 1.]

Walton, K. 1984: 'Transparent Pictures: On the Nature of Photographic Realism'. *Critical Inquiry*, 11, pp. 246–77.

—— 1997: 'On Pictures and Photographs: Objections Answered'. In *Film Theory and Philosophy*, R. Allen, (ed.). New York: Oxford University Press.

Warburton, N. 1988: 'Seeing Through "Seeing Through Photographs" '. *Ratio*, 30, pp. 64–74.

—— 1996: 'Individual Style in Photographic Art'. *British Journal of Aesthetics*, 36, pp. 389–97.

Wicks, R. 1989: 'Photography as a Representational Art'. *British Journal of Aesthetics*, 29, pp. 1–9.

3

Everybody Gets a Cut:
DVDs Give Viewers Dozens of
Choices – and that's the Problem

Terrence Rafferty

A kiss, all moviegoers know, is just a kiss, and a sigh, by the same inexorable logic, is just a sigh, but I'm starting to wonder whether in the age of the DVD a movie – even one as indelibly stamped on the collective memory as *Casablanca* – can ever again be just a movie. The DVDs that have been piling up in the vicinity of my TV seem to be telling me that a movie is not a movie unless it arrives swaddled in "extras": on-set documentaries, retrospective interviews with cast and crew, trailers, deleted scenes, storyboards, even alternate endings. These days, any film for which a studio's marketing department has sufficiently high commercial expectations is issued on DVD in a "special" or "limited" or "collector's" edition that makes an Arden Shakespeare look skimpy by comparison. The extras on the new double-disc Director's Edition of Brett Ratner's *Red Dragon* include such indispensable material as hair and wardrobe tests and one of the auteur's NYU student films, and take as long to watch as the movie itself. We all, in our 21st-century paradise of leisure, have too much time on our hands. But not that much.

Should some scholar of the future be insane enough to take an interest in *Red Dragon*, however, the annotated variorum edition of this deeply mediocre picture could be useful. And the as yet unborn author of *Unfaithful Cinema: The Art of Adrian Lyne* (2040) will need to consult the Special Collector's Edition DVD of *Fatal Attraction*, which contains the film's original ending as well

as the one moviegoers saw. It also includes the director's own helplessly revealing comment on the radical difference between the conclusion he chose and the one he discarded: "You can make up your mind which you like better."

I've always thought it was the *artist's* job to make that sort of decision, but as I watched Lyne smugly leaving it up to the viewer, I realized with a jolt that I had fallen behind the times. I still think of a film as a unified, self-sufficient artifact that, by its nature, is not interactive in the way that, say, a video game is. To my old-media mind, the viewer "interacts" with a movie just as he or she interacts with any other work of art – by responding to it emotionally, thinking about it, analyzing it, arguing with it, but not by altering it fundamentally. When I open my collected Yeats to read *Among School Children*, I don't feel disappointed, or somehow disempowered, to find its great final line ("How can we tell the dancer from the dance?") unchanged, unchanged utterly, and un-encumbered with an "alternate." For all I know, Yeats might have written "How can we tell the tailor from the pants?" and then thought better of it, but I'm not sure how having the power to replace the "dance" version with the "pants" version would enhance my experience of the poem.

And although *Among School Children* is divided into eight numbered stanzas and therefore provides what DVD's call "scene access," I tend to read them consecutively, without skipping, on the theory that the poem's meaning is wholly depen-

Terrence Rafferty, "Everybody Gets a Cut," *The New York Times Magazine*, May 4, 2003: 58, 60–1.

dent on this specific, precise arrangement of words and images. If you read *Among School Children* in any other way, would it still be *Among School Children*? Would it be a poem at all?

The contemporary desire for interactivity in the experience of art derives, obviously, from the heady sense of control over information to which we've become accustomed as users of computers. The problem with applying that model to works of art is that in order to get anything out of them, you have to accept that the artist, not you, is in control of this particular package of "information." And that's the paradox of movies on DVD: the digital format tries to make interactive what is certainly the *least* interactive, most controlling art form in human history.

When you're sitting in a movie theater, the film is in absolute, despotic control of your senses. It tells you where to look and for how long, imposes its own inarguable and unstoppable rhythm, and your options for interaction are pretty severely limited. You can wise off quietly to your companion or loudly at the screen, or, in extremis, you can walk out, but nothing you can do, short of storming the projection booth, will affect the movie itself: it rolls on serenely without you, oblivious as the turning world.

It's that imperious, take-it-or-leave-it quality that, in the early days of cinema, aroused the suspicions of devotees of the traditional arts, who would argue that watching a film denied the audience some of the freedoms available to readers – who could set their own pace rather than meekly submit to a rhythm imposed on them by the creator of the work – and to theatergoers who were at liberty to look wherever they wanted to at the action on stage and whose reactions could actually affect the play's performance. Eventually, we all learned to stop worrying and love the art form, but the skeptics and reactionaries had a point: the techniques of film are unusually coercive, a fact quickly grasped both by the art's early masters, like D.W. Griffith, Fritz Lang, Sergei Eisenstein and Alfred Hitchcock, who reveled in their ability to manipulate the viewer's responses, and by the leaders of totalitarian states, who recognized cinema's potential as an instrument of propaganda.

The manipulative power of cinema is neither a good nor a bad thing; it is what it is, and all movies partake of it in varying degrees. The films of Jean Renoir, for example, are markedly freer than those of Hitchcock, but the freedom they offer is relative; although the long takes, deep focus and im-provisatory acting style of Renoir's *Rules of the Game* (1939) allow the viewer's imagination more room to roam, the director is nonetheless in complete control of what we see and what we hear. In fact, just about the only way a film artist can subvert his or her own authority is by significantly limiting the use of the medium's expressive resources, as, for example, Andy Warhol did in the mid-60s. His eight-hour-long *Empire* (1964), a single shot of the Empire State Building, with no cuts, no camera movement and no sound, is about as uncoercive as a film can be. It's the most interactive movie ever made.

All I'm saying, really, is that watching a film is, and should be, an experience different from that of playing Myst or placing an order on Amazon. I suspect that many DVD owners use their players exactly as I do, as a way of recreating as nearly as possible at home the experience of seeing a film in a theater. The DVD picture is sharp, the sound is crisp and the film is almost invariably presented in its correct aspect ratio – i.e., letterboxed for movies made in wide-screen process, as all but a few since the mid-50s have been. The DVD player is, by common consent, the best-selling new device in consumer-electronics history. It's said that the "market penetration" of DVD players (which were introduced in 1997) into American homes is progressing at a rate twice that of the VCR. And the unprecedented "penetration" of this format cannot be attributed solely to the Rohypnol of advertising hype; the DVD is a distinct improvement over the videocassette, and even over the extinct laserdisc.

But the DVD is a gift horse that demands to be looked squarely in the mouth, because it has the potential to change the way we see movies so profoundly that the art form itself, which I've loved since I was a kid, is bound to suffer. What does it mean, for example, when a director recuts or otherwise substantially alters the theatrical-release version of his or her film for the DVD, as Peter Jackson did for the four-disc Special Extended Edition of *The Lord of the Rings: The Fellowship of the Ring*? This cut, half an hour longer than the film that was shown in theaters and that sold millions of copies in its first two-disc DVD incarnation just four months earlier, is obviously the definitive version of *Fellowship*: clearer, fuller, richer emotionally and kinetically. Better late than never, I guess, but I still felt a little cheated at having to watch this grand, epic-scale adventure on the small screen. And don't the hardy souls who every now and then peel themselves off their Barcaloungers, trek to the multiplex, stand in line for $4 sodas and dubious popcorn and then subject themselves to the indignity of sitting in a room with hundreds of rank strangers – don't *they* deserve the best version of the movie? At least when Steven Spielberg reedited and digitally rejiggered his *ET: the Extraterrestrial*, he had the decency to give it a brief stopover in movie theaters on the way to its final destination as a multidisc Limited Collector's Edition DVD.

It's thoughtful of Spielberg, too, to include in the DVD package, alongside the spiffy new *ET*, a disc containing the original 1982 theatrical version of that justly beloved movie, which is not only the sole extra worth watching in the whole overstuffed grab bag of goodies – what viewers, I wonder, are thrilled to discover therein a two-hour film of John Williams conducting the score at the Shrine Auditorium? – but is also a stern warning to filmmakers who might be tempted to tinker with their past work: in almost every respect the old version is better. Although the two brief scenes Spielberg has restored to the picture are nice, you wouldn't miss them if they weren't there (as the filmmaker evidently didn't when he left them on the cutting-room floor two decades ago), and the digital removal of the guns carried by the government agents in the original's climactic chase just seems silly.

What's most damaging to *ET* is the way Spielberg has tampered with the movements and facial expressions of the eponymous alien itself. A team of computer wizards has labored mightily to make ET cuter – an undertaking that, as even those of us who admire the picture would have to agree, has a distinct coals-to-Newcastle quality.

I'm sure most filmmakers occasionally look at their past movies and wish they'd done one thing or another differently, but before the rise of the DVD, they rarely received much encouragement (i.e., financing) to roll up their sleeves, get under the hood and fine-tune or soup up their vintage machines. That state of affairs changed when the consumer-electronics industry discovered, to its delight, that many members of its affluent and highly penetrable market could be induced to buy the same entertainment product, with variations, over and over again. (One day you wake up to find you have 17 ways of listening to Elvis's *Heartbreak Hotel*.) For movie lovers, a new DVD

Director's Cut of *The Fellowship of the Ring* or *ET* or *Apocalypse Now* or even *X-Men* can be a powerful incentive to reach for the wallet yet one more time.

The restoration of older films that were mutilated before their theatrical release or that have suffered from disfiguring wear and tear is, of course, welcome. There's every reason to shell out for the DVD's of David Lean's *Lawrence of Arabia*, Hitchcock's *Vertigo* and *Rear Window*, with their images and sounds, which had faded badly over the years, now buffed by crack restorers, and Orson Welles's baroque 1958 noir *Touch of Evil*, which replaces the distributor's release cut with a version that conforms more closely to the director's own extensive notes on the editing of the film. (Like the new *ET*, all those restorations played briefly in theaters.) In each of those cases, the DVD allows us to see the film as its maker wanted it to be seen.

But most of the current mania for revision appears to be driven by motives other than a burning desire for aesthetic justice. It's not that I don't believe Steven Spielberg when he says that his "perfectionist" impulses were what spurred him to rework *ET*; it's that I don't believe that without the financial incentive of DVD sales he would have given in to those impulses – or, perhaps, felt them at all. Although the film's 20th anniversary, last year, supplied a pretext for revision, nothing in the finished new version argues very strongly for its *necessity*. God knows, there are DVD packages far crasser than the Limited Collector's *ET*. (For an especially pungent recent example, see *X-Men 1.5*.) I'm picking on Spielberg here because he's a great filmmaker and a man who loves and respects the history of his art; if even he can be seduced into tampering with his own work, then the innocent-looking little DVD is rolling us down a very steep slope indeed.

Revisiting past work is almost never a good idea for an artist. Every work of art is the product of a specific time and a specific place and, in the case of movies, a specific moment in the development of film technology. Sure, any movie made before the digital revolution could be "improved" technically, but the fact is that the choices the director made within the technical constraints of the time *are* the movie. It wasn't so long ago, maybe 15 years, that filmmakers took up arms against Ted Turner and his efforts to "modernize" old black-and-white films by computer-coloring them. Colorization was an easy target, both because the process was surpassingly ugly and because it was inflicted on films without the consent of their makers. But would the principle have been any different if the colorization technology had been better, or if the directors had somehow been persuaded to perform the evil act themselves, on their own movies, of their own apparent free will? If Georges Méliès, the wizardly animator of silent cinema, were alive today, would he boot up his computer and take another crack at *A Trip to the Moon*? Would we think more highly of him if he did?

That's kind of where we are with DVDs today. We're all well past the point of being shocked at the compromises people make in the name of commerce, but I still wonder why filmmakers have been so meekly compliant with the encroaching revisionism and interactivity of the digital format. For many, I suppose, it's simply a matter of taking the bad with the good. The huge upside of the DVD, for filmmakers, is that it makes their work widely available, in a form that more or less accurately reflects their intentions: they long ago learned to live with the reality that ultimately more people would see their films on a small screen than on a large one – the directors of Spielberg's generation themselves received a fair amount of their movie education from television – and at least on DVD the movies aren't interrupted by commercials or squashed into a "full-frame" presentation. So the filmmakers tell themselves, I guess, that the more insidious features of the format don't really matter: that the making-of documentaries don't make them sound like hucksters and blowhards; that the deleted scenes and alternate endings don't subtly impinge on the formal unity of the work; that all the revisions and digital tweaks they agree to don't undermine the historical integrity of the picture; that voice-over commentaries don't drown the movie in a torrent of useless information; that scene access doesn't encourage viewers to rearrange the film to their own specifications; that the user-friendly conventions of the format will not steadily erode the relationship between movies and their audience.

The men and women who make films need to put up more resistance to the rising tide of interactivity, because, *Casablanca* notwithstanding, there's no guarantee that the fundamental things will continue to apply as time goes by. The more "interactive" we allow our experience of art – any art – to become, the less likely it is that future generations will appreciate the necessity of art at

all. Interactivity is an illusion of control; but understanding a work of art requires a suspension of that illusion, a provisional surrender to someone else's vision. To put it as simply as possible: If you have to be in total control of every experience, art is not for you. Life probably isn't, either. Hey, where's the alternate ending?

There's not much point speculating on what the ending will be for the strange process of DVD-izing cinema. Many suspect that the DVD is already the tail wagging the weary old dog of the movies. Will the interactive disc ultimately become the primary medium, with film itself reduced to the secondary status of raw material for "sampling"? Maybe; maybe not. The development of digital technology, along with the vagaries of the marketplace, will determine the outcome, and neither of those factors is easily predictable. What's safe to say, I think, is that the DVD – at least in its current, extras-choked incarnation – represents a kind of self-deconstruction of the art of film, and that the DVD-created audience, now empowered to take apart and put together these visual artifacts according to the whim of the individual user, will not feel the awe I felt in a movie theater when I was young, gazing up at the big screen as if it were a window on another, better world.

I no longer look at movies with quite that wide-eyed innocence, of course, but it's always there somewhere in the background: an expectation of transport, as stubborn as a lapsed Catholic's wary hope of grace. Perhaps the DVD generation, not raised in that moviegoer's faith, will manage to generate some kind of art from the ability to shuffle bits and pieces of information randomly – the aleatory delirium of the digital. It just won't be the art of D.W. Griffith, Jean Renoir, François Truffaut, Sam Peckinpah, Andrei Tarkovsky and Roman Polanski.

Feeling slightly melancholy, I call up David Lynch, who is not only a director whose works – *Blue Velvet, Mulholland Drive* – demand a pretty high level of surrender on the part of the viewer, but also one who has in recent years refused to allow voice-over commentary or scene access on the DVDs of his movies. "The film is the thing," he tells me. "For me, the world you go into in a film is so delicate – it can be broken so easily. It's so tender. And it's essential to hold that world together, to keep it safe." He says he thinks "it's crazy to go in and fiddle with the film," considers voiceovers "theater of the absurd" and is concerned that too many DVD extras can "demystify" a film. "Do not demystify," he declares, with ardor. "When you know too much, you can never see the film the same way again. It's ruined for you for good. All the magic leaks out, and it's putrefied."

He's not opposed to DVD per se. Lynch just finished supervising the DVD of his first feature, *Eraserhead* (1976), which, while eschewing the usual commentary and chapter stops, will contain a few extras (the nature of which he declines to reveal). We spend a few minutes discussing one of his favorite DVDs, the Criterion Collection's *Complete Monterey Pop*, and agree that D. A. Pennebaker's groundbreaking concert film is the sort

of movie the format serves well; even the scene access is, in this case, mighty useful. But Lynch says that filmmakers need to be very careful about the way they present their delicate, tender creations on DVD. "Don't do anything to hurt the film, and then you're rockin'."

I hang up, leaving David Lynch to rock on, and find that I'm feeling more hopeful that the relationship between movies and their audience will survive the current onslaught of interactivity – that this need not be the beginning of the end of a beautiful friendship. So I dig out the no-frills DVD of *Mulholland Drive*, slide it into its little tray and pick up the remote. And I tell the machine to play it.

PART II

What Is Film?

Introduction

The main topic of this section is the ontology of film. "Ontology" is a forbidding-sounding word, but it need not be. "Ontology" is the study of being. The ontology of film, then, is an inquiry into the being of film, or, to say it a bit less awkwardly, an inquiry into the *kind* of being, the kind of *thing*, a film is. To what category does it belong or, alternatively, under which concept do we classify it?

Asked what a tiger is, we answer "an animal." Similarly, philosophers are concerned with how to classify film. For example: is it basically photography? is it art? is it a little bit of both? or is it neither?

The ontology of film interrogates the mode of existence of film – the kind of thing it is essentially. The ontologist attempts to identify the nature or essence of film – its manner of existing (of being). In short, he endeavors to answer the question: what is film?

The philosophy of any practice strives to clarify the concepts indispensable to carrying on that practice. The philosophy of mathematics, for instance, attempts to define what a number is, asking whether it is something real or only a logical fiction. Likewise, the philosophy of law analyzes what a law is, along with clarifying other concepts crucial to the practice, like intention and voluntariness. So, in like manner, the philosophy of film, among other things, aspires to an account of that which we call film.

The concern with defining cinema arose within the first two decades of the advent of moving pictures. One reason for this was simply that film was a new thing under the sun and, therefore, needed to be fitted into our scheme of things –

where, as the intellectual division of labor would have it, situating items into our biggest picture of the way things are is the job of the philosopher (specifically, the task of the metaphysician or ontologist).

Secondly, as we saw in Part I, it was felt that a specification of the nature of film was in order, if film was to be defended from its detractors. That is, lovers of film longed to prove that film is not essentially or necessarily a mere slavish, mindless, mechanical technology of reproduction such that its every instance is, by definition, precluded from classification under the concept of art. But this, in turn, required an examination of the nature of film which could demonstrate that film possesses the inherent capacity to discharge the responsibilities – such as the expression of thought and/or emotion – of a mature artform. In other words, showing that films can be artworks required the elaboration of a certain sort of ontology of film.

One of the earliest systematic philosophies of film was developed by Hugo Munsterberg, a member of the Harvard philosophy department, in his 1916 treatise, originally entitled *The Photoplay*.[1] Munsterberg argued that film – in virtue especially of some of its editing devices – was an objectification of the human mind, and, therefore, not sheerly a mechanical reproduction, but something in principle able to convey thoughts and feelings.[2]

Perhaps due to the fact that early philosophers and theorists of film were so vexed by the threat of having the claims of film to art status dismissed peremptorily by the accusation that film was *nothing but* photographic reproduction, editing was frequently the card they played in the film-as-art debate. And, as we saw in the introduction to Part I, this is still a serviceable gambit.

Early philosophers and theorists were not simply interested in identifying the nature of film in order to differentiate it from its ostensible neighbors, like theater and painting. They were also in search of what might be called the "cinematic." The cinematic is the feature or features of the medium that not only distinguish film from adjacent media, but which, in addition, enable film *qua* film to produce art – that is, specifically filmic or *cinematic* art (as opposed to theatrical art that is merely preserved on celluloid).

Since these features were putatively precisely the ones that enabled films to acquit their artistic function, once they were identified, it was presupposed that they could also serve as evaluative criteria. That is, the more a film exploited these features, the more artful the film; the less a film took advantage of the relevant features, the less artful it would be. Or, to be blunt, a cinematic film, all things being equal, was good – good as a film; but an uncinematic film was, in the same sense, bad.

Such theorists assumed that accentuating the relevant (cinematic) features of the medium would make a film better, while neglecting them would make it worse. Just as knowing that the function of a knife is to cut alerts one to the fact that sharpness is the evaluative feature we care about with such utensils, film theorists, committed to art as the function they prized of film, believed that cinematicity was the key to evaluating anything pretending to the status of film art.

However, as the theoretical discussion of film evolved over time, different philosophers and theorists staked out different candidates for that which counts as cinematic. In the earlier stages of the debate, emphasis on the ways in which film diverges from the bare replication of whatever stands before the camera dominated film theory; particularly favored were those departures from brute reproduction/mechanical recording that were available through editing. Authors such as Rudolph Arnheim, Roman Jakobson, and the Soviet school of montage-theory are eloquent exemplars of the tendency that celebrates film as a means to *create* "realities" rather than baldly to record them. Call this approach "creationism."

But as history moved forward, a reaction formation caught on, represented by figures such as André Bazin and Siegfried Kracauer. Called realists, they argued that the art of film depended fundamentally on its photographic element. Cinematic accomplishment rested on being true to the photographic nature of film. However, they did not – like the early detractors of cinema – believe that film forfeited its claim to art status because it was photographic. Rather, they asserted that photography made possible a new kind of art – an art of the real – of which film was in the vital forefront. Thus, by boldly exploiting the photographic aspect of film – its cinematic identity, so to speak – in order to penetrate reality, filmmakers, it was argued, could tap into the essence of cinema, fulfilling film's destiny as a realist art and thereby securing the highest order of cinematic excellence *qua* film art. The essay by Lopes in Part I of this volume also participates in this tendency.

For the realists, relying on photography was the key to cinematic success; disrespecting the photographic element was a recipe for disaster. Contrariwise, many of the creationists felt the same way about editing. The Soviet montagists thought editing was the way to cinematic achievement; the photographic contribution was of secondary importance and, if overplayed, was downright detrimental. Each camp regarded their own criterion for cinematic accomplishment as exclusively *the* correct one, since each camp claimed to derive their criteria of cinematic excellence from an ontological inquiry into the essence of film – a.k.a. the cinematic.

But it hardly seemed credible that both the realists and the creationists could be right on their own terms. On the one hand, to the theoretically unaligned observer, cinematic masterpieces in the styles endorsed by both the realists and the creationists appeared to be widely in evidence. Thus, inasmuch as each side claimed to have an exclusive purchase on the truth, the achievement of montage masterpieces presented counterexamples to the realists, while realist accomplishments – Renoir's *Rules of the Game* is possibly the greatest film ever made – were the flies in the ointment of creationist theory. How could either side in the debate have located the sort of functional essence of film they were after, if their candidates, respectively, left so much cinematic value unexplained?

The sort of style championed by realists and that advocated by the creationists are, in certain respects, practically incompatible. That is, the two styles cannot be maximally exploited in the same film at the same time. One cannot, for example, combine long-take, depth-of-field shots (a realist technique) and vigorous montage (a creationist technique) to the advantage of both devices in the same sequence. The two styles, if pushed to the hilt, get in the way of each other's most pointed effects, thereby canceling each other out. But surely deciding which style to elect in a particular sequence cannot be adjudicated by invoking the nature of cinema. The choice, rather, calls for a consideration of what the filmmaker hopes to accomplish.

Style, in other words, is not dictated by the nature of the medium, but by the purposes of the filmmaker. The medium – truth be told – has no inherent purposes of its own (how could it?), and, therefore, the so-called medium dictates no preferred style. It suffers them all.

The error of early realist and creationist ontologists of film is that they presupposed that the medium had a built-in purpose or function. But in reality, they "discovered" the *nature* of the medium by zeroing in on those features of the medium that facilitated the implementation of the uses of the medium of which they approved on antecedent grounds. Of course, the "nature" of the medium suited their preferred style, since it was the commitment to the style (and its attendant effects) in question that served as the optic through which the theorists in question selected out and anointed the pertinent features alleged to be the essence of the medium. It was no surprise that the styles esteemed to be the most cinematic could be traced back to the nature of the medium, then, since the "nature" of the medium had been gerrymandered from the get-go to facilitate exactly the styles that excited the relevant theorists.

The problem with this way of conducting inquiry into the ontology of film is that it fails to acknowledge the normative dimension actually involved in designating a style as cinematic. It pretends to deduce the appropriate style of film from the nature of the medium. But, in fact, the ontologist in this case has begged the question by unconsciously and precedently projecting onto the medium the style or use of cinema that he favors as his candidate for the essence of film. He finds the style of film he deems cinematic inherent in the nature of cinema because he has, so to speak, put it there.[3]

Recent explorations into the ontology of film generally no longer assume that discovering the distinguishing features of the medium will grant insight into the most (cinematically) excellent way of making film. Ontologists do not presently believe that we can know a priori what will work or

not work in film just by knowing what makes a performance of Paul Scofield's *King Lear* a work of theater and a performance of Roman Polanski's *King Lear* a work of cinema.

However, the fact that we can no longer have faith in the promise that the ontology of film will show us the royal road to cinematic success does not mean that the project of film ontology is no longer of any interest. For we still would like to have a sense of where film lies in the overall scheme of things. How is film different from related practices like theater and painting, and, for that matter, photography? We have an insatiable curiosity about the cartography of our concepts. Inquiring minds want to know what goes where, and it is the vocation of philosophy to satisfy this appetite.

The philosophers in this section all make stabs at the ontology of film, or, as some of them wish to call it, the moving *such-and-such* (either picture or image). None of them argues that their hypotheses about the nature of film entail or preclude a particular style of filmmaking. But all undertake to map out the place of film on the landscape of artistic media. In the selections that follow, the major answers to the question "What is film?" will be discussed, though not always endorsed; these include the realist answer (Cavell), the film-as-dream answer (Langer and Sparshott), the film-as-language answer (Currie), and the view that film is best classified as a moving something (Danto and Carroll).

The first selection has been excerpted from *The World Viewed: Reflections on the Ontology of Film* by Stanley Cavell. Like Hugo Munsterberg, Cavell is also a former member of the Harvard philosophy department. But unlike Munsterberg, who might be categorized as a creationist, Cavell is a realist; indeed, he is probably the subtlest realist ontologist of film to date.

By labeling Cavell a realist, we intend to signal his commitment to the idea that photography is the basic element in film. However, unlike Bazin and Kracauer, Cavell does not appear to believe that film's photographic origin imparts an a priori privilege to any particular style or subject matter.[4] Cavell does not offer an argument for his conviction that photography is the basic element of cinema, but seems to take it as an hypothesis on the authority of Erwin Panofsky and Bazin. But Cavell develops this suggestion with far greater depth than any previous realist.

Like Leo Tolstoy – for whom the question "what is art?" had to be answered in such a way as to explain why art is important – Cavell intends to answer the question "what is film?" in a manner that will account for why film in all its various genres and styles is so significant for so many people. Because film appeals almost universally and because it is all sorts of film that compel interest, Cavell presupposes that the feature of film that will account for this will have to be fairly generic – a feature, that is, that all films will have irrespective of genre.

Perhaps because it appears so generic, it is the photographic dimension that Cavell battens upon as key to the power of film. He proceeds to investigate what distinguishes film-as-photography from painting and theater with an eye not only to differentiating these media, but also in order to tease out clues about the distinctive human needs satisfied by cinema. For he presupposes that the virtually universal attraction of cinema can be explained by the *generic* needs, if any, that film satisfies.

Contrasting film with painting, Cavell reaches a conclusion that is also embraced by Scruton and Lopes, viz., that the photographic/filmic image is transparent. He says: "[a photograph] presents us, we want to say, with the things themselves."

Cavell then bolsters this phenomenological observation by proposing a disjunctive argument. The photographic image is either the copy of the sight or appearance or look of whatever it is photograph of, *or* it is in some sense a presentation of the thing itself. However, he contends, the photograph cannot be the reproduction of the sight of the object because, for the sake of ontological parsimony, we should be chary of the temptation to postulate that things have sights that can be re-represented. Put simply, if we include sights in our ontological inventory of that which exists, our metaphysics will swell to an inordinate largeness, since every object that exists will also be connected to an indefinitely huge number of sights, i.e., ways the object appears from virtually limitless angles and distances. But if there are no sights for photographs to re-present to viewers, then it must be the things themselves that photographs re-present to us – Uncle George and Aunt Harriet. Or, to use the terminology favored by Lopes, photographic images are transparent.

So photographs give us transparent access to things past, putatively unlike painting. In addition, photography is said to be automatic, thereby excluding subjectivity from the process mechanically. Paintings are hand-made; photos are ma-chine-made in a fashion that acquires an unavoidable aura of objectivity unattainable in painting. And lastly, in contrast to figurative painting, photography is *of* the world, whereas a painting is a *world* – that is to say, a supposedly self-sufficient world of a work of art.

What this last distinction largely rests upon is the claim that a photograph is lifted out of the spatial continuum;[5] we always assume that there was something adjacent to the frame of a photograph. It always makes sense to ask about a closely cropped photograph of Hitler delivering a speech – "Who was standing next to him, just off-camera?" On the other hand, it is fruitless to ask who is standing nearby Bacchus in the portrait. No one was, since it is an imaginary confection. As well, as we saw in Part I, emphasis on photography as a causal process versus an intentional one is meant by Cavell to dispose us to regard the photograph as inextricably bound up with the actual world, albeit past, in opposition to a painting which can contrive a world unto itself.

The contrast between painting and photography yields the conclusion that film, as a creature of photography, is a series of transparent, automatic projections of the world past. Moreover, the relation of the spectator to the world past that is automatically projected on film can be further delineated by comparing cinema with its other near neighbor, theater. In theater, the spectator is in the presence of the actor, whereas, in film, the spectator is now absent from the actor and the world he inhabited. So, a film is a series of automatic projections of the world past from which the spectator is metaphysically absent.

For Cavell, these features not only serve to define film and to differentiate it from painting and theater. They also supply suggestions as to why film is significant – that is, why people of all sorts value a vast variety of different types of films. According to Cavell, cinema as such is important to us for three reasons, all related to the essential features of photographic film as just enumerated. They are: (1) that film enables us to escape the burden of response; (2) that film overcomes subjectivity; and (3) that film relieves the anxiety of solipsism.

Because we are absent from the world of the screen and because we are metaphysically debarred from entering it, we need not respond to what we see there. We are not obligated to right the wrongs we observe on the screen, because we cannot. There is, therefore, no pressure to act. Film viewing is a vacation *sans* recrimination – of necessity.

Because film is an automatic process, it purportedly releases us from the oppressive and debilitating – or, at least, tiresome – suspicion that everything is subjective. According to Cavell, it is part of the plight of modern man to be unable to escape the specter of all-encompassing subjectivity. We long for something objective. Film, in virtue of being an automatic, mechanical process, to a certain extent, purportedly satisfies this wish.

In a related vein, Cavell also thinks that we are plagued by the fear of solipsism – by the worry that I am the only thing that exists, that I am alone, and that everything else and everyone else is just a product of my mind. But since I am absent from the world re-presented by the film – from the world viewed – film gives me a symbol or talisman to ward off the anxiety that I am all there is. For the world re-presented in the film is independent from me; I am, by definition, absent from it. Film shows a world past of which I am not a part – a world that is separate from me at the moment I view it. This, on Cavell's reading, serves as a powerful symbol of the possibility that the world could exist without my presence in it. And it reassures me that I can hope for at least a limited kind of immortality. Since the world is independent of me – since there are other people – I can be remembered by them, whereas solipsism would consign me to oblivion once I expire.

Of course, film does not offer a philosophical refutation of solipsism. After all, the friend of solipsism will be quick to point out that a solitary consciousness could imagine a world with films in them – films from which I appear to be absent – just as the solipsist imagines that other people exist (though they only appear to do so). Nevertheless, Cavell is not claiming that film is important because it philosophically defeats solipsism, but only that it gives us a vivid, needful, experientially rooted symbol of the possibility of the world existing independently of my mind in a way analogous to Kant's speculation that beauty gives us a powerful intuitive symbol or metaphor for the possibility of morality.

Cavell not only derives an account of the significance of cinema from its photographic provenance. He also explores the implications of the photographic element of film in order to develop several intriguing conjectures about the nature of movie acting and, thence, a theory about the origins of motion picture genres.

Contrasting acting on stage with acting on film, Cavell, like others before him, suggests that "for the stage, an actor works himself into a role; for the screen, a performer takes the role onto himself." This alleged difference, moreover, may be attributable to photography in virtue of which the actor may be said to lend his being to the character. Thus, every tic of Clint Eastwood, including the rasp of his whisper, goes into the constitution of Dirty Harry to the point at which we are willing to say "Dirty Harry is Clint Eastwood." Dirty Harry's identity, so to speak, is fixed on film – fixed in film in a way that is, so to say, fused with the identity of Clint Eastwood. That is why when we describe movies to our friends we generally use the name of the actor, rather than the character. By dint of photographic realism, theorists like Cavell suggest, the two congeal.

Of course, what we are talking about here is the phenomenon of movie stars. Due to photography, Cavell suggests, movie stars merge their own being with the characters they portray. In a certain sense, the character is John Wayne or Marilyn Monroe, personae that exist across films. Theater actors, in contrast, might be thought to wear masks, so to speak, that they easily shed from role to role. But the movie star brings her public personality to each role.

Furthermore, that public personality finds itself best expressed in certain situations and certain stories. Douglas Fairbanks Sr., for example, thrived in narratives where he is in constant motion – constantly laughing at death, running, climbing, swinging, and so forth. According to Cavell, it is from such star personalities that genres are born – successful genres being story types, situations, and moods that best showcase the celestial chemistry of the celebrities that populate them. Movie genres are the dwelling places of movie stars; genres become cycles when they are able to function as a habitat, or, more precisely, a home for a compelling series of star personalities.

Whereas previous film theorists thought that they could deduce what was possible and impossible – aesthetically advisable, permissible, and/or forbidden – from an *a priori* account of the nature of the medium, Cavell contends that the possibilities of film – that is, what will work on film – can only be discovered as filmmakers experiment with different projects, notably in the form of genres. Kracauer thought that he could legislate which genres suited the realistic inclination of the film medium by reference to the essence of cinema. Tragedy, on his account, was destined to fail. Cavell is far more sensible, adopting the attitude that we must wait and see what works and what doesn't by attending to which films actually succeed. The possibilities of the medium will be revealed as various genres take hold, thereby illuminating what it is possible to achieve in film *a posteriori*. The proof of the pudding is in the tasting, in other words. One cannot determine what is possible or impossible in film abstractly.

Cavell's attitude toward the possibilities of the medium is surely sage. However, some of his other proposals are more controversial. It does not seem that film acting and theater acting are as categorically distinct as Cavell maintains. There have been theater stars who have lent their personalities to their characters to the point that they appeared to merge with their roles. Gilette was identified with Sherlock Holmes; Eugene O'Neill's father with the Man in the Iron Mask. Moreover, there are film stars who transform themselves from role to role – chameleons who do not imprint their own personality or being on their character: Laurence Olivier from yesteryear comes to mind, while today one thinks of Meryl Streep and Daniel Day-Lewis.

Nor do all genres appear to originate as vehicles for star personalities. For example, the two science fiction cycles of the 1950s did not. Actors like Richard Denning and Philip Carlson appeared in a number of them, but they were not really stars in the strong sense of the word. For instance, they were not household names. Indeed, they were rather bland, perhaps purposefully so, given the type of characters they portrayed. Moreover, the kinds of roles they undertook could be performed by other equally bland actors, like Peter Graves and others even less memorable and more nondescript.

Furthermore, as we saw in Part I, the presupposition that film is essentially photographic is contestable. Granted, barring animated films, until quite recently, most film images were produced via photography. However, given the resources of computer processing, it is now possible to create motion pictures without using photography. There is no reason to think that in the future there will not be films concocted entirely through digital means.[6] In fact, there is every reason to think that this is likely, since computer-generated characters do not command the salaries that flesh-and-blood movie stars do.

Perhaps some traditionalists will claim that these are not films, properly so-called, since they are not mediated by celluloid – not mounted upon film stock. But we predict that people will still call them movies. After all, no one hesitates to call the computer-generated mattes and the armies generated by multiplier functions "movie" images today. There is no reason to think that this willingness will slacken when the proportion of digitally created imagery expands to the point where it could be the whole ball of wax. And, in any event, such digitally produced extravaganzas are indisputably *motion pictures*. Thus, we predict, the old label *film* will probably carry over to them, even if somewhat anachronistically.

But, of course, the issue here is not merely a matter of words. Cavell is claiming that film is important to large numbers of people because it is photographic – because it presents people with the world past, the world from which they are ontologically excluded. Yet we foresee that motion pictures will remain important to people in the same way as they have in the past when they become increasingly digitized – to the point where the extent to which they can be said to present views of the world past will be utterly negligible. People will remain in love with film – or, more accurately, motion pictures – because what grips them, when it grips them, is that these are *visualized narratives* and not because they afford a glimpse of the world past. Indeed, that opportunity which weighs so heavily for Cavell is a rather *recherché* one compared to the fascination that folks derive from watching stories unfold before their very eyes. That is what is important to them about movies, rather than the service films might be thought to provide as occasions to view the world past.

It is hard to accept the notion that our passion for film is based in our recognition that the image is technically of the world past. This is doubtful not only because most films are fictions and the provenance of the image scarcely preoccupies the consciousness of most viewers as they watch. But we also wonder if it is even necessary to understand how the image was made in order to fall under the sway of cinema. Most of us are bitten by the motion picture bug before we know how photography works. And surely a great many people, especially illiterate individuals in more remote and rural areas, have taken to film without knowing how the image was produced.[7] But if that is so, it seems unlikely that it is their knowledge about the provenance of the motion picture in the world past which is the source, in any way, of the importance they find in movies. Rather, they are captivated by the moving visual narratives that come to them via film.

Realists in general appear to place far too much emphasis on photography as a recording device. The reason that photography has proven so attractive to film artists is that it is a fast way of producing the basic ingredients of moving fictions – namely, moving images – cheaply and quickly. It is a great deal more efficient to shoot scenes than it is to draw cartoons by hand. Admittedly, it is the recording capacity of cinema that does the work here – as the camera records enacted scenes. But what drives the process is not the desire to produce recordings as recordings but rather recordings that can function as parts of fiction. For both viewers and filmmakers, what is primarily of importance about cinema, most of the time, is its capacity to convey moving fictions visually. Thus, we will consider it the same artform if and when the relevant images are generated by computers rather than photographed by cameras. Just as photography was more efficient than manually crafted animation, computer generation is more efficient than photography. The handwriting is already on the screen, so to speak. And because our devotion to motion pictures is unlikely to diminish under this new dispensation, realists like Cavell are on the wrong track when they theorize that the importance of cinema lies in its connection to the world past. For it is the way in which photography (and comparable media, some awaiting invention) can be used to produce *moving* fictions, in both senses of that term, that, for the most part, accounts for the nearly universal significance of film.

In arguing for the transparency of the photographic image, Cavell presents us with a choice – either the film image reproduces or re-presents the appearance of the object it is a photo of, or it is a reproduction or re-presentation of the object itself. Cavell invites us to go with the latter half of the disjunction, since he is convinced that it is metaphysically profligate to posit the existence of sights or appearances. But there is a question here of whether or not Cavell's argument is too powerful.

Recall that Cavell is concerned at this point in his argument to demarcate the boundary between the photographic and the painterly image. Supposedly, the photographic image is transparent; the painting is not. We see the object itself through the photograph and this is why film has the capacity to show us the world past. However, isn't it the case that the argument for the transparency of

the photographic/filmic image can be impressed to reach identical conclusions about painting?

Consider: paintings since the time of Plato, if not before, have been said to traffic in the appearances of things. If it is problematic to speak about appearances, for metaphysical reasons, when it comes to photography, it should be equally problematic to do so with respect to paintings. So if paintings do not represent the appearances of the objects that they are paintings of, what do they represent? The only alternative Cavell offers us is "the objects themselves." But then paintings are transparent pictures too. This would appear to be a counterintuitive result for most people.[8] But, in addition, it is an unhappy one for Cavell since he appears to need transparency to pertain uniquely to photography, not only to distinguish it from painting, but to pave the way for his "world-viewed" hypothesis. Is there a way out of this objection? We leave that puzzle for the reader's delectation.

The realist answer to the question of the nature of cinema has been one of the most enduring. It was voiced at the onset of cinema and has reverberated ever since. The realist is struck by the way in which its reliance upon photography forges a close link between film and the world. However, as already noted, most of the films that most people care about are not sought after for being recordings of the actual world, but for being departures therefrom. Most audiences do not swarm to movie theaters to see documentaries, but to see fictions. They are not after something real, but something made up. Even a deliriously lucrative documentary like *Fahrenheit 9/11* was dwarfed by the box office receipts of *Spiderman 2* one week later. For audiences are not looking for reality at the movies, but something unreal.

This has been the case since the magician, storyteller Georges Méliès knocked the documentarian, Lumière brothers off the top of the charts around the turn of the nineteenth to twentienth century. Moreover, it is that craving for unreality – which the cinema nourishes so readily – that induces theorists to think of film as an analog to dream. For what experience is more "unreal" than dreaming?

In her "A Note on the Film," Susanne K. Langer is attempting to find a place for film in her larger, systematic philosophy of art. For Langer, all art is a form of feeling. That is, every artwork is a symbol that externalizes something structurally isomorphic to some internal affective state. For example, she writes:

The tonal structures we call "music" bear a close logical relation to the forms of human feeling – feelings of growth and of attenuation, flowing and stowing, conflict and resolution, speed, arrest, terrific excitement, calm or subtle activation and dreamy lapses, – not joy and sorrow perhaps, but the poignancy of either and both – the greatness and brevity and eternal passing of everything vitally felt. Such is the pattern or logical form of sentience; and the pattern of music is that same form worked out in pure measured sound and silence. Music is a tonal analogue of emotive life.[9]

On Langer's view, an artwork objectifies (makes into an object) the patterns and rhythms of inner states of feeling. The forms of internal feelings are cast, so to speak, into the external world where they can be inspected. Our interest in art involves our desire to have our inner life clarified and shown forth in a way that permits us to examine it and to understand, for instance, how certain feelings hang together. Artworks perform this function by resembling the structure of various emotive states – by being isomorphic to them. A piece of music may have the tempo of longing.

Furthermore, Langer believes that, though artforms all share the generic purpose of embodying the forms of feelings, artforms also differ from each other by specializing in the objectification of different aspects of our affective lives. There is a division of labor amongst the arts; different artforms make manifest the structures of different types of inner experiences.

Since film is an artform, it too must be in the business of externalizing something of our inner lives. Langer conjectures that it is the inner experience of dreaming that is the domain of film to externalize and body forth. She arrives at this conclusion by noting what she takes to be three formal similarities between films and dreams. They are: (1) that the dreamer is always at the center of her dreams and the film viewer is always in the middle of the action onscreen; (2) both the film and the dream are marked by a sense of immediacy – a sense that everything that comes into view is of pressing importance; and (3) the "logic" of both film and dream can proceed on the basis of emotional association rather than in terms of more *natural* relations like causation and proximity.

For example, at the end of Frank Borzage's *A Farewell to Arms*, as Henry carries Catherine's dead body from the bed, there is a cutaway to the sky, full of flying doves. The doves soaring upwards is not a causal effect of Catherine's death, nor are they flying above the hospital. The image, in other words, is not linked to what precedes it either causally or geographically. What justifies the cut? It is a kind of emotional punctuation. It makes sense – emotional sense. That is, the logic – the order of the images – in film need not be organized with regard to either causation, geography, or even chronology – but like the sequence of apparitions in a dream it may unfold in accordance with affective promptings.

Langer's interest in film is that of a systematic philosopher. She has an overarching theory of art, and she wants to situate film in the appropriate niche in her system. But one might be attracted to the film-as-dream persuasion for different reasons. For example, in his "Vision and Dream in the Cinema," Francis Sparshott finds the analogy intriguing because he thinks that it might provide a way to explain how it is that we are so facile at comprehending the conventions of cinema.

Why doesn't an example of editing like that just cited from *A Farewell to Arms* leave us utterly baffled? How is it that people not previously exposed to cinema, including young children, can understand so quickly what is going on in a film? When you pause to think carefully about the typical ordering of images in films – with flashbacks, flashforwards, parallel editing, symbolical editing, and so forth – it can only strike you as a pretty bizarre and jumbled affair. How is it that we come to master it almost effortlessly?

Sparshott suggests that it may be something with which we are already familiar – a "logic" we already know from our dreams. That is, dreaming is rather like a psychic prototype for the conventions of film. We grasp those conventions so readily because film is so like a dream.

Whether one is drawn to the film-as-dream hypothesis for reasons of systematic philosophy, like Langer, or in order to explain an anomaly, like Sparshott, the logical structure of the argument is the same. It rests upon amassing a number of similarities between film and dream to the point where it seems plausible to regard them as cognate phenomena. Langer finds three nodes of similarity; Sparshott adds another – that we are disconnected from the space in film; that the spaces we see in a film are discontinuous with the space our bodies inhabit. This, Sparshott observes, is something that can happen in a dream. When you witness your own funeral in a dream, you are weirdly outside the event; it is as though you were watching it from another world. In film, this is always the case; with film viewing, we are always viewing a world (Cavell's "world viewed") from which we are ontologically alienated.

So far then we have discussed four analogies between films and dreams. For the film-as-dream theory to be compelling, there must be a sufficient number of analogies to convince us. Moreover, those alleged analogies must really obtain; they must be similarities that pertain distinctively to film and dreaming (they should not equally pertain to film and painting); and there should be no striking disanalogies between film and dream such that they outweigh the analogies.[10] How do the analogies in our readings fare in terms of these desiderata?

Not well. With regard to the requirement that the analogies actually obtain, the claim that the viewer and the dreamer are always at the center of the imagery would appear to be literally false. It is false because usually the film viewer is not in the center of the array. She is typically off to one side. That is, she is not normally seated in the theater in such a way that her line of sight is perfectly aligned with the place at the center of the image where the camera stood before the pro-filmic event. Indeed, this is one of the factors that gives rise to the discontinuity, noted by Sparshott, between our vision and the alienated "vision" manifested on screen. For we are always at the center of our own visual field, whereas we are standardly off-center with respect to the angle of vision of the movie camera; at any given film showing, most of us are seated to the left or to the right of the central line of sight that emanates from the lens of the photographic apparatus.[11]

Langer also analogizes film and dream on the basis of immediacy and what she calls the "rhythm of the thought stream," whose principles of sequential ordering are affective in dreams and can be in film. But these analogies do not pertain uniquely to the film-and-dream couplet. In a play, we think that everything we are shown is of pressing importance – everything is there for a reason. Recall Scribe's law: the gun that appears in the first act goes off in the third (just as no character appears who will not, sooner or later, add something to the action). Likewise, we take it that every object in a painting has a contribution to make to the whole. The sense of importance and urgency that everything we see in film acquires does not seem different

in kind from comparable feelings of immediacy derivable from theater and painting, i.e., from other visual arts.

Furthermore, film's capacity to develop its stories by means of affective logic faces criticisms on two fronts. First, though some films, such as Buñuel's *Andalusian Dog* and *Age of Gold*, may be as disjunctive as dreams, most films are far more rationally sequenced. This analogy, therefore, is not really an irresistible or unqualified one. Moreover, even were it more solid than it is, it would nevertheless fail to mark off a distinctive correlation between film and dream, since the reliance on so-called affective logic or emotive association is also available in other artforms, including poetry, the novel, painting (think of Surrealism), and theater (think of Symbolism).

That leaves us with one analogy standing, scarcely sufficient grounds for regarding film as a manifestation of dream forms. But even if one could assemble more analogies than canvassed so far, there is still a problem with the film-as-dream approach that neither Langer, Sparshott, nor any other thinker in this tradition has confronted, namely the existence of several awesome disanalogies between films and dreams.

The first is noted in our selection from Cavell's *The World Viewed*. It is this: only the dreamer can recall his dream; in fact, whether he is remembering it or imagining it when he tells some other person about it cannot be determined, since dreams are absolutely subjective experiences. Not so movies. If I do not remember how the character died in a movie, I can ask someone else who saw the film what happened, and she can tell me. Films are public; they are objective. Others have access to the movies I see, whereas no one but me has access to my dreams. And because films are interpersonally available, others can refresh my film memories, though no one can refresh my dream memories. In this way, experiencing a film is more like experiencing reality than it is like experiencing dreams, a point that a realist like Cavell is happy to point out.

Another disanalogy is developed by Cavell later in his book. He argues:

Here is an obvious reason not to be quick about equating films with dreams. Most dreams are boring narratives (like most tales of neurotic or physical symptoms), their skimpy surface out of all proportion with their riddle interest and their effect on the dreamer.[12]

That is, in dreams quotidian events, like trying to find one's notes before a talk, may be charged with electrifying emotion, so much so that once we awaken, we wonder what all the fuss was about. The situation was so ordinary. In films, on the other hand, the events typically are anything but mundane and the emotions they call for are completely proportionate – a three-headed alien lizard is about to conquer the world and we are, understandably, horrified. Films usually comprise extraordinary happenings; dreams frequently trade in bland events, no matter how incongruously burdened by affect they appear. Admittedly, some dreams may contain movie-like motifs – chases, falling from high places, and even monsters. But most dreams are not the stuff that movies are made of. Most dreams are not anywhere as interesting as films.

Given these disanalogies, it is difficult to credit the film-as-dream approach. Moreover, it is not clear even if the theory had legs that it would be profitable to run with it. For we do not really understand much about dreaming. Consequently, do we really learn anything about film by analogizing it to dreams? For a comparison to be informative, you need to know more about the thing – in this case, dream – that you are juxtaposing to the object of your curiosity (in this case, film). Otherwise you have nothing to learn. How can comparing something A of which you have next to no understanding to something B that you would like to know something about be in any way illuminating? From nothing, nothing comes.

We know next to nothing about dreams. Indeed, we probably know more about films and filmmaking than we know about dreams and dream-making. So the film-as-dream view can provide us with no insight into the ways of cinema. We can learn more about film by examining it directly than we can by examining it through the metaphor of dream.

Sparshott, on the other hand, does suggest one thing that the film-as-dream analogy might elucidate, viz., how it is that we are able to catch onto the conventions of film so quickly. *Ex hypothesi*, insofar as those conventions are extrapolations from the principles of dream construction, we have an inkling of how they work before we enter our first movie theater. However, as Sparshott candidly acknowledges, there are enticing alternative accounts to this view. One is that we also become acquainted with narrative very early on. And since we are exposed to the conventions of

storytelling virtually as soon as our care-givers start to talk to us, we are being prepared to assimilate those conventions as they occur in film as we hear our first fairytales. Thus, it may be that it is our narrative capacity, nurtured in tandem with the acquisition of language, that gives us a handle on the narrative conventions of film. Until that hypothesis is eliminated, there seems scant cause to invoke the dream analog.

In addition to the associations of film with reality and dream, there is a third approach to the ontology of film which is probably as longstanding as the other two. It is the notion of film-as-a-language. This idea became prominent at least by the 1920s. Silent filmmakers especially were wont to think of film as a kind of universal visual language – one that transcended the borders erected by natural languages such as French or Japanese. Filmmakers, such as F. W. Murnau, aspired to make films that could be shown anywhere in the world and yet be greeted with understanding by peoples so diverse that they understood almost nothing of each other's languages. Films would communicate pictorially by gesture; since they were silent films, the audiences would hear no speeches, and intertitles, ideally, would be kept to a minimum. Such filmmakers thought of film as an international idiom, a celluloid Esperanto, one structured analogously to a language, but a language that was thought to be accessible to all.

For example, the great Soviet filmmaker and theoretician V. I. Pudovkin wrote: "Editing is the language of the film director. Just as in living speech, so one may say in editing: there is a word – the piece of exposed film, the image[, and] a phrase – the combination of pieces."[13] Perhaps people like Pudovkin were confident that film could be a universal language because they thought that almost everyone has access to the basic vocabulary of film; everyone, that is, can recognize a moving picture of a dog, if they can already recognize a dog in "real life" (though, as we shall see, this perceptual accessibility of the filmic image may really be one reason to think that film images are *not* at all like words).

The film-as-language motif has had great influence in the history of film and on film pedagogy. Film classes and film textbooks often have titles like "The Language of Cinema" or "Elements of Film Language." Perhaps this is often meant only metaphorically. Maybe the implicit claim here amounts to nothing more than that film is broadly like a language because it communicates. If this is all that is intended by the notion that film is language-like, then the metaphor is harmless enough, since we can all agree that film communicates and is like a language, at least to that very limited extent. But a correlation like this is not sufficient to warrant calling film a language, since things other than language, like facial expressions, also communicate without being, strictly speaking, linguistic. (Indeed, a footprint could be used to communicate. I might intend to alert my friends that I am walking north by making deep imprints in the ground so that my tracks are unmistakable and patently meant to be that way. But we do not typically think of muddy footprints as linguistic.)

However, at least some theorists have taken the analogy more seriously than those who merely mean it as a colorful way of saying films communicate. For such theorists, film *is* a language. This, in turn, puts them at least within striking distance of delivering an answer to Sparshott's question about how we are able to master the disjunctions of film editing so easily. We master them as we master the conventions of any language. Humans are born with a capacity to learn languages. That capacity kicks in when we are exposed to film, just as it does when the biologically prepared child assimilates the words and combinatory rules of the discourse that surrounds him.

Thus, the film-as-language view may be a tempting one. Yet, as Gregory Currie shows in his devastating "The Long Goodbye: the Imaginary Language of Film," the film/language hypothesis cannot sustain close scrutiny. Currie conscientiously sets out the formal requirements of anything that we should be ready to call a language and points out that film, as it is currently practiced, falls far short of these criteria. Currie's dissection of the film-as-language analogy is so detailed and exacting that we have been unable to field anything representing the other side of the debate of comparable perspicuity. Due to the force of Currie's arguments, the burden of proof in this debate now clearly belongs to him who, without metaphorical intent, asserts that film is a language. (Perhaps it is an exercise that some readers may find provocative.)

Currie shows that given the structure of actual languages, film cannot be one. The relation of words to their referents, for example, is different than that of pictures, including moving ones, to their referents. The linguistic relation is conventional in the strong sense of being arbitrary. But as noted earlier, the relation between a motion pic-

ture image and what it is an image of is not arbitrary; if you can recognize dogs in daylight, then you can see them in the projector light too. The word "dog," all by itself, if you do not understand English, gives you no instructions as to how to pick dogs out; but you can use a moving picture of a dog to find one.

This, moreover, should remind us of how differently we acquire access to actual languages versus how we come to understand films. With actual languages, we learn the words one at a time. Knowing the word "dog" does not help us learn the rest of the vocabulary of English, except possibly for a few more words (like "doghouse" and "dogfight" and so on). But once we see a motion picture image of a dog, and catch onto the basics of cinematographic symbolism (viz., that shots represent that of which they are shots), then we are able to understand every other symbol in cinema in one fell swoop.

It is like being able to know the entire Hungarian language after learning only three or four words. But, of course, we can't learn a language that way because the elements of its vocabulary are associated with its referents in an arbitrary and conventional way that requires step-by-step, piece-by-piece, word-by-word acquisition. That film does not involve anything appreciably similar should warn us that it is a different animal altogether from language. And this is an immense disanalogy between film and language.

Cinematic images do not communicate after the fashion of words, but, as Currie indicates, they are naturally generative of meanings. And to the extent that cinematic images are naturally generative, models based on the conventionality of linguistic communication will be of little service.

As indicated during our discussion of the film/dream hypothesis, the way to criticize the film-as-something-else approach is to emphasize striking differences between films and their alleged analogs. As these disanalogies gather strength, they undermine the force of the attempted connection between film and that other category (dream, mirrors, language, and so on). Currie points out a number of other ways, in addition to the one just cited, in which film is palpably not like a language. A useful exercise is to read his article, pencil in hand, and to jot down all the disanalogies Currie adduces.

One problem with the film/language analogy that Currie does not develop at length is that the combination of film images by editing is not, as is often suggested, governed by a grammar. But if film has no grammar, then it is no language, since grammar is a hallmark of language.

Film sequences are not constructed after the manner of sentences.[14] Admittedly, there are conventional ways of articulating film sequences in the sense that there are provisional rules of thumb based upon what has done well or badly in the past regarding how to proceed and what to avoid. For example, there are prohibitions against crossing the one-hundred-and-eighty-degree line (which will flip the direction of character movement) and against cutting together shots from nearly the same camera set-up (jump-cuts). But these are advisory, and not genuinely grammatical.

Why? Because these rules can be flouted and the results will not be counted "wrong" or "incorrect" in any sense of the word. If a shot interpolation works, there is no talk of its being ungrammatical. The aforesaid "rules" can be successfully waived, as John Ford and Jean-Luc Godard have done. Of course, one transgresses these recommendations at one's own risk. Usually doing so has turned out nasty. But in some contexts, the risk may pay off aesthetically. Breaking with the customary way of doing things can have artistic dividends. Ignoring the so-called rules is not wrong, unless it undercuts the filmmaker's purposes, and it is right if it advances them. Thus, these rules are not grammatical in the strictest sense. For in the strictest sense, film editing does not have a grammar. But again, if there is no grammar, then there is no language.

Moreover, the reason for this lack of a grammar in this case is that editing is not a language, but an art. English has a grammar, but English poetry *qua* poetry does not. What is right as poetry is not what abides by strict grammatical conventions, but that which, when executed, proceeds in cognizance of how things are usually done, but which nevertheless works with or against traditional procedures in order to move the reader in the way the poet intends. If an infinitive needs to be split, so be it. This is not poetically ungrammatical. For poetry has no grammar. Ditto film editing. And likewise all the other arts.

Traditionally, editing has always had the best claim to be language-like of all the elements of film. It is combinatory. And as Currie points out, there is little hope for the correlation that Pudovkin advertises between the shot and the word. So editing looks to be the best hope for the language analogy.

But because film editing is an art and not a language, the only relevant test for its correctness is whether the editing in question works in terms of the way the filmmaker intends to move spectators. Sentences, on the other hand, are ungrammatical, even if they get the job their speakers intend done. So, film editing lacks a grammar in that respect, and if it lacks a grammar, it is not a language, which, among other things, implies that the language model is ultimately of little or no use in explaining how we come to understand the significance of the way in which a series of shots is ordered. For that we need some sense of the story the filmmaker intends to tell or, if the film is not narrative, whatever other point or purpose she means to convey.

Rather than analogize film to something else – to a mirror, as some realists do, or to dreaming or to language – the essays by Arthur C. Danto and Noël Carroll emphasize a feature that distinguishes cinema from its neighbors in the realm of images, namely, movement. That movement is the mark of film is, of course, already suggested by ordinary language, where it is common to call films moving pictures or motion pictures. And, of course, the most common term for film in American culture is "movie," i.e., something that moves. The association of film with movement, as well, is quite old. One early label for film was *bioscope*, where *bio* alluded to life, where life, in turn, is associated with that which is animate, that which can move.

In his article "Moving Pictures," Arthur Danto elegantly demonstrates that a necessary condition or essential condition for film is that it deliver the impression of movement. Danto makes his case by inviting us to imagine two indiscernible objects – a page from a Tolstoy novel and a film of the same. In both cases, what is before our eyes does not move (let us assume that there is no discernible shakiness in the film image). That is, the two images look the same. Nevertheless, they are ontologically different; they belong to two distinct categories. But what is the differentia that determines that difference. Danto suggests a hypothesis – to wit, the page of the book will not move, if we do not move it, but the page onscreen might move in all sorts of ways – for example, the letters on the page could start moving like little insects or pair off and dance, or the page could "magically" turn, with no apparent human intervention, or, it could ignite and burn up, again with no visible human intervention. Things move in movies. That's why we call them moving pictures. In this regard, they are categorically or conceptually distinguishable from pictures that don't move – photographs, slides, paintings, drawings, and suchlike – what, colloquially, we refer to as still pictures. What are films, then? Danto argues that they are moving pictures.

The kind of argument Danto uses in this case is a hypothesis to the best explanation. He introduces a peculiarity – a vexation. Why, inasmuch as the two pages of the Tolstoy novel look exactly the same, do we feel that they are different? On what does this nagging intuition rest? Danto explains it by hypothesizing that there is a difference here, one that awaits articulation. And he zeroes in on it in terms of the distinction between movement and non-movement. This kind of argument is called a hypothesis to the best explanation – the explanation that best explains our conviction of difference is the leading candidate for how we sort the pertinent indiscernibilia into different classes. This kind of argument is also sometimes called a transcendental deduction. Danto is a philosopher who favors this style of argumentation more than any of his contemporaries. He holds a virtual copyright on it and has even suggested that this is the style of argument that shows us that what we are doing is philosophy and not something else. In "Moving Pictures," he quite effectively uses his method of indiscernibles to hypothesize that what makes a picture a cinematic one is that it is a *moving* picture rather than a *still* picture.

In his "Defining the Moving Image," Carroll builds on Danto's insight that movement, or, at least, the physical possibility of the impression of movement in the image, is a necessary feature of what is alternatively called film, or cinema, or the movies. Carroll modifies Danto's discovery slightly by speaking of moving *images* rather than moving *pictures* in order to accommodate the case of abstract films. Carroll also appropriates Sparshott's observation that "vision" in the cinema is alienated, or, as Carroll prefers to put it, the image is a "detached display."

For Carroll, the fact that the cinematic image is a detached display distinguishes what we see on film from what we see in reality. And, insofar as the image is a moving image, film is categorically different from painting, photography, drawing, etching, and any other form of still imaging. But what hives off cinema from theater? Carroll says, somewhat baroquely, that something belongs to the class of moving images only if its token performances are generated by a template that is a token *and* only if performance tokens of it are not artworks in their own right.

The bizarre-sounding condition – that the token performances of the moving image are generated by templates that are themselves tokens – is explained in the text. But the idea behind it is easy to understand. Performances of a film, say *Puppetmaster* – that is, film screenings of *Puppetmaster* – are generated from a template, a film print, a video cassette, a DVD of *Puppetmaster* which is a token of the type, the masterpiece made by Hou Hsiao-Hsien. The DVD in my hand is one of multiple copies of the film; it is a token of the film; it is a material thing that can be destroyed, though if my copy or token of *Puppetmaster* is destroyed, the type is not. Moreover, a performance or showing of *Puppetmaster* is a purely mechanical affair; I pop it into my DVD player and, if all the settings on the machine are correct, we get a perfect showing of the film.

But this is radically different from the performance of a play. It can only be executed by actors who are actively interpreting the lines of the play. There is nothing automatic or mechanical here. The actor conveys Shakespeare's *As You Like It* to us by interpreting how to say, how to deliver, how to interpret this or that speech of Rosalind's. That is, the performance of a play is mind-mediated, whereas the performance of a film is mediated automatically by the routine operation of a mechanical apparatus on a template. Moreover, since the operation of this machinery can be fully automatized – think of all those projectors in the cineplex that are, for the most part, running themselves – there is no temptation to think of the performance (the screening) of a film as an artwork in its own right, whereas the interpretively mediated performance of a play surely is.

But even with the enumeration of all these features, Carroll still worries that his definition of the moving image is too broad. For it encompasses all sorts of what might be called "moving sculptures," for example, the "dancing figures" on top of music boxes that circle each other in a perpetual waltz and the robots in Disneyworld who "do" such things as deliver the Gettysburg Address. To forestall such counterexamples, Caroll adds another condition to his definition of the moving image. He requires that it be two-dimensional.

But is there a problem here? Does the addition of the criterion of two-dimensionality render

Caroll's definition of the moving image too exclusive? Why think so? Suppose that we could produce moving holographs. Imagine that we could project a scene from *Gladiator* three-dimensionally. We would sit around a virtual arena, like the Roman populace in the past, and we would watch Maximus duel his opponents in three dimensions. Should not such a spectacle count as a moving image? But doesn't Carroll's requirement that moving images be two-dimensional block this? Does this show that Carroll's two-dimensionality cannot be a necessary condition for something to count as a moving image? For putatively our holographic *Gladiator* is a moving image but it is not two-dimensional.[15]

In order to meet this objection, Carroll might attempt to deny that the holograph is really two-dimensional. After all, it is not a solid figure. If you try to strike Maximus, your hand will pass right through him. But even if the image is insubstantial, it still seems correct to say that it is three-dimensional. Maximus has girth, even though he has no bulk. He may have no weight, but he has height, width, and depth. It is not clear that solidity is really a necessary condition for three-dimensionality.

Alternatively, it may be argued that just because the holograph is three-dimensional, it is not a moving image. Recall – the criterion of two-dimensionality was introduced in order to distinguish what we call moving images from moving sculptures. Since the moving sculpture has three dimensions, it is natural to call a moving holograph a moving sculpture.

Is this merely an ad hoc solution – one that basically invokes a new category to avoid an embarrassing theoretical predicament? And yet many classic sculptures have moving parts. Many fountains involve sculptural ensembles in which moving water represents moving water. There is one in Holland where the urination of a young boy is represented by a spout in the appropriate place shooting liquid forth. Some fountains, indeed, might be thought of entirely as abstract moving sculptures – volumes crossing in mid-air and then diffusing. That is, the category of moving sculpture has not been made up on the spot. There are such things. Why shouldn't moving holographs be classified in this way, if they are in fact three-dimensional? Or is the idea of a moving sculpture just a sophistry? We leave it to the reader to determine the answer.

And after contemplating that objection, here is another. Danto and Carroll talk about moving images. But in doing so, aren't they changing the subject? The notion of a moving image is broader than the term *film* as it is traditionally understood. "Film" refers to the photographic film stock on which motion-picture images are fixed. It is a very specific kind of material. Moving images, on the other hand, do not require such a base. They can be made via video or computer generation. For that matter, they can be produced via paper, as in the case of a cartoon flip book. But when we speak of film in ordinary parlance, we do not have children's flip books in mind. Rather we are talking about something that is mounted on celluloid. Therefore, the notion of the moving image as elaborated by Danto and then Carroll is really besides the point. They have left off talking about cinema and are onto something else – something that includes film, but also much more.

This is the sort of rebuke that a realist might level especially at Carroll. In response, the friends of the moving image are likely to respond that cinema never was only the name of moving images generated by cinematography. There has long been the use of all sorts of optical effects, composite shots integrating drawing and animation, lab effects, the use of blue screens, and so on that are not reducible to straight photographic shooting. The label "film" has always been shorthand for much more, much more that was not literally photographic. The widespread use of computers in movie production makes the heterogeneous nature of the image even more evident. Film is just one way of producing movie images. Since it was arguably the first way, the name has stuck. But what it really signifies is that the images in question move. Thus, it is more in keeping with the nature of the practice that we call the art of film (or cinema or movie-making) to bring our nomenclature up-to-date by rechristening it as the art of the moving image. Calling it film, where this is thought to require that it is a necessary condition for membership in the class, is not a philosophical discovery, but a misnomer. The proponents of the concept of the moving image are not changing the subject, but rather they are finally getting it into the right ontological framework.

Or are they? If movies in the future are wholly computer-generated, will we regard them in the same way that we regard photographic films made by once living and breathing human actors? Will it be the same practice as the one we currently call movie-making? Is the difference between animation and live-action movie production an ontological difference? What if you could not tell them apart by looking? What if instead of comparing Minnie Mouse with Sophia Loren, you had two films of *Two Women* that looked exactly alike, but one was the classic made by photography and the other was CGI from one end to the other with no resort to photography? Do they belong to the same or different artforms? Do you think it is better to continue talking about film, in the manner of the realist, or is it better to speak of the moving image?

N.C.

Notes

1 Hugo Munsterberg, *Film: A Psychological Study* (New York: Dover Publications, 1970).

2 For further discussion, see Noël Carroll, "Film/Mind Analogies: The Case of Hugo Munsterberg," in *Theorizing the Moving Image* (Cambridge: Cambridge University Press, 1996), pp. 291–304.

3 For further elaboration of this argument, see Noël Carroll, "Forget the Medium!" in *Engaging the Moving Image* (New Haven, Connecticut: Yale University Press, 2003).

4 This may not be completely accurate inasmuch as Cavell appears to reject the prospects of film as a modernist art.

5 Cavell stresses that the photograph frames a space that is continuous with the rest of the actual world because this will be crucial to his claim that part of the power of film is that it relieves the anxiety of solipsism by exposing us to the *whole world* from which we are absent. That is, what is on the other side of the rectangle of the motion picture frame is the rest of the entire actual world. That is what the motion picture image is continuous with. On the other hand, the same, putatively, cannot be said of the painting, since its subject may be entirely imaginary in a way that does not permit us to say that anything is adjacent to the picture frame. But with a photographic/filmic image, since it is *of* the world, it also makes sense to ask what stands next to what is seen onscreen. For there is always something there.

6 Nor would such spectacles need to be delivered to movie houses on film reels; they could be conveyed by satellite feeds.

7 Indeed, many of us from literate and industrialized societies first fall in love with the moving image upon exposure to television. But how many youngsters and even adults can really explain how the TV image is produced and relayed?

8 It would not, however, disturb Dominic Lopes, an author you encountered in Part I. Nevertheless, Lopes is decidedly in the minority on this issue.

9 Susanne K. Langer, *Feeling and Form* (New York: Scribners, 1953), p. 27. (See also ch. 5 in this volume.)

10 Because Langer's defense of the film-as-dream analogy is connected to her systematic philosophy of art, she is open to an objection that many other proponents of the analogy are not. To wit: why suppose that film is to be associated with any form of inner life whatsoever? If you are committed to the view that every artform, such as film, is connected to some internal form of feeling, then you might be attracted to dream as the likeliest candidate. But if you do not think that the art of film requires a psychic analog, would the three glancing correlations Langer adduces seem at all compelling? Another way to develop this criticism is to challenge outright the idea that every artform is connected to some generic stratum of feeling.

11 If, as just noted, we are normally at the center of our everyday, waking visual experiences, why does Langer choose to analogize what she (mistakenly) takes to be the nature of film perception with dream perception, rather than waking perception? Even had she been correct about film perception, she would not have picked out a distinctive correlation between film perception and dream perception, since the central positioning she has in mind is also a feature of waking perception.

12 Cavell, *The World Viewed: Reflections on the Ontology of Film* (New York: Viking Press, 1971), p. 67.

13 V. I. Pudovkin, *Film Technique and Film Acting*, trans. I. Montagu (New York: Evergreen Press, 1970), p. 100.

14 Obviously, since it has been established that film as film is not wordlike, it follows that it does not have syntax – the rules that recursively combine words into well-formed formulae. This too is a major disanalogy with language.

15 This counterexample was proposed by Tom Wartenberg.

4

The World Viewed

Stanley Cavell

What is film?

Sights and Sounds

The beginning of an answer is given by the two continuously intelligent, interesting, and to me useful theorists I have read on the subject. Erwin Panofsky puts it this way: "The medium of the movies is physical reality as such."[1] André Bazin emphasizes essentially this idea many times and many ways: at one point he says, "Cinema is committed to communicate only by way of what is real"; and then, "The cinema [is] of its essence a dramaturgy of Nature."[2] "Physical reality as such," taken literally, is not correct: that phrase better fits the specialized pleasures of *tableaux vivants*, or formal gardens, or Minimal Art. What Panofsky and Bazin have in mind is that the basis of the medium of movies is photographic, and that a photograph is *of* reality or nature. If to this we add that the medium is one in which the photographic image is projected and gathered on a screen, our question becomes: What happens to reality when it is projected and screened?

That it is reality that we have to deal with, or some mode of depicting it, finds surprising confirmation in the way movies are remembered, and misremembered. It is tempting to suppose that movies are hard to remember the way dreams are, and that is not a bad analogy. As with dreams, you do sometimes *find* yourself remembering moments in a film, and a procedure in *trying* to remember is to find your way back to a characteristic mood the thing has left you with. But, unlike dreams, other people can help you remember, indeed are often indispensable to the enterprise of remembering. Movies are hard to remember, the way the actual events of yesterday are. And yet, again like dreams, *certain* moments from films viewed decades ago will nag as vividly as moments of childhood. It is as if you had to remember what happened *before* you slept. Which suggests that film awakens as much as it enfolds you.

It may seem that this starting point – the projection of reality – begs the question of the medium of film, because movies, and writing about movies, have from their beginnings also recognized that film can depict the fantastic as readily as the natural.[3] What is true about that idea is not denied in speaking of movies as "communicating by way of what is real": the displacement of objects and persons from their natural sequences and locales is itself an acknowledgment of the physicality of their existence. It is as if, for all their insistence on the newness of the medium, the antirealist theorists could not shake the idea that it was essentially a form of painting, for it was painting which had visually repudiated – anyway, forgone – the representation of reality. This would have helped them neglect the differences between representation and projection. But an immediate

Stanley Cavell, excerpts from *The World Viewed: Reflections on the Ontology of Film* (New York: Viking Press, 1971): 16–41. Reprinted by permission of Stanley Cavell.

fact about the medium of the photograph (still or in motion) is that it is not painting. (An immediate fact about the *history* of photography is that this was not at first obvious.)

What does this mean – not painting? A photograph does not present us with "likenesses" of things; it presents us, we want to say, with the things themselves. But wanting to say that may well make us ontologically restless. "Photographs present us with things themselves" sounds, and ought to sound, false or paradoxical. Obviously a photograph of an earthquake, or of Garbo, is not an earthquake happening (fortunately), or Garbo in the flesh (unfortunately). But this is not very informative. And, moreover, it is no less paradoxical or false to hold up a photograph of Garbo and say, "That is not Garbo," if all you mean is that the object you are holding up is not a human creature. Such troubles in notating so obvious a fact suggest that we do not know what a photograph is; we do not know how to place it ontologically. We might say that we don't know how to think of the *connection* between a photograph and what it is a photograph of. The image is not a likeness; it is not exactly a replica, or a relic, or a shadow, or an apparition either, though all of these natural candidates share a striking feature with photographs – an aura or history of magic surrounding them.

One might wonder that similar questions do not arise about recordings of sound. I mean, on the whole we would be hard put to find it false or paradoxical to say, listening to a record, "That's an English horn"; there is no trace of temptation to add (as it were, to oneself), "But I know it's really only a recording." Why? A child might be very puzzled by the remark, said in the presence of a phonograph, "That's an English horn," if something else had already been pointed out to him as an English horn. Similarly, he might be very puzzled by the remark, said of a photograph, "That's your grandmother." Very early, children are *no longer* puzzled by such remarks, luckily. But that doesn't mean we know why they were puzzled, or why they no longer are. And I am suggesting that we don't know either of these things about ourselves.

Is the difference between auditory and visual transcription a function of the fact that we are fully accustomed to hearing things that are invisible, not present to us, not present with us? We would be in trouble if we weren't so accustomed, because it is the nature of hearing that what is heard comes *from* someplace, whereas what you can see you can look *at*. It is why sounds are

warnings, or calls; it is why our access to another world is normally through voices from it; and why a man can be spoken to by God and survive, but not if he sees God, in which case he is no longer in *this* world. Whereas we are not accustomed to seeing things that are invisible, or not present to us, not present with us; or we are not accustomed to acknowledging that we do (except for dreams). Yet this seems, ontologically, to be what is happening when we look at a photograph: we see things that are not present.

Someone will object: "That is playing with words. We're not seeing something not present; we are looking at something perfectly present, namely, a *photograph*." But that is affirming something I have not denied. On the contrary, I am precisely describing, or wishing to describe, what it means to say that there is this photograph here. It may be felt that I make too great a mystery of these objects. My feeling is rather that we have forgotten how mysterious these things are, and in general how *different* different things are from one another, as though we had forgotten how to value them. This is in fact something movies teach us.

Suppose one tried accounting for the familiarity of recordings by saying, "When I say, listening to a record, 'That's an English horn,' what I really mean is, 'That's the *sound* of an English horn'; moreover, when I am in the presence of an English horn playing, I still don't literally hear the horn, I hear the sound of the horn. So I don't worry about hearing a horn when the horn is not present, because *what* I hear is exactly the same (ontologically the same, and if my equipment is good enough, empirically the same) whether the thing is present or not." What this rigmarole calls attention to is that sounds can be perfectly copied, and that we have various interests in copying them. (For example, if they couldn't be copied, people would never learn to talk.) It is interesting that there is no comparable rigmarole about visual transcriptions. The problem is not that photographs are not visual copies of objects, or that objects can't be visually copied. The problem is that even if a photograph were a copy of an object, so to speak, it would not bear the relation to its object that a recording bears to the sound it copies. We said that the record reproduces its sound, but we cannot say that a photograph reproduces a sight (or a look, or an appearance). It can seem that language is missing a word at this place. Well, you can always invent a word. But one doesn't know what to pin the word *on* here. It isn't that there aren't sights to see, nor even that a sight has by definition to be especially *worth* seeing (hence could not be the sort of thing we are *always* seeing), whereas sounds are being thought of here, not unplausibly, as what we always hear. A sight *is* an object (usually a very large object, like the Grand Canyon or Versailles, although small southern children are frequently held, by the person in charge of them, to be sights) or an extraordinary happening, like the aurora borealis; and what you see, when you sight something, is an object – anyway, not the sight of an object. Nor will the epistemologist's "sense-data" or "surfaces" provide correct descriptions here. For we are not going to say that photographs provide us with the sense-data of the objects they contain, because if the sense-data of photographs were the same as the sense-data of the objects they contain, we couldn't tell a photograph of an object from the object itself. To say that a photograph is of the surfaces of objects suggests that it emphasizes texture. What is missing is not a word, but, so to speak, something in nature – the fact that objects don't *make* sights, or *have* sights. I feel like saying: Objects are too *close* to their sights to give them up for reproducing; in order to reproduce the sights they (as it were) make, you have to reproduce *them* – make a mold, or take an impression. Is that what a photograph does? We might, as Bazin does on occasion, try thinking of a photograph as a visual mold or a visual impression. My dissatisfaction with that idea is, I think, that physical molds and impressions and imprints have clear procedures for getting *rid* of their originals, whereas in a photograph, the original is still as present as it ever was. Not present as it once was to the camera; but that is only a mold-machine, not the mold itself.

Photographs are not *hand*-made; they are manufactured. And what is manufactured is an image of the world. The inescapable fact of mechanism or automatism in the making of these images is the feature Bazin points to as "[satisfying], once and for all and in its very essence, our obsession with realism."[4]

It is essential to get to the right depth of this fact of automatism. It is, for example, misleading to say, as Bazin does, that "photography has freed the plastic arts from their obsession with likeness,"[5] for this makes it seem (and it does often look) as if photography and painting were in competition, or that painting had wanted something that photography broke in and satisfied. So far as photography satisfied a wish, it satisfied a wish not confined to painters, but the human wish, intensifying in the

West since the Reformation, to escape subjectivity and metaphysical isolation – a wish for the power to reach this world, having for so long tried, at last hopelessly, to manifest fidelity to another. And painting was not "freed" – and not by photography – from its obsession with likeness. Painting, in Manet, was *forced* to forgo likeness exactly because of its own obsession with reality, because the illusions it had learned to create did not provide the conviction in reality, the connection with reality, that it craved.[6] One might even say that in withdrawing from likeness, painting freed photography to be invented.

And if what is meant is that photography freed painting from the idea that a painting had to be a picture (that is, *of* or *about* something else), that is also not true. Painting did not free itself, did not force itself to maintain itself apart, from *all* objective reference until long after the establishment of photography; and then not because it finally dawned on painters that paintings were not pictures, but because that was the way to maintain connection with (the history of) the art of painting, to maintain conviction in its powers to create paintings, meaningful objects in paint.

And are we sure that the final denial of objective reference amounts to a complete yielding of connection with reality – once, that is, we have given up the idea that "connection with reality" is to be understood as "provision of likeness"? We can be sure that the view of painting as dead without reality, and the view of painting as dead with it, are both in need of development in the views each takes of reality and of painting. We can say, painting and reality no longer *assure* one another.

It could be said further that what painting wanted, in wanting connection with reality, was a sense of *presentness*[7] – not exactly a conviction of the world's presence to us, but of our presence to it. At some point the unhinging of our consciousness from the world interposed our subjectivity between us and our presentness to the world. Then our subjectivity became what is present to us, individuality became isolation. The route to conviction in reality was through the acknowledgment of that endless presence of self. What is called expressionism is one possibility of representing this acknowledgment. But it would, I think, be truer to think of expressionism as a representation of our *response* to this new fact of our condition – our terror of ourselves in isolation – rather than as a representation of the world from within the condition of isolation itself. It would, to that extent, not be a new mastery of fate by creating selfhood against no matter what odds; it would be the sealing of the self's fate by theatricalizing it. Apart from the wish for selfhood (hence the always simultaneous granting of otherness as well), I do not understand the value of art. Apart from this wish and its achievement, art is exhibition.

To speak of our subjectivity as the route back to our conviction in reality is to speak of romanticism. Perhaps romanticism can be understood as the natural struggle between the representation and the acknowledgment of our subjectivity (between the acting out and the facing off of ourselves, as psychoanalysts would more or less say). Hence Kant, and Hegel; hence Blake secreting the world he believes in; hence Wordsworth competing with the history of poetry by writing out himself, writing himself back into the world. A century later Heidegger is investigating Being by investigating *Dasein* (because it is in *Dasein* that Being shows up best, namely as questionable), and Wittgenstein investigates the world ("the possibilities of phenomena") by investigating what we say, what we are inclined to say, what our pictures of phenomena are, in order to wrest the world from our possessions so that we may possess it again. Then the recent major painting which Fried describes as objects of *presentness* would be painting's latest effort to maintain its conviction in its own power to establish connection with reality – by permitting us presentness to ourselves, apart from which there is no hope for a world.

Photography overcame subjectivity in a way undreamed of by painting, a way that could not satisfy painting, one which does not so much defeat the act of painting as escape it altogether: by *automatism*, by removing the human agent from the task of reproduction.

One could accordingly say that photography was never in competition with painting. What happened was that at some point the quest for visual reality, or the "memory of the present" (as Baudelaire put it), split apart. To maintain conviction in our connection with reality, to maintain our presentness, painting accepts the recession of the world. Photography maintains the presentness of the world by accepting our absence from it. The reality in a photograph is present to me while I am not present to it; and a world I know, and see, but to which I am nevertheless not present (through no fault of my subjectivity), is a world past.

Photograph and Screen

Let us notice the specific sense in which photographs are of the world, of reality as a whole. You can always ask, pointing to an object in a photograph – a building, say – what lies behind it, totally obscured by it. This only accidentally makes sense when asked of an object in a painting. You can always ask, of an area photographed, what lies adjacent to that area, beyond the frame. This generally makes no sense asked of a painting. You can ask these questions of objects in photographs because they have answers in reality. The world of a painting is not continuous with the world of its frame; at its frame, a world finds its limits. We might say: A painting *is* a world; a photograph is *of* the world. What happens in a photograph is that *it* comes to an end. A photograph is cropped, not necessarily by a paper cutter or by masking but by the camera itself. The camera crops it by predetermining the amount of view it will accept; cutting, masking, enlarging, predetermine the amount after the fact. (Something like this phenomenon shows up in recent painting. In this respect, these paintings have found, at the extremest negation of the photographic, media that achieve the condition of photographs.) The camera, being finite, crops a portion from an indefinitely larger field; continuous portions of that field could be included in the photograph in fact taken; in principle, it could all be taken. Hence objects in photographs that run past the edge do not feel cut; they are aimed at, shot, stopped live. When a photograph is cropped, the rest of the world is cut *out*. The implied presence of the rest of the world, and its explicit rejection, are as essential in the experience of a photograph as what it explicitly presents. A camera is an opening in a box: that is the best emblem of the fact that a camera holding on an object is holding the rest of the world away. The camera has been praised for extending the senses; it may, as the world goes, deserve more praise for confining them, leaving room for thought.

The world of a moving picture is screened. The screen is not a support, not like a canvas; there is nothing to support, that way. It holds a projection, as light as light. A screen is a barrier. What does the silver screen screen? It screens me from the world it holds – that is, makes me invisible. And it screens that world from me – that is, screens its existence from me. That the projected world does not exist (now) is its only difference from reality.

(There is no feature, or set of features, in which it differs. Existence is not a predicate.) Because it is the field of a photograph, the screen has no frame; that is to say, no border. Its limits are not so much the edges of a given shape as they are the limitations, or capacity, of a container. The screen *is* a frame; the frame is the whole field of the screen – as a frame of film is the whole field of a photograph, like the frame of a loom or a house. In this sense, the screen-frame is a mold, or form.[8]

The fact that in a moving picture successive film frames are fit flush into the fixed screen frame results in a phenomenological frame that is indefinitely extendible and contractible, limited in the smallness of the object it can grasp only by the state of its technology, and in largeness only by the span of the world. Drawing the camera back, and panning it, are two ways of extending the frame; a close-up is of a part of the body, or of one object or small set of objects, supported by and reverberating the whole frame of nature. The altering frame is the image of perfect attention. Early in its history the cinema discovered the possibility of *calling* attention to persons and parts of persons and objects; but it is equally a possibility of the medium not to call attention to them but, rather, to let the world happen, to let its parts draw attention to themselves according to their natural weight. This possibility is less explored than its opposite. Dreyer, Flaherty, Vigo, Renoir, and Antonioni are masters of it.

Audience, Actor, and Star

The depth of the automatism of photography is to be read not alone in its mechanical production of an image of reality, but in its mechanical defeat of our presence to that reality. The audience in a theater can be defined as those to whom the actors are present while they are not present to the actors.[9] But movies allow the audience to be mechanically absent. The fact that I am invisible and inaudible to the actors, and fixed in position, no longer needs accounting for; it is not part of a convention I have to comply with; the proceedings do not have to make good the fact that I do nothing in the face of tragedy, or that I laugh at the follies of others. In viewing a movie my helplessness is mechanically assured: I am present not at something happening, which I must confirm, but at something that has happened, which I absorb (like a memory). In this, movies resemble novels,

a fact mirrored in the sound of narration itself, whose tense is the past.

It might be said: "But surely there is the obvious difference between a movie house and a theater that is not recorded by what has so far been said and that outweighs all this fiddle of differences. The obvious difference is that in a theater we are in the presence of an actor, in a movie house we are not. You have said that in both places the actor is in our presence and in neither are we in his, the difference lying in the mode of our absence. But there is also the plain fact that in a theater a real man is *there*, and in a movie no real man is there. That is obviously essential to the differences between our responses to a play and to a film." What that means must not be denied; but the fact remains to be understood. Bazin meets it head on by simply denying that "the screen is incapable of putting us 'in the presence of' the actor"; it, so to speak, relays his presence to us, as by mirrors.[10] Bazin's idea here really fits the facts of live television, in which the thing we are presented with is happening simultaneously with its presentation. But in live television, what is present to us while it is happening is not the world, but an event standing out from the world. Its point is not to reveal, but to cover (as with a gun), to keep something on view.

It is an incontestable fact that in a motion picture no live human being is up there. But a human *something* is, and something unlike anything else we know. We can stick to our plain description of that human something as "in our presence while we are not in his" (present *at* him, because looking at him, but not present *to* him) and still account for the difference between his live presence and his photographed presence to us. We need to consider what is present or, rather, since the topic is the human being, *who* is present.

One's first impulse may be to say that in a play the character is present, whereas in a film the actor is. That sounds phony or false: one wants to say that both are present in both. But there is more to it, ontologically more. Here I think of a fine passage of Panofsky's:

Othello or Nora are definite, substantial figures created by the playwright. They can be played well or badly, and they can be "interpreted" in one way or another; but they most definitely exist, no matter who plays them or even whether they are played at all. The character in a film, however, lives and dies with the actor. It is not

Stanley Cavell

the entity "Othello" interpreted by Robeson or the entity "Nora" interpreted by Duse, it is the entity "Greta Garbo" incarnate in a figure called Anna Christie or the entity "Robert Montgomery" incarnate in a murderer who, for all we know or care to know, may forever remain anonymous but will never cease to haunt our memories.[11]

If the character lives and dies with the actor, that ought to mean that the actor lives and dies with the character. I think that is correct, but it needs clarification. Let us develop it slightly.

For the stage, an actor works himself into a role; for the screen, a performer takes the role onto himself. The stage actor explores his potentialities and the possibilities of his role simultaneously; in performance these meet at a point in spiritual space – the better the performance, the deeper the point. In this respect, a role in a play is like a position in a game, say, third base: various people can play it, but the great third baseman is a man who has accepted and trained his skills and instincts most perfectly and matches them most intimately with his discoveries of the possibilities and necessities of third base. The screen performer explores his role like an attic and takes stock of his physical and temperamental endowment; he lends his being to the role and accepts only what fits; the rest is nonexistent. On the stage there are two beings, and the being of the character assaults the being of the actor; the actor survives only by yielding. A screen performance requires not so much training as planning. Of course, both the actor and the performer require, or can make use of, experience. The actor's role is his subject for study, and there is no end to it. But the screen performer is essentially not an actor at all: he *is* the subject of study, and a study not his own. (That is what the content of a photograph is – its subject.) On a screen the study is projected; on a stage the actor is the projector. An exemplary stage performance is one which, for a time, most fully creates a character. After Paul Scofield's performance in *King Lear*, we know who King Lear is, we have seen him in the flesh. An exemplary screen performance is one in which, at a time, a star is born. After *The Maltese Falcon* we know a new star, only distantly a person. "Bogart" *means* "the figure created in a given set of films." His presence in those films is who he is, not merely in the sense in which a photograph of an event is that event; but in the sense that if those films did not exist,

Bogart would not exist, the name "Bogart" would not mean what it does. The figure it names is not only in our presence, we are in his, in the only sense we could ever be. That is all the "presence" he has.

But it is complicated. A full development of all this would require us to place such facts as these: Humphrey Bogart was a man, and he appeared in movies both before and after the ones that created "Bogart." Some of them did not create a new star (say, the stable groom in *Dark Victory*), some of them defined stars – anyway meteors – that may be incompatible with Bogart (e.g., Duke Mantee and Fred C. Dobbs) but that are related to that figure and may enter into our later experience of it. And Humphrey Bogart was both an accomplished actor and a vivid subject for a camera. Some people are, just as some people are both good pitchers and good hitters; but there are so few that it is surprising that the word "actor" keeps on being used in place of the more beautiful and more accurate word "star"; the stars are only to gaze at, after the fact, and their actions divine our projects. Finally, we must note the sense in which the creation of a (screen) performer is also the creation of a character – not the kind of character an author creates, but the kind that certain real people are: a type.

Types; Cycles as Genres

Around this point our attention turns from the physical medium of cinema in general to the specific forms or genres the medium has taken in the course of its history.

Both Panofsky and Bazin begin at the beginning, noting and approving that early movies adapt popular or folk arts and themes and performers and characters: farce, melodrama, circus, music hall, romance, etc. And both are gratifyingly contemptuous of intellectuals who could not come to terms with those facts of life. (Such intellectuals are the alter egos of the film promoters they so heartily despise. Roxy once advertised a movie as "Art, in every sense of the word"; his better half declaims, "This is not art, in any sense of the word.") Our question is, why did such forms and themes and characters lend themselves to film? Bazin, in what I have read of him, is silent on the subject, except to express gratitude to film for revivifying these ancient forms, and to justify in general the legitimacy of adaptation from one art to another. Arnold Hauser, if I understand him, suggests wrong answers, in a passage that includes the remark "Only a young art can be popular,"[12] a remark that not only is in itself baffling (did Verdi and Dickens and Chaplin and Frank Loesser work in young arts?) but suggests that it was only natural for the movies to pick up the forms they did. It *was* natural – anyway it happened fast enough – but not because movies were destined to popularity (they were at first no more popular than other forms of entertainment). In any case, popular arts are likely to pick up the forms and themes of high art for their material – popular theater naturally *burlesques*. And it means next to nothing to say that movies are young, because we do not know what the normal life span of an art is supposed to be, nor what would count as a unit of measure. Panofsky raises the question of the appropriateness of these original forms, but his answer is misleading.

> The legitimate paths of evolution [for the film] were opened, not by running away from the folk art character of the primitive film but by developing it within the limits of its own possibilities. Those primordial archetypes of film productions on the folk art level – success or retribution, sentiment, sensation, pornography, and crude humor – could blossom forth into genuine history, tragedy and romance, crime and adventure, and comedy, as soon as it was realized that they could be transfigured – not by an artificial injection of literary values but by the exploitation of the unique and specific possibilities of the new medium.[13]

The instinct here is sound, but the region is full of traps. What are "the unique and specific possibilities of the new medium"? Panofsky defines them as dynamization of space and spatialization of time – that is, in a movie things move, and you can be moved instantaneously from anywhere to anywhere, and you can witness successively events happening at the same time. He speaks of these properties as "self-evident to the point of triviality" and, because of that, "easily forgotten or neglected." One hardly disputes this, or its importance. But we still do not understand what makes these properties "the possibilities of the medium." I am not now asking how one would know that these are *the* unique and specific possibilities (though I will soon get back to that); I am asking what it means to call them possibilities at all.

Why, for example, didn't the medium begin and remain in the condition of home movies, one shot just physically tacked on to another, cut and edited simply according to subject? (Newsreels essentially did, and they are nevertheless valuable, enough so to have justified the invention of moving pictures.) The answer seems obvious: narrative movies emerged because someone "saw the possibilities" of the medium – cutting and editing and taking shots at different distances from the subject. But again, these are mere actualities of film mechanics: every home movie and newsreel contains them. We could say: To make them "possibilities of the medium" is to realize what will give them *significance* – for example, the narrative and physical rhythms of melodrama, farce, American comedy of the 1930s. It is not as if film-makers saw these possibilities and then looked for something to apply them to. It is truer to say that someone with the wish to make a movie saw that certain established forms would give point to certain properties of film.

This perhaps sounds like quibbling, but what it means is that the aesthetic possibilities of a medium are not givens. You can no more tell what will give significance to the unique and specific aesthetic possibilities of projecting photographic images by thinking about them or seeing some, than you can tell what will give significance to the possibilities of paint by thinking about paint or by looking some over. You have to think about painting, and paintings; you have to think about motion pictures. What does this "thinking about them" consist in? Whatever the useful criticism of an art consists in. (Painters before Jackson Pollock had dripped paint, even deliberately. Pollock made dripping into a medium of painting.) I feel like saying: The first successful movies – i.e., the first moving pictures accepted as motion pictures – were not applications of a medium that was defined by given possibilities, but the *creation of a medium* by their giving significance to specific possibilities. Only the art itself can discover its possibilities, and the discovery of a new possibility is the discovery of a new medium. A medium is something through which or by means of which something specific gets done or said in particular ways. It provides, one might say, particular ways to get through to someone, to make sense; in art, they are forms, like forms of speech. To discover ways of making sense is always a matter of the relation of an artist to his art, each discovering the other.

Panofsky uncharacteristically skips a step when he describes the early silent films as an "unknown language . . . forced upon a public not yet capable of reading it."[14] His notion is (with good reason, writing when he did) of a few industrialists forcing their productions upon an addicted multitude. But from the beginning the language was not "unknown"; it was known to its creators, those who found themselves speaking it; and in the beginning there was no "public" in question; there were just some curious people. There soon was a public, but that just proves how easy the thing was to know. If we are to say that there was an "unknown" something, it was less like a language than like a fact – in particular, the fact that something is intelligible. So while it may be true, as Panofsky says, that "for a Saxon peasant of around 800 it was not easy to understand the meaning of a picture showing a man as he pours water over the head of another man," this has nothing special to do with the problems of a moviegoer. The meaning of that act of pouring in certain communities is still not easy to understand; it was and is impossible to understand for anyone to whom the practice of baptism is unknown. Why did Panofsky suppose that comparable understanding is essential, or uniquely important, to the reading of movies? Apparently he needed an explanation for the persistence in movies of "fixed iconography" – "the well-remembered types of the Vamp and the Straight Girl . . . the Family Man, and the Villain," characters whose conduct was "predetermined accordingly" – an explanation for the persistence of an obviously primitive or folkloristic element in a rapidly developing medium. For he goes on, otherwise inexplicably, to say that "devices like these became gradually less necessary as the public grew accustomed to interpret the action by itself and were virtually abolished by the invention of the talking film." In fact such devices persist as long as there are still Westerns and gangster films and comedies and musicals and romances. *Which* specific iconography the Villain is given will alter with the times, but that his iconography remains specific (i.e., operates according to a "fixed attitude and attribute" principle[15]) seems undeniable: if Jack Palance in *Shane* is not a Villain, no honest home was ever in danger. Films have changed, but that is not because we don't need such explanations any longer; it is because we can't *accept* them.

These facts are accounted for by the actualities of the film medium itself: types are exactly what carry the forms movies have relied upon. These

media created new types, or combinations and ironic reversals of types; but there they were, and stayed. Does this mean that movies can never create individuals, only types? What it means is that this is the movies' way of creating individuals: they create *individualities*. For what makes someone a type is not his similarity with other members of that type but his striking separateness from other people.

Until recently, types of black human beings were not created in film: black people were stereotypes – mammies, shiftless servants, loyal retainers, entertainers. We were not given, and were not in a position to be given, individualities that projected particular *ways* of inhabiting a social role; we recognized only the role. Occasionally the humanity behind the role would manifest itself; and the result was a revelation not of a human individuality, but of an entire realm of humanity becoming visible. When in *Gone With the Wind* Vivien Leigh, having counted on Butterfly McQueen's professed knowledge of midwifery, and finding her as ignorant as herself, slaps her in rage and terror, the moment can stun us with a question: What was the white girl assuming about blackness when she believed the casual claim of a black girl, younger and duller and more ignorant than herself, to know all about the mysteries of childbirth? The assumption, though apparently complimentary, is dehumanizing – with such creatures knowledge of the body comes from nowhere, and in general they are to be trusted absolutely or not at all, like lions in a cage, with whom you either do or do not know how to deal. After the slap, we are left with two young girls equally frightened in a humanly desperate situation, one limited by a distraction which expects and forgets what it is to be bullied, the other by an energetic resourcefulness which knows only how to bully. At the end of Michael Curtiz' *Breaking Point*, as the wounded John Garfield is carried from his boat to the dock, awaited by his wife and children and, just outside the circle, by the other woman in his life (Patricia Neal), the camera pulls away, holding on the still waiting child of his black partner, who only the unconscious Garfield knows has been killed. The poignance of the silent and unnoticed black child overwhelms the yarn we had been shown. Is he supposed to symbolize the fact of general human isolation and abandonment? Or the fact that every action has consequences for innocent bystanders? Or that children are the real sufferers from the entangled efforts of adults to straighten out their lives? The effect here is to rebuke Garfield for attaching so much importance to the loss of his arm, and generally to blot out attention to individual suffering by invoking a massive social evil about which this film has nothing to say.

The general difference between a film type and a stage type is that the individuality captured on film naturally takes precedence over the social role in which that individuality gets expressed. Because on film social role appears arbitrary or incidental, movies have an inherent tendency toward the democratic, or anyway the idea of human equality. (But because of film's equally natural attraction to crowds, it has opposite tendencies toward the fascistic or populistic.) This depends upon recognizing film types as inhabited by figures we have met or may well meet in other circumstances. The recognized recurrence of film performers will become a central idea as we proceed. At the moment I am emphasizing only that in the case of black performers there was until recently no other place for them to recur in, except just the role within which we have already met them. For example, we would not have expected to see them as parents or siblings. I cannot at the moment remember a black person in a film making an ordinary purchase – say of a newspaper, or a ticket to a movie or for a train, let alone writing a check. (*Pinky* and *A Raisin in the Sun* prove the rule: in the former, the making of a purchase is a climactic scene in the film; in the latter, it provides the whole subject and structure.)

One recalls the lists of stars of every magnitude who have provided the movie camera with human subjects – individuals capable of filling its need for individualities, whose individualities in turn, whose inflections of demeanor and disposition were given full play in its projection. They provided, and still provide, staples for impersonators: one gesture or syllable of mood, two strides, or a passing mannerism was enough to single them out from all other creatures. They realized the myth of singularity – that we can still be found, behind our disguises of bravado and cowardice, by someone, perhaps a god, capable of defeating our self-defeats. This was always more important than their distinction by beauty. Their singularity made them more like us – anyway, made their difference from us less a matter of metaphysics, to which we must accede, than a matter of responsibility, to which we must bend. But then that made them even more glamorous. That they should be able to stand upon their singularity! If

one did that, one might be found, and called out, too soon, or at an inconvenient moment.

What was wrong with type-casting in films was not that it displaced some other, better principle of casting, but that factors irrelevant to film-making often influenced the particular figures chosen. Similarly, the familiar historical fact that there are movie cycles, taken by certain movie theorists as in itself a mark of unscrupulous commercialism, is a possibility internal to the medium; one could even say, it is the best emblem of the fact that a medium had been created. For a cycle is a genre (prison movies, Civil War movies, horror movies, etc.); and a genre is a medium.

As Hollywood developed, the original types ramified into individualities as various and subtle, as far-reaching in their capacities to inflect mood and release fantasy, as any set of characters who inhabited the great theaters of our world. We do not know them by such names as Pulcinella, Crispin, Harlequin, Pantaloon, the Doctor, the Captain, Columbine; we call them the Public Enemy, the Priest, James Cagney, Pat O'Brien, the Confederate Spy, the Army Scout, Randolph Scott, Gary Cooper, Gable, Paul Muni, the Reporter, the Sergeant, the Sheriff, the Deputy, the D.A., the Quack, the Shyster, the Other Woman, the Fallen Woman, the Moll, the Dance Hall Hostess. Hollywood was the theater in which they appeared, because the films of Hollywood constituted a world, with recurrent faces more familiar to me than the faces of the neighbors of all the places I have lived.

The great movie comedians – Chaplin, Keaton, W. C. Fields – form a set of types that could not have been adapted from any other medium. Its creation depended upon two conditions of the film medium mentioned earlier. These conditions seem to be necessities, not merely possibilities, so I will say that two necessities of the medium were discovered or expanded in the creation of these types. First, movie performers cannot project, but are projected. Second, photographs are of the world, in which human beings are not ontologically favored over the rest of nature, in which objects are not props but natural allies (or enemies) of the human character. The first necessity – projected visibility – permits the sublime comprehensibility of Chaplin's natural choreography; the second – ontological equality – permits his Proustian or Jamesian relationships with Murphy beds and flights of stairs and with vases on runners on tables on rollers: the heroism of momentary survival, Nietzsche's man as a tightrope across an abyss. These necessities permit not merely the locales of Keaton's extrications, but the philosophical mood of his countenance and the Olympic resourcefulness of his body; permit him to be perhaps the only constantly beautiful and continuously hilarious man ever seen, as though the ugliness in laughter should be redeemed. They permit Fields to mutter and suffer and curse obsessively, but heard and seen only by us; because his attributes are those of the gentleman (confident swagger and elegant manners, gloves, cane, outer heartiness), he can manifest continuously, with the remorselessness of nature, the psychic brutalities of bourgeois civilization.

Ideas of Origin

It is inevitable that in theorizing about film one at some point speculate about its origins, because despite its recentness, its origin remains obscure. The facts are well enough known about the invention and the inventors of the camera, and about improvements in fixing and then moving the image it captures. The problem is that the invention of the photographic picture is not the same thing as the creation of photography as a medium for making sense. The historical problem is like any other: a chronicle of the facts preceding the appearance of this technology does not explain why it happened when and as it did. Panofsky opens his study of film by remarking, "It was not an artistic urge that gave rise to the discovery and gradual perfection of a new technique; it was a technical invention that gave rise to the discovery and gradual perfection of a new art." We seem to understand this, but do we understand it? Panofsky assumes we know what it is that at any time has "given rise" to a "new art." He mentions an "artistic urge," but that is hardly a candidate to serve as an explanation; it would be about as useful as explaining the rise of modern science by appealing to "a scientific urge." There may be such urges, but they are themselves rather badly in need of explanation. Panofsky cites an artistic urge explicitly as the occasion for a new "technique." But the motion picture is not a new *technique*, any more than the airplane is. (What did we use to do that such a thing enables us to do better?) Yet some idea of flying, and an urge to do it, preceded the mechanical invention of the airplane. What is "given rise to" by such inventions as

movable type or the microscope or the steam engine or the pianoforte?

It would be surprising if the history of the establishment of an artistic medium were less complex a problem for the historical understanding than (say) the rise of modern science. I take Bazin to be suggesting this when he reverses the apparent relation between the relevant technology and the idea of cinema, emphasizing that the idea preceded the technology, parts of it by centuries, and that parts of the technology preceded the invention of movies, some of it by centuries. So what has to be explained is not merely how the feat was technically accomplished but, for example, what stood in the way of its happening earlier. Surprisingly, Bazin, in the selection of essays I have read, does not include the contemporary condition of the related arts as a part of the ideological superstructure that elicited the new material basis of film. But it is certainly relevant that the burning issue during the latter half of the nineteenth century, in painting and in the novel and in the theater, was realism. And unless film captured possibilities opened up by the arts themselves, it is hard to imagine that its possibilities as an artistic medium would have shown up as, and as suddenly as, they did.

The idea of and wish for the world re-created in its own image was satisfied *at last* by cinema. Bazin calls this the myth of total cinema. But it had always been one of the myths of art; each of the arts had satisfied it in its own way. The mirror was in various hands held up to nature. In some ways it was more fully satisfied in theater. (Since theater is on the whole not now a major art for us, it on the whole no longer makes contact with its historical and psychological sources; so we are rarely gripped by the trauma we must once have suffered when the leader of the chorus stopped contributing to a narrative or song and turned to face the others, suffering incarnation.)

What is cinema's way of satisfying the myth? Automatically, we said. But what does that mean – mean mythically, as it were? It means satisfying it without *my* having to do anything, satisfying it *by* wishing. In a word, *magically*. I have found myself asking: How could film be art, since all the major arts arise in some way out of religion? Now I can answer: Because movies arise out of magic; from *below* the world.

The better a film, the more it makes contact with this source of its inspiration; it never wholly loses touch with the magic lantern behind it. This suggests why movies of the fantastic (*The Cabinet* of *Dr Caligari, Blood of a Poet*) and filmed scenes of magic (say, materialization and dematerialization), while they have provided moods and devices, have never established themselves as cinematic media, however strongly this "possibility" is suggested by the physical medium of film: they are technically and psychologically trivial compared with the medium of magic itself. It is otherwise if the presented magic is itself made technically or physically interesting (*The Invisible Man, Dr Jekyll and Mr Hyde, Frankenstein, 2001: A Space Odyssey*), but then that becomes another way of confirming the physicality of our world. Science presents itself, in movies, as magic, which was indeed one source of science. In particular, projected science retains magic's mystery and forbiddenness. Science-fiction films exploit not merely certain obvious aspects of adventure, and of a physicality that special effects specialize in, but also the terrific mumbo-jumbo of hearsay science: "My God, the thing is impervious to the negative beta ray! We must reverse the atom recalcitration spatter, before it's too late!" The dialogue has the surface of those tinbox-and-lever contraptions that were sufficiently convincing in prime *Flash Gordon*. These films are carried by the immediacy of the fantasy that motivates them (say, destruction by lower or higher forms of life, as though the precariousness of human life is due to its biological stage of development); together with the myth of the one way and last chance in which the (external) danger can be averted. And certainly the beauty of forms and motions in Frankenstein's laboratory is essential to the success of *Frankenstein*; computers seem primitive in comparison. It always made more sense to steal from God than to try to outwit him.

How do movies reproduce the world magically? Not by literally presenting us with the world, but by permitting us to view it unseen. This is not a wish for power over creation (as Pygmalion's was), but a wish not to need power, not to have to bear its burdens. It is, in this sense, the reverse of the myth of Faust. And the wish for invisibility is old enough. Gods have profited from it, and Plato tells it at the end of the *Republic* as the Myth of the Ring of Gyges. In viewing films, the sense of invisibility is an expression of modern privacy or anonymity. It is as though the world's projection explains our forms of unknownness and of our inability to know. The explanation is not so much that the world is passing us by, as that we are displaced from our natural habitation within it, placed at a distance from it. The screen overcomes our fixed distance; it makes displacement appear as our natural condition.[16]

What do we wish to view in this way? What specific forms discover this fundamental condition of the medium of film?

Notes

1 Erwin Panofsky, "Style and Medium in the Moving Pictures," in Daniel Talbot, ed., *Film* (New York: Simon and Schuster, 1959), p. 31.
2 André Bazin, *What is Cinema?*, trans. Hugh Gray (Berkeley: University of California Press, 1967), p. 110.
3 Certainly I am not concerned to deny that there may be, through film, what Paul Rotha in this *The Film Till Now* (first published in 1930) refers to as "possibilities... open for the great sound and visual [i.e., non-dialogue sound, and perhaps non-photographically visual] cinema of the future." But in the meantime the movies have been what they have been.
4 Bazin, *What is Cinema?*, p. 12.
5 Ibid.
6 See Michael Fried, *Three American Painters* (Cambridge, Mass.: Fogg Art Museum, Harvard University, 1965), n. 3; and "Manet's Sources," *Artforum*, March 1969, pp. 28–79.
7 See Michael Fried, "Art and Objecthood," *Artforum*, June 1967; reprinted in Gregory Battcock, ed.,

Minimal Art (New York: E. P. Dutton, 1968), pp. 116–47.
8 When painting found out how to acknowledge the fact that paintings had shapes, shapes became forms, not in the sense of patterns, but in the sense of containers. A form then could *give* its shape to what it contained. And content could transfer its significance as painting to what contains it. The shape *pervades*, like gravity, or energy or air. (See Michael Fried, "Shape as Form," *Artforum*, November 1966; reprinted in Henry Geldzaher's catalogue, *New York Painting and Sculpture: 1940–1970* [New York: E.P. Dutton, 1969].)

This is not, as far as we yet know, a possibility of the film or screen frame – which only repeats the fact that a film is not a painting. The most important feature of the screen format remains what it was from the beginning of movies – its scale, its absolute largeness. Variation of format – e.g., CinemaScope – is a matter determined, so far as I can tell, by questions of convenience and inconvenience, and by fashion. Though perhaps, as in painting, the declaration of color as such required or benefited from the even greater expanses of wider screens.

The idea may seem obviously false or foolish that the essential ontological difference between the world as it is and as it is screened is that the screened world does not exist; because this overlooks – or perhaps obscurely states – a fully obvious difference between them, viz., that the screened world is two-dimensional. I do not deny the obscurity, but better a real obscurity than a false clarity. For *what* is two dimensional? The world which is screened is not; its objects and motions are as three-dimensional as ours. The screen itself, then? Or the images on it? We seem to understand what it means to say that a painting is two-dimensional. But that depends on our understanding that the support on which paint is laid is a three-dimensional object, and that the description of *that* object will not (except in an exceptional or vacuous sense) be the description of a painting. More significantly, it depends on our understanding of the support as *limiting* the extent of the painting in two dimensions. This is not the relation between the screen and the images projected across it. It seems all right to say that the screen is two-dimensional, but it would not follow that what you see there has the same dimensionality – any more than in the case of paint, its support, and the painting. Shadows are two-dimensional, but they are made by three-dimensional objects – tracings of opacity, not gradations of it. This suggests that phenomenologically the idea of two-dimensionality is an idea of either transparency or outline. Projected images are not shadows; rather, one might way, they are shades.

9 This idea is developed to some extent in my essays on *Endgame* and *King Lear* in *Must We Mean What We Say?* (New York: Scribener's, 1969).

10 Bazin, *What is Cinema?*, p. 97.

11 Panofsky, "Style and Medium in the Moving Pictures," p. 28.

12 "The Film Age," in Talbot, *Film*, p. 74.

13 Panofsky, "Style and Medium in the Moving Pictures," p. 18.

14 Ibid., p. 24.

15 Ibid., p. 25.

16 Within that condition, objects as such may seem displaced; and close-up of an object may render it *trouvé*. Dadaists and surrealists found in film a direct confirmation of their ideologies or sensibilities, particularly in film's massive capacities for nostalgia and free juxtaposition. This confirmation is, I gather, sometimes taken to mean that Dadaist and surrealist films constitute the *avant-garde* of film-making. It might equally be taken to show why film made these movements obsolete, as the world has. One might say: Nothing is more surrealist than the ordinary events of the modern world; and nothing less reveals that fact than a surrealist attitude. This says nothing about the value of particular surrealist films, which must succeed or fail on the same terms as any others.

Ideas of displacement (or contrasted position), of privacy, and of the inability to know are linked in my study of the problem of other minds, "Knowing and Acknowledging," in *Must We Mean What We Say?*

5

A Note on the Film

Susanne K. Langer

Here is a new art. For a few decades it seemed like nothing more than a new technical device in the sphere of drama, a new way of preserving and retailing dramatic performances. But today its development has already belied this assumption. The screen is not a stage, and what is created in the conception and realization of a film is not a play. It is too early to systematize any theory of this new art, but even in its present pristine state it exhibits – quite beyond any doubt, I think – not only a new technique, but a new poetic mode.

Much of the material for the following reflections was collected by four of my former seminar students,[1] at Columbia Teachers College, who have kindly permitted me to use their findings. I am likewise indebted to Mr Robert W. Sowers, who (also as a member of that seminar) made a study of photography that provided at least one valuable idea, namely that photographs, no matter how posed, cut, or touched up, must *seem factual*, or as he called it, "authentic." I shall return later to that suggestion.

The significant points, for my purposes, that were demonstrated by the four collaborating members were (1) that the structure of a motion picture is not that of drama, and indeed lies closer to narrative than to drama; and (2) that its artistic potentialities became evident only when the moving camera was introduced.

The moving camera divorced the screen from the stage. The straightforward photographing of stage action, formerly viewed as the only artistic possibility of the film, henceforth appeared as a special technique. The screen actor is not governed by the stage, nor by the conventions of the theater; he has his own realm and conventions; indeed, there may be no "actor" at all. The documentary film is a pregnant invention. The cartoon does not even involve persons merely "behaving."

The fact that the moving picture could develop to a fairly high degree as a silent art, in which speech had to be reduced and concentrated into brief, well-spaced captions, was another indication that it was not simply drama. It used pantomime, and the first aestheticians of the film considered it as essentially pantomime. But it is not pantomime; it swallowed that ancient popular art as it swallowed the photograph.

One of the most striking characteristics of this new art is that it seems to be omnivorous, able to assimilate the most diverse materials and turn them into elements of its own. With every new invention – montage, the sound track, Technicolor – its devotees have raised a cry of fear that now its "art" must be lost. Since every such novelty is, of course, promptly exploited before it is even technically perfected, and flaunted in its rawest state, as a popular sensation, in the flood of meaningless compositions that steadily supplies the show business, there is usually a tidal wave of particularly bad rubbish in association with every important advance. But the art goes on. It swallows everything:

Susanne K. Langer, "A Note on the Film," *Feeling and Form: A Theory of Art Developed from Philosophy in a New Key* (New York: Charles Scribner's Sons, 1953), 411–15.

dancing, skating, drama, panorama, cartooning, music (it almost always requires music).

Therewithal it remains a poetic art. But it is not any poetic art we have known before; it makes the primary illusion – virtual history – in its own mode.

This is, essentially, *the dream mode*. I do not mean that it copies dream, or puts one into a daydream. Not at all; no more than literature invokes memory, or makes us believe that *we* are remembering. An art mode is *a mode of appearance*. Fiction is "like" memory in that it is projected to compose a finished experiential form, a "past" – not the reader's past, nor the writer's, though the latter may make a claim to it (that, as well as the use of actual memory as a model, is a literary device). Drama is "like" action in being causal, creating a total imminent experience, a personal "future" or Destiny. Cinema is "like" dream in the mode of its presentation: it creates a virtual present, an order of direct apparition. That is the mode of dream.

The most noteworthy formal characteristic of dream is that the dreamer is always at the center of it. Places shift, persons act and speak, or change or fade – facts emerge, situations grow, objects come into view with strange importance, ordinary things infinitely valuable or horrible, and they may be superseded by others that are related to them essentially by feeling, not by natural proximity. But the dreamer is always "there," his relation is, so to speak, equidistant from all events. Things may occur around him or unroll before his eyes; he may act or want to act, or suffer or contemplate; but the *immediacy* of everything in a dream is the same for him.

This aesthetic peculiarity, this relation to things perceived, characterizes the *dream mode:* it is this that the moving picture takes over, and whereby it creates a virtual present. In its relation to the images, actions, events, that constitute the story, the camera is in the place of the dreamer.

But the camera *is* not a dreamer. We are usually agents in a dream. The camera (and its complement, the sound track) is not itself in the picture. It is the mind's eye and nothing more. Neither is the picture (if it is art) likely to be dreamlike in its structure. It is a poetic composition, coherent, organic, governed by a definitely conceived feeling, not dictated by actual emotional pressures.

The basic abstraction whereby virtual history is created in the dream mode is immediacy of experience, "givenness," or as Mr. Sowers calls it, "au-thenticity." This is what the art of the film abstracts from actuality, from our actual dreaming.

The percipient of a moving picture sees with the camera; his standpoint moves with it, his mind is pervasively present. The camera is his eye (as the microphone is his ear – and there is no reason why a mind's eye and a mind's ear must always stay together). *He takes the place of the dreamer*, but in a perfectly objectified dream – that is, he is not in the story. The work is the appearance of a dream, a unified, continuously passing, significant *apparition*.

Conceived in this way, a good moving picture is a work of art by all the standards that apply to art as such. Sergei Eisenstein speaks of good and bad films as, respectively, "vital" and "lifeless"[2]; speaks of photographic shots as "elements,"[3] which combine into "images," which are "objectively un-presentable" (I would call them poetic impressions), but are greater elements compounded of "representations," whether by montage or symbolic acting or any other means.[4] The whole is governed by the "initial general image which originally hovered before the creative artist"[5] – the matrix, the commanding form; and it is this (not, be it remarked, the artist's emotion) that is to be evoked in the mind of the spectator.

Yet Eisenstein believed that the beholder of a film was somewhat specially called on to use his imagination, to create his own experience of the story.[6] Here we have, I think, an indication of the powerful illusion the film makes not of things going on, but of the dimension in which they go on – a *virtual* creative imagination; for it *seems* one's own creation, direct visionary experience, a "dreamt reality." Like most artists, he took the virtual experience for the most obvious fact.[7]

The fact that a motion picture is not a plastic work but a poetic presentation accounts for its power to assimilate the most diverse materials, and transform them into non-pictorial elements. Like dream, it enthralls and commingles all senses; its basic abstraction – direct apparition – is made not only by visual means, though these are paramount, but by words, which punctuate vision, and music that supports the unity of its shifting "world." It needs many, often convergent, means to create the continuity of emotion which holds it together while its visions roam through space and time.

It is noteworthy that Eisenstein draws his materials for discussion from epic rather than dramatic poetry; from Pushkin rather than Chekhov,

Milton rather than Shakespeare. That brings us back to the point noted by my seminar students, that the novel lends itself more readily to screen dramatization than the drama. The fact is, I think, that a story narrated does not require as much "breaking down" to become screen apparition, because it has no framework itself of fixed *space*, as the stage has; and one of the aesthetic peculiarities of dream, which the moving picture takes over, is the nature of its space. Dream events are spatial – often intensely concerned with space – intervals, endless roads, bottomless canyons, things too high, too near, too far – but they are not oriented in any total space. The same is true of the moving picture, and distinguishes it – despite its visual character – from plastic art: *its space comes and goes*. It is always a secondary illusion.

The fact that the film is somehow related to dream, and is in fact in a similar mode, has been remarked by several people, sometimes for reasons artistic, sometimes non-artistic. R. E. Jones noted its freedom not only from spatial restriction, but from temporal as well. "Motion pictures," he said, "are our thoughts made visible and audible. They flow in a swift succession of images, precisely as our thoughts do, and their speed, with their flash-backs – like sudden uprushes of memory – and their abrupt transition from one subject to another, approximates very closely the speed of our thinking. They have the rhythm of the thought-stream and the same uncanny ability to move forward or backward in space or time.... They project pure thought, pure dream, pure inner life."[8]

The "dreamed reality" on the screen can move forward and backward because it is really an eternal and ubiquitous virtual present. The action of drama goes inexorably forward because it creates a future, a Destiny; the dream mode is an endless Now.

Notes

1 Messrs Joseph Pattison, Louis Forsdale, William Hoth, and Mrs Virginia E. Allen. Mr Hoth is now Instructor in English at Cortland (New York) State Teachers College; the other three are members of the Columbia Teachers College staff.
2 *The Film Sense*, trans. and ed. Jay Leyda (London, 1968), p. 17.
3 Ibid., p. 4.
4 Ibid., p. 8.
5 Ibid., p. 31.
6 Ibid., p. 33: "...the spectator is drawn into a creative act in which his individuality is not subordinated to the author's individuality, but is opened up throughout the process of fusion with the author's intention, just as the individuality of a great actor is fused with the individuality of a great playwright in the creation of a classic scenic image. In fact, every spectator ... creates an image in accordance with the representational guidance, suggested by the author, leading him to understanding and experience of the author's theme. This is the same image that was planned and created by the author, but this image is at the same time created also by the spectator himself."
7 Compare the statement in Ernest Lindgren's *The Art of the Film* (London, 1948), p. 92, apropos of the moving camera: "It is the spectator's own mind that moves."
8 *The Dramatic Imagination* (New York, 1941), pp. 17–18.

6

Vision and Dream in the Cinema

F. E. Sparshott

(The following is a strictly lay view of some of the main topics in the aesthetics of cinema. I have no special knowledge of any aspect of film, and the material I present is essentially what is to be found on any book on the subject. It is in the interpretation of these familiar observations that I hope to have found something to say that will be new enough and true enough to be worth presenting.[1])

Film seems to be unlike any older art in the way it depends on illusion. In fact, it is by definition an art of illusion, because you can only explain what a film is by saying how it works, and how it works is by creating an illusion. A sample definition might go something like this: 'A film is a series of images projected on a screen so fast that anyone watching the screen is given an impression of continuous motion; such images being projected by a light shining through a corresponding series of images arranged on a continuous band of flexible material.'

From the beginnings of film, its makers and critics have diverged in their attitudes to this basic illusoriness. One school has fastened on film's ability to create a semblance of reality, seemingly to recreate the very look and quality of people and things in their physical presence and vitality: to this school, the mission of film is not merely to record but to celebrate the physical world and redeem it from temporality. The opposing school has noted that the illusion in question results from the projection not necessarily of a series of images duplicating a natural event, but of any such series whose succes-sive members are sufficiently like each other; and this school has seen in film the world's first means of creating convincing fantasies. The illusoriness of film seems to carry with it both the possibility of fidelity and the possibility of freedom. Like Hesiod's Muses, it tells the best truths and the best lies too.

The positions of these two schools are not really so directly opposed as I have made them sound. It seems likely that for a fantasy to be convincing it must observe fidelity to precisely the weight and texture of the real world: in Robert Enrico's *Occurrence at Owl Creek Bridge*, we are drawn into the dream by the conviction of the photography, the clumsy struggle of a booted man under water, the light on a spider's web. And Siegfried Kracauer, the great spokesman for the realist wing, insists that what matters to him is not that a film happens to have been shot on location, but that it contrives to convey the sense of the real world. Both realists and fantasists may be thought of as combining against films that convey a sense of contrivance, actors looking like actors and scenery looking like cardboard, and above all against films that make one conscious of an intelligence directing the course of events. Where realists and fantasists part company is that the latter would insist, and the former deny, that the proper province of cinema includes the imparting of the sense of reality to things that could not exist and events that could not happen. The fantasist would also argue that the conviction that comes from fidelity to the

F. E. Sparshott, "Vision and Dream in the Cinema," *Philosophical Exchange*, Summer 1971: 111–22. Reprinted by permission of F. E. Sparshott.

texture of the real world of objects can be replaced by the subtler convincingness that an imaginary world derives from fidelity to its own laws. The expressionist sets and lurid lighting of *Caligari* are accepted by the fantasists because they create a consistently hallucinatory world in which the fancy can dwell; they are rejected by the realists because it is a nightmare world.

You may have noticed that my argument has already gone adrift. The illusory conviction of reality that attends the worlds of cinema is not, as I seem to have implied, the same as the primary illusion whereby an apparently moving image is engendered on a screen. That illusion concerns the presented image as a moving shadow; the secondary illusions that realists and fantasists exploit have to do not with what is there on the flat screen but with the status of what that image represents. Of course, this second level of illusion depends on the first – it is because of the way the screened image is constituted that it can be manipulated in the interests of faithfulness or fraud. None the less, they are two separate strata of illusion. That confronts us with a problem: why should the screened image be referred to any particular kind of original? Why should we not take it, as we would take a drawing, as a representation of something whose ontological status is a matter of indifference? No more than when attending a stage play does any film-goer feel as if a real event were actually taking place before his eyes. Yet there is a sense in which a film can and often does make you believe in the reality of what you see in a way that a play never does. Why should there be such illusions of provenance? The answer seems to lie in the complex relations between cinematography and photography, and in the peculiar nature of photographic images themselves. For realists and fantasists alike assume that films are normally photographed; but you may have noticed that my sample definition of a film made no reference to photography at all.

The images whose successive projection makes a film are most easily produced by photography; but they *can* also be drawn directly on the film stock. A photograph to represent an object is most easily made by aiming a camera at one, but what is photographed *may* also be a model or a drawing or even another photograph. A photograph of an event or happening of a certain sort is most simply made by finding one and photographing it, but it is *possible* to enact scenes and build sets for the purpose. The required succession of images is most readily produced by using a mechanical de-

vice that will take a lot of photographs in rapid succession and fix them in the right order; but it *can* be photographed, or even drawn, frame by frame. And the obvious way to work a film camera (though, this time, not the easiest, because synchronization requires care) is to run it at the same speed as you will run your projector; but it *can* be run as much faster or slower as the sensitivity of your film allows. The effect of all these facilities, with their countervailing possibilities, is that film has a strong though not irresistible bias toward its simplest form, that in which the projector repeats a camera event. Film-goers who are not on guard tend to assume, wherever they can, that what is shown on the screen results from such a repetition; and, if something in the film precludes this assumption, they tend to assume that what they see departs from a camera event as little as possible. It is as if we took the projector to be copying a camera that enacted a spectator's eye.

An eye is not a camera, and photographic images do not show what eyes see.[2] A roving eye constantly adjusts its iris as brightness varies, and alters its focus as depth changes. Because we have two eyes, everything on which we are not at the moment focusing yields a vague, doubled image, so that whatever one sees takes on a shifting and unstable character. The eye is restless before nature. But before a photograph, all in one plane and with a relatively small range of luminosity, the eye is spared much of its labor. In its stability, singleness and consistency, a photographic images is not at all like the visual world. But there is something that it is like. It has precisely the quality that theorists used to ascribe to that venerable phantom of optics, the 'retinal image.' This was thought of exactly as if it were a photograph imprinted on the back of the eye and serving in some mysterious sense as the true object of vision. In other words, what a photographic image represents is a sort of ideal projection, the way our imaginations normalize what we see. When photography was invented it was hailed as reproducing vision, but that is not what it did. What it really accomplished was the realization of an *ideal* of vision. A photographic image is not so much a true one as a superlatively convincing one. Photographs carry an overwhelming sense of authenticity. And that their doing this does not depend on their being just like what they are photographs of is clear from Peter Ustinov's famous remark, that he filmed *Billy Budd* in black and white because it was more realistic than color. The world is not black and white, but a news photograph is. The authenticity is not that of a duplicate but that of a faithful record.[3]

Taken by itself, the primary filmic illusion of movement gives an impression not of reality but of a sort of unattributed vivacity. That this is so becomes clear when one watches an animated cartoon. Verisimilitude adds nothing to the lifelikeness of such films, and the elaborate equipment used in Disney's heyday to simulate the third dimension has mostly been abandoned as no less futile than expensive. The sense of reality elicited by such films seems akin to that of figurative painting: we attribute the actions we see neither to the real world nor to the screen image, but to Donald Duck and the cartoon world in which alone he is alive. In ordinary films, then, it cannot be the illusion of movement that makes us attribute what we see to the world of everyday experience; rather, it is the photographic character of the image itself that, so far as it is present and is not contradicted by the nature of what is shown, entices us to take what we see as the record of something that took place in the way that we see it taking place. After all, each of us knows what it is to take a photograph and then look at the snap he has taken. The film medium, then, has this characteristic bias of exposition, providing a direction in which we normalize our perceptions of films made in the most diverse ways.

The realists and fantasists of whom I spoke at first are best understood as expressing attitudes not merely to the technical possibilities of their medium but even more to this tendency of every film to look much more like a faithful record than it is. Other theorists adopt variants of the same attitudes. Eisenstein and other Soviet film makers of the twenties claimed that the whole art of film lay in exploiting the bias of exposition by associative or contrastive cutting, joining strips of photographed film from various sources in such a way as to synthesize in the spectator's mind an experiential reality that went beyond the presented imagery. In the opposite direction, some contemporary makers of 'underground' film urge that to cut at all is to falsify. Since film looks like a record, a record is what it should be. The finished film should consist of all that the camera took in the order it was taken in, and if the result is that some shots are out of focus, ill-exposed, or irrelevant, they will thereby be all the truer to the film experience. On this way of thinking, a film records not what happened *in front of* the camera but what happened to the film *in* the camera.

That the realism of film is that of a graphic record and not that of an illusive actuality becomes apparent in the peculiar nature of film space: the actual and suggested spatial relations between elements of a film and between a film and its viewers. Some writers imply that film-goers ordinarily feel themselves to be in the same spatial relation to the filmed scene as the camera was (or purports to have been). On this basis, such trick shots as those which show a room through the flames of a fire in its fireplace are condemned not as silly gimmicks but on the ground that no observer would be in that position. I cannot reconcile this thesis with my experience. I find that I usually identify myself with the camera viewpoint only if some such process as Cinerama is used, in which the screen is magnified to the point where it becomes almost the whole visual environment. Experienced film-goers are not disoriented or nauseated by rapid changes in camera position, or made giddy by shots taken looking straight down.[4] If we really accepted a change in camera viewpoint as a change in our own position, rapid intercutting between different viewpoints would obviously be intolerable; but in fact we hardly notice it. And yet there is certainly a sense in which one does have a feeling of spatial presence at the filmed scene. This is not to be confused with psychological involvement in the action: one actually construes the scene as a three-dimensional space in which one is included and has a definite viewpoint. This depth and inclusiveness of cinema space owes much to parallax, the differential motion and occlusion of distant objects as one's viewpoint changes. The importance of parallax becomes obvious when, as is often done nowadays, action is interrupted by stop-motion. As soon as we become aware that this has happened, the whole nature of the space in which the action takes place is transformed, it goes flat and remote. This little-noted factor is important. Without such a change of spatiality, stop-motion might make it seem that the world had come to a halt. As it is, it confronts us rather with a transition to a different mode of representation. Momentarily, a different game is being played.

The more I reflect on my sense of cinema space, the more peculiar to cinema it seems. For instance, the use of a zoom lens increasing the (objective) size of the image does have the effect of bringing the action nearer; but getting up and walking towards the screen, though it produces a (subjectively) larger image and does of course bring the screen nearer, does not bring the action nearer at all. One's sense of spatial inclusion in a scene does not depend on one's occupying any particular seat, but only on one's being neither too close nor too far to see the screen properly. Similarly with all the distortions of space that result from the use of various lenses. We accept the resulting plasticity of space relations as a narrative device or as an invitation to an imaginary viewpoint. It does not disorient us. Thus David Lean's use of a deep-focus lens for Miss Havisham's room in *Great Expectations* certainly has a magnifying effect, but a curious one: we do not feel that we are in a big room, but that 'This is how it must have seemed to Pip.' Again, take those banal telephoto shots of people running towards or away from the camera and of course not making much visible headway. Such shots answer to no possible real spatial relationship between viewer and event. There is a viewing angle, but no possible viewpoint. Yet this disturbs no one. For instance, in the scene where the girl runs toward the airplane in *Zabriskie Point*, the scale relations between girl and low horizon are such that we may (and I did) accept what we see for a moment or two as an ordinary medium shot; then we notice how slowly the girl is receding, and realize that it is a telephoto shot. But the effect of this recognition on me was not to alter my feeling of where I was in relation to the scene, but to change my interpretation of that relation.

Such phenomena as I have been mentioning suggest that in film our sense of space is somehow bracketed or held in suspense: we are aware of our implied position and accept it, but are not existentially committed to it. We do not situate ourselves where we see ourselves to be. One simple explanation of this detachment is that most of the time we are simultaneously aware of a film, as we are of a painting, both as a two-dimensional arrangement on a flat surface and as a three-dimensional scene. Except in moments of excitement or disaffection, neither aspect achieves exclusive domination of the mind.[5] Perhaps a subtler explanation is that cinema vision is alienated vision. A man's sense of where he is at depends largely on his sense of balance and his muscular senses, and all a filmgoer's sensory cues other than those of vision and hearing are related firmly to the theater and seat in which he sits. For instance, in the scene with the epileptic doctor in *Carnet du Bal*, which is taken with a consistently tilted camera, one's eyes insist that they are off balance but one's body insists that it is not; and the effect on me was the one that Duvivier surely intended, a feeling of malaise ac-companied by a sense of *vicarious* disorientation on behalf of the protagonist.

Some of the spatial ambiguities of film are shared with still photography. No matter how one moves a photograph around in relation to oneself, it continues to function as a faithful record implying a viewpoint from which it was taken, and in a sense one continues to be 'at' this viewpoint no matter what angle one looks at the photo from. Film differs from still photography not only in the sense of vivacity that motion imparts and the sense of depth that parallax gives, but also in the great size and contrasting illumination of the screened image in the darkened theater, which enable it to dominate the visual sense, and in the relatively invariant relationship between screen and spectator. A director determines the audience's spatial relationship to his film. But what he determines remains an imaginary space: we are within the film's space without being part of its world, and observe from a viewpoint at which we are not situated.

The alienated space of film is not the only experienced space in which the spectator participates without contact, and which he observes from a vantage point that contrives to be at once definite and equivocal or impossible. The spatiality of dreams is somewhat similar. Or perhaps, since different people seem to have very different dream perceptions, I should only say that my own spatial relationship to my dream worlds is like nothing in waking reality so much as it is like my relationship with film worlds. In my dreams, too, I see from where I am not, move helplessly in a space whose very nature is inconstant, and may see beside me the being whose perceptions I share. But however many ways there are in which filmgoing is like dreaming, there are vital differences. Films, like dreams, involve us in a world we cannot control; but we have no sense of effort and participation in their world, as we do in that of our dreams. Filmed reality shares with dreamed reality (as nothing else does) its tolerance of limitlessly inconsequent transitions and transformations; but it lacks that curious conceptual continuity of dreams in which what is a raven may become a writing desk or may simultaneously be a writing desk, and in which one knows that what looks like one person is really someone else. Film-makers do indeed essay equivalences, as when Eisenstein in *October* equated Kerensky with a peacock, by intercutting shots of the two entities to be equated. But these are more like literary similes than they are like the fusions of dream. In the film, the interpretation cannot be made unless it is suggested by the percept itself, or by something else in the film, or by current convention. In the dream, the interpretation is imposed *a priori* – the dreamer simply knows without evidence that the two things are the same.[6]

The analogy between films and dreams has perhaps been less often noted than that between films and daydreams. Daydreams of course are utterly unlike real dreams, and unlike them in just the ways in which dreams are like films. But there is one quite fundamental way in which the film-goer is like the daydreamer and unlike the dreamer. That is, he is awake. However caught up he may be in the world of the film, he retains control of his faculties, is capable of sustained and critical attention, and above all can rationally direct his interest. A dreamlike inconsequentiality is thus far from typical of film, although it does remain among filmic possibilities, and the film-going public at large acquiesces in a degree of cheerful incoherence (as in *Casino Royale*) that in other arts is acceptable only to the sophisticate.

I suggested that writers on film are often so bewitched by the plausible but untenable dogma of the camera eye that they overlook the ambiguous and dreamlike character of film space. In the same way, many of them adopt an equally dubious dogma about film time: because the eye is the camera on the spot, they urge that film time is always present time; in watching a film one seems to see things happening *now*, as though one were present not at the film but at the filmed event. But this contention is vulnerable to the same sort of objection that was brought against the doctrine of the camera eye. In one sense it is true but trivial: of course, whatever one sees is always here and now, because the terms 'here' and 'now' are defined by one's presence. But in any other sense it is false, or we should not be able to take in our stride the flash-backs and flash-forwards, the accelerations and decelerations, that are part of film's stock in trade. Rather, it is as though we were spectators of the temporality of the films we see. Film time has a quality analogous to that dreamlike floating between participation and observation, between definite and indeterminate relationships, that gives film space its pervasive character. It is certainly true that the fundamental illusion of motion combines with the convincingness inherent in any photographic record to ensure that we ordinarily read the presented motion as continuous and as taking just as much time to

happen as it takes us to observe it; but this supposition is readily defeated by any counter-indication. When D.W. Griffith was challenged on his early use of spatio-temporal discontinuities, he justified his procedures by appealing to the example of Dickens; and surely he was right to do so. We accept a fiction film as a narrative. The time of a novel is filmic as its space is not: events can be filmed, as they can be narrated, with equal facility in any order, at any speed, with any degree of minuteness. But the film-maker, unlike the novelist, uses a language without tenses. He has no device proper to his medium with which to signify any temporal relations other than immediate succession and interruption. He may use titles, trick dissolves, a superimposed narrator's voice, or datable visual cues (such as calendar leaves) to establish his temporal orientations; but some directors seem to feel that such devices are clumsy or vulgar, and prefer (like Bunuel in *Tristana*) to trust the public's acumen or simply to leave the relations indeterminate.

The dream-relationships of film space combine with the narrative nature of film time to encourage an ambiguity that may be fruitful or merely irritating. One often does not know what one is seeing: part of what is supposed actually to take place in the film, or only what is passing through the mind of one of the characters. This ambiguity becomes acute whenever there is a temporal leap; for time, as Immanuel Kant observed, is the form of subjectivity. A flash-back may represent a character's memory, or it may be just a narrative device. The anticipation in a flash forward may be that of the film-maker, or it may be a character's premonition – or even merely his hope; and when temporally displaced scenes are recalled or anticipated, they may be taken as standing either for an event as it really was or would be in the film's reality, or for the way it is (perhaps erroneously or mendaciously) conjured up. And as soon as we admit this last possibility we must acknowledge that what we see on the screen may simply be imagined by one of the characters without any implied temporal reference at all. Still worse, it may have been inserted by the director neither as objective nor as subjective content, but merely as an 'objective correlative,' an evocative image with no other purpose than to show what he, or we, or someone, is or should be feeling.

The status of film events thus readily becomes equivocal. Many modern novelists exploit a similar ambiguity: Robbe-Grillet would be an obvious instance even if he had not done the scenario for *L'année dernière à Marienbad*. But in a novel it is an artifice, even an affectation, a withholding of information one would naturally give; in a film it is the automatic result of the most straightforward use of the medium. In fact, its novelistic use is often ascribed to the influence of film – or more precisely, as Andre Bazin insists, of the novelists' ideas about film. So I think it is legitimate to treat the equivocal status of events as characteristic of the medium of cinema, but not peculiar to it. Such uncertainty may pervade an entire film. The stock example of this pervasive uncertainty is Fellini's *8½*, in which some scenes are remembered, some dreamed, some imagined, and some belong to the reality of the film's story. There are many scenes whose status is unclear at the time, and some whose status never becomes clear. Does the opening scene of the closed car in the traffic jam show a man undergoing a seizure which makes his cure necessary, or is the seizure dreamed by a man already sick and undergoing treatment? Or is it even a parable, portraying with its fantastic sequel the dimensions of Guido's dilemma? In the version of the film I saw, there was nothing to determine either answer. In *Occurrence at Owl Creek Bridge* the case is different. Almost the whole of this film consists of a sequence of events whose status remains unresolved until the very end of the film. If we think of the hanged man's escape as real, we may take his repeated endeavors to reach his wife's welcoming arms simply as the director's way of emphasizing the emotion involved in his arrival;[7] or we may take them as symbolizing the hope that drives the fugitive on. Only when he slips through her arms to hang at the end of his rope can we be sure that the whole sequence is the delusive vision of a man at the moment of death. As for the shots of the insects in sunlight, despite the accompanying song we are not sure whether these celebrate the fugitive's gladness in his escape from death, or express the director's sense of the sweetness of life. Perhaps only if we refer to Bierce's original story does a third possibility occur to us. This is what the fugitive sees with his 'preternaturally keen and alert' senses:

"He looked at the forest on the bank of the stream, saw the individual trees, the leaves and the veining of each leaf – saw the very insects upon them, the locusts, the brilliant-bodied flies, the grey spiders stretching their webs from twig to twig. He noted the prismatic colors in all the dewdrops upon a million blades of grass."

When confronted with such ambiguities, one need not assume that there is some one right way of taking the scene – perhaps, in our examples, the way Fellini describes the scene in his shooting script, or, more remotely, the version that answers to Bierce's original story. All the director has done is splice celluloid. If the resulting sequence of images does not furnish enough clues to determine a reading, then no reading is determined. What the director had in mind is not enough, for what he had in mind may not be what he put on film. Besides, directors quite often have nothing at all in mind. The flexibility of film technique is a standing invitation to meaningless trickery, and the complexities of production involve limitless risks of inadvertent incoherence.

The time and space of film combine in a characteristic type of motion which inherits their quality of dreamlike plasticity. But there are other aspects of film motion that do not make for dreamlikeness but enhance the sense of actuality. This is an endlessly complex topic, and all I will do now is mention a few facts not implicit in what I have said already.

In the earliest movies, each scene was taken with a fixed camera, so that movement was presented as taking place within a fixed frame and against an unchanging background. A scene in a more recent film is likely to be enriched or muddled with three different kinds of camera motion.[8] The camera may be shifted from place to place, turned horizontally or vertically to alter its field of reception, or modified by changing the focal length of its lens to take in a greater or smaller area.[9] This third kind of camera movement is often dismissed as the equivalent of a tracking shot, moving the camera viewpoint towards or away from the scene. But it is not quite the same. It retains much of the sense of getting a different view from the same position.

The free combination of all the kinds of film motion can give a single scene a kind of dancing beauty that is at once abstract and realistic and that has no parallel in any other medium. Some of you will be familiar with a kind of kaleidoscope in which an image is formed by multiplying segments of whatever in your surroundings you aim the tube at. This enchanting device achieves an abstract beauty of great intensity, simply by the symmetrical arrangement of arbitrary portions of the visual field. This abstraction is won at the price of sacrificing all the reality of what is seen, which is reduced to mere pattern. The formal beauty of film is quite different. While entering into the

F. E. Sparshott

visual dance, the filmed elements of the world do not lose their reality but have it greatly enhanced. The eye dwells without restraint on ever new aspects of what is truly there to be seen: the abstract element comes from the form of its dwelling. It is the spectator, not what he sees, that becomes *unreal*.

Camera mobility gives the filmed image a shifting frame that combines with the camera's notorious neglect of natural boundaries to make the edge of the screen function like a window frame through which we glimpse part of a world that stretches to infinity. This produces a marked contrast between the actions of cinema and theater. The stage world is closed. An actor who leaves the stage loses all determinate existence for the audience. On the other side of the scenery there is nothing.[10] But beyond the edge of the cinema screen is the whole wide world, through whose endless continuity the camera may move at will – though not, of course, at the *spectator*'s will.

Because film time and space are rather observed than lived, film motion can be speeded up or slowed down within scenes in a way that cannot be matched in the live theater, where events have to take their proper time as determined by the human rhythms of the actors' bodies.[11] Variations in the speed of filmed actions do not always have the same effect, but vary in a way that becomes easier to understand if we reflect that motion photography was invented to serve not one realistic purpose but two: not only to observe and record movements, but also to study and examine them. And, of course, very fast movements are best studied by slowing down their representation, very slow ones by speeding it up. Nature films are quite regularly made at unnatural speeds, accelerating plant growth and decelerating bird flight to something approaching the rhythms of human activity. In such studious contexts the spectator has no sense of unreality at all: his anticipatory set is one of discovery, and he feels simply that he is getting a better look at what he wants to see. But in narrative contexts things are different. Acceleration was early discovered to have a reliably comic effect: Buster Keaton's two-reeler *The Haunted House* (1921), for instance, gives the impression of having been taken at continuously varying camera speeds, slowing down to natural speed only for a few seconds at a time. The effect of deceleration in narrative films is more variable. It may give an impression of joy, of unreality, of obsessiveness, of solemnity, of ponderous force, or of inevitability.

But though its effects are so various and often evade brief description, film directors must find that they are perfectly reliable in their various contexts, for they use them regularly. In fact, more than one cliché has hardened in this practice. One such is the flash-back reverie (as in *The Pawnbroker*), where the slowed motion seems to work by suggesting weightlessness and hence ethereality. Another is the use of this same weightlessness as a metaphor for lightheartedness, as in countless TV commercials. A third is the slow-motion death by shooting, most notably in *Bonnie and Clyde*: largely an appeal to voyeurism, but partly perhaps an equivalent for shock, and partly also a symbolization of death, as the unreal speed transposes the action into another key of reality.

One can think of acceleration and deceleration as a kind of pre-editing, the same as adding or subtracting frames in a film shot at projector speed. It is basic to film that editing can produce an impression of movement by intercutting suitably spaced shots of the same object in different positions. The impression does not depend on the primary film illusion of continuity: all that is needed is that the object should appear to be the same, that its position in successive shots should appear to be different, and that the mind can somehow supply a possible trajectory to connect the successive positions. Such inferred motions are neither possible nor felt to be possible. We tend not to believe in them even while we see them, referring them to the film as artifact and not to the film as record.

My main purpose in reminding you of all these peculiarities of film experience has merely been to ask you if they don't strike you as extremely odd. Least odd are the last item and the first, the primary film illusion of movement and the impression of movement produced by cutting. These testify only to aspects of the mind's familiar tendency to smooth things over, interpreting whatever confronts it in terms of the simplest pattern to which it can be made to conform. But the other things I spoke about do strike me as really strange; I mean the whole sense of film reality, in which we accept, not only without difficulty but even without any sense of mystery, a complex fictional experience whose spatio-temporal character is quite unlike that of ordinary life. How is this possible? It is as though the mind had an inbuilt capacity to live in an indefinite number of possible worlds, just as according to Noam Chomsky it is born with a capacity to learn an infinite number of languages.

But according to Chomsky there are basic grammatical conditions which a language must fulfil to be learnable; perhaps too there are limits on the distortions and discontinuities acceptable by a human mind as compatible with a world of which the experience is continuous. However, it may be a mistake to represent the cinematic phenomena as not merely strange but unexampled. E. H. Gombrich has shown in *Art and Illusion* how a sense of reality in the visual arts can be satisfied through the most arbitrary conventions – though here, too, we may suspect that there are limits beyond which stylistic transformations cease to carry conviction. Perhaps film adds nothing to this situation with which we have become familiar in painting, other than a number of superficial complications and the seductive verisimilitude of the photographic image. All the same, I keep coming back to the feeling that the way a film-goer's brain can accommodate disorganizations and reconstitutions of its principles of order borders on the uncanny. I do not think we find any adequate analogue for it in those psychological experiments which show how perceptual constancy is maintained and restored when vision is distorted or disoriented through inverting lenses and the like. What those experiments show is how a normal awareness of the real world is retrieved in difficult conditions, not how one accepts as perceptually normal a world that never takes on the aspect of everyday reality. As I said before, the closest analogy seems to be with dreaming. It has always seemed uncanny to me that although my waking self is quite unable even to make a convincing drawing of the simplest shapes, my sleeping mind not only composes continuous and coherently organized visual fields that are completely lifelike, but combines them with appropriate sound to make a fictive world in which events can be recognized and provided with interpretations that themselves constitute a plausible simulacrum of thought. Perhaps it is simply the dreamer's skill at constructing alternative realities that film-makers and their public employ. Well, perhaps. But there are other possibilities. Some people would say that films are actually lifelike in most of the ways we have described.[12] Often we doubt whether we imagine or remember, whether we wake or dream; our experience of space varies with atmospheric and other conditions; time slows down when we are bored, speeds up when we are absorbed, seems to stand still

when we are shocked. There is truth in this contention, but it needs to be qualified. It assumes that our experience is measured against some norm of physical space and time. But for us as we live it, lived time is natural and normal. The variations we spoke of correspond to our own involvement in events. In film, on the other hand, the changes occur in what is seen by an observer whose attention is assumed constant. The variations and dislocations in film space and time have nothing to do with that other phenomenon whereby a tedious film seems to take longer than an exciting one of the same footage. The truth that lies in this contention is perhaps no more than that our knowledge of how lived space and time can vary is among the things that enables us to accept the variations in film space and time as expressive narrative devices.

No doubt the true explanation of the intelligibility of the fictive worlds of film is the simple one we gave before. Film-goers take films as narratives. A film-maker works from a script, sometimes 'in his head' but usually written down, in which ample stage directions prescribe how each image should be interpreted. Film-goers know this. They know that the film-maker is up to something, and that if they are patient and attentive they stand a good chance of making out what it is. They start with the knowledge that the film is something made, and made for people to see, and (unless they have rashly exposed themselves to the assaults of the avant-garde) made for them to make sense of and enjoy. One can at least guess what the missing stage directions are.

It is comparatively seldom, after all, that we learn about any event in real life from hearing a straightforward account of it. More often we must actively piece our knowledge together from hints and allusions, received in no particular order and colored by error, bias, and fabrication. Perhaps the character of film is only that of our ordinary sources of information transposed into a single medium, with all the distortions, compressions, expansions, dislocations, ambiguities, gaps, false clues, and subjective interpretations transformed into properties of the moving image. Our ability not only to follow films but to live imaginatively in their worlds would then be no more than the realization in this novel and specialized field of our general capacity to live in a world largely reconstructed from unsatisfactory hearsay.

Notes

1 This article is an altered and expanded version of an article on 'Basic Film Aesthetics,' *The Journal of Aesthetic Education*, 5.2, April 1971. Research was facilitated by a Leave Fellowship from the Canada Council.

2 The verb 'see' is not of course here used as an 'achievement' word, as in everyday intercourse it usually is. Perhaps what the camera records is indeed what one sees in this sense: it represents a sum of visual successes, as the end of the paragraph suggests in other terms.

3 That this is indeed the kind of authenticity a film has may be gathered from Truffaut's *L'Enfant Sauvage*, in which an old-fashioned system of articulation (iris-in and iris-out) and old-fashioned looking photography are used to give the impression that we are seeing something that really happened, but happened a long time ago. For a different account of photographic credibility, see André Bazin, *What Is Cinema?* (Berkeley: University of California Press, 1967), pp. 12–14.

4 Unless, of course, the viewer happens to be susceptible to vertigo. Different individuals will respond variously to a given stimulus, and so will the same person at different times; the statements in the text can only refer to a supposed 'average' or 'normal' response, that on which the film-maker seems to rely for the success of his devices.

5 This is not an isolated spatial phenomenon, but is connected with our overall acceptance or rejection of the film's world. A comparable polarity was observed in connection with stage reality by the German psychological aestheticians of the late nineteenth century.

6 Analytically minded philosophers may ask, 'The same WHAT? The "same" in what sense?' The same dream-entity: and the sameness, and perhaps even the sense of the word 'same,' are peculiar respectively to dreams and to talk about dreams.

7 This device would then be analogous to that whereby in *Potemkin* a young sailor's action in smashing a dish is protracted in time by being split up between a number of shots, each of which begins at a moment earlier than that in which the previous shot ends.

8 I am told that the regular use of camera motion as a creative resource was established by Murnau in *The Last Laugh* (1924).

9 Cameras may also be bounced, joggled, rotated on their focal axes etc.; but never mind about that.

10 This non-existence of the offstage world forms the theme of Tom Stoppard's play *Rosencrantz and Guildenstern are Dead*.

11 Conversely, theater has a way of achieving temporal plasticity that cinema lacks, by exploiting the unreality of the offstage world: in theater, but not in cinema, unseen actions are often performed in the course of a scene in an impossible short time, without any sense of incongruity.

12 'Resnais aims to construct a purely mental time and space and to follow the mind which goes faster, or skips, doubles back, lingers, repeats, and creates imaginary scenes, parallels and possibilities.' – Ralph Stephenson and J. Debrix. *The Cinema as Art* (Baltimore: Penguin Books, 1965), p. 106, speaking of *L'Année Dernière à Marienbad*. This account is acceptable if the authors are thinking specifically of *Daydreaming* as the paradigm of mental activity. Otherwise, they (and perhaps Resnais and Robbe-Grillet) are making the fundamental mistake of omitting what since Brentano has been called the 'intentionality' of thought. A mental image is not just a picture floating before the mind's eye: it is always essential to it that it is related in a specific way to some real or fictive entity, it is always a desire for, or in some other such definite way *about*, something or other.

7

The Long Goodbye: The Imaginary Language of Film

Gregory Currie

When future historians of ideas name our age the age of language, they will have two kinds of reasons for their choice. The reasons creditable to us have to do with the discoveries we have made concerning the structure of language, the mechanism of its acquisition, its role in thought and communication. The discreditable reasons have to do with our insistence that every humanistic discipline is founded upon some linguistic or quasi-linguistic structure.

So entrenched is this principle of the ubiquity of language that expressions such as 'the grammar of stories', 'the vocabulary of modernism' and 'the language of film' do not seem strange to us.[1] Sometimes, indeed, they are not seriously meant: talk of the vocabulary of a style often means just whatever devices are standardly employed within that style. But sometimes the usage suggests possession of a theory that can turn casual connoisseurship into a powerful technique of analysis. That suggestion is spurious. Art, architecture, film and the rest have little in common with any of the uncontroversial examples of language that have shaped linguistic theorizing. It is not likely, therefore, that language will help us explain how it is we use, interpret and appreciate any of these things. So I claim, and so I shall argue with respect to the case of film – a case with certain complexities that make it especially interesting in this regard.

This much is entirely negative. But we shall learn something important about film and the comprehension of film by comparing its communicative aspect with that of language.

I

The hypothesis that there is a language of film is not the true but uninteresting claim that the language of *Citizen Kane* is English and that of *Rashomon* is Japanese. It is the hypothesis that there is a specifically cinematic language that can and sometimes does apply when there are no accompanying words or sounds. It is the hypothesis that there is a language of cinematic images, their modifications and their juxtapositions.[2]

Enthusiasm for the hypothesis seems to be on the decline. Christian Metz, for example, has said that there is nothing in the cinema corresponding to 'a language-system's characteristics and internal organization'.[3] But he has continued to apply the categories, or at least the terminology, of linguistic analysis; he says, for example, that photographs lack the 'syntactic components of discourse so numerous in cinema', and he describes optical effects as 'clauses of speech'.[4] And while the emphasis in film theory has moved away from the straightforwardly linguistic to the psychoanalytic, the

Gregory Currie, "The Long Goodbye: The Imaginary Language of Film," *British Journal of Aesthetics* 33(3), July 1993: 207–19. Reprinted by permission of Oxford University Press Journals.

impetus for this move seems not to have come from a rejection of the linguistic model, but from the thought that psychoanalytic models are themselves language-like. Thus one of the leading ideas of the theorist to whom so much credit in this area is given, Lacan, is that the unconscious is structured like a language. Perhaps talk of film language is the nostalgic rhetoric of a ritual that no longer commands belief. If that is so, let us acknowledge it, and say goodbye at last to an idea we should never have embraced.

There may be another hypothesis to consider: that cinema is to be analysed not as a language but as an example of the broader category of semiotic systems. It will seem natural, if the hypothesis that cinema is a language is to be rejected, that we should consider the weaker position of the semioticists (weaker, that is, because the hypothesis that cinema is a language entails but is not entailed by the hypothesis that it is a semiotic system). But I shall not confront the semiotic hypothesis in any detail. One reason is that the generality aimed for in semiotics – including, according to one author, everything from aesthetics texts to 'zoosemiotics'[5] – has resulted, rather predictably, in a great deal of taxonomizing but little that could be identified as theory. Nor has it ever been made clear what a 'code' is supposed to be, though codes are what semioticians are apparently most interested in finding.[6] But there is no need to tackle semiotics separately, for some of what I shall say in relation to the hypothesis that there is a language of cinema will count against semiotics as well. Semioticists seem to be committed to the *conventionality* of the sign systems they investigate.[7] And in the course of arguing against the idea of a language of film I shall be arguing that cinematic images are not conventional signs.

II

W. J. T. Mitchell described the idea of a language of images as 'an institutionalized violation of common sense', though he did not seem to think that this was an argument against it.[8] But there is more at stake here than common sense, which is anyway notoriously revisable in the light of successful theory. What do we hope to *gain* by supposing that there is a language of cinema? One thing the cinema-language theorists seem to have hoped for is an explanation of our comprehension of cinematic images and their combinations in terms of the capacities we exercise in interpreting language.[9] I claim that the most plausible account of our comprehension of those things uncontroversially described as languages cannot help us explain our understanding of cinema, because the central concepts employed in explaining linguistic comprehension have no application to cinema. Arguing in this way, we may sidestep those potentially confusing and sterile questions of definition. If someone agrees with my conclusions and still wants to say that the cinema is a language, I shall not argue with his choice of words. All that matters will have been conceded: that there is insufficient similarity between this 'language' and any natural language for us to expect progress to be made in understanding the cinema by applying to it our hard won knowledge of how paradigmatic languages work.

III

Let us specify some salient features of natural language: salient, that is, from the point of view of explaining comprehension. Since one of the reasons the concept of cinema language has been able to thrive is that it is never discussed with any precision, I shall try to be as precise as I can be – and that may be more precise than the phenomenon before us strictly warrants – in describing what I take to be theoretically important aspects of that supposed language. This will have at least the virtue that those who want to defend the concept of cinema language will have to specify exactly where and how my description goes wrong, or where I go wrong in claiming that there is nothing in cinema that corresponds to the description. The account will be somewhat compressed, but the concepts appealed to should be familiar, and compression will facilitate an overview; it is the logical relations between these concepts that I want to emphasize.

Natural languages such as English display the features of *productivity* and *conventionality*. Productivity means that there is an unlimited number of sentences of English that can be uttered, and in fact many of the sentences we utter and comprehend have never been uttered before. It is evident, then, that whatever learning English involves, it does not involve learning meanings sentence by sentence; otherwise we would need instruction every time we heard a new sentence.

English is conventional in that what words and sentences of English mean is determined, not by relations of naturalness or affinity between words and meanings, nor because the human mind is specially apt to associate certain words with certain meanings, but by adventitious uniformities of practice that are adhered to because they facilitate communication. The differences between the various natural languages are very largely accounted for as differences between these uniformities of practice. A convention, as David Lewis has argued, need not have its origin in *agreement*.[10] There is a convention to the effect that a word has a certain meaning when there is a certain *regularity* of use among members of the speech community; they use that word intending thereby to mean something, and they do so because they know that others do the same, and desire to continue the regularity because by doing so they are able to achieve a co-ordination between what they mean by it and what hearers will take them to mean: a co-ordination necessary for successful communication. It does not much matter what word we use to express a given meaning; what matters is that most of us use it most of the time to express the same meaning. That way we have some idea about what meaning others use it to express, and they have some idea about our use. And that way we are able to co-ordinate our communicative activities.

Conventionality and productivity combine to set further requirements on the shape of language: conventionality requires that language has to be learned, productivity precludes it being learned sentence by sentence. If meanings in our language are to be learned, they must be specifiable *recursively*: starting with a set of conventions that assign meanings to a finite stock of words, we combine words into further meaningful units (e.g., sentences) by rules of composition, which tell us how the meaning of the whole depends on the meanings of the parts.[11] Thus our language is *molecular*: its sentences are built out of independently meaningful units – what I shall call *meaning-atoms* – by rules that assign meaning to complexes as a function of the meanings of the atomic parts, together with the rules of compositional structure. The words are our atoms; they are meaningful, and they contribute by their meaning to the meanings of larger units to which they belong, but they themselves have no meaningful parts.

Since the atoms – words in English – are assigned meanings individually,[12] and since the composition rules make the meaning of the whole a function of the meanings of the parts, we can say that meaning in our language is *acontextual*. The meaning of a given word is determined by its

meaning-convention, not by the meanings of other words, and not by anything else; the meanings of sentences depend only on the meanings of the words in them.[13]

In sum, our language is productive and conventional, so its meaning-determining conventions are recursive, so it has meaning atoms, so it is molecular, so it is acontextual.[14] A great deal in the argument that follows will depend heavily on these entailments.

IV

So far we have been discussing the meanings of words and sentences in the common language: *semantic* meaning. Semantic meaning needs to be distinguished from *utterance* meaning: what it is reasonable to suppose the utterer meant by uttering that sentence in the context it was uttered in.[15] As the definition suggests, utterance meaning depends partly on context. An utterance of 'Harold is a snake', performed while witnessing some particularly discreditable action of Harold's and as part of a conversation about Harold's character, might mean that Harold is given to scheming self-aggrandizement. But the sentence 'Harold is a snake' does not mean that.

The meaning of a particular utterance depends in part also on the meaning of the sentence uttered, which depends on convention: your utterance about Harold would probably have had a different meaning if you had said 'Harold is an aardvark'. But it is an error to think that utterance meaning is itself conventional. As our example makes plain, semantic conventions alone don't determine utterance meaning, and it cannot be supposed that the meaning of an utterance is determined by conventions of the form 'An utterance of sentence S in context C means M'. There is an unlimited number of values for C, and contexts are not constructed recursively from a finite set of context constituents. We figure out utterance meaning by applying the conventions of semantic meaning, together with *non-conventional* rules of rationality. We assume the speaker understands the language and the relevant features of the speech-context, and is able to act appropriately – to choose appropriate words – so as to get us to realize what it is he intends to get across. The best hypothesis about that intention gives us the utterance meaning. This assumption of rationality is not a convention, because it is not an assumption to which there is any alternative. We cannot choose to regard a speaker as rational and so interpret his utterance one way, or choose to regard him as irrational and interpret it another. If we do not assume him at least minimally rational we have no way of deciding between countlessly many interpretations.

It is important to recognize that utterance meaning can occur where the utterance in question does not involve a use of language; gestures, facial expressions and acts of all kinds can have an utterance meaning. I take this to be uncontroversial. It is controversial as to whether the category of utterance meaning is conceptually or historically prior to that of semantic meaning, but we do not need to make a judgement about that. We might hold that utterance meaning is not prior to semantic meaning, but that it is possible for there to be specific acts with utterance meaning that are not semantically based.

As we shall see, a failure to distinguish semantic and utterance meaning has confused both sides of the argument over cinema language.

V

Our question, then, is this: is meaning conveyed by cinematic images in anything like the way that (semantic) meaning is conveyed by words and sentences? I shall assume that we are dealing with cinematic images that are made photographically. Not all the things we call cinematic images are made that way; there are cartoons and the less familiar practice of marking directly onto the film strip. I will consider only photographic films because they present an interesting and distinctive class, and because it is photographic films that are most often discussed in the context of film language. I shall also assume that we are dealing with cinematic images that function to present a fictional narrative, rather than, say, a documentary. In that case, we can sharpen our question a little further, for the kind of meaning we shall be concerned with here must be meaning that contributes in some way to our understanding of the fiction the film presents. It is clear, pre-theoretically, that cinematic images present meanings that do so contribute; let us call any meaning of that kind *story meaning*. And now our question is this: Does any of the story meaning that cinematic images convey possess the communicative features that we have attributed to the meanings of words and sentences?

One tempting but unsound strategy would be to argue that, with film, story meaning is conveyed in a way that is context sensitive, thus violating the acontextuality condition which, as we have seen, is a feature of semantic meaning. Thus George Wilson argues that the meaning we give a particular sequence of shots depends on how coherently that sequence, so interpreted, fits into the rest of the film. Whether, in *The Lady from Shanghai*, the juxtaposition of a hand pressing a button and a car crashing is to be taken as signifying a causal relation between the two depends on whether there is elsewhere in the film evidence for this peculiar causality. This suggests, says Wilson, 'the holistic character of all interpretive work'.[16]

Wilson is right to say that what the cinematic images tell us about the story depends on the surrounding context of other images. But that is true also of words and sentences in a text, where there is no dispute about the presence of a language. What kind of relation between described events is suggested by one bit of text depends upon the role that bit of text is seen to have in the context of all the other bits. If the texts says 'her hand pressed the button just before the car crashed' it is then a matter of interpretation, that will have to take account of the rest of the text, as to whether it is part of the story that the pressing caused the crash. So the context-dependence of interpretation applies to literature as much as to film, and it cannot on its own be an argument against there being a language of the cinema.

Plainly, we are mixing up semantic and utterance meaning. Semantic meaning is determined by the conventions of the language, and these conventions provide, as we have seen, for the acontextuality of meaning. What those words suggest about the structure of the story told is just what that choice of words with those meanings suggests about the story the teller *intended* to tell; this kind of meaning does not depend on convention. It depends on context, together with assumptions about rationality.[17]

So perhaps the defenders of cinema language can meet Wilson's objection by drawing a parallel distinction for cinematic images. In that case the defender will say, of Wilson's example and the countless others like it: 'What we may infer about the story from these images and their juxtaposition is, of course, a contextually sensitive matter. But we should not conclude from this that the meaning *intrinsic* to the images themselves is contextually determined – no more than we should conclude that the semantic meanings of words and sentences is contextually determined.' What we require of the defender is that he tell us what this intrinsic, acontextual meaning possessed by cinematic images is, and that he shows (i) that this meaning is story-meaning, and (ii) that this meaning has the explanatory features of semantic meaning.

I shall argue that there are two plausible candidates for such an intrinsic meaning of cinematic images, that the first one fails to satisfy condition (i), and that the second one, while it meets condition (i), fails to satisfy condition (ii).[18] So the case for a language of cinema is not made out. Of course, this argument depends for its force on my having correctly identified the plausible candidates, and my result could be overturned by the discovery of some other candidate that meets conditions (i) and (ii). But I have no idea what this other candidate would be.

VI

My first candidate is what the cinematic image records, which I shall call *photographic meaning*. What the image typically records is actors performing actions among props on a set. This sort of meaning is acontextual: it does not depend on relations between images, because it is locally determined by the conditions of the take. And by juxtaposing images one simply gets an accretion of meaning: if the meaning of image A is $M(A)$ and that of image B is $M(B)$, then image A followed by image B just means $M(A)$ & $M(B)$, where the order of juxtaposition is irrelevant to meaning; showing B after A does not mean, in the sense of meaning at issue here, that the events that A records occurred before the events that B records. The meaning, in this sense, of a complex of images is just the logical sum of the meanings of its constituent images.

But photographic meaning cannot be story meaning. There are several reasons for this, and I shall mention just one of them.

If photographic meaning were story meaning, it would always be true that a viewer who did not grasp the photographic meaning of the image would lack knowledge relevant to understanding the story – just as one who does not know the meanings of the words and sentences on the page lacks knowledge relevant to understanding the story told in the novel. But photographic meaning

is not like that. A shot may involve a trick of some kind; it may seem to show a man falling a distance that no man involved in the relevant profilmic events ever did fall. It may seem to show a fantastic creature, or a man walking on water. Or it may be a shot that seems to be a distant or blurred view of the main actor but is actually a photograph of a stand-in. In such cases the members of the audience will seldom have any idea about the photographic meaning of the shot in question. But if there is a doubt in the minds of the audience about what is happening in the story, or a disagreement between them about what is happening, it is implausible to suppose that it will be resolved by teaching them more about the cinematographer's tricks of the trade. By learning those tricks they might learn something about cinema in general, but they would not be put in a better position to work out what is happening in the story.

While it may not be relevant to interpreting the story what events the cinematic image actually records, it is relevant what event the image *seems* to record. Because of the use of mattes and other devices, the image may not record a man falling off a building; but it may very well seem to record such an event, and anyone who viewed the image in standard conditions would be able to say that that was what it seemed to record. And its seeming to record this would be a relevant piece of evidence for someone watching the film and trying to work out what the story is – though it would be a too hasty conclusion to say, on the basis of watching the image, that it is part of the story that one of the characters really does fall off a building; it might turn out that the image presents something which, within the story, is a dream, a hallucination or a mere possibility (deciding which would require taking into account the rest of the film's images, together with sound and other features). So this kind of meaning – call it *appearance meaning* – is a kind of story-meaning. It is also acontextual, in the sense that one can generally say at least something about what an image appears to record without knowledge of the surrounding context of other images. There may be images to which this kind of meaning does not have application, and we shall say of them that any story meaning they have is context dependent; I am thinking of examples such as the uniformly dark screen that begins and ends Ford's *The Searchers*; it is only in the context of other images that one could say that this dark image represents the dark interior of the home-stead; out of context it does not seem to represent anything at all.[19] But the fact that there are exceptions to the general rule that images have appearance meanings does not show that appearance meaning is an irrelevant or unimportant feature of those images; there are occasional sequences of letters and words occurring in literature that have no (semantic) meanings, but that has no tendency to show that literal meaning is irrelevant or unimportant for literature.[20]

Appearance meaning is story meaning; but it is certainly not conventional meaning: it is not possible to identify any set of conventions that function to confer appearance meaning on cinematic images in anything like the way in which conventions confer (semantic) meaning on language. This is the fundamental disanalogy between language and all pictorial modes of representation. We saw from the case of language that where meaning is both productive and conventional it must also be recursive and so molecular. But the appearance meaning of a cinematic image is non-molecular. There are no atoms of meaning here; every temporal and spatial part of the image is meaningful down to the limits of visual discriminability. To suppose otherwise would be to embrace an absurd epistemology of the image according to which we understand the meaning of a cinematic image by identifying certain elements of it from a list of meaning atoms, building up the meaning of the whole by rules of composition. The understanding of cinematic and generally pictorial images manifestly does not work like that. On the other hand, appearance meaning is productive: there is an unlimited number of situations that cinematic images can appear to record, and we generally have no trouble understanding the appearance meanings of cinematic images we have never seen before. So appearance meaning cannot be conventional.

It is conventionality that allows linguistic meaning to be productive. Where meaning is productive and non-conventional, as it is with the meaning of cinematic images, we have what Flint Schier called 'natural generativity': the characteristic of certain kinds of representations to enable us to go on from a few samples to understand and interpret novel representations of the same kind.[21] We cannot do that with the meanings of English words; we cannot explain 'red' and 'blue' to a novice and expect him then to form a reliable belief about what colour it is we call 'green' (unless he can make an informed guess on the basis of his knowledge of the conventions for some other, suitably related language). But with cinematic images, as with pictorial images of other kinds, we do catch on, once the confusions provoked by novelty have passed. Of course natural generativity is something that wants explaining; it is scarcely credible that a system of communication would be naturally generative without there being something *in virtue of which* it is naturally generative – though that something might be highly complex and disjunctive. I happen to believe that cinematic images are naturally generative in virtue of their similarity to real things. In that case it is *likeness* that plays the role for cinematic images that conventionality plays for language: both, in their different ways, make for productive systems of communication. But this is not something I am concerned to argue for here. I am arguing only for the non-conventionality of cinematic images.

VII

It is time to answer some objections.

To say, as I do, that the appearance meaning of an image is non-conventional is not to say that this kind of meaning *has nothing to do* with convention or with intention. For example, there are causal relations between intentions, conventions, and the appearance meanings of pictures. Intention plays its part in guiding the camera, and how things are placed before the camera is usually influenced by social institutions such as styles of dress, composition and decor, as well as by considerations of decorum. But this is not grounds for saying that the meaning of the image is *itself* conventional in the sense that meaning in natural language is conventional. To be conventional in that sense there would have to be a set of conventions governing the meanings of all the image-atoms, and since there are no image-atoms there are no such conventions.

The distinction between meaning that is determined by convention (and that is therefore conventional) and meaning that is merely connected to convention is overlooked by those who appeal to a vague, impressionistic and all-purpose notion of convention to support their claims about the conventionality of images. Umberto Eco has argued for the conventionality of images generally on the grounds that our images tend to be, and perhaps inevitably are, affected by our social practices: a picture of a lion, once praised for its lifelikeness, owes much, we can now see, to the conventions of heraldic representation.[22] Again, this argument simply conflates two kinds of conventions: conventions that affect meaning and conventions that determine meaning. From the fact that the characteristics of a sign are affected by convention it does not follow that the sign is a conventional sign. A sign is conventional only if there is a convention which determines its meaning.

It can sound as if I am winning this argument by stipulation, insisting that images are not conventional in a quite idiosyncratic sense. Not so. You may give 'convention' any sense you please, but please use it only in one way, and make sure you have in your vocabulary other words, one for each distinguishable concept we need in this inquiry. One of those concepts is what I have called 'conventionality', and it is a concept that applies to words in English because their meanings are determined by a co-ordinated practice based on mutual expectation. That is the target concept, call it what you will, for anyone who wants to argue that the comprehension of cinematic images has much in common with the comprehension of language. I have been arguing that this target concept does not, and could not, apply to the relation between cinematic images and their meanings, and the whole argument could be restated without using the word 'convention' at all.

VIII

Someone might agree with all I have said so far, and claim that it is an elaborate irrelevance, that the analogy between cinema and language takes hold not at the level of individual images but at the level of their combination; that there are identifiable patterns of combination between images, and that these combinations have a meaning that is partly dependent on the manner of their combination, just as sentences are meaningful partly in virtue of their syntactic structure. But at this level the analogy between film and language is utterly superficial. First, as many theorists have noted, the representational content of an image cannot be equated with that of a name, predicate or other sub-sentential part of speech. If these images line up with anything in language it is with sentences, since both represent states of affairs. So we cannot hope to find in the articulation of images anything like the internal syntactic structure of a sentence. The most we can hope for is to latch onto the linguistic model at the point where sentential connectives are introduced:

the familiar truth functions, together with the intensional operators such as 'because', 'causes', 'in spite of', etc. Even if there were a genuine parallel discoverable at this point (I shall argue that there is not) it would hardly constitute a vindication of the idea that a theory of language comprehension will explain the comprehension of cinematic images; by the time we have introduced these operators into our account of language, we have done nearly all the hard work of explaining how language is comprehended in terms of conventions of word meaning and the recursive rules of grammar – things that we have seen have no counterpart for in film.

In fact, there is no significant parallel between the connectedness of images in film, and the sentential connectives of language. Consider a piece of standard shot–reverse–shot editing, in which the second shot is understood to represent the view as seen by the character shown in the first shot, and compare this with sentential connection displayed in the construction 'P because Q'. In the latter case we can point to conventions of meaning and rules of grammar that determine for this construction a literal meaning: that P occurred because Q occurred. But with the shot–reverse–shot construction we cannot speak in the same way of conventions and literal meanings; there is no convention that says that a shot of a character face-on followed by a different shot means that the second shot is from the point of view of the character – there are too many cases where a shot of the first kind is followed by a shot that is not subjective. Rather, we infer the connection between the two shots from the context of surrounding shots, together with assumptions we have made about the course of the story so far, the likely location of the character, and the rationality of the film-maker: we assume that shots and their combinations are chosen by the maker so as to facilitate our comprehension of the story rather than that they succeed one another in an arbitrary fashion. We arrive at a judgement that this is a shot–reverse–shot combination not, as the model of our comprehension of semantic meaning would have it, by understanding a rule of cinematic grammar, but by applying the constitutive rules of rationality discussed earlier in connection with our comprehension of speaker's meaning.

Should we say, then, that there are no specifically cinematic conventions? My argument does not require that. Perhaps there are a few such conventions. Perhaps it is 'by convention', or something like it, that the slow fade out and fade in signifies a significant passage of time. Anyhow, it will do no harm to my thesis to admit that there are occasionally in cinema conventions of meaning at work. If there are, they do not amount to anything like the systematic, articulated, bottom-up set of conventions that govern a natural language. The most they manage to do is to enrich the meaning of an already non-conventionally meaningful structure. The conventions of cinema are islands in a stream driven by the force of natural generativity; they may improve the view, but they have a marginal effect on the direction of flow.

IX

If my argument is right, the project of explaining our comprehension of cinema on the model of our comprehension of natural language cannot succeed. It does not even come close, employing as it does quite the wrong concepts. We must abandon the way of language, convention and code, and think about cinema narrative in terms of natural generativity and intentional, rationalistic explanation.[23]

Notes

1 On the myth of 'story grammar', see R. Wilensky 'Story Grammars Revisited', *Journal of Pragmatics*, 6 (1982), pp. 423–32.

2 Sometimes advocates of cinema language seem to be asserting that there are many different such languages. The arguments I shall bring forward will be just as effective against that hypothesis as they are against the hypothesis that there is one such language. So I shall not bother to consider the multiple-languages hypothesis separately.

3 'On the Notion of Cinematographic Language', in *Movies and Methods*, ed. Bill Nichols (Berkeley and Los Angeles: University of California Press, 1976).

4 '*Trucage* and the Film', in *The Language of Images*, ed. W. J. T. Mitchell (Chicago University Press, 1980), p. 158 and p. 165. Metz's theorizing, with its movement from language proper, to *grand syntagmatique*, to a vast proliferation of codes, bears the marks of a degenerating research programme.

5 Umberto Eco, *A Theory of Semiotics* (Bloomington: University of Indiana Press, 1976), p. 13.

6 Eco says that a code is 'a repertoire or system of sign-functions' – somewhat unhelpful as a definition ('On the Contribution of Film to Semiotics', in *Film Theory and Criticism*, eds. M. Cohen and G. Mast, third edition, Oxford University Press, 1985), p. 196). And no characterization can be read off from the ragbag of examples on offer. Among cinematic codes there are, we are told, 'the complex system according to which the cinematic equipment (recording camera, film strip, projector) "reproduces movement" ' (Christian Metz, *Language and Cinema* (The Hague and Paris: Mouton, 1974), p. 191), and 'the representational code of linear perspective' (Jean Louis Comolli, 'Machines of the Visible', in *The Cinematic Apparatus*, eds. Stephen Heath and Teresa de Lauretis (London: Macmillan, 1980), p. 135). There is no natural way to 'go on from there', unless it be just to say that everything is a code.

7 'Signs are correlated with what they stand for on the basis of a rule or convention', Umberto Eco, 'On the Contribution of Film to Semiotics', p. 196.

8 Editorial introduction to *The Language of Images*, p. 3.

9 'The concepts of linguistics can be applied to the semiotics of the cinema only with the greatest caution. On the other hand, the methods of linguistics . . . provide . . . a constant and precious aid in establishing units that, though they are still very approximate, are liable over time . . . to become progressively refined', Christian Metz, 'Some Points in the Semiotics of Cinema', in *Film Theory and Criticism*, third edition, p. 176.

10 See David K. Lewis, *Convention* (Harvard University Press, 1968).

11 It is not claimed that we learn our language entirely from the bottom up. No doubt we start with simple sentences, shake out the word meanings by decomposition, and zigzag back and forth, continually expanding our competence in a way governed partly by trial and error. But if the meanings of linguistic units could not, in principle, be stated recursively, the language would not be learnable.

12 Not every word is an atom, as when a single word has a meaning that is a function of the meanings of other words and operators, as with 'invalid'.

13 Notice how this account of meaning in natural language contradicts the structuralist's claim that linguistic meaning is wholly a matter of a sign's relations to other signs. That is as it should be; a change in the meaning of one term does not induce a change in the meanings of all terms.

14 This theory, sometimes called 'compositional semantics', still seems to me the only straw floating, despite the arguments of Stephen Schiffer, *Remnants of Meaning* (Cambridge, Massachusetts, 1987). See the papers by Mark Johnston and Bar-

bara Partee in the Symposium on Schiffer's book, *Mind and Language*, 3:1 (1988).

15 Note that this might be a different thing from what the speaker *did* mean by uttering it, sometimes called 'speaker's meaning'.

16 *Narration in Light* (Baltimore: Johns Hopkins University Press, 1986), p. 203.

17 This is not Davidsonian charity, which would have us regard the speaker's utterances as (largely) true – clearly a pointless injunction in the case of a fictional utterance.

18 The first candidate fails, incidentally, to satisfy condition (ii). But since it fails to satisfy condition (i), we need not argue for this further conclusion.

19 This illustrates the difference between a dark and a blank screen, for in these shots the screen is not, so it turns out, blank.

20 Appearance meaning certainly requires further analysis and explanation. Here, I will say only that the appearance meaning of an image is not to be thought of as typically giving rise to a judgement that things really are as the appearance meaning of the image suggests – a suggestion in line with the currently popular but false hypothesis that cinema is deceptive. Rather, we might say, the image gives rise to an experience with a *representational content* corresponding to that appearance meaning. See Christopher Peacocke, *Sense and Content* (Oxford University Press, 1983), Chapter 1.

21 See his *Deeper into Pictures* (Cambridge University Press, 1986). See also Crispin Sartwell, 'Natural Generativity and Imitation', *British Journal of Aesthetics*, 31 (1991), pp. 58–67, especially pp. 62–4. Schier, I think, wanted to *define* pictures (and icons generally, of which pictures are in his sense a subset) in terms of natural generativity. I have no such ambition. Richard Wollheim employs a very similar concept, which he calls 'transfer', as the basis for a telling criticism of semiotic theories of art in *Painting as an Art* (London: Thames and Hudson, 1987), p. 77.

22 *A Theory of Semiotics*, p. 205. See also Ernst Gombrich, *Art and Illusion* (fifth edition, Oxford: Phaidon Press, 1977), p. 68.

23 Something I attempt in *Imagination and the Image: A Philosophical Essay on Film and other Pictorial Arts*, forthcoming. An earlier version of this paper was read by Jerrold Levinson, who made important suggestions for revision. Thanks are also due to Paisley Livingston for discussion.

8

Moving Pictures

Arthur C. Danto

Section I

Perhaps there is no serious reason to consider film as especially nearer of artistic kin to drama than to painting. Indeed, the expression "moving pictures" implies an evolutionary expansion of representational possibilities of much the same order as we would find were painting to have developed out of drawing, and the new forms called "colored drawings" (though we ought to be cautious in regarding any artistic genre as a progressive step beyond an established one, inasmuch as a colored drawing is not thereby demoted to the stature of a painting, any more than a black-and-white painting is demoted by monochromy to drawing).

Possibly a basis for considering film and drama together lies in the fact that both are viewed in theaters by a seated audience focused on a common spectacle. But this may be adventitious, inasmuch as concert-halls and opera houses are not remarkably different at this level from theaters; nor, for the matter, are hippodromes, circus tents, sports arenas or even churches – there being *some* basis, I suppose, for regarding theaters as mutations of churches and audiences as secularized congregations. The race-track and the basilica were equally charged with religious energy in Byzantine culture, where supporters of different teams were divided along lines of theological partisanship. In any case, it is not essential to films that they be projected onto screens; early films were viewed in peepboxes. I do not wish to deny that our response to film is in some

measure a function of our being members of an audience, since some of our feelings are doubtless collective and due to contagion, and I doubt anyone would be very deeply moved by something seen through a hole while assuming the compromised posture of a voyeur. Or if there *is* a special artistic experience to be had here, it is due less to *what* is seen than to the fact that it is seen *in a box*: for the box encloses and transforms a space encapsulated in, but distinct from, real space – the space of the spectator – like a holy object deposited in the real world but not of it, belonging to another domain of reality.

That there should be a space we can see into but cannot enter explains in part the uncanny power of Joseph Cornell's boxes or the perspective boxes of seventeenth century Holland or the looking-glass world – all of which give a kind of literal exemplification of something essentially true of art; namely, that it logically excludes its spectators from the space and often the time it occupies. We can see in a play, for instance, the transpiration of events in which we have no possible point of intervention. I can stab the man who plays Hamlet, but only Laertes can stab Hamlet; Juliet is logically restricted to the embraces of Romeo, even if the woman who plays her is in fact a rake. I own a crystal paperweight, vintage Baccarat, scarred by a hammerblow which I cherish for its philosophical meaning. Some child must once have been frustrated by the distance he thought physical, which in truth is metaphysical between himself and the spun-glass flowers embedded in

Arthur C. Danto, "Moving Pictures," *Quarterly Review of Film Studies* 4(1), Winter 1979: 1–21.

the transparent hemisphere, and he tried to collapse it by shattering the glass, not realizing that the value of those colored bits lay precisely in the fact that they escaped his touch. The invention of the projector enabled the audience to *enter* the box, which then receded into the mere walls of the theater, and some different method for marking the space between audience and spectacle was required: but this way a lot of people could see the same show at once, with measurable economic advantages to the impresario, chairs being cheaper than optical contraptions like Reynaud's praxinoscopes.

Proust, who practiced voyeurism to the point of genius and who sought to transfigure his life into art by taking a stand outside it from which to look in on it as a whole (and who almost literally stopped living in order to do so), imagined as a child (or at least his narrator imagined) that the theater was a kind of elaborate peepshow: a columbarium of matched spectacles. And I suppose if we bred actors for smallness, like bonsai trees, plays could be mounted in boxes for Gulliver-type spectators. But there would still be a difference to draw between film and drama, which we may see if we elaborate Proust's fancy, in which *chaque spectateur regardait comme dans un stereoscope un decor que n'était que pour lui, quoique semblable au milliers d'autres, chacun pour soi, le reste des spectateurs.* I wish to stress the phrase '*quoique semblable au milliers d'autres*' since '*quoique*' would have no application to the different showings of the same film in the same peepbox at different times or different peepboxes at the same time. The set of performances of the same play stands to the latter in something like the relationship in which the set of platonic particulars stands to the same archetype, or as the various interpretations of it stand to the same sonata, while the showings of the same film stand to one another somewhat as copies of the same newspaper do (hence Wittgenstein's joke), so that there is no relevant difference between reading the same paper twice or two papers one time each.

A missed inspired performance of a certain play or opera is unrecoverable, but I have no idea what a man might mean who tells me that I missed something marvelous if I did not see *Last Tango in Paris* at the Trans-Lux 85th Street on Friday at 8:00 p.m. I don't mean to deny the possibility of a kind of perversion of connoisseurship of the sort which animates stamp-collectors, but conceptually I shall have to suppose he is not talking about *Last Tango*, since nothing stands to it as a playing by Alicia stands to a piece by Granados, the relationship between negative and print being too mechanical to count. Showings of the same film stand to one another in the manner of classes as conceived of by Aristotle rather than Plato, with the basis of similarity *in rebus* rather than *ante rem*. Whether this difference is deep enough to subvert a natural comparison between film and drama may be questioned, and it in any case equally subverts a comparison between film and paintings. If we have two paintings which resemble each other as much as two showings – or two performances – this will either be a coincidence or more likely a matter of one being a copy of the other, while two showings of a film are not copies of another at all, and though one actor may imitate another, it is not part of the concept of performances that they should be copies of each other in the sense in which A is a copy of B only if B explains A.

A fresh performance of one of Goldoni's plays may not be explained at all by earlier ones, and we may indeed have no idea *how* such plays were first put on. And neither, save adventitiously, are two showings of the same films related as copy to original. We may appreciate this more profoundly if we recognize that our experience of a painting is seriously compromised when we are told it is a copy – certain historical presuppositions regarding provenance and history having a deep relevance even if copy and original should exactly resemble each other. But nothing remotely parallel compromises our appreciation of a showing which happens exactly to resemble another one, since matters of provenance and history are irrelevant here; and neither does it compromise our appreciation of a *performance* of it, were we to learn this performance was copied from another – unless its being copied was an artistic ingredient in the performance, as when we are told that a certain performance is exactly like the performances of Shakespeare's day and the result of hard antiquarian research.

In the end, showings are related to one another more or less as closely as are prints from the same plate – each being members of what we might pay homage to Walter Benjamin by terming "Mechanically Reproducible Classes" it not mattering conceptually if by accident or decision there is only one showing or only one print drawn from a given plate.

But to use this as a basis for drawing serious artistic parallels between prints and films would be

Arthur C. Danto

to use taxonomic principles with the same crazy accuracy with which Ucello used those of linear perspective; to produce something distorted to the point of parody. Prints seem vastly more to belong to the same artistic phylum as do paintings, as may be seen from the fact that historical beliefs function here as well – our experience of a print being compromised by the knowledge that it did not come from the same plate as an original it exactly resembles. And nothing like this matters with films at all, so far as I see – not that historical beliefs are irrelevant to their appreciation, but that they enter at a different point in their ontology. It is difficult to see that "an original" has any artistic significance in the appreciation of films, even though there are originals and epigones amongst the filmmakers. And films still seem to have some more natural affinity to plays than either has to paintings or to prints.

Possibly this felt parity has less to do with dramatic form than to the way in which each involves *events* in some special temporal way. "Some special temporal way" is a makeshift way of saying that there will remain a difference with paintings, even though paintings may involve time in the sense of showing an *event*, e.g., the Rape of the Sabine Women or The Drunkard's Farewell. We mark this to a degree with verbs of perception, for while we indifferently speak of seeing or watching a show (as of hearing or listening to a piece), we do not *watch* paintings, save in senses irrelevant to experiencing them as art, e.g., guarding them against theft, or observing them disintegrate, as with the frescos in *Roma*. We don't, because everything to happen is already before us; there is nothing further to watch *for*. The most energized baroque figures will never move a step, but stand locked in logically immutable postures like the personages on Keats's urn: "Bold lover, never, never canst thou kiss,/Though winning near the goal...."

This is so even if there are films in which nothing happens. Imagine, for instance, if inspired by Warhol, I produce a film called "War and Peace," based on the novel. It consists of *eight hours* of footage – a saga! – of the title page of Tolstoi's novel. Or suppose an ill-advised avant garde dramatist mounts a play consisting of an actor seated on the stage through three acts. "Lessness" by Beckett has an immobile figure this way. Nothing happens either in the film or the play in the sense that what happens *is* nothing. But the contrast remains even so with a painting

even of the most energetically deployed figures: for a person who stood before such a painting in anticipation, say, of an event – like the dancers in Breugel taking some step – would be mad, or hoping for a miracle of the sort which earned Pygmalion a place in mythology: whereas one has every right, however frustrated, to expect an event in the monotonous film or play just described. It would be a sardonic concession to the legitimacy of this expectation if the title-page burned up to end the film, or the seated man scratched his ear in act three.

Film and drama seem essentially temporal in a way somewhat difficult to pin down directly, though perhaps one way to do it indirectly would be to mark the difference between projecting a *slide* of the title-page for eight hours and running a *film* of the "title page" for eight hours. There is a considerable difference here in the circumstances of projection – none of which need be reflected as an element in the image projected on the screen – and we can imagine matters so arranged that there *is* no difference there, so one could not tell by patient visual scrutiny whether it were a slide or a film. Even so, though *what* they experience will be indiscernible as between the two cases, *knowledge*, however arrived at, that there is a difference, should make a difference. Although nothing happens in either case, the truth of this is logically determined in the case of the slide whereas it is only a matter of a perverse artistic intention in the case of the film, where something could happen if I wished it to. So a perfectly legitimate right is frustrated in the case of the film, whereas there is no legitimate expectation either to be frustrated or gratified in the case of the slide. Again, at the end of eight hours, the *film* will be over, but not the slide. Only the session of its dull projection will have come to an end – but not it – since slides logically lack, as do painting, beginnings and endings. Our viewing of a painting may indeed have beginning and ends, but we don't view the beginning and endings of paintings.

The same contrived contrast may be drawn between a *tableau vivant*, in which living persons are frozen in certain positions, and a play, in which by artistic design the actors do not move. Again, though no difference may meet the eye, there is a difference conferred by the logical differences of the two genres. We have, in brief, to go outside what is merely viewed to the categories, which define the genre in question, in order to establish differences, and to understand what is philosophically distinctive of more natural artistic examples. Finding the difference between pictures and moving pictures is very much like finding the differences between works of art and real objects, where we can imagine cases in which nothing except knowledge of their causes and of the categories which differentiate works of art from real things make the difference between the two, since they otherwise *look* exactly alike. It is this initial foray into categorical analysis that has given us some justification for considering films together with plays, since both seem subject to descriptions which, though in fact false, are not *logically* ruled out as they are in the case of pictures. If in a film "bold lover" does not succeed in kissing "maiden loth," this will not be because the structure of the medium guarantees these works of art to be a joy forever in consequence of logical immobility. Here, immobility has to be *willed*.

Section II

Let us stand back, for a moment, from this proliferation of cases and ponder the methodology which generates them. I am not engaged in botanizing, in seeking for a new classification of the arts. Rather, I am seeking for what may be philosophically relevant in film as an art. And one method for isolating philosophical relevance is to look for principles which must be invoked if we are to distinguish between things which are otherwise exactly alike.

Consider epistemology. The skeptic supposes that our experiences might be exactly as they are, only, in fact, the product of a dream. Then the difference between dream and veridical experience is that experiences are caused by what they are *of*, but causality and reference are relations at right angles to the experiences, which the experiences then underdetermine. Thus there is no possible hope for finding – *within* the experiences in question – whether these external connections hold or not. But the method of matching experiences in this manner is certainly a method of conceptual discovery, for without it we might never have appreciated how complex the analysis of experience must be, and how dependent, finally, it is on factors logically external to what we experience, on what does not meet the eye.

Or consider, again, induction, where a body of data supports not only a natural hypothesis, but also an immense set of unnatural ones (this is

Goodman's "New Riddle of Induction"). Because the data underdetermine the set of possible hypotheses, we plainly have to look outside the body of our data in order to determine which is the correct inference and, more importantly, what are the factors other than consistency with known data that have to be invoked in order to identify an inductive inference as correct.

In art, an important sort of case arises with fakes. We are asked what difference it makes if a work is produced exactly like the genuine one. Obviously, the distinction between *genuine* and *fake* must be established with reference to factors external to the works themselves – for example, with reference to their histories. However, the serious question is whether knowledge of these differences in any way impinges upon our appreciation of a work whose structure underdetermines the difference between authenticity and trumpery, or whether it makes no difference. I think one cannot say in advance whether it makes a difference or not. Consider for example, the possibility of duplicating persons. Suppose a man is killed in an automobile accident, but the widow is promised delivery in say three weeks of someone exactly like her husband in all obvious respects. Would it matter? Is she required to love, honor, and obey the exact simulacrum of her husband, or what? Would the *known* history of this reconstituted mate make a difference or not? I am certainly unprepared to say, but my feeling is that it would make an *enormous* difference, and my philosophical point is that the possibility of doubles, in which the pairs are exactly alike relative to some schedule of descriptions, may reveal factors outside this set with reference to which our attitudes toward one or the other of the counterparts may differ. The method of philosophical duplication is a powerful lever for lifting factors into consciousness which otherwise never would have been alive – presuppositions upon which our attitude toward the world has always depended though we might not have realized their crucial role since it never had been challenged. These factors will alway be logically external to the thing in question.

The most striking contribution to have been made to our understanding of art by the artworld itself has been the generation of objects – in every manifest regard like perfectly ordinary objects – things like bottle-racks, snow-shovels, Brillo boxes, and beds. We are (1) to regard these "things" as artworks, and not as the sort of mere real objects from which they are indiscernible: and (2) to say what difference it makes that they should be art-works and not mere real things. Indeed, I regard the matter of furnishing answers to these questions the central issue in the philosophy of art. But since it hardly can have been a question before the possibility arose, philosophers of art who merely studied artworks would have been blind to just the sorts of factors with which a philosophy of art must deal; for these factors would be logically external to the objects in question, which under-determine the difference between artworks and real things.

In times of artistic stability, one might have learned to identify artworks inductively and to distinguish them from other things (much in the way we learn to distinguish cabbages from carrots) and to think the essence of art must then lie in the differentiable features. Theory of art which is based upon such induction has necessarily to fail if something can be an artwork but share all the manifest features of an erstwhile ordinary object, and to understand what art then is requires us to avert our eyes from the manifest appearances of things and ask what it is that does *not* meet the eye, which makes the difference between art and real-ity: where knowledge of this difference then makes the difference in our experiences of objects as artworks or as real things. Think, after all, of the difference it makes whether the man in the lobby is threatening the woman or – using the same words he would use were he to be threatening her – is merely going over his lines as he waits for the elevator to carry him to his audition. It is not merely a difference in attitude in which the differ-ence consists: the difference is ontological and between things which otherwise are indiscrimin-able.

This is my purpose in manufacturing cases in which things – though they may appear the same – are seriously different, and it is what animates my preoccupation in section I between slides and films. Usually the differences are obvious, but we don't learn much philosophically by sticking to obvious differences. It is with this in mind that I want to explore some differences between film and drama.

Section III

Although there are many ways in which one can directly modify a strip of film to produce a cine-matic image (through the techniques of the photo-gram, by actually drawing or painting on the film and using the latter after the manner of a micro-scopic slide, or even by gluing things onto film), I shall primarily be concerned with photography, largely because photographs stand in interesting relations to the real world (almost as interesting as the relations in which perceptions do) and be-cause the camera has so many remarkable analogies to the eye. Consider, for example, what is involved in identifying a photograph as being *of* something – *of* the Cathedral of Rouen, for example, or *of* Prin-cess Anne. Here I believe we have an almost spontaneous representationalist theory of photo-graphic content which almost precisely resembles a parallel theory of perception. Something is a photograph *of* x when it is caused by what it denotes, so that if the causal condition fails, the semantical identification fails as well, in that it no longer is *of* x if x does not enter into a causal explanation of the state of the photograph we speak of as the picture, and in a natural sort of way.

It seems to follow that there are no *false* photo-graphs; that is, photographs which retain a con-stant semantical content invariantly as to their semantical value. Unlike a sentence, the meaning of which does not vary with variations in truth-value, a photograph has its closest linguistic peer in the "proper name," (if Russell is right that names without bearers are noises and if Kripke is right that a name denotes only what it is causally connected with). Thus something exactly like a photograph of Rouen Cathedral is itself not *of* Rouen Cathedral if not caused by *the* Cathedral of Rouen. I am thinking here of exposing a sensi-tized surface to the light in some random way, developing and fixing the result, and finding that one has produced a pattern of darks and lights exactly of the sort one would identify as *of* Rouen Cathedral had it a proper causal history. This has nothing to do with the sharpness of the image. A blurred snapshot of Rouen has this identity, and a sharp but fortuitously-caused pattern does not; or to suppose the latter after all to be of Rouen is to suppose Rouen after all to explain its prov-enance. To see the most sharply articulated pat-tern as *of* Rouen when uncaused *by* Rouen is like seeing faces in clouds: a cloud can look exactly like the profile of Voltaire – as much so as the bust of him by Houdon – but this is merely the result of an uncanny happenstance, a lucky bit of nebular con-figuration which is to be explained by whatever are the forces which account for cloud-formation, not Voltaire! We refer to Voltaire only with reference to why *we see* the cloud as we do, not with reference to why the cloud is the way we see it.

So photographs are very tightly linked to their causes when construed representationally rather than as abstract patterns of light. Indeed, they are linked in just the way in which ideas are in a Lockian or Cartesian view of representation: (1) as *of* their causes, in the respect that their having any real content at all is put in question the moment we have doubts as to their provenance; (2) if my ideas are caused by some condition of myself rather than, as I would spontaneously believe, by things in the external world, they directly lose their representational qualities and have just the sort of content clouds do, which is to say none; (3) as ideas they become meaningless, even if they exactly resemble what would be representations of the world on the routine assumptions of causality and denotation.

Suppose a drunken driver has a car which leaks oil, and you notice that the erratic trail of drips has just the shape of an English sentence, for example, "Your dog is pregnant." Are you, if a dog owner, going to *heed* this and treat it as a message? And suppose you do, and the dog indeed – and to your surprise – is pregnant? Will this still be anything but an accident? I am not going to advise you regarding signs and strange portents, but *if* you regard the marks as a sentence, with truth and meaning, you are going to have to suppose a very different causal structure than the one I have just described, concerning the way those marks get deposited in the world. In this case, all the signs are evidence for is that something is wrong with the driver and something amiss with his engine.

We can, of course, liberate ourselves from these severe constraints by letting a photograph be *of* something other than its cause, if we transform the cause into a model and (1) let *it* acquire a semantical structure of its own; (2) let it stand for something ulterior – in which case we require a rule of interpretation. Reynolds painted a portrait of Mrs Siddons as the Muse of Tragedy, and the subject of the painting was Mrs Siddons who was got up as the tragic muse. The subject was not the tragic muse *tout court*. But imagine an alternative history for Mrs Siddons – a possible world (if you like that sort of semantics) in which Mrs Siddons, rather than having become a famous actress, instead became merely an artist's model whom Reynolds happened to use as a model for a painting of the muse of tragedy. Then the subject of the painting would be not Mrs Siddons – she was only the model – but the Tragic Muse herself, though the painting looks exactly like "Portrait of Mrs Siddons as Tragic Muse" does. The model here would become a vehicle of meaning through which we see the muse as we see *L'embarquement à Cythere* as an allegory of love, rather than a group portrait of some of Watteau's chums, although indeed they were his models.

Much the same thing is available to photography. The famous 1857 collodion print of Henry Peach Robinson's 'Fading Away' is *of* a dying virgin, a bit of Victorian "saccharinity." However, he was not *documenting* a touching demise; he instead used models who stood for the dying girl, the grieving parents, and the like. The model becomes the subject only of pictures of models, whether the pictures be photographs or paintings; whereas the model becomes, as it were, semantically opaque and stands this once for nothing, or for itself. Leonardo may have used a bit of available majolica in setting up the Last Supper, but it *stands* for the vessel of the Lord, and the vessel is the subject of that portion of the fresco, not the crockery itself. Leonardo was not painting still lifes.

Let us resurrect the term *motif* from the vocabulary of yesterday's art schools, where something was a motif if *an occasion for painterly representation*, for example, an old fisherman's shack – and the identical object may be motif or model – the latter, if by dint of some rule of interpretation, is to stand for something other than itself. Then in Reynold's portrait, Mrs Siddons as tragic muse is motif, whereas in the other possible world she is model, and the tragic muse herself is subject. Of course, we may learn a good deal about florentine ceramics by studying the dishes Leonardo used as models by disinterpreting them and viewing them as motifs. And this will be remarkably and inevitably the case with photography, whatever the interpretive intentions of the photographer. A tremendous amount of sheer reality – simply in consequence of the physical circumstances of the process – is recorded through the blank uninterpreting eye of the camera, which simply transcribes whatever is before it, discounting for retouching, which raises problems of its own. The objects that we see in old movies have often far greater interest as motifs than as models, and the films themselves have a greater interest as inadvertent documentaries than as screenplays. They stand as testimonials to vanished realities. But this takes us considerably ahead of our analysis. In any case any representational form has the option of treating objects as motifs, in which case it is documentary, or as models, in which case it is anagogic. What is immediately important to us in photography is that it is inescapably dependent upon the objects it records, a limitation which may be overcome in cinema by the other sorts of techniques for modifying film I began this section by mentioning, where spontaneous reference to an external reality is considerably more elastic and less direct than in the photographic case, and where the option of documentarity is compromised if not lost. This is part of the reason I am making photography so central. We would lose considerable interest in the so-called photographs of the Earth taken from outer space were we to discover they were painted on film – unless the astronaut were painting what he *saw* and had adequate mimetic gifts.

Let us utilize these somewhat gross semantical distinctions to differentiate between a *film of a play* and what we might speak of as a *screenplay proper*, where the play, so to speak, is in the film, but there is in reality no play which is actually photographed; for example a film version of *Hamlet*, say, and the filming of a stage-version of *Hamlet* (before the advent of the medium of cinema, we could not have spoken of stage versions since plays were *only* staged, this being a case where the advent of new genres create boundaries for old ones). Filming a staged play may employ specifically cinematographic techniques by showing the action from angles not normally available to a fixed and seated audience (though science fiction theaters might be imagined in which the spectator is moved around: sometimes seeing the spectacle from the "normal" vantage point of the fixed seat, sometimes from above the stage, sometimes being literally brought up to where a closeup would place him, etc.) But even so, it is a staged play which is being filmed, an external event having an existence external to the film, which could in principle take place whether recorded or not, much in the way in which, on a realistic epistemology, we regard the world as there and determinate invariantly as to whether we perceive it or not. Of course, the knowledge that they are being filmed may have some effect in transforming the reality we think of the film as recording, much in the way in which the knowledge that we are being perceived (or observed) may alter the way in which we behave: the presence of an eye – or a camera – may precipitate a kind of *pour autrui* different through the

fact of perception from the stolid *en soi* the realist intends, but this intervention, however interesting, leaves the semantics of the situation unaffected: even if the fact that it is being filmed modifies the reality the film itself records, the play in question is an external, ongoing event, there whether filmed or not, and the same perturbations of consciousness would, for instance, occur if the actors merely believed they were being filmed, or if the director forgot to put film in his cameras, and believed he were making a film, falsely as it happens. In any case, the film here is a documentary, as much so as a newsreel, and the play in question is what the film is about, as much so as a newsreel of the events of May 1968 in Paris is about those events. The difference, of course, in the subjects here mentioned is that the events themselves were not *about* anything in the way in which the play happens to be about something rotten in the state of Denmark, or whatever *Hamlet* is about: but a photograph of a piece of New York *graffiti* remains about the piece of graffiti even though the latter may be itself about something, and have a content in its own right. And as denoted by its filmic representation, the film of a play in this sense is subject to the rigid semantical structures of photography as such. It is about a particular performance of a particular play, whatever may be the subject of the play itself. Of course, we may, in seeing the film, get caught up in the play, just as we may read the piece of graffiti; however, the play remains the motif of the film, even if we happen spontaneously to treat it as model. In a screenplay proper, by contrast, the film is not about what is photographed, any more than Delacroix's *Liberty at the Barricades* is about a certain woman, whatever her identity, whom Delacroix happened to pose in a phrygian cap with a flag in her hand in his atelier in the Place Furstenbourg. Delacroix meant us to see through that woman to what she stood for, which is the subject of the painting. A film of the play is about actors, whereas a screenplay is not about actors, except in the special sense in which what the actors play is actors, as in a certain Hollywood genre in which films were made about struggling young actors or skaters or singers or whatever; it continues to be not about the persons who play the roles, but about the persons whose roles they play, and even if the film should actually show the play in which they get their break and become stars, the play is in the film and the film itself is not documentation of the play. Of course, the inverse possibility to the one we noted before is a danger here: just as we may treat the actors in a filmed play as models rather than as motifs, see Hamlet rather than the man playing Hamlet, so in screenplays we may see the actors as motifs rather than as models, refuse to see Hamlet but rather Olivier: which is one of the problems of the star system, in which the actor becomes so autographic a cultural artifact as to render himself opaque. Which perhaps explains the motivation for finding anonymous actors, or just ordinary passersby. This is supposed to enhance realism, whereas what it does in fact is to enhance artifice, for the very naturalness of the persons 'playing themselves' renders them transparent in a way in which Garbo or Gable never could be. Or Elizabeth Taylor, who is to movies in which she plays, like Mrs. Siddons was in Reynold's portrait. These movies provide mixtures of document and anagogy, and about Elizabeth Taylor as . . . , hence compromising the illusion since we are always aware of the actor as actor: something which Proust's Berma managed to overcome. One wonders, for example, if in the typical Hollywood film, the audience even remembered the name of the characters their favorite stars played: for in describing the film they speak not of what, say, Diana Medford did, but what Joan Crawford did in *Our Dancing Daughters*. The movie star is a metaphysically-complex personality, retaining an identity so strong as to swamp the role he or she plays to the point that we speak of Eliot Gould rather than Philip Marlowe as doing this or that, as though roles were like lives through which a Hindu soul transmigrates, which is false of opera stars or stage stars, nor merely because the roles in the dramatic or operatic repertoires have a strong identity of their own, whereas film roles are often ephemeral, but also because the same role may in opera or theater be played by different actors, and we can compare their performances of films in the same respect, and the role is exclusively preempted by one person who plays it in a movie, so much so that we almost cannot separate the person from the role. Of course, different versions of the same thing are possible in films, but if someone today decides to do the *Thin Man*, it would not be like a new staging of *A Midsummer Night's Dream*, with its largely invariant lines and scenes, but a whole new work – like a version by Giraudoux of the same general story also but differently done by Euripides and Racine. In a movie, a role belongs to the person who plays it in the sense that were another to play the so-called same role, it would

be in a different *work*. So the fact that films use actors ought not to mislead us into thinking of film as an essentially performative art inasmuch as nothing counts as a different performance of the same work. So the star is intimately woven into the substance of the film, almost in the way in which Mrs. Siddons' appearance is woven into her portrait; but even so, the film is not *about* its actors or stars, any more than a play is. And this returns me to my subject.

Let us consider once more the difference between a film about a play in the documentary sense, and a film in which a play is put on. Imagine a film in which the famous star Delilah De Lillo plays the role of Mary Mutt, a struggling actress waiting for a break, which she gets at the climax of the movie. And we see her in her moment of triumph, playing the role of Blossom Beauchamps in the Broadway hit *Tepid Latitudes* – the name of the film is *Our Daughters, Our Dreams*. *Tepid Latitudes* can be a play, if you wish, about Blossom Beauchamps's moment of triumph as an actress in a play called *Broken Playthings*, in which she plays the role of Susan Seaward, a debutante who achieves erotic redemption. The high-point of the film shows Delilah-Mary-Blossom-Susan leaving her fiancé, a stock-broker, and embarking towards orgasmic authenticity with someone named Brian. *Tepid Latitudes* is in the film much as *Broken Playthings* is in *Tepid Latitudes*. Neither is in real life, and the film is never documentary. But the point I wish to make is that the difference is considerable between seeing a play and seeing a play of a play – as considerable as the semantical distinction between use and mention. Consider the Second Act of *Ariadne auf Naxos* in which a play is presented which is discussed in Act One. In a recent staging of this at the New York Opera, the second act did not so much present the play, but presented instead a play *of* it, putting a small stage onto the stage along with some people playing the part of the audience. So what *we* saw were some people seeing a play, along with seeing the play they saw; however, we saw the latter as a play. The play itself was then what the act was about, rather than whatever the play itself, were we to see it, would have been about. Thus, instead of seeing the characters, Ariadne, Zerbinetta, and the like, we saw actresses and actors *playing these parts*: hyphenated personages, which complicates identification of the dramatic object. In a staging of *Ariadne* in Rome, by contrast, we were actually presented with the play, rather than the play of the play, and so saw Ariadne and Zerbinetta directly. The difference is astonishing. Since in the New York production, we saw actors, there was nothing strange but only something comical in seeing *commedia del arte* actors on the same stage with classical tragedians. But in the Rome production, where we saw Ariadne on her island, singing out her heart, it was an artistic shock to see *commedia del arte* figures occupying the same *dramatic* space. How could they *be on that island*? How could figures from eighteenth century Italy be contemporary with a figure out of Greek mythology? Someone may represent Ariadne next to someone representing Zerbinetta, with no more shock than seeing a painting of Ariadne next to a painting of the Italian Comedians. What we cannot see without shock is Italian comedians in the same painting with Ariadne; it would be like seeing one of Picasso's cubist women being carried off on one of Titian's bulls. So in the documentary film of a play, we are supposed to see actors playing roles, whereas in a screenplay – apart from the complexities introduced by the star concept – that there are actors is not part of what the film is about. There being actors is not supposed to be part of what we see, or something which, if we fail to see, we will have misidentified what the film is about. It would, then, be consistent with a film which documents a play that it should also show members of the audience without in the least inducing aesthetic shock. But there is no room for shots of an audience in a screenplay except in the sort of contrived genre I sketched above. What a nondocumentary film is about cannot be photographed. Nondocumentary films stand to documentary ones – a common photographic base notwithstanding – in the relationship in which perception stands to imagination.

And this strong conclusion holds even if the director decides that the way he is going to proceed in making a film version of *Hamlet* is to have his actors actually *put Hamlet on*, which he then shoots, so that there would be no internal difference between the film he produces and the film a man might make who is documenting a performance of *Hamlet*. Of course this is not the ordinary way in which movies are made. Scenes can be shot anywhere; the man who plays Hamlet can recite his soliloquies in New York and stab Polonius at *Cinecitta*. In a parallel way, Leonardo might have painted the *Last Supper* by setting up a table in Milan with twelve models for the disciples and a thirteenth for Christ, in which case a documentary

painting of Leonardo's model setting might in fact be indiscernible from the *Last Supper*. Of course, Leonardo did not do it this way at all, so far as we know, and drew his models from here and there, and perhaps there was no such table as the one we see in the *Cenecolo*. At the same time, it would be an interesting fact were we to learn that he painted Christ from a model who happens to have had very broad shoulders. Then the fact that Christ *in the painting* has very sloping shoulders – supposing we can discount draftsmanly ineptitude on Leonardo's part – acquires iconographic or at least expressionistic content. But the *History of Models*, alas, is yet to be written.

It would be instructive at this point to discuss such matters as space and time in films; how the space of a photographed setting differs from the space of the action; and the time of the photographed scene differs from the time of the action meant. I recall how striking it was to recognize that in *Avventura*, Antonioni used *real time* as *artistic time*. (In *Simon Boccanegra* twenty-five years lapses between Prologue and Act One.) But I want to say a few words about movement, which the decision to treat films as *moving pictures* appears to demand.

Section IV

Moving pictures are just that: *pictures* which move, *not* just (or necessarily at all) pictures *of* moving things. For we may have moving pictures of what are practically stolid objects, like the Himalayas and nonmoving pictures of such frenetically-motile objects as Breugel's reeling peasants and Rosa Bonheurs's rearing horses. Before the advent of moving pictures, it would not have been illuminating to characterize nonmoving pictures as nonmoving; there would have been no other sort. With statues, of course, because they already existed in a full three dimensions, the possibility of movement was an ancient option, with Daedelus being credited with the manufacture of animated statuary, and not just statuary of moving things. Any good carver was up to that (though possibly not Daedelus's contemporaries, it being difficult to know how to characterize the content of archaic sculptures in terms of the presence or absence of overt kinesis). Calder introduced movement into sculpture as an artistic property of them, but it is not plain that his mobiles are *of* anything, even if they are so interpreted, it seems almost foreclosed that they would be of moving things: of branches in the wind or bodies in orbit or graceful spiders or whatever. Calder invented the striking predicate "stabile" to designate his non-moving statues, but I suppose all statues, even such dynamic representations of movement as Bernini's *David* or Rodin's *Icarus* would retrospectively be stabiles or at least nonkinetic as such. Keats's observation holds true of these works. *David* remains eternally flexed in his gigantocidal posture in the Villa Borghese, though the slinger he represents could not have maintained that position, given the reality of gravity. He is represented at an instant in a gesture where a next and a preceding instant would have to be anatomically marked, in contrast with Donatello's or even Michaelangelo's *David*, whose models could have held their pose: subjects for a dageurreotype, on which Bernini's model would have registered a blur. But Keats's observation would not have been logically true of sculptures or pictures as such, as mobiles and moving pictures demonstrate: things of beauty can be joys just for a moment.

In a philosophically stinging footnote to the *First Critique*, Kant observes that a representation of permanence need not be a permanent representation, and comparably a representation of motion need not be a moving representation – conspicuously in descriptions of motion, which do not swim about the page. But even with pictures, it had long been recognized that the properties of the thing represented need not also be properties of the representation itself. This was obviously so in one main triumph of representational art, the mechanism of perspective rendering where it would not have been the trivially present third dimension in a canvas which accounted for the depth in the painting. Though I suppose an artist could have introduced real depth as Calder introduced real movement; for example, by using boxes in which figures were deployed and one real space to represent another. But, in fact, it is not clear that this would have enhanced his powers of representation, and might have had in fact the opposite effect, just as animation of Bernini's *David* might have reduced or severely altered its representational power, resulting in something more like a toy than a man, more like the fetish of Abraham Lincoln delivering the Gettysburg Address as misbegotten by Walt Disney. We are struck with the *discrepancies* between representation and subject which we have learned to overlook, unless technicians, in routine examples of representational art.

On the other hand, the first movies used moving pictures to represent motion, and despite Kant's dictum, it is difficult to think that this is not a breakthrough of sorts of representation, much in the way in which it would have been a breakthrough to use colors to represent colored things, heretofore represented only in white and black (in contour drawings, for example) and perhaps the difference can be brought out this way. Chiang Yee told me of a celebrated Chinese painter of bamboo who, having repeatedly been importuned to make a drawing for a certain patron, decided to comply, but had at hand only the red ink normally used for seals. The patron thanked him, but asked where had he ever seen *red bamboos*, to which the artist replied by asking where the patron had ever seen *black* ones. Why infer from the fact that if the representation is red, the subject must be red, if we don't infer from the fact that if the representation is black that the subject is black? In a way, it may be a matter merely of convention. We handle sanguine and grisaille drawings in stride. However, there is more to the matter than that, since the *shape* of the image is the shape of the subject, and if the artist had painted his bamboos *zigzag*, he would hardly have been in position to counter the obvious question by asking where had the patron ever seen *straight* ones. So some properties one feels must be shared by representation and subject; some structural parities must hold, for at least this class of representation.

So perhaps the difference is this. In describing our experience with *David*, we might say that we see he is in movement, but we don't see him move. And with the bamboos, we see that they are yellow, but we don't see their yellowness. "Seeing that he moves," or "seeing that they are yellow" are declarations of inference, supported by an initial identification of the subject and some knowledge of how such things in fact behave. To paint the bamboos in color reduces the inference, and there is always a serious question as to whether, say, the use of red ink is merely a physical fact about the medium, or if it is to have *representational* (or, today, *expressional*) properties in its own right. Obviously, we have to learn. An emperor was fond of a concubine and commissioned that her portrait be done by a jesuit painter in China who was master of chiaroscuro. She, however, was horrified at the result, believing that the artist showed her with a face half-black, not able to see yet that he was representing shadows rather than hues and that the portrait showed solidity rather than coloration. But the problem remains and is as much a function of our antecedent knowledge of the world as of our mastery of pictorial convention: a painting of a tapir could appear, I suppose, to the zoologically ignorant as of a monocrome animal half in shadow, rather than a dichromatic animal in full illumination. In any case, with the movies, we do not just see *that* they move, we see them *moving:* and this is because the pictures themselves move, the way the pictures themselves must be colored when we would correctly describe ourselves as seeing the colors of what they show.

The earliest moving pictures, then, also showed things moving: not trains as such shown as moving, such as we see in Turner, but moving trains we see move: not just moving horses but horses moving, and the like. Of course, photography is not required for this, but a series of pictures moving past at a certain speed, which can be drawings, as in the Zoopraxinoscope, or for that matter the animated cartoon, where the several representations are synthesized into one, in a manner strikingly anticipated in the First and Second Analogies of the Critique of Pure Reason, and which requires the viewer to see these as pictures of the same thing in different stages of a movement, which the optical mechanisms we are born with spontaneously smooth out to continuity. That the matter is conceptual as well as perceptual is illustrated, I think, by the fact that if the pictures are of different things, or of the same thing but not at different stages of the same movement, we would simply register a quantized stream of images rather than a smooth motion – as we do in a way with some of Brakages' films in which, though the pictures move, they do not show movement, since the discontinuities are so abrupt. So we have, as it were, to synthesize the images as of the *same* thing at different moments of the *same* motion or the optic nerve will not help us at all. As students of Descartes's bit of wax would know, however ignorant they might be of the physiology of perception.

At the level of kineperception, I think, the distinction between photography and drawing comes to very little. Indeed, photography was originally less satisfactory in certain ways. The problem Leland Stanford's cameraman had was how to make it look like the horse was moving when in fact what the eye registered was the background moving and the horse deployed statically before rushing trees, disconcerting in something like the way it ought to be to us that the wagon's wheels turn backward as the wagon goes forward; we have learned to live with the eye and mind being in a conceptual antagonism.

Where photography opens up a new dimension is when, instead of objects moving past a fixed camera, the camera moves amongst objects fixed *or* moving. Now to a degree we could do the same thing with drawings. We could have a sequence of drawings, say, of the Tower of Pisa, displayed in increasing order of size; of the Cathedral of Rouen, seen from different angles. And we know as a matter of independent fact that buildings are not easily rotated or brought across a plain. Still, though we may describe our experience here in terms of seeing the Tower closer and closer up, or seeing the Cathedral from all sides, phenomenologically speaking is our experience of the Tower's being brought closer to us or ourselves closer to the tower: of the Cathedral's turning before us or ourselves circling the Cathedral? I tend to feel that when the camera moves the experience is of *ourselves* moving, which the phenomenon of Cinerama dramatically confirms. And on this I would like to say a few words which will bring us back to the semantical preoccupations of the last section.

An experience of kinesis need not be a kinetic experience. The experience itself based on rather natural cartesian assumption, is a kinetic – neither kinetic nor static – but beyond motion and stasis, these being only the content of experience, like colors and shapes, and logically external to the having of the experiences as such. It would be wholly natural to treat the camera in essentially cartesian terms, logically external to the sights recorded by it – detached and spectatorial. When the early cameraman strapped his apparatus to a gondola and rolled the film while riding through the canals of Venice, it was his philosophical achievement to thrust the mode of recording into the scenes recorded in a remarkable exercise of self-reference.

At this point cinema approaches the proper apprehension of architecture, which is not something merely to be looked at but moved through, and this, in turn, is something the architect will have built into his structure. I think, in a way, the kinetification of the camera goes some way toward explaining the internal impact films make upon us, for it seems to overcome, at least in principle, the distance between spectator and scene, thrusting us like movable ghosts into scenes which a-kinetic photography locates us outside of, like disembodied cartesian spectators. We are within scenes which we also are outside of through the fact that we have no dramatic location, often, in the action which visually unfolds, having it both ways at once, which is not an option available to the audiences of stageplays. Or this at least happens to the degree that we are not conscious of the mediation of the camera, and transfer its motion to ourselves, inversely to our deepseated geostatic prejudices. Whether, of course, the film actually achieves instillation of kinetic illusion – in contrast with the illusion of kinesis, which is the commonplace form of cinematic experiences – is perhaps doubtful, especially if the film is in black and white and manifestly representational; e.g., in contrast with holographs in which it is difficult to believe we are *not* seeing three-dimensional objects, even if we *know* better.

Even so, I think the chief innovation the moving camera introduces is to make the mode of recording part of the record, and thus thrusts the art of cinema into the image in a singularly intimate way. This happens when, for instance, the swinging of the image through an abrupt angle is to be read as a movement not of it but of the camera, for instance in a mob scene where the camera is, as it were, "jostled," or where, more archly, the camera literally climbs the stairway with an eye and a lubricity of its own, and pokes into one bedroom after another, in search of the lovers, as in one of Truffaut's films. In such cases, the movement of the camera is not our movement, and this has precisely the effect of thrusting us outside the action and back into our metaphysical cartesian hole. When this *happens*, however, the subject of the film changes; it no longer is the story of young lovers, but of their being observed and filmed which the movie is then about, as though the story itself were but an occasion for filming it, and the latter is what the film itself is about. Film becomes in a way its own subject, the consciousness that it is film is what the consciousness is *of*, and in this move to self-consciousness cinema marches together with the other arts of the twentieth century in the respect that art itself becomes the ultimate subject of art, a movement of thought which parallels philosophy in the respect that philosophy in the end is what philosophy is about. As though the director had become jealous of the characters who heretofore had absorbed our artistic attention to the point that we had forgotten if we ever thought about art as such, and at his ontological expense. Of course, we have to distinguish a film about the making of a film – which is

merely another form of the Hollywood genre of films in which the making of a play is what the film is of – from films whose *own* making is what they are about, only the latter, I think *graduating* (if that is the term) from art to philosophy. But of course a price is paid, and a heavy one. When, instead of transforming real objects into artworks or parts of artworks, the transformation itself is what we are aware of, the film becomes a documentary with the special character of documenting the making of an artwork, and it is moot if this will be an artwork in its own right, however absorbing. For the artwork which is being made is not in the end what the film is about when the film is about its making, and if this were perfectly general there would be no artworks at all.

Or perhaps the model is wrong. Perhaps films are like consciousness is as described by Sartre with two distinct, but inseparable, dimensions, consciousness of something as its intentional object, and a kind of non-thetic consciousness of the consciousness itself: and it is with reference to the latter that the intermittent reminders of the cinematic processes as such are to be appreciated.

Then a film achieves something spectacular, not merely showing what it shows, but showing the fact that it is shown; giving us not merely an object but a perception of that object, a world and a way of seeing that world at once; the artist's mode of vision being as importantly in his work as what it is a vision of. This is a deep subject, with which I end this paper, and I cannot hope to treat it here. I wonder, nevertheless, of the degree to which we are ever conscious of a vision of the world when it is ours. We are aware of the world and seldom aware, if at all, of the *special way* in which we are aware of the world. Modes of awareness are themselves transparent to those whose they are. And when they become opaque then, I think, they no longer are ours.

Atget was recording the city of Paris. His photographs are precious for their documentary value, preserving a reality which has achingly dissipated, but they also reveal a way of seeing that reality which, I am certain, Atget was not aware of as a *way* of seeing. He *simply* saw, as do we all. What is precious in old films is often not the "gone" artifacts and the dated modes of costume and acting. The people who made those films did not see their dress as a "mode of costume" but merely as *clothes*, nor their gestures as modes of acting, but as acting, tout court. A way of viewing the world is revealed when it has jelled and thickened into a kind of spiritual artifact, and despite the philosophical

Arthur C. Danto

reminders our self-conscious cineastes interpose between their stories and their audiences, their vision – perhaps in contrast with their style – will take a certain historical time before it becomes visible. In whatever way we are conscious of con-sciousness, consciousness is not an *object* for itself; and when it becomes an object, we are, as it were, beyond it and relating to the world in modes of consciousness which are for the moment hopelessly transparent.

9

Defining the Moving Image

Noël Carroll

I Background: The Problem of Medium-Essentialism

"What is cinema?" has been one of the presiding questions that has agitated many film theorists throughout much of the twentieth century. The aim of this essay is to try to provide one sort of answer to this question. Namely, I shall attempt to defend a definition of the class of things – moving images – to which film belongs and in which, I believe, film is most appropriately categorized. My reasons for preferring the idiom of "moving images" over "cinema" or "film" will emerge as my argument proceeds. Moreover, I should also warn the reader that though I intend to define the moving image, my definition is not what is called a "real" or an "analytical" or an "essential" definition – i.e., a definition in terms of necessary conditions that are jointly sufficient. Instead, my definition comprises five necessary conditions for the moving image. I do not claim joint sufficiency for them. For I suspect that would involve more precision than the subject will bear. And, like Aristotle, I think that it is advisable to respect the limits of precision available in a given domain of inquiry.

If you have read the preceding articles in this book, it may appear peculiar to you that I should now embark upon the enterprise of attempting to answer the question "What is cinema?" or, at least, a question very much like it. For the question "What is cinema?" is generally taken as a request

for an essentialist answer, and my position has been stridently anti-essentialist. Am I now contradicting my earlier position? Not really. The sort of essentialism that film theorists have traditionally sought is misguided, as I hope I have shown. But that does not preclude the possibility that film has some necessary, general features whose explicit acknowledgment is useful in locating (though perhaps not pinpointing) the place of film among the arts. Thus, I intend to approach the question "What is cinema?" while at the same time avoiding an essentialist answer to that question.

Of course, saying only this is somewhat obscure, since essentialism comes in many shapes and sizes. So in order to clarify my own approach, I should be overt about the varieties of essentialism that I wish to eschew. First and foremost, in answering the question "What is cinema?" I want to avoid the pitfalls of what might be called medium-essentialism, which is the variety of essentialism to which I believe film theorists have been most prone. My answer to the question "What is cinema?" also falls short of what might be called real-definition essentialism, on the one hand, and Grecian essentialism, on the other hand. But more on that later. For now it is most instructive to indicate how my approach grows out of a response to medium-essentialism, since it is medium-essentialism that has been of primary concern for film theorists.

What is medium-essentialism? Roughly it is the doctrine that each artform has its own distinctive

Noël Carroll, "Defining the Moving Image," *Theorizing The Moving Image* (New York: Cambridge University Press, 1996): 49–74. Reprinted by permission of Cambridge University Press.

medium, a medium that distinguishes it from other forms. This is a general doctrine, espoused by many theorists across the arts. Perhaps it was especially attractive to film theorists because it began to suggest a way in which to block accusations that film was merely a subspecies of theater.

Furthermore, essentialists of this ilk regard the medium as an essence in the sense that it, the medium/essence, has teleological ramifications. That is, the medium *qua* essence dictates what it is suitable to do with the medium. A weak, negative version of this is the "limitation" view that maintains that in virtue of its identifying medium, certain artforms should not aspire to certain effects. Thus, Lessing reproached the attempt to simulate hyperactivity in stolid, unmoving stone.

Alternatively, a stronger version of medium-essentialism holds that the medium dictates what will function best – in terms of style and/or content – for artists working in that medium, and that artists ought to pursue those and only those projects that are most efficiently accommodated by or even mandated by the nature of the medium. For example, it might, on this basis, be urged that painters specialize in representing still moments rather than events.[1]

Medium-essentialism is an exciting idea. For it promises not only a means for differentiating artforms, but also for explaining why some artworks fail and others succeed. Some fail, it might be said, because they do not heed the limitations of the medium, often by attempting to do something that some other medium is more essentially suited to discharge; while other artworks in a medium succeed because they do what the medium is essentially suited to do – they realize the telos inherent in the medium. Medium-essentialism may also be enticing because it addresses artists where they live. This is not dry philosophy cataloguing what is after the fashion of some ontological bureaucrat. Medium-essentialists give the artist helpful advice about what the artist should and should not do.[2] Medium-essentialism is not a bland, pedantic exercise in definition. It has explanatory and pragmatic value. Unfortunately, it is false.

Medium-essentialism depends on a number of presuppositions, many of which are extremely controversial. Some of these include the following: that each artform has a distinctive medium; that the material cause, so to speak, of an artform – its medium – is also its essence (in the sense of its telos); that the essence of an artform – its medium – indicates, limits or dictates the style and/or

content of the artform; and, finally, that film possesses such an essence.

The view that every artform has a distinctive medium appears false on several counts. First, it is not clear that every artform has a medium at all. Does literature have a medium? Words, you might say. But are words the right sort of thing to constitute a medium? Aren't media, in the most straightforward sense, physical, and are words physical in any interesting way? But put that set of questions aside for heuristic purposes. Even if words can be taken to constitute the medium of literature, would they amount to a distinctive artistic medium? For words are shared with all types of speech and writing, on the one hand, and with other artforms like theater, opera, song, and even some painting and sculpture, on the other hand. Likewise, if one says that the medium of literature comprises human events, actions and feelings, that, for similar reasons, would be hardly distinctive.

So, as a general theory of the arts, medium-essentialism is false in its first premise. Not all artforms have distinctive media. Literature does not – nor do its various parishes, including the novel, poetry, and the short story. But perhaps the position can be qualified in a useful way as merely stating that some artforms have distinctive media and those that do, in fact, possess the teleological structure that medium-essentialism describes. Then, the question for us becomes whether film is such an artform? And that, of course, depends on what one takes the medium of film to be. If it is identified as light and shadows, then film has no distinctive medium, since light and shadow are also arguably the medium of painting, sculpture, photography, magic lantern shows, and so on. Similarly, and for the same reason, light and shadow could dictate nothing by way of film-specific style and content.

Of course, yet another reason that the premise that each medium has its own distinctive medium is mistaken is that – in the most literal senses of what a medium might be – many artforms (most? all?) possess more than one media, some of which are hardly distinctive. That is, the view that each and every artform must have a single medium that is uniquely and distinctively its own must be erroneous, since artforms generally involve a number of media, including frequently overlapping ones.

For example, if we think of the medium as the material stuff out of which artworks are made, then painting comprises several media: oil paints, water color, tempera, acrylic, and others. Also, in this rather straightforward sense of media, sculpture comprises a wide range of media, including at least bronze, gold, silver, wood, marble, granite, clay, celluloid, acrylic (again), and so on.

On the other hand, if we think of a medium as an implement used to produce an artwork, painting can be made by brushes, palette knives, fingers, and even human bodies (remember Yves Klein); while sculptures can be made by means of chisels, blowtorches, casts, and, among other things, fingers. Perhaps every musical instrument is a discrete musical medium in this sense, but, then, so is the human voice, and, once again, so are fingers.

Thus, it cannot be the case that every artform has its own distinctive medium since many (most? all?) artforms possess more than one medium, many of which themselves have divergent and nonconverging potentials. Nor, as these examples should suggest, are these media always distinctive of one and only one artform. Plastic acrylic figures in painting and sculpture; celluloid in film and sculpture; bodies in painting, sculpture and dance; and fingers, in one way or another, everywhere. Furthermore, if we think of the medium of an artform in terms of its characteristic formal elements, then the cause is altogether lost. For features like line, color, volume, shape, and motion are fundamental across various artforms and unique to none.

Obviously, what is meant by the phrase "artistic medium" is highly ambiguous, referring sometimes to the physical materials out of which artworks are constructed, sometimes to the implements that are used to do the constructing and sometimes to the formal elements of design that are available to artists in a given practice. This ambiguity alone might discourage us from relying on the notion of the medium as a theoretically useful concept. Indeed, I think that we might fruitfully abandon it completely, at least in terms of the ways in which it is standardly deployed by aestheticians. Be that as it may, it should be clear that most artforms cannot be identified on the basis of a single medium, since most artforms correlate with more than one medium.

Film is certainly like this. If we think of the medium on the basis of the materials from which the images are made, our first impulse might be to say that the medium is obviously a film strip bearing certain photographic emulsions. But flicker films, like Kubelka's *Arnulf Rainer*, can be made by alternating clear and opaque leader, sans

photographic emulsion. And one can paint on a clear film strip and then project it. Moreover, in principle, video may be developed to the point where in terms of high definition, it may be indiscernible from film, or, at least, to the point where most of us would have little trouble calling a commercial narrative made from fully high-definition video a film. And, of course, if films can be made from magnetized tape, film would share a medium with music.

If we think of the film medium in terms of the implements typically employed to make cinema, cameras undoubtedly come to mind. But as our previous example of flicker films and painted films indicate, cinema can be made without cameras, a point reinforced by the existence of scratch films. And one could imagine films constructed completely within the province of CD-ROM; while, at the same time, formal features of film – such as line, shape, space, motion, and temporal and narrative structures – are things that film shares with many other arts. Consequently, it should be clear that, strictly speaking, there is no single medium of film from which the film theorist can extrapolate stylistic directives; at best there are film media, some perhaps which await invention even now.

It may seem counterintuitive to urge that we think of media where heretofore we have referred to the medium. But it shouldn't. There can be little question that photography is comprised of many media such as the daguerreotype and the tintype, on the one hand, and the polaroid, on the other. How fine grained we should be in individuating media may be problematic. Are panchromatic and orthochromatic film stocks different media? Are nitrate and ascetate both film? Is the fish-eye lens a different medium than the so-called normal lens? One can imagine respectable arguments on both sides of these questions. But such disputes notwithstanding, the observation that artforms involve multiple media, which, in turn, may be frequently mixed, is incontrovertible. Talk of *the* (one and only) medium with respect to an artform, then, is generally a misleading simplification or abstraction. Indeed, it seems to me that there is no way to stipulate selectively (from the various media that comprise a given artform) an hypostatized medium for the artform at the physical level of media that would not be guided by a notion of the proper function of the artform, a notion, moreover, that is informed by one's stylistic interests.

Of course, by denying that artforms possess a medium in the way that idea is standardly used, I do not intend to say that artworks lack a material basis or that they are not fashioned by physical implements. My point is simply that artworks in a given artform may employ different media, sometimes simultaneously, and that they may be constructed through various implementations. To hypostatize this diversity under the rubric of something called *The Medium* obscures the richness and complexity of the relations of the artform to its material base(s). Undoubtedly some might resist my skepticism about the medium here on the grounds that my construal of medium talk is far too narrow. However, at this point in the dialectic, the burden of proof rests with them to come up with a concept of the medium that is immune to my objections.

So far I have been challenging two pre-suppositions of medium-essentialism, viz., that each artform has a unique, singular medium and that this is so of film. But the other presumptions of medium-essentialism are also worthy of scrutiny, often for reasons connected with the issues we have already broached.

The medium-essentialist thinks that the so-called medium of an artform is also the essence of the artform in the sense that it carries within it the distinctive telos of the form, somewhat in the manner of a gene. This is a surprising doctrine because many of the candidates for the medium that one encounters are not only shared by different artforms, but because in many cases – like oil paint or celluloid – the candidates seem to underdetermine the uses to which they might be put.

But the doctrine can also be challenged when one recalls that artforms do not generally possess a single medium but are better thought of in terms of media. For if artforms possess several media, there is no reason to suppose that they will all converge on a single effect or even a single range of effects. The media that comprise a single artform may sustain different, nonconverging potentials and possibilities. There is no antecedent reason to think that all the media that comprise an artform gravitate toward the same range of effects. Indeed, the more media that comprise an artform, the more likely statistically it will be that their assortment of effects may diverge. Thus, the fact that the media of an artform are multiple tends to undermine the supposition that a single medium (out of all the media) of the artform in question could define the telos of the artform as a whole. This is not to deny

that even a single medium might have a nonconverging range of effects such that it might fail to specify a single coherent end for the artform. Rather when that possibility is added to the problem that artforms are composed of multiple media, the probability that the putative medium might correspond to an essence or telos of an artform becomes immensely dubious.

In commenting on the multiplicity of the media that may comprise an artform, I noted that some of the relevant media may not have been invented yet. Media are added to artforms as times goes by. Bellini could not have known that plastic would become a medium of sculpture. Moreover, it almost goes without saying, when media are added to an artform they may bring with them unexpected, unprecedented possibilities, ones that may not correspond to the already existing effects familiar to artists. Drum machines and samplers have recently been added to the arsenal of musical media in order to imitate existing sounds, but it was soon discovered that they could also be used creatively to produce heretofore unimagined sounds. For example, with a sampler one can combine the attack of a snare drum and the sustain of a guitar by means of a careful splice. That an artform is not static – at least because it can acquire new media with unpredictable, nonconverging possibilities – indicates that one cannot hope to fix the telos of an artform on the basis of one of its constituent media.

It may be that artforms do not possess coherent essences in the way in which the tradition has supposed. But even if they did, no single medium constitutes the essence or telos of an artform. Perhaps theoreticians in the past have missed this because they have tended to select out one medium of a given artform and treat it (or, as they say, "privilege" it) as *the* medium. This maneuver at least superficially makes the derivation of a coherent telos for the artform appear more plausible. But this ignores the fact that artforms are constantly expanding their productive forces. New media are, in principle, always available to artforms, thereby opening new possibilities to the practice. One can no more shackle these developments by means of theories that privilege a single medium in a given artform than one can shackle the means of production by means of ideology.

One does not identify the essence or telos of an artform such as film, on the basis of something called the medium, nor does this alleged medium indicate or mandate the legitimate domain of exploration in terms of style or content with respect to an artistic practice. One way to see the inadequacy of the medium-essentialist's view in this regard is to compare the implications of the medium-essentialist's view for stylistic development with reality.

The strongest version of mediumistic essentialism appears to regard artforms as natural kinds outfitted with gene-like programs that mandate stylistic developments. The artform has an unalterable nature – inscribed in the medium – and this unalterable nature dictates style. But this is clearly a false idea. An artform is not analogous to a natural kind. Artforms are made by human beings in order to serve human purposes. Artforms are not unalterable; they are frequently adapted, altered and reinvented, often to serve preordained stylistic purposes. And this, moreover, is exactly the opposite course of events from that predicted by the medium-essentialist.

Consider musical instruments. They have a fair claim to be considered artistic media in the sense that they are physical implements used to construct artworks. They are media in the same sense that chalk and crayon are media. Furthermore, new musical instruments are constantly being invented and readapted. And, in many cases, these developments are driven by stylistic interests. The piano, for example, was introduced at a time when composers were becoming increasingly interested in sustained crescendos. Here, stylistic interests figure in the alteration of the very shape of the medium. Likewise, individual musicians adapt musical media to suit their stylistic aims as did the jazz performer Jack Teagarden when he took the slide off his trombone and cupped the horn with a whiskey glass. In such cases, the medium does not fix the parameters of style, but stylistic ambitions dictate the production or reinvention of media.

Nor is this phenomenon unique to music. In film, the move to various wide-screen processes was undertaken, to a certain extent, in order to facilitate certain "realistic" stylistic effects that practitioners had observed imperfectly realized in earlier formats.[3] Likewise, in the late 1910s and early 1920s, as Kristen Thompson has shown, filmmakers introduced the use of portrait lenses and gauze over the lens to create noticeably soft images for certain stylistic effects.[4] And there is also the case of the reintroduction of the use of arc lamps for black-and-white cinematography that Welles and Toland pioneered for stylistic effects

involving depth of field in *Citizen Kane*, which others picked up in the 1940s. In such cases, the "medium" is modified or reinvented in order to serve stylistic purposes. The so-called medium is physically altered to coincide with the dictates of style, rather than style docilely following the dictates of some fixed medium.

What cases like this suggest, of course, is that, contra the medium-essentialist, stylistic developments need not follow the "directives" of the so-called medium (even if one could identify said "directives") because in many cases, it is stylistic considerations that influence the invention, adaptation and reinvention of artistic media. This is not to deny that sometimes artists arrive at their distinctive stylistic choices by contemplating features of the medium (or "the media," as I prefer to say). I only wish to dispute the crucial premise of the medium-essentialist, who maintains that style is determined by the structure (notably the physical structure) of the medium. That must be false because sometimes it is style that determines the very structure of media.

I hypothesize that medium-essentialism derives a great deal of its appeal from its association with the apparently common-sensical view that artists should not attempt to make a medium do what it cannot do. Once the medium-essentialist secures agreement with this negative prognostication, he then goes on to suggest that one can also specify certain determinate things that an artist ought to do with the medium. But two points are worth noting here.

First, there is no way logically to get from the truistic, negative prognostication to some robust, positive prescription of any determinateness about what artists should do with the medium. Second, the negative prognostication itself is idle. It is an empty admonition for the simple reason that if something truly cannot be done with a certain medium, then no one will do it. No one can do the impossible. The case is closed. But also, again, from the vacuous warning that no one should do what it is impossible to do with the medium, nothing follows about what live possibilities of the medium an artist ought to pursue. Medium-essentialists who leave the impression that their positive recommendations are implied by the negative injunction to refrain from making a medium do what it cannot are simply trading in non sequiturs.

I have spent so much time disputing the presuppositions of medium-essentialism because of my conviction that this approach has unfortunately dominated previous attempts to answer the question "What is cinema?" Thus, in what follows, I will define film, or what I call the moving image without reference to a specific physical medium, and, furthermore, my definition will not have stylistic ramifications for what film artists should and should not do. The problems of medium-essentialism become, in other words, constraints on my theory, demarcating certain areas of speculation where I shall not tread. By way of preview, what I intend to produce are five necessary conditions for what I call the moving image. Moreover, as I will try to explain, this does not amount to the assertion of a new kind of essentialism – of either the real-definition or Grecian variety – for reasons that I shall defend in my concluding remarks.

II Revisiting Photographic Realism

In this section, I shall attempt to introduce one necessary condition for what I call the moving image. I shall try to argue on behalf of this condition dialectically by showing how a case for it can emerge in the process of demonstrating the shortcomings of one traditional view of the essence of cinema, namely photographic realism (a view discussed in the preceding essay in this volume).

As is well know, André Bazin answered the question "What is cinema?" by stressing the photographic basis of film. For him, photography was what differentiates the film image from other sorts of pictorial art, such as painting. He maintained that whereas handmade pictorial practices like painting portrayed objects, persons, and events by means of resemblance, machine-made pictures, like photographs and films, literally presented or re-presented objects, persons and events from the past to viewers. If the relation of paintings to their objects is resemblance, then the relation of photos and, by extension, film images to their referents is identity. The photo of Woodrow Wilson is Woodrow Wilson presented again in his visual aspect to contemporary witnesses. Film and photography provide us with telescopes, so to speak, into the past. Bazin says: "The photographic image is the object itself. . . . It shares by virtue of the process of its becoming, the being of the model of which it is a reproduction; it is the model."[5]

Among other things, what Bazin intends to achieve by emphasizing the photographic basis of film is to mark the essential difference between film and other picture-making processes like painting. Those traditional picture-making processes are representational, and what is distinctive about representation, in Bazin's opinion, is that it is rooted in resemblance. But film, like photography, is presentational, not representational, according to Bazinians. It presents objects, persons and events again, and, in consequence, there is some kind of identity relation between photographic and cinematographic images of x and x itself. Moreover, this distinction between presentational images, on the one hand, and representational images, on the other, is connected for Bazin to the fact that photographic and cinematographic images are machine-made whereas more traditional images are handmade.

Is there really such a vast difference between a machine-made picture and a handmade picture? In order to bolster the intuition that there is a deep difference lurking here, the Bazinian can invite us to consider the following comparison.[6] Quite frequently, objects that the photographer never noticed in the profilmic event appear in photos and cinematic images. This can be quite embarrassing when, for example, a Boeing 707 turns up in the background of a shot from El Cid or a telephone pole appears in First Knight. But even when it isn't embarrassing, photographers often admit finding things in photos of which they were unaware when they snapped the shutter and exposed the film. The reason for this is simple. Photography is a mechanical process. The apparatus will record everything in its field of vision automatically, whether or not the photographer is alert to it.

But, on the other hand, the Bazinian might suggest that such an occurrence is impossible in painting. One simply can't imagine a painter returning to her canvas and being shocked at finding a building there. Painting is an intentional action such that every object portrayed in the painting is there because the painter intended it to be there. There will be no surprises of the sort that photographers typically encounter when the painter looks at her painting – unless she has amnesia or unless someone else has tampered with it – because every person, object or event in the painting is there as a result of her intentions.

Because a painting is man-made, or woman-made, in a way that is dependent upon the maker's intention to portray this or that, it is, so the story goes, impossible that a painter could be shocked by the discovery of a Boeing 707 in her portrait of the Cid. But that very sort of shock is not only possible, but fairly routine when it comes to photography. Many scenes from movies must be reshot when things from the profilmic situation – which no one noticed at the time of shooting – wander into the frame. A director may demand to know "How did *that* get into my shot?" when she reviews the dailies. But the painter never has to ask. She knows already since she put it there – whatever it is.

Thus, the Bazinian surmises that the difference between machine-made and handmade pictures is not a trifling matter of alternative techniques. It is situated on an ontological fissure that goes deep into the very structure of the world at the level dividing what is possible from what is impossible. And since what is possible in film (because it is machine-made) is impossible in painting (because it is handmade), the Bazinian photographic realist believes that he has discerned a fundamental differentiating feature that separates traditional pictorial representations from photographic presentations.

Undoubtedly, the photographic realist can marshall some very powerful intuitions on his side. But until recently, as we argued in the previous article in this volume, this position has also been encumbered by a number of liabilities. One of these is that Bazin himself was never very helpful in explaining how we are to understand the supposed identity relation between a photo or shot of *x* and *x* itself. Patently, a shot of Denzel Washington is not the same thing as the man himself. So, in what sense *is* the image its model? Unless a reasonable answer can be supplied to this question, photographic realism seems dead in the water.[7]

Secondarily, photographic realism, as advanced by Bazin, represents a variation on the medium-essentialist refrain, and, therefore, involves many of the shortcomings rehearsed a moment ago in this essay. Consequently, added to its potentially incoherent account of the relation between the cinematic image and its referent, Bazinian photographic realism is also open to the charge that it attempts to mandate aesthetic choices on the basis of spurious ontological claims.

Yet these problems may not be so daunting. On the one hand, the photographic realist may detach his position from the medium-essentialist biases of Bazin. He may agree that his position has no stylistic implications about what must or must not be done by way of cinematic style at the same time that he maintains that cinema is essentially photographic. That is, photographic realists can argue that the photographic basis of film is the essential feature of the cinema without committing themselves to the idea that this logically implies a determinate style or range of styles for filmmakers.

Moreover, turning to photographic realism's other problem, a number of philosophers – including Roger Scruton, Kendall Walton and Patrick Maynard – have begun to work out the sort of identity claims which were only obscurely hinted at by Bazin in a way that makes them intelligible, if not compelling.[8] Thus, if they are able to provide a coherent account of the way in which photography is a presentational, rather than a representational art, then it may once again be plausible to ask whether or not photography is an essential feature of cinema, one that sets it off from traditional forms of pictorial representation, like painting.

A new defense of photographic realism could begin by analogizing film to telescopes, microscopes, periscopes and to those parking-lot mirrors that enable you to look around corners. When we look through devices like these, we say that we see the objects to which these devices give us access. We see stars through telescopes; bacteria through microscopes; aircraft carriers and atomic blasts through periscopes; and oncoming traffic through parking-lot mirrors. Such devices are aids to vision. As such, we may regard them as prosthetic devices.[9] Moreover, these prosthetic devices enable us to see things themselves, rather than representations of things.

When I look through my theater glasses at the ingenue, I see the ingenue, rather than a representation of the ingenue. Devices like these glasses, and the ones mentioned above, enhance my visual powers. They enable me to see, for example, what is faraway or what is small. Indeed, they enable us to see the things themselves, not merely representations of these things. These devices are not, in principle, different from the eye glasses we use to correct our vision. They enable us to overcome visual shortcomings and to make direct visual contact with objects otherwise unavailable to us.

But if we are willing to speak this way about microscopes and telescopes, the photographic realist asks, why not regard photography in the same light? Photography and cinematography are prosthetic devices for vision. They put us in direct visual contact with persons, places and events from the past in a way that is analogous to the manner in which telescopes put us in direct visual contact with distant solar systems. A photograph enables a wife to see her dead husband on their wedding day once again. A shot from an old news-reel enables one to see Babe Ruth at bat.

The argument here takes the form of a slippery slope. If a periscope enables us to see directly over a wall into an adjacent room, why not say that a video set-up does the same thing? One's first response is to say "But we don't see the contents of the adjacent room directly when we look at a video monitor." But what does it mean "to see directly?"

One thing that it means is that our perception is counterfactually dependent on the visible properties of the objects of our perception – i.e., had the visible properties of those objects been different, then our perceptions would have been different. There is a causal chain of physical events between the objects of our perception and our perception such that if the starting point in that network had been different, our perception would have varied accordingly. For example, I see the redness of the apple because the apple was red, but had the apple been green, what I would have seen would have been green. And had the object been a banana, rather than an apple, what I would have seen, all things being equal, would have been a banana.

Similarly, when I look through the periscope, what I see is also counterfactually dependent on the objects that give rise to my perception. This is why I am willing to say that what I see through a periscope or through a pair of opera glasses is seen directly. These devices boost the powers of direct perception. They are on a continuum with unaided sight inasmuch as what they give us access to possesses the property of counterfactual dependence. What we see through them would have been different if the visible properties they are aimed at were different. The causal chain of physical events involved in looking through a pair of opera glasses may have an added step when contrasted to un-aided vision. But the step is not different in kind. It is still a causal process that preserves the feature of counterfactual dependence. It is on a par with prosthetically unaided vision and so we are willing to say that opera glasses, like unaided vision, put us in direct (counterfactually dependent, causal) contact with objects.

But, then again, is the situation so different with photography and cinematography? Photographic and cinematographic "visions" and unaided, "nor-mal" vision are as strikingly analogous as opera glass "visions" and "normal" vision insofar as all three exhibit the relation of counterfactual de-pendence with respect to the objects of which

they are "visions." We expect a photograph of x to present the visible properties of x in such a way that if x's visible properties had been altered, the photograph would have been altered in corresponding respects. For example, we expect a photograph or a cinematic image of a white church to be white, though if, counterfactually, the church had been black, then we would have expected the photographic depiction to show it as black, at least in cases of straight shooting.

This, of course, once again correlates with pros-thetically unaided visual experiences of x where it is presumed that my visual experience of x depends on the visible features of x in such a way that had the visible features of x been different, my visual experience would differ – had the tan lion been red, I would have seen a red lion. Both prosthetically unaided vision and photography are counterfactually dependent on the visible proper-ties in the same way because of the particular physico-causal pathways between these sorts of vision and that of which they are "visions." We say that we are in direct visual contact in the case of vision unaided by opera glasses and vision aided by opera glasses because of the kind of physico-causal processes involved. Since the same kind of physico-causal processes are involved in photo-graphic and cinematic vision, we have no reason, in principle, to say that they do not directly show us those things to which they give us visual access – such as JFK's assassination.

One might say "Not so fast; what about the temporal difference between the events in news-reels and the events themselves?" But the photo-graphic realist can respond that this is not really so different theoretically than the case where the images of stars delivered to us by telescopes – through which we see directly – come from the past.

Given this argument, the photographic realist maintains that photographic and cinematic images are transparent – we see through them to the ob-jects, persons, and events that gave rise to them.[10] It is this species of transparency, one conjectures, that Bazin had in mind when he talked about the relation between the photographic image and its referent in terms of identity. By means of trans-parency, we see through the photograph to that of which it is a photograph. The photograph is a transparent presentation of something from the past which we see directly in the sense of counter-factual dependence – i.e., had the relevant objects been different, the photography would have been different in corresponding ways as a result of the kinds of physical processes involved in photography.

Furthermore, traditional picture-making practices, like painting, are not transparent in this way. Paintings need not be counterfactually dependent upon the visible properties of what they portray. They are dependent on the beliefs the painter holds about those objects. The chain of events from objects to paintings of objects are not physico-causal chains like those found in what I have called unaided, "normal" vision. The relation is mediated by the beliefs and intentions of painters. A green apple in a painting would have been blue had the painter intended the apple to be otherwise; something other than "natural" physico-causal chains of events are involved. This is why drawings are not accepted as evidence in court in the way that videotapes are. A drawing of Rodney King being beaten would not have possessed the evidential power of the videotape for this reason.

We do not see directly through paintings. Paintings are representations. They are mediated by intentions. They are not transparent presentations. A painting offers us a representation of an object, whereas a photograph, and, by extension, a cinematic image, provides us the object that gave rise to the image in the same way that a microscope boosts our perceptual powers in a way that is continuous with "normal" vision so that we directly see tiny things. What photography and cinematography enable us to see transparently are the very things from the past that started the mechanical processes that caused the images in question.

In order to "see through" a picture, it is a necessary condition that the photographic process put us in contact with its object by purely mechanical means. But though this is a necessary condition for something to count as a transparent photographic presentation, it is not sufficient. Why not? Well, imagine a computer that was capable of scanning a visual array and then printing out a description of it. It need not be a complicated visual array; it might be comprised of very simple geometric shapes. Surely, there would be no problem in constructing a computer that could recognize such shapes and correlate them to simple descriptions. Yet in such circumstances, it would appear that we are in the sort of mechanical contact with the array that warrants attributions of transparent seeing. But something is wrong here, since descriptions are not transparent pictures for the simple reason that they are not pictures at all. So what

then must be added to mechanical contact to differentiate between computer-generated descriptions of the sort imagined here and the kind of image that we might be able to see through?

One way to get at this difference is to note some of the ways in which we might be confused by a picture versus the ways in which we might be confused by a description. Reading, for example, we might confuse *mud* for *mut* because the lettering is so similar; such a mistake might come quite easily if we are confused or hasty. However, when out in the world, viewing objects in nature, so to speak, it appears nearly impossible to mistake an unsculpted mud puddle for a mongrel canine, if the light is good, our eyes reliable, our distance from the objects in question reasonable and our command of visual categories in place.

On the other hand, when it comes to seeing in nature, it may be easier to mistake the back of a garage for the back of a house, whereas even when fatigued it is difficult to mistake the word "garage" for the word "house." What accounts for these differences? One very plausible hypothesis is that confusions between objects in the case of natural seeing is rooted in real similarities between the objects in question, whereas the confusions between the words is based on similarities in lettering which is, in one sense, perfectly arbitrary. Thus, the photographic realist may say that seeing through a photographic process obtains only where confusion over the object in the photographic or cinematic image is a function of real similarity relations. Descriptions, even if mechanically generated, do not provoke visual confusion on the basis of the real similarities between the objects that they refer to, but only through confusion over lettering, which lettering is arbitrary. Transparent presentations, in contrast, traffic in real or natural similarities, whereas descriptions do not.

Consequently, in order to block counter-examples like mechanically generated descriptions, the account of transparent seeing or seeing through pictures must be supplemented by the stipulation that the presentations in question preserve real similarity relations betwixt the photo and that of which it is a photo.

So, summarizing: x is a transparent presentation only if (1) x puts us in mechanical contact with its object, and (2) x preserves real similarity relations between things. These conditions are individually necessary and jointly sufficient conditions for transparent pictures or transparent presentations.

Moreover, the first condition provides the crucial differentia between *representations*, like painted pictures, and transparent presentations like photographs.

We have traveled this rather long and winding path in order to indicate that, unlike Bazin, the contemporary photographic realist can give an intelligible account of what it is to see through a photograph to its referent. The photographic realist, thus, can advance the claim that transparent seeing is the essential feature of photography or, at least, a necessary feature. And arguing that the photographic basis of cinema is an essential feature of film, the photographic realist could, if he wished, then go on to argue that transparent seeing is the essential feature of film or, at least, a necessary feature, thereby reinstalling something like Bazin's insight, albeit in a theoretically more sophisticated framework.

But even if the claims of photographic realism can be rendered intelligible in the way indicated, it does not seem that transparent seeing can be accepted as an essential or necessary condition of cinema or even photography. For photography is not the only medium of film. Cinema (and photography) can be computer generated, as the stampeding dinosaurs of *Jurassic Park* amply demonstrate. These images are certainly cinema, but there is nothing for the viewer to see directly by means of them. The first computer-generated sequence appeared in major motion pictures, like *Star Trek II* in the eighties and computer simulations have been deployed increasingly since then, as in Roger Corman's *The Fantastic Four*. Since the eighties, some shots in films have been wholly composited: several matte paintings, animation and so on have been "jigsawed together," without any photography of three-dimensional objects having been involved. The array we see, in such cases, corresponds to no independently existing spatial field, in part or whole.

Perhaps, the photographic realist will protest that every constructed image must have some photographic elements through which we see directly. But surely we are on the brink of completely digitally synthesized films. Matt Elson's animation short *Virtually Yours*, starring the completely constructed Lotta Desire, substantiates this possibility.[11] Moreover, the exorbitant costs of film actors nowadays provides an awesome financial incentive for film to turn toward the development of fully computerized characters.[12]

The future of film may become, in large measure, the future of digitally synthesized images, where the notion of seeing directly has little or no purchase, since such images need not possess a model in nature that we can see directly. There is no reason in principle why this cannot come about.[13] The epoch of photographic film, then, may represent nothing but a brief interlude in the artform. But even if these prophecies fall on fallow ground, seeing directly is neither an essential or a necessary feature of film even now, since we already have *some* fully computer-generated images. Nor need the only source of our counter-examples be contemporary. Hollywood has used matte shots – another technique that problematizes the notion of direct seeing – for decades, and though these shots are often only partially constructed, there is no reason in principle why a fully constructed matte shot or "composite" should not count as an instance of film as we know it.[14] In this case, as in the case of computer-generated images, film approaches the status of painting.

But what of earlier intuition pumps that suggested that film shots and paintings must be essentially different, since filmmakers could be surprised at finding Boeing 707s in their images, but painters could not? In truth, the intuition was premature. There is no principled difference between film shots and paintings here. Picasso tells the story of finding the outline of a squirrel in a painting by Braque.[15] Braque was unaware of the presence of the squirrel, since it inhabited the "negative" space in the image, rather like the vase that inheres in some pictures of facing profiles. Switch images like these – and the duck/rabbit and the old woman/young woman – are well known, and we have no problem imagining a painter who, while knowingly drawing one of the aspects of such an image, also unknowingly draws the other aspect. Something like this apparently happened to Braque. As Picasso tells the story, it is comical. But it is also theoretically important. For in documenting the possibility, Picasso shows how a painter could be as surprised as a cinematographer at finding some creature or object, that he had not intended to be there, lurking in his picture.

For the photographic realist, the cinematic image is a presentation, not a representation in the standard sense of that term as it pertains to things like paintings. The cinematic image presents us with things that we see directly; it is a transparent presentation. It is a transparent presentation because it puts us in mechanical contact with what we see and it preserves real similarity relations between things. But one wonders whether this is really sufficient for calling something a presentation rather than a representation (in the standard sense of that term).

Imagine a railyard. Suppose we build a point-by-point model of the railyard. Suppose also that we link every square inch of the railyard to a super computer so that every change in the surface of the railyard registers a change in the model. Next imagine that we interpose the model between us and the railyard so that we do not see any part of the railyard directly and so that the model occupies our field of vision at the angle and scale the railyard would, were the model not standing in the way between us and the railyard. In such a case, we would be in direct mechanical contact with the railyard, and every change we perceived in the model would notate a change in the railyard. Moreover, where we might tend to confuse objects (like spades and hoes) in the railyard, we will also tend to confuse objects in the model, because the model preserves real similarity relations between things.

Will we be disposed to call the model a presentation of the railyard, rather than a representation (in the standard sense) of it? Will we say that we see the railyard directly through the model? The answer to both questions, I predict, will be no. Thus, the conditions that the photographic realist proposes to identify a class of transparent presentations that are ontologically discrete from the class of representations are not adequate to the task, which, in turn, implies that the story the photographic realist has told so far about transparent presentation is insufficient to bear out claims about the uniqueness of photographic and cinematic images.

The photographic realist maintains that cinematic images are transparent presentations, not representations (in the standard sense of that term). We see through them. This conclusion is advanced by analogies between photographs and film, on the one hand, and microscopes and telescopes, on the other. If we are willing to say that we see through the latter, why should we be hesitant about saying the same thing with respect to the former? The photographic realist has us on a slippery slope. Do we have any principled reason for regarding telescopes as visual prosthetic devices while withholding the same status from photographic and cinematic images? I think that we do.

If I look through a pair of binoculars at a brace of horses racing to the finish line, the visual array I obtain, though magnified, is still connected to my own body in the sense that I would be able to find my way to the finish line, were that my wish. That is, when I use binoculars, I can still orient myself spatially to the finish line. My bodily orientation to the things that I perceive is preserved. The same story can be told about typical microscopes and telescopes. When I look through them, I can still point my body approximately in the direction of the bacteria and the meteors that they reveal to me.

But the same cannot be said of photographic and cinematic images. Suppose that I am watching *Casablanca* and what I see on the screen is Rick's bar. I cannot, on the basis of the image, orient my body to the bar – to the spatial coordinates of that structure as it existed some time in the early forties in California (nor could I orient my body by means of the image to the putative fictional locale [in North Africa] of the film). Looking at the cinematic image of the bar, I will not know how to point my body toward Rick's bar (the set) or away from it. That is, I would not know, looking at the image on the screen, how to point my body in the direction that I would have to take in order to walk, or drive or fly to Rick's bar (i.e., some set on a sound stage in LA). The image itself would not tell me how to get to the set, presuming that it still exists, nor how to get to the place in the world where, if it no longer exists, it once did. For the space, so to speak, between the set of Rick's bar and my body is discontinuous; it is disconnected, phenomenologically speaking, from the space that I live in.[16]

Following Francis Sparshott, we might call this feature of viewing cinema "alienated vision."[17] Ordinarily, our sense of where we are depends on our sense of balance and our kinesthetic feelings. What we see is integrated with these cues in such a way as to yield a sense of where we are situated. But if we call what we see on the silver screen a "view," then it is a disembodied view. I see a visual array, like Rick's bar, but I have no sense of where the portrayed space really is in relation to my body. On the other hand, with prosthetic devices like binoculars, telescopes and microscopes – at least in the standard cases – I can orient my body in the space I live in to the objects these devices empower me to see. Indeed, I submit that we do not speak literally of seeing objects unless I can perspicuously relate myself spatially to them – i.e., unless I know (roughly) where they are in the space I inhabit.

Yet if this requirement is correct, then I do not literally see the objects that cause photographic and cinematic images. What I see are representations in the standard sense or displays – displays whose virtual spaces are detached from the space of my experience. But insofar as cinematic images are to be understood as representations in the standard sense of the term or what I call "detached displays," they are better categorized with paintings and traditional pictures, rather than with telescopes and mirrors.

Photographic realism, then, is mistaken. Photographic and cinematic images are not instances of transparent presentations that afford direct seeing. Photographic and cinematic images cannot be presumed to be on a par with binoculars as devices through which the sight of remote things is enhanced. For authentic visual, prosthetic devices preserve a sense of the body's orientation to the objects that they render accessible; whereas photographic and cinematic images present the viewer with a space that is disembodied or detached from her perspective. Nor can we speak of direct seeing here either, for the same reasons.

Undoubtedly the photographic realist will respond by saying that the feature of "normal" vision and of prosthetic vision that I have stressed as essential is an adventitious feature that should not be used to block the analogies the photographic realist underscores. However, I cannot agree. Surely it is the fact that normal vision connects us spatially with its objects that accounts for its evolutionary value. That vision informs us how to move toward what we want and away from what threatens us explains, in part, why vision, as we know it, is an adaptively selected attribute. Apart from the pressure of common sense, then, another reason to think that the feature of vision that I have emphasized in order to draw a brake along the photographic realist's slippery slope is not an avoidable one is that the feature in question plays a significant role in the evolutionary theory of vision. Nor can the photographic realist object that the analogy does not hold because mirror-vision is direct and yet there are some arrangements of mirrors where light is relayed along such a complicated pathway that we could not locate the source in nature of the image reflected before us. For though we may be said to see directly through some mirrors, I see no reason to believe that we see directly before any imaginable arrangement of mirrors. The mirror arrangements that make spatial orientation implausible, indeed, are just the ones we do not see through.

I have spent a great deal of time disputing the photographic realist's candidate for an essential or necessary feature of film.[18] But though the argument has been primarily negative so far, the outcome has had at least one positive result. For in the course of challenging the photographic realist's account, we have discovered a necessary condition of the cinematic image: all photographic and cinematic images are detached displays. It is this feature of such images that block the claim that photographic images are not representations in the standard sense of the term, but rather are transparent presentations that enable us to see through them to the objects they display. But this feature, insofar as it blocks the photographic realist's account across the board, also reveals a telling attribute of all film images – that they all involve alienated visions, disembodied viewpoints, or, as I prefer to call them, *detached displays*. That is, all cinematic images are such that it is vastly improbable and maybe effectively impossible that spectators, save in freak situations, be able to orient themselves to the real, profilmic spaces physically portrayed on the screen.

What of a situation where a video monitor shows us what is going on in a room on the other side of a wall? Isn't this a counterexample to our thesis concerning detached displays? No: because it is not the image itself that provides the orientational information, but our knowledge of the placement of the camera in addition to the information available in the image. We might be easily deceived in such cases, were the image of an identical room being broadcast to our monitor from a remote location.

One necessary feature of a motion picture image, then, is that it is a detached display. Something is a motion picture image only if it is a detached display. Such an image presents us with a visual array whose source is such that on the basis of the image alone we are unable to orient ourselves toward it in the space that is continuous with our own bodies. We are necessarily "alienated" from the space of detached displays whether those displays are photographs or cinematic images.

However, though this feature of film – that it projects detached displays – is a plausible necessary condition for motion picture images, it does not yet provide us with the conceptual wherewithal to distinguish film from other sorts of visual representation, such as painting. To that end, we must introduce consideration of another necessary condition of film.

III   The Moving Image

Even if it is a necessary condition of a film image that it be a detached display, this feature does not enable us to draw a distinction between motion pictures and paintings. For a painting of a landscape is typically a detached display or a disembodied viewpoint in the same sense that a moving picture is. For we cannot orient our bodies spatially to the vista in nature that the painting portrays on the basis of the painting. That is, sitting in my study in Madison, Wisconsin and looking at a painting of a street scene in Mexico City, I do not know, on the basis of the painting, how to walk to that street. Like a cinematic image, the painting is a detached display. So what then differentiates paintings from film images?

A useful clue is already available in ordinary language, where we call the phenomena in question *motion* pictures or *moving* pictures.[19] But we should be careful in the way that we exploit that clue. Roman Ingarden, for example, maintained that in films things are always happening whereas paintings, drawing, slides and the like are always static.[20] But this is not perfectly accurate. For there are a number of films in which there is no movement, such as Oshima's *Band of Ninjas* (a film of a comic strip), Michael Snow's *One Second in Montreal* (a film of photos) and his *So Is This* (a film of sentences), Hollis Frampton's *Poetic Justice* (a film of a shooting script on a tabletop with a plant), Godard and Gorin's *Letter to Jane* (another film of photos), and Takahiko Iimura's *1 in 10* (a film of addition and subtraction tables).

A perhaps better-known example than any of these is Chris Marker's *La Jetée*, a film of almost no movement whose time-travel narrative is told primarily through the projection of still photographs. Of course, there is one movement in Marker's film, but it should be easy to imagine a film just like *La Jetée* but with no movement whatsoever.

Some may respond to cases like these by saying that surely the prospect of such movies without movement is oxymoronic or perhaps even self-contradictory. Such experiments, it might be charged, are little more than slide shows mounted on celluloid, maybe for the purpose of efficient projection.

But there is a deep difference between a film image of a character, say from our imagined version of *La Jetée*, and a slide taken of that character from *La Jetée*. For as long as you know that what you are watching is a film, even a film of what appears to be a photograph, it is always justifiable to entertain the possibility that the image *might* move. On the other hand, if you know that you are looking at a slide, then it is categorically impossible that the image might move. Thus, if you know what you are looking at is a slide and you understand what a slide is, then it is unreasonable – indeed, it is conceptually absurd – to suppose that the image can move.

Movement in a slide would require a miracle; movement in a film image is an artistic choice which is always technically available. Before *Band of Ninjas* concludes – that is, until the last image flickers through the projection gate – the viewer may presume, if she knows that she is watching a film, that there may yet be movement in the image. For such movement is a permanent possibility in cinema. But if she knows that what she is looking at is a slide, it would be irrational for her to entertain the possibility that it might move. It would be irrational, of course, because if it is a slide, it is impossible for the image to move, and if she knows what a slide is, then she must know this.

Furthermore, the difference between slides and films applies across the board to the distinction between every species of still picture – including paintings, drawings, still photos and the like – and every sort of moving picture – including videos, mutoscopes, and movies. When it comes to still pictures, one commits a category error, if one expects movement. It is, by definition, self-contradictory for still pictures to move. That is why they are called *still* pictures. Thus, to watch what one understands to be a painting with the expectation that it will move is absurd. But it is eminently reasonable – and never irrational – to expect to see movement in films because of the kind of thing – a moving picture – that a film is. Even with a static film, like *Poetic Justice*, it is strictly reasonable to wonder whether there will be movement until the last reel has run its course.

With a film like *Poetic Justice*, it is an intelligible question to ask why the filmmaker, Hollis Frampton, made a static film, since he had movement as a genuine option. But it makes no sense to ask why Raphael foreswore literal movement in his *School of Athens.* Unlike Frampton, he had no other alternative. Asking why Raphael's philosophers don't move is like asking why ants don't sing *The Barber of Seville.*

Of course, once one has seen a static film from beginning to end, then it is no longer justifiable to anticipate movement in repeated viewings, unless you suspect that the film has been doctored since your initial viewing. On first viewing, it is reasonable, or, at least, not irrational to wonder whether there will be movement on the screen up until the film concludes; on second and subsequent viewings, such anticipation is out of place. However, on first viewings, one can never be sure that a film is entirely still until it is over. And this is what makes it reasonable to stay open to the possibility of movement throughout first viewings of static films. But to anticipate movement from what one understands to be a slide or a painting is conceptually confused.

Why categorize static films as films rather than as slides or as some other sort of still picture? Because, as I've already noted, stasis is a stylistic choice in static films. It is an option that contributes to the stylistic effect of a film. It is something whose significance the audience contemplates when trying to make sense of a film. It is informative to say that a film is static; it alerts a potential viewer to a pertinent lever of stylistic articulation in the work. Contrariwise, there is no point in saying of a painting that it is a literally still painting. It is thoroughly uninformative. It could not have been otherwise. To call a painting or a slide a still painting or a still slide is redundant.

Indeed, one can imagine a slide of a procession and a cinematic freeze frame of the exact same moment in a parade. The two images may, in effect, be perceptually indiscernible. And yet they are metaphysically different. Moreover, the epistemic states that each warrants in the spectator when the spectator knows which of the categories – slide or film – confronts him are different. With motion pictures, the anticipation of possible future movement is reasonable, or, at least, conceptually permissible; but with still pictures, such as slides, it is never conceptually permissible. The reason for this is also quite clear. Film belongs to the class of things where movement is a technical possibility, while paintings, slides and the like belong to a class of things that are, by definition, still.

Ordinary language alerts us to a necessary feature of films by referring to them as *"moving pictures."* But the wisdom implicit in ordinary language needs to be unpacked. It is not the case that every film image or every film leaves us with the impression of movement. There can be static films. However, static films belong to the class of things where the possibility of movement is always technically available in such a way that *stasis* is a stylistic variable in films in a way that it cannot be with respect to still pictures. Perhaps the label, "moving pictures," is preferable to "film" since it advertises this deep feature of the artform.

Of course, the category of *moving pictures* is somewhat broader than that which has traditionally been discussed by film theorists, since it would include such things as video and computer imaging. But this expansion of the class of objects under consideration to moving pictures in general, in my opinion, is theoretically advisable, since I predict that in the future the history of what we now call cinema and the history of video, TV, CD-ROM and whatever comes next will be thought of as of a piece.

Nevertheless, there is at least one limitation in calling the relevant artform *moving pictures.* For the term "picture" implies the sort of intentional visual artifact in which one recognizes the depiction of objects, persons and events by looking. But many films and videos are abstract, or nonrepresentational, or nonobjective. Consider some of the work of artists like Eggeling and Brakhage. These may be comprised of nonrecognizable shapes and purely visual structures. Thus, rather than speaking of moving pictures, I prefer to speak of moving *images,* as the title of this article indicates. For the term *image* covers both pictures and abstractions. Whether the image is pictorial or abstract is less pertinent for this investigation than that it is moving imagery in the sense that it is imagery that belongs to the class of things where movement is technically possible.

So far then, we have not only recommended a change in the domain of investigation for film theory – from cinema to moving images – but we have also identified two necessary conditions for what is to count as a moving image. In answer to the question, "What is a moving image?" we argue that x is a moving image (1) only if it is a detached display and (2) only if it belongs to the class of things from which the impression of movement is technically possible. The second of these conditions enables us to distinguish film, or, as I call it, the moving image from painting, but this will not discriminate it from theater, since theatrical representations also warrant the expectation of movement. So what, then, differentiates moving images from theatrical representations?

IV   Performance Tokens

A theatrical performance is a detached display. Watching a theatrical performance of *A Streetcar Named Desire*, we cannot orient our bodies – on the basis of the images onstage – in the direction of New Orleans. The space of the play is not my space. It is not true of the play that Hamlet dies three feet away from me, even if I am sitting in the first row. Nor can I point my body toward Elsinor on the basis of the theatrical image before me.

Furthermore, though there may be literally static theater works – performances bereft of movement, such as Douglas Dunn's *101*[21] – in such cases, as in the case of moving pictures, it is reasonable for the audience to suppose that movement might be forthcoming up until the conclusion of the performance. For movement is a permanent possibility in theater, even in works that do not exercise it as a stylistic option. Thus, theater meets the two conditions that we have so far laid down for the moving image. Are there some other ways in which to signal the boundary between these two artforms?

Roman Ingarden locates the border between theater and film by arguing that in theater the word dominates while spectacle (as Aristotle would have agreed) is ancillary; whereas in film, action dominates and words subserve our comprehension of the action. But this ignores films like *History Lessons* and *Fortini-Cani* by Jean-Marie Straub and Daniele Huillet, and Yvonne Rainer's *Journeys from Berlin*, as well as Godard's videotapes, not to mention pedestrian TV shows such as *Perry Mason*.

Some photographic realists have attempted to draw the line between film and theater by focussing on the performer.[22] Due to the intimacy between the photographic lens and its subjects, some, like Stanley Cavell, think of film acting primarily in terms of star personalities, whereas stage performers are actors who take on roles. For Erwin Panofsky, stage actors interpret their roles, whereas film actors, again because of the intimacy of the lens vis-à-vis the actor, incarnate theirs. When it comes to movies, we go to see an Eastwood film, whereas with theater we go to see a Paul Scofield interpretation of Lear.

But this contrast does not seem to really fit the facts. Surely people go to the theater to see Baryshnikov dance and Callas sing no matter what the role, just as they did to see Sarah Bernhardt or Fanny Elssler. We may say that "Sam Spade *is* Bogart," but only in the sense that people once said that Gilette was Sherlock Holmes or O'Neill was the Man in the Iron Mask.

The difference, then, does not appear to reside in the performers in film versus those in theater. But it may reside in the token performances of the two artforms. Both theater and film have performances. On a given evening, we might choose to go to a live performance of Ping Chong's *Kindness* or a performance (a screening) of Robert Altman's *Ready to Wear*. Both might begin at eight. In both cases, we will be seated in an auditorium, and perhaps both performances start with a rising curtain. But despite the similarities, there are also profound differences between a theatrical performance and a film performance.

Undoubtedly, this hypothesis will seem strange to some philosophers. For they are likely to divide the arts into those that involve unique singular objects (e.g., paintings and sculptures) versus those arts that involve multiple copies of the same artwork – there are probably over a million copies of *Vanity Fair*.[23] And having segregated some artforms as multiple, philosophers frequently go on to characterize the multiple arts – like novels, plays and movies – in terms of the type/token relation. But on the basis of this distinction, theatrical performances and film performances do not look very different; in both cases, the performance in question is a token of a type. Tonight's film performance is a token of the type *Ready to Wear* by Robert Altman, whereas tonight's dramatic performance is a token of *Kindness*, a play of Ping Chong. Consequently, it might be concluded that there really is no deep difference between theatrical performances and film performances.

But, though the simple type/token distinction may be useful as far as it goes, it does not go far enough. For even if theatrical performances and film performances may both be said to be tokens, the tokens in the theatrical case are generated by interpretations, whereas the tokens in the film case are generated by templates. And this, in turn, yields a crucial aesthetic difference between the two. The theatrical performances are artworks in their own right that, thereby, can be objects of artistic evaluation, but the film performance itself

Noël Carroll

is neither an artwork nor is it a legitimate candidate for artistic evaluation.

The film performance – a film showing or screening – is generated from a template. Standardly, this is a film print, but it might also be a videotape, a laser disk, or a computer program. These templates are tokens; each one of them can be destroyed and each one can be assigned a temporal location. But the film – say *Toni* by Renoir – is not destroyed when any of the prints are destroyed. One might think that the master or negative is privileged. But the negative of Murnau's *Nosferatu* was destroyed as the result of a court order, and yet *Nosferatu* (the film, not the vampire) survives. Indeed, all the prints can be destroyed and the film will survive if a laser disk does, or if a collection of photos of all the frames does,[24] or if a computer program of it does whether on disk, or tape or even on paper or in human memory.[25]

To get to a token film performance – tonight's showing of *Pulp Fiction* – we require a template which is itself a token of the film type. Whereas the paint on Magritte's *Le Château des Pyrénées* is a constituent part of a unique painting, the print on the page of my copy of the novel *The Mill on the Floss* conveys George Eliot's artwork to me. Similarly, the film performance – the projection or screening event – is a token of a type, which token conveys *Pulp Fiction*, the type, to the spectator.

The account, however, is both different and more complicated when it comes to plays. For plays have as tokens both objects and performances. That is, when considered as a literary work, a token of *The Libation Bearers* is a graphic text of the same order of my copy of *The Warden*. But considered from the viewpoint of theater, a token of *The Libation Bearers* is a performance which occurs at a specific place and time. Unlike the film performance, the theatrical performance is not generated by a template. It is generated by an interpretation. For when considered from the perspective of theatrical performance, the play by Aeschylus is akin to a recipe that must be filled in by other artists, including the director, the actors, the set and lighting designers, costumers, and the like.

This interpretation is a conception of the play and it is this conception of the play that governs the performances from night to night. The interpretation may be performed in different theaters; it may be revived after a hiatus. For the interpret-

ation is a type, which, in turn, generates performances which are tokens. Thus, the relation of the play to its performances is mediated by an interpretation, suggesting that the interpretation is a type within a type. What gets us from the play to a performance is not a template, which is a token, but an interpretation, which is a type.

One difference between the performance of a play and the performance of a film is that the former is generated by an interpretation while the latter is generated by a template. Furthermore, this difference is connected to another, namely, that performances of plays are artworks in their own right and can be aesthetically evaluated as such, whereas performances of films and videos are not artworks. Nor does it make sense to evaluate them as such. A film may be projected out of focus or the video tracking may be badly adjusted, but these are not artistic failures. They are mechanical or electrical failures. That is, a film projectionist may be mechanically incompetent, but he is not artistically incompetent.

In theater, the play, the interpretation, and the performance are each discrete arenas of artistic achievement. It is to be hoped, of course, that they will be integrated. And in the best of all cases, they are. Nevertheless, we recognize that these are separable stratas of artistry. We often speak of a good play interpreted badly and performed blandly; or of a mediocre play, interpreted ingeniously and performed brilliantly; and every other combination thereof. This manner of speaking, of course, presupposes that we regard the play, the interpretation, and the performance as separate levels of artistic achievement – even where the play is written by someone who directs it and acts in it as well. The play by the playwright is one artwork, which is then interpreted like a recipe or set of instructions by a director and others in the process of producing another artwork or series of artworks.

But our practices with regard to motion pictures are different. If in theater, the play-type is a recipe that the director interprets, and the recipe and the interpretation can be regarded as different though related artworks, in film both the recipe and the interpretations are constituents of the same artwork. When the writer produces a play, we appreciate it independently of what its theatrical interpreters make of it. But in the world of moving pictures, as we know it, scenarios are not read like plays and novels, but are ingredients of moving pictures (or, more accurately, moving images).

That is, to speak metaphorically, with movies, the recipe and its interpretation come in one indissoluble package.

Sometimes people say things like "many actresses can play Rosalind and the performance will still be a performance of the play type *As You Like It*, but it would not be an instance of the movie type *White Heat* without James Cagney." The reason for this is that Cagney's performance of Cody – his interpretation – in concert with the director Raoul Walsh is a nondetachable constituent of the film. The interpretation is, so to speak, etched in celluloid. The interpretation in the case of film is not separable from the film type in the way that interpretation is separable from the play type.

Whereas film performances are generated from templates which are tokens, play performances are generated from interpretation types. Thus, whereas film performances are counterfactually dependent on certain electrical, chemical, mechanical and otherwise routine processes and procedures, play performances are counterfactually dependent upon the beliefs, intentions and judgments of people – actors, lighting experts, make-up artists and so on. Though in modern Western theater, there is typically an overarching directorial interpretation of the playwright's recipe, the realization of the token performance on a given night depends on the continuous interpretation of that play, given the special exigencies of the unique performance situation. It is because of the contribution that interpretation makes in the production of the performance that the performance warrants artistic appreciation; whereas the performance of a film – a film showing – warrants no artistic appreciation, since it is simply a function of the physical mechanisms engaging the template properly. Or, in other words, it is a matter of running the relevant devices correctly.

A successful motion picture performance – the projection of a film or the running of a video cassette – does not command aesthetic appreciation, nor is it an artwork. We do not applaud projectionists as we do violinists. We are likely to complain and to perhaps demand our money back if the film emulsifies in the projector beam, but that is a technical failure, not an aesthetic one. If it were an aesthetic failure, we would expect people to cheer when the film doesn't burn. But they don't. For the happy film performance only depends on operating the apparatus as it was designed to be operated, and since that involves no more than often quite minimal mechanical

savvy, running the template through the machine is not regarded as an aesthetic accomplishment. On the other hand, a successful theatrical performance involves a token interpretation of an interpretation type, and inasmuch as that depends on artistic understanding and judgment, it is a suitable object of aesthetic appreciation.

Moreover, if this is right, then we may conjecture that a major difference between motion picture (or moving image) performances and theatrical performances is that the latter are artworks and the former are not, and, therefore, that performances of motion pictures are not objects of artistic evaluation, whereas theatrical performances are. Or, another way to state the conclusion is to say that, in one sense, motion pictures are not a performing art – i.e., they are not something whose performance itself is an art.

This sounds bizarre and is apt to call forth counterexamples. Here are three. First, before motors were installed in projectors, film projectionists hand-cranked the performance, and audiences were said to come to prefer some projectionists over others. In these cases, it might be argued, the projectionists were performers whose performances elicited artistic appreciation. Second, the avant-garde filmmaker Harry Smith sometimes accompanied some of his film screenings by personally alternating colored gels in front of the projector lens. Was he in this case any less a performing artist than a violinist? And lastly, Malcolm LeGrice presented a piece in the early seventies which he called *Monster Film*. In it, he walked – stripped to the waist – into the projector beam, his shadow becoming progressively larger (like a monster), while a loud crashing sound dominated the space. If *Monster Film* is a film, then surely its performance is an artwork.

However, these counterexamples are not compelling. Since the early projectionists who are usually cited are also said to have cranked the films they thought were tedious in such a way that the action was comically sped up, I doubt that their performances were actually performances of the film types advertised, rather than travesties or parodies thereof – that is to say comic routines in their own right. On the other hand, both Smith and LeGrice seem to me to have produced multimedia artworks in which film or the film apparatus play an important role, but which cannot be thought of as simply motion pictures.

What may be disturbing about my denial that moving pictures (and/or images) are instances of the performing arts is that motion picture types are generally made by people whom we standardly think of as performing artists – actors, directors, choreographers, and so on. But it is essential to note that the interpretations and the performances that these artists contribute to the motion picture type are integrated and edited into the final product as constituent parts of the moving image type.

When we go to see *Moby Dick*, we do not go to see Gregory Peck perform, but to see a performance of *Moby Dick*. And while Gregory Peck's performance required artistry, the performance of *Moby Dick* – the showing of it – does not. It requires nothing above and beyond the proper manipulation of the template and the apparatus. A performance of a play, contrariwise, involves the kind of talents exhibited by Gregory Peck prior to the appearance of the first template of *Moby Dick*. That is why the performance of a play is an artistic event and the performance of a motion picture is not.

Thus, there are important differences between the performance of a motion picture and the performance of a play. Two of them are that the play performance is generated by an interpretation that is a type, whereas the performance of the motion picture is generated by a template that is a token; *and* the performance of a play is an artwork in its own right and is an appropriate object of aesthetic evaluation, whereas the performance of the motion picture is neither. Moreover, the first of these contrasts helps us explain the second. For it is insofar as the performance of the motion picture is generated by engaging the template mechanically that it is not an appropriate object of artistic evaluation in the way that a performance generated by an interpretation or a set of interpretations is. These two features of film performance are enough to differentiate performances of moving images from performances of plays, and, furthermore, the two differentia under consideration apply to all films, videos and the like, whether they are artworks or not.

V   Two-Dimensionality

So far we have identified four necessary conditions for the moving image. Summarizing our findings, we can say that *x* is a moving image (1) only if *x* is a detached display, (2) only if *x* belongs to the class of things from which the impression of movement is technically possible, (3) only if performance

tokens of *x* are generated by a template that is a token, and (4) only if performance tokens of *x* are not artworks in their own right. Moreover, these conditions provide us with the conceptual resources to discriminate the moving image from neighboring artforms like painting and theater.

However, these conditions also seem vulnerable to at least one sort of counterexample. Consider what might be called moving sculptures of the sort exemplified by music boxes. Once wound up, the box plays a tune while mechanical figurines shaped like ballerinas cavort in a semblance of pirouettes. This is a detached display; the virtual space of the ballerinas is not our space. The image moves. It is manufactured from a template, and the mechanical dancing is not an artwork. But clearly this is not the sort of thing that we customarily think of as a moving picture or even a moving image.

In order to forestall cases like this we need to add a fifth condition to the preceding four, namely, that *x* is a moving image only if it is two-dimensional. Perhaps, it might seem unnecessary to supplement the preceding formula this way, since some may contend that two-dimensionality is already entailed by the fact that we are talking about moving pictures and moving images which are, by their very nature, two-dimensional. This may be right when it comes to pictures, but it surely cannot hurt to make it explicit that the images we have in mind, when speaking of moving images, are two-dimensional.

Here, of course, the weary reader may complain "Why wasn't two-dimensionality introduced earlier, since it would have given us the boundary between film and theater at a stroke?" "Why do we need all that extra paraphernalia about tokens generated by templates?" The answer I think is simple: theater can be two-dimensional. Consider the shadow-puppet plays of Bali (the Wayang Kulit), and of China. In order to count them as theater rather than motion pictures, we will require recourse to the notion that film, in particular, and the moving image, more broadly, are tokens generated by templates that are themselves tokens.

Concluding Remarks

I have proposed five necessary conditions for the phenomena that I am calling moving images. Of course, once one has accumulated so many necessary conditions, it is natural to wonder whether or not they might not be jointly sufficient conditions for what we typically call motion pictures. But they are not, for treated as a set of jointly sufficient conditions for what it is to be a motion picture, they are overly inclusive. Consider for example, the upper-right-hand page corners of Arlene Croce's *The Fred Astaire and Ginger Rogers Book*.[26] There you will find photographs of Astaire and Rogers dancing. If you flick the pages quickly enough, you can animate the dancers after the fashion of a flip book. Although the third condition of my theory – that token motion picture performances are generated by templates – excludes handmade, one-of-a-kind flip books from the category of moving images, the Astaire/Rogers example clearly meets the condition in question, as would any mass-produced flip book, whether it employed photographs or some other kind of mechanically produced illustrations. Similarly, Muybridge-type photographs of horses animated by the nineteenth-century device known as the zoetrope fit the formula. But these do not seem to be the kind of phenomena that one has in mind when speaking of moving pictures in ordinary language, or of moving images in my slightly regimented language.

You might attempt to preempt this species of counterexample by requiring that moving pictures (and/or images) be projected. But that would have the infelicitous consequence of cashiering early Edison kinetoscopes from the domain of motion pictures. Obviously, it will be hard to draw any firm boundaries between motion pictures (and images) and the protocinematic devices that led to the invention of cinema, without coming up with difficult cases; indeed, we should expect to find problematic border cases in exactly this vicinity. But in any event, it does not seem obvious to me that we can turn the preceding five necessary conditions into jointly sufficient conditions for what is commonly thought to be a motion picture, without doing some severe violence to our everyday intuitions.

Thus, the characterization of moving pictures (or moving images) proposed in this essay is not essentialist in the philosophical sense that presup-poses that an essential definition of cinema would be comprised of a list of necessary conditions that are jointly sufficient. That is, my account is not an example of real-definition essentialism. Nor is it what I earlier called Grecian essentialism.

By a Grecian essence, I mean a necessary condition for x whose citation a theorist believes is useful for understanding x. When Plato speaks of drama as essentially mimetic, he does not suppose that this is a unique feature of drama, but only that it is a necessary feature of drama (as he knew it) to which it is useful to draw our attention, if we wish to understand how drama works. However, though I have pointed out what I think are five necessary features of moving pictures, I do not think that they are particularly central to our understanding of how moving images function. For example, we don't – at least as far as I can see at present – derive any deep insights into the effects of movies or into film style by contemplating these five conditions.

And lastly, my position is not that of what I earlier called medium-essentialism. For, among other things, my analysis is not connected to any specific medium. Moving images, as I call them, can be instantiated in a variety of media. The moving image is not a medium-specific notion for the simple reason that the artform that concerns us, though born in film, has already undergone and will continue to undergo transformation as new media are invented and integrated into its history.

Furthermore, my position is not that of a medium-essentialist since the five conditions that I have enumerated have no implications for the stylistic directions that film and/or video and/or computer imaging should take. The preceding five conditions are compatible with any motion picture style, including styles that may conflict with each other. Thus, if I have indeed managed to set out five necessary conditions for moving pictures (and images), then I have also shown that contrary to previous traditions of film theory, it is possible to philosophize about the nature of moving images without explicitly or implicitly legislating what film, video, and computer artists should or should not do.[27]

Notes

1   The idea that each art has its own province and, thus, possesses unique features goes back at least to the Renaissance and the tradition of the paragone. It was also a prominent feature of turn-of-the century mod-ernism. Thus, it may seem reasonable that theorists who were interested in justifying film as a fine art would naturally draw on premises already endorsed by the tradition of high-art.

2 This, at least, is how artists may regard mediumistic essentialist when they are enamored of it. Once disenchanted, they are apt to scorn it as a narrow-minded, unimaginative, intrusive, and altogether inappropriate exercise in proscription.

3 Such an interpretation is suggested by Charles Barr in his "Cinemascope: Before and After," in *Film Theory and Criticism: Introductory Readings*, second edition, edited by Gerald Mast and Marshall Cohen (New York: Oxford University Press, 1979). Of course, I don't mean to suggest that stylistic considerations were either the only reasons or even the most important reasons behind the adoption of realism. But they were, for the reasons Barr suggests, one motivating factor. At the same time, it should be noted that Barr's "realist/essentialist" reading of his preferred use of cinemascope can be readily challenged by considering the use that Sergio Leone makes of those cinemascope close-ups of Clint Eastwood's and Lee Van Cleef's eyes in the dazzling edited arrays in his spaghetti westerns.

4 See David Bordwell, Janet Staiger and Kristen Thompson, *The Classical Hollywood Cinema: Film Style and Mode of Production to 1960* (New York: Columbia University Press, 1985), pp. 287–93.

5 André Bazin, *What is Cinema?*, vol. I, translated by Hugh Gray (Berkeley: University of California Press, 1967), p. 14. See also pp. 96–7. In conversation, David Bordwell has argued that the quotation above is a bad translation. However, even if this is true, the position represented by the translation is still worth debating, since it has given rise to what might be called a Bazinian position. And that position needs refuting, even if it is not Bazin's.

6 The shift to the idiom of the "Bazinian" here is meant to indicate that the following argument was not developed by Bazin himself, though I believe that if Bazin had thought of this "intuition pump," he would have been happy to use it.

7 For challenges to the coherence of Bazin's claims about the identity of the photograph to its model, see my essay "Concerning Uniqueness Claims for Photographic and Cinematographic Representation," in *Theorizing the Moving Image* (New York: Cambridge University Press, 1996).

8 Roger Scruton, "Photography and Representation," in *The Aesthetic Understanding* (London: Methuen, 1983) [see also this volume, ch. 1]; Kendall L. Walton, "Transparent Pictures: On the Nature of Photographic Realism," *Critical Inquiry* 11, no. 2 (December 1984); Patrick Maynard, "Drawing and Shooting: Causality in Depiction," *Journal of Aesthetics and Art Criticism* 44 (1985). In "Looking Again through Photographs," Kendall Walton defends his position against Edwin Martin's objections in "On Seeing Walton's Great-Grandfather"; both articles appear in *Critical Inquiry* 12, no. 4 (Summer 1986).

9 See David Lewis, "Veridical Hallucination and Prosthetic Vision," in *Philosophical Papers*, vol. 2 (Oxford: Oxford University Press, 1986) and E. M. Zemach "Seeing, 'Seeing' and Feeling," *Review of Metaphysics* 23 (September 1969).

10 This view should not be confused with the view of transparency employed by Althusserian-Lacanian film theorists. For them, viewers mistakenly take cinematic images to be transparent, but they really are not. Photographic realists, on the other hand, are committed to the view that photographic and cinematic images – or, at least, most of them – are actually transparent in pertinent respects.

11 See "Computer Technology and Special Effects in Contemporary Cinema" by Robin Baker in *Future Visions: New Technologies of the Screen*, edited by Philip Hayward and Tana Wollen (London: BFI Publishing, 1993).

12 See "Virtual Studio: Computers Come to Tinseltown," *The Economist* 333, no. 7895 (December 24, 1994–January 6, 1995), p. 88.

13 At this point, the photographic realist may argue that, nevertheless, there are some transparent pictures and that is really the bottom line in his theory. But if this is the view, then transparency cannot count as a necessary condition of cinematic images.

14 On mattes, see Fred M. Sersen, "Making Matte Shots," in *The ASC Treasury of Visual Effects*, edited by George E. Turner (Hollywood: American Society of Cinematographers, 1983); and Christopher Finch, *Special Effects: Creating Movie Magic* (New York: Abbeville, 1984).

15 Reported in *Life with Picasso* by Françoise Gilot and Carlton Lake (New York: Anchor Books, 1989), p. 76.

16 This disanalogy has also been noted by Nigel Warburton is his "Seeing Through 'Seeing Through' Photographs," *Ratio*, New Series 1 (1988), and by Gregory Currie in his "Photography, Painting and Perception," *Journal of Aesthetics and Art Criticism* 49, no. 1 (Winter 1991).

17 F. E. Sparshott, "Vision and Dream in the Cinema," *Philosophic Exchange* (Summer 1975), p. 115. [See also this volume, ch. 6.]

18 The reason for using the singular here – e.g., *an* essential feature of film – is that the photographic realist will have to introduce at least one further feature in order to differentiate film from photography. Perhaps he might avail himself of the feature I defend in the next section, called "The Moving Image."

19 Here, and throughout this section I have been profoundly influenced by Arthur Danto's brilliant article "Moving Pictures," *Quarterly Review of Film Studies* 4, no. 1 (Winter 1979). [See also this volume, ch. 8.]

20 Roman Ingarden, "On the Borderline between Literature and Painting," in *Ontology of the Work of Art: The Musical Work, The Picture, The Architectural Work, The Film*, translated by Raymond Meyer and J. T. Goldwait (Athens: Ohio University Press, 1989), pp. 324–25.

21 For descriptions of this piece see Sally Banes, *Terpsichore in Sneakers* (Boston: Houghton Mifflin Company, 1980), p. 189, and Noël Carroll, "Douglas Dunn, 308 Broadway," *Artforum* 13 (September 1974), p. 86.

22 See, for example, Stanley Cavell, *The World Viewed: Reflections on the Ontology of Film*, the enlarged edition (Cambridge, Mass.: Harvard University Press), pp. 27–28 [See also this volume, ch. 4]; and Erwin Panofsky, "Style and Medium in the Motion Pictures," in *Film Theory and Criticism*, edited by Gerald Mast and Marshall Cohen (New York: Oxford University Press, 1985).

23 See Richard Wollheim, *Art and Its Objects* (Cambridge University Press, 1980), sections 35–38.

24 This would be true of a silent film. If we are talking about a sound film, the soundtrack would have to be retrievable as well.

25 If you can print the code out, then it is theoretically possible for it to be memorized, if not by one person, then by a group – like the population of China. It is at least imaginable, therefore, that we might run something like the *Fahrenheit 451* scenario for film, with groups of guerrilla film buffs learning the programs of forbidden films in defiance of totalitarian censors.

26 Arlene Croce, *The Fred Astaire and Ginger Rogers Book* (New York: Vintage, 1972).

27 This paper represents a substantial rewriting and expansion of my "Towards an Ontology of the Moving Image," in *Film and Philosophy*, edited by Cynthia Freeland and Tom Wartenberg (New York: Routledge, 1995). I would also like to thank David Bordwell, Arthur Danto, Stephen Davies, Jerrold Levinson, and Alan Sidelle for their comments on an earlier version of this paper.

PART III

Documentary

Introduction

The definition of "documentary" has long been a hot site for theoretical debate – not only in the philosophy of film, but also in film studies in general. Postmodernists, including Brian Winston, question whether we can draw a sharp distinction between fiction and non-fiction films and underline the fact that the latter are just as constructed as the former. Against the common conception of documentary as revealing truth about the world, and depicting the unmediated reality that unfolds in front of the camera, postmodernists underscore the fact that a documentary, like a fiction film, is a product of the filmmaker's specific intentions in guiding or persuading the viewer's conception of the world.

Postmodernists argue that in representing reality, the filmmaker can intervene at any moment – before, during, and after shooting. Filmmakers not only decide the subject matter of their films before shooting, but also preplan the location, time, and film style, including whether to incorporate re-enactments or use archival footage. Shooting itself inevitably involves selection on the filmmaker's part, since filmmakers cannot possibly capture everything that takes place in front of the camera. The same applies to the post-production phase: filmmakers assemble and edit footage with a specific purpose in mind – how to get their messages across to the viewer. Furthermore, aestheticization in documentary, such as that in Errol Morris's *The Thin Blue Line* (1988), blurs the distinction between documentary and fiction film at the level of style. Documentary films can be just as stylized as fiction films, and fiction films can also incorporate a "documentary look" for their own purposes. All of these considerations make us reconsider whether documentary is indeed a feasible category to hold on to: documentary seems a lot closer to fiction film than was originally supposed.

Two essays collected in this section, Gregory Currie's and Noël Carroll's pieces on documentary, contest such a postmodernist challenge. Both claim that the distinction between fiction and non-fiction is still a legitimate one. However, the two represent rather divergent approaches. If Currie's approach to documentary represents a medium-specific one, emphasizing the mechanical nature of the photographic medium, Carroll's employs a communication model, basing his definition on the assertoric stance of both the filmmaker and the audience as directed toward the content of film.

In "Visible Traces: Documentary and the Contents of Photographs," Currie defines documentary film as a film in which: (1) the narrative is asserted, and (2) the narrative predominantly consists of visual traces of elements – objects, people, or events – that form the narrative. With the first condition, Currie excludes fiction films from the category of documentary. Unlike fiction films, which invite the viewer to imagine a world depicted, a documentary mandates that the viewer assume the world depicted is true or factual. The second condition also distinguishes documentary from fiction film in a significant way by virtue of the relationship held between the narrative and photographic images. That is, the narrative of a documentary relies on the capacity of photography to mechanically reproduce images of the object or the event in front of the camera, and thereby serves as their visual traces. In a fiction film, such as *North by Northwest* for example, an image of Cary Grant is a literal trace of Grant. But it also has an additional function in representing the fictional character Roger Thornhill. In contrast, a photographic image in a documentary lacks this additional function. A photographic image of Stephen Hawking in Morris's *A Brief History of Time* (1991) is merely that of Hawking and nothing further.

In the second condition above, Currie attempts to preserve the epistemic privilege often attributed to documentary by appealing to the idea of "trace." A photographic image is, in principle, rendered independently of the operator's belief or perception of an object or an event recorded. Currie does not deny that a photographer or filmmaker chooses the object of a photographic image, nor does he ignore that one can even emphasize certain aspects of the object in question. Currie underscores the fact that once such choices are made, an image of the object is mechanically and causally induced, independently of the operator's perception of the object. Currie contrasts the notion of "trace" with that of "testimony," which necessarily involves an agent's perception of the object or event in question: verbal testimony and other representational media, such as painting, are necessarily mediated through the agent's mental state – be it perception or belief – directed toward the object that she or he witnesses or sees.

A few questions arise. As Carroll points out, the correspondence between photographic images and the narrative, which Currie requires in his definition, is often violated within documentary practice.[1] Filmmakers often replace a genuine image of an object – e.g., a specific submarine under discussion – with a generic image of an object – e.g., a submarine. Another problem with Currie's definition lies in the fact that he suggests that the decision as to whether a film is a documentary depends upon the "predominant" use of literal traces of the objects or events that comprise the narrative. Such a quantitative claim, however, always gives rise to a question of the threshold. Exactly how much counts as "predominant"? Moreover, should we count specific shots of actual footage or just measure screen time?[2]

Carroll proposes to replace the term documentary with a neologism, "film of presumptive assertion," a subset of non-fiction film. One of the reasons for such a replacement, Carroll claims, can be found in the vagueness and equivocation of the term "documentary." The referent of "documentary" has changed over time and has broadened to include films that John Grierson, who coined the term, did not originally intend. Carroll claims that better terminology covering the scope and characteristics of films currently classified as "documentary" is in order, to wit: "film of presumptive assertion."

We rarely encounter a film without having at least the slightest information about it. We are often aware ahead of time of the category that the film belongs to, whether it is a documentary or fiction film. Both the filmmaker and the audience have a mutual understanding of the communication process in which they partake. In the case of a film of presumptive assertion, Carroll argues, the filmmaker intends for the viewer to entertain the film's content assertively as a result of the audience's recognition of the filmmaker's intention. The audience, in turn, brings in a set of relevant expectations and measures to comprehend and evaluate a film of presumptive assertion.

Carroll's definition of "film of presumptive assertion" contrasts well with Currie's definition, a version of what Carroll terms "film of the presumptive trace." Currie rules out from the category of documentary a film that heavily relies on re-enactments or animation – since animation is not a literal trace of anything. On the other hand, under Carroll's definition, such a film counts as an instance of "documentary" insofar as the filmmaker's intention is assertoric – the filmmaker's intention is for the audience to entertain the content of a film assertively. The scope of Carroll's definition of the film of presumptive assertion is broader than that of Currie's in that what is crucial in determining the status of a documentary film is the filmmaker's assertoric intention rather than the kind of film images comprising the narrative.

Another difference between Currie's and Carroll's definitions can be found in the concern of whether narrative is a necessary condition of documentary. According to Carroll's definition, a film of presumptive assertion does not need to involve any strictly conceived narrative, since the audience is intended to entertain assertively the "propositional contents" of the film. Moreover, the propositional contents need not necessarily constitute a narrative. Narrative consists of a set of states of affairs that are causally linked in space and time. Carroll claims that Currie's definition of documentary is too narrow, since some of Lumière's actualités do not involve any strictly conceived narratives.[3] Furthermore, causality is only one of the ways in which a documentary can be constructed. Poetic documentaries, including *Berlin:*

Symphony of a City (Walter Ruttman, 1927), are often organized in terms of visual parallelisms or contrasts rather than in strict causal sequences.

Despite their theoretical differences, Carroll, like Currie, endorses the possibility of the objectivity in films of presumptive assertion. Postmodern skeptics not only blur the distinction between fiction and non-fiction, but also question the supposed objectivity and epistemic reliability of documentary as a vehicle to convey truth about the world. In Carroll's view, however, it is too hasty to dismiss a film of presumptive assertion altogether as merely subjective or relative. It is true that a film of presumptive assertion is not intrinsically veridical. Filmmakers do misguide and misinform the audience. However, this does not mean that such films can never be objective. Filmmakers are not free of any responsibility to commit to either the truth or the plausibility of content in their films. They should be more responsible and committed to preserving a documentary's tie to the world, because of the audience's general expectation of characteristics for a film of presumptive assertion. In addition, the viewer is capable of applying a set of standards of evidence and logic relevant to the subject matter in order to evaluate the objectivity or plausibility of an argument embedded in the film.

J.C.

Notes

1 See Noël Carroll, "Photographic Traces and Documentary Film: Comments for Gregory Currie," *The Journal of Aesthetics and Art Criticism* 58, no. 3 (2000), pp. 303–6.
2 Jinhee Choi, "A Reply to Gregory Currie on Documentaries," *The Journal of Aesthetics and Art Criticism* 59, no. 3 (2001), pp. 317–19.
3 Carroll, "Photographic Traces."

10

Visible Traces: Documentary and the Contents of Photographs

Gregory Currie

*I think of it as . . . an entertaining movie like So-
phie's Choice [or] any Charlie Chaplin film that
dealt with social commentary.*
Michael Moore, on Roger and Me[1]

*Documentary is a clumsy description, but let it
stand.*
John Grierson[2]

I Ways to Misunderstand

Slogans and dictionary entries are often too context dependent to be of much use to an outsider.
An alien, keen to comprehend *documentary*, would
do especially badly from these sources. It is not
merely that they will not give the intension; dictionary entries, after all, fix reference more often
than they fix sense. The problem is that they are
not even extensionally correct, suggesting either
that the filmic documentary is any transcription,
or recording, of events, or that it is an interpreted
representation of the factual. Thus, while the
Oxford English Dictionary illustrates the concept
with "a transcription of real life, a bit of what
actually happened," Grierson, who introduced
the term "documentary," at least into English, is
famous for having called it "the creative treatment
of actuality." Neither of these is remotely credible:
the first allows any piece of exposed film to be
documentary, since all film is film *of* something
actual, and the second conflates documentary with

"dramatic reconstruction," a category I shall say
more about later on.[3] Inadequacies of this kind
encourage the view, suggested by the quotation
from filmmaker Michael Moore above, that documentary is a merely rhetorical category you can
slip out of at will, especially when faced with
embarrassing revelations about the unreliability
of your work.[4]

I say we can obtain a robust account of documentary by playing these two approaches against
one another.[5] Each, alone, is massively overinclu-
sive; together, they correct each other's faults and
neatly cover the target without harm to innocent
bystanders. Lumière-style *actualités*, straight-faced
Griersonian products, and Moore's whimsical effort referred to above all fall in, as they should.
And we shall not tolerate items that are merely
documentary in style or subject, like *Culloden* (1964)
and *Cathy Come Home* (1966).[6] Style and subject
might be indicators of documentary status, as clarity
and potability are indicators of water, but they are
not defining features. Just as there can be fool's
water, there can be a fool's documentary. And just
as the underlying structure of water is of substantive
rather than merely semantic interest, so the nature of
documentary is a matter that concerns us qua artists,
aestheticians, and philosophers. I shall have time
here only for the third of these aspects.

Perhaps this sounds overly prescriptive. But
I welcome categorizations that cut across the docu-
mentary/nondocumentary boundary as I draw it;

Gregory Currie, "Visible Traces: Documentary and the Contents of Photographs," *The Journal of Aesthetics and Art Criticism* 57(3), Summer 1999: 285–97. Reprinted by permission of Blackwell Publishing.

Gregory Currie

I merely insist that my way of dividing up the territory is legitimate and, given certain purposes, interesting. Also, I acknowledge a great deal of vagueness and uncertainty about what we call "documentary." I am going to concede that much of what we call documentary is in fact a mixture of documentary and nondocumentary elements. But that does not undermine the significance of the concept *documentary*. If samples of water are agglomerations of H_2O molecules, very few objects in this world are pure water samples. But that has no tendency to show that the concept of water is one we ought to get rid of. It is just that we should allow that there is a loose (but legitimate) sense in which many things are water samples, and that this loose sense derives from a stricter sense in which not many things are. Many things, I shall argue, are partly documentaries, and some things are very largely so. I need claim no more.

In accounting for documentary we are going to take in some fundamental issues about representation, and in particular about the nature of photographic representation. One thing I shall suggest that might be of interest even to those who reject my theory of documentary will be that the duality of content possessed by film images is a duality of *kinds* of content: conceptual and nonconceptual.

I shall begin by saying something about a notion I take to be central to that of filmic documentary itself, namely the method of cinematic (and more broadly photographic) recording, and why it is that such methods have results that belong to a kind I call *traces*. Traces carry information, but they do so in ways different from the ways that what I shall call *testimony* carries it. I shall say something about the epistemic and other implications of this distinction. The first substantive point will then be that a documentary must involve traces of its subject, and not merely testimony of it. But since fiction films and dramatic reconstructions give us traces also, we need to say more in order to characterize documentary. At that point I shall appeal to a distinction between two ways that film images can represent: that will be the key to our first attempt at saying what a documentary is.

We shall then recognize the need for a finer level of analysis: to talk about documentary and nondocumentary *elements* within a documentary. But then it will turn out that we cannot just take a compositional approach, defining a documentary whole as the sum of its documentary parts. We are caught in a hermeneutical circle: we cannot define the parts of documentary without reference to the whole, nor the whole without reference to the parts. So we have to define both in one go, and say what it is for something to be a documentary part of a documentary whole.

II Traces and Testimonies

To understand the contrast between trace and testimony, compare a painting and a photograph. The painter may make a likeness of her subject so vivid and detailed that one could take it for a photograph. But photography is not just a device to make paintings by cheaper and quicker means; a photograph is a *trace* of its subject, while a painting is *testimony* of it. It is that thought which André Bazin, the French film theorist, was struggling to express when he likened photographs to footprints, to death masks, and, more problematically, to mummified remains.[7]

Leaving mummies out of it for the moment, what is the similarity between the photograph, the footprint, and the death mask? All these things are traces left on the world by their subjects themselves. A painting, on the other hand, is not a trace, however much it tells us about the appearance of its subject and however reliable what it tells us is. Nor is an equally detailed and reliable written description of the subject a trace of it. Traces of all kinds are, as Kendall Walton has pointed out, in a certain sense *independent of belief*;[8] they are independent of it in a way that paintings and descriptions are not. A camera records what is in front of it, and not what the photographer thinks is in front of it, if there is a difference between them. But the painter paints what he or she thinks is there. An hallucinating painter will paint the pink elephant he thinks he sees, and an hallucinating diarist will describe the same, but an hallucinating photographer will be surprised when his photograph reveals an empty room.

When I say that photography is belief independent, I mean that in this precise and restricted sense: the photographer or cinematographer who sets out to record the scene in front of him will record what is there; the painter with the same intent will paint what he thinks is there. I do not mean that how or whether a film image gets to be created is wholly independent of belief; that is not usually the case. But significantly, an accidental photograph is possible: I trip, the shutter button is depressed, and a picture of my foot results.

142

An accident in a paint shop may result in something startlingly reminiscent of Chartres, but no portrait of that cathedral is produced by the spillage. There might even be photograph-producing plants or animals, whose surfaces hold an imprint of focused light (perhaps our brains are a bit like that). But there cannot be paintings that are the product of nature below the threshold of intentionality.

As with photographs, so with footprints and death masks. These are traces left by things on the world. Anything about the person's appearance that the footprint or death mask manages to record is belief independent in the way that the photograph is: what is recorded depends on the morphology of the foot or face; not on what someone thinks the morphology of the foot or face is. In the same category fall the cross-sections of trees, considered as records of the age of the trees, seismographs, time-slices of thermometers, and so on. Paintings and drawings fall into a different category of representations on account of their being in the first instance records of what someone thought the facts of the matter were. They belong with chronicle, history, journalism, and like activities that are similarly mediated by producer's intention. Things in this category I say are testimonies, and their representational natures contrast with those of traces. Note that the pictorial/linguistic distinction cuts right across this one; testimony can be verbal or pictorial, and a sophisticated thermometer that generates a written description of the weather is still a trace.

Testimonies differ from traces also in what I shall call their primary representational range: we can draw and write about things that never happened or have not happened yet, but only real things can leave traces of themselves, and a trace can be only of something in the past and never of anything in the future (assuming the direction of causation and the direction of time are one). But as we shall see, we must not confuse this point with the false claim that photographs never mislead.

Do traces and testimonies exhaust the field? There are hybrids, of course, like hand-painted photographs, where testimony and trace are literally superposed. But is there anything else? I think so. Between traces and testimonies lie *simulations*. The detective, lacking both a reliable testimony and a film of the murderer's movements, may wonder how the murder was carried out. Suspecting that a shot was fired from the conservatory, she may go there and try firing a shot to the position where she knows the victim was struck down, then run to the library to see whether she can get there in the time she knows the murderer would have needed, etc. At every step of the process we have intention-driven activity on the part of the agent, but the result may be surprising information not contained in or implied by anything in the agent's mental state: yes, the murderer could have gotten back in time, unlikely though it seems at first sight. And crucial to the reliability of the information is the assumption of causal isomorphism between the simulation and the process it simulated, an isomorphism that would not hold if it turned out, for instance, that the murderer walked with a limp. Thus simulations are at their most reliable when you can get the criminal to simulate his own behavior, as happens, rather implausibly, in Wilkie Collins's *The Moonstone*.[9]

III Ways to Misrepresent

Let us leave simulations to one side, and return to documentaries and their relations to traces. Documentaries use photographic, cinematographic, or similar trace-inducing methods, and depend heavily – though as we shall see, not exclusively – for their status as documentaries on doing so. To probe this further we need to understand the ways that photographs and film images can represent, and a useful way to do that is to consider misrepresentation.

Documentaries can mislead, and they often do because their makers either have mistaken beliefs about the events being documented, or actively wish to mislead us about them. Suppose the history of technology were somewhat different, and that there was a film crew recording various events during the collapse of the Roman Empire. The filmmaker might have believed that citizens of the Empire were falling sick at this time because the barbarians were poisoning the water supply. He might, accordingly, show us a film of sick people, stating in the commentary that these people were victims of this act of poisoning. We, watching the film, might believe him. But if the filmmaker was wrong, and the reason the people were sick was because of the lead in the water pipes, then his film does not record people who have become sick as a result of deliberate poisoning. It records people who have become sick because of inadvertent poisoning. That is because photographs are traces, and events that do not happen – like barbarians poisoning the Roman water – cannot leave traces. So the documentary film cannot present us with a record of events the filmmaker thinks occurred but which did not in fact occur, though the events can be recorded and presented to us in a way that misleads us about, say, their antecedents and consequences.

So it is no part of my argument to claim that the documentary film, in virtue of being a trace, is always or even usually a more reliable source of knowledge than a written history, which is testimony. But we can say this: if a documentary is misleading, it is not intrinsically misleading. That is, it is not misleading because the representations that constitute the documentary material itself are representations of things that did not exist or of events that did not happen. For those representations, being traces, cannot misrepresent in that fashion. If the documentary is misleading it is because we have made some inference from the representations to something, and that inference was a wrong one, though it might be a very natural one for us to make, and one that the filmmaker clearly wants us to make. But a written history can be intrinsically misleading: its constitutive representations – the words and sentences that make it up – can be representations of things that do not exist and events that did not occur. The sentence "Barbarians were poisoning the water supply" is like that. And a painting of barbarians poisoning the water supply is like that also.

But do not photographs – and certainly films – represent fictional things? I think they do: those images from *Casablanca* represent Rick and Ilsa as well as representing Bogart and Bergman. But they do so only secondarily: *by* representing the real. That way the asymmetry between these representations and paintings is retained; a painting can represent the mythical without having along the way to represent the real. And if photographs represent the fictional, they are not photographs *of* fictional things. There is a difference between what a photograph is of, and what it is about; a photograph can be about things other than the things it is of. What it is of is just the thing it is a trace of, something we can identify by examining brute causal connections. But if the photograph is part of a fiction, then it may also be about things – fictional things – other than the things it is of.

I shall say more about these representational differences between traces and testimonies when I tell you what a documentary is, but now I shall say a little more about the significance of photographs and film images being traces of things. Without that, my attempt to show that documentaries involve traces leaves it unclear why documentary is a category of any interest.

IV Photographs and Knowledge

Photographs can be sources of information in ways that paintings cannot. That is why Antonioni's *Blow Up* (1966) is about a photographer and not about a painter; no painter could reasonably hope to find, by vastly enlarging small sections of his own painting, evidence for the existence or occurrence of something he or she did not know about at the time the painting was made. But a photograph may well give us a minute clue to something we, including the maker, did not suspect. A painter can, of course, make various mistakes. She can think she has represented an X when in fact she has represented a Y, and she can fail to see the significance of, or relations between, the things she has painted (perhaps this is the idea behind *The Draughtsman's Contract* [Greenaway, 1982]). But a painter cannot represent an object she did not see and did not intend, under any description, to represent.

What holds of photographs in this regard holds also of cinematic images made by photographic means (thus excluding, for instance, animated cartoons, about which more in a moment). The difference between the photograph and the cinematic image is merely that the film image is capable of revealing *more* things the photographer did not expect, for the film image records movement as well as the things a still photograph records. Someone might recall the movement of a horse, and commit it to posterity by producing an animated cartoon that reproduces the movement as remembered. But if the maker remembers wrong, it is his mistaken impression that goes in the archives. By contrast, the cinematographer's image records what the movement was really like. And by analyzing, frame by frame, the filmed record of Kennedy's assassination, we can hope to learn things about the origin and number of shots fired that we cannot learn by similarly analyzing a dramatic recreation of the same event.

In addition to this epistemological point, some writers have wanted to go further. Bazin and, following him, Roger Scruton and Kendall Walton have claimed that photography and cinematography do not provide us merely with a distinctive form of representation: rather, they *reproduce* reality for us.[10] On this view, photographs are not related to paintings and drawings even to the extent of belonging to adjacent subgroups, for photographs are not representations at all. Rather, they are like windows, mirrors, and telescopes: aids to sight. All these things help us see things we could not otherwise see, and photographs extend our visual powers so that we can see people no longer alive. As Walton puts it, photographs are transparent.

I am not prepared to put photographs in the same class as windows, mirrors, and telescopes.[11] But we need not have this debate here, for nothing in what follows will depend on how you decide this issue. I mention it partly because the arguments I have been giving for regarding photographs as essentially different from paintings are sometimes used to draw the stronger conclusion that they are transparent, and so I want to make it clear that I am not going that far. And I mention it also because it is going to come up, briefly, in my next paragraph.

We can make epistemic contact with things and people, but we can also make emotional or affective contact with them. And photographs seem to have an affective capacity that handmade pictures lack. Other things being equal, we are likely to be more offended or disturbed by an offensive or disturbing photograph than by a painting. Walton cites this as support for the transparency thesis: we are more offended or disturbed by photographs and films because when we see them we are actually seeing the offensive or disturbing events themselves. But while photographs and films may affect us more than paintings do, they surely affect us less than witnessing the offensive or disturbing acts *directly* would. This suggests that photographs somehow lie midway between the handmade image and the reality itself. That photographs are more able to affect us than handmade pictures are is therefore best explained in terms of the photograph's being a trace. Traces of things bear particularly direct relations to those things: things leave their traces on other things. Possessing a photograph, death mask, or footprint of someone seems to put me in a relation to that person that a handmade image never can.

By now we have some material with which to explain the significance we attach to documentaries – assuming that documentaries are, or involve, traces. By virtue of being traces of things, they offer us special epistemic and emotional access to the things they are documentaries of.

V From Trace to Documentary: Two Kinds of Representations

I have said that to be a documentary the thing in question must be a trace. But *all* films made by photographic and analogous means are traces: *Casablanca* is a trace left on the world by the activities of Humphrey Bogart, Ingrid Bergman, and a lot of other people as they went about the business of making the fiction film by that very name. But surely it would be a misunderstanding to suppose that *Casablanca* is a documentary. So being a trace cannot be sufficient for something to be a documentary, though it might be necessary.

I allow a sense (a weak sense) in which *Casablanca* is a documentary: a documentary record of those people's activities as they made *Casablanca*. So I admit that every film – every *piece* of film – is documentary in one sense. What is important is that we should be able to distinguish within this class of cinematic works those that correspond to a stronger, more recognizable notion of documentary: the class containing items like *Drifters*, *The Plough that Broke the Plains*, and *Roger and Me*, but not containing *Star Wars*, *Casablanca*, and *Culloden*. And I think we can.

As we have seen, a photograph or film image has, potentially, at least two representing functions. It represents in virtue of being a photograph, and in thus representing, it represents the things and events of which it is a trace. But a photograph can also have another representing role: a role imposed on it by its association with some narrative. That is how it is with photographs and film images that function to present to us either fictional stories or recreations of actually occurring events. The film images in *Casablanca* that are traces of Bogart and Bergman also represent the fictional characters Rick and Ilsa; the film images in *All the President's Men* that as traces represent Hoffman and Redford also represent the real but absent persons Woodward and Bernstein. Armed with this distinction between representational roles, I can make my first substantive point about documentary. *It is a condition on a film being documentary that its constitutive images have only that first, causally induced, representing role.* They may not represent things and events other than the things and events they are traces of.

That is not to say that documentary can be disconnected from narrative; on the contrary, I shall argue that narratives are constitutive elements of documentaries. But their narratives must not be such as to induce the film's images to represent in any way other than in virtue of their being photographic traces of things. Those images must be suited, through their causal origin, to convey or help convey the meaning of whatever narrative they are associated with.

So let us distinguish between a cinematic image *contributing* meaning to a narrative, and such an image *obtaining* meaning from a narrative. The images of Flint, Michigan in *Roger and Me* contribute to the meaning of that film's narrative in virtue of representing Flint. The images of Chico, California used in *The Adventures of Robin Hood* obtain, from the narrative of that film, the property of representing Sherwood Forest. In the first case the content that concerns us is photographic content, in the second case it is narrative content.

It follows immediately from this – and even before we get to the full, official account of what documentary is – that standard fictional cinema is not documentary by my lights. To be a documentary, the narrative of *Bringing up Baby* would have to be supported by images that, in virtue of being photographic traces, represented a paleontologist, an escaped leopard, an incompetent sheriff, etc. But in fact the images that support this narrative do not photographically represent any such things; instead they represent those things in the second way I described above: through their association with that very narrative. And the same argument establishes the nondocumentary status of *Culloden* and *Cathy Come Home*.

VI Conceptual and Nonconceptual Content

I have said that film images, potentially at least, possess two kinds of contents: photographic and narrative. These two contents might be of the same kind, or of different kinds. Which? I say they are different – very different. We can see this if we take seriously another distinction that has recently been influential in the philosophy of perception.

Perceptions and beliefs are representational states. Some people used to say that perceptions just *are* beliefs.[12] Now there is more inclination to draw a sharp distinction between the two on the grounds that beliefs must have conceptual content and perceptions need not. On this view, to credit someone with a belief is to credit them with the concepts necessary for a description of how that belief represents the world. But someone can have a perceptual experience that represents the world as a certain way, yet lack the concepts necessary to say in *what* way the world is thus represented.[13] Thus we can say that the contents of beliefs are conceptual, while the contents of perceptions are nonconceptual.

We can find something like this difference when we look at the case of, on the one hand, the purely photographic, or causally induced, representational content of a film image and, on the other, the distinct narrative content of the image, if it has one. A typical case of this is in the fiction film, where images of actors and sets also represent fictional characters and locations. I say that in such a case, the content the image has in virtue of its photographic origin is nonconceptual, while the content it has in virtue of representing things and events in the fiction is conceptual.

We cannot straightforwardly take over definitions of conceptual and nonconceptual content from the case of mental representation, because beliefs and perceptions are states of a person, while pictures are not. But we can come up with a distinction very much in the spirit of the one appropriate for mental states:

> For any picture, S, with representational content, S has conceptual content P iff a subject X's having made S entails that X possesses the concepts that appear in a specification of what it is that S represents. Otherwise, the picture has nonconceptual content.[14]

It is easy to see that on this criterion photographs do not have conceptual content, because it is true of any photograph that it could have had the content it does have without the person who took the photograph being able to conceptualize that content in any way. This is because the content of the photograph is determined wholly by brute causation. But if we say that the photograph or film image has also a distinct narrative content, that must be because there is some association between the image and the narrative, and that association must be an intended one. Nonintentional causation cannot induce such a relationship, nor can it create any narrative. But then the content of the narrative is describable only in terms constrained by information about the concepts possessed by or at least available to the agent.[15]

A long tradition of film theorizing associates the film image with subjective experience. In all sorts of ways this view is wrong, but we have now discovered one similarity between perception and the film image: both carry nonconceptual content.

VII Ideal Documentaries

We have seen that documentaries can mislead. The narratives of some documentaries tell us (often by artful implication, rather than directly) that things happened which in fact did not happen, or did not happen in that way or for that reason. When they do, there is a tension within the film of a kind that is not possible in a fiction or dramatic reconstruction, as long, at least, as its narrative is internally coherent. If the fictional narrative of *Casablanca* has it that Rick kills Major Strasser, then there cannot be anything represented within the film's images which is inconsistent with that, though there might be things – dream sequences or "lying flashbacks," for example – that appear, at first sight, to be inconsistent with it. And if the dramatic reconstruction, as with *All the President's Men*, is undertaken by people who have false beliefs about the events they are trying to reconstruct, then the film that results will accord with that narrative, representing things as existing and occurring that did not exist or occur. But in a *documentary* that is misleading, the film images represent simply what they are traces of, however much the maker may believe and/or want us to believe things inconsistent with the filmic record. This is another reason for classing documentaries as separate not only from fictions but from dramatic reconstructions. Documentaries have a special capacity to undermine themselves.

I can now say, in a preliminary way, what a documentary is. This is preliminary, because what I am going to characterize is an ideal documentary – something that, as we shall see, not every documentary is. An ideal documentary is a filmically sustained narrative the constitutive film images of which represent only photographically: they represent only what they are of. Thus in *Roger and Me*, the only things that the film images represent are the events and their constitutive objects recorded by the camera in Flint, Michigan. And in thus representing, those images help to sustain the film's narrative about Flint and its industrial troubles.[16] But in *Casablanca* the images sustain the fictional narrative there presented by

representing the nonexistent Rick and Ilsa. And in *All the President's Men* the images sustain the factual narrative about the Watergate break-in by representing the certainly existent Woodward and Bernstein, though those people are not the objects these images are traces of.

Talking this way requires us to have certain views about the individuation of films, views that I had better make explicit. A film has various constitutive features. Among them is its sequence of film images. There may also be a soundtrack plus odors, vibrations, electric shocks, and other sensory accompaniments, assuming the makers want to go so far. All these things are the sensible elements of the film. But they are not the whole film. There is the narrative they sustain. And that narrative makes an independent contribution to the film's identity; it does not supervene on those other things. Two films with the same sensible components can sustain different narratives if they occur in contexts where those sensible elements will bring about different implicatures; what one group will reasonably take as serious assertion may constitute irony for another group. Thus films sustain narratives only in the context of specific community-wide expectations and beliefs.

So much on documentaries as a whole. The problems, or some of them, emerge when we consider their internal structures.

VIII Parts and Wholes

Even a pure documentary can be a misleading documentary: it is so if there is a tension between its narrative and its photographic content (though there are other ways for a documentary to be misleading). Conversely, a reliable documentary can be impure: there might be a reliable documentary about Disneyland in which Mickey Mouse acts as the narrator. Assume we see Mickey on screen, as he takes us through the location. Here, it is fictional that Mickey Mouse is telling us various things, but what he tells us is intended as serious assertion and turns out to be, we will assume, reliable. In particular, there is no attempt to mislead us into thinking that Mickey is real and really narrating. If not every part of a documentary is documentary, this suggests that we need the concept of a documentary *part* of a documentary.

Another kind of case confirms this idea: documentaries can mislead by containing spurious or "fake" material. I am thinking of cases like *Night*

Gregory Currie

Mail (Basil Wright, 1936) where, notoriously, shots purporting to record the sorting of mail in the train carriage were in fact studio recreations.

Fake material, or some of it, does seem different from material presented in a qualitatively misleading way (though we may not be able to draw a sharp distinction between the two categories).[17] It is one thing to present shots of postal workers sorting the night mail and to suggest, by some means, that the postal workers are happier and more devoted to their tasks than is in fact the case; it is another to present shots of nonpostal workers not sorting mail in a film studio, and to suggest that these are postal workers sorting mail on the night train.

With the material that is merely misleading, the problem seems not to lie in the images themselves but in what the narrative suggests about those images; material crosses the boundary into the realm of fakes when it is the images themselves that are out of place. If my documentary about Nixon involves, for convenience, a number of shots of my brother-in-law who, from a distance and in poor lighting, looks like Nixon, then these shots surely are not documentary material *on Nixon*. Similarly with the studio-bound shots of actors in *Night Mail:* the film is a documentary, but those shots are not documentary parts of it. So what we call a "documentary film" can be a mixture of the truly documentary and the nondocumentary fake. Our use of "documentary" to apply to a whole film is therefore a rough-and-ready one, based on a judgment that the film is preponderantly documentary.

Films sometimes go beyond the inclusion of mere fake detail; they can consist wholly of fake elements. *No Lies* (1972) purports to record a conversation between a female rape-victim and her increasingly aggressive (male) interlocutor, who tries to suggest her complicity in the assault; the credits at the end reveal the whole thing to have been staged with actors, scripts, and weeks of rehearsal.[18] *No Lies* is no documentary. Why not? Because none of its images support, through their role as traces of things, the narrative: the events recorded on film and the events asserted in the narrative (but without, note, any explicit commentary) are completely at odds. The images seem to support the narrative only so long as we have false beliefs about them.

Go back to the less extreme case of the documentary that contains fake elements. This suggests that we need a notion of documentary more discriminating than that which applies to whole films: a notion of the documentary parts. As an approximation, we might take the *shot* as our documentary

unit (though later I shall suggest problems with this). But if we take the shot as our unit, we must not fall into the trap of supposing that a shot, in isolation, can be said to be (or not to be) documentary. Parodying Frege, we can say: it is only in the context of the film that the shot has documentary status. Those shots of my shifty-looking brother-in-law are not documentary in the film about Nixon, but they surely are in the film I make about my brother-in-law and his propensity for posing as Nixon. But context does not determine merely whether the unit is documentary or fake; it can also make the difference between documentary and fiction. In the context of *Casablanca*, those shots of Bogart and Bergman are fiction rather than documentary; in the context of a documentary about the acting style of Ingrid Bergman, they are genuine documentary, and not merely fictions interpolated within the documentary, as with the Mickey Mouse material.

So we have something like a hermeneutic circle: to be worthy of the name, a documentary film has to be made up of a preponderance of documentary shots, but the shot's status as documentary depends on the documentary status of the film it is a part of. In that case, the notion we have to specify is a relational one: *being a documentary part of a documentary whole* (D^2 (x,y)). I suggest the following as a first step:

(1) D^2 (A,B) iff (i) A is a filmic part of B and (ii) A is a trace of P, and as such contributes to the provision of information about P in the narrative of B.

But this will not do, because shots of the (real) Eiffel Tower often serve to set the scene in a fiction film. We might try to avoid the difficulty by insisting that the whole must be substantially, perhaps predominantly, composed of parts like A, parts that contribute similarly to the narrative:

(2) D^2 (A,B) iff (i) A is a filmic part of B and (ii) A is a trace of P, and as such contributes to the provision of information about P in the narrative of B and (iii) the filmic parts of B consist predominantly of parts like A in this respect.

But this will not do either, for slightly less obvious reasons. There might be a fiction film in which the fictional characters *never* appear; all we see is real locations and real people, understood to be just background to the events of the story, which is told in a voice-over.[19] The problem can be avoided by distinguishing between narratives that are asserted (as they are in both documentary and docudrama) and those that are not (as in a fiction):

(3) D^2 (A,B) iff (i) A is a part of B; (ii) A is a filmic trace of P, and as such contributes to the provision of information about P in the (asserted) narrative of B; (iii) the filmic parts of B consist predominantly of parts like A in this respect.

Here I have retained clause (iii) from the failed (2), because otherwise we would have included many dramatic recreations within our definition: a dramatic recreation of Watergate involves an asserted narrative (or so I am assuming for the moment) and might contain shots of the Watergate building, the White House, etc., in the service of the narrative telling us things about these places germane to the events of the break-in and its aftermath. But with the "predominantly" clause in place, I am happy to accept under the banner "documentary" films that contain *some* degree of reconstruction: they count as documentaries (though not pure ones), as Ludovic Kennedy's television film about Lord Lucan is a documentary with reconstructive interludes.

Let me summarize the argument so far. In a weak sense, any film is a documentary, as is any shot in isolation: it is a documentary record of that of which it is a trace. But in a stronger sense of "documentary," not every film is a documentary. Those that are, are so because they consist substantially of filmic parts that support an asserted narrative, in virtue of those parts being traces of things and not in virtue of their having any other representational role. Some shots are not documentary shots, and some shots are documentary with respect to one film and nondocumentary with respect to another. To decide whether shots/films are documentary in this stronger sense we have to look, not merely at their status as traces, but at the intentionally produced narratives and their constituent assertions, which those shots/films support.

IX   Things That are Both Trace and Testimony

To be a trace and to be testimony are different things. But a thing that is a trace can also be testi-

mony. If something is both, then its status as a trace does not immediately qualify it as a documentary element within a given documentary context. This is notably the case where we are dealing with *auditory* traces: recordings of people's voices, for instance. The recording is a trace of the voice, and not testimony of that voice, for the tape recorder records the sounds that impact on its receiving equipment, and not the sounds the person recording believes are being made (thus de Palma's *Blow Out*, a transposition into auditory mode of the mystery described in Antonioni's *Blow Up*). Documentaries typically contain auditory traces as parts, but they, like other parts, are not always documentary parts of the documentary. A documentary about Hitler may present us with both visual and auditory traces of him, and the recording of his voice should count as a documentary part of the documentary. But if the commentary is spoken by Laurence Olivier, the trace of *his* voice is not a documentary part of the documentary – assuming that the focus of the narrative is Hitler and not Olivier. For the recording of Hitler's voice cannot be a recording of words he did not utter (though the sound quality might be so distorted that we draw a wrong conclusion about what his words were). It cannot intrinsically misrepresent the documentary's focus. But Olivier's words can, and those words represent actual things and occurrences if the beliefs of the person who wrote them were true, and not otherwise. So things are complicated: the recording of Olivier is a trace of his speech, but it is testimony of Hitler and his activities. Because Hitler is the focus of the documentary, and because the Olivier-trace is testimony concerning Hitler, the Olivier-trace is not a documentary part of this documentary, however informative it may be. But that same trace of Olivier could be a documentary part of another documentary: if it were recycled and used as part of a documentary about the speaking powers of Olivier, for instance.

So just as the question whether a shot is documentary needs resolution by context, so – sometimes – does the question whether the item we are considering falls exclusively into the trace category or, at the same time, into the testimony category as well. A trace of A can be testimony of B, and if the narrative focus of the documentary is B and not A, that trace functions, in that context, as testimony, as the trace of Olivier functions as testimony in the documentary about Hitler.

Now this observation – that a trace of one thing can function as testimony of another – suggests a problem for my theory. Take a "documentary" about Napoleon. No filmic traces here of Napoleon – nor, let us assume, of things to which Napoleon was closely related, which would complicate the picture. Rather, there are traces of Napoleon experts, drawings of Napoleon, models of battlefields, etc. If, as it seems we should, we say that the film's narrative is about Napoleon and closely Napoleon-related things and events, then this is no documentary, because the things of which the filmic parts are traces are not the things that are the focus of the narrative. We could identify a kind of subnarrative that the film presents, concerning Napoleon-experts, drawings of Napoleon, models of battlefields, etc., but the most that gets us is the conclusion that this is a documentary about those things, not about Napoleon.

I choose to tough this one out. If this film is not a documentary about Napoleon, it is not surprising that we would casually label it as one. In medium, form, and technique it is very like things that are documentaries about, say, current or recent heads of state. In some sense it is also clearly about Napoleon; at least that is the focus of its narrative. Let us use the phrase "A is a documentary-about-B" to mean that A is a documentary that tells a narrative about B and does so to a significant extent through its use of traces of B and closely B-related things. But let us use "A is a B-relevant documentary" to mean that A is a documentary (and hence a documentary-about-something) from which you could learn, and perhaps are intended to learn, things about B. On my theory, the imagined documentary is a documentary-about-various-things (none of them Napoleon) and is a Napoleon-relevant documentary. One would not in that case be surprised to hear it called a "documentary about Napoleon."

But if I have struggled out of one difficulty, I am immediately caught in another. The documentary I just imagined turned out to be about the things of which its constitutive filmic elements were traces, as all documentaries are. In the imagined case they were traces of Napoleon-experts and other things. Imagine a new case that provides traces of just one eminent historian telling us about Napoleon. This sounds as if it ought to be described as a "television lecture" and not as a documentary about anything. But on my account it is a documentary about the historian, just as game-shows turn out to be documentaries about their participants, chat-shows documentaries about the interviewer and interviewees, sports

programs documentaries about the activities of the athletes, etc.

Though we do not normally count these things as documentaries, they are hard to exclude from that category in any principled way.[20] For example, we have no difficulty accepting Ichikawa's *Tokyo Olympiad* (1965) as a documentary, which in all ways except its visual and narrative quality is simply sports coverage. Yet quality cannot surely be the difference between documentary and nondocumentary, since many things accepted as documentary have few or none of the qualities of the kind that distinguish *Tokyo Olympiad*.

But this line of thought may open up an abyss comparable to that revealed by the "defining art" debate, where quality seems to be what makes for art in some cases and not in others, with no one able convincingly to tell a general story about where the boundaries lie. At this point people may say that I have failed to see that *documentary*, like *art*, is an historical concept. But since I do not believe that art is an historical concept, I am not attracted to this line of thought.[21] There may be more to documentary than I have been able to excavate, but I hope I have uncovered at least part of its structure.

X   The Docudrama

I began by saying that we could not say simply that the documentary is the nonfiction film, because this would not distinguish between the documentary and the docudrama: the re-creation, by dramatic means, of certain actually occurring events.

If there are any genuine docudramas, they are certainly not documentaries. There might be docudramas, and their possibility ensures the intensional nonequivalence of documentary and nonfiction film. But are there actually any docudramas? I suggest that there are few if any, and that the things we are most inclined to place in the docudrama category are in fact fictions, or at least things with substantially fictive content.

Consider *All the President's Men*. This film is based on fact; it contains many characters who are real people and depicts many events that (I assume) actually happened. But so are many other films we happily call fiction. In the film, a vast number of things are depicted that did not occur, that it is not intended that the audience will believe occurred, and that the audience will not in fact believe occurred. Woodward is depicted as having a certain appearance, namely that of Robert Redford. Redford, Hoffman, and the other actors speak certain words and speak them in certain ways with certain intonations. They move in certain ways in certain settings, all this plainly visible on screen. None of this is attributed or intended to be attributed to Woodward and Bernstein. These are fictional things; we are to imagine them happening, we are not intended to believe they happened. At times we are intended to assume that what the film depicts really did occur, but only in general outline. Each morsel of assertion is thickly coated with fictional detail.

All this is traceable to the nature of the medium. An historical text can tell us just as much as the author wants to tell us, and no more, because its sentential structure is discriminating. But film is not discriminating. Without incredible and self-defeating artifice, it cannot be confined to that which is reliably believed by the maker, or to what the maker expects the audience to believe. The actor playing the character has to look, speak, and move in a certain way. And we watchers know that none of this (or very little of it) is intended to be believed to be true of the character, and we consequently believe very little of it. Rather, we imagine the events that the screen portrays in all their specificity. So even the most faithful and restrained docudrama contains a vast amount of fictional material: material the appropriate response to which is imagining rather than belief. Moreover, in the documentary film, this fictional material is largely presented via the photographic process (or the comparable process of sound recording), and therefore makes a break with assertion at the very point where the documentary is at its most reliably assertive. One thing that a documentary detailing the activities of Woodward and Bernstein could be expected to do very well is to offer reliable information about what Woodward, Bernstein, and the other protagonists look like. The docudrama's divergence from the documentary is thus not merely a matter of the quantity of assertions it fails to make, but of the way in which the kind of assertion here lacking is central to the documentary project. A docudrama – unless it is a very unusual one – is best counted along with the fictions.[22]

XI The Parts of the Documentary

There is a problem I do not know how to solve. I said that we ought to distinguish documentary and nondocumentary parts within a documentary whole. I also said that the purely cinematic parts would naturally be thought of as shots. In that case the separation into shots ought to be fine grained enough to segregate documentary from nondocumentary elements. But sometimes that is not so. Take the Disney documentary narrated by Mickey Mouse. Assume for the sake of simplicity that Mickey appears in every shot. Exactly which bits are documentary proper and which bits fiction? No shot is wholly documentary. Should we imagine cutting Mickey's image out of each frame, or drawing a boundary round it, thereby denoting the place where documentary begins and fiction ends? That would get us nowhere. Much else in the image consists of things that Mickey looks at, comments on, points to – or rather, it is fictional, of those things, that Mickey looks at, comments on, and points to them: they have distinctly fictional properties in virtue of Mickey's activities. At least within the visual pattern we see before us, there does not seem to be any natural segmentation into the fictional and the nonfictional.

XII Conclusion

While problems remain, the broad outline is this. Documentaries are filmic narratives, the images of which support the narrative in virtue (mostly) of their being photographic representations. Putting it somewhat loosely, in a documentary meaning passes from image to narrative, while in nondocumentary meaning goes the other way. *Documentary* is not a rhetorical, empty, or confused category, though it is an essentially vague one. But all this stands or falls with a certain conception of what is distinctive about photographic and other trace-inducing media, and with the consequent distinction between conceptual and nonconceptual content. That is why I have spent so much time on issues of representation, and no time at all on the aesthetics, or the politics, of documentary.[23]

Notes

1 Michael Moore, in an interview with Harlan Jacobson, "Michael and Me," *Film Comment* 25, no. 6 (1989): 16–26.

2 John Grierson, "First Principles of Documentary," in Forsyth Hardy ed., *Grierson on Documentary* (London: Faber and Faber, 1966), p. 145.

3 The reconstruction is sometimes called the *docudrama*, and I shall use that term myself below. *The Oxford Dictionary of New Words*, in its entry on "docudrama," says that the term "is used to show that a film or entertainment contains an element of documentary (or at least that real events have formed the basis for it)." In my view this does not do enough to distinguish docudrama and documentary, but the parenthetical comment has at least the merit of suggesting that having real events as the basis of the film is not sufficient for documentary status. I am grateful to Frank Jackson and Richard Holton for having pressed the issue of definition.

4 Moore's *Roger and Me* telescopes events of two decades into an imagined industrial holocaust a fraction of that duration. The issue over that film is *not* "whether the order of the filming was the order of the film," as Brian Winston supposes (*Claiming the Real: The Documentary Film Revisited* [London: British Film Institute, 1995], p. 206), adding in a rather lame footnote that "It is possible that [the] critics were not so absurdly naive as this suggests" (p. 274). The issue is whether the order of the film constitutes an implication that events had one kind of cause when in fact their actual time of occurrence made such causation impossible.

5 By and large, film theorists have been skeptical of the category "documentary." See Bill Nichols, *Representing Reality* (Indiana University Press, 1991), pp. 5–6. See Noël Carroll, "From Real to Reel: Entangled in Nonfiction Film," in his *Theorizing the Moving Image* (Cambridge: Cambridge University Press, 1996), for critical scrutiny of contemporary film-theoretic approaches to documentary (also his "Nonfiction Film and Postmodernist Skepticism," in *Post-Theory: Reconstructing Film Studies*, eds. D. Bordwell and N. Carroll [University of Wisconsin Press, 1996]). For Carroll's own positive theory – somewhat at odds with mine – see his "Documentary and the Film of Presumptive Assertion," in *Film Theory and Philosophy*, eds. Richard Allen and Murray Smith (New York: Oxford University Press, 1997).

6 As does the *Oxford Companion to Film* (Oxford University Press, 1976); see the entry "documentary."

7 See André Bazin, "The Ontology of the Photographic Image," in *What is Cinema?* trans. Hugh Gray (University of California Press, 1971), vol. 1.

8 See Kendall Walton's fascinating essay "Transparent Pictures: On the Nature of Photographic Realism," *Critical Inquiry* 11 (1984): 246–277. Walton acknowledges a debt to the work of Paul Grice.

9 Sherlock Holmes simulates the criminal in "The Musgrave Ritual."

10 See Bazin, "Ontology of the Photographic Image"; Walton, "Transparent Pictures"; and Roger Scruton, "Photography and Representation," in *The Aesthetic Understanding: Essays in the Philosophy of Art and Culture* (London: Methuen, 1983) [see also this volume, ch. 1].

11 See my *Image and Mind: Film, Philosophy, and Cognitive Science* (Cambridge: Cambridge University Press, 1995), chap. 3.

12 For criticism of this view see Frank Jackson, *Perception: A Representative Theory* (Cambridge: Cambridge University Press, 1977), pp. 38–48.

13 See Gareth Evans, *The Varieties of Reference* (Oxford: Clarendon, 1982), especially p. 123. For dissent, see John McDowell, *Mind and World* (Harvard University Press, 1994), chap. 3.

14 I base this formulation on the one in Tim Crane, "The Nonconceptual Content of Experience," in *The Contents of Experience*, ed. T. Crane (Cambridge: Cambridge University Press, 1992). Crane records a debt to Adrian Cussins, "The Connectionist Construction of Concepts," in *The Philosophy of Artificial Life*, ed. M. Boden (Oxford: Oxford University Press, 1990).

15 This line of thought is complicated, but not ultimately subverted, by consideration of the issue of interpretative realism: should we think of the agency behind the narrative as the real, flesh and blood author with real and possibly misfiring intentions? Or should we think of her as a construct – the personality that seems to be behind this work? I take the latter option. See my "Interpretation and Objectivity," *Mind* 102 (1993): 413–428.

16 This is a simplification, since I am here treating *Roger and Me* as if it were an ideal documentary, which it is not. Nothing hangs on the simplification.

17 Take a film about Smith, who sometimes sleeps in a coffin. Suppose I make use of footage of Smith rising from his coffin within a narrative that suggests that Smith rose from the dead. I am not sure whether this footage is fake or merely misleading. Perhaps there is no answer. I owe the example to Keith Lehrer, though I am using it in a way different from that intended by Lehrer.

18 Thanks to Julia Erhart for drawing cases of this kind to my attention.

19 Mike Walsh suggested Chris Marker's *Sans Soleil* as an example of this.

20 Indeed, in the early days of film, people would have had no trouble classifying them as "*documentaires*" or "*actualités*."

21 See my "Aliens, Too," *Analysis*, n.s., 53 (1994): 116–118.

22 Though it can be *fictional* of a docudrama that it is a documentary. In Peter Watkin's *Culloden*, the battle is recreated through the fictional presence of a film crew there to record the event, and we see what purports to be their documentary record of it, and hear their commentary. But since, in fact, the battle is being re-enacted, what we see is a trace of that re-enactment, of which it is fictional that it is the battle itself.

23 Earlier versions of this paper were read at the Adelaide-Flinders Research Seminar and at the Research School of Social Sciences, Australian National University. Thanks are due to both audiences, especially to Hugh Clapin, Frank Jackson, Alan Lee, Chris Mortensen, and Ian Ravenscroft. Thanks also to Noël Carroll and Tim Crane for discussion. Research on this paper was supported by the Australian Research Council and by the Institute for Advanced Study, Australian National University.

11

Fiction, Non-Fiction, and the Film of Presumptive Assertion: A Conceptual Analysis

Noël Carroll

I   Introduction

In both film studies and the culture at large, there is an area of practice which is typically labelled 'the documentary', or perhaps less frequently, 'non-fiction film'. These labels are roughly serviceable for practical purposes, but they are not always as theoretically precise as they might be. Therefore, in this chapter, I will propose another label for the field – namely, 'films of presumptive assertion' – and I will attempt to define it.[1] In response to this statement of intent, some may worry that my new label and its accompanying definition are stipulative and revisionist. However, I will argue that they track the extension of films that film scholars want to talk about and refer to better than the alternative candidates do.

Current usage of the term 'documentary' to denominate the field in question appears to stem from John Grierson. It was his preferred name for his own practice, and it has been extended by many to cover all work in what might be provisionally earmarked as the non-fiction film. However, when Grierson introduced the term, he had something rather specific in mind. He defined the documentary as 'the creative treatment of actuality'.[3] The notion of *creative treatment* in this formula had a very particular function. It was intended to distinguish the Griersonian documentary from things like the Lumière *actualité* and newsreels.[4]

In contrast to the *actualité* and the newsreel, the Griersonian documentary had a creative dimension by virtue of which it was explicitly conceived to be artistic. In this, Grierson's ambitions paralleled those of other film-makers and theoreticians of the silent and early sound periods who wished to defeat the prejudice that film could merely function as the slavish and mechanical reproduction of whatever confronted the camera lens. They argued that film could be more than a record of the flow of reality. It could shape reality creatively and, therefore, it deserved to be taken seriously in virtue of its artistic dimension.[5]

One can certainly sympathize with Grierson's aims. However, once we see what is behind his definition of the documentary, I think it is pretty clear that the notion will not serve to demarcate the area of study that often bears its name today. For Grierson's concept is too narrow. It excludes such things as Lumière *actualités* and the videotape of the Rodney King beating – things that most of us, I conjecture, think belong legitimately in the curriculum of courses with titles such as *Introduction to the Documentary Film*.

Needless to say, this is not a criticism of Grierson. He meant to exclude candidates like these from the class of things he called 'documentaries'. And it is his privilege to call what he was doing whatever suits him. Rather, I mean to criticize those who carelessly try to stretch Grierson's

Noël Carroll, "Fiction, Non-Fiction, and the Film of Presumptive Assertion: A Conceptual Analysis," *Film Theory and Philosophy*, eds. Richard Allen and Murray Smith (New York: Oxford University Press, 1997): 173–202. Reprinted by permission of Oxford University Press.

notion to cover the whole field. For Grierson's notion of documentary picks out an extension of objects far more narrow than that referred to by most subsequent authors of books on the so-called documentary.

One might say 'so what?' Grierson meant one thing by 'documentary', and now we mean something else by it. But there is at least this problem. Whatever *we* might mean by it is obscure and perhaps equivocal. Thus, we find ourselves in a situation where we have, on the one hand, the relatively precise notion of the documentary that Grierson has bequeathed us, and, on the other hand, another more ambiguous idea. This at the very least courts confusion. I propose to relieve that confusion by granting Grierson his definition for what he was talking about and by introducing a new concept for what we wish to speak about.

Here it might be thought that we already have an alternative ready to hand in the concept of non-fiction. But if the Griersonian label of the documentary is too narrow for our purposes, the notion of non-fiction is too broad. Consider the way in which the couplet fiction/non-fiction divides up a book shop. The novels, short stories, and perhaps plays will be found in the fiction section. Everything else is non-fiction, including children's drawing manuals. But when we consider what is discussed under the prevailing rubric of the documentary film, interactive lessons about the way to draw a flower are not what we have in mind.

Moreover, films like J. J. Murphy's *Print Generation*, Peter Kulbelka's *Arnulf Rainer*, and Ernie Gehr's *Serene Velocity* are not fictions. They tell no imagined story. So, they are non-fiction. But, once again, they are not included in histories of, nor classes concerning, the so-called documentary. Thus, I take it that the suspicion that the category of non-fiction is too broad for our purposes is well motivated.

If I am right in supposing that our presiding labels and concepts are inadequate to our purposes, then the best solution, it seems to me, is to devise a new label, accompanied by a rigorous definition. This sounds very reformist. However, I think that my proposal in terms of films of presumptive assertion – which might more tendentiously be called 'films of putative fact' – does a better job of locating the body of work that concerns those who currently signal their domain of discourse by means of the idiom of the documentary or non-fiction film.

How might one substantiate this claim? One way is to argue that the notion of films of presumptive assertion makes more sense out of the debates that people have in this area of enquiry. For example, major debates over the so-called non-fiction film involve claims about the objectivity of the relevant films and about whether they can refer to reality. But if what we want to talk about includes films like *Arnulf Rainer* – a flicker film – then questions of objectivity and reference to reality fall by the wayside, since it makes no sense to ask of *Arnulf Rainer* whether it is objective or even subjective in its reference to reality. Its images are not fictional, but they are not referential either. It is a non-fiction film, but it stands outside the epistemic questions that obsess documentary film studies. On the other hand, the notion of films of presumptive assertion would not encompass works like *Arnulf Rainer* to begin with, but only films that play what we might call the assertion game, a game wherein epistemic questions of objectivity and truth are uncontroversially apposite. – what does this mean?

I will pursue the analysis of films of presumptive assertion in stages. First, I will try to draw a distinction between fiction and non-fiction. Then, I will go on – exploiting what has been said about the fiction/non-fiction couplet – to propose an analysis of films of presumptive assertion (as a subcategory of the non-fiction film). Once I have subcategory worked out my analysis of films of presumptive assertion, I will then contemplate a series of problems or questions that my theory is likely to raise.

2 Fiction and Non-Fiction

The first step in defining the film of presumptive assertion is to draw a distinction between fiction and non-fiction, since the film of presumptive assertion, on my account, is a subcategory of non-fiction. However, many film scholars are likely to regard even this first step as quixotic. For they are persuaded that there is no viable distinction between fiction and non-fiction. They are convinced that it has been, as they say, 'deconstructed';[6] all films can be shown to be fictional.

Christian Metz, for example, has argued:

> At the theater Sarah Bernhardt may tell me she is Phèdre or if the play were from another period and rejected the figurative regime, she might say, as in a type of modern theater, that she is Sarah Bernhardt. But at any rate,

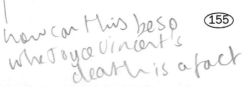

how can this be so when Joyce Vincent's death is a fact.

I should see Sarah Bernhardt. At the cinema she could make two kinds of speeches too, but it would be her shadow that would be offering them to me (or she would be offering them in her own absence). Every film is a fiction film.[7]

Another reason why some film scholars suppose that the distinction between fiction and non-fiction is inoperable is that non-fiction and fiction films share many of the same structures – flashbacks, parallel editing, cross-cutting, point-of-view editing, and the like. And certain mannerisms found in non-fiction films, like grainy footage and unsteady camera movements, have been appropriated by fiction films in order to achieve certain effects – like the impression of realism or authenticity. Thus, on the grounds of formal differentiae, one cannot distinguish fiction films from non-fiction films.[8]

There is also another way to argue for the view that the distinction between fiction films and non-fiction films is unsupportable. Friends of this view, whom we will call 'deconstructionists' for convenience, might suggest the following intuition pump. Presented with a film, it is at least conceivable that an informed viewer – i.e. a viewer fully knowledgeable of film techniques and their histories – might not be able to identify it correctly as a fiction or non-fiction film. All the formal information in the world would not be conclusive. Perhaps the dissection segments of the notorious *Alien Autopsy* are a pertinent example in this respect.

But let us start with Metz's position first. Metz's argument seems to me to be clearly fallacious. In effect, it not only denies the distinction between fiction and non-fiction, but it undermines the distinction between representation and fiction as well. If the reason that a film of Sarah Bernhardt saying that she is Sarah Bernhardt is a fiction is because Sarah Bernhardt is not in the screening room, then an aerial photograph of a battlefield will count as a fiction. But clearly it is not a fiction. It does not represent an imaginary configuration of forces due to the fact that the enemy is not in the room as our General Staff examines said aerial photographs. Armies do not plan counter-attacks on the basis of novels. But that is tantamount to what they would be doing if the aerial photographs were fictions.

Perhaps the proponent of Metz will counter that, even though all representations are fictions, there are different kinds of fictions. The aerial photographs belong to one sort and *All that Heaven Allows* to another sort. But what then distinguishes these different sorts of fiction? Without further argument, it would appear that something like the fiction/non-fiction distinction needs to be reintroduced.

Perhaps it will be said that there are *fictional* non-fictions (the class to which the aerial photographs and *Hoop Dreams* belong) and *fictional* fictions (the class to which *Seven* belongs). But this seems to reinscribe the fiction/non-fiction distinction, rather than to dismiss it. And, furthermore, the aforesaid *fictional* prefixes to these alleged categories do no conceptual work – i.e. make no meaningful contrast conceptually – and, therefore, are theoretically dispensable.

But an even deeper criticism of Metz's argument is that it contradicts the logic of representation. Representations are not equivalent to whatever they represent. This is why we have representations. It is one of the reasons they are so useful. If a map had to be the very terrain it is a map of, it would be of no added pragmatic value when we are lost on the terrain in question. Representations standardly are *not* what they represent. But in requiring Sarah Bernhardt in the screening room for a film of her *not* to count as fiction, Metz is forgetting (and, indeed, contradicting) what a representation is, as well as conflating representation and fiction.

In response, one might say that what Metz has done is to discover that all representations are really fictions. But one wants to question the nature of this discovery. It certainly does not reflect the way in which we typically deploy these concepts. Maybe Metz is assuming some stipulative redefinition of these concepts. But can Metz defend his stipulative redefinition of these concepts on the grounds that it is useful to construe these concepts his way? I doubt it. Indeed, Metz's reconstrual of these concepts is more likely to cause more confusion than anything else. Imagine how counter-productive it would be to be told that the pictures on a wanted-poster are fictional?

Metz reminds us that when Bernhardt plays Phèdre, there is a person, Bernhardt, standing before us, whereas when we see a movie of the same event, Bernhardt is not present. Fair enough. But what Metz ignores is the fact that the actress, Bernhardt on-stage, is a representational vehicle, indeed a fictional representational vehicle. She represents Phèdre. And there *is* also, in fact, a representational vehicle present in the screening room with us, namely the cinematic apparatus projecting the film of Bernhardt/Phèdre. So far there is no significant theoretical difference between the stage case and the film case in terms of the presence of representational vehicles. Moreover, in neither case is what we literally see a fictional character. What we literally see is a representational vehicle which may present either a fiction or non-fiction. Therefore, the question of the presence or absence of a representational vehicle is irrelevant to deciding a difference in the fictional/non-fictional status of the two cases.

Furthermore, what Metz vaguely calls absence would appear to be an essential characteristic of representations, irrespective of whether the representations are fictional or non-fictional. Thus, Metz seems guilty of a conceptual confusion inasmuch as he conflates representation and fiction.

Let us now turn to the second line of dissolving the distinction between fiction and non-fiction. This 'deconstructionist' attack begins with a series of reasonable observations. Many of the structures of the fiction film are shared by the non-fiction film. It is certainly true that non-fiction film-makers have imitated narrative devices that originated in the fiction film. And fiction film-makers have imitated non-fiction stylistics. Nevertheless, the lesson that those who favour the view that every film is fictional draw from these observations is too quick. They surmise that these considerations indicate that there is no difference between fiction and non-fiction. But another conclusion, equally consistent with the relevant observations, is that the distinction between fiction and non-fiction *does not rest* on a principled difference between the stylistic properties of fictional and non-fictional films.

Consider the analogous case of literature. There are no textual features – linguistic structures, writing styles, or plots – that mark something as a fiction. You might suppose that there are certain structures that could appear only in fiction, such as internal monologues. But, in fact, you can find them in non-fictions such as *Armies of the Night*. Moreover, this problem is necessarily insurmountable, since any linguistic structure, writing style, plot device, or other textual feature that characteristically appears in a fiction can be imitated by the non-fiction writer for a wide range of aesthetic effects.

And, of course, there is the mirror-image problem regarding the fiction writer. He can imitate any of the textual features characteristically associated with non-fiction writing for a broad assortment of purposes, including that of imbuing his fiction with a sense of heightened verisimilitude. So, since non-fiction and fiction authors alike can appropriate any of the formulae or devices associated with fiction and non-fiction respectively, we are compelled to the unavoidable conclusion that fiction and non-fiction cannot be differentiated by pointing to some linguistic or textual features that belong to all and only fiction or non-fiction respectively.

Of course, this is a theoretical rather than a practical problem, since we rarely encounter texts not knowing their status as fiction or non-fiction. Generally, we know before we start reading a text whether it is fiction or non-fiction. We do not adopt the role of detectives, trying to determine whether the story we are reading is fictional or non-fictional. Typically the story comes to us labeled one way or the other. Thus, the issue is theoretical and not practical.

Admittedly, it might be a problem which, though rarely arising, nevertheless could arise. We might find a text from the distant past, about which we possess no contextual information. In such a case, we might look at stylistic and textual features for some evidence about whether the work is fictional or non-fictional. But though this is a way in which we might proceed, such speculation is neither the only evidence we would look for,[9] nor would it be conclusive. Such evidence is at best probable and contingent because of what has already been said – namely, that any non-fictional device can always be imitated by the fiction writer, and vice versa for the non-fiction writer. But the distinction between fiction and non-fiction is ultimately not a matter of probability; it is a conceptual matter.

Yet even the preceding case does not show that there is no distinction between fiction and non-fiction, but only that nothing is conclusively fiction or non-fiction writing on the basis of the textual or linguistic features that it possesses. A text does not, for example, have the status of a fiction by virtue of the textual features it has or has not got. The fictional status of a text is not constituted by its textual features, even if, to a limited extent, the textual features, in some circumstances, might provide us with *some* evidence or clues that we might use to hypothesize its status where it is otherwise unknown.

Another way to make the point is to say that the fictionality of a text is not constituted or determined by its *manifest* textual properties. That is, you cannot tell whether a text is a fiction simply by looking at its linguistic, stylistic, or other textual features. You cannot tell for sure whether a text is fictional by reading it in a decontextualized way, where the only permissible information involves the consideration of its linguistic and textual features. Whether or not a text is fictional depends on its non-manifest (relational) properties (which I will specify further anon). You cannot tell whether a text is fictional in virtue of its manifest properties, inspected in isolation. You have to consider the text in relation to something else – something else that is not manifest in the text; something else that cannot be read off the surface of the text.

As it is with literature, so it is with film. One does not conclusively identify something as either a fiction or a non-fiction film by looking at its manifest structural features. This is not what film-goers do. Like the readers of literature, film-goers generally know whether the film they are about to see has been labelled one way or the other. This information circulates in the film world before the work is seen – in the form of advertisements, distribution releases, reviews, word of mouth, and the like. This is why the previous intuition pump is so contrived and unilluminating. We do not go to films and attempt to guess whether they are fictions or non-fictions. In the largest number of cases, we know ahead of time how to categorize the films in question. Moreover, it is hard to see what motivation practitioners in the institution of film would have to replace the current system with guessing games.

Film scholars are correct in noting the overlapping stylistics of the fiction and non-fiction film. However, they are wrong to understand this as entailing that there is no distinction between fiction films and non-fiction films, and that all films are fictional. Their error is logical. For they presume that if there is no stylistic differentia between fiction and non-fiction films, then there is no differentia whatsoever. But this is baldly a non sequitur. For they have not foreclosed the possibility that there may be differentiae other than stylistic or formal considerations in virtue of which the distinction can be drawn.[10]

Of course, revealing the lacuna in the argument for the reduction of all film to fiction on the grounds that it has failed to preclude the possibility that it has not eliminated all the potential candidates for drawing the distinction, though logically correct, is unlikely to be persuasive, un-

less it is possible to come up with a plausible alternative candidate for distinguishing fiction from non-fiction. Thus, in order to carry my case across the finish line, it is incumbent upon me to show that there are eminently reasonable grounds for thinking that there is a viable way to make the distinction that the 'deconstructionists' have overlooked, and to defend it.

By denying that one can demarcate fiction from non-fiction on the basis of stylistics, the 'deconstructionist', in effect, is denying that one can determine whether a candidate film is a fiction, for example, on the basis of the intrinsic, manifest properties of the work. I agree. But this does not mean that the distinction cannot be crafted by considering certain non-manifest, relational properties of the works in question. This is the line of argument that I want to pursue. Specifically, I want to argue that we can draw a distinction between fiction and non-fiction on the basis of certain authorial intentions.[11] The authorial intentions I have in mind may, of course, not be manifest in the work, and, moreover, they are relational properties of the work – i.e. properties of the work in relation to the author, and, as we shall see, in relation to spectators as well.

Furthermore, if the analysis in terms of authorial intentions can be defended, then, from the perspective of logic, the burden of proof falls to the 'deconstructionists'. That is, if they still wish to maintain that there is no distinction between fiction and non-fiction, it falls to them to show the error in my proposal.

As I construe the problem, we begin with a presumption in favour of a distinction between fiction and non-fiction. There is a presumption in favour of it because it is deeply embedded in our practices and it is at the centre of our conceptual scheme. It is difficult to see how we can get along without it. But a presumption is not a proof. The presumption must be backed up by compelling reasons. Moreover, as we have seen, the presumption cannot be defended on stylistic grounds. We can imagine fiction films that are stylistically indiscernible from non-fiction films, and vice versa. We cannot 'eyeball' the distinction between the two. That is one indication that the problem before us is philosophical.[12]

Because we cannot 'eyeball' the distinction by looking at a given film, the distinction, if there is one, must rest upon some non-manifest, relational properties of fiction films and non-fiction films respectively. But what can that distinction be?

In order to answer that question, I shall take advantage of what might be called an intention-response model of communication. This approach is frequently employed nowadays by philosophers in order to develop theories of art as well as fiction.[13] The approach is broadly Gricean in its inspiration. Applied to art, it presupposes that an artist or an author, such as a film-maker, communicates to an audience by way of indicating that the audience is intended to respond to his or her text (i.e. any structure of sense-bearing signs) in a certain way, where the reason that the audience has for mobilizing the response or the stance in question is the audience's recognition of the sender's intention that they do so.

This approach is social, at least in the sense that it depends upon certain relations, rooted in our communicative practices, between the senders and receivers of sense-bearing signs. Moreover, if this approach can be applied to the cases of fiction and non-fiction, it will propose a non-manifest, relational property of the texts in question as that which determines the status of the text as fictional or non-fictional. And that is just the sort of property that we are looking for in our endeavour to distinguish fiction and non-fiction films.

Since the Gricean-type intention-response model of communication has provided insights already to philosophers, psychologists, and linguists alike, it seems a reasonable theoretical option to try out, at least hypothetically, though, of course, the hypothesis must be defended subsequently. Thus, applying the intention-response model to the case of fiction, we may begin by hypothesizing that a structured set of sense-bearing signs, such as a novel or a film, is fictional only if presented by an author, film-maker, or sender who intends the audience to respond to it with what we might call the fictive stance on the basis of recognizing the author's, film-maker's, or sender's intention that the audience do this on the basis of recognizing what we might call the sender's fictive intention. A compact, jargonistic statement of the theory, then, is that a structure of sense-bearing signs is a fiction only if it is presented by a sender with the fictive intention that the audience respond to it by adopting the fictive stance on the basis of recognizing the sender's fictive intention that they do so.[14]

Of course, this definition is pretty obscure. It needs to be unpacked – more needs to be said about what is involved in a fictive stance and a fictive intention. What is a fictive intention? It is the intention of the author, film-maker, or sender of a structure of sense-bearing signs that the audience imagine the content of the story in question on the basis of their recognition that this is what the sender intends them to do.

Suppose we are buying a can of lemonade from a vending machine. After we put our money in the machine, we then press one of the selection buttons. Why do we do this? Because we realize that this is what the designer of the machine intends us to do, presupposing that we wish to use the machine in the way it was designed to be used. Similarly, there is a design intention when it comes to fiction – namely, that we imagine the content of the story in question. Moreover, we adopt this attitude when consuming a fiction because we recognize that this is what the sender intends us to do, presupposing that we wish to use the story in the way in which it was designed to be used. So, when we read that Sherlock Holmes lives on Baker Street, we imagine that he lives on Baker Street. Moreover, our mental state or attitude here is one of imagining, rather than, say, one of believing, because we recognize that Conan Doyle intends us to imagine rather than to believe that Sherlock Holmes lives on Baker Street.

Undoubtedly, there may be epistemological questions about the way in which we come to recognize whether the sender's intention is fictive or non-fictive. But we can put them to one side for the moment and come back to them later. For our concern now is ontological, not epistemological, since what we are pursuing is the question of the nature of fiction. It is one thing to say that fiction is constituted by an authorial fictive intention, and another thing to say how we go about recognizing that intention.

In *Metaphor and Movement*, the dance historian Lincoln Kirstein intends us to believe that *The Sleeping Beauty* ballet was produced in 1890, when he presents us with propositions to that effect, whereas in the novel *The Moor's Last Sigh*, Salman Rushdie intends us to imagine that Aurora is a great Indian painter. Moreover, Rushdie does not intend us to adopt this mental state as the result of magic or drugs. He intends that we adopt this mental state on the basis of the recognition that this is what he, the designer of the text, intends us to do with the novel.

With respect to *The Moor's Last Sigh*, one of Rushdie's fictive intentions is that we imagine that Aurora is a great Indian painter. I say *one* of his *relevant to Morley.*

intentions because he has others – for example, he also intends that we imagine that Aurora is married to Abraham. Furthermore, all these fictive intentions can be subsumed under one, overarching fictive intention – namely, that the reader imagine all the objects, persons, actions, and events that comprise the story of *The Moor's Last Sigh*. In publishing *The Moor's Last Sigh*, Rushdie intends that the reader shall imagine the persons, actions, objects, and events of the story.

Shall here is normative, not predictive. That is, Rushdie's fictive intention prescribes or mandates how we should take his story in order to use it as it was designed to be used. Someone might, of course, mistake it for a history book and come to believe, rather than to imagine, that Aurora was a great Indian painter. Yet that only shows that to prescribe certain behaviour is not to predict behaviour, a fact brought home to God more than once since the time he promulgated the Ten Commandments.

But, in addition, Rushdie's fictive intention does not simply involve a prescriptive component – that the reader shall imagine the content of the story. It also contains what we might call a reflexive, reason-giving component – that the reader imagine the content *for the reason* that he recognizes that this is what Rushdie intends him to do. Thus, Rushdie's fictive intention is that the reader imagine the propositional content of *The Moor's Last Sigh* for the reason that the reader recognizes that this is what he is intended to do.

We have already effectively described what is involved in the fictive stance in the preceding discussion of the fictive intention. The notion of the fictive intention looks at the matter from the author's side of the transaction; the notion of the fictive stance refers to the audience's part of the bargain. The author intends the audience to adopt a certain attitude toward the propositional content of the story. That attitude is the audience's stance.[15] Where the work is a fiction, the attitude or stance is one of imagining. The fictive stance, then, is a matter of the audience's imagining the propositional content of a structure of meaning-bearing signs whether they be of the nature of words, images, or something else.

So far, our analysis says that a structure of sense-bearing signs is a fiction only if it involves the audience's adoption of the fictive stance on the basis of its recognition of the author's fictive intention. However, the analysis contains at least one major obscurity. The fictive stance involves im-

how do we consider performances?

agination. But what is meant by the notion of *imagining*? This problem is compounded by the fact that the histories of literature, psychology, and philosophy are littered with many different, often non-converging notions of the imagination. So how are we to understand that term in a formula such as: *x* is a fiction only if the sender intends the audience to imagine the propositional content of *x* for the reason that the audience recognizes that this is what the sender intends?

The way in which we conceive of imagining here is crucial to the attempt to defeat the 'deconstructionist'. For certain concepts of the imagination are likely to encourage 'deconstruction' rather than to thwart it. For example, one concept of the imagination, found in Descartes's *Meditations* and echoed by Kant in *The Critique of Pure Reason*, is that the imagination is the faculty that unifies perceptions. That is, I have the discrete perception of the front of a building, and another discrete perception of the back of the building. But my mind unifies them as parts of the same building. How is this done? By what we might call the imagination.

But if this is the concept of the imagination that we bring to the preceding analysis of fiction, the prospect of 'deconstruction' looms again, since both the historian and the novelist intend us to mobilize what can be called the *constructive* imagination. Indeed, if Kant is right, the constructive imagination is always in play so its operation cannot serve to distinguish anything involving cognition from anything else.[16]

Of course, there are other major notions of the imagination. One is that it is the capacity for mental imagery. But this will be of no use to us in defining fiction, since the audience's prescribed response to a fiction does not require mental imaging. I can imagine the proposition that Aurora is a great Indian painter, even if I do not have a mental image of her. And as well, it is possible for the reader of a history book to have mental images on the basis of the text.

The imagination has received a great deal less philosophical attention than mental states such as belief. As a result, the notion has often served as a catch-all category of last resort. Thus, we have inherited a mixed bag of faculties and mental functions under the rubric of the imagination. Consequently, if we intend to use the concept of the imagination in our formula for fiction, we must specify what exactly we take *the imagination* to refer to. We cannot have either the constructive imagination or the mental-imaging imagination in mind in our formula for the reasons already given. Instead, my claim is that the relevant sense of *imagination* for my formula is what I will call the *suppositional imagination.*[17]

Often in the course of a discussion, we may say something like, 'I'll grant you *x* for the purposes of the argument.' Or, in a mathematical proof, we may begin by saying, 'Suppose *x*.' These are examples of what I mean by the *suppositional imagination*. In such cases we are entertaining a certain thought or propositional content – namely, that *x* – without committing ourselves to it by way of belief. We hold *x* in our mind as, so to speak, a hypothesis, rather than as an assertion. Or we can say that we are entertaining that *x* as an unasserted thought. To believe *x*, on the other hand, is to entertain *x* as an asserted thought. The idea here is that we can entertain thoughts or propositional contents – such as that Aurora is a great Indian painter – as either asserted or unasserted. To entertain a thought or a propositional content as unasserted is to imagine it in the sense of the *suppositional imagination*. And it is suppositional imagining that is pertinent to the analysis of fiction advanced above.

Fictions, then, in this sense are communications that authors intend the audience to imagine on the grounds that the audience recognizes that this is what the author intends them to do. That is, in making fictions, authors are intentionally presenting audiences with situations (or situation-types) that we are meant to entertain in thought.[18] The author, in presenting a novel as a fiction, in effect signals to the reader 'I intend you to hold these propositions (*p*) before your mind unasserted' – that is, 'suppose *p*', or 'entertain *p* unasserted', or 'contemplate *p* as a supposition'.

Of course, it needs to be added that when an author invites you to imagine the propositional content of a story, he is not providing you with a *carte blanche* to imagine whatever you wish. He is inviting you to imagine *his* story – its propositional content, including what it presupposes and implies. The audience's suppositional imagination is to be controlled imagining, normatively speaking. That is, it is supposed or meant to be constrained by what the author mandates by way of presenting his text. The details of the text control what it is legitimate for the audience to imagine in response to the author's fictive intention.

With this conception of the imagination under our belt, we can say that a structure of sense-bearing signs *x* by sender *s* is fictional only if *s* presents *x* to an audience *a* with the intention that *a* suppositionally imagine the propositional content of *x* for the reason that *a* recognizes this as *s*'s intention. This is the core of our proposal of what it is for a text – filmic or otherwise – to be fictional. It constitutes a necessary condition for fictionality, though further conditions would have to be added to bring the formula to sufficiency.[19]

Moreover, once we have the crucial defining condition of fiction in our possession, the formula for non-fiction is also within our reach. We can generate it by negating the core defining feature of fiction. So, a structure of sense-bearing signs *x* is non-fictional only if sender *s* presents it to audience *a* with the intention that *a* not suppositionally imagine *x* as a result of *a*'s grasp of *s*'s intention. That is, a non-fiction *x* is such that it is presented by an author to an audience with the intention that the audience recognize that it, the audience, is *not* mandated to entertain the propositional content of the relevant structure of sense-bearing signs as unasserted. This, of course, is only an essential, defining, necessary condition of non-fiction; the complete formula would have to be more complicated.[20]

Inasmuch as this account of non-fiction is simply a negation of the core defining feature of fiction, it encompasses a great many structures of sense-bearing signs, indeed it includes any structure of sense-bearing signs that is not a fiction. Any film, for example, that does not authorially prescribe that viewers entertain its propositional content as unasserted falls into this category. And that will incorporate not only films that mandate that their propositional content be entertained as asserted, but also films that lie outside the assertion game, like Kubelka's *Arnulf Rainer* or Gehr's *Serene Velocity*.

But *Serene Velocity*, I submit, does not tell us anything about how we are to entertain the shots of the hallway that comprise it. Are we to imagine there is such a hallway, or are we to believe it? It really makes no difference to the effect of the film one way or another.[21] It does not mandate that we entertain as unasserted the thought that there is such and such a hallway, since the film-maker is neutral or perhaps indifferent to how the images of the hallway are to be entertained by us. Thus, it is non-fiction, since, for the reasons given, it does not mandate that we imagine that there is such a hallway. The shots of the hallway function purely as stimuli. So *Serene Velocity* is *not* fiction. But as

Noël Carroll

I claimed earlier, *Serene Velocity* is not at the same time the sort of film that people in the field of the so-called documentary film have in mind. We need a more fine-grained concept than non-fiction in order to capture that narrower extension of films.

3 Films of Presumptive Assertion

Against 'deconstructionists', we have introduced a principled distinction between fiction and non-fiction. However, as we have seen, the concept of non-fiction that we have defined is broader than what we need for film studies. Nevertheless, I think that we can locate a category, suitable to the purposes of film studies, which is a subcategory of the preceding concept of non-fiction.

We derived our concept of non-fiction by negating the fictive stance component of our concept of fiction. In effect, we characterized non-fiction as the logical contradictory of fiction – that the audience *not* entertain as unasserted the propositional content of the structure of sense-bearing signs in question. That is, the non-fictive stance involves not imagining the propositional content of the text, or, summarily: non-fiction = not the fictive stance. So, we might generate a narrower concept than non-fiction by producing the logical contrary of the fictive stance.

The fictive stance involves entertaining as unasserted the propositional content of the text. An alternative, logically contrary stance, then, is that the audience entertain as asserted the propositional content of the text. In plain English, the mandated audience response to fiction is that the audience imagine the propositional content of the text. An alternative audience attitude is mandated when the author intends the audience to believe the content of the text.

Our concept of non-fiction was essentially negative. It was based on specifying what the author intended the audience to refrain from doing, namely, imagining the propositional content of the text. Our present suggestion is a positive characterization. It specifies what the author intends the audience to do with the propositional content of the pertinent structure of sense-bearing signs. To wit: we are to entertain the propositional content of the relevant structure as asserted thought. This characterization is key to defining the film of presumptive assertion.[22]

With the film of presumptive assertion the film-maker intends that the audience entertain the propositional content of his film in thought as asserted. Thus, in the CBS *Twentieth Century* instalment entitled *Born to Kill*, the audience is not only mandated *not* to imagine that Jeffrey Dahmer and Ted Bundy were found guilty, but, in addition, the film-makers prescribe that the audience should entertain this proposition in thought as asserted. We might say that in contrast to the case of fiction, the sender of a structure of sense-bearing signs of this sort possesses an assertoric intention which prescribes that the audience adopt an assertoric stance toward the propositional content of the text on the basis of their recognition that this is what the sender intends them to do.

This is a necessary condition for the species of cinema that I am calling films of presumptive assertion. I call them films of *presumptive* assertion not only because the audience presumes that it is to entertain the propositional content of such a film as asserted, but also because such films may lie. That is, they are presumed to involve assertion even in cases where the film-maker is intentionally dissimulating at the same time that he is signalling an assertoric intention. Moreover, in light of this presumption, the films in question are assessed in terms of the standard conditions for non-defective assertion, including: that the film-maker is committed to the truth (or plausibility, as the case may be) of the propositions the film expresses *and* that the propositions expressed in the film are beholden to the standards of evidence and reasoning appropriate to the truth (or plausibility) claims that the film advances.[23]

In the case of the film of presumptive fact, the film-maker presents the film with an assertoric intention: with the intention that the viewer entertain the propositional content of the film as asserted. In order for the film-maker's assertoric intention to be non-defective, the film-maker is committed to the truth or plausibility of the propositional content of the film and to being responsible to the standards of evidence and reason required to ground the truth or plausibility of the propositional content the film-maker presents.

Recognizing the film-maker's assertoric intention, the audience entertains the propositional content of the film as asserted thought. This means that the audience regards the propositional content of the film as something that the author believes to be true, or, in certain circumstances, that the author believes is plausible, and as something that is committed to the relevant standards of evidence and reason for the type of subject-matter

162

being communicated. If the audience believes that the film-maker does not believe the propositional content of the film, despite the fact that the film-maker signals an assertoric intention, they suspect that the film-maker is lying. If the audience member thinks that the film is not committed to the relevant standards of evidence, he suspects that the film is apt to be mistaken, and, in any case, that it is objectively unjustified. Such audience expectations are part of what it is to take the assertoric stance – to entertain the propositional content of the film in thought as asserted.

sharpest definition → Stated compactly, then, a crucial, defining condition of the film of presumptive assertion is that it involves an assertoric intention on the part of a film-maker that the audience adopt an assertoric stance to the propositional content of the film, where the audience adopts this stance on the basis of its recognition of the film-maker's assertoric intention. This gives us the core ingredients of the film of presumptive assertion. However, more is required to define the film of presumptive assertion completely. For not only does the audience have to discern and respond to the film-maker's assertoric intentions. It must also grasp the meanings communicated by the film. That is, the maker of a film of presumptive assertion not only intends that the audience adopt the assertoric stance to his film, but he also intends that the audience understand his film. So a complete definition of the film of presumptive assertion involves not only an assertoric intention on the part of the film-maker, but a meaning-intention as well.

In order to accommodate this requirement, let us adopt a Gricean account of what is involved when an utterer means something by x. Let us say that 'a sender means something by x' is roughly equivalent to 'the sender intends the presentation of x to produce some effect in an audience by means of this intention'.[24] Applying this pattern, then, to the film of presumptive assertion, I contend that:

x is a film of presumptive assertion if and only if the film-maker s presents x to an audience a with the intention (1) that a recognizes that x is intended by s to mean that p (some propositional content), (2) that a recognize that s intends them (a) to entertain p as an asserted thought (or as a set of asserted thoughts), (3) that a entertains p as asserted thought, and (4) that 2 is a reason for 3.[25]

Or to put the matter more succinctly, something is a film of presumptive assertion if and only if it involves a meaning intention on the part of the film-maker which provides a basis for meaning pick-up on the part of the audience as well as an assertoric intention on the part of the film-maker which provides the grounds for the adoption of the assertoric stance on the part of the audience.[26]

In order to appreciate what is involved in this theory of the film of presumptive assertion, it is instructive to compare it to an alternative theory of the way in which we might characterize the so-called 'documentary' film. Using the intention-response model, we might hypothesize a category which can be called 'the film of the presumptive trace'. On this account, the relevant structure of sense-bearing signs is such that the film-maker intends that the audience regard the images in the films as historic traces as a consequence of the audience's recognition that that is what the film-maker intends them to do. Regarding the images as historic traces, in turn, involves entertaining the thought as asserted that the images in the film have originated photographically from precisely the source from which the film claims or implies they originated. Nevertheless, these are called 'films of the *presumptive* trace', since, of course, the film-maker may be dissimulating.

In a fiction film, we see an image of a house and we imagine that it is Tara, the home of Scarlet O'Hara. In the case of the film of the presumptive trace, when we see an image of a tree and we are told something about trees in the Amazon rainforest, we entertain as asserted – so the theory of the film of the presumptive trace goes – that the image of the tree we are seeing is the photographic trace of some tree in the Amazon rainforest. We do not regard the image as the historic trace of some tree in a botanical garden in Brooklyn. We regard it as the historic trace of some tree in the Amazon; nor do we use the image to imagine that there is such a tree. We take the image as having been produced by a camera aimed at a specific tree in the Amazon rainforest.

Moreover, we regard the image in this way because we recognize that the film-maker intends us to regard the image of the tree as an authentic historic trace. In effect, we recognize that the film-maker intends that we regard as asserted the proposition that this image of a tree was photographically produced by some actually existing tree which does or did luxuriate in the Amazon rainforest.

compared to overlay "downplay"

Traces

Noël Carroll

The concept of the film of the presumptive trace is different from that of the film of presumptive assertion. The film of presumptive assertion, for the most part, is broader, since it refers to works where the film-maker possesses any sort of assertoric intention, whereas the film of the presumptive trace refers only to films where the makers have a very particular assertoric intention, namely, that the images be entertained in asserted thought as being historic traces. The notion of films of the presumptive trace captures the 'document' dimension that many associate with the so-called documentary film. One might even regard it as deriving inspiration from the *actualité*. Films of presumptive assertion, on the other hand, not only include *actualités*, but any film made with an assertoric intention, including an animated simulation of the trajectory of a satellite.

Given these two contrasting concepts, the question arises which one we should prefer? Both seem perfectly intelligible. Is one more attractive than the other? Needless to say, in order to answer this, we have to consider the use we wish the concept to serve. If we wish to define the *actualité*, the notion of the film of the presumptive trace does a better – more precise – job of tracking the phenomenon. However, if we want to capture what film scholars generally have in mind when they talk about documentaries or non-fiction films, I think that the notion of the film of presumptive assertion is superior. The reason for this is that scholars in this field have always talked about films where the audience was clearly not intended to regard every shot as the historic trace of its subject.

Consider, for example, the History Channel's film *Nautilus*. Quite clearly not all of the images are historic traces, nor are they intended to be taken as such. In the first part of the film, there is a discussion of nineteenth-century submarines. As the narrator discusses a progression of these early submersibles, we see outline drawings of them superimposed over water; we also see a model of Fulton's submarine, in living colour, likewise superimposed over water. These are not historic traces of antique submersibles, nor are they intended to be so taken. The audience realizes that they are merely illustrations of them. Audience members understand that they are being shown these images in order to gain a sense of what these contraptions looked like.

Similarly, when the narrator of *Nautilus* recounts the sinking of the cruiser HMS *Cressy* by a German U-boat in the First World War, we are shown a shot in colour – of palpably contemporary origin – of a sailor's cap floating to the bottom of Davy Jones's locker. Later, when we are told that a U-boat sank a merchant ship, we see another colour shot, this time of a life-preserver labelled *Falada*, the name of the doomed ship. But the audience does not take these shots as historical documents.

Nautilus is clearly what scholars, and film distributors, are prone to label a 'documentary', but its makers do not intend that the aforesaid shots be regarded as historic traces of the naval engagements in question. The audience understands that they are at best factually based illustrations of something that plausibly happened when, respectively, the *Cressy* and the *Falada* sunk. What the audience is intended to entertain in thought as asserted is simply that the *Cressy* and the *Falada* were torpedoed with lethal effect.

Throughout *Nautilus*, we are shown maps sketching the journeys of various submarines. The audience correctly regards these as informational, but nothing indicates that one is to take these shots as historic traces of actual submariners plotting their courses on authentic naval charts. Moreover, the film has some re-enactments, in colour footage, of what was involved in life in the close quarters of a U-boat. The audience understands that this is not actual archival footage, but only presumptively accurate visual information bringing home concretely to the viewers what the narrator means when he tells them how very cramped the space in a vintage submarine was.

I submit that *Nautilus* is a film that falls into the category that everyone in the field of the so-called documentary wants to talk about. But if we are employing the notion of the film of the presumptive trace to model that category, *Nautilus* would be excluded.[27] Of course, the issue is not simply whether *Nautilus* should be included. Rather, the point is that the techniques to which we have drawn attention in *Nautilus* are pretty common in the so-called documentary film. Thus, if we are trying to capture conceptually what people generally mean by 'documentary' today, then the film of the presumptive trace is too narrow a concept.

The concept of the film of presumptive assertion is a better idea. For it allows that the films in question can involve re-enactment, animation, the use of stock footage, and the like. In fact, a film of presumptive assertion could be comprised completely of animation or computer-generated imagery. For the notion of the film of presumptive assertion merely requires that the structure of sense-bearing be presented with the assertoric authorial intention that we entertain the propositional content of the film as asserted thought. It does not require that we regard the images as authentic historic traces. The notion of the film of presumptive assertion countenances a state of the art, computer-generated programme on the life of dinosaurs as falling under its rubric, whereas it seems to me that such a programme could not be contained in the class of things denominated as films of the presumptive trace.

Unlike Grierson's notion of the documentary, the concept of the film of presumptive assertion encompasses the *actualité*. But in contrast to the concept of the film of the presumptive trace, it also covers much more. It includes every sort of film of putative fact, irrespective of whether those facts are advanced by means of authentic archival footage or by other means. And in so far as it captures this wider domain, it better suits the purposes of film scholars, film-makers, film distributors, and the general public than does the idea of the film of the presumptive trace.

4   Some Objections

In developing the concept of both the film of presumptive assertion and the film of the presumptive trace, I have taken advantage of the intention-response model of communication. Both concepts require that the audience recognize a certain intention of the film-maker. However, many film scholars are apt to reject this type of theorizing, since, like their confrères in other humanities departments, they do not believe that we can have access to authorial intentions, and, therefore, they do not believe that theories of this sort are practicable.

Perhaps the very first thing to say in response to this objection is that it misses the point, since the theory of the film of presumptive assertion is an ontological theory – a characterization of the nature of a certain type of film – and not an epistemological theory about the way in which to identify such films. However, having said that, let me also add that I do not believe that the theory would be impracticable if used to distinguish different sorts of film. And so even though the objection misses the mark, I will attempt to show that the allegation of impracticability is also mistaken.

If film scholars think that the concept of the film of presumptive assertion is compromised because they presuppose that intentions are always unfathomable, then they need to be reminded that we constantly attribute intentions to others with an astoundingly high degree of success. When someone holds a door open, I take this as a signal of their intention that I walk through it. And most of the time when I make this inference, I am not mistaken. When someone at the dinner table hands me a plate of potatoes. I infer that they intend that it is my turn to take some potatoes. And again I am almost always correct in this. Likewise, when the notice comes from the electrical company, I always recognize that they intend me to pay my bill. And every time I pay my bill in response, it turns out that I was right. Or, at least, they never send my cheque back.

Social life could not flourish if we were not able to discern the intentions of others. We could not understand the behaviour or the words and deeds of others if we could not successfully attribute intentions to them. This is not to say that we never make mistaken attributions of intentions to others. But we are all more successful in this matter than we are unsuccessful.

Consequently, the film scholar who is sceptical of the practicability of the category of the film of presumptive assertion on the grounds that we are incapable of correctly attributing intentions to others, including film-makers, is immensely unconvincing. We do not typically have any principled problems in discerning the intentions of others. The social fabric could not cohere, unless we were *generally* successful in attributing intentions to others. The social fabric does cohere because we are so adept at discerning the intentions of others, including even film-makers. There are no grounds for thinking that, in principle, the intentions of others are unfathomable. For in fact, they are not.

Moreover, our ability to attribute intentions to others successfully is not restricted to living people. Historians scrutinize the words and deeds of the dead with an eye to determining their intentions. And there is no reason to suppose that they do not often do so successfully. Are historians wrong when they hypothesize that by early 1941 Hitler intended to invade the Soviet Union, or that in 1959 Kennedy intended to run for the presidency? Perhaps Hitler and JFK took some of their intentions to the grave with them. But some of their intentions are certainly accessible to historians. Not all the intentions of historical agents, including film-makers, are ontologically obscure. Historians, including film historians, confront no unscalable barriers when it comes to surmising the intentions of past persons.

Scholars in film studies and the humanities in general distrust talk of authorial intentions because they believe that powerful arguments with names like the 'intentional fallacy' and 'the death of the author' have demonstrated that authorial intentions either are inaccessible or should be treated as such. These arguments are inconclusive, and I, and others, have attempted to show at length why they are mistaken.[28] However, rather than enter that debate once again, let me now point out that even if the preceding arguments were uncontroversial, they would still not provide grounds for scepticism with regard to the assertoric intentions required for films of presumptive assertion, since the intentional fallacy and the death of the author argument pertain to the interpretation of the meaning of texts,[29] not to their categorization. Thus these arguments, even if they were sound (which they are not) are irrelevant to the question at hand.

According to the intentional fallacy and the death of the author argument, invocation of authorial intention is either illicit, impossible, or impermissible when we are interpreting the meaning of a text. The meaning intentions of the author are, so to speak, out of bounds. But when presenting a work, meaning intentions are not the only intentions at issue. There are also what we might call *categorical intentions* – i.e. intentions about the category to which the relevant work belongs. And these are hardly inscrutable in the way that friends of the intentional fallacy and the death of the author allege the meaning intentions of the author to be. Can anyone doubt that Stanley Kubrick intended *A Space Odyssey* to be regarded as at least belonging to the category of the science fiction film or that John Ford intended *My Darling Clementine* as a western? What grounds are there to suppose that these attributions of intention are mistaken? Surely the reasons for scepticism about the attribution of meaning intentions do not cut against such attributions of categorical intentions.[30] We might argue about the intended meaning of the Star Child in *A Space Odyssey*; but we do not think that the attribution of categorical intentions raises the same kind of epistemological problems. It would take something like the postulation of a Cartesian demon to be seriously sceptical

about the attribution of the preceding categorical intentions to Stanley Kubrick and John Ford.

The force of the intentional fallacy and the death of the author argument is that the reference to authorial meaning intentions is either irrelevant or prohibited when interpreting the meaning of a poem. But it is one thing to interpret a poem on the basis of a hypothesis of what an author intends to mean, and another thing to identify a poem on the basis of a hypothesis that poetry is the category in which the author intended to write. Indeed, it may be that in order to be agnostic about authorial meaning intentions even requires that an interpreter know (as he almost always does) that what he is dealing with is intended to be a poem and not a laundry list.

The relevance of this discussion of categorical intentions, I hope, is clear-cut. The assertoric intention of the maker of a film of presumptive assertion is a categorical intention. It is not, therefore, the kind of intention at which either the intentional fallacy or the death of the author argument is directed. Categorical intentions are at the very least more publicly determinable than meaning intentions are supposed to be according to proponents of the intentional fallacy and the death of the author argument. Personally, I do not believe that meaning intentions are as inaccessible as these fashionable arguments allege. But even if (*a big if*) meaning intentions were, that would provide no reason to be suspicious concerning the categorical assertoric intentions of the makers of films of presumptive fact.

Of course, this defence of the practicability of reference to the assertoric intentions of film-makers is rather abstract. It provides a very theoretical reassurance that the assertoric intention is not, in principle, inaccessible. But the conscientious film theorist will want to know in some detail how we go about recognizing the film-maker's assertoric intentions before he or she is willing to grant that my formula is feasible for identifying films of presumptive assertion. So how do we determine that the film-maker has the assertoric intention that we adopt the assertoric stance when we see a film?

Actually, the answer to this question is so obvious that only a film theorist could miss it. Films come labelled, or indexed, as to the type of films they are, and where these labels index the films as 'documentaries' or 'non-fiction films' the audience has access to information about the assertoric intentions of the film-maker.[31] The way in which a

[handwritten annotation at top of page: how could we decide if the film had no context at all.]

film is indexed is a perfectly public matter; there is nothing occult or obscure about it. We have access to the film-maker's assertoric intentions through many routes. There are press releases, advertisements, television interviews, film listings and TV listings, previews, critical reviews, and word of mouth. Moreover, information in the title cards of the film may also be relevant, as in the case of the *National Geographic Society Special – Rain Forest*.

Through many redundant, public channels of communication, the typical viewer knows the kind of film he is about to see. When one chooses to see a film, one generally knows that it is what is called a 'documentary' ahead of time because the film has been indexed and circulated that way. And knowing this much, the film viewer knows that he is intended by the film-maker to adopt what I have called the assertoric stance.

Of course, it is possible that while channel surfing we come across a film whose indexing is not already known to us. Perhaps we ask ourselves, what kind of film is this supposed to be? But we can figure this out pretty quickly – by fairly reliable inference if it is on the Discovery Channel or the History Channel, or, more directly, by looking it up in a TV guide. And we can also wait for the end credits which will generally reiterate information pertinent to indexing the film. Needless to say, we may also use the content, the look, or the sound of the film as evidence about the category to which the film belongs. And this generally works, but, for reasons discussed earlier, a conclusive determination hinges on ascertaining the film-maker's intention through indexing.

Another apparent problem case might be the situation of the film historian who discovers film footage in an archive and wonders what kind of film it is. He cannot be sure by just looking at the film. And let us suppose that the titles are missing. What is he to do? Well, probably what he will do is attempt to find some paper record of it. He will look at newspapers, film histories, memoirs, the records of distributors and film-makers, and the like to find a description of something like the footage he has discovered. He will attempt to identify the footage by appealing to historical data. And in searching for the identity of the film, he will also be searching for its indexing.

Historians have to evaluate, identify, and authenticate documents all the time. Very often they are successful in their endeavours. There is no principled reason to think that a film historian

searching for the indexing of a film need be any less successful than any other historian dealing with primary sources of uncertain origin.

Admittedly, it is logically possible that our film historian may never discover the way in which a given film was indexed. Thus, it may turn out that in such cases the assertoric intentions of the film-maker are lost to us forever. What would be the consequences of such cases for the theory of films of presumptive assertion? Not much. First of all, it would not compromise the theory as a definition of films of presumptive assertion because that is an ontological theory. Our inability to determine whether or not the film in question was a film of presumptive assertion would not challenge our claim that the film falls in that category just in case its makers were possessed by an assertoric intention. That we are uncertain of the relevant intention is compatible with the fact that the maker had an assertoric intention, but that we do not know it. The film is or is not a film of presumptive assertion, whether or not we know it is.

Moreover, the practicability of our formula is not unhorsed by the fact that sometimes our formula will leave us with undecidable cases. For, given the phenomenon of indexing, our definition will give us a *generally reliable* way of sorting films of presumptive assertion from other types of film. If there are some cases where there are empirical obstacles to applying the theory, then that does not show the theory is not generally practicable. The theory does not guarantee that we can ascertain with every case whether a given film is a film of presumptive assertion or not. But, nevertheless, it gives us the wherewithal to tell most of the time, and, more importantly, there are not principled reasons to suppose that the formula is not generally reliable. The only problems that may arise are with possible isolated cases where the record of the indexing of the film has been completely obliterated. But this is not likely to occur very often.[32]

In general, then, by virtue of the way a film of presumptive assertion is indexed we recognize the maker's assertoric intention that we entertain the propositional content of the film as asserted thought on the basis of his intention. Thus, when I go into a Blockbuster video outlet and peruse a cassette of *Reptiles and Amphibians*, by Walon Green and Heinz Sielmann, I recognize that it is intended to be a film of presumptive assertion, not only because it is in the section labelled 'documentary', but because the information on the sleeve of the cassette iterates this indexing. Moreover, when

I put it in my VCR, the title cards indicate that it is a National Geographic Society presentation. As a result, I know that, *ceteris paribus*, the film-makers intend that I entertain the propositional content of *Reptiles and Amphibians* as asserted thought.

Thus, when the film shows and/or tells me that the vine snake of south-east Asia lives in trees, that the Komodo dragon is really a monitor lizard and that it sometimes eats small goats, that the sea snake's venom is the most toxic, and that, before engaging in ritual mating combat, male tortoises bob their heads, I entertain these propositions as asserted thought, I presume that Walon Green and Heinz Sielmann believe these things to be true, and that they are committed to the probity of these propositions in accordance with the canons of evidence and reason-giving appropriate to this type of information.

Were I to learn that Green and Sielmann did not believe that these things were true, I would accuse them of lying, even if, unbeknownst to them, these things were actually true. Moreover, if the film-makers were not committed to the appropriate canons of evidence and reason-giving – if they came up with all this stuff about reptiles and lizards by reading tea-leaves – I would have grounds for criticizing the film as a nature film of presumptive assertion. Likewise, the fact that *Roger and Me* knowingly plays fast and loose with the evidence is a bad-making feature of that film, just as if it knowingly advanced propositions that could not be supported by the relevant canons of evidence and reason-giving.

That films of presumptive assertion are beholden to the interpersonal canons of evidence and reason-giving appropriate to the kind of information they convey entails that such films are committed to objectivity. This, of course, does not mean that all, or even most, films of presumptive fact are objective, but only that they are committed to it, which, in turn, entails that their failure to respect the requirements of objectivity provides us with reasons to criticize them *qua* films of presumptive assertion. We may have further reasons to commend such a film – perhaps, its editing is bravura. Nevertheless, the failure to meet its commitment to objectivity, entailed by the assertoric intention that we take an assertoric stance toward it, is always *a* bad-making feature of a film of presumptive assertion, even if, in addition, the film possesses other good-making features. A film of presumptive assertion that fails to meet our expectations with respect to objectivity,

which are based on our recognition of the film-maker's assertoric intention that we adopt the assertoric stance, can never receive anything but a mixed critical verdict. If *Roger and Me* is acclaimed as effective anti-capitalist propaganda, outrageous street theatre, or comic high jinks, it should also at the same time be criticized for its failure to respect the evidentiary record.

Of course, in arguing that according to the theory of films of presumptive assertion such films are necessarily committed to objectivity, I am courting rebuke by film scholars. For they believe that it has been conclusively demonstrated that objectivity is impossible in the sort of films I am talking about. Thus, if I maintain that such films are necessarily committed to objectivity, they are likely to respond that, inasmuch as 'should implies can', there is something profoundly wrong with my theory. That is, I contend that makers of films of presumptive assertion, in virtue of their assertoric intention and what it entails, should abide by canons of objectivity. But film scholars are apt to counter that this must be wrong because it is well known that such films necessarily cannot be objective.

Of course, I disagree with this presupposition, and I have argued at great length against it elsewhere.[33] It is not true that such films necessarily always fall short of objectivity because they are selective – a popular argument among film theorists – since selectivity is an essential, non-controversial feature of all sorts of enterprises, such as sociology, physics, biology, history, and even journalistic reportage. Thus, if selectivity presents no special problem for the objectivity of these areas of enquiry, then it is not an a priori problem for makers of films of presumptive fact either. Film-makers, like physicists and historians, may fail to meet their commitments to objectivity. But where that happens it is a matter of individual shortcomings and not of the very nature of things.

Moreover, postmodern theorists who contend that objectivity is impossible in the film of presumptive assertion because it is impossible to achieve in any form of enquiry or discourse champion a position that is inevitably self-refuting. For such theorists act as if they are presenting us with objective reasons that support the truth or the plausibility of their conjectures about knowledge claims in general. But how is that possible if the notion of objective reasons is to be regarded with suspicion? For if all reasons fail to be objective that includes their reasons. So why are they advancing them as objective reasons, and why should anyone believe them?

Likely grounds for rejecting the theory of films of presumptive assertion involve scepticism about the accessibility of authorial intentions and scepticism about the prospects for objectivity. In this section, I have tried to undermine both these anxieties. If my efforts in this regard have been successful, then the theory of films of presumptive assertion is provisionally creditable, and the burden of proof falls on the sceptics to show otherwise.

5 Conclusion

In this chapter I have advanced a theory of what I call films of presumptive assertion. It is my claim that this concept captures what people mean to talk about when they speak informally of 'documentaries' and 'non-fiction films'. Whether the theory is successful depends, in part, on how well it picks out the extension of films we have in mind when we use terms like 'documentary'. Undoubtedly, it is up to the reader to see how well my theory tracks usage.

I began developing this theory with the presumption that there is a real distinction in this neighbourhood. I tried to defend this presumption by (1) criticizing the plausibility of 'deconstructionist' arguments to the contrary, and (2) showing that we could develop persuasive theories of fiction, non-fiction, and films of presumptive assertion by employing the intention-response model of communication. In effect, my argument is transcendental in nature. I take it, after clearing away various sceptical arguments, that there are genuine distinctions here to be drawn and then I propose candidates for what I argue are the best ways of making those distinctions. Thus, at this point in the debate, it is up to others (such as the 'deconstructionists') to show either that my distinctions are flawed (logically, empirically, or pragmatically), or that there are better ways of drawing the distinction than mine. Until that time, I propose that what has heretofore been regarded as documentary film in common, contemporary parlance be reconceived in terms of films of presumptive assertion.

Of course, 'films of presumptive assertion' is quite a mouthful. And it does not have a nice ring to it. So, I am not suggesting that we attempt to make ordinary folk replace 'documentary' with this cumbersome locution. We would not succeed, even if we tried. Rather, I am suggesting that for technical or theoretical purposes, we understand that what is typically meant by saying that a film is a 'documentary' is really that it is 'a film of presumptive assertion', unless we have grounds for thinking that the speaker is using the term in the Griersonian sense. The reform I am suggesting is not primarily a linguistic reform, but a theoretical one. Moreover, if other film theorists think that this reform is ill advised, it is up to them to say why.

Notes

1 Though I constantly refer to film in this chapter, this is really a *façon de parler*. For I also mean to be talking about TV, videotapes, and computer imaging. A more accurate way to talk about the extension of visual media I have in mind would be to speak of *moving images*. But that would not only be cumbersome and perhaps confusing. It would also add even more jargon to an essay that already uses quite enough. Nevertheless, when I refer to film in general in this chapter, it should be understood as referring to moving images of all sorts including TV, video, and CD-ROM. For an account of what I mean by *moving images*, see Noël Carroll, 'Defining the Moving Image', in *Theorizing the Moving Image* (New York: Cambridge University Press, 1996) [see also this volume, ch. 9].

2 According to Chuck Wolfe, by way of Carl Plantinga, the term *documentaire* was widely used in France in the 1920s before Grierson used its English translation to refer to *Moana*.

3 Paul Rotha, *Documentary Film*, 2nd edn. (London: Faber, 1952), 70. This book was originally published in 1935.

4 Brian Winston, *Claiming the Real* (London: British Film Institute, 1995).

5 Showing just this was a pressing issue for early filmmakers and film theoreticians. For an account of this ambition, see Noël Carroll, *Philosophical Problems of Classical Film Theory* (Princeton: Princeton University Press, 1988), ch. I.

6 Throughout this chapter, I have placed terms like 'deconstructed' and 'deconstructionists' in scare quotation marks in order to signal my recognition that some may charge that what I refer to is not strictly Derridean deconstruction. I call the practitioners

I have in mind 'deconstructionists' because they wish to erase the distinction between fiction and non-fiction. However, in dismissing this distinction in favour of calling everything 'fiction', these practitioners might be accused by Derrideans of *privileging* fiction.

7   Christian Metz, 'The Imaginary Signifier', *Screen*, 16: 2 (Summer 1975), 47.

8   Michael Renov suggests an argument like this one – among other arguments – in 'Introduction: The Truth about Non-fiction', in his anthology *Theorizing Documentary* (New York: Routledge, 1993). For criticism of Renov's overall position, see Noël Carroll, 'Nonfiction Film and Postmodern Skepticism', in David Bordwell and Noël Carroll (eds.), *Post-Theory: Reconstructing Film Studies* (Madison: University of Wisconsin Press, 1996).

9   Other evidence that we would look for might include the search for mention of this work by historical commentators who might identify it one way or the other, or, at least, suggest the appropriate identification, given information about the context of the work (in terms of its production and/or reception).

10 It also pays to note that there is a second logical error in their argument. For even if it were demonstrated that there is no differentia between fiction and non-fiction films, it would not follow that all films are fictional.

11 Trevor Ponech explores a similar line of argumentation in 'What is Non-Fiction Cinema?' in Richard Allen and Murray Smith (eds.), *Film Theory and Philosophy* (New York: Oxford University Press, 1997).

12 This view of the nature of philosophical problems is defended by Arthur Danto in his book *Connections to the World* (New York: Harper & Row, 1989).

13 Examples of the intention-response model with respect to art theory include: Monroe Beardsley, 'An Aesthetic Definition of Art', in Hugh Curtler (ed.), *What Is Art?* (New York: Haven 1983), and Jerrold Levinson, 'Defining Art Historically', in his *Music, Art, and Metaphysics* (Ithaca, NY: Cornell University Press, 1990). Examples of the intention-response model with respect to fiction include: Gregory Currie, *The Nature of Fiction* (Cambridge: Cambridge University Press, 1990), and Peter Lamarque and Stein Haugom Olsen, *Truth, Fiction and Literature* (Oxford: Clarendon Press, 1994).

14 The notion of a 'fictive intention' derives from Currie's *The Nature of Fiction*. 'Fictive stance' is used both in Currie's book and by Lamarque and Olsen in *Truth, Fiction and Literature*.

15 I use the notion of propositional content in its technical sense. It does not refer narrowly to sentences. Propositional content is what is conveyed by a structure of sense-bearing signs, where the sense-bearing signs need not be restricted to sentences of natural or formal languages.

16 It seems to me that a move like this, which film 'deconstructionists' might attempt to emulate, is made by Paul Ricœur in his 'The Interweaving of History and Fiction'. However, I think that this move is mistaken because Ricœur is trading on the notion of what I call the 'constructive imagination', whereas I maintain that the relevant sense of the imagination for this argument should be what I call the 'suppositional imagination'. See Paul Ricœur, *Time and Narrative*, vol. iii (Chicago: University of Chicago Press, 1985), 180–92.

17 In this I disagree with Kendall Walton, who employs the notion of make-believe. Walton and I might appear to be in agreement, since we both think that fiction involves mandating that the audience imagine. But we have different concepts of imagination. Mine is the suppositional imagination, whereas Walton thinks of the relevant function of the imagination in terms of make-believe. For some of my objections to Walton's notion of make-believe, see Noël Carroll, 'The Paradox of Suspense', in P. Vorderer, M. Wulff, and M. Friedrichsen (eds.), *Suspense: Conceptualizations, Theoretical Analyses and Empirical Explorations* (Mahwah, NJ: Lawrence Erlbaum, 1996), 88; id., 'Critical Study: Kendall L Walton, Mimesis as Make-Believe', *Philosophical Quarterly*, 45: 178 (Jan. 1995), 93–9; and id., 'On Kendall Walton's *Mimesis as Make-Believe*', *Philosophy and Phenomenological Research*, 51: 2 (June 1991), 383–7. Walton's view is stated most elaborately in his book *Mimesis as Make-Believe: On the Foundations of the Representational Arts* (Cambridge, Mass.: Harvard University Press, 1990).

18 Kendall Walton objects to the assimilation of the imagination to the notion of 'entertaining thoughts'. He contends that entertaining thoughts restricts us to occurrent imaginings, whereas in order to follow a narrative fiction the non-occurrent imagination must be employed as well in order to deal with such things as the presuppositions and implications of the fiction. But I worry that this is a matter of quibbling over words. For if I ask you to entertain the thought (unasserted) that Taras Bulba is a man, then, *ceteris paribus*, I am also asking you implicitly to entertain all the presuppositions and implications of that thought. I am asking you to entertain the propositions (unasserted) that he has a heart, a circulatory system, that he requires oxygen, and so on. *Pace* Walton, not everything that you are invited to suppose and that you implicitly suppose need be in the spotlight of the theatre of the mind.

19 One reason that this analysis requires more conditions is because, as stated, nothing has been said about the audience's understanding of the meaning of the structured, sense-bearing signs in question. Thus, a fuller account that takes heed of this would be:

A structure of sense-bearing signs x by sender s is fictional if and only if s presents x to audience a with the intention (1) that a recognize that x is intended by s to mean p (a certain propositional content), (2) that a recognize that s intends a to suppositionally imagine p, (3) that a suppositionally imagine that p, and (4) that 2 is the reason for 3.

Undoubtedly this analysis could be further refined. For example, see Currie's *Nature of Fiction*, 33. Though Currie and I disagree on some important points, the structure of my analysis was inspired by his.

20 The complications derive from the same considerations found in the preceding note. A more complete definition of non-fiction would look like this:

A structure of sense-bearing signs x is non-fictional if and only if x is presented by sender s to audience a where s intends (1) that a recognize that x is intended by s to mean p, (2) that a recognize that s intends them not to entertain the propositional content of p as unasserted, (3) that a does not entertain p as unasserted, (4) that s intends that 2 will be one of a's reasons for 3.

21 I would not wish to deny that *Serene Velocity* might be involved in providing something like an object lesson concerning the impression of movement in film. But it is not material to that object lesson whether the images of the hallway be entertained by way of the suppositional imagination or belief. The object lesson will obtain either way. Thus, since Gehr does not prescribe that we entertain the propositional content of his shots – that here is a hallway – as unasserted, *Serene Velocity* is not a fiction; therefore, it is non-fiction.

22 Though from here on I talk about the film of presumptive assertion, it should be clear that the analysis could be applied more broadly to what we might call either 'texts of presumptive assertion' – like history books or newspaper articles – or what we might call, even more commodiously, 'structures of sense-bearing signs of presumptive assertion'.

23 For a discussion of assertion, see John Searle, *Expression and Meaning: Studies in the Theory of Speech Acts* (Cambridge: Cambridge University Press, 1979), 62.

24 This is the Gricean way of putting it, but, as Richard Allen points out, the relevant effects that the reader should have in mind here are what might be called 'meaning effects'.

25 I say *a* reason here because there may be other reasons as well having to do with the verisimilitude of the image.

26 This analysis shares a number of points with the one proposed by Carl Plantinga in his article 'Defining

Documentary: Fiction, Non-fiction, and Projected Worlds', *Persistence of Vision*, 5 (Spring 1987), 44–54. I suspect that, despite the difference in language, our theories are compatible. Plantinga expands on his view in *Rhetoric and Representation in Non-fiction Film* (New York: Cambridge University Press, 1997).

27 Perhaps the defender of the notion of the film of the presumptive trace would deny this, claiming that the makers of the film intend the audience to regard all the footage in the film as historic, but that, in addition, they are lying. I, however, can find no grounds to suppose that the film-makers are trying to mislead the audience about the provenance of the footage described above.

28 See Noël Carroll, 'Art, Intention, and Conversation', in Gary Iseminger (ed.), *Intention and Interpretation* (Philadelphia: Temple University Press, 1992); id., 'Anglo-American Aesthetics and Contemporary Criticism: Intention and the Hermeneutics of Suspicion', *Journal of Aesthetics and Art Criticism*, 51: 2 (Spring 1993).

29 Of course, the intentional fallacy also pertains to the evaluation of texts. But, once again, evaluation is not categorization.

30 Interestingly, Monroe Beardsley, one of the leading progenitors of the intentional fallacy, uses the intention-response model in order to present his theory of art. He, at least, thinks that reference to an artist's categorical intentions is not problematic, while also arguing that reference to an artist's meaning intentions falls foul of the intentional fallacy. He believes that being open to categorical intentions while rejecting meaning intentions is logically consistent, and this leads him to a mixed view – accepting the invocation of authorial intentions for the purpose of categorizing a work, but disallowing it in the interpretation of a work. See Beardsley, 'An Aesthetic Definition of Art'.

31 Indexing is discussed in Noël Carroll, 'From Real to Reel: Entangled in Nonfiction Film', in *Theorizing the Moving Image*.

32 The reader may wonder about a case where a film-maker dissimulates by presenting cooked-up footage, but indexes the film as a documentary. My view is that we regard it as presented with an assertoric intention, since the film-maker has prescribed that the audience entertain its propositional content as asserted thought. It does not become a fiction film because the film-maker has counterfeited the footage. It is still a film of presumptive assertion. But it is a *bad* film of presumptive assertion because the film-maker has failed to live up to his commitments to the standards of evidence and reasoning appropriate to the subject-matter of the film.

33 See Carroll, 'From Real to Reel: Entangled in Nonfiction Fiction Film', and 'Postmodern Skepticism and the Nonfiction Film'.

PART IV

Film Narrative/Narration

Introduction

Most of the films that most people see most of the time are narrative films. Probably even most of the documentaries that people watch are narratives. And, of course, most people most likely consume more fiction films than they do documentaries, and fiction films are, of course, narrative. Though cinema and narrative are not necessarily conjoined, they are so often enough that narrative is an unavoidable concept for the practice of film, and, therefore, it is a predictable topic for the philosophy of film.

Since narration entails a narrator, one question that arises for the philosopher of film concerns the nature of that narrator. This might seem peculiar to you. The answer may seem obvious: the narrator is the filmmaker or filmmakers who have constructed the narration. If we are talking about the silent film *Our Hospitality*, then the narrator is Buster Keaton. Who else would it be?

However, some philosophers suspect that this response is too hasty. They think that things are more complicated. George M. Wilson's article "*Le Grand Imagier* Steps Out: The Primitive Basis of Film Narration" adroitly reviews some of these complications and also proposes a rather surprising suggestion about the nature of film narration.

In the discussion of literature, frequently distinctions are drawn between the actual author, an implied author, and a narrator. The actual author is someone whose hand you can shake, if she is still alive. The implied author is the author as he or she manifests herself in the text. The implied author may be a manifestation of the actual author with all her beliefs, desires, attitudes, allegiances, and commitments intact, or the implied author may be a persona that the actual author takes on – that is,

she may pose as a cynic, whereas the actual author is really a romantic. Cynicism is merely a mask she puts on for the story. In any event, the implied author is the agent who is responsible for the way the fiction is written – its structures, emphases, etc. *qua* fiction.

But in addition to the actual and implied authors of a literary text, there are also what may be called narrators. These are fictional creatures. They are part of the fictional world presented by the text. Indeed, they are the fictional presenters of the text. Such narrators can be explicit, as is the case with *Wuthering Heights*, where a named character tells the story. Similarly, Watson is the explicit narrator of the Sherlock Holmes stories, Gulliver of his travels, Ishmael of *Moby Dick*, and Roger Ackroyd of the novel of the same name. These figures are all explicitly introduced narrators of the fictions we read. It is fictional in the stories they inhabit that they are presenting the story, telling the tale.

But, as well as *explicit* fictional narrators, some literary theorists hold that there are also implicit narrators, fictional beings who, as it were, are responsible for the tale being told as it is. Why believe this? A fiction is something that we are mandated to imagine. We are mandated to imagine the events in the fiction as true – as obtaining, that is, in the world of the fiction. Where an explicit fictional character is telling the tale, we imagine that what is reported is true (in the world of the fiction). But where there is no explicit character in view, isn't there still some agency in the fictional world who is reporting the events of the narrative to be true? Remember: no narrative without a narrator. Putatively, the actual author is not telling us that the content of his fiction is true; the actual author typically includes a disclaimer in the front of his book that states that none of the characters or events is intended to correspond with existing ones. So, we must posit an implicit fictional teller of the tale; it is the implicit narrator who believes the characters exist and who relates their trials and tribulations to us as fact.

Whereas the implied author is the agency responsible for the construction of the fiction *qua* fiction, where there is no explicit narrator, the *implicit* narrator is, allegedly, the agency responsible for narrating the tale as true in the fictional world. If it is the author and/or the implied author who makes it fictional that Hans Castorp stayed in a sanitarium, it is the implicit narrator (or narrator) who speaks from inside the fiction and *asserts* that Hans Castorp stayed in a sanitarium. Just as Ishmael tells us that Ahab did thus-and-so – i.e., presents Ahab's doings as something that actually happened (which we then go on to imagine) – where there is no explicit narrator, there still must be an implicit one narrating (that is, asserting) that it is the case that *x*, albeit from inside the fiction operator (it is fictional that *it is the case that x*). Moreover, the implicit narrator is part of the fiction, although he/she/it is not someone acknowledged to exist by the other fictional characters in the text.

One question that arises about film narration then is: which of the preceding distinctions regarding narration apply to film and which don't? Clearly, films have actual authors whose manifestation in the text may be implied or not. Films may also have fictional narrators, such as Walter Neff in *Double Indemnity* or Scout in *To Kill a Mockingbird*. And, in addition, movies may have a fictional narrator who, though not a player in the storyworld itself, is the fictional presenter of the story – for example, the voice-over narration by Spencer Tracy in *How the West Was Won*. In this case, Spencer Tracy is not speaking as Spencer Tracy, but as the fictional narrator supposedly responsible for recounting the stories of frontier life that comprise the film.

So far all seems well. Yet, the question remains as to whether films have completely implicit narrators – fictional narrators whose voice we never hear, but, who, nevertheless, are posited as presenting the images we see. As is well known, a framing story was added to the classic silent film *The Cabinet of Dr. Caligari* involving the explicit fictional narrator Francis, a madman. Had that framing story not been added, would *Caligari* still have had a fictional narrator, though an implicit one?

And if there are such narrators lurking in films, how extensive are they? Do they appear in some films, all films, or none at all? As is often the case in philosophy, one side says they occur in no films, whereas the other side says they occur in all. In "*Le Grand Imagier* Steps Out," Wilson flirts with the possibility that they may inhabit all fictional film narratives, and he attempts to defend this alternative.

Why would anyone suspect that all fiction films possess implicit narrators? One argument would be the same as that which we encounter with respect to literature: narration requires narrators. So, there must be implicit narrators in film. But this is not conclusive. Why not say that the actual author is the narrator or that the implied author is? After all, the narrator in nonfiction narratives is the actual author.[1] Why not say the same of fiction?

Perhaps the response will be that, though the actual author constructs the fiction, the story as narrated from inside the fiction must be narrated by a fictional being. Nonfiction narratives typically have no fictional assertions nested inside them. So all the work of narration can be attributed to the actual author of a nonfiction narrative.

But, supposedly, things stand differently with fictions. The actual author of a fictional narrative can tell the tale as fictional, but cannot tell the tale as true, which is what we are mandated to imagine (we are not mandated to imagine that it is fictional that Katie loves Hubbel in *The Way We Were*; we are asked to imagine – to entertain in thought – *that* Katie loves Hubbel). So, there must be some agency presenting the facts of the fictional world as true, and that, allegedly, is the implicit narrator.

But why? If signaling that such-and-such is fictional instructs the audience to imagine it as true, why isn't the fictive intention of the author (that we imagine such-and-such) adequate to warrant supposing that such-and-such is true in the fictional world? Maybe it will be said that if such-and-such is asserted, there must be an agency doing the asserting. But is "that Katie loves Hubble" a genuine assertion? "It is true in the fiction that 'Katie loves Hubble' " is an assertion; but is "that Katie loves Hubble" really an assertion, or merely a propositional content?

Another reason to suspect the postulation of ubiquitous implicit narrators is that they would quickly find themselves enmeshed in self-contradiction. In some fictions, the audience is told how things turned out, but it is also given as true in the fiction that no one ever learnt how things turned out. Yet, if there is an implicit narrator who is party to the fictional world, then there is some agent in the fictional world who does know how things turned out. So the implicit narrator contradicts himself when avowing that no one ever learnt what really happened at the same time that he tells us what happened. Perhaps we should save him this embarrassment by denying his existence.

So far our skepticism about the existence of implicit narrators has been motivated by considerations that would cut equally against their existence in literature as well as film. But perhaps there is something about film that would favor positing ubiquitous implicit narrators. In order to find this claim persuasive, we need to back up one step.

Many will not find it too strained at all to say, when a tank rolls onscreen in a fiction film, that "I imagine seeing a tank." When I read in a story that Sherlock Holmes lives on Baker Street, I am intended by the storyteller to entertain the thought that Sherlock Holmes lives on Baker Street. That is, I imagine it. When I get an establishing shot of Sherlock's Baker Street digs in Graham Cutts's film *The Sign of the Four*, similarly I say that I imagine *seeing* Sherlock Holmes's apartment building. This does not seem to be an unnatural way of speaking.

And yet some philosophers will ask, if I am being shown something from the fictional world, who is responsible for showing it to me? There must be some fictional presenter doing it. There must be some narrative agency that is situated in the fictional world that is drawing my attention here and then there in such a way that I imagine seeing this and then that. Putatively it cannot be the actual author. How could the actual author display anything from the fictional world for me to see imaginarily? He can bring our attention to an existing apartment building perhaps by pointing toward it; but he cannot point toward Sherlock Holmes's apartment building, since it does not exist. Some other agency must be guiding our attention through the sights and scenes of the fictional world. There must be an implicit narrator – an implicit, fictional presenter – of the views that we audience members are thereby enabled to see imaginarily.

I am to imagine seeing that it is the case that Sherlock Holmes's apartment building is a certain number of stories tall. This is a fact in the world of the fiction. But the actual author does not present us with facts, but with fictions. The height of Sherlock Holmes's apartment building will only stand as a fact to someone inside the world of the fiction. And the actual filmmaker is not so situated. So there must be some fictional narrator who is exhibiting the fictional world to us in a certain way, and, thereby, empowering us to see it imaginarily.

Or, to put it differently, if there are these fragments of a fictional world being presented to us, how are they being presented to us? The real author is presenting us with photographic shots of real actors in actual places. But who, then, is drawing our attention to these scenes in the world of the fiction? Perhaps it is an implicit fictional narrator, a postulated *metteur en scène* who shows us this and then that in order that we may imagine seeing them.

As we view a fiction film, we are being presented with visual information from the fictional world. On reflection, we must ask ourselves how this is being accomplished. The most plausible hypothesis is, allegedly, that some fictional agency, the implicit narrator, is making this information available to us. That is, we are being shown people and things in the fictional world. Reason enjoins us to ask how this is possible. That we are being shown these things by a fictional presenter is our best answer.[2]

The argument for the existence of an implicit narrator in film – or, more awkwardly, a fictional presenter – is: because we imaginarily see events and actions, persons and things in films, there must be an implicit, fictional presenter. Otherwise, we would not be able to make perceptual contact with the world of the fiction. To make fictional contact requires a fictional intermediary. Therefore, there must be an implicit narrator, the agency that presents us with sights from hither and yon in the fictional world.

But as Wilson and others point out, this argument is liable to the objection that, despite the fact that it may seem natural to say we imagine seeing Ethan face-to-face in *The Searchers*, we do not really do so. Seeing imaginarily – at least seeing imaginarily as if we were face-to-face with the characters – is not really a plausible way of characterizing our experience of film. So there is no reason to hypothesize the existence of a fictional presenter or narrator who guides our imaginary seeing. For reasons about to be rehearsed in what follows, it cannot be the case that I am imagining seeing a character in the flesh or a scene "live." I cannot be imagining being situated in the midst of a battle scene, viewing the combatants tooth-by-jowl, lest I would also have to imagine the bullets going through me. But who does that? Thus, seeing imaginarily seems dubious, and so, if such alleged seeing imaginarily is the grounds for positing the implicit fictional presenter, then we may dispense with the presupposition that such narrators are ubiquitous in fiction films.

What is wrong with the notion of imaginarily seeing of the aforesaid face-to-face variety? One problem is that it frequently asks us to imagine discharging physically improbable and/or impossible actions. Consider a shot of a room taken from inside a fireplace; the flames are roaring. Are we supposed to imagine that we are seeing what is happening from that perspective? But then shouldn't we also imagine that we are burning up? Or, the camera is positioned on the ceiling. Are we to imagine that we are hanging from the rafters?

Furthermore, if we are to imagine seeing what is happening from the perspective of the camera lens, then won't we also have to imagine how we got there as well as whether it is plausible to suppose we could be there – hanging from the rafters, or on an open fire? And what are we to imagine when the camera is in the middle of a raging torrential rainstorm, but we are not wet? How did that happen? What should we imagine? Do you imagine anything?

And what are we to imagine we are seeing when there is a wipe or a lap dissolve on screen? That there is a ripple or a fissure in the universe of which we imagine ourselves to be witnesses? To the extent that these questions pose absurdities, one may be skeptical of the notion of seeing imaginarily "up close and personal" the sights in the fictional world.

Problems with the idea of seeing imaginarily exacerbate when we think about film editing. Recall the most famous cut in *2001*: a hairy primate triumphantly hurls a bone into the air and then there is a cut to a space station. In one twenty-fourth of a second, the camera has traversed thousands of years and thousands of miles. If we are to imagine seeing first the bone mid-air and then the space station, don't we also have to imagine that we have somehow gotten ourselves from prehistory to the future in rather short order? How did we do it? How many of us have imaginations so

spry as to come up with an answer to that question, and, even for those who do, can they mobilize it at the speed of a splice? Isn't it more reasonable simply to deny the idea that we are seeing imaginarily?

And finally, even if these practical absurdities could be rendered coherent by some kind of story, there is still the logical problem that we encountered in our discussion of fictional narrators in literature – namely, that postulating motion picture equivalents to these agents would provoke contradictions. At the end of the first episode of the fourth season of the TV series *Six Feet Under*, the character Nate Fisher buries his wife under a tree in the desert. In the fiction, it is ostensibly given that no one sees him. But if there is an implicit presenter in the fictional work who prompts us to see imaginarily Nate bury his wife, then it both is and is not the case that no one saw Nate bury his wife.

Therefore, if it is presumed that we could only see events imaginarily if there were an implicit agency guiding our attention, insofar as the existence of that agency courts contradiction, there is no imaginary seeing, and, hence, no cause to posit the agency that allegedly makes it possible.

Moreover, it cannot be the case that the actual author is metaphysically debarred from granting us access to the fictional world and that we need a fictional intermediary to relay that which is fictional to us. For if the contents of the fictional world are inaccessible directly to actual authors and audiences, why would that not apply to our access to the alleged fictional presenters as well as to the named fictional characters in the film? If there is any problem with making contact with the fictional world, that problem would persist with respect to making contact with an implicit fictional narrator and/or presenter.

That is, if we need a fictional intermediary to secure access to whatever is fictional, and the implicit narrator/presenter is fictional, then in order to make contact with the first implicit narrator, we will need a second implicit narrator, and then, for the same reason, a third implicit narrator to make contact with the second, and so on. The postulation of an implicit narrator on the grounds that only a fictional being can link actual audiences to the fictional world threatens to open an infinite regress. Positing an implicit narrator for this reason would make it impossible for us to gain access to the fictional world. But we do have access to fictional worlds.

Therefore, at least with respect to the notion that there is an otherwise impassable ontological chasm that only an implicit narrator can cross, we should reject the notion of an implicit narrator and presume that the actual author can connect us to the fictional world.[3] How? By mandating that we imagine it.

Wilson reviews many of these arguments against the imaginary-seeing-implicit-narrator hypothesis. But, unpredictably, this does not lead him to reject the view entirely. He thinks it can be saved with appropriate modifications. He notes that many of the arguments against seeing imaginarily are based on the idea that we are said to be imagining seeing persons and things in the fictional world face-to-face. That is, we are thought to be imagining seeing the events in question as if we were present to them. Wilson concedes that it is extremely doubtful that we are imagining seeing lava flows rising around us. If we were, would we not also have to imagine how it is that we are unscathed? For if reason dictates that we have an explanation of the way in which we have access to these fictional sights, shouldn't it also require that we be able to explain how it is that we are not singed by the molten magma?

But who wastes their time imagining such an account? Consequently, it is improbable that we are imagining seeing the lava "in person," since we are not also imagining how this is possible. Likewise, remembering the case of *2001*, it is dubitable that we imagine seeing – "live" – the bone hurled skyward and then the space station, since no one imagines how it is feasible to have close encounters of the third kind with these two sights back-to-back in less than a second's duration. So seeing imaginarily – what Wilson thinks of as the face-to-face variety – needs to be abandoned.

However, that is not the end of the story, because, Wilson maintains, there is another sort of seeing imaginarily that avoids the preceding objections and which is available to the friends of ubiquitous implicit narrators. One need not presume that one is seeing the people and places in the fictional world directly. Instead, what one imagines seeing are *images* of the fictional world. One need not imagine hanging from the rafters when one imagines seeing a room from the perspective of a fly on the ceiling, nor must one imagine being incinerated when one is shown the same room from inside the fireplace. One has only to imagine that one is seeing an image taken by some kind of image-making device, like a camera, which shows us what we would have seen were we positioned as that device was. We can imagine seeing a moving image taken of a room taken from somewhere on the ceiling without asking ourselves how we got up there, and we can imagine seeing a moving image of a room as recorded from inside a fireplace without asking ourselves why we are not aflame. For we are simply imagining that we are seeing images of these situations being projected for us. We need not imagine that we have left the comforts of a movie theater.

How is this possible? Well, we could imagine that we are seeing a documentary made by the implicit narrator in the fictional world. Of course, this is not quite right. When we see a fiction film like *The Crusades*, it is implausible to imagine that we are seeing a documentary, since motion picture cameras had not been invented in the Middle Ages. Nor is it plausible to imagine seeing documentaries when it comes to many films set in contemporary times. It strains credulity to imagine that with a film like *Touching the Void* we are seeing a documentary record. Who shot it and, if there was a camera team present, why didn't they lend a helping hand? Or consider the old *Twilight Zone* episode "Two." The fiction tells us that only two people are left on earth – a modern Adam and Eve. So where did the camera crew come from?

Also, is it plausible that much of what we see in fiction films was shot by an implicit documentary crew? Lovers share intimacies and criminals make deals that it is unlikely they would ever suffer a film crew to record. In the film *The Secret Window*, Mort kills his wife and her lover. Are we to imagine that he let a film crew record the murder? Some of the close-ups, shot with a normal lens, are so close that Mort could not have missed the camera in his face. He's insane, but he's not that insane. So it is implausible to maintain that we imagine seeing documentaries when we watch films.[4]

But Wilson is aware of this sort of objection. So he conjectures that what we imagine seeing is not a nonfiction film as we typically understand that phrase. Rather we imagine seeing a *naturally iconic representation or image*. What is that? Remember that in the introduction to Part I of this volume, we conjured up the idea of a naturally occurring camera. We speculated that it was logically possible that there could be a puddle of photographic salts on the floor of a cavern such that when light seeped through a crack overhead, the cave acted like a pin-hole camera and an image was fixed on the floor of the cave. Here the picture was the result of natural processes, *sans* any human manipulation. Wilson is suggesting that we imagine that some such natural process could obtain, without violating any of the laws of logic, which process could account for the moving images we see of the fictional world.

Imagining seeing such moving images would evade many of the objections that were just leveled against the notion that we are imagining seeing man-made documentaries. Naturally iconic images could have occurred at any time – even way before the Middle Ages. Lovers and criminals would not resist being documented by naturally iconic images, since such images do not involve witnesses and, it may be supposed, their subjects might not even know they were being recorded anyway. Moreover, naturally iconic images would not require any addition to the population of the fictional world of "Two." And, interestingly, for the same reason, naturally iconic images may avoid some of the problems of self-contradiction bruited earlier. For a naturally iconic image of something that no *person* saw is a perfectly coherent, even if weird, idea.[5]

One might respond to Wilson's proposal by saying that imagining naturally iconic images would involve us in contemplating something as improbable as many of the implications of seeing imaginarily face-to-face. How do these naturally iconic image-forming devices work? Exactly what are we supposed to imagine? Just that there are such things? But is that any less outlandish – or, at least, any less "magical" – than imagining that we travel from prehistoric earth to futuristic outer space in less than a second? If the consequences of face-to-face imaginary seeing strain the bounds of sense, shouldn't the notion of a naturally iconic image-maker have us shuddering as well?

Also, if the naturally iconic image-maker is said to be the implicit narrator, then shouldn't it be an agent of some kind, even if not of human kind? But then the possibility of self-contradiction still looms. For there may be science fictions in which it is given that *nothing* witnessed or recorded the events recounted; but, of course, the natural iconic image maker/implicit narrator did.

Wilson responds to these criticisms by contending that when we are mandated to imagine such-and-such regarding a fiction, we are not mandated to imagine everything that such-and-such might involve. We are invited to imagine that Tarzan can communicate with the apes; we are not required to

imagine how this is done, though we suppose it is done somehow. Anyone hit squarely on the head by a brick dropped from a high place should be suffering severe trauma; but we need not take that implication seriously while watching a slapstick comedy. Fictions leave much about that which we are mandated to imagine indeterminate, and, though mandated to imagine that certain things happen, we are not thereby mandated to imagine everything their occurrence would ordinarily involve. So we are not required to imagine how the images we see from the fictional world are contrived.

In the old Flash Gordon serials, there was a viewing device that enabled one to see anywhere with no cameras in evidence. Ours was not to reason why or how. We just imagined that such machines existed in the fictional world of Flash Gordon. Similarly, Wilson suggests we can imagine that the implicit presenter has an equally unexplained and narratively underdeveloped mechanism which allows us to see imaginarily the pictures it produces though we know not – and even cannot imagine – how.

Some fictions mandate our imagining nagging incongruities – for example, that Marty in *Back to the Future* remains unchanged in every respect despite the fact that his journey into the past has altered virtually everything else in the fictional world. Isn't this very strange? Nevertheless, according to Wilson, we need not worry about how this anomaly could have eventuated. It is given to us that thus-and-so is the case. We are not mandated to concern ourselves imaginarily with what this presupposes or entails. Let that remain indefinite or undetermined.

Just as one may imagine being in bed with one's favorite movie star, without imagining how one got there, so we may imagine seeing all sorts of images imaginarily without imagining, as well, how it is possible that we see them. If such images provoke anomalies – such as recordings of murders that have putatively gone unrecorded – that are implications of what has been shown in conjunction with the implicit presenter hypothesis, we are not mandated to imagine everything that is implied by what we have been prompted to imagine.

Wilson argues that we need not imagine how naturally iconic image-makers work – we may leave that indeterminate in our imagining – but only imagine that they work and imagine that we see their results. Nor are we mandated to imagine everything their existence might entail. If they imply incongruities, we are not enjoined to imagine either those incongruities or possible *ad hoc* resolutions thereof.

Nevertheless, it is not clear that Wilson can banish these problems so quickly. When processing a fiction, we need to fill in many of the details that the creator of the story has left out. That is, in the normal course of affairs, we are mandated to imagine things that are presupposed or implied by the fiction, but which are not stated outright or shown in it. For example, we are mandated to imagine that Sam Spade has a heart and that if shot through said heart at point blank range, he will die.

This supplemental imagining is governed by a default assumption: unless otherwise instructed by the fiction, we initially assume that the world of the fiction is like our world and imagine accordingly. This default assumption can be overridden. Some genres presuppose things at odds with the way of the real world – for example, that there are werewolves. And stories from other cultures and other times may presuppose things at variance with the way we believe the actual world to be; and this will force us to adjust our imagining in their direction so that we do not impose our beliefs on these alien fictional worlds. But, our first response to a fiction is to fill it in in terms of our beliefs about how the actual world works. Call this the realist heuristic.

Insofar as there is such a realistic heuristic, Wilson is wrong in maintaining that we are not mandated to imagine that which has not been said or shown by the fiction. We are mandated to imagine that Sam Spade has a heart, though it is never said, and, likewise, that a bullet can stop it. Consequently, if we are to employ the realistic heuristic, then any implications involved in the postulation of the iconic image-maker that fall afoul of it raise genuine problems for the view. Wilson might respond that the realistic heuristic is not ironclad; it may be overridden. If we are told explicitly that Sam Spade is invulnerable, we should accept this and not ask any questions about how this is physically possible. The same is true of that viewing device from the Flash Gordon serial. However, note that in these cases the realistic heuristic can be retired because the fiction has explicitly told us to do so. Flash Gordon's viewing machine has been introduced straightforwardly in the fiction and we are overtly reassured that it works in the story. That it seems to be physically impossible is not something we are concerned

about, since we have been told that it is a given in the relevant fictional world.

But, by definition, no fiction tells us that it possesses an implicit narrator/presenter nor that there is an implicit iconic image-maker. So we have no reason to think that such a device is in operation in the fictional world. Moreover, since the realistic heuristic has not been waived, if we are told by some theorist that there is such a device in some fictional world, we may legitimately wonder how just such a device is viable. And, furthermore, if the device presupposes or entails any absurdity – such as that an event given as unrecorded has been recorded – the contradiction cannot be evaded by appealing to the principle that we need not imagine that which the putative device entails *because*, without explicit instructions to do otherwise, we are to imagine that the kinds of logical, physical, and psychological implications that obtain in the actual world obtain in the fictional world.

Moreover, it would appear that the implicit narrator/presenter and his/her/its naturally iconic image-maker does force us to imagine wild improbabilities and absurdities with no warrant from the text. Consequently, for this reason, the implicit narrator/presenter, the naturally iconic image-maker, and the connected notion of imaginary seeing propose a package of concepts that we should avoid postulating.[6]

But even if there were not the preceding problems plaguing the version of ubiquitous implicit narration that Wilson sketches, it still seems an unlikely posit. Notice how carefully Wilson has crafted this theoretical entity. Since he realizes the conceptual conundrums that imagining seeing a documentary would involve, he "invents" naturally iconic imaging as a way to deflect counterexamples. Not only is a naturally iconic image-maker an unlikely thought to occur to most viewers – let alone a thought they would entertain in imagination without explicit prompting – it is also a thought that it takes a shrewd metaphysician to conceive. It is an ingenious strategy for dodging the logical and ontological objections launched against earlier variants of the idea of the implicit narrator/presenter. It may not be an entity only a metaphysician can love, but it is certainly the type of entity that only a metaphysician can manufacture.

But how likely is it that ordinary viewers mobilize such a conception in the process of responding imaginatively to films? Isn't the naturally iconic image-maker too sophisticated a posit to attribute to most viewers? It may be possible that some viewers – especially ones with expertise in logic and metaphysics – imagine films relayed to them in the way that Wilson suggests. Yet it cannot be the way that most viewers process fiction films.[7] It would require that most of us be far more clever and more learned in the ways of metaphysics than we are simply in order to access the most unassuming movies.[8]

Another problem with the naturally iconic image-maker – one which Wilson acknowledges – is that even if there were some imaginable natural process that could give rise to individual images of a movie, what conceivable natural process could edit them into a coherent story? The implicit presenter does not just display pictures; those pictures get organized into stories. They are edited into sequences; selections are made. By what miraculous process does a neatly structured story arise? Can we imagine that? If we imagine that, won't some gesture in the direction of imagining how it could happen nag at us? Even if naturally iconic images are conceivable, can naturally produced film narratives be as readily imaginable?

Defenders of ubiquitous implicit narrators in film contend that if we get visual information about the fictional world from a film, rationality compels us to ask how we get it. The implicit narrator is their answer. But why do we stop there in our quest to learn about the provenance of that information?

Positing the agency of an implicit narrator may lead us to ask what appear to be totally silly and irrelevant questions about the fiction – such as: how does the implicit narrator know what happened, when it is indicated that no one knows this in the fictional world? In order to forestall such questions, the friends of implicit narration declare that our questioning about the way in which we learn about the fictional world stop as soon as we surmise that the implicit narrator has informed us. But isn't stopping just here arbitrary? Why has reason suddenly become so complacent? If we really feel driven to know how we get the relevant information, won't we want an account of how the implicit narrator gathered it? But if this leads on to what we agree are silly questions, perhaps we should stop them before they start by refraining from postulating the implicit narrator from whom these absurdities flow.

So far the case has been made against the ubiquity of implicit narrators/presenters in film. This leaves open the possibility that there may be *some* implicit narrators. One circumstance in which it is often felt that it is necessary to hypothesize the activity of implicit storytellers is that of unreliable narration in film.

As we have just seen, the case for there being implicit narrators in film is not strong. However, when there is no explicit narrator in a film, but where the narration appears unreliable, aren't we forced to infer the work of an implicit narrator, one whose presentation of the fictional world is false or misleading? Who is responsible for the misdirection and dissembling, if not some implicit narrator? According to George Wilson's well-known analysis of Lang's *You Only Live Once*, the audience is led to believe that Eddie is innocent, though a thoughtful review of the evidence will indicate that this conclusion is far from certain.[9] There is a disjunction between what is true in the fictional world – as that is fixed by the intentions of the implied author – and the story as presented. But given this disjunction, ostensibly it cannot be the implied author who is responsible for this misleading presentation. Who is? The implicit narrator is the usual suspect.

In "Unreliability Refigured: Narrative in Literature and Film," Gregory Currie, perhaps the leading opponent of the notion of the implicit narrator/presenter,[10] argues that we are not forced to postulate the operation of such agents, even in the case of unreliable narration. Instead, he maintains that unreliable narration can be understood solely by reference to the implied narrator, taken to be either the actual author or a hypothetical author.

On Currie's view, unreliable narration in an example like *You Only Live Once* is exclusively the function of a *complex* intention on the part of the implied author. The author in this instance presents the visual and auditory information in such a way that it causes an initial impression that he intends to indicate that Eddie is innocent, but he includes enough peculiarities in the array to entice a second, more scrupulous review of the evidence that results in the mindful audience member's suspension of her earlier opinion. Attributing a two-tiered structure of intention to the implied author, then, can account for cases of unreliable narration without forcing the imputation of an implicit author who is otherwise nowhere to be seen (or heard from). Currie also goes on to suggest interesting connections between unreliable narration and ambiguous narration.

Currie's discussion of unreliable narration rounds out the debate about the existence of implicit narrators/presenters in film in an important way. For the most part, the postulation of an implicit narrator/presenter in all fiction films seems to involve taking on a lot of excess, unmotivated metaphysical baggage. Why suppose that we are compelled to admit such beings into our ontology in all cases? However, perhaps there are reasons to posit them in some cases. The case of unreliable narration – where there is no explicit narrator upon whom to pin it – seems to provide an occasion where inferring the activity of an implicit narrator/presenter appears most pressing. But in handling this case by resorting only to the implied author, Currie scotches that opportunity and, thereby, puts another nail in the coffin of the implicit narrator.

One exercise, then, for the ambitious reader is to come up with some reason that demands the invocation of the implicit narrator/presenter which reason has not yet been foreclosed by the argumentation so far. It is up to you to reanimate him/her/it.

N.C.

Notes

1 Paisley Livingston, "Narrative," in *The Routledge Companion to Aesthetics*, ed. Berys Gaut and Dominic McIver Lopes (London: Routledge, 2001), p. 279.
2 Jerrold Levinson, "Film Music and Narrative Agency," in *Post-Theory: Reconstructing Film Studies*, ed David Bordwell and Noël Carroll (Madison, Wisc.: University of Wisconsin Press, 1996), p. 251.
3 Andrew Kania says that proponents of the implicit narrator/presenter advance what he calls the "ontological gap argument" which maintains that there is no bridge from the actual world to the fictional world such that the artist can reach down and show us something from the fictional world. But Kania notes that if there is no way the artist can reach down into the fiction, then there is no way that the implicit presenter/narrator can reach "up" and make contact with us in the actual world. Yet, despite this alleged gap, some kind of contact between viewers and the fictional world is secured. Consequently, there does not really appear to be an ontological gap after all is said and done. See Andrew Kania, "Against the Ubiquity of Fictional Narrators", *The Journal of Aesthetics and Art Criticism*, 63(1), Winter 2005: 47–54.
4 There are also other reasons why it is implausible to suppose that audiences are, in general, imagining that they are seeing documentaries. First, I suspect that many initially encounter film fictions rather than film documentaries. They follow the story and they know it is make-believe, but they do not yet have the concept of a documentary at their disposal. I know that this was true of me as a small child. I could not have imagined seeing a documentary, because I didn't know what a documentary was. I do not think that I was an unusually uninformed child in this respect. Also, might it not also be the case that many first-time viewers in technologically undeveloped areas may also be in the position I found myself as a child? Isn't it likely that a first-time viewer in a poor rural village in Kashmir in 1940 might have seen a fiction film and known it to be made up, but not known that there were such things as documentary films? Such a viewer could not be imagining that he is seeing a documentary, since he does not know what a documentary is.

In a related vein, if I were imagining seeing a documentary, then it seems to me that that would require that I have some rudimentary knowledge of the way in which films are made. Yet, once again, it seems to me that many of the first-time viewers – both youngsters and adults – described in the previous paragraph may have no working knowledge of how films are made and yet be able to follow the story in a fiction film and even know that it is make-believe. But if they do not know how films are made, how can they imagine that what they are seeing is the result of a fictional making of a documentary film? For they have no basis upon which to imagine anything. And it is even more unlikely that they are imagining that they are seeing the results of a video documentary when they see a fiction on videotape, since it is even more improbable that they understand how video images are produced than that they understand how film images are produced.

Of course, another objection to the idea that people are imagining that they are seeing a documentary is that it adds an entirely extra layer of imagining to their mental processing of the fiction. It encumbers the ongoing fiction with another, barely articulated, parallel fiction. Though it may be possible that some viewers engage in such additional imagining, what compels us to infer that all of the rest of us are also riding on this fictional epicycle? Nothing, as far as I can tell.
5 On the other hand, the implicit narrator/presenter is supposed to be some sort of agent. It need not be human, but it is putatively an agent. But is a naturally iconic representation an agent in any meaningful sense? Recall that the proponent of the implicit narrator is relying on the entailment from narration to

narrator which itself depends on the supposition that since narrating is an action, it implies an agent (in this case, a narrator). But is a natural iconic image an agent or a random freak of nature?

6 See Berys Gaut, "The Movies: Cinematic Narration," in *The Blackwell Guide to Aesthetics*, ed. Peter Kivy (Oxford: Blackwell, 2004), p. 245.

7 My own view is that there is no seeing imaginarily involved. Spectators see cinematographic images onscreen which they then use to imagine what is fictionally the case. Watching *The General*, they see a moving photographic picture of a locomotive chugging out of a station stop and they imagine that the engine, The General, has been hijacked by Union spies. They do not imagine seeing the event; but they do imagine or suppose the event. The actual filmmaker, Buster Keaton, presents us with images – images of actors and props – which we then go on to use to imagine what is fictional in the world of the General. We do not imagine seeing Johnnie Gray and his locomotive. We see images of Buster Keaton doing this and that, and imagine that Johnnie Gray is doing thus and so.

8 It may be that Wilson is only attempting to show that the ubiquity of the implicit narrator/presenter is a logically possible posit. I am not sure that it is, given our previous objections, but it does seem that Wilson wants to say something stronger than that the implicit narrator is at least conceivable.

9 Wilson develops this interpretation of *You Only Live Once* in his book *Narration in Light* (Baltimore, Maryland: Johns Hopkins University Press, 1986). It should be noted that not everyone accepts Wilson's interpretation. There is some debate over his descriptions of certain shots, notably the shot from inside the car during the robbery. David Bordwell has suggested to the editors that Wilson's characterization of this image is inaccurate. Nevertheless, for the purposes of argument, we, like Currie, are supposing Wilson's account, since if it is apt, then it would be one of the rare examples of unreliable narration in film where there is no explicit narrator in sight to take the blame.

10 See especially Gregory Currie, *Image and Mind: Film, Philosophy, and Cognitive Science* (Cambridge: Cambridge University Press, 1995).

12

Le Grand Imagier Steps Out: The Primitive Basis of Film Narration

George M. Wilson

It was Christian Metz who first introduced me to *le grand imagier*, or, at least Metz first introduced him to me under that elegant description. Here is the famous passage in which Metz evokes the mysterious figure in question:

> The spectator [of a narrative film] perceives images which have been obviously selected (they could have been other images) and arranged (their order could have been different). In a sense, he is leafing through an album of predetermined pictures, and it not he who is turning the pages but some "master of ceremonies," some "grand image-maker"... situated somewhere behind the film, and representing the basis that makes the film possible.[1]

Metz is endorsing the view that narrative films routinely have "filmic narrators," the counterparts, in cinema, of the more familiar "verbal" narrators in works of literature. The filmic narrators, he tells us, conduct their business by selecting and arranging film images instead of sentences in a linguistic text.[2]

However, this apparently appealing idea has set off an explosion of controversy and debate in film studies. A number of distinguished writers have worked out elaborate theories about the nature of cinematic narrators and their proper job description.[3] Despite the energetic theorizing, it seems

fair to say that there is precious little agreement among the different theories and a plethora of confusion on the subject. Indeed, some authors have maintained that cinematic narrators do not exist, at least in standard movies.[4] And these debates have sputtered on for a long time and over many pages.

It is not my ambition in this paper to side with friends of the grand image-maker or with his enemies. In fact, I think that the literature on this topic has tended to mix together different issues that ought to be kept distinct. In what follows, I will try to do some disentangling – to set out certain questions that need to be settled first before we speculate (or refuse to speculate) about the leading attributes a cinematic narrator might have. By the end of the discussion, I will identify a simple conception of what narration in film might be which has attracted little notice despite the fact that it has merits which should be explored further.

I The Ontological Status of Film Narration

In his book *Coming to Terms,* Seymour Chatman has argued that fairly minimal considerations establish that all fictional stories, whether they are told, shown, or enacted, imply the occurrence of a "narration" of the relevant fictional events, and, correlatively, imply the existence of a narrator

George M. Wilson, "Le Grand Imagier Steps Out: The Primitive Basis of Film Narration," *Philosophical Topics* 25(1), 1997: 295–318. Reprinted by permission of George M. Wilson.

– the agent of the narration.[5] Chatman allows that, if the terms "narration" and "narrator" carry too strongly the connotation of *verbal* tellings and tellers of fictional tales, then, in cases where the fictional story has been shown, we can speak instead of a "show-er" or "(visual) presenter" of the fictional narrative. Nevertheless, it is his position that the show-er of a fictional story plays the same functional role within a primarily visual work as verbal tellers play in literary works of fiction. Therefore, both are properly subsumed under a general category of "narrator." For instance, Chatman states, "It stands to reason that if shown stories are to be considered narratives, they must be 'narrated,' and only an overly restrictive definition of 'to narrate' – identifying it solely with telling – keeps that observation from being self-evident. To 'show' a narrative, I maintain, no less than to 'tell' it, is to 'present it narratively' or to 'narrate' it."[6] Subsequently, he adds, "I would argue that every narrative is by definition narrated – that is, narratively presented – and that narration, narrative presentation, entails an agent even when the agent bears no sign of human personality."[7] The argumentation in these and surrounding passages is not entirely clear (as we will see), but the following is a plausible reconstruction of Chatman's line of thought. If an audience is presented with a "text" which visually or verbally conveys a series of fictional occurrences, then the text serves as a medium or instrument by means of which the events and situations of the story are progressively shown or told. Thus, the text is understood to be the product of an *activity* of either showing or telling the events that constitute the story, an activity that proceeds in a certain temporal order. Moreover, given that such a narrating activity is presupposed, there must be an *agent*, also presupposed, who performs the relevant activity of showing or telling. Chatman is at pains to insist that the narrating agency need not be human or humanlike, but that claim is not one that will concern us in the present discussion.

What needs to be investigated, from the very outset, is the notion that a narrative text is to be conceived as the product and instrument of a narrating activity. In the case of literary works of fiction, the claim is ambiguous in a familiar way, and the ambiguity is important when one turns, as Chatman does, to the narration of fiction films. The text of the novel *David Copperfield* conveys the fictional story of David's early adventures. But, in writing the novel, Charles Dickens *told* (verbally constructed) the story of David's adventures, and the text is the actual product of his writing. But, in the novel itself, it is fictional that David *tells* (recounts) the story of his own adventures, and it is fictional for the reader that the text is the product of his activity of telling. This distinction between the *actual* telling of the Copperfield story by Dickens and the *fictional* telling of that story by the narrator, David, is, as noted, well established.

However, this distinction does not simply concern, as it were, actual and fictional instances of the same kind of activity. We should observe that the type or force of an actual telling of a fictional tale is typically different from the type or force of the fictional telling that supervenes upon it. Characteristically, in the work *David Copperfield*, it is fictional that the narrator asserts that such and such events (actually) took place, while, in writing the relevant parts of the text, Dickens does not, actually or fictionally, assert these same propositions. Indeed, very often, he is not asserting any propositions at all. If Dickens is directly performing any type of "illocutionary act," it is this: he is using his words to make it fictional in the novel both that David asserted the propositions and, in most instances, that those very propositions are true. On the other hand, if the narrator is a story-telling narrator, then it is fictional that the narrator is using the words to make it fictional in his/her story that certain things took place.[8] By contrast, the author of *The Exhaustive Cliff Notes for David Copperfield* also tells in full detail the story of David's adventures, but his telling consists of actual assertions about what is fictional in the Dickens novel.[9] Clearly, we have to be careful about what sort of activity any particular "telling" of a fictional story specifically amounts to.

In the case of fictional tellings, the text both represents the narrative events and is itself implicitly represented in a certain way. Very roughly, the sentences of the text, in virtue of their semantic properties, represent types of situations or events. But those same sentences are implicitly represented – are correctly imagined by the reader – as utterances or inscriptions of someone who thereby asserts that an event or situation of the designated type actually took place. Hence, the text makes it fictional that the utterer or inscriber asserted that thus-and-so, and typically, either by convention or reasonable inference, it also makes it fictional "in the story" that thus-and-so obtains. In the standard case, the text fictionally describes the narrative events, while, "in the same breath," it "scripts" the narrator's fictional speech-act performance. It will emerge shortly that similar discriminations have to be made in connection with fictional showings.

It has become normal practice, when we speak of "the narration" and/or "the narrator" of a work of literary fiction, to be referring to the fictional telling of the story and to the fictional or fictionalized agent of that telling. Thus, one assumes that Chatman intends to be maintaining that a text which shows a fictional story gives rise, as a part of the total work, to a *fictional* activity of showing the depicted narrative events, and that the existence of such a fictional showing implies that there is a *fictional* or *fictionalized* show-er of the story. At the conclusion of his positive arguments, he affirms that he has been concerned with "the someone or something *in the text* [my emphasis] who or which is conceived as presenting (or transmitting) the set of signs that constitute it."[10] However, it is hard to see how the considerations he adduces support his stated conclusion. On the face of things, the most that Chatman's considerations show is that there cannot be an actual activity of showing the events of a fictional story in the absence of an actual agent who performed the activity. This claim can also be questioned, but let it stand. It still does not follow from this thesis that the showing of a fictional narrative invokes a fictional activity of showing (in any sense) the relevant series of narrative events. In the remainder of this essay, I will be primarily concerned with the thesis that fiction films presuppose the existence of some narrative-establishing activity of fictional showing. The problems that this claim engenders are surprisingly delicate. Therefore, I will largely leave aside the question that most vexes Chatman and many other writers, i.e., given the assumption that there *is* a presupposed activity of fictional showing, does that imply that there is also a fictional or fictionalized cinematic narrator? I will explore the more restricted topic: is there even a primitive basis for a fictional activity of cinematic narration?

II Fictional Showing and Showing the Fictional

I believe that Chatman does not see how there can be an issue about the existence of fictional showings. He thinks, in effect, that the concept of "a

fictional story that is shown" somehow implies the concept of "a fictional showing of the story." Nevertheless, it is doubtful that any such relatively direct connection exists. Grounds for doubt are illustrated by the following rudimentary form of visual representation. Nixon presents, by means of the production of certain hand shadows, a fictional story in which a certain hawk attacks and kills a hapless mole. The hand shadows, occurring in a field of light, depict the hawk, the mole, and their respective actions, and *Nixon* is the agent who actually produces the shadow "text." However, there is no obvious reason to postulate that the hand shadows are themselves the fictional product of some fictional activity of "showing-as-actual" the elements of the depicted tale. Indeed, the very idea that this might be so appears to lack a determinate sense, and, at a minimum, one would want some explanation of and justification for the claim. It is wholly unclear what type of "showing" could be fictionally instanced in such a case. The only showing that appears to be involved in "The Hawk and Mole Story" is the actual showing by Nixon of the pertinent fictional events. In this example at least, the "text" does not instantiate the crucial property of representing and being represented at one and the same time. And yet, it is just this status of the text as both means and object of representation that is basic to the creation of fictional tellings in literary fiction.

The hand shadow example illustrates an important point about the showing of fictional events. If I want to show you what *actually* happened in certain historical circumstances, then I might do so in at least one of two ways. If we are appropriately present at the circumstances in question, I can direct your perceptual attention to the events themselves as they take place. But, alternatively, I might show you the events by displaying to you a picture or series of pictures that visually record, accurately and in enough detail, the historical episode of interest. Similarly, if I want to show you a fictional episode, I can show you a series of fictional events by exhibiting to you a suitable series of pictures in which it is fictional that events of the envisaged kinds take place. My showing you those pictures is sufficient to present the story, and there need not be facts about the pictures, and about the context of their imaginative reception, that make it fictional or make-believe for the viewer that the pictures are the products of some additional "fictional showing."[11] It is for this reason that a special argument needs

George M. Wilson

to be given to justify an inference from "T depicts the fictional incidents in a narrative N" to the conclusion "T involves a fictional showing of the incidents in N."

Similar thoughts apply to the visual presentation of a fictional story in a standard comic strip or comic book, although this case illustrates an additional complication. The story is primarily transmitted by presenting to the reader a sequence of cartoon drawings, each of which depicts a fictional event or situation in the unfolding narrative.[12] Here, as before, it seems that the frames that make up the strip are not imagined to be the upshot of some kind of fictional showing. As in the hand shadow example, it is doubtful that there are any general grounds for positing such a fictional showing and obscure what sort of activity one could be positing. However, we should not state the conclusion too broadly. It is easy to think of possible comic strips in which a fictional showing would be implicated. The frames of the comic strip could be rendered in such a fashion that they are themselves represented as being, say, photographs taken by a witness to the events depicted. Going a step further, one can conceive of ways in which the represented character of the frames and the nature of their selection could convey fictional facts about the personality and sensibility of the "implied" photographer. In this example, there plainly is a fictional activity of showing the story that the viewer is to imagine, i.e., the fictional activity of taking and assembling the photographs. And here there *is* a fictional agent of that activity, i.e., the fictional eyewitness and photographer. Various other more subtle and sophisticated strategies would give rise to analogous fictional results.

The example of comic strips suggests a couple of cautionary morals. First, we should not ask, in the absence of further qualification, whether showings of fictional stories do or do not engender fictional showings or (visual) presentings. The answer is: some do and some do not. Moreover, the same mixed answer generally holds for narrower categories of texts, e.g., the comic strip. Second, when a text that shows its fictional story does involve a fictional showing, it does so in virtue of some relatively clear-cut representational strategy implicit in and appropriate to the imaginative context of the text's reception. Detailed facts about the particular nature of the text and facts about the proper mode of apprehending that text serve to prompt us to imagine about the text that it is the product of an appropriate kind of fictional showing. Naturally, in the case of writing and reading works of literary fiction, the basic components of the implicit representational strategies are highly familiar, ubiquitously deployed, and almost automatically invoked for the reader on the basis of pretty minimal cues. But in other cases – the comic strip is a good example of this – rather special strategies of implicit representation of the text have to be more distinctly set in place.

These conclusions would not be accepted by Chatman, and there is a line of argument against them which is hinted at in some of his discussions. Consider, for example, these remarks: "[W]e must avoid the metaphor that the camera 'sees' *the events and existents in the story world* [my emphasis] at such and such a distance, from such and such an angle. Rather it *presents* them at those distances and angles." Or a bit later: "The convention [in fiction films] is that the particular rectangle of visible material constitutes a 'favored view,' a selection of the implied author which the cinematic narrator is delegated to present."[13] The import of these and related passages is murky, but I believe that we can articulate the basic idea behind them in the following fashion.

First, we are concerned with cases in which a fictional story has been shown by means of a text which either is a single picture or consists of a series of pictures. Let us suppose, in addition, that we are dealing with visual representations that determine an implied vantage point upon the scene. That is, we suppose that these are visual representations each of which determine a position in the implied space of the picture, a position such that the scene depicted is represented as if viewed from that fictional location. This added supposition will cover all of the cases which we will henceforth be investigating. When we are looking at "perspectival" representations of this sort, viewers normally imagine and are intended to imagine seeing the objects and events depicted in the image, and, moreover, they imagine seeing these contents from a reasonably distinctive visual perspective.

Second, from these suppositions we can construct the relevant argument as follows. In imagining that they actually see the depicted scene, a part of what viewers thereby imagine is that the contents of the scene are being displayed or exhibited to their perception. In the case of fiction film, they imagine the movie shots before them as offering a perspectival view of those contents, and it is the function of the shots to prescribe an imagining of this kind. So, it is in this sense that the shots of a film *present* a view of or perspective on some spatio-temporal slice of the "story world" and *show* us what that view contains. Of course, it is only a fiction that "the events and existents" in that world have been presented and shown in this manner. Both the constituents of the story and the visual exhibition of them are fictional constructions of the work, although the items thus presented belong to the world of the narrative while the "presentings" of them belong to the "world" of the narration. Still, these considerations should be enough to convince us that fiction films *do* incorporate a series of "fictional showings" in their narration, i.e., the fictional presentation of views of characters, actions, and circumstances which are themselves merely fictional. This argument, if correct, would demonstrate that any or almost any showing of a fictional scene or story involves a fictional showing (to the viewer) of the represented elements. Moreover, given the generality of the considerations deployed in the argument, it should work for comic strips as well and would undercut the remarks I made earlier.

A similar argument is developed in Jerrold Levinson's article "Film Music and Narrative Agency."[14] Levinson affirms there his broad agreement with the claims of Chatman sketched above. But Levinson is more careful and explicit than Chatman is about the distinction between fictional showings of fictional events in movies, on the one hand, and actual showings of the movie images, on the other. Having correctly highlighted the distinction, he maintains that there *is* a coherent conception of what *fictional* showings in standard movies consist of. He says, for example,

> The presenter [show-er] in a film presents, or gives perceptual access to, the story's sights and sounds; the presenter in film is thus, in part, a sort of *perceptual enabler.* Such perceptual enabling is what we must implicitly posit to explain how it is we are, even imaginarily, perceiving what we are perceiving of the story, in the manner and order in which we are perceiving it. The notion of a presenter, whose main charge is the providing of perceptual access on the fictional world, is simply the best default assumption available for how we make sense of narrative fiction film.[15]

Notice that Levinson asserts that a fictional activity of giving the viewer "perceptual access to the story's sights and sounds" is needed to explain the viewer's fictional activity of perceiving the sights and sounds in question. There is some vagueness in Levinson's description of what the presenter *does* by way of enabling the viewer's perception of narrative events, but this quotation and other remarks in his article certainly suggest something like the reasoning delineated above. Let us call this proposal "the Fictional Showing Hypothesis."

However, Levinson's statement of the hypothesis seems crucially schematic at a certain point, as does my earlier extrapolation from the Chatman quotations. What is the activity of the presenter by means of which the audience is given perceptual access to portions of a fictional world? What kind of displaying or exhibiting of fictional constituents is supposed to be in play? I mentioned earlier that there are different ways in which I can provide you with perceptual access to a certain range of actual sights and sounds. If the sights and sounds are in our immediate vicinity, I may be able to single them out ostensively. Otherwise, I may be able to supply you with adequate recordings of them. Levinson simply does not specify which of these means of affording perceptual access (or others) are constitutive of the fictional showings of stories on film that he is prepared to postulate. Nevertheless, it seems unlikely that his visual "presenter" shows us recorded images of the story world. The actual filmmakers have already pre-empted that task.[16] The most natural interpretation of Levinson's proposals takes him to be arguing that the movie's image track leads viewers to imagine that they are seeing the events of the narrative, as we may put it, "face to face."

After all, if it is fictional for the viewer that she is seeing a scene in the story, then, apparently, it should be correlatively fictional for her that the items in the scene are located, at a viewable distance and a suitable angle, before her gaze. This means, in other words, that it is fictional in her perceptual game of make-believe that she has somehow been situated in the picture's implied space and has had her visual attention directed from that vantage point to the objects and events that it encompasses. On this interpretation, the work of the film narration (in its visual dimension) is to effect a fictional placing of the scene in front of the viewer's receptive and attentive eyes so that she may see it from just that place. Naturally, it is not fictional *in the work* that the viewer occupies such a position and is present as an observer on the scene. It is fictional only in the viewer's imaginative perceptual engagement with the film that this is so. I will call this interpretation "the Face to Face Version" of the Fictional Showing Hypothesis and assume, at least tentatively, that it is the position that Levinson has in mind. Similarly, I will take him to be urging that the movie's soundtrack prompts viewers to imagine being "within earshot" of the characters and their circumstances and hearing the diegetic speech and other sounds in that direct fashion. Certainly, whether either Levinson or Chatman would endorse this version of the Fictional Showing Hypothesis, it can seem, as explained above, the almost inevitable elaboration of their explicit claims.[17]

III Fictional Seeing from a Perspective

The Face to Face Version is, however, implausible. It is true that when people actually see a scene from a certain visual perspective, they are, in fact, located in a position which, given the circumstances, offers them that perspective. But it does not follow that if a person *imagines* seeing a scene from a certain perspective, then he thereby also imagines being at a place which offers him that view. Similarly, when, in viewing a perspectival visual representation, a person imagines seeing a scene from the visual perspective established by the pictorial field,[18] he usually does not imagine himself occupying a point in the picture's implied space that would yield this visual perspective and seeing the scene from that place. As a rule, I think that it is false that we ordinarily imagine ourselves being anywhere in the depicted or implied space of the image. Speaking specifically of movie images, Gregory Currie has registered the intuitive objection forcefully.

> For me the most striking thing about the view ... is that it seems to me to misdescribe the *experience* of movie watching. Do I really identify my visual system, in imagination, with the camera, and imagine myself to be placed where the camera is? Do I imagine myself on the battlefield, mysteriously immune to the violence around me, lying next to the lovers, somehow invisible to them, viewing Earth from deep space one minute, watching the dinner guests from the ceiling the next? None of this corresponds to my own experience of movie watching.[19]

Despite lapses on this question in an earlier work of mine, I think that Currie is right about this.[20] In general, when one views a movie, one does not imagine oneself to be present within the depicted and/or off-screen space of the story.

Our ordinary ways of describing our perceptual connections to story space provoke confusion on this topic. Often we do say things like "In viewing that shot from *Rear Window*, I saw Thorwald's threatening gesture from Jeff's apartment window in the building across the court." But we need to distinguish two distinct claims that can be naturally conveyed by formulations of the form,

> (1) In viewing picture A, I imagine seeing X from position P,

where P is a place in the space depicted or implied by the picture. One claim we could be making is the following:

> (1a) In viewing A, I imagine being situated at P and seeing X from that position.

But, the same words could also be used to say,

> (1b) In viewing A, I imagine seeing X from the visual perspective one would have if one were situated at P.

When we make statements like the one about the shot from *Rear Window*, we are likely to intend the (1b) version of our utterance and not, it seems to me, the version in (1a). This is a case in which the face-value proposition expressed by the words is not the message we normally aim to convey. Understood in the manner of (1b), such statements often report our experience correctly. Movie advertisements sometimes promise to place us "in the middle of the [depicted] action," but we recognize that this is simply hyperbole and hype. Currie correctly insists that readings of instances of (1) along the lines of (1a) would usually misdescribe what we imagine in seeing films and other perspectival visual representations.

However, Currie also wants to draw a further, much stronger conclusion, and his conclusion depends upon denying, in effect, that there is a substantive distinction between (1b) and (1a). Currie contends, plausibly enough, that

> (2) If in viewing a picture A, I imagine seeing X, then I thereby imagine seeing X from

the visual perspective established by the pictorial field of A.

But, as before, let P be the depicted or implied position in the fictional space of A which a person would have to fictionally occupy in order to see X from the visual perspective in question. Call this "the [fictional] vantage point in [the implied space of] A."[21] Currie maintains that if, in viewing picture A, I imagine seeing X from the visual perspective established by A, then I thereby imagine being at P and seeing X from that vantage point. In other words, Currie holds that

(3) If (1b) is the case, then (1a) also obtains.

Since he holds, as the previous quotation indicates, that viewers never (or very rarely) imagine being at the vantage point in the picture and seeing from there, he infers from this and thesis (3) that there is never (or almost never) a visual perspective from which viewers imagine seeing the depicted contents of a picture. Then, from this step, in conjunction with (2), he goes on to conclude that we never (or almost never) *imagine seeing* the depicted contents of the picture at all. Naturally, if Currie's line of argument is sound, then *no* version of the Fictional Showing Hypothesis could succeed. There cannot be a fictional process or activity of giving perceptual access to viewers of the picture if it is generally not fictional for viewers that they perceive the depicted scenes in the first place.

Here is Currie's own formulation of the point: "To see *is* to see from a point of view: there is no such thing as nonperspectival seeing. You cannot imagine, of a certain scene represented to you on screen, that you are seeing it, but not that you are not seeing it from any point of view. To imagine seeing it is to imagine seeing it from the point of view defined by the perspectival structure of the picture."[22] Currie has made precisely the mistake that the conflation of (1a) and (1b) so readily encourages. Not only is it possible for a viewer of a picture to imagine seeing the pictured prospect from a certain visual perspective without, at the same time, imagining being at the vantage point in the picture, but normally this is just what viewers do. They imagine having perspectival visual perceptions of the contents of the picture from, as we might say for brevity, an unoccupied perspective.

In looking at a picture, the viewer imagines having a veridical visual experience of the items in a certain scene, and those elements, as the

viewer imagines seeing them, have what Currie here calls "a perspectival structure." That is, various of the items are presented as foreshortened, as overlapping one another, and as having appropriate relative occlusion sizes.[23] Thus, the viewer imagines seeing the scene from the visual perspective defined by that network of properties and relations. The visual perspective may well be the one a viewer would or might have if he were located at a certain site in relation to that scene, but the identity of a perspectival view is not constituted by its relation to a vantage point from which it could have been secured. Hence, the question is: Can one imagine seeing the scene from a specified perspective without imagining that one is at the vantage point and obtaining his visual perspective from that position? In the final sentence of the quotation above, Currie illegitimately forecloses the pertinent option by running the two concepts together under the dangerous rubric of "point of view." The question here is a complex one and deserves more space than I can give it, but the following reflections provide grounds for answering it in the affirmative.

Just as I can imagine romping in the buff on Neptune without imagining anything about how I came to do so or about what makes it possible for me to be dancing on that distant planet, so also I can imagine having a (veridical) visual experience of a scene without imagining anything about how I came to have the experience or about what enables me to have it. In particular, I may imagine nothing about whether I am having that experience *because* I am situated face to face with what I see. These further matters, normally essential either to visiting other planets or to seeing a scene, are simply left *indeterminate* in my imagining.[24]

Perhaps the following thought experiment will help to establish that the concept of "visual experience from an unoccupied perspective" is at least minimally coherent. We seek to conceive of *one* way in which I might imagine seeing a scene from a certain visual perspective without imagining, as part of this, that I am seeing from the implied vantage point. (1) I can imagine in detail the qualitative and perspectival character of the kind of visual experience I would (or might) have if I were to look at a scene S from a "face to face" position P. (2) I can imagine having a visual experience of just that character while imagining that I am *not*, as I have the experience, situated at the vantage point P. Maybe, in the broader context of my imagining, I imagine that a devious neurophysiologist is causing me to have that very visual experience while I am sitting in his laboratory. (3) Finally, I can imagine having this same experience while, nevertheless, imagining of the experience that it constitutes an instance of my *seeing* S. Thus, it may be a part of the broader context of my imagining, that the processes whereby the neurophysiologist induces this visual experience (and others) in me are such that my having the visual experiences he produces count as a kind of "prosthetic" seeing of S and other scenes. Here, then, is a case in which I imagine myself seeing a scene from an unoccupied visual perspective.

I hasten to add that in ordinary cases when we imagine having a visual experience from an unoccupied perspective, my imaginings are *not* contextualized in this manner. First, I do not imagine that I am *not* at P – imaginatively, it is indeterminate where, if anywhere, I am. And, second, I do not imagine anything about the causes and conditions of my having the relevant visual experience – it is imaginatively indeterminate how this came about. Still, the fact that all these important matters are left indeterminate in what I imagine does not preclude me from imagining seeing S from a P-like perspective while I am not at P. The content of such an imagining has the same kind of minimal coherence as the content "running naked on the surface of Neptune," and each content specifies something I can imagine.

Similarly, when looking at a representational picture, we usually imagine having a (veridical) visual experience of the scene depicted, where the qualitative and perspectival character of the experience corresponds in detail to the pictorial field of the picture we are viewing. And we do this without imagining that we are somehow present at the vantage point in the picture. As before, we can imagine this perception from an unoccupied perspective because we imagine nothing about the potential fictional circumstances that would have enabled us to have the visual experience we imagine. Of course, we know a great deal about what it is before our eyes which is actually cueing our experience. The pictorial field prompts and guides our imagining of the visual experience (e.g., determines a certain perspectival structure for it) without establishing much of anything about the causal conditions of the imagined experience. This, I believe, is the standard case when we view perspectival visual representations.

It is the *standard* case, but not the only one possible. For it *is* possible for a perspectival

image (a painting, say) to lead the viewer to imagine himself being at the vantage point in the picture and seeing from that place. The artistic strategies that are meant to elicit such an imagining are not frequently deployed, but when they are, they represent an important aspect of how we comprehend the visual significance that the painting offers us. Richard Wollheim, in *Painting as an Art*, describes a class of paintings that involve what he calls "internal spectators," and it partially defines the class that these paintings are visually and dramatically so constituted that they are intended to induce the spectator into imagining himself at the vantage point in the picture.[25] Wollheim carefully delineates the different ways that various classic paintings rely upon the imaginative endeavor in question. For example, he argues that Manet's *Bar aux Folies-Bergere* is a striking instance of the category.[26] A viewer of the painting is encouraged by a panoply of its key features to imagine himself as standing before the bar and as seeing the barmaid with her eyes averted from him. However, one can also conceive of a painting, broadly similar to the Manet both in subject matter and angle of depiction, in which we imagine seeing the barmaid standing behind the bar with her averted eyes, but one for which we have no inclination and are not meant to have any inclination to imagine *ourselves* standing in front of the bar. This example and others like it underscore the point that, in looking at a perspectival representation, imagining seeing a scene from a visual perspective is one kind of imaginative achievement, while imagining seeing from the picture's vantage point is of a different and somewhat more complicated kind. If so, it is a mistake to identify, as Currie does, the state of affairs described by (1a) with the one described in (1b).

Confusion about (3) is endemic in these debates. I have just argued that Currie's acceptance of (3) leads him to argue wrongly against the existence, or at least the prevalence, of imagined seeing in our viewing of images. But, if we look back to my reconstruction of the background considerations for the Face to Face Version of the Fictional Showing Hypothesis, we observe that the acceptance of (3) plays a crucial role in that argument as well. As Levinson correctly points out, in viewing perspectival pictures, we imagine seeing the scene from a certain visual perspective, and it seems to follow by way of (3) that we thereby imagine ourselves having been placed at a vantage point in the picture space and seeing the prospect from that site. But both parties to the disagreement are mistaken. It is (3) itself that should be rejected. It is hard to keep in focus that (3) is false, because, given our understandable temptation to waver between (1a) and (1b) interpretations of (1), the equivocal character of (3) lends it the deceptive guise of a tautology.

IV The Incoherence of Some Founding Fictions

It is natural, especially for philosophers, to feel discomfort with the position outlined above. Let Q be a possible condition whose realization is obviously essential for it to be the case that P. I have claimed that it is possible for it to be fictional, in a work or game of make-believe, that P, despite the fact that it is not fictional in either the work or game that Q. Worse yet, it can be fictional that P even though, if we were to take the first steps toward imagining how P could have come about, then the supplemented fiction would be paradoxical or otherwise incoherent. Troubling as these claims may be, I think that we will have to learn to live with the discomfort. Kendall Walton has done a lot to support this somewhat severe prescription.[27]

It is not at all uncommon for it to be fictional for a reader or viewer that she is Fing and not fictional for her that she is in condition G, even though being in G is obviously required as means to make it possible for her to F. In other words, what she imagines is *merely* minimally coherent. In many "Old Dark House" movies, it is fictional that the ghosts are completely invisible to human eyes, but audience members imagine seeing them as glowing, diaphanous creatures gliding among the furniture. Still, it is no part of the viewers' imaginings that they have special powers that permit them, unlike other human beings, to see ghosts. There are numerous similar examples, but I suspect that the threat of imminent paradox looms as most threatening when the coherence of the foundations of representational and/or narrational practices appear to be at risk – as in the domain of perspectival pictures discussed before. However, the tensions which exist in that case are hardly unique.

When a person reads the text of a work of literary fiction, she imagines herself to be reading the very words (word types) that fictionally were produced by the narrator of the tale. But paradox or incoherence easily impinges in this case also. To illustrate, we begin with what is admittedly a special kind of example, i.e., cases in which the reader imagines herself reading the narrator's own words despite the fact that there are propositions fictional in the work which imply that this should be fictionally impossible for her to do so. Thus, it might be fictional for the reader that she is reading the narrator's diary even though it is clearly indicated, at the end of the work, that this diary must have been consumed in a story-culminating fire. When a reader steps back from the fiction and focuses upon the relevant facts, the situation will strike her as paradoxical. But in the course of reading the work, this same reader is likely to ignore or discount the conflict, and she surely will not stop imagining that what she is reading are the words of the diarist/narrator.

A more common and more subtle conflict of narrational background assumptions is the following. Again, it is usually fictional for the reader that the words she is reading were produced by the narrator, but it is often fictionally indeterminate how those words were initially produced by that narrator. That is, it is indeterminate whether fictionally the narrator originally uttered them out loud or only in his mind or, alternatively, set them down in writing. Moreover, in these same cases, it will also be fictionally indeterminate for the reader how those words came to be *transmitted* to her or to a readership in general. Nothing will fictionally connect an original production by the narrator of the words (whatever mode of production may have been involved) with the appearance "in print" of the text of which the narrator's activity is fictionally the source. The reader will imagine nothing whatsoever about how the words came to be transcribed into a publicly distributed version.[28] Thus, the reader imagines reading a transcription of the narrator's own utterances or inscriptions, but her imagination does not specify anything about what makes it possible for her to do this. Fictionally, it is indeterminate how the reader can be acquainted, as she is, with the product of the narrator's storytelling performance.

Such indeterminacies at the core of the fictions that ground some types of literary narration open up the possibility that a related indeterminacy underlies our fictional perception of narrative events in film and that it does so deeply and extensively. This possibility suggests in turn a serious challenge to the *overall* approach of the Fictional Showing Hypothesis. Chatman and Levinson hold, and I have agreed with this, that it is fictional for movie viewers that they imagine seeing (on screen) the fictional activities of the characters portrayed. This fundamental fact, they conclude, implies that it is fictional for the viewer that the movie's image track is the product of an "activity" that somehow enables the viewer to see the narrative fictions. I have rejected the Face to Face Version of the Fictional Showing Hypothesis which says that the fictional activity of perceptual enabling is achieved by situating the viewer face to face with the story scenes. But now, our recent discussion demonstrates that it could be altogether fictionally indeterminate for movie viewers what, if anything, permits them to see episodes in cinematic worlds. There needs to be an argument to establish that such a fictional enabling activity is to be recognized as part of the work, an argument to rule out the hypothesis that audiences imagine seeing movie fictions without being expected to imagine a means by which such seeing would be achieved. Neither Chatman or Levinson supplies the missing argument.

So far, then, we have no plausible reason for supposing that the showing of a fictional film story involves the fictional showing of the events related in the film. However, we have, in this discussion, bypassed an obvious dimension of fiction film which is potentially crucial to the topic. We have concentrated on the fact that cinematic images in fiction films depict fictional characters and situations, but we have ignored the fact that they do this by showing us actors and actresses in real places – cast members who play the characters and places that represent the narrative locales. If we factor in this extra dimension, an alternative conception emerges of what narration in fiction films might be.

Our discourse about movies wavers between reference to shots which are *of* the cast and their performances and reference to shots said to be *of* the characters and the fictional actions they perform. Normally, these vacillating forms of description cause no confusion, but plainly there is an ambiguity in our talk about the "content" of shots in fiction film. Let us signal the rough distinction by saying that a shot is a *motion picture shot* of the actual objects and events before the camera and that the same shot is a *movie story shot* of the fictional characters and their fictional behavior. Naturally, any movie story shot (in a given film) is also a motion picture shot, but not conversely. In fact, let X be a shot in movie M, a shot in which it is fictional that a certain character C performs an action A. Shot X, in M, is also a motion picture shot of the actor who portrays C making the movements that represent the action A. But, if X were edited into a documentary, *The Making of Movie M*, then, in the altered context, it would not be a movie story shot in which C does A. It would merely be a motion picture shot of the actor in the course of playing C. It is not a simple task to give an adequate positive account of the further conditions required for such a motion picture shot to be, in the full sense, a movie story shot, and I will not try to construct one here. Intuitively, a movie story shot is one which has as a primary function, in its filmic context, the role of making it fictional in the movie that P, where its being fictional that P sustains or elaborates the movie's narrative progression.

In any case, we start with the following proposal. If X is a movie story shot in M of a fictional scene S, then *it is fictional for the viewer of M that X is a motion picture shot of that same scene S*. In other words, it is fictionally for the viewer as if the scene S actually took place, there exist motion picture shots of S, and X, as it occurs in M, is one of these. Viewers imagine that the events of the fictional narrative have been registered directly, without dramatic mediation, and that these events are exhibited to us "on screen" in the projection of the film.

There are many potential questions about how exactly this proposal is to be construed, but let us set them aside for now. We have here the basis for an alternative account of the type of narrational activity which movies might implicitly invoke. That is, the fictional showing involved in a fiction film would be the fictional exhibition and sequential arrangement, by means of editing, of *motion picture shots* of the occurrences that constitute the story. On this view, although an image track actually consists, as we well know, of a selection of motion picture shots of actors and actresses acting, we imagine and are intended to imagine that we are shown a selection of motion picture shots of fictional characters and their deeds. If one hears an echo of Metz in all of this, the fact is not surprising. Our new alternative sounds like a description of the business his great image-maker regularly conducts.

If one further aesthetic component were added to the proposal, the result would be, so to speak, a "Mediated Version" of the Fictional Showing Hypothesis. Suppose that we accept the thesis, developed and defended by Kendall Walton, that still photographs and motion picture shots are *transparent*.[29] Walton argues that, in seeing, e.g., a motion picture shot of a real scene S, viewers actually *see* the photographed scene, although, naturally, they see S in a rather special, mediated way; they see S *through* or *by means of* the motion picture photographs. Just as an observer can see a scene by means of mirrors or through a telescope or on live TV, so, in the same natural sense of the word, viewers see photographed objects and events through or by means of photographs. If the transparency of photography is genuine, then our new account of the nature of film narration entails that when a viewer sees a movie story shot of a (fictional) scene S, then it is thereby fictional for her that she is actually seeing S by means of a motion picture shot. Thus, the presentation and ordering of actual motion picture shots in a fiction film have the function of fictionally enabling the viewer to see the progression of the fictional narrative, albeit to see this "photographically."

Gregory Currie gives glancing notice to the Mediated Version of the Fictional Showing Hypothesis, although he states it in a misleading manner. He says, "[T]he only candidate [for an alternative to the Face to Face Version] seems to be this: that we imagine someone to be filming the action as a documentary, and that we are seeing the visually restricted result." Currie, however, thinks that the supposed alternative can be dismissed quickly. He goes on to object that "[b]ut to imagine this (something I have never been aware of imagining) would be to imagine that the fiction contains as a part the assumption that the action is being filmed by a camera crew and that we are watching the result. Occasionally, as with *Culloden* (Peter Weir, 1964) this would be an appropriate piece of imagining, but it certainly would not be for most fiction films."[30] In other words, it cannot be that, in watching a fiction film, the viewer imagines seeing a motion picture shot of the portrayed events, because imagining this would entail imagining that it is fictional, in the movie or for the viewer, that a motion picture camera was present in the fictional circumstances and that it photographed the events before its lens. But, in the standard case, it is not fictional, in the movie or for the viewer, that a camera was at the scene. In fact, if anything, it is fictional that no camera was there at all.

This objection can seem devastating, but it is really just another instance of a philosophical outlook we have had ample reason to repudiate. It is true that if an actual scene is filmed, then a motion picture camera must be present to do the filming. It is the operation of the camera that enables that scene to be photographed and incorporated into a motion picture. However, we should not conclude from this unquestioned fact that if spectators imagine that a motion picture shot of a scene exists and has been displayed to them, they must also be imagining that the real world means for producing that type of state of affairs are realized as well. For all that has been said thus far, it should be an open question whether or not it is wholly indeterminate for a movie viewer how it is that S came to exist and to be selected for the film. I have already pointed out that narration in works of literary fiction may rest on indeterminacy about how the narrator's words became available for us to read. The reply to Currie's objection is that a related truth applies to movie story shots construed as fictional motion picture shots. It is fictional that they were not taken by a camera at the fictional scene, and it is otherwise indeterminate how fictionally they came to be.

And yet, is this even minimally coherent? Isn't what we are supposed to imagine, on this proposal, a blatant contradiction? For what can it mean to imagine, of the film shots, that they are motion picture shots, without thinking of them as images formed by a motion picture camera? Are we supposed to imagine that the shots were produced, in some indeterminate fashion, by a motion picture camera which was nowhere in the vicinity of the fictionally photographed scene? Are we supposed to imagine motion picture shots that were *magically* created?

The last two rhetorical questions miss the point. It is not that it is fictional that motion picture shots of fictions are imagined to have bizarre or supernatural enabling conditions. As I have stressed throughout this section, we do not imagine anything in particular about what makes their existence possible. For the rest, the problem posed here is at least partly terminological. If "being a motion picture shot" is taken to entail "photographed by a motion picture camera," then perhaps we should say something like this: viewers imagine the motion picture shots in fiction films "as naturally iconic images," where this new concept is explained in terms of aesthetically salient attributes of motion picture shots that do not directly implicate the property of being made by a particular kind of picture-generating device.

Thus, an actual motion picture shot exhibits several fundamental and characteristic features.

George M. Wilson

One of these, discussed by both Walton and Currie, is that motion picture shots have a kind of *natural counterfactual dependence* on the rich collection of elements and their properties found within the photographed situation.[31] To call this kind of counterfactual dependence "natural" is, at least in part, to say that it does not itself depend upon an intervening counterfactual dependence between the array of items and features in the image, on the one hand, and the beliefs, desires, and intentions of the human image-maker, on the other. In reality, this natural counterfactual dependence arises in virtue of the mechanical operations of the motion picture camera, the film stock, the projection, and so on, but the same kind of dependence could have been achieved in some different way.

So this is one basic characteristic of motion picture images, and here is another. Because motion picture images are formed on a fixed screen by means of the projection of light, they, unlike paintings, do not exhibit the sort of worked surface produced, for example, by strokes of paint on a canvas. As a consequence, film images do not have the same potential for eliciting the experience of seeing the drawn or painted scene *as arising out of* the fine-grained configurations of material on the displayed surface – an aspect of our total experience of painting whose aesthetic importance Richard Wollheim has done so much to elucidate.[32] The absence in film images of this property, foundational for representational painting, both enhances our impression of the "immediacy" of their depictive power and denies to them the special artistic possibilities of well-crafted facture.

Now we can simply stipulate that we will say that a visual representation is a *naturally iconic representation (or image)* just in case: (1) It is one whose production depends essentially on a process involving the kind of natural counterfactual dependence just mentioned. (2) The process in question is of a type which has been designed to store and/or transmit the visual information in the resulting images. And (3), the image lacks the sort of worked surface that characteristically supports the impression of the pictorial field as supervening upon it. No doubt the envisaged definition could be, in various ways, expanded and emended. But, for present purposes, it is the strategy of introducing such a concept which is important and not the details. However any possible revisions might go, we are in a position to state the Mediated Version with much less conceptual stress and

strain. What we rightly imagine of the shots, when we watch a movie, is that they are naturally iconic shots of the fictional events in question. And it is fictionally indeterminate for us what specific sort of mechanism caused those naturally iconic shots to be produced and assembled as they are. It may be that what we are thereby intended to imagine is only minimally coherent, but this does nothing to establish that we do not imagine these things as we view fiction films.[33]

David Hills has reminded me that it is not uncommon for us to be asked to imagine, as a part of particular fictional worlds, the transmission of such naturally iconic images whose mode of operation is largely indeterminate. He observes,

> Consider the viewscreens that were standard equipment in the old *Flash Gordon* serials. Here, perspectival visual access to a distant scene is afforded by means of an image whose structure is somewhat photograph-like, but the process giving rise to these images is not imagined to involve, and in some instances may be actively imagined not to involve, the processing of causal inputs collected at the point in space on which the image is centered.[34]

Similarly, in the later Oz books, Ozma has a "Magic Picture" which can show her contemporaneous happenings anywhere in Oz, although, presumably, there is no device at the site of happenings that sends signals back to Ozma's wonderful screen.[35] If we are ordinarily untroubled by imagining these and similar contraptions as the *subject* of fiction, it seems likely that we may well cheerfully imagine motion picture image tracks as naturally iconic but causally ungrounded in a similar manner.

It should be clear what is so misleading about Currie's statement of the proposal under scrutiny. On the most natural way of understanding the phrase, to imagine a film as being a *documentary* is to imagine that its shots are motion picture shots of fictional events, shots which were made by a camera present at the fictional scenes. And, of course, there are movies in which this fiction is adopted. In *This Is Spinal Tap* (Rob Reiner, 1984), and, apparently, in *Culloden*, it is a part of the total fiction that a camera was present to shoot the narrative situations and that (most of) the shots in these movies were fictionally created by that camera. As Currie remarks, these are exceptional cases, but it is also not the type of case which the

Mediated Version describes. That account, properly understood, is not subject to such easy refutation.

V Conclusion

The Mediated Version of the Fictional Showing Hypothesis offers a novel account of the primitive basis of cinematic narration, and it deserves to be investigated thoroughly. It will be hard to make a serious assessment of the position unless and until it is more fully stated and imbedded in a larger, multifaceted theory of how movies present fictional narratives. As it has been stated above, this version only tells us something about how we imaginatively construe motion picture images in movies. That hardly counts as an explication of the purported activity of visual presentation of film stories.

A more or less random series of events does not constitute a narrative, and a series of movie shots depicting a mélange of unconnected events does not constitute a narration. But the Mediated Version focuses on individual shots and does not address the question of how they come to show an articulated story. The little that has been said in this connection about, for instance, film editing is extremely general and relatively insubstantial. According to the Mediated Version, editing in fiction films is construed by the viewer as a selection and arrangement of motion picture shots of fictional scenes. However, there are several kinds of editing transitions (straight cut, fade, dissolve, etc.), and there are many distinctive structures of editing employed in whole sequences and larger units. It needs to be shown that the Mediated Version allows us to make good sense of how viewers imagine the storytelling patterns that these devices help establish for them. For that matter, something would have to be said about the imaginative effects of camera movement within a single shot. Moreover, even if we assume that the Mediated Version adapts successfully to the presentation of diegetic sound, that adapted account will have to be extended, in some form, to fit sound-track music and voice-over narration.[36] In fact, the use of intertitles and other written documents in film would need to be considered here as well. A genuine analysis of cinematic narration based on the Mediated Version calls for careful elaboration and defense.

Nevertheless, even the limited proposal we have before us has significant attractions. We have seen that it avoids the implausibilities of the Face to Face Version without denying that movie audiences imagine seeing the fictional action on screen. It does not ask us to believe that we *actually* see the movie fictions (just as we see the actual motion picture shots), through a kind of magical window that opens, from the theater, onto the fictional prospects of the story. Film theorists have been tempted by all these options and by others, but each of them has led pretty directly to conceptual disaster. The Mediated Version promises, at a minimum, to hold the more familiar disasters at bay.

In trying to work out a full-scale theory of cinematic narration, various authors have embraced various theses about how we imagine motion picture shots in fiction films. According to the Face to Face Version, we imagine movie images as objective views of fictional situations perceived from an internal vantage point. Semioticians have tended to treat movie shots as statements which are iconically encoded. Others have favored the idea that the image track implicitly represents the visual experience of a camera observer. And, finally, in recent theory, the shot is often described as if it were a kind of subjectless apparition – a mirage-like visual field – with which the spectator "identifies" in fantasy-driven perception. Compared with any of these, the Mediated Version gives a rather deflationary account. "No," it replies, "we imagine motion picture shots as motion picture shots [or as naturally iconic images], but as motion picture shots for which the fictions they construct are real."

But what is the force and content of imagining the image track in this way? An answer to this question will not be trivial, and, indeed, it will not be easy to supply. For it simply refers us back to other questions and puzzles concerning the epistemics and aesthetics of (nonfiction) photography and filmmaking. These, of course, are major topics on their own. However, if the Mediated Version is correct, much of what we know or will come to learn about these topics will bear critically upon the nature of our special imaginative relations to visual narration in fiction films.[37]

Notes

1 "Notes Toward a Phenomenology of the Narrative," in *Film Language: A Semiotics of the Cinema*, trans. Michael Taylor (New York: Oxford University Press, 1974), 20–1. In fact, Metz credits the concept and the phrase to the French phenomenologist Albert Laffay.

2 In this passage, Metz makes reference only to the image track and not to the soundtrack. Many other writers on film narration speak only of the visual aspects of "the primitive basis" of film narration. For simplicity, the hypotheses I formulate and my discussion of them will largely conform to this practice. However, I assume in these discussions that the chief views under scrutiny can readily be reformulated as counterpart hypotheses about *diegetic* sound.

3 The literature on this subject is immense. For a useful survey, see part 3, "Film-narratology," in Robert Stam, Robert Burgoyne, Sandy Flitterman-Lewis, *New Vocabularies in Film Semiotics* (London: Routledge, 1992), 95–117. This section was written by Burgoyne. Of course, movies have "narrators" in a number of more restricted senses of the term. The voice-over narrator is probably the most familiar of these. I will not be discussing these more restricted concepts of "narrator" and "narration" in this essay, but the omission is not meant to suggest that questions about the nature and roles of the more specialized narrators are unimportant. Their importance and interest is amply documented in Avrom Fleishman, *Narrated Films: Storytelling Situations in Cinema History* (Baltimore: Johns Hopkins University Press, 1992).

4 David Bordwell, *Narration in the Fiction Film* (Madison: University of Wisconsin Press, 1985), 61–6, and my *Narration in Light: Studies in Cinematic Point of View* (Baltimore: Johns Hopkins University Press, 1986), 132–7. My views on this topic have changed, as the present essay will reveal.

5 Seymour Chatman, *Coming to Terms: The Rhetoric of Narrative in Fiction and Film* (Ithaca, N.Y.: Cornell University Press, 1990).

6 Ibid., 113.

7 Ibid., 115.

8 For the concept of a "storytelling narrator," see Kendall L. Walton, *Mimesis as Make-Believe: On the Foundations of the Representational Arts* (Cambridge, Mass.: Harvard University Press, 1990), 368–71.

9 This is not one of the more popular or helpful works in the Cliff Notes series.

10 Chatman, *Coming to Terms*, 116.

11 In this essay, I understand the concept of "being fictional (in a work or in a game of make-believe)" and the concept of "being make-believe (for a viewer or reader)" along the general lines that are set out in Walton's *Mimesis as Make-Believe*.

12 Of course, even the case of comic strips is more complicated than this. Usually, they will include some verbal narration in their frame insets. And this is not to mention the representation of the characters' speech in "word balloons."

13 Chatman, *Coming to Terms*, 155–6.

14 Levinson's fine essay is in *Post-Theory: Reconstructing Film Studies* (Madison: University of Wisconsin Press, 1996), 248–82.

15 Ibid., 252.

16 However, we will have reason to reconsider this assumption later.

17 Chatman, in particular, makes several remarks that can be interpreted as repudiating the Face to Face Version. For example, he says, "The cinema frame, too, presents events and characters from a post this side of the story world; there is never any question about what is included and what excluded from our perception" (*Coming to Terms*, 156). If these and similar comments are directed against the Face to Face Version, then it continues to remain quite unclear what his fictional showings amount to. On the other hand, he may be insisting that (as I would put it) it is fictional only in the viewer's game of make-believe that she sees the objects and events in the story and it is not fictional in either the narration (discourse) or the narrative that she sees these items. The second point is correct, but it is not incompatible with the position of the Face to Face Version.

18 I take this use of "pictorial field" from Malcolm Budd, *Values of Art: Pictures, Poetry, and Music* (London: Penguin Books, 1995), 64. Briefly, he states that the pictorial field is "the visible nature of a picture's surface."

19 *Image and Mind: Film, Philosophy, and Cognitive Science* (Cambridge, UK: Cambridge University Press, 1995), 171.

20 See *Narration in Light*, 55. Currie is here responding to this passage in my book. The passage he quotes was intended as metaphorical, but he is right in judging that it is best taken as a metaphor for what he calls the "Imagined Observer thesis."

21 Very often, we are able to specify the vantage point only in pretty rough terms. We can do no better than, e.g., "I see the contents of the picture from such-and-such a distance and from so-and-so an angle," where "such-and-such" and "so-and-so" are vague. Especially in paintings, it is only sometimes that anything substantial is suggested about the specific character of the "place" in question. In films, where earlier or later shots may have established the spatial layout of the scene in considerable

detail, we typically can describe our "vantage point" in a more determinate way.

22 Currie, *Image and Mind*, 178.

23 For a helpful summary account of perspective in painting and of some notions upon which depicted perspective depends, see the entry on "Perspective" by John Hyman in *A Companion to Aesthetics*, ed. David Cooper (Oxford: Basil Blackwell, 1992), 323–7.

24 Walton offers much the same response to Currie in "On Pictures and Photographs – Objections Answered," in *Film Theory and Philosophy*, ed. Richard Allen and Murray Smith (Oxford: Oxford University Press, forthcoming).

25 *Painting as an Art: The A. W. Mellon Lectures in the Fine Arts in 1984* (Princeton: Princeton University Press, 1987), chap. 3. There are some nice questions about how precisely Wollheim's position is best formulated, and he might object to aspects of my (very brief) statement of his views. However, I believe that nothing relevant to present concerns turns on any possible divergences.

26 For his discussion of Manet's use of "the spectator-in-the-picture," see ibid., 141–63.

27 See especially the section on "Silly Questions" in *Mimesis as Make-Believe*, 174–83.

28 David Hills, in correspondence, offers the following beautiful example of the point. He says, "*The Adventures of Huckleberry Finn* . . . represents itself as a carefully crafted 300 page memoir by its title character, a barely literate young man getting ready to light out for the territories because the prospect of any work that requires him to sit still terrifies him."

29 "Transparent Pictures," *Critical Inquiry* 11 (Spring 1984): 246–77, and "Looking Again Through Photographs: A Response to Edwin Martin," *Critical Inquiry* 12 (Summer 1986): 801–6, and the article cited in n. 24 above.

30 Currie, *Image and Mind*, 173.

31 See Walton, "Transparent Pictures," and Currie, *Image and Mind*, 182–3.

32 See his "Reflections on *Art and Illusion*" and "On Drawing an Object" in *On Art and the Mind* (Cambridge, Mass.: Harvard University Press, 1974), and *Painting as an Art*, esp. 46–7 and 72–5.

33 The Mediated Version of the Fictional Showing Hypothesis is the conjunction of the thesis that viewers imagine movie image tracks as selections of motion picture (naturally iconic) shots of fictional events *and* the thesis that photographs are transparent. The first thesis is of interest even if it were to be divorced for the second, so it deserves a name of its own. Call it, then, "The *Grand Imagier* Hypothesis."

34 Quoted from private correspondence.

35 See, for example, L. Frank Baum, *The Emerald City of Oz* (New York: William Morrow and Company, 1993), 192–96. However, the *Flash Gordon* example is better because, in Oz, the mediation of magic is naturally to be suspected.

36 Levinson, "Film Music and Narrative Agency," discusses this question extensively. His remarks suggest that the best case for recognizing "cinematic narrators" may rest upon the viewer's proclivity to imagine an agent who co-ordinates all the different dimensions of film to serve a unifying, e.g., narrative-constructing, function.

37 I am deeply grateful to David Hills for a marvelously detailed commentary on an earlier version of this paper. His criticisms, queries, and examples have greatly improved the essay, and it could have been additionally strengthened had I been able to accommodate fully all of the suggestions that he offered me. Thanks also to Jerry Levinson for helpful and clarifying comments.

13

Unreliability Refigured: Narrative in Literature and Film

Gregory Currie

As consumers of fiction, we have become skilled at recognizing unreliable narratives; as theoreticians, we are less well able to say what constitutes unreliability and how it is detected. I aim to improve our understanding of the theoretical issues. In the process, I hope to show four things:

1 that narrative unreliability is a concept separable from the concept of an unreliable *narrator*;
2 that narrative unreliability requires for its explanation the concept of an *implied author*;
3 that narrative unreliability bears close and interesting connections to the importantly distinct concept of an *ambiguous* narrative;[1]
4 that we can explain the prevalence of certain devices in narrative in terms of the ease or difficulty of the reader's task in figuring out whether and how those devices are being used.

Another theme that runs through the discussion is the relation between narration in literary fictions and in film. Indeed, the central example of narrative unreliability I shall use is an example from film. Part of the problem of developing an adequate general theory of narrative has been the tendency to fix on narrative *literature* as the central explanatory target, and to apply the theory so generated to other representational modes: a method which often leads to strained and implausible results.

I shall be assuming throughout that the comprehension of narrative is essentially a matter of intentional inference; the reader or viewer has to infer, on the basis of her reading or viewing, the complex and sometimes covert intentions that seem to lie behind the words and images the work presents. But while I shall not be arguing directly for this hypothesis, what follows will constitute a test of it. For the worth of the hypothesis is directly proportional to its success in explaining those particular devices which make up the repertoire of narrative. Unreliability is one of them. The fact that our theory does well in explaining the mechanisms of unreliability tells strongly in its favor.

I Fictions Misdescribed

A newspaper article can be unreliable, meaning that it misleads us about what actually happened, or would mislead us if we found it credible. Being misleading in this sense requires a disparity between the world as it is and the world as it is represented to be, in this case by a newspaper. Is there then, in the case of the unreliable fictional narrative, a disparity between the world of the novel and the claims that someone – we might very naturally call her a narrator – makes about that world? That this is always and necessarily the explanation of unreliability in narrative is an idea I want to challenge. Before I do, it is worth noting that, even from the point of view of one who thinks

Gregory Currie, "Unreliability Refigured: Narrative in Literature and Film," *The Journal of Aesthetics and Art Criticism* 53(1), 1995: 19–29. Reprinted by permission of Blackwell Publishing.

that narrators are always the source of unreliability, the idea of "fictional reality misdescribed" is hardly one we can appeal to in explanation of that unreliability. You may believe that there are fictional worlds.[2] But if you do, you must be careful not to fall into a quasi-magical mode of explanation, whereby you "explain" what happens in the fiction by appeal to what happens in the corresponding world. For how does a particular fictional world, *w, get to be* the fictional world of *The Good Soldier*? Not because of any straightforward fit between the meaning of the text and world *w*; we want to say that, since this is an unreliable narrative, the text *misdescribes w*. So what extratextual mechanism links the text to this world and no other? More than one answer is possible, but whatever answer is favored, the locus of our interest in the nature of unreliability must surely be the mechanism itself and not the world that mechanism locates. For it is in the workings of that mechanism that we shall find the justification for saying, "The text is a misdescription of this world, rather than a correct description of that one." Since I hold that this mechanism is intention, and the recognition of intention on the part of the audience, I hold that intention is the key to narrative unreliability.

But that, we may suppose, is a lesson well learned. For the standard account of narrative unreliability is one that appeals, exactly, to the mental economies of agents – though these agents are typically thought of as hypothetical or imaginative constructs rather than living beings. The standard account says that narrative unreliability is a product of a discrepancy between what we might call internal and external perspectives. The external perspective is that of the so-called "implied author," a figure who in a sense may herself be fictional or imagined, because her mental economy does not necessarily correspond to that of the actual author, but who is not to be thought of as occupying a position within the work itself. Rather she is conceptualized as the agent responsible for the story qua fiction.[3] The internal perspective is that of a narrator; a creature who is conceptualized as a product of the work itself, rather than as the work's producer. In a moment I shall describe how the conflict between these two perspectives creates unreliability. But we need first to note that narrators come in a variety of kinds, of which two shall be distinguished at once.

The narrator may be internal (or *intradiegetic*): a character within the story itself, to be thought of as telling what is in fact fiction as if it were known fact – or as lies or deluded ravings, but not, anyway, as fiction (then she is internal not only to the work but to the fictional story that work has to tell). Or she may be an external (*extradiegetic*) narrator, who announces herself as telling the story as fiction, but where there is some reason to think of this narrator's voice as distinct from and dependent on that of the implied author. While it may be possible for narrators of both kinds to count as unreliable, rather different kinds of unreliability attach to each, and it is not altogether easy to state the difference between them. But I shall not enquire more deeply into the difference between these two kinds of unreliability, because I shall be asking: What happens to the concept of unreliability *when there is no narrator*? Merely for the sake of simplicity, and not because it favors my argument, I shall speak only of intradiegetic narrators in what follows: they are more commonly the source of narrative unreliability, and their role in opposition to the implied author is easier to conceptualize, since it is often very difficult to distinguish between a case where implied author and extradiegetic narrator are distinct, and a case where the implied author is simply speaking ironically.

The implied author is epistemically dominant over the narrator in this sense: that the intentions of the implied author *determine* what is true in the story, while the mental economy of the narrator is thought of simply as a part of the story itself and not as authoritative – not, at least, automatically so. The narrator's role is to tell us what is true in the story, and, like tellers in real life, she may have it wrong, or wish to tell us other than what she believes is true. On this model, we perceive narrative unreliability when we perceive a disparity between the (determining) intentions of the implied author concerning what is true in the story and the (reporting) intentions of the narrator concerning what she would have the reader believe occurred.[4] And because the implied author is authoritative, this amounts to recognizing a disparity between what is true in the story and the intentions of the narrator concerning what she would have the reader believe occurred. This view is expressed in a summarizing remark of Wayne Booth's: "I have called a narrator *reliable* when he speaks for or acts in accordance with the norms of the work (which is to say, the implied author's norms), *unreliable* when he does not."[5] That, roughly, is how it is in Ford's *The Good*

Soldier, in Camus's *The Fall*, in Ishiguro's *The Remains of the Day*, and in many other narratives we commonly describe as unreliable.

But what of those narratives which are intuitively unreliable, but where the unreliability is not, or at least not obviously, attributable to a narrator? In the literary case you might insist that there always is a narrator to blame for the unreliability, however unobvious her presence may be (and there are some notably unobvious narrators). This seems rather ad hoc; it is worth asking whether there is some more elegant solution to the difficulty. And with film, the idea of a hidden narrator such as would be postulated in order to save the Boothian definition of unreliability strains the bounds of coherence. It will take a moment to see why.

II   The Asymmetry Between Literature and Film

I want now to introduce two further distinctions between kinds of narrators, and these distinctions will play an important role in the argument that follows. (Remember: we are ignoring external narrators, and the distinctions I am now making are, for our purposes, distinctions within the class of internal narrators.) These new distinctions cut across one another. First, I draw a distinction between a *foregrounded* and a *backgrounded* narrator. A foregrounded narrator is one whose presence is signaled in the work itself, a backgrounded one is a narrator whose presence has to be inferred (I do not claim that there is a sharp boundary between these two kinds, but indeterminacy of boundary is, of course, no argument against their distinctness).[6] The second distinction is one between *controlling* and *noncontrolling* narrators. Narrators are characters within the world of the fiction who are to be thought of as telling us facts, or lies, or deluded ravings – but not as telling us a fictional story.[7] Narrators tell by making utterances, and we can speak of the text of that utterance, whether written or not. Now that text – the text of which it is fictional that it is uttered by the narrator – may coincide with the text we are reading when we read the work. In that case, we imagine the narrator to be controlling; he or she is the source of the text before us. We know, of course, that the text is fictional, and we probably know the identity of its real author, but we may think that it is part of the fiction itself that the narrator is the source of this

text and accept the fiction's implicit or explicit invitation to imagine exactly that. In this sense, Watson is a controlling narrator of the Holmes stories and to some extent an unreliable one in the sense of Booth.[8] But sometimes narrators are noncontrolling. That occurs when the narrator is *embedded:* when her own text is not the text we read but a text described or reported in the text we read (which may also describe the embedded narrator's telling of it).[9]

As I have said, our two distinctions cut across one another. That gives us four options: foregrounded/controlling, foregrounded/noncontrolling, backgrounded/controlling, and backgrounded/noncontrolling. But it will be seen that there is a difficulty in the last of these combinations. A backgrounded narrator is a shadowy figure whose characteristics are hard to identify in detail, and everything about her that can be inferred has to be inferred on the basis of very tenuous evidence – otherwise she would not count as backgrounded. In reasoning about the characteristics of such a narrator, as with other kinds of evidentially underfunded reasoning, we rely very heavily on default assumptions; if a decision has to be made about the possession of some characteristic and there is no evidence either way, we tend to favor the answer that is simpler or otherwise preferable on a priori grounds. And it is simpler to assume that a backgrounded narrator is controlling than that she is not; to suppose that she is not is to see her appearing as told about in the text, rather than as the source of the text itself. But if she is told about in the text, there ought to be some evidence in the text for her existence, which, by assumption of her backgroundedness, there is not. In that case, backgrounded narrators are almost bound to be controlling – it being relatively unproblematic that the agent responsible for a text might not signal her presence within the text itself. And I certainly am not aware of any actual cases of works where we could point with any conviction to a backgrounded but non-controlling narrator.

Now there is something awkward – indeed, something close to incoherence – about the idea of a controlling narrator in film. With literature it is often natural to imagine that what one is reading is a true account of certain events witnessed or otherwise known about by someone, who then went to the trouble of setting it all down for us in writing; some of John Buchan's adventure stories, we are to imagine, are the product of a careful editor who has heard from the parties concerned and has created a judicious account on paper from their reports; it is that account, we imagine, that we are now reading, and its imagined author counts as a controlling narrator. But what are we to imagine that would be analogous to this in the filmic case – that the person in the know has gone to the trouble of recreating it all for us on camera, spending millions of dollars, employing famous actors and a vast army of technicians? That seems implausible, especially in cases where the narrator, if there is one, would most naturally be thought of as living in the pre-cinematic age. The same argument tells against the hypothesis that the narrator is a documentary filmmaker who went to the trouble of recording the events of which he has knowledge on film at the time; it would also seem to leave no room for narrative *unreliability*, which is after all what we are trying to account for.[10] But if controlling narrators in film are ruled out, and backgrounded narrators are almost inevitably controlling, we may conclude that backgrounded narrators in film are very rare, if possible at all.[11] In that case, it will not do simply to insist on their presence whenever we encounter a film narrative that is unreliable but where there is no foregrounded narrator. Better to say simply that in such a case we have unreliable narrative without a narrator.[12]

Perhaps the argument just given merely shows that the only unreliable film narratives there can be are those which involve noncontrolling, and therefore probably foregrounded narrators – as with *Rashomon, Stage Fright*, and most of the other filmic narrations we think of as unreliable. The trouble with that conclusion is that there seems to be a counterexample to it. At any rate, George Wilson claims to have found one: Fritz Lang's *You Only Live Once*.[13] Wilson argues that the natural interpretation of the film, according to which the young man Eddie is innocent of the crime for which he is due to be executed, is on closer examination not supported by, and is in fact at certain crucial points undermined by, the film's narration and its studiedly selective presentation of events. On Wilson's view, a right interpretation of the film would have us withhold judgment as to Eddie's guilt or innocence. But that is certainly not what most viewers of the film have done; generations of critics and lay viewers have accepted the view that Eddie is an innocent victim.[14] Notably, there is no foregrounded narrator in the film, and no evidence, so far as I can see, for the existence of that very rare bird, the backgrounded, noncontrol-

ling narrator either. In that case we seem bound to conclude that we have unreliable narrative without a narrator.[15]

I should say that I am not entirely convinced by Wilson's interpretation, and it seems to me that some of the evidence that Wilson cites in support of it – in particular a crucial shot inside the getaway car – does not in fact support it. But Wilson's interpretation does mesh very finely with certain parts of the film which are otherwise hard to understand. And if Wilson's interpretation does not apply in all detail to Lang's film, it is not difficult to imagine a film, different from Lang's in minor ways, to which it does. So we may conclude that it is *possible* for there to be unreliable narration in film where no foregrounded narrator is present – and when it comes to definitions, possible counterexamples are as telling as actual ones. In that case we really will have to look for another definition of narrative unreliability. Anyway, I shall assume, for the sake of the argument, that Wilson is right.

How might narrative unreliability occur other than as a result of a disparity between the viewpoints of the narrator and the implied author? It can occur, I claim, as a result of there being a certain kind of *complex intention* on the part of the implied author. I shall explain. An agent can do something with an intention of the following complex kind: she creates or presents something which she intends will be taken as evidence of her intentions, and she intends that superficial evidence will suggest that her intention was X, whereas a better, more reflective grasp of the evidence will suggest that her intention was Y. Trivial example: Frieda compliments Fred on his sophisticated sense of humor. Her flattery is a little disturbing; this is not the Frieda we know. But now we see: it was all ironic and intended to be recognized, ultimately, as more of the abuse she usually heaps upon Fred. Frieda's performance was unreliable, and there may be people, Fred among them, who didn't get to the second stage, because that took just a little more calculating than some of us can be relied on to make.

That seems to be what is going on in *You Only Live Once*; we take the images and sounds that go to make up the film as intended one way. But if we are scrupulous in our examination of those images, we find peculiarities, incongruities, and apparently unmotivated elements that start to fall into place when we see that it can be interpreted in another. Their falling into place consists in their being seen as intended to suggest that second, less obvious interpretation. Narratives which are the product (or which seem to be the product – remember that it is the *implied* author who concerns us here) of this kind of two-tier system of intentions constitute a distinctive and especially challenging class of narratives, and I do not think that they are very well understood. I hope to change that somewhat in the rest of this paper. Before I begin, a methodological remark.

In appealing to the notion of an implied author here I leave behind those intentional realists who insist that the work must be interpreted in the light of the real author's intentions – where those intentions are to be understood as "embodied" or "made effective" in the text. While there seem to me to be great difficulties in the realist's position, the present focus of our attention need not be the occasion for a dispute between us.[16] The realist may take over my definition of unreliability and say that it applies in those cases where a complex intention of the kind I have described is possessed by the real author and is embodied in the text by her storytelling actions.

III Which Definition?

Defining unreliable narrative in terms of complex intentions attributable to an implied author allows us to count a narrative as unreliable even when there is no narrator who we can identify as the source of unreliability. What, then, are the relations between this kind of unreliability and the cases that are covered by Booth's narrator-centered definition? Certainly, some of the cases that are unreliable on Booth's definition would not be unreliable on mine. In Lardner's "Haircut," for example, we have an internal narrator whose outlook (his "norms" as Booth puts it) is different from, and undermined by, that of the implied author. But this is not a case, I believe, where we would attribute a complex intention to the implied author. The disparity of outlooks is too obvious in this case for us to be warranted in concluding that the implied author has intentions that can be grasped only on a significantly deeper level of reflection. The warranted conclusion is surely that the implied author intends us to see, straight off, the moral idiocy of the narrator.

That is not to say that the extensions of Booth's definitions and mine are disjoint, for it is possible for a work to satisfy both of them. In such a work

there is a disparity of outlooks between the implied author and the internal narrator, but the disparity is not obvious, and it is only on deeper reflection that we realize that it was intended that we find the narrator unreliable.[17] Then we have an instance of our complex intention.[18] So there is overlap, but not sameness, for the extensions of these concepts – mine was introduced, after all, to cover cases that Booth's does not cover – and so the definitions characterize different concepts.

But I am afraid I shall not be able to endorse the comfortably ecumenical position that these definitions are merely different: different but equal. I believe that my characterization of unreliability in terms of a complex intention – call it unreliability$_2$ – is of greater theoretical and critical interest than the familiar Boothian characterization in terms of a disparity of outlook between the narrator and the implied author – call it unreliability$_1$. There are of course interesting cases of unreliability$_1$, but they tend also to be cases of unreliability$_2$; they tend to be cases where the narrator's unreliability is to some degree unobvious. We are past the point where a narrator's unreliability is *intrinsically* interesting, because we are past the point where we bring to the work a strong presumption that narrators will be reliable. Without that presumption, narratorial unreliability is, of itself, no more significant than the mendacity of a dramatic speaker: no more significant, that is, from the point of view of a theory of narrative. But unreliability that is to some degree hidden is of theoretical interest because its operation depends on delicately balanced inferential strategies that the reader must undertake. For the rest of this essay I want to concentrate on unreliability$_2$ and on the structure of our inferences to it. For reasons to do with the structure of those inferences, unreliability$_2$ is less frequently encountered than its Boothian rival. To see why will require the introduction of another kind of narrative that I want to call *ambiguous*.

IV Ambiguity and Unreliability

An ambiguous narrative is one which does not enable us to answer all the significant questions which arise concerning the story. Significance is an important condition here, since no narration can possibly provide complete information about the characters and events it describes. When is a question significant? One answer is this: when it is a question that members of the audience are (normally) inclined to ask concerning that narrative. But this will not do. Sometimes there are questions we as audience are inclined to ask at the end of the work and which the work does not answer, but which would not be grounds for calling it ambiguous. Many people are inclined to wonder what will happen to Rhett and Scarlet at the end of *Gone with the Wind* (as the recent and long-awaited sequel indicates). But this would not be grounds for saying that the narrative (either the book or the film) is ambiguous in the sense I am interested in here. Questions about the continuation or noncontinuation of relationships are ones we are almost always inclined to ask – at least they arise fleetingly in our minds – at the end of the work. This proposal is going to make too many narratives ambiguous.

A proposal with a similar defect has it that the narrative is ambiguous if it is a narrative that leads us to expect an answer to a question when in fact it does not provide an answer; though this would at least explain the intuition that *Gone with the Wind* is not ambiguous, since that narrative does not lead us to expect that an answer will be given to the question "What happens to them after the narrative breaks off?" But this proposal is neither necessary nor sufficient for ambiguity: the narrative might make it clear right from the start that a certain question is not going to be answered (in the case of a film that might require a voice-over to be convincing). So we are not led to expect an answer, and indeed the question may not be answered by the narrative, yet the question may be one such that, in not answering it, the narrative takes on the intuitive character of ambiguity. So satisfaction of the proposed criterion is not necessary for ambiguity. And a question may arise to which we expect an answer, but where we put down failure to provide an answer to incompetence in the construction of the narrative. In that case we would be doing the work a favor it does not deserve by calling it ambiguous.

But the case of narrative incompetence is the clue to solving our problem. When a question arises which is not answered in the narrative, but where we ascribe the nonanswer to incompetence, we do not think that a question has been deliberately raised by the implied author, and deliberately left unanswered; we think, exactly, that either the raising or the failure to answer were due to some oversight or other failure of execution. So I propose the following as the criterion of when a nar-

ration is ambiguous: when it raises a question in the viewer's mind which it fails to answer, and where the raising and the nonanswering seem to have been intentional. This proposal gives the result that *Gone with the Wind* is not ambiguous; while readers and viewers may wonder about the future of Rhett and Scarlet, and the makers may have expected that they would wonder about it, and while all this may be common knowledge between audience and maker, the question does not seem to be intentionally raised and intentionally left unanswered by the narrative.[19]

It is easy at the level of theory to see the differences between unreliable and ambiguous narratives. But it is not always easy to say which kind a particular work belongs to. Is *Rashomon* an ambiguous or an unreliable narration? If there figure within it embedded narrators who are unreliable, we may grant that it is unreliable in the sense of Booth (unreliability$_1$). It would be ambiguous if it left it an open question which of the conflicting accounts is true. But is it unreliable in the sense that I defined above (unreliability$_2$), viz., that it is possible to detect in its making the influence of a complex intention of the kind I have described in connection with *You Only Live Once*? That would be so if we thought of *Rashomon* this way: as intended, first, to suggest to us that the problem is to decide which account is true, and second, to suggest on deeper reflection the relativity of truth and, in consequence, the falsity of our first question's presupposition, that there is a right answer. For some of us, the easy relativism of the last option is too banal to be a plausible candidate for interpretation, but this may be just an indication that there is sometimes no neutral perspective from which to choose between ambiguity and unreliability, a situation we sometimes experience with other interpretive choices.[20]

But while ambiguity and unreliability are distinct interpretive options, they are compatible, not merely in the sense that there is sometimes no principled choice between them, but in the stronger sense that a single interpretation of the work may require the application of both. We might, for instance, take *Rashomon* as unreliable$_2$ in this way: that at first glance the options are between the explicit accounts of the various narrators, while on reflection we see that there is another option – the relativistic one – and that the story is ambiguous between those collected at the first round and this one. (I would count that as only marginally less banal than straightforwardly opting for relativism, but it might still be the best thing we can come up with.) On that view, *Rashomon* is both ambiguous and unreliable$_2$.

Note that *You Only Live Once* is, on Wilson's account, both ambiguous and unreliable$_2$. At first the question: "Is Eddie guilty of murder?" seems to be answered by the narrative. But we see, on closer inspection, that it is left open by it. In that case might there be some internal connection between unreliability$_2$ and ambiguity? I believe there is, though the connection is not a straightforward logical one. It is not that unreliability$_2$ necessitates ambiguity; rather, unreliability$_2$ is an easier effect to achieve when it goes with ambiguity than when it does not. The reason is this: it is easier to persuade the reader or viewer that a question has been answered when it has not than it is to persuade her that a question has been answered one way when in fact it has been answered in another. The task of the author of an unreliable$_2$ narration is a difficult one. It is to set clues at two levels: at level one where the clues are more obvious but only superficially persuasive, and at level two where they are less obvious but more weighty when reflected upon. But the degree of difficulty of the task varies from case to case, and one determinant of its degree of difficulty is what we might call the *epistemic distance* between the two levels; increase the distance and you increase the difficulty. By "distance" I mean the disparity between what you want to convey as a first impression and what you want the audience to catch on to on further reflection. The greater the distance in this sense, the greater the subtlety and complexity of the reasoning that the audience will have to go through to cover the gap, and the less likely it is that they will succeed. And trying to raise the probability of success in such a case by reinforcing the clues at level two may simply undermine the whole project by making the inference to level two more obvious and natural than that to level one.

It will generally be the case that there is a greater distance, in this sense, between the two levels if at one level we are given, say, a yes answer, and at the other a no answer, than there will be if at one level we are given an answer (yes or no) and at the other we are told that no answer is forthcoming. In the first case one has to persuade the audience to abandon a position and adopt the opposite one; in the second one has merely to do the first of those two things. So the second is an easier thing to do than the first. And if Wilson is right, the second of these two things is what Lang

(or his implied surrogate) seeks to do with *You Only Live Once*. Ambiguity is also probably the best thing that advocates of the delusional interpretation of *The Turn of the Screw* can hope for. Reflection doesn't show that there are no ghosts; at best it shows that another hypothesis does about as well as the supernatural one when it comes to explaining the text.

When an unreliable narrative is one that seems, superficially, to close a certain issue but reveals on reflection that the question is left open, as in *You Only Live Once*, let us say that we have a "transition to openness." Consider a transition in the opposite direction – a "transition to closure" – where the narrative seems, superficially, to leave a certain issue open but is seen on reflection to answer the question one way or another. Would a transition to closure be easier or more difficult to effect than a transition to openness? Taking into account only what I have called epistemic distance suggests that it would be neither more nor less difficult, since distance is symmetrical – the distance between two things is independent of the order in which they are taken. However, I think there are grounds for saying that it would, other things being equal, be more difficult to effect a transition to closure than a transition to openness. The problem, in creating an unreliable narration, is to suggest one hypothesis by means of more obvious but ultimately less convincing evidence, and to suggest another by means of less obvious but more convincing evidence. The difficulty is to ensure that the more convincing evidence will in fact be less obvious, without having it disappear entirely from view. And that difficulty will be the greater, the stronger the hypothesis that it is evidence for. After all, it takes more evidence to get us to believe a strong conclusion than a weak one. It's not hard to convince me that either Oswald shot Kennedy or someone else did; it's much harder to convince me that someone else did. So, other things being equal, one will have to provide stronger evidence to support a definite conclusion than to support a mere ambiguity. But then the transition to closure requires stronger evidence at the level of the less obvious, and that kind of transition is going to be more difficult to effect than is a transition to openness. On that assumption, we would expect to find transitions to openness more frequently in literature and other narrative forms than transitions to closure. And that, I believe, is exactly what we do find.[21]

V   Implied Author and Narrator

I have been arguing that narrative unreliability in literature and film can occur in the absence of a narrator, but not in the absence of an implied author. There are two kinds of theories that clash with that idea: theories that deny the necessity of an implied author, and theories that assert the necessity of a narrator. Such theories have been advocated by, respectively, David Bordwell and Seymour Chatman.

David Bordwell has argued that in film we have narration without a "sender." Part of the way I can agree with him. He argues, as I have argued, that narrators in film must be embedded: they are "invariably swallowed up in the overall narrational process of the film, which they do *not* produce."[22] But I have argued that while narrators are optional elements in film (and noncontrolling when present), the implied author is not dispensable, that the interpretation of film is crucially dependent on our seeing the images and other elements of the film as the products of intention. Here we disagree:

> ...literary theory may be justified in looking for a speaking voice or narrator. But in watching films we are seldom aware of being told something by an entity resembling a human being. As for the implied author, this construction adds nothing to our understanding of filmic narration. No trait we could assign to an implied author of a film could not more simply be ascribed to the narration itself: it sometimes suppresses information, it often restricts our knowledge, it generates curiosity, it creates a tone, and so on. To give every film a narrator or implied author is to indulge in an anthropomorphic fiction.... [Filmic] narration is better understood as the organization of a set of cues for the construction of a story. This presupposes a perceiver, but not any sender, of a message.[23]

Bordwell may be right to say that when watching a film, we are seldom aware of being told something by a human being. But that is no argument against the dependence of interpretation on the idea of an intentional agent as sender. The mechanisms whereby we arrive at the interpretation of films and other works are no more likely to be continually present to consciousness in their operation

than are the mechanisms of, say, arithmetical calculation. And it is unclear how some of the functions that Bordwell assigns to narration could be accounted for outside the scope of assumptions we make about a sender; he speaks, for instance, of a narration which "suppresses information." Without recourse to the idea of intention, you can speak of a system that fails to deliver all the information you want, but not of a system that suppresses information. And, of course, the idea of suppression (rather than just of informational incompleteness) is essential to an adequate description of filmic narration and our reaction to it; we feel, in some cases, that we are being deliberately deprived of information (as when we see only the hands of the murderer), that we are being deprived of it for some dramatic or emotional purpose, that our expectations are being played with. None of this would make sense unless we understood the narration as something communicated to us by someone.[24] In particular, unreliable narratives of the kind exemplified in *You Only Live Once* depend, for their interpretation, on our perception of a certain kind of complex intention on the implied maker's part.

But while it is an error to dispense with the notion of an intelligence that communicates the story to us, we must not confuse the need for such an intelligence with the requirement that every story have a narrator. Seymour Chatman tells us that the idea that stories, or some of them, might not be communicated by a narrator leads to a conclusion that "contradicts both logic and common sense" – "that narratives just appear unannounced."[25] We can agree that no narrative "just appears"; the question is whether its appearance requires a narrator rather than simply an implied author. Chatman, who distinguishes narrators from authors, both real and implied, thinks it does: the narrator is "someone or something in the text who or which is conceived of as presenting (or transmitting) the set of signs that constitutes it." But there is certainly no violation of logic, and probably none of common sense, when we deny that every text contains such a being. The implied author is responsible for the story, what she intends to be true in the story is true in it, and the text she writes (or the film she makes) is our guide to what she does intend. She may intend it to be true in that story that someone other than her is telling it, perhaps as known fact. In that case we have a narrator. But she may not intend this; she may simply intend to tell a tale in which it is

fictional that this and that occurred, but not fictional that anyone is telling that it occurred. (Of
course she herself tells the story, but her doing so
does not make it *fictional* that she, or anyone, does
so.) Where in all this are there violations of logic
and common sense?

While the view Chatman rejects is unproblematic, his own theory faces problems of a kind to
which our discussion has rendered us sensitive.
"Only the narrator can be unreliable," he tells
us, and the duplicitous flashback in *Stage Fright*
is the product of the character Johnny who "is
'responsible' for the lying images and sounds that
we see and hear."[26] But Johnny, like the other
characters, exists within the story, and it is no
part of that story that he produced and edited
cinematic images in order to convince his fictional fellows (and us?) of his innocence – anyway
a transparently self-defeating enterprise. (Chatman's scare-quotes indicate an unease about this
notion of responsibility, but they do nothing to
solve the problem.) Rather, the deceptive images
and their juxtaposition must be thought of as
representations of Johnny's account, though we
begin by taking them also to be representations
of what is real within the fiction itself. They are
thus attributable to the film's implied maker. What

Chatman would have the narrator do can be done
by the implied maker, at considerably lower cost to
common sense and its educated cousin, theory.

VI Conclusion

I have suggested that there are cases – certainly
possible and possibly actual – of a kind of narrative
unreliability not covered by the standard account.
I have given a general characterization of this kind,
and suggested how it might supersede the more
familiar, Boothian, kind of unreliability. I also
described what I call ambiguous narrative, and
suggested that there is a close connection between
this and the kind of unreliable narrative I defined –
a connection forged by the difficulty readers face
in making the inferences to the implied author's
intentions that are necessary if unreliability is to be
detected. I have argued, finally, that unreliability
in narrative makes no sense without appeal to the
concept of an implied author, but that the concept
of a narrator is required only by one kind of
unreliability. The implied author, we may say, is
an absolute presupposition of unreliability, the
narrator a merely conditional one.[27]

Notes

1 My terminology only partly coincides with that of
other writers on narrative, and some of the deviations
are noted and discussed in these notes. Sometimes I
find their terminology inappropriate; sometimes
I find that their terminology marks distinctions in
the wrong places. Anyway, there is not much uniformity of usage evident in writing on narrative.
2 If commitment to them is nothing more than a commitment to sets of propositions, I believe in them
myself.
3 So the implied author, as I use that notion, is always
"extradiegetic" in Genette's sense (Gerard Genette,
Narrative Discourse, English translation [Oxford:
Blackwell, 1972]). See text immediately below.
4 So narrator and implied author occupy quite distinct
functional roles, and we should not attribute properties of the one to the other. Narrators may be (but
need not be) omniscient, but implied authors never
are; their perspective on the story is not one of
knowledge but of determining choice.
5 Wayne Booth, *The Rhetoric of Fiction*, 2nd ed.
(New York: Viking Books, 1983), pp. 158–9, emphasis
in the original, and in the first edition thereof, 1961.
One misleading feature of this remark is

the implication that narrative unreliability is always
and exclusively a matter of value (Booth's "norms"),
which is certainly not the case, as many of
Booth's examples attest. Booth's definition is taken
over, more or less, by Seymour Chatman, *Story and
Discourse* (Cornell University Press, 1978), p. 233, and
is repeated in Gerald Prince, *A Dictionary of Narra-
tology* (University of Nebraska Press, 1987), p. 101.
6 Foregrounding a narrator may not require an explicit
statement in the text of the work that there is such a
narrator, though that is certainly one way to achieve
foregrounding. There are various ways that stop
short of explicit statement in which texts make features of the stories they tell obvious.
7 This, of course, is a simplification, since there are
stories within stories where a narrator internal at one
level is external at another; in these stories it is
fictional that the narrator is telling us that it is fictional that ... Inclusion of such cases into our present
taxonomy would further complicate an already complex structure, and ignoring them will not affect the
argument.
8 F. K. Stanzel supposes that all "first-person" narrators (in my terms: internal narrators) are necessarily

unreliable, because of the limitations on their knowledge (*A Theory of Narrative*, trans. Charlotte Goedsche [Cambridge: Cambridge University Press, 1984], p. 89). But failure to be omniscient is one thing and failure to be reliable another. Perhaps the thought here is that a non-omniscient narrator could not be certain of the truth of any of his beliefs. But it is an error of the Cartesian tradition to suppose that lack of certainty translates into unreliability.

9   The term "embedded narrator" is sometimes used to refer to any character-narrator. This strikes me as misleading usage; a character-narrator who is controlling in my sense is not necessarily embedded in the story. He tells the story, but he does not tell of his own telling. See, e.g., Wallace Martin, *Recent Theories of Narrative* (Cornell University Press, 1986), p. 135.

10 Chatman, I think, sees the difficulty here. See his discussion of the famous "lying flashback" in Hitchcock's *Stage Fright* in *Story and Discourse*, p. 237. But in more recent writings Chatman describes this case in much more problematic terms; see below, text to note 26.

11 I think I agree with Christian Metz here: "the explicit enunciators in the film are always embedded," "The Impersonal Enunciation, or the Site of Film," *New Literary History* 22 (1991): 747–72, (p. 768).

12 A referee suggested that there is another argument against narrators in film: narrators must be utterers, and the audio-visual representation of film is not utterance. But we Griceans have no problem taking "utterance" in a broad sense that includes, for example, showing people pictures and making gestures. Filmic narrative is just utterance of a complex kind.

13 George M. Wilson, *Narration in Light* (Johns Hopkins University Press, 1986).

14 Recently shown here on a local TV station, Lang's film was advertised with a quotation from William Farr: "a damning indictment of the injustice, prejudice and brutality that can be directed, in the name of justice, against an excriminal."

15 Perhaps you think it analytic that narrative must have a narrator (as does Sarah Kozloff: "Because narrative films are narrative, someone must be narrating," *Invisible Storytellers: Voice-Over in American Fiction Film* [University of California Press, 1988], p. 115, quoted approvingly in Seymour Chatman, *Coming to Terms* [Cornell University Press, 1990], p. 133). But then you simply object to my terminology, and I could avoid the objection by using another term to refer to the vehicle of narratorless storytelling. Consider it done.

16 See my "Interpretation and Objectivity," *Mind* 102 (1993): 413–28.

17 In that case we have a "seductive" unreliable narrator; the classic case is *The Turn of the Screw*. Where

Booth's definition applies and mine does not, we have an unseductive one (see James Phelan, "Narrative Discourse, Literary Character and Ideology," in James Phelan, ed., *Reading Narrative* [Ohio State University Press, 1989], p. 137). Sometimes cases of unobviously unreliable narratives are described as "ambiguous" (e.g., by Shlomith Rimmon-Kenan, *Narrative Fiction* [London: Methuen, 1983], p. 103), but I wish to use this term for another purpose. See below, Section IV.

18 We should not forget that *all* unreliability must ultimately be traceable to the intentions of the implied author; we see the narrator as unreliable because we think that words have been put into her mouth by the implied author so as to signal the narrator's unreliability.

19 There may be other grounds for saying that *Gone with the Wind* is ambiguous in the sense favored here. The film narratives used by David Bordwell and Kristin Thompson to illustrate ambiguity (*Day of Wrath* and *Last Year at Marianbad*) would count as ambiguous on my definition. Bordwell and Thompson associate ambiguity closely with causality (*Film Art* [Reading, MA: Addison-Wesley, 1980], p. 250). Their idea seems to be that the work is ambiguous to the extent that the causes or effects of narrative elements are unclear. Since most narrative events, like most events in real life, have many distinct partial causes and many distinct effects, we shall need to distinguish the significant from the non-significant causes and effects. My proposal above can be read as doing that.

20 See my "Interpretation and Objectivity." An interesting case of the relation between unreliability and ambiguity is Jack Clayton's *The Innocents*, a film version of *The Turn of the Screw*. One difficulty the filmmakers had to contend with was that a significant proportion of the film's audience would bring with them their knowledge of the unreliability in James's story, which would make it virtually impossible for the film to achieve the same effect; the audience would be primed for the discovery of the higher level clues from the start. As I understand the film, their solution, intelligently enough, was to give the film an ambiguous rather than an unreliable narrative.

21 George Wilson argues that Ford's *The Searchers* employs what I have called a transition to closure (*Narration in Light*, pp. 46 ff.). But I find Wilson less persuasive on this than on *You Only Live Once*. For more on this, see my *Image and the Mind* (Cambridge: Cambridge University Press, 1995).

22 David Bordwell, *Narration in the Fiction Film* (University of Wisconsin Press, 1985), p. 60, emphasis in the original.

23 Ibid., p. 62.

24 See Seymour Chatman, *Coming to Terms*, chap. 8 for criticism of Bordwell on this point.

25 Seymour Chatman, *Coming to Terms*, p. 116. For somewhat different reasons I argued that same view in *The Nature of Fiction* (New York: Cambridge University Press, 1990), chap. 2. I now think that we can explain fictional truth in terms, not of the beliefs of a narrator, but the intentions of an implied author. This is well argued in Alex Byrne, "Truth in Fiction: The Story Continued," *Australasian Journal of Philosophy* 71 (1993): 24–35. See also my "Interpretation and Objectivity."

26 Ibid., p. 132.

27 Thanks to Jerrold Levinson and Paisley Livingston for discussion, and to the suggestions of a referee. Apologies to Mark Johnstone for having stolen (part of) his title.

PART V

Film and Emotion

Introduction

The emotions directed toward fiction/film have long puzzled philosophers. The question regarding such emotions is twofold. First, how on earth do we emotionally engage with fictional characters whom we know for certain do not exist? Second, granted that we are emotionally involved with fictional characters, why do we continue consuming fiction or watching films? Is there anything irrational about such a phenomenon? This puzzle is often called "the paradox of fiction." The five essays collected in Part V explore ways in which to solve this paradox.

Noël Carroll's essay, "Film, Emotion, and Genre," provides us with an overview of how to approach and map out the paradox of fiction. Carroll starts by examining the term "emotion," and suggests limiting "emotion proper" to affective responses caused by cognitive states. "Emotion" in everyday use encompasses a wide range of affective states, from reflex responses such as the startle response (which does not, strictly speaking, include a cognitive state), to more complex and long-lasting emotional states such as loyalty (which requires a cognitive assessment of a situation in order to give rise to such an emotion). For this reason, Carroll claims, there is a need to separate out "emotion proper," by which he means emotions that combine cognitive states and feeling states – more specifically those in which cognitive states cause feeling states to occur.

Unlike the common-sense view that holds emotion to be opposite to cognition or rationality, cognition is an essential component of emotion, one that gives rise to emotion. The cognitive component of emotion not only causes the affective elements of emotion, but also provides us with a typology of emotion. In order to have an emotion, one must subsume the object in question under an appropriate category or criterion, and each emotion is mapped onto a different category or criterion. For example, my anger is caused by my awareness that harm has been done to me and is directed toward the object or person causing such harm. Disgust is caused by and directed toward impurity. This view can be identified as "the cognitive theory of emotion."

Emotion construed this way helps us to illuminate how we emotionally engage with film. Fictional situations and characters provide us with objects that fall under emotive categories, which then cause corresponding emotions. In this respect, emotions directed toward film are parallel to real-life emotions. However, this alone is insufficient to explain emotional responses to fiction film. As Carroll correctly points out, in order to engage emotionally with fiction we should care about the protagonists. One may either share with fictional characters certain traits or admire the merits of the character whose wishes one wants to obtain. Thus one cares about the fictional outcome that befalls the protagonist. We, as viewers, take what Carroll calls a "pro-attitude" toward the protagonists.

Granted, as Carroll suggests, that the same kind of emotional mechanism is employed for both everyday-life emotion and fiction-directed emotion, is there any significant difference between the two kinds of emotions? Carroll claims that an important distinction to be noted between the two is that the film text is designed to evoke or mobilize specific types of emotions in the first place and, in that respect, the film text is prefocused. The film text, via its narration process and redundant cues, guides the viewer's perception and attention more efficiently than everyday events. Furthermore, although every film evokes a range of emotions, for certain genres their main function is to give rise to a specific type of emotion: horror films give rise to fear and disgust, melodramas give rise to sadness and admiration, and crime-thrillers give rise to suspense.

Cognitivists such as Carroll, Gregory Currie, Susan Feagin, and others all claim that cognition is a constituent of emotion directed to fiction. Among cognitivists, however, there is disagreement regarding exactly what kind of cognitive mechanism is employed and how to classify fiction-directed emotion. In his immensely influential essay, "Fearing Fictions," Kendall Walton argues that fiction-directed emotions are of a different kind from everyday emotions. Walton foregrounds the fact that the viewer neither believes the content of a fiction film, nor does he or she manifest the usual behaviors associated with certain types of emotions during the film viewing process. For instance, the viewer neither believes that the monster in a horror film exists, nor does he or she flee the theatre when a monster approaches the camera.

How exactly, then, is the viewer so often caught up during film viewing? Walton claims that in watching, say, a movie about green slime, the viewer participates in a game of make-believe with the fictional world. The viewer interacts with characters in the fictional world, but he or she does so in make-believe. For instance, one makes believe that there exists green slime, and that the green slime is on the loose. The question is, then, what exactly does it mean to "make-believe"? Walton distinguishes "make-believe" from the suspension of belief, or half-belief, or even belief at a gut level. The former two assume a kind of uncertainty regarding the object of one's belief – as the phrases such as "almost believe" or "half-believe" imply – while "make-believe" does not presuppose such an uncertainty on the viewer's part. The viewer knows for a fact that monstrous slime does not exist. Nor can "make-believe" be assimilated to belief at the gut level, since the former does not manifest any of the deliberate actions that are often found in the latter case. For example, if one believes that flying is safe in one's mind, but is still afraid of flying at a gut level, one would avoid flying if possible. Quite to the contrary, the viewer of the slime movie does not show comparable behaviors. One willingly goes to see horror films over and over again despite being terribly horrified.

One might notice that in articulating his theory of make-believe, Walton makes frequent reference to the child's game of make-believe as a model. Similarities exist between the two in that both the child's game of make-believe and that of the viewer are implicit rule-following activities, and both rely on the participant's imaginary activity in engaging with what is fictional. But one must also consider how far such an analogy can hold. Certainly, in a child's game of make-believe, the child is often the protagonist, but in the viewer's game, he or she is only an onlooker. There are cases in which films do directly address the viewer – as in the slime example, when the slime heads toward the camera – but these are exceptions rather than the norm. Most of the time, we as viewers feel for the characters, not for ourselves. So the next point, then, is to explain how we feel for others, viz. the fictional protagonists.

Two essays, by Alex Neill and Berys Gaut, provide some answers. Both attempt to revive the notion of identification, a major concept employed by film scholars of the psychoanalytic bent. Psychoanalytically inclined film scholars such as Jean Baudry and Christian Metz explain the viewer's pleasure in watching films by recourse to the notion of identification; the viewer identifies with the camera, and then with characters. Cognitivists such as Carroll, however, are suspicious of relying on such a concept. In Carroll's view, "identification" is vague at best and contradictory at worst. If by "identification" one means a literal identification with the character on screen, this is metaphysically impossible, for two separate people cannot merge their identities into one. If by "identification" one means the viewer's "care for" or "concern about" a character, the concept cannot explain the phenomenon in question – i.e., why or how do we care about them – and more importantly, as mentioned above, the viewer's emotional responses to the fiction film often diverge from that of characters in the fictional world due to the disparity between their ranges of knowledge. Suppose the viewer sees a shark that slowly approaches the protagonist in the ocean. In such a case, the character may obliviously continue to enjoy swimming in the ocean, while the viewer would feel suspense and fear, anticipating the immanent attack of the shark. Is there any room for recourse to the notion of "identification"?

While Neill focuses on a sub-set of identification, i.e., empathy, Gaut provides a typology for the umbrella term "identification." Neill claims that the notion of empathy still is a viable option to explain our emotional engagement with fiction. According to Neill, empathy differs from sympathy – another type of emotion directed toward another's plight – in that the viewer feels with, not for, characters. In watching and experiencing fiction film, the viewer's emotional responses are assimilated to those of characters. More importantly, the viewer feels an emotion of the same kind as that of a character, *because of* the character's response. As in the example on which Neill draws, in watching a scene from *The Haunting*, the viewer feels terrified precisely because the characters in the film feel this way when they hear the pounding noises from outside followed by a woman's laughter. The viewer imaginatively projects him or herself into the character's shoes, and feels emotions comparable to that of the character. Neill emphasizes the function of empathy, not only in its contribution to apprehend and understand others whose perspectives and experiences are foreign to oneself, but also in its ability to cultivate one's own emotions and morals by broadening one's purview via having such an experience.

Unlike the way psychoanalytic film scholars characterize identification, Gaut claims that identification is not an all-in-one concept. Instead, identification is aspectual. Film invites, as well as encourages, the viewer to identify with *specific* aspects of a character. Gaut divides "identification" into four different kinds: perceptual, affective, motivational, and epistemic identification. To identify perceptually with a character is to imagine seeing from the character's point of view; to identify affectively with a character is to imagine feeling what the character feels; to identify motivationally with a character is to imagine wanting what the character wants; lastly, to identify epistemically with a character is to imagine believing what the character believes.

Gaut argues that one type of identification may foster – or trigger – another type of identification, but there is no law-like correlation among these four types of identification. One can identify with a character epistemically but not affectively if a character is the major source of narrative information about a fictional world, but is not the main focus of the emotive arena of the film. By refining the concept of identification, Gaut avoids the pitfall of a reductionist approach that connects identification directly to specific film techniques, such as point-of-view shots. Among psychoanalytically inclined film scholars, point-of-view shots, which

consist of a glance shot (a shot of a character looking) and a content shot (a shot of what the character sees), are allegedly the main carrier of character identification. However, such an approach is neither able to point out specific characteristics with which the viewer identifies, nor is it able to trace out the identification processes that take place. According to Gaut, point-of-view shots can provide the viewer with occasions to identify with characters perceptually, since the viewer imagines what the character sees from his or her point of view, but point-of-view shots also provide occasions for the viewer to identify characters epistemically, since the viewer attributes what he or she sees to what a character sees. These types of identification, then, can further be followed by affective identification with a character, if the character is worthy of the viewer's concern.

Although empathy and sympathy are often primary examples of identification in everyday discourse as well as scholarly literature, Gaut distinguishes identification from both empathy and sympathy. He claims that identification is imaginative – more precisely, imaginative projection – in its nature, be it perceptual, affective, motivational or epistemic. On the contrary, both empathy and sympathy require the viewer's *actual* feeling directed toward fictional characters in their situation. The question, then, comes down to whether it is possible to feel "actual emotions" toward something fictional: fictional characters in fictional situations.

Although Gaut himself does not further explore this question in his essay, as we have seen, Walton is hesitant to classify fiction-directed emotions in the same category as real-life emotions, since the cognitive mechanism involved in the engagement with fiction is of the "make-believe" kind and thus its output, however intense it is, should be classified as "quasi" emotions. On the contrary, Neill emphasizes a greater similarity between empathy with a real person and that with a fictional character. Neill claims that empathy in both situations involves a second level of assessment and engagement – both cognitive and affective – for those who empathize; one feels the way he or she feels by reflecting on how the target person feels that way. In Neill's view, the fact that fictional characters do not "really" feel – fictional characters are not real entities – does not entail that the viewer does not need to form a meta-level belief regarding character psychology. Neill argues that such a formation of beliefs and knowledge at the meta-level are, in fact, a prerequisite to successful empathy, as well as imagination.

Deborah Knight, in her essay "In Fictional Shoes: Mental Simulation and Fiction," questions the validity of the recent adoption of "simulation theory" in explaining fiction-directed emotion – to what extent is simulation theory, which has emerged as a popular solution to the paradox of fiction, applicable to an explanation of our emotional responses to fiction? To what extent are we warranted to apply the simulation model from cognitive psychology, which primarily aims to explain real people in real-life scenarios, to fictional scenarios? Knight's answer to this question is: not much.

Simulation theory, which is proposed against the "theory-theory" in cognitive psychology, assumes that in order to predict another's behaviors and understand another's emotions and feelings, we employ our *own* decision-making mechanism, adopting other people's beliefs and desires as input, run our own decision-making system off-line, and attribute our own decisions and/or responses to the person whose behavior we attempt to predict. Knight's objection is aimed at two different realms: (1) whether the simulation theory is useful in explaining the viewer's prediction of a character's *behavior* and (2) whether the same theory illuminates the viewer's *emotional engagement* with fiction.

According to the simulation model, especially when applied to fiction, the viewer tends to treat fictional characters as if they were real persons. However, Knight argues that it often ignores the obvious fact that fictional characters are not real people: they do not *really* have mental states and attitudes. If fictional characters do not possess "real" psychological states, how can we simulate them? Nevertheless, there are some among those who endorse the simulation model who can avoid such criticism. For example, Gregory Currie, one of the proponents of the simulation theory in aesthetics, does not presuppose that we simulate character's beliefs and desires – not the same as those of real people, but something analogous to

those. Knight's second criticism, which seems more relevant to the simulation theory, is that the viewer often has extra-fictional knowledge concerning such elements as generic conventions and star persona, which make it redundant for the viewer to simulate characters' psychological states to predict how they would behave. In romantic comedy, for example, the romantic couple seldom falls in love in the first scene, nor will they be united until the final minutes of the film. Knowing this, rather than simulation, is what enables the viewer to predict character behavior.

Is, then, the simulation theory appropriate for explaining our emotional engagement with fictional characters? Knight argues that it is not. First of all, the viewer's physiological responses – tightness felt in the neck and shoulder while watching a horror film or tears running down the cheek while watching *Stella Dallas* – are not imaginative but real, even if they may result from the viewer's imaginative identification with fictional characters. If so, the alleged simulation process is not completely "off-line." Second, the object of the viewer's emotions is fundamentally different from that of fictional characters. The viewer's emotions are directed toward fictional characters themselves, while those of fictional characters are either self-directed or directed toward peers within the fictional world. Such an asymmetry makes the viewer's response more or less a sympathetic, not an empathic, one.[1]

The cognitive theory of emotion and fiction has contributed to explain how we emotionally engage with fiction and fictional characters. However, the scope of such an inquiry is still limited. The viewer's experience of fiction film is not confined merely to the content or story of a film; it is more holistic. If so, proponents of the cognitive theory should broaden their inquiry to include other stylistic elements of film, and question how such elements contribute to or prohibit the viewer from engaging the film as a whole.

J.C.

Note

1 For futher discussion of simulation, see Noël Carroll, "Simulation, Emotion, and Morality," in *Beyond* *Aesthetics* (Cambridge: Cambridge University Press, 2001), pp. 306–16.

14

Film, Emotion, and Genre

Noël Carroll

Film and Affect

A nasty, largish beast rushes at the camera, backed by a pounding score and crushing sound effects, and the audience flinches. The villain abuses the innocent heroine and our jaws clench in anger; our longing for revenge keeps us pinned to the screen, awaiting the moment when the loutish brute is dealt his due. The young lovers are separated by the callous vagaries of fate, or the child dies long before his time, and we weep. Or perhaps the camera pans over a vernal landscape of rolling gentle greenery and a feeling of serenity wells up in us. These are very common movie events. They bear testimony to the hardly controversial observation that, in large measure, affect is the glue that holds the audience's attention to the screen on a moment-to-moment basis.

I have said "affect" here rather than "emotion," even though it might be acceptable in ordinary language to label all the preceding examples as instances of emotional response. My reason for this way of speaking is that the ordinary notion of *emotion* can be exceedingly broad and elastic, sometimes ranging so widely as to encompass hard-wired reflex reactions (like the startle response), kinesthetic turbulence, moods, sexual arousal, pleasures and desires, as well as occurrent mental states like anger, fear and sorrow.

The everyday usage of *emotion* can be rather catch-all, referring to quite a lot of heterogeneous phenomena. It is not clear – indeed, it is very unlikely – that this conception of emotion, which can be found in everyday speech, captures a natural kind, like gold; therefore, using it in a discussion of film and something called "the emotions" is likely to be a barrier to the construction of precise, theoretical generalizations. As a result, in what follows I will use the notion of *affect* where everyday speech might talk of the emotions, reserving the term *emotion* to name a narrower subclass of affect, namely, what might be even more accurately called *cognitive emotions* (i.e., affects that include cognitive elements).

By subdividing the affective life – what might be called the "life of feeling" – in this way and putting to one side many of the phenomena that comprise it, I do not mean to privilege one sort of affect over others. I would not deny that many of the affects that I am ignoring are integral to the experience of film. Through the manipulation of sound and image, filmmakers often address audiences at a subcognitive, or cognitively impenetrable, level of response. Loud noises – either recorded effects or musical sounds – can elicit instinctual responses from spectators as can the appearance of sudden movement. The movie screen is a rich phenomenal field in terms of variables like size, altitude, and speed, which have the capacity to excite automatic reactions from viewers, while the display of certain phobic and sexual material may also call forth

Noël Carroll, "Film, Emotion, and Genre," *Passionate Views*, eds. Carl Plantinga and Greg M. Smith (Baltimore: Johns Hopkins University Press, 1999): 21–47, 260–2 (notes). Reprinted by permission of The Johns Hopkins University Press.

responses barely mediated by thought. Such transactions certainly need to be studied and analyzed.[1] By hiving these affects off from the category of the emotions, I do not mean that we can neglect the cognitively impenetrable affects. I only intend, for methodological purposes, to bracket consideration of them for the time being in order to focus upon the subclass of affect that I am calling the emotions.

Though I may be departing somewhat from certain ordinary usage in this matter, since I am not leaving everyday speech altogether behind me, I hesitate to say that I am *stipulating* what shall count as an emotion. For ordinary language has broader and narrower ideas of the emotions. I am certainly eschewing the broader usages in favor of the term *affect*. However, there are narrower senses of *emotion* in everyday speech and my account stays fairly close to those.

Certain phenomena, such as fear, anger, patriotism, horror, admiration, sorrow, indignation, pity, envy, jealousy, reverence, awe, hatred, love, anxiety, shame, embarrassment, humiliation, comic amusement, and so on, are paradigms of what counts as emotion in ordinary language, even if sometimes ordinary language also stretches farther afield.[2] These garden-variety emotions are the sorts of phenomena that I will regard as emotions proper in this essay. In this, I do not think that I am doing great violence to ordinary language.

Moreover, inasmuch as these garden-variety emotions are not only paradigmatic but also exhibit common structural features, I think that I am merely pushing ordinary language in a direction toward which it already inclines, rather than stipulating a brand-new concept of the emotions. That is, by treating certain states as paradigmatically emotional, ordinary usage perhaps already regards them as composing a core class of like phenomena. In this respect, my analysis may be regarded as a rational reconstruction of some already existing intuitions rather than as the invention of a new concept that, in fact, tracks a somewhat unified field of phenomena.

In this chapter, I attempt to develop some generalizations about film and what might be called "emotions proper" or "core emotions" or "garden-variety emotions." This requires that I provide a characterization of the emotions that I have in mind as well as suggesting their relevance to film analysis. In the concluding section, I discuss the applicability of my approach to film and the emotions to certain genres, including melodrama, horror, and suspense.

Film and the Emotions

Though I do not consider film in relation to every kind of affective state, it should be clear that the affective states I intend to look at – garden-variety emotions, like anger, fear, hatred, sorrow, and so on – are central constituents of the film experience as we know it. Often it is our hatred of certain characters, like the redneck boyfriend in *Sling Blade* (1996), that keeps us riveted to the screen. Our mounting anger at his treatment of his lover and her son, along with the way he continually insults and torments the gay store manager and the retarded giant, stoke our indignation and encourage us to anticipate hopefully and vindictively his downfall and even his death. A primitive feeling for retributive justice shapes the way that we attend to *Sling Blade*, along with so many other films. That is probably why most of the time astute filmmakers wait until near the end of the film to kill their villains off. If the characters that we love to hate die too soon, there may be little left on-screen to hold our interest.

It is surprising to what extent darker emotions like anger, hatred, and revenge provide the cement that holds our attention on the popular movies we consume. But more socially acceptable emotions can do the job as well. A certain *tristesse* pervades our experience of *Letter from an Unknown Woman* (1948). And, of course, most movies elicit a gamut of garden-variety emotions over the duration of the narrative. *God Is My Witness* (1992) engenders, among other emotions, both feelings of revenge toward figures like the bandit chief, and sadness for those other central characters who have been separated from their loved ones. The pleasure that attends the conclusion of the film is a function of the desires that subtend these different emotions being finally satisfied.

The garden-variety emotions underwrite our experience of most films, especially popular movies. Undoubtedly, the degree to which our experience of movies is emotional is so extensive that we may lose sight of it. Emotion supplies such a pervasive coloration to our movie experience that it may, so to speak, fly in under the radar screen. But a little apperceptive introspection quickly reveals that throughout our viewing of a film we are generally in some emotional state or other, typically one prompted and modulated by what is on screen.

Nor is it only the case that a great deal of our experience of films is saturated with emotion; it is also that our emotional engagement constitutes, in many instances, the most intense, vivid, and sought-after qualities available in the film experience. Perhaps that is why the Dutch film psychologist Ed S. Tan subtitles his recent important book *Film as an Emotion Machine*.[3]

Clearly, then, it is crucial for a theoretical understanding of film that we attempt to analyze its relation to the emotions. But in order to do that we first need a clearer sense of what constitutes an emotion proper.

If one reflects on the states that we paradigmatically think of as emotional, one is first struck by the fact that they involve feelings – sensations of bodily changes, like muscle contractions, often attended by phenomenological qualities, such as being "uptight." Such states are very apparent with respect to violent emotional states like fear, but they can also be detected in what Hume called the calm emotions. Thus, a first, albeit reductivist conception of the emotions is that they are nothing more than bodily feelings. Moreover, this position might be bolstered by noting that in English the term *emotion* is interchangeable with the term *feeling*.

In fact, a theory very close to this was quite popular in psychology for some time. William James claimed that an emotional state was just a perception of a bodily state.[4] For James, I notice myself crying and then label the state sadness. Since C. G. Lange proposed a similar theory at roughly the same time, the view is often called the James-Lange theory of the emotions.[5]

But neither of these views – the emotion-as-bodily-feeling view nor the emotion-as-bodily-feeling-plus-perception view (the James-Lange theory) – is adequate. The problem with the first view is that it excludes cognition from the emotional complex and the problem with the James-Lange view is that, in a manner of speaking, it puts the relevant cognitive states in the wrong place. In order to explain these objections, let's indulge in a little science fiction.[6]

First, if an emotion were simply a bodily feeling, marked by certain sensations, then if a person were presently in a bodily state that resembled exactly the bodily state she was in the last time she was angry, then we should be prepared to say that she is angry now. But that doesn't sound quite

right. For imagine that we have enough pharmacology at our disposal that we can induce any bodily state along with any phenomenological quality in anyone we wish. The last time our subject was angry was when she discovered that her lover was cheating on her. We can provoke the same bodily state and the same phenomenological qualia in her now that she felt back then. Suppose we do it? Shall we say that she is angry?

I suspect not. Why not? Well, the last time that she experienced this bodily state and its attendant qualia, she was angry at her lover. But that was a while ago. She no longer has a lover, and if the truth be told, she's forgotten the old one. Thus, *ex hypothesi*, there is no one for her to be angry with now. But if there is no one for her to be angry with – if there is no object to her emotional state – can she really be said to be in an emotional state?

She is in a bodily state, probably an uncomfortable and even confusing bodily state. But is she angry? No – because there is no one or no thing with whom or with which she is angry. You can't be angry, unless there is someone or something that serves as the object of your anger. Emotional states are directed. You hate Marvin or you are afraid of the smog. This is what it means to say that emotions take objects.[7]

But sheer bodily states do not take objects; they are not directed. They are internal events with no external reference. Thus, the subject of our science-fiction experiment is not in an emotional state. For her disturbed visceral state is not directed, nor does it have an object. Therefore, the view that emotions are simply bodily states cum some phenomenological qualia is wrong. Emotions may always involve bodily states and phenomenological qualia. However, something must be added to the mix if the state is to count as a full-fledged emotion.

What has to be added? Something that functions to connect the relevant bodily states and phenomenological qualia to some object. When I am angry at my lover for betraying me, I am racked by inner bodily turmoil. What is the bridge between that inner turmoil and my lover? Presumably, it is some cognition that I have about my lover. That is, I either believe or imagine that my lover has betrayed me. Of course, I can be mistaken in this. But in order to be angry with my lover in this case, I must believe or imagine that my lover has done me wrong *and* that cognitive state must be the cause of the inner consternation that buffets me. Together the cognitive state in causal conjunction with the bodily state and its phenomenological qualia comprise the emotional state of anger. This state can take objects and be directed – can have intentionality – because the cognitive states that are necessary constituents of the overall emotional states possess intentionality.

Emotions cannot simply be bodily feelings, since sheer bodily feelings lack intentionality. But if cognitions are necessary constituents of emotional states, this lacuna disappears. Thus, if adding cognition to bodily feeling is the right way to solve the preceding problem, then the reductivist theory that emotions are just bodily feelings is false, since emotions also require cognitive components (either beliefs or belief-like states such as thoughts and imaginings). This gets rid of the emotion-as-bodily-feeling view. But what about the James-Lange theory?

According to the James-Lange theory, emotions have a cognitive component. My brother is hit by a car; I choke up and I weep; I perceive these bodily changes and I interpret or cognize them as sadness. Here, the bodily state causes the relevant cognitive state. But the causal order seems backwards. The cognitive state appears epiphenomenal.

Undeniably, there are some occasions where a loud noise, say a firecracker, makes us frightened and where upon reflection we say, "I guess that really frightened me." But this is not paradigmatic of garden-variety emotional states. When I am jealous of a rival, that is *because* I believe that he is stealing affection that belongs to me; it is not because I observe myself overwhelmed by the phenomenology of the green-eyed monster and surmise that I must be jealous. To return to our science-fiction example once again, one can imagine pharmacologically counterfeiting the sensations of my last episode of jealous rage where it makes no sense to say that I am jealous now – perhaps because I have become a spiritual adept who has successfully renounced all earthly attachments.

Thus, our thought-experiment suggests that what we are calling emotions proper at least involve both cognitions and feeling states where the two are linked inasmuch as the former cause the latter.[8] In this account, certain affects – like the churning stomach sensations that viewers reported resulted from watching the car chases in *Bullitt* – are not examples of emotions proper. Emotions proper require a cognitive component. Admittedly, not all of the affects that are important to the analysis of cinema fall into this category. What might be called cognitively impenetrable affects – like the startle

response – don't. Nevertheless, a great many of the affects experienced in response to film are of the nature of emotions proper. To get a handle on them, we must now say a little more about the way in which the cognitive component in these emotions operates.

I am angry at Leslie because he is telling everyone that I failed my first driving test. I told this to Leslie in strictest confidence, but Leslie has broadcast this all around the neighborhood. When I learn and come to believe that Leslie has divulged my secret, my blood pressure skyrockets and I feel hot under the collar. My cognitive state, in other words, causes a spate of bodily disruption. How does this come about?

Notice that though in this case my anger is caused by Leslie's indiscretion, indiscretion is not the only thing that can function to elicit an emotional response. If someone smashed my car or if someone ruined my print of *The General*, I might also find myself in an angry state, if I believed that these things were done to me wantonly or inexcusably. That is, I will be angry where I subsume the events in question under the rubric of wrongs done to me or mine and where that formation of that belief functions in provoking some bodily disturbance in me. Cognitions, in other words, play not only a causal role in emotions in that they figure in the etiology of bodily alterations; they also play a role in identifying what emotional state we are in when we are in one. My response to Leslie is anger because I have subsumed or assessed Leslie's indiscretion under the category of a wrong done to me or mine, and forming that belief has caused the pertinent bodily upset.

What this example suggests is that emotional states, like anger, are governed cognitively by criteria of appropriateness. Where the cognitions in a given emotional state come about through the subsumption of a person or event under the category of wrongs done to me or mine, the emotional response is apt to be anger. Moreover, other emotional states are also like this. The harmful or the dangerous is the criterion (or the category appropriate to) fear; thus when I subsume the object of my state under the category of the harmful, I am, other things being equal, apt to undergo fear. That is to say, for example: I cognize the scorpion next to my hand under the harmful, that cognition causes my blood to freeze, and the overall state is fear.

Similarly, in order for me to feel pity for x, I must believe that x has suffered some misfortune;

the criterion for pity, in other words, is misfortune, just as in order to envy y I must believe that y has something that I have not. If y cannot move and I know this, then I cannot envy y's athletic prowess. For in order to envy y I must be able to form the belief that y possesses some advantage that I lack, or some degree of advantage over and above what I take myself to command. Envying y signals that I have subsumed y under the category of someone who possesses more than I do.

Emotions require cognitions as causes and bodily states as effects. Moreover, among the cognitions that are essential for the formation of emotional states are those that subsume the objects of the state under certain relevant categories or conceive of said objects as meeting certain criteria. In fear, the object must meet the criterion of being harmful or, at least, of being perceived to be harmful. Anger requires that the object be perceived as meeting the criterion that it has wronged me or mine.

What "criterion" means above, functionally speaking, is that in order to be an appropriate object of the emotion in question, the relevant object must meet certain necessary conditions, or, alternatively, must be thought to be subsumable under certain essentially defined categories. For x to be the object of pity, x must be thought to meet the necessary criterion of having suffered some misfortune; for y to be the object of my envy, I must cognize y as at least meeting the necessary condition of possessing something I lack (indeed, generally something that I lack that I would prefer to have, if only upon learning that y has it).

Thus, when we speak of emotions as requiring cognitions, the cognitions that we have in mind – first and foremost – involve subsuming the objects of the emotion under certain categories or, alternatively, perceiving that the object meets certain criteria of appropriateness (harmfulness, for example, in the case of fear; wrongfulness in the case of anger).

Of course, this is not the whole story of what it is to be in an emotional state. Emotional states are temporal affairs; they endure over time intervals; they are episodes. When we detect the object of our emotional state and the relevant cognitions ensue, our perception becomes emotionally charged. It casts the cause or the object of our state in a special phenomenological light; it fixes our attention upon it and alerts us to its significance (e.g., x is dangerous).

The emotions gestalt or organize perception. They call our attention to those aspects of the situation that are pertinent by selectively guiding perception to the features of the stimulus that are subsumable under the criteria of the reigning emotional state.

There is also a feedback mechanism in operation here. Once in an emotional state, the prevailing state further structures our perception by drawing our attention to further elements in the array that are pertinent to sustaining the emotional state that we are in. Alerted by fear to the potential that there is someone or something prowling around our campsite, we scope out the scene in search of further signs of threat which, if found, reinforce both the state we are in and its related feedback processes. In this way, the emotions manage attention over time. The form that this perceptual management takes is to focus our attention upon those elements in a situation that are relevant to (that mesh with the criteria that govern) the presiding emotional state (e.g., dangers with respect to fear; slights with respect to anger).

The emotions can be analogized to searchlights. They direct attention, enabling us to organize the details before us into significant wholes or gestalts. Where the emotional state is one of fear, we scan it for details highlighted as dangerous; where the state is pity, it battens on elements subsumable under the category of misfortune. The emotions foreground such relevant details in what might be called a special phenomenological glow.

Furthermore, once we are in the grip of a given emotional state, we not only stay fixed upon the details it has selected out in the first instance; we scan the array for more details with a similar pertinence to our initial emotional assessment of the situation. The emotions manage our attention, guiding both what we look at and what we look for. Moreover, that process of attention management undergoes changes of adjustment. First our emotions alert us to certain gestalts (whose structure of inclusion and exclusion is governed by the criteria relevant to the ruling emotional state), and then the presiding emotion encourages further elaboration of our attention, prompting us to form expectations about the kinds of things that we should watch for as the situation evolves (where the pertinent kinds of things are those that fall into the categories that criterially determine our prevailing emotional state).

So far we have been talking about the emotions and their relation to perception in a pretty abstract way. How applicable is any of this to film viewing?[9] Can this abstract characterization of the emotions tell us anything about the relation of the garden-variety emotions to standard fictional films? I think it can, although in order to see how we must take note of one very large and obvious difference between the activation of emotional responses with respect to events in everyday life versus events in narrative film fictions.[10]

In life, in contrast to fiction, our emotions have to select out the relevant details from a massive array of largely unstructured stimuli. We are sitting in a room reading the newspaper. We hear sirens nearby, alerting us to potential danger. An incipient sense of fear prompts us to rise and to go to the window to search for indications of danger. We smell fire. Warily, we look down to see if it is coming from our apartment building. If it is, we rush to the hallway in order to see if the flames have reached our floor. Our mounting sense of fear, in other words, shapes our perceptual itinerary. It organizes the situation for us in a way pertinent to action, which, in this case, all things considered, will probably eventuate in flight.

But with respect to fiction, things stand differently. The emotions are not called upon to organize situations de novo. To a much greater extent than in everyday life, situations in fiction films have already been structured for us by filmmakers. We do not usually rely upon the emotions to organize fictional film events for us as much as we rely upon the emotions to perform this task for us in ordinary life because, in the main, fiction film events have been emotionally predigested for us by filmmakers. That is, the filmmakers have already done much of the work of emotionally organizing scenes and sequences for us through the ways in which the filmmakers have foregrounded what features of the events in the film are salient. In contrast to the way that emotions focus attention for us in everyday life, when it comes to films the relevant events have already generally been prefocused emotively for us by the filmmakers. The filmmakers have selected out the details of the scene or sequence that they think are emotively significant and thrust them, so to speak, in our faces. The means that the filmmakers have to secure this end include camera position and composition, editing, lighting, the use of color, and, of course, acting and the very structure of the script or narrative.[11]

Very frequently in everyday life, when an acquaintance or colleague slights us – perhaps by a passing remark – we are not immediately angry, even if we are hurt, because we may wonder whether the insult was an intentional wrong rather than merely carelessness. But as such remarks recur, anger takes hold and we come to recognize a discernible pattern of nastiness directed at us. In typical fictional films, on the other hand, we rarely have to waver so long. So often, characters wear the meanness of their actions on their sleeve and, if that were not enough, we also have access to the disapproving judgments of the people around them. We not only have a pretty unmistakable gestalt of wrongness thrust in bold relief before us, but we also have the reaction of surrounding characters to reflect and to reinforce our assessments of the situation.

Thus, it is hard not to respond (initially) with anger to the father in *Shine* (1996) when he refuses to allow his son to accept various scholarships. Generally in fiction films, that is, the detection work that our emotions need to do for us is somewhat minimized because the scenes and characters in such films have very frequently already been made or designed from, so to speak, the point of view of anger to begin with; or, to say it differently, they have been emotively prefocused or predigested for us.[12]

But how is it possible for a character, a scene, or a sequence to be emotively prefocused? Here it is useful to advert to the general picture of the emotions that we developed previously. The emotions, we argued, are governed by criteria of appropriateness. To be angered, the object of our emotional state must be perceived as a wrong done to me or mine. I was angry with Leslie because I regarded his gossip as a wrong done to me. Likewise, if I am angry with a broker because I believe he has squandered my mother's savings, it is because I perceive it as a wrong done to mine (where mine can extend to friends, countrymen, and anyone else, including a fictional character, to whom I bear a pro attitude).

But just as emotions must meet certain criteria of appropriateness in everyday life, so must emotions in response to fictions be governed by criteria of appropriateness. Thus, a film text can be emotively prefocused by being *criterially prefocused* – that is, by being so structured that the descriptions and depictions of the object of our attention in the text will activate our subsumption of the relevant characters and events under the categories that are criterially apposite to the emotional state in question.

Once we recognize the object under the criterially relevant categories – like the harmful for fear or the wrongful for anger – the relevant emotion is apt (under certain conditions to be discussed shortly) to be raised in us. That is, as a result of entertaining the appropriate cognitions, we will be likely to undergo some physical changes: with comic amusement, ideally, we laugh; as we will see in the next section, with horror films our skin may crawl; with suspense films, we tense up; and with melodramas, we may shed a tear.

As well, our attention becomes emotively charged. Our emotional states fix our attention and illuminate it in a special phenomenological glow. Our attention is glued to those features of the object of the emotion that are appropriate to the emotional state we are in. Our emotional state prompts us to survey the event for further features that may support or sustain the presiding emotional state in which we find ourselves. And, protentively, our emotively charged state shapes our anticipation of what is to come by priming us to be on the watch for the emergence of further details that are also subsumable under the categories of the dominant emotional state – our anger at a character in the first scene alerts us to be on the lookout for more churlishness from him in later scenes. Or, in summary, a criterially prefocused film text gives rise, in the right circumstances, to *emotive focus* in the audience, where by "emotive focus" I am referring both to the way in which the emotional state of the viewer fixes *and* then shapes her attention.

Central, then, to a theoretical understanding of the relation of the garden-variety emotions to film are the notions of the *criterially prefocused film text* in relation to the *emotive focus* of the audience. On our account so far, a criterially prefocused film text is a standard condition for securing emotive focus. However, it should be obvious that merely presenting viewers with criterially prefocused film texts, no matter how well designed, does not guarantee that spectators will respond emotionally. A criterially prefocused film can be viewed dispassionately. What makes for a passionate response? The notion of a criterially prefocused film text needs to be supplemented, if we hope to propose a theoretical model of the arousal of garden-variety emotions by narrative fiction films.

I hypothesize that what that supplement comes to is a concern or a pro attitude on the part of the viewer with respect to the way in which the depicted situation in the fiction is or is not going. That is, in addition to being criterially prefocused, the narrative must invest the viewer with certain concerns about the fictional characters and events (and their prospects) in the film. These concerns or pro attitudes function like the desires that are found in many everyday emotions, and when added to the mental content or conception of the object, derived from the criterially prefocused text, the combination, all things being equal, should elicit an emotional response (including emotive focus) from viewers in accordance with the criterial features of the film text that the filmmakers have made salient.

The structure of our emotional involvement with narrative fiction films, then, typically comprises a criterially prefocused film text plus certain concerns or pro attitudes, and together, in the standard case, these are apt to elicit broadly predictable responses (including emotive focus) in standard audiences (which, by stipulation, bars sociopaths). The criterially prefocused film text embodies a conception of a situation from an emotively relevant point of view. But a conception of a situation may not alone be sufficient to motivate an emotional response, if the audience is otherwise indifferent to what is going on. To prompt an emotional response and to secure emotive focus require that the audience be engaged by concerns – certain pro and con attitudes – about what is going on in the story.

This hypothesis presupposes that film narratives can enlist audiences in preferences about the way in which a story might go. This assumption should not be problematic. *Potemkin* (1925) enlists a pro attitude in the audience toward the crew of the battle cruiser which leads them to prefer that the fleet not destroy them. In *High Noon* (1952), the intended audience prefers that the sheriff survive. This is not to say that films always defer to the preferences that they engender in audiences. With *You Only Live Once* (1937), we may prefer that Eddie (Henry Fonda) escape, but he doesn't. Nevertheless, the special emotional *frisson* that attends the end of this film is a function of the fact that the filmmakers encouraged viewers to form a pro attitude toward another outcome.

Typically, narrative fiction films develop in such a way that spectators have a structured horizon of expectations about what might and what might not happen. And in addition to a sense of the possible outcomes of the ongoing courses of events, one also, generally under the guidance of the filmmakers, has convictions about what outcomes one would, in a certain sense, prefer to obtain in the world of the fiction versus those one would prefer not to obtain. In some cases, the preferred course of events correlates with the express goals and plans of the protagonists of the story; what they want to happen – say, delivering life-saving medical supplies – is what the audience wants to happen. However, in a great many other cases, the film may proffer preferred outcomes independently of the express goals and plans of any of the characters. That is, the film may have its own agenda, as in the cases of all those fictional lovers who never wanted to fall in love in the first place.

But however motivated, audiences evolve concerns regarding the situations portrayed in films, and when those concerns are threatened, we tend to react with dysphoric (or discomforting) emotions, whereas when the concern in question is abetted by narrative developments, our emotions tend to be euphoric.[13] Which particular dysphoric or euphoric emotion is engaged, of course, depends upon the way that the film text is criterially prefocused. For example, considering some dysphoric emotions, if a character toward whom I bear a pro attitude is wronged – as when the character Zane, played by Charlie Sheen, in *The Arrival* (1996) is fired – in such a way that the injustice of the event is made criterially salient, then, all things being equal, I will feel anger; whereas if presented with the criterially prefocused misfortune of a group that has elicited my concern – say the victims in a disaster movie – then I am apt to feel pity for them.

Similarly, euphoric emotions of different sorts are also likely to evolve in accordance with the way in which the film text is criterially prefocused in those cases where our concerns or desires about the direction of the relevant courses of events are satisfied. When a character toward whom we bear a pro attitude overcomes obstacles, saliently posed in the film – as when the sheriff finally defeats the shark in *Jaws* (1975) – then we are likely to respond with admiration; whereas the manifestation of virtually limitless power by an agency of which we approve – for instance, nature or a god – will tend to evoke reverence.

My proposal, then, for analyzing our emotional response to fiction films is that a criterially prefocused film text is apt to elicit an emotional response from audiences where the audiences are encouraged to adopt pro attitudes to certain developments in the story. Where story developments mesh with those preferences, the response is likely to be euphoric; where they clash, the emotional response is apt to be dysphoric. Moreover, the emotional response involves engendering emotive focus in the audience and this emotive focus guides our reception of ongoing and anticipated screen events on a moment-to-moment basis.

Furthermore, if this hypothesis about our emotional involvement with fiction films is roughly correct, it suggests a certain direction for cinema research. To analyze the way in which a film arouses an emotional response from viewers, one needs to first determine the way in which the film or film segment is criterially prefocused. Here the critic, using herself as a detector, begins by noting the emotion the film has elicited in her. Perhaps she feels a global sense of pity. Next, using the criteria of the emotion in question as a hypothesis, she can review the way in which the filmic material is articulated in order to isolate the pertinent depictions or descriptions in the film that instantiate the concept or meet the criteria of the pertinent emotion.

Additionally, she will want to determine which features of the film are designed to engender pro attitudes in viewers, along with determining what those pro attitudes are. By following this procedure, one can pith the emotive structure of the film.

To "pith the emotive structure of the film" here means finding the aspects of the depictions or descriptions of the object of the emotion that satisfy the necessary criteria for being in whatever emotional state the audience is in. This is what explaining the emotional state of the audience generally amounts to (along with identifying the depictions or descriptions that give rise to the concerns and preferences the audience is meant to bear to developments in the narrative).

Of course, this order of research may not always be practicable. In some cases, the analyst may not be able to identify with precision his or her emotional response to a film or film segment. In that event, the analyst is better advised to take up the salient depictions or description in the text with an interest in seeing what they foreground. Then, after evolving some hypotheses or questions in this regard, the analyst can compare what the film has foregrounded with the criteria for the better-known emotional states. This may lead to a clarification of the emotional address of the film or film segment under examination.

Needless to say, the emotional address of some films may be designedly ambiguous, while other films may introduce novel emotional timbres. But even in these cases the methodology that I am recommending is still somewhat serviceable, since it will enable us systematically to get a rough sense of the general contours of the emotional ambiguities and novel emotional timbres of the films in question.

Undoubtedly, often when we are watching films that are remote from us in time and place, we will not be able to depend on our own emotional responses to the film because we do not have the appropriate cultural background. This is exactly where film history and the ethnographic study of film have an indispensable role to play. Film historians and ethnographers can supply us with the background necessary to make the emotive address of films from other cultures and other periods in our own culture emotionally accessible to us.

Emotion and Genre

The framework for analyzing the relation of film and the emotions advanced above is general in the sense that it is supposed to be useful for analyzing responses to characters, sequences, scenes, and whole films. A great deal of our experience of film viewing is attended by garden-variety emotions in response to many different units of film articulation, ranging from single gestures and looks to the sorts of chase sequences that can last for half the length of a film. Attempting to illustrate the feasibility of the preceding method for every kind of case would require more detail than an essay allows. But perhaps empirical credibility for my theoretical proposals can be derived by illustrating what these hypotheses might facilitate with respect to the analysis of certain genres.

As I have said, emotion is engaged on a moment-to-moment basis throughout much (if not most) of our experiences of film. We track much of the unfolding action in films via what I have called emotive focus. My theory is intended to be instructive in analyzing virtually every instance of our emotional engagement and emotive tracking of cinema. However, there are certain dimensions of cinematic articulation, notably genre films of various sorts, where emotive address is particularly pronounced and obvious. Thus, at the very least, my theory should have something informative to contribute to the study of the relevant genres.

Some genres seem to traffic in certain specifiable emotions essentially. That is, certain genres appear to have as their abiding point the elicitation of specifiable emotional states in audiences. For

example, Aristotle thought that the arousal of pity and fear was an essential feature of Greek tragedy.

Of course, all popular film genres engage emotions, generally a range of emotions. However, some genres appear dedicated to raising particular, predetermined emotional states in audiences just as Aristotle thought that Greek tragedy was predicated upon provoking pity and fear. That is, whereas all genres tend to evoke anger, joy, hatred, and the like, in addition to these emotions some genres also aim at arousing specific emotions in spectators as a condition of being an instance of the very genre in question. Or, to put it differently, raising various preordained emotions in spectators is the *sine qua non* of certain film genres. In these cases, the genres in question aim at the production of a particular emotion whose tincture colors the film as a whole.

Sometimes these genres are named by the very emotion it is their purpose to arouse. Suspense and horror are examples here. Moreover, other genres, like melodrama, though they are not named by the emotion whose point it would appear they are predicated upon provoking, nevertheless aim at arousing a roughly specifiable, preordained emotional response from spectators. This emotional response is dominant in the sense that it lends its aura to the film as a whole.

Suspense, horror, and melodrama, then, are three genres where films count as instances of the relevant genre only if they are dedicated to eliciting certain specifiable kinds of emotions from spectators. If my theory is to be even minimally convincing, it should have something to say about genres like these. Thus, for the remainder of the chapter, let me quickly review some of the applications of my theory to these genres.

Melodrama

The first step in applying our theoretical framework to a genre is to identify the dominating emotion that the genre aims to instill in audiences.[14] The term *melodrama* is perhaps an unwieldy one, and it may be difficult to isolate a single package of emotions that applies to everything that someone might be willing to classify under this notion. However, there is a relatively clear class of melodramas, often called "tearjerkers," that take as their subject matter what are loosely called "interpersonal relationships" and that appear to call forth certain massively recurring emotional responses. Three examples are *An*

Affair to Remember (1957), *Back Street* (1932), and *Stella Dallas* (1937).

The fact that melodramas like these are often referred to as *tearjerkers* gives us an initial clue concerning their emotive domain. It should be something, all things being equal, that should warrant crying. Of course, crying can be elicited by many stimuli and can accompany many emotional states. Two such related states are sorrow and pity. Moreover, it should come as no surprise to the informed viewer that pity is the relevant tear-producing state that comes into play in the vast majority of melodramas.

Pity, of course, requires as a criterion of emotive appropriateness that its object be persons – we do not pity snowstorms – who have suffered misfortune. Thus, we expect from such melodramas that they be saliently comprised of misfortunes *suffered* by the protagonists.

I emphasize suffering here because the protagonists must feel the pain of their circumstances. Indeed, part of their misfortune is the pain that they feel as a result of their circumstances. Moreover, this misfortune – including the pain that, in part, comprises it – should not be seen as a matter of just desserts. We do not usually feel pity for villains who deserve to be annihilated. Melodramatic pity involves bad things happening to good people, or, at least, disproportionately bad things happening to people of mixed character.

It seems to me that the melodramatic emotion is not merely pity in the typical case of film melodrama. The standard film melodrama is not just a study in victimology. As already indicated, the ill-fortuned characters we weep for in many melodramas are of a certain sort. They are not victims pure and simple. They are people whom we admire; indeed, often we admire them for the way in which they negotiate their misfortune.

One important, recurring motif here is that the victim of melodramatic misfortune often accepts her suffering in order to benefit another, often at the expense of satisfying her own personal desires and interests. Sometimes, in fact, the character's misfortune is a result of the sacrifices she has made on behalf of others. For example, Stella Dallas's (Barbara Stanwyck) misfortune is the loss of her daughter, though she, in fact, has herself engineered this state of affairs on the basis of her belief that this will guarantee her daughter the best possible life.

Thus, we do not merely pity Stella Dallas. We admire her as well. The emotion that wells up in us as she watches her daughter's wedding from afar is not merely a result of pity, but is compounded of admiration as well. Often such emotions are called bittersweet. Perhaps the part that is pity is bitter (or dysphoric), but the part that we feel in response to Stella's noble self-sacrifice is sweet (or euphoric). To attempt to reduce our emotional states in cases like this to pity alone ignores the euphoric component in the response. We don't just feel bad about Stella, we feel good about her, too. That is because the dominating emotional response to the typical melodrama involves admiration – often motivated by a display of self-sacrifice – in addition to pity.

Were melodrama only a matter of pity – of witnessing horrible things happen to people – it might strike us as a particularly sadistic genre. It does not, I think, because typically the misfortunes in melodramas also provide the occasion for characters to exhibit noble virtues amid adversity, encouraging the spectator to leaven pity with admiration. A film of suffering unrelieved by virtue would be more likely an exercise in avant-garde realism than a melodrama. Melodramas are not all dark from the perspective of our emotional responses. Triumph is blended with tribulation so that pity comes in tandem with admiration.

In *An Affair to Remember* the female protagonist, Terry (Deborah Kerr), is struck down by a car on her way to a long-awaited rendezvous with her lover Nicky (Cary Grant). Their meeting, atop the Empire State Building, is supposed to symbolize their commitment to each other. Terry fails to make the appointment because of her accident. Terry's old boyfriend (Richard Denning) wants to tell Nicky what has happened, but Terry won't allow him. She feels that if Nicky learns that she has become disabled, his reaction will be pity, not love. Her silence is, in other words, principled. She does not want to take advantage of Nicky's sense of obligation. We may feel that Terry's course of action is ill-advised. But we admire her for her principles at the same time we pity her. Meanwhile, Nicky is becoming more and more embittered.

Perhaps the most emotionally wrought scene in the film comes at the end. Nicky still does not realize that Terry is disabled. He visits her apartment to deliver a shawl to her that his grandmother has bequeathed to Terry. He is still very hurt and angry. But just as he is about to leave, he realizes that Terry is disabled, that that's the reason why she missed their rendezvous, and, we presume, he also realizes that she didn't inform him because of a self-sacrificing desire to "protect him."

None of this is said. The audience infers that this is what is going on in Nicky's mind. Compactly, in a few seconds of screen time, this device encourages the audience to review the whole saga of Terry's adversity and nobility, jerking tears from man and woman alike. (I'm sniffling even as I write – and I don't have a cold.)

Similar scenes of recognition and acknowledgment are frequent in melodramas. The most moving scene in *Back Street* (1932), I think, occurs when the son learns the sacrifices his father's mistress made in order to sustain their relationship, while in *What's Eating Gilbert Grape?* (1993) the "viking funeral" of Gilbert's mother stands as a commemoration to her ultimate maternal integrity, despite all her other limitations. As in the case of *An Affair to Remember*, recognition/acknowledgment scenes like these serve to remind the audience not only of the bad things that have befallen the protagonists, but of their virtues as well. Pity attaches to the misfortunes, while admiration attaches to the virtues.

Even the ending of *Letter from an Unknown Woman* concludes on a note of admiration. Once the pianist learns of the self-sacrificing love of the unknown woman, he no longer acts the cad; he rides off to a doomed duel, shedding his selfishness and recognizing that, since the best thing in his life has just passed away, the only appropriate action is to join her in death. We pity their demise, but admire their willingness to die for their love.

Melodrama, then, frequently is rooted in engendering a compound emotion, comprising pity and admiration. The depictions and descriptions in a film like *An Affair to Remember* are criterially prefocused by making, on the one hand, misfortune, and, on the other hand, character virtues – especially self-sacrifice – salient to the audience. This, in turn, prompts spectators to be moved to feel pity and admiration, at least in cases where the audience has a pro attitude toward the characters. In *An Affair to Remember*, this is secured by portraying Terry and Nicky not only as very attractive and desirable people, but by establishing them to be persons of superior wit and culture (this is done especially in the voyage section of the film).

Once this pro attitude is in place, misfortune strikes, encouraging us to pity them, especially Terry, while at the same time providing a dramatic forum for Terry to exhibit her self-sacrificing no-

bility (finally to be joined by Nicky's when his recognition of that nobility leads him to love her all the more).

Horror

Like melodramas of the tearjerking variety, horror films are also designed to elicit a compound emotion.[15] And also like the tearjerker, one of the constituents of this emotional response is pretty evident. If melodramatic tearjerkers can be said uncontroversially to be aimed at eliciting pity from spectators, little argument seems required to establish that horror films are designed to provoke fear. Harmfulness, of course, is the criterion for fear. Thus, the depictions and descriptions in horror films are criterially prefocused to make the prospects for harm salient in the world of the fiction. The relevant harms here take the form of threats – generally lethal threats – to the protagonists in the horror film, and the locus of these threats is standardly a monster, an entity of supernatural or sci-fi provenance whose very existence defies the bounds of contemporary scientific understanding.

These monsters possess powers or propensities that make them threatening to human life. Most often, they are also hostile to the human protagonists in the relevant films. Usually they are bent on destroying or enslaving the humans. Moreover, they have certain capacities or advantages – such as great strength, cunning, indomitable technologies, supernatural abilities, or even invisibility – that are not easily deterred. This makes them particularly dangerous and fearsome. Here the fear that the audience emotes with regard to the monster is not fear for its own survival. Our fear is engendered on behalf of the human characters in the pertinent films. We cringe when the Werewolf of London stalks his prey, not because we fear that he will trap us, but because we fear for some character in the film. When the outsized arachnid in *Earth vs. the Spider* (1958) awakens to the beat of rock 'n' roll music, we fear for the teenagers, not for ourselves.

But though fear is a necessary condition for horror, it is not sufficient. Many films conjure up fear on the basis of scientific improbabilities without counting as horror films. Examples include time travel films where merciless fascists from the future are arriving in the here and now to gain a foothold, or *When Worlds Collide* (1951).

Fear, in short, is not the whole of horror, just as pity is not the whole of melodrama.

Though fearful, our emotive response to the oncoming planet in *When Worlds Collide* is different from our reaction to the monster in *Species* (1995), *Xtro* (1983), or *The Relic* (1997). For we not only find those latter entities fearsome, they are also disgusting. Were a part of their anatomy to find its way into our mouth, like the tentacles of so many slimy aliens, we would want to gag and to spit it out.[16] The thought of ingesting a piece of such creatures invites nausea. If we touched one of them, we would try to scrub our hands clean at the soonest opportunity. Think of the zombies in *Night of the Living Dead* (1968), or the giant, dribbling snails in *The Monster that Challenged the World* (1957).

We find the monsters in horror films repulsive and abhorrent. They are not only fearsome, they are somehow unclean, reviling, and loathsome by their very nature. Vampires, for example, are frequently associated with vermin and disease.

Monsters generally fall into the category that the Bible calls abominations. Even if such monsters were not dangerous, their very being is such that we would wish to avoid them and to refrain from touching them. The very thought of them is repelling – enough to make our flesh crawl, our spine tingle, and our throat choke shut. The most suitable expletives for them are "Ugh" and "Yuck!"

Thus, the objects that comprise the objects of our emotional response in horror films elicit a compound reaction in terms of fear and disgust. The fear component of our response is grounded in the fact that in the world of the fiction these monsters constitute clear and present dangers. They are harmful. But they are also disgusting, and the emotive criterion for disgust is impurity. Thus, the depictions and descriptions in horror films are criterially prefocused in terms of foregrounding the harmfulness *and* the impurity of the monsters.

The harmfulness of the monsters is usually exhibited readily in their behavior. They are killing people, eating them, dismembering them, or taking possession of either their minds or their souls. But in addition to their evident harmfulness, horror-film monsters are also impure. Their impurity, in turn, can be manifested by means of several generally recurring strategies, usually involving the violation of standing cultural categories in various ways.

For example, horror-film monsters may be categorically hybrid, mixing different biological or ontological orders. The creature in *The Relic* blends various species, being part reptile, part human, and part (?) water buffalo. As the very title of the film signals, the zombies in *Night of the Living Dead* appear to be members of an ontologically self-contradictory set of things – creatures that are both living *and* dead at the same time. Many horror-film monsters violate defining characteristics of the categories they supposedly belong to. The giant spider alluded to earlier is at least a thousand times bigger than the largest possible spider.

Moreover, many horrific monsters are incomplete examples of their category – they are so often missing parts like arms, legs, eyes, and even heads. Or sometimes they are heads or just brains without bodies. And last, some horrific beings are altogether so formless that it would be hard to assign them to any category. The Blob is formless throughout the film of the same name. But, of course, many horrific creatures, like vampires, can assume formlessness at will or start out formless before they take over someone else's body.

The monster in *From Beyond* (1986) is designed in such a way that it exploits a number of these strategies for projecting horrific impurity. Edward Praetorius (Ted Sorel) has developed a machine whose sonic vibrations give him access to another dimension inhabited by noxious, ill-tempered creatures that resemble lampreys. During his first penetration of this alternative dimension, his head is bitten off. The police assume he is dead and they arrest his assistant as a suspect. Encouraged by a psychiatrist to work through his trauma, the assistant restages Praetorius's experiment. As the alternative dimension becomes manifest, it turns out that Praetorius is not dead. He has gone over to live on the other side.

However, as is par for the course in mad-scientist movies, all is not well with Praetorius. His mind has melded with that of some other-dimensional being. He is evolving into a new kind of hybrid or composite entity. On Praetorius's second manifestation, much of his human body has disappeared into a mass of tissue. He is half a face attached to a gelatinous, decomposing mound of flesh. Not only is he mostly amorphous, but he can dissolve at will into oozing goo. Part of his horrific signature is his ability to go in and out of formlessness, formlessness of a sort that is all the more sickening for being sticky and saliva-like.

Praetorius cannot merely transform himself from bodily articulateness to formlessness, he can also take on parts of different genera. So the sucker of a giant leech can burst through his human forehead. Thus, in addition to exploiting the line between form and formlessness, Praetorius is also a categorically hybrid creature – sometimes displaying parts of several species simultaneously and sometimes changing from one kind of creature into another sequentially.

The categorical distinction between inside and outside is also contradicted and breached in Praetorius's biology; his extended pineal gland waves about externally like an antenna. Sometimes Praetorius has one arm, sometimes two. In addition to all his other problems, then, he is also at times categorically incomplete.

The creature Praetorius has been designed by the filmmakers of *From Beyond* as if in an attempt to touch all the bases when it comes to horrific impurity. There is something to disgust virtually everyone in Praetorius's makeup (both biological and dramaturgical).

And, perhaps needless to say, Praetorius is also quite dangerous. Like so many other mad scientists he, in concert with other-dimensional creatures who also inhabit his body, take it into his (their?) head(?) to conquer the world. His great intelligence, amplified by his experience of other dimensions, poses a great threat to humanity as does his superhuman strength and telekinetic prowess. He represents the greatest potential harm humanity has ever known, so the film avows, and the portal he has opened to the other world must be closed.

Looking at a horror film like *From Beyond* from an analytic point of view requires dissecting, so to say, the way in which the monster has been designed to engender a horrified emotional response from audiences. One proceeds by noting how the monster has been composed and set into action in accordance to the criteria appropriate to the emotion of horror. In *From Beyond*, Praetorius's attributes rehearse the themes of impurity and danger in many dimensions. By saliently posing these criterially prefocused attributes, the filmmakers encourage the audience to subsume or to assess them under the categories of the impure and the harmful in a way that is apt to promote emotive focus of a horrific variety. Moreover, if my hypothesis is correct, once this sort of emotive focus takes control, the audience keeps surveying the image of Praetorius for further evidence of

impurity and danger, thereby sustaining the operation of their ongoing emotional processes.

Suspense

Suspense is not exactly a genre unto itself, since suspense is an emotion that is often elicited in many other genres.[17] In *An Affair to Remember*, we feel suspense about whether or not Nicky will see that Terry never abandoned her love for him. And in so many horror films, suspense is engendered over the question of whether or not Earth can be saved from the onslaught of flying saucers, rampaging zombies, pod people, birds, or whatever. In *The Arrival*, which is a science-fiction horror film, suspense is generated over the question of whether the alien attempt to transform ("terraform") the atmosphere of earth can be unmasked. Suspense, it would appear, is a genre classification that cuts across other genre classifications.

Nevertheless, we do talk of suspense films. These, roughly speaking, are films, perhaps of almost any other genre, that either contain arresting or memorable suspense scenes as major parts of the narrative, or that conclude with a rousing suspense sequence, or, maybe most paradigmatically, films that are organized virtually in their entirety around resolving certain dominant, suspenseful questions, such as "can the assassination be averted?"

Suspense is a future-oriented emotion. In everyday life, we don't normally feel suspense about what happened in the past. I don't feel suspense about the outcome of World War II, since I already know it. Suspense is a posture that we typically adopt to what will happen, not to what has happened.

But suspense is not an emotion that takes possession of us with respect to just any future event. I do not feel suspense about whether or not I will go to work tomorrow because I think that it is highly probable that I will go and, moreover, I want to go. In everyday life, suspense takes over where the odds are against – or at least up in the air – concerning something that I want to happen, or, conversely, where something that I do not want to happen seems probable. If it looks like the candidate whom I oppose is either likely to win or has just as good a chance of winning as the candidate I support, then I feel suspense over the outcome of the election. But if the candidate I oppose cannot possibly win and the candidate

I favor cannot possibly lose, then there is little room for me to feel suspense.

Suspense concerns probabilities. It is not simply a matter of uncertainty. I am uncertain about the outcome of many future events, but I do not feel suspense in regard to them. Suspense only takes hold where the probabilities seem to be running against some outcome that I prefer, or, to put it the other way around, where the probabilities are running in favor of some outcome that I would rather not obtain. Moving from everyday life to film fiction, for example, as the townspeople are savaged by the outlaws, we feel suspense, since what we want – the rescue of the villagers – is unlikely because the cavalry is still miles away.

The emotion of suspense takes as its object some future event whose desired outcome is improbable, or, at least, no more probable than the undesired outcome; indeed, with suspense, the undesired outcome is characteristically much more probable than the desired outcome. That is to say that the emotive criteria appropriate to regarding an event with suspense is such that the event promises that an undesired outcome appears likely, while the desired outcome seems unlikely. Thus, in constructing suspense episodes, filmmakers must criterially prefocus their depictions and descriptions in such a way that the audience's desires and the probabilities that attach to them come apart.

Perhaps the ways in which filmmakers structure events so that certain outcomes appear probable and others improbable require little more explanation than the ways in which they make the plights of the characters in melodramas pitiable, or the monsters in horror films fearsome. The rescue of the heroine in the burning building is so unlikely because the flames are so high and the hero is so far away and anyway he is engaged in a losing battle with four implacable villains. Her life hangs on a slender thread, stretched to the breaking point. However, the answer to the question of how filmmakers dispose audiences to prefer certain outcomes over others may be less obvious.

In order to mobilize suspense in an audience, a fiction filmmaker has to get the audience to care about one of the outcomes of the course of affairs she is narrating. She has to engender the audience's concern in such a way that the audience desires the outcome that the narrative depicts as vastly improbable, or, at least, no more probable than the countervailing alternative. But is there any fairly reliable way for the filmmaker to do this? After all, the filmmaker is designing her

movie for an audience most of whose members she does not know personally. She has no access to their private preferences and desires. How can she be fairly certain that by characterizing a situation one way rather than another, she will enlist the audience's concern in the way that she needs to in order to make the scene work in terms of suspense? This is a general problem that confronts all suspense filmmakers. Moreover, it has a straightforward solution that is in evidence in virtually every suspense film ever made.

In order to encourage the kind of concern that is requisite for suspense, the filmmaker has to locate some shared stratum of interests and preferences in diverse audiences about whom she has little or no personal knowledge. That is, she has to find some common interests or preferences in the audience such that they will support the suspense response. Here, morality turns out to be the card that almost every suspense film plays. Morality supplies a fairly common set of sentiments that are apt to be shared by most typical viewers. Thus we find in most suspense films that the object of the emotion is an event whose *evil* outcomes are probable and whose *righteous* outcomes are improbable, or, at least, no more probable than the evil ones.

When the train is no more than ten feet away from the heroine strapped to the tracks, the evil machinations of the villain seem inevitable. Likewise, in *Secret Agent* (1936) when "the General" is about to push the kindly old gentleman, misidentified as a spy, over the cliff, we find ourselves in the grip of suspense because averting the murder seems impossible (Ashenden [John Gielgud], the only person who could stop the event, is half a mile away in an observatory, watching the assassination, in anguish, through a telescope) at the same time that we regard the deed as immoral (in part because we share Ashenden's scruples and perhaps, in part, because we realize that the evidence that the old man is a spy is not only slim, but contradicted by his altogether generous, open demeanor). Similarly, in *Speed* (1994) suspense takes over for much of the film because there seems to be no way that the hurtling bus won't be blown to smithereens, killing all of the innocent passengers. In films like *Ransom* (1996), suspense seems to become most excruciating just when it appears that the villain is going to get away.

Of course, the sense of morality that operates in such films is not always the same as the morality that rules our everyday affairs. Often we feel inclined toward projects in films that we would never endorse in "real life." For example, caper films represent persons involved in perpetrating crimes that we do not usually condone. However, it is often the case that films shape our ethical responses to them in a way that diverges from our everyday moral judgments.

Perhaps the most important lever that filmmakers possess for influencing our assessment of the morality of scenes in suspense films involves character portrayal. That is, we tend to accept the projects of characters in suspense films who strike us as virtuous. With caper films, for example, we find that the protagonists in such fictions are standardly possessed of certain striking virtues; and in the absence of countervailing virtues in their opposite number, or possibly given the emphasis on the outright vice of their opponents, we tend to ally ourselves morally with the caper. The virtues in question here – strength, fortitude, ingenuity, bravery, competence, beauty, generosity, and so on – are more often than not Grecian, rather than Christian. But it is because the characters exhibit these virtues – it is because we perceive (and are led to perceive) these characters as virtuous – that we cast our moral allegiance with them.

If the protagonists are represented as possessed of some virtues and their opponents are less virtuous, altogether bereft of virtue, or downright vicious, suspense can take hold because the efforts of the protagonists are morally correct in accordance with the ethical system of the film. Of course, it is probably the case that generally the actions of the protagonists in typical films are morally correct in accordance with some prevailing ethical norms shared by the majority of the audience. However, in cases in which this consensus does not obtain, the protagonist's possession of saliently underlined virtues will project the moral valuations of the fiction and, indeed, incline the audience toward accepting that perspective as its own. Thus it turns out that sometimes even an antagonist can serve as the object of suspense, as long as he or she is presented as possessed of some virtues. In fact, at the limit, I suspect that even a vicious character and his plight can become the object of suspense when he is portrayed as an utterly helpless victim, since the audience's sense of rectitude recoils at the prospect of harming truly helpless victims.

Typically the criteria that an event in a fiction film will meet in order to serve as an appropriate object of suspense involve morality and probability. The depictions and descriptions in suspense films criterially prefocus the events they characterize in terms of outcomes in which the triumph of evil is likely while the prospects for righteousness are slight. Making these features of the courses of events in a fiction film salient is apt to elicit emotive focus in accordance with the criteria appropriate to suspense. Thus, spectators in the grip of suspense fix their attention on the details that contribute to the probability and morality rankings of the unfolding actions in the story. Moreover, once in the thrall of suspense, their emotive focus avidly tracks the fluctuating probabilities in the contest between moral good and evil on the screen.

Analyzing a suspense sequence or a suspense film, then, involves isolating the thematic and stylistic choices that play a role in the criterial prefocusing of the film text. With suspense, those will be the elements of depiction and description that lead the audience to make the relevant assessments concerning the probabilities and moral values of the alternative outcomes of the unfolding action.

Analyzing the ways in which horror films elicit the emotion after which the genre is named also involves attending to the way in which the film text is criterially prefocused. However, in this case, the relevant emotive criteria are not probability and morality, but harm and impurity, and the object of the emotion in question is a being, the monster, and not an event, as it is with respect to suspense. Thus, the horror analyst will attend to the way in which the monster is structured to bring properties in accordance with the criteria of harm and impurity to the fore, and to the way that the plot affords opportunities both to allow the monster to display these properties and to permit the human characters an occasion to talk about and to describe them.

With melodrama, criterial prefocusing is again crucial, though the criteria appropriate to what we might call the melodramatic emotion – a compound of pity and admiration – are misfortune and virtue (generally of an other-regarding and often of a self-sacrificing sort). Pithing the structure that gives rise to the melodramatic emotion involves attending to incidents that set forth the misfortunes and virtues of characters and to the ways in which these are emphasized dramatically, narratively, and cinematically.

Concluding Remarks

In this chapter I have proposed a sketch of a theoretical framework for analyzing the relation between film and what I have called the emotions proper (or, alternatively, the garden-variety emotions). I have also attempted to show the significance of this program for the analysis of various genres that are universally acknowledged to traffic in certain well-known emotional states.

Throughout, I have repeatedly stressed the importance of criterial prefocusing for eliciting emotive focus. My hypothesis has been that by criterially prefocusing the film text – where the criteria in question are the ones appropriate to certain emotions – filmmakers encourage spectators to assess or to subsume the events onscreen under certain categories, namely the categories pertinent to the excitation of the relevant emotional states.

Through criterial prefocusing we could say that the filmmaker leads the horse to water. But the circuit is not completed until the audience drinks. In order for that to occur, the audience must cognize the film text in the ways that the filmmaker has made salient through criterial prefocusing. That means subsuming the onscreen events under the intended criterially governed categories or, alternatively, assessing the onscreen events in light of the intended emotive criteria. But whichever way you prefer to put it, the audience's faculties of cognition and judgment are brought into play in the process of eliciting an emotional response to film. Thus we see that even when it comes to analyzing the relation of film to the emotions, a cognitively oriented approach to film theory has much to offer.

Notes

1 By only alluding to cognitively impenetrable affects here, I do not want to suggest that other states – such as pleasure and desire – do not warrant study. I consider those to be topics for future research. I have even attempted some preliminary work on desire in my book *A Philosophy of Mass Art* (Oxford: Clarendon, 1998).

2 When I say that ordinary language treats these examples as paradigmatic, what I have in mind is that, when asked, competent language users will tend to offer phenomena like these – especially fear, anger, sadness and love – as central instances of emotional states.

3 Ed S. Tan, *Emotion and the Structure of Narrative Film: Film as an Emotion Machine*, trans. Barbara Fasting (Mahwah, NJ: Erlbaum, 1996).

4 William James, "What Is an Emotion?" in *Mind* 9 (1884): 188–205.

5 Robert Solomon, "The Jamesian Theory of Emotion in Anthropology," in *Culture Theory: Essays on Mind. Self and Emotion*, ed. Richard A. Shweder and Robert A. LeVine (Cambridge: Cambridge University Press, 1984), 214.

6 Though the case that follows is made up, it is not entirely fanciful, since experiments like it have been run. A classic example in the literature is Stanley Schachter and Jerome E. Singer, "Cognitive, Social, and Physiological Determinants of State," excerpted in *What Is An Emotion?*, ed. Cheshire Calhoun and Robert C. Solomon (Oxford: Oxford University Press, 1984), 173–83.

7 Here it might be argued that there are some emotional states, like free-floating depression, that do not take objects. Rather than deny that there are such states, I prefer to take advantage of the distinction I drew earlier between affects broadly construed and paradigmatic emotional states. Perhaps free-floating depression is just not a core case of the emotions proper. Maybe it is an affective state brought about by chemical imbalances in the body.

8 Some garden-variety emotions may also include – in addition to cognitions and bodily feelings – desires as a typical or even a necessary component.

9 In this, I will restrict myself to the case of viewing narrative fiction films rather than to abstract and/ or nonnarrative films. I have made this methodological decision not only because it makes the job easier, but because I think that we will be in a better position to understand the operation of the emotions in the latter when we understand it in relation to the former. Unfortunately, in this paper, I only have space to deal with the case of the fictional narrative.

I will also not be considering the role of music in engendering movie emotion in this paper, However, I have made a stab at that topic in Noël Carroll, "Notes on Movie Music," in my *Theorizing the Moving Image* (Cambridge: Cambridge University Press, 1996).

10 With respect to the arguments in this paper, see also Noël Carroll, "Art, Nature and Emotion," in *The Emotions and Art*, ed. Mette Hjort and Sue Laver

(Oxford: Oxford University Press, 1997); and my *Philosophy of Mass Art*, esp. chap. 4.

11 I address the use of point-of-view editing to prefocus audience attention emotively in my "Toward a Theory of Point-of-View Editing: Communication, Emotion and the Movies," in *Theorizing the Moving Image*.

12 I talk of what is "generally" or "very frequently" the case in fiction films here because sometimes a character or a scene in a film may be emotively marked in an initially ambiguous way. This is a *standard* deviation from the norm whose existence I would not wish to deny. However, above I am talking about the norm in order to illustrate what I mean by talking about the emotive prefocusing of scenes, sequences and characters. Moreover, even where the filmic phenomena are ambiguously marked, that too is generally (barring cases of ineptitude) a function of the filmmakers' design and prefocusing activity.

13 The notion of dysphoric and euphoric emotion here comes from Keith Oatley, *Best-Laid Schemes* (Cambridge: Cambridge University Press, 1992), 107–9, 174–7.

14 This section has been inspired by an important article by Flo Leibowitz. See her "Apt Feelings, or Why 'Women's Films' Aren't Trivial," in *Post-Theory: Reconstructing Film Studies*, ed. David Bordwell and Noël Carroll (Madison: University of Wisconsin Press, 1996).

15 The account of horror derives from Noël Carroll, *The Philosophy of Horror, or Paradoxes of the Heart* (New York: Routledge, 1990). See also Noël Carroll, "Horror and Humor," in *Beyond Aesthetics* (New York: Cambridge University Press, 2001).

16 See David Pole, "Disgust and Other Forms of Aversion," in his *Aesthetics, Form and Emotion*, ed. George Roberts (New York: St. Martin's Press, 1983).

17 For further discussions of suspense, see Noël Carroll, "Toward a Theory of Film Suspense," in *Theorizing the Moving Image* (Cambridge: Cambridge University Press, 1996); and Noël Carroll, "The Paradox of Suspense," in *Suspense: Conceptualizations, Theoretical Analyses, and Empirical Explorations*, ed. Peter Vorderer, Hans J. Wulff, and Mike Friedrichsen (Hilldale, NJ: Erlbaum, 1996).

15

Fearing Fictions

Kendall Walton

*[T]he plot [of a tragedy] must be structured
...that the one who is hearing the events unroll
shudders with fear and feels pity at what happens: which is what one would experience on
hearing the plot of the Oedipus.*

Aristotle, Poetics[1]

I

Charles is watching a horror movie about a terrible
green slime. He cringes in his seat as the slime oozes
slowly but relentlessly over the earth destroying
everything in its path. Soon a greasy head emerges
from the undulating mass, and two beady eyes roll
around, finally fixing on the camera. The slime,
picking up speed, oozes on a new course straight
toward the viewers. Charles emits a shriek and
clutches desperately at his chair. Afterwards, still
shaken, Charles confesses that he was "terrified"
of the slime. *Was* he?

This question is part of the larger issue of how
"remote" fictional worlds are from the real world.
There is a definite barrier against *physical* interactions between fictional worlds and the real world.
Spectators at a play are prevented from rendering
aid to a heroine in distress. There is no way that
Charles can dam up the slime, or take a sample for
laboratory analysis.[2] But, as Charles's case dramatically illustrates, this barrier appears to be psychologically transparent. It would seem that real
people can, and frequently do, have psychological

attitudes toward merely fictional entities, despite
the impossibility of physical intervention. Readers
or spectators detest Iago, worry about Tom Sawyer and Becky lost in the cave, pity Willy Loman,
envy Superman – and Charles fears the slime.

But I am skeptical. We do indeed get "caught
up" in stories; we often become "emotionally involved" when we read novels or watch plays or
films. But to construe this involvement as consisting of our having psychological attitudes toward
fictional entities is, I think, to tolerate mystery
and court confusion. I shall offer a different and,
in my opinion, a much more illuminating account
of it.

This issue is of fundamental importance. It is
crucially related to the basic question of why and
how fiction is important, why we find it valuable,
why we do not dismiss novels, films, and plays as
"mere fiction" and hence unworthy of serious attention. My conclusions in this paper will lead to some
tentative suggestions about this basic question.

II

Physical interaction is possible only with what
actually exists. That is why Charles cannot dam
up the slime, and why in general real people cannot have physical contact with mere fictions. But
the nonexistence of the slime does not prevent
Charles from fearing it. One may fear a ghost or

Kendall Walton, "Fearing Fictions," *Journal of Philosophy* 75(1), January 1978: 5–27. Reprinted by permission
of the Journal of Philosophy, Columbia University.

a burglar even if there is none; one may be afraid of an earthquake that is destined never to occur.

But a person who fears a nonexistent burglar *believes* that there is, or at least might be, one. He believes that he is in danger, that there is a possibility of his being harmed by a burglar. It is *conceivable* that Charles should believe himself to be endangered by the green slime. He might take the film to be a live documentary, a news flash. If he does, naturally he is afraid.

But the situation I have in mind is the more usual and more interesting one in which Charles is not deceived in this straightforward way. Charles knows perfectly well that the slime is not real and that he is in no danger. Is he afraid even so? He says that he is afraid, and he is in a state which is undeniably similar, in some respects, to that of a person who is frightened of a pending real-world disaster. His muscles are tensed, he clutches his chair, his pulse quickens, his adrenalin flows. Let us call this physiological/psychological state "quasi-fear." Whether it is actual fear (or a component of actual fear) is the question at issue.

Charles's state is crucially different from that of a person with an ordinary case of fear. The fact that Charles is fully aware that the slime is fictional is, I think, good reason to deny that what he feels is fear. It seems a principle of common sense, one which ought not to be abandoned if there is any reasonable alternative, that fear[3] must be accompanied by, or must involve, a belief that one is in danger. Charles does not believe that he is in danger; so he is not afraid.

Charles might try to convince us that he was afraid by shuddering and declaring dramatically that he was "*really terrified.*" This emphasizes the intensity of his experience. But we need not deny that he had an intense experience. The question is whether his experience, however intense, was one of fear of the slime. The fact that Charles, and others, call it "fear" is not conclusive, even if we grant that in doing so they express a truth. For we need to know whether the statement that Charles was afraid is to be taken literally or not.

More sophisticated defenders of the claim that Charles is afraid may argue that Charles *does* believe that the green slime is real and is a real threat to him. There are, to be sure, strong reasons for allowing that Charles realizes that the slime is only fictional and poses no danger. If he didn't we should expect him to flee the theater, call the police, warn his family. But perhaps it is *also* true that Charles believes, in some way or "on some

level," that the slime is real and really threatens him. It has been said that in cases like this one "suspends one's disbelief," or that "part" of a person believes something which another part of him disbelieves, or that one finds oneself (almost?) believing something one nevertheless knows to be false. We must see what can be made of these notions.

One possibility is that Charles *half* believes that there is a real danger, and that he is, literally, at least half afraid. To half believe something is to be not quite sure that it is true, but also not quite sure that it is not true. But Charles has *no* doubts about whether he is in the presence of an actual slime. If he half believed, and were half afraid, we would expect him to have *some* inclination to act on his fear in the normal ways. Even a hesitant belief, a mere suspicion, that the slime is real would induce any normal person seriously to consider calling the police and warning his family. Charles gives no thought whatever to such courses of action. He is not *uncertain* whether the slime is real; he is perfectly sure that it is not.

Moreover, the fear symptoms that Charles does exhibit are not symptoms of a mere suspicion that the slime is real and a queasy feeling of half fear. They are symptoms of the certainty of grave and immediate danger, and sheer terror. Charles's heart pounds violently, he gasps for breath, he grasps the chair until his knuckles are white. This is not the behavior of a man who realizes basically that he is safe but suffers flickers of doubt. If it indicates fear at all, it indicates acute and overwhelming terror. Thus, to compromise on this issue, to say that Charles half believes he is in danger and is half afraid, is not a reasonable alternative.

One might claim that Charles believes he is in danger, but that this is not a hesitant or weak or half belief, but rather a belief of a special kind – a "gut" belief as opposed to an "intellectual" one. Compare a person who hates flying. He realizes, in one sense, that airplanes are (relatively) safe. He says, honestly, that they are, and can quote statistics to prove it. Nevertheless, he avoids traveling by air whenever possible. He is brilliant at devising excuses. And if he must board a plane he becomes nervous and upset. I grant that this person believes at a "gut" level that flying is dangerous, despite his "intellectual" belief to the contrary. I grant also that he is really afraid of flying.

But Charles is different. The air traveler performs *deliberate* actions that one would expect of someone who thinks flying is dangerous, or at least he is strongly inclined to perform such actions. If he does not actually decide against traveling by air he has a strong inclination to do so. But Charles does not have even an inclination to leave the theater or call the police. The only signs that he might really believe he is endangered are his more or less automatic, nondeliberate, reactions: his pulse rate, his sweaty palms, his knotted stomach, his spontaneous shriek.[4] This justifies us in treating the two cases differently.

Deliberate actions are done for reasons; they are done because of what the agent wants and what he thinks will bring about what he wants. There is a presumption that such actions are reasonable in light of the agent's beliefs and desires (however unreasonable the beliefs and desires may be). So we postulate beliefs or desires to make sense of them. People also have reasons for doing things that they are inclined to do but, for other reasons, refrain from doing. If the air traveler thinks that flying is dangerous, then, assuming that he wants to live, his actions or tendencies thereto are reasonable. Otherwise, they probably are not. So we legitimately infer that he does believe, at least on a "gut" level, that flying is dangerous. But we don't have to make the same kind of sense of Charles's automatic responses. One doesn't have reasons for things one doesn't *do*, like sweating, increasing one's pulse rate, knotting one's stomach (involuntarily). So there is no need to attribute beliefs (or desires) to Charles which will render these responses reasonable.[5] Thus, we can justifiably infer the air passenger's ("gut") belief in the danger of flying from his deliberate behavior or inclinations, and yet refuse to infer from Charles's automatic responses that he thinks he is in danger.

Someone might reply that at moments of special crisis during the movie – e.g., when the slime first spots Charles – Charles "loses hold of reality" and, *momentarily*, takes the slime to be real and really fears it. These moments are too short for Charles to think about doing anything; so (one might claim) it isn't surprising that his belief and fear are not accompanied by the normal inclinations to act.

This move is unconvincing. In the first place, Charles's quasi-fear responses are not merely momentary; he may have his heart in his throat throughout most of the movie, yet without experiencing the slightest inclination to flee or call the police. These long-term responses, and Charles's propensity to describe them afterwards in terms of "fear," need to be understood even if it is allowed

that there are moments of real fear interspersed among them. Furthermore, however tempting the momentary-fear idea might be, comparable views of other psychological states are much less appealing. When we say that someone "pitied" Willy Loman or "admired" Superman, it is unlikely that we have in mind special moments during his experience of the work when he forgot, momentarily, that he was dealing with fiction and felt flashes of actual pity or admiration. The person's "sense of reality" may well have been robust and healthy throughout his experience of the work, uninterrupted by anything like the special moments of crisis Charles experiences during the horror movie. Moreover, it may be appropriate to say that someone "pities" Willy or "admires" Superman even when he is not watching the play or reading the cartoon. The momentary-*fear* theory, even if it were plausible, would not throw much light on cases in which we apparently have other psychological attitudes toward fictions.

Although Charles is not really afraid of the fictional slime depicted in the movie, the movie might nevertheless produce real fear in him. It might cause him to be afraid of something other than the slime it depicts. If Charles is a child, the movie may make him wonder whether there might not be real slimes or other exotic horrors *like* the one depicted in the movie, even if he fully realizes that the movie-slime itself is not real. Charles may well fear these suspected actual dangers; he might have nightmares about them for days afterwards. (*Jaws* caused a lot of people to fear sharks which they thought might really exist. But whether they were afraid of the fictional sharks in the movie is another question.)

If Charles is an older movie-goer with a heart condition, he may be afraid of the movie itself. Perhaps he knows that any excitement could trigger a heart attack, and fears that the movie will cause excitement, e.g., by depicting the slime as being especially aggressive or threatening. This is real fear. But it is fear of the depiction of the slime, not fear of the slime that is depicted.

Why is it so natural to describe Charles as afraid of the slime, if he is not, and how *is* his experience to be characterized? In what follows I shall develop a theory to answer these questions.

III

Propositions that are, as we say, "true in (the world of)" a novel or painting or film are *fictional*.

Thus it is fictional that there is a society of tiny people called "Lilliputians." And in the example discussed above it is fictional that a terrible green slime is on the loose. Other fictional propositions are associated not with works of art but with games of make-believe, dreams, and imaginings. If it is "true in a game of make-believe" that Johnnie is a pirate, then fictionally Johnnie is a pirate. If someone dreams or imagines that he is a hero, then it is fictional that he is a hero.

Fictional truths[6] come in groups, and each of these groups constitutes a "fictional world." The fact that fictionally there was a society of tiny people and the fact that fictionally a man named "Gulliver" was a ship's physician belong to the same fictional world. The fact that fictionally a green slime is on the loose belongs to a different one. There is, roughly, a distinct fictional world corresponding to each novel, painting, film, game of make-believe, dream, or daydream.

All fictional truths are in one way or another man-made. But there are two importantly different ways of making them, and two corresponding kinds of fictional truths. One way to make a proposition fictional is simply to imagine that it is true. If it is fictional that a person is a hero because he imagines himself to be a hero, then this fictional truth is an *imaginary* one. Imagining is not always a deliberate, self-conscious act. We sometimes find ourselves imagining things more or less spontaneously, without having decided to do so. Thoughts pop into our heads unbidden. Dreams can be understood as simply very spontaneous imaginings.

Fictional truths of the second kind are established in a less direct manner. Participants in a game of mud pies may decide to recognize a principle to the effect that whenever there is a glob of mud in a certain orange crate, it is "true in the game of make-believe," i.e., it is fictional, that there is a pie in the oven. This fictional truth is a *make-believe* one. The principles in force in a given game of make-believe are, of course, just those principles which participants in the game recognize or accept, or understand to be in force.

It can be make-believe that there is a pie in the oven without anyone's imagining that there is. This will be so if there is a glob in the crate which no one knows about. (Later, after discovering the glob, a child might say, "There was a pie in the oven all along, but we didn't know it.") But propositions that are known to be make-believe are usually imaginary as well. When kids playing mud pies do know about a glob in the crate by virtue of which it is make-believe that a pie is in the oven, they imagine that there is a pie in the oven.

Principles of make-believe that are in force in a game need not have been formulated explicitly or deliberately adopted. When children agree to let globs of mud "be" pies they are in effect establishing a great many unstated principles linking make-believe properties of pies to properties of globs. It is implicitly understood that the size and shape of globs determine the make-believe size and shape of pies; it is understood, for example, that make-believedly a pie is one handspan across just in case that is the size of the appropriate glob. It is understood also that if Johnnie throws a glob at Mary then make-believedly Johnnie throws a pie at Mary. (It is *not* understood that if a glob is 40 per cent clay then make-believedly a pie is 40 per cent clay.)

It is not always easy to say whether or not someone does accept, implicitly, a given principle of make-believe. But we should notice that much of the plausibility of attributing to children implicit acceptance of a principle linking the make-believe size and shape of pies to the size and shape of globs rests on the dispositional fact that if the children should discover a glob to have a certain size or shape they would imagine, more or less automatically, that a pie has that size or shape. The children are disposed to imagine pies as having whatever size and shape properties they think the relevant globs have. In general, nondeliberate, spontaneous imagining, prompted in a systematic way by beliefs about the real world, is an important indication of implicit acceptance of principles of make-believe. I do not claim that a person disposed to imagine, nondeliberately, that p when he believes that q *necessarily* recognizes a principle of make-believe whereby if q then it is make-believe that p. It must be his understanding that whenever it is true that q, *whether he knows it or not*, it will be fictional that p. It may be difficult to ascertain whether this is his understanding, especially since his understanding may be entirely implicit. But the spontaneity of a person's imagining that p on learning that q strongly suggests that he thinks of p as having been fictional even before he realized that q.

A game of make-believe and its constituent principles need not be shared publicly. One might set up one's own personal game, adopting principles that no one else recognizes. And at least some of the principles constituting a personal

Kendall Walton

game of make-believe may be implicit, principles which the person simply takes for granted.

Representational works of art generate make-believe truths. *Gulliver's Travels* generates the truth that make-believedly there is a society of six-inch-tall people. It is make-believe that a green slime is on the loose in virtue of the images on the screen of Charles's horror movie. These make-believe truths are generated because the relevant principles of make-believe are understood to be in force. But few such principles are ever formulated, and our recognition of most of them is implicit. Some probably seem so natural that we assume them to be in force almost automatically. Others we pick up easily through unreflective experience with the arts.[7]

IV

[The actor] on a stage plays at being another before a gathering of people who play at taking him for that other person.

Jorge Luis Borges[8]

Compare Charles with a child playing an ordinary game of make-believe with his father. The father, pretending to be a ferocious monster, cunningly stalks the child and, at a crucial moment, lunges viciously at him. The child flees, screaming, to the next room. The scream is more or less involuntary, and so is the flight. But the child has a delighted grin on his face even while he runs, and he unhesitatingly comes back for more. He is perfectly aware that his father is only "playing," that the whole thing is "just a game," and that only make-believedly is there a vicious monster after him. He is not really afraid.

The child obviously belongs to the fictional world of the game of make-believe. It is make-believe that the monster lunges, not into thin air, but at the child. Make-believedly the child is in grave and mortal danger. And when the child screams and runs, make-believedly he knows he is in danger and is afraid. The game is a sort of theatrical event in which the father is an actor portraying a monster and the child is an actor playing himself.

I propose to regard Charles similarly. When the slime raises its head, spies the camera, and begins oozing toward it, it is make-believe that Charles is threatened. And when as a result Charles gasps

and grips his chair, make-believedly he is afraid. Charles is playing a game of make-believe in which he uses the images on the screen as props. He too is an actor impersonating himself. In this section I shall explain this proposal in detail. My main arguments for it will come later.

Charles differs in some important respects from an ordinary on-stage, self-portraying actor. One difference has to do with what makes it make-believe that Charles is afraid. Facts about Charles generate (*de re*) make-believe truths about him; in this respect he is like an actor portraying himself on stage. But the sorts of facts about Charles which do the generating are different. Make-believe truths about Charles are generated at least partly by what he thinks and feels, not just by how he acts. It is partly the fact that Charles is in a state of quasi-fear, the fact that he feels his heart pounding, his muscles tensed, etc., which makes it make-believe that he is afraid. It would not be appropriate to describe him as "afraid" if he were not in some such state.[9]

Charles's quasi-fear is not responsible, by itself, for the fact that make-believedly it is the *slime* he fears, nor even for the fact that make-believedly he is afraid rather than angry or excited or merely upset. Here Charles's (actual) beliefs come into play. Charles believes (he knows) that make-believedly the green slime is bearing down on him and he is in danger of being destroyed by it. His quasi-fear results from this belief.[10] What makes it make-believe that Charles is afraid rather than angry or excited or upset is the fact that his quasi-fear is caused by the belief that make-believedly he is in danger. And his belief that make-believedly it is the slime that endangers him is what makes it make-believe that the slime is the object of his fear. In short, my suggestion is this: the fact that Charles is quasi-afraid as a result of realizing that make-believedly the slime threatens him generates the truth that make-believedly he is afraid of the slime.[11]

An on-stage actor, by contrast, generates make-believe truths solely by his acting, by his behavior. Whether it is make-believe that the character portrayed is afraid or not depends just on what the actor says and does and how he contorts his face, regardless of what he actually thinks or feels. It makes no difference whether his actual emotional state is anything like fear. This is just as true when the actor is playing himself as it is when he is portraying some other character. The actor may find that putting himself into a certain frame of mind makes it easier to act in the appropriate ways. Nevertheless, it is how he acts, not his state of mind, that determines whether make-believedly he is afraid.

This is how our conventions for theater work, and it is entirely reasonable that they should work this way. Audiences cannot be expected to have a clear idea of an actor's personal thoughts and feelings while he is performing. That would require knowledge of his off-stage personality and of recent events that may have affected his mood (e.g., an argument with his director or his wife). Moreover, acting involves a certain amount of dissembling; actors hide some aspects of their mental states from the audience. If make-believe truths depended on actors' private thoughts and feelings, it would be awkward and unreasonably difficult for spectators to ascertain what is going on in the fictional world. It is not surprising that the make-believe truths for which actors on stage are responsible are understood to be generated by just what is visible from the galleries.

But Charles is not performing for an audience. It is not his job to get across to anyone else what make-believedly is true of himself. Probably no one but him much cares whether or not make-believedly he is afraid. So there is no reason why his actual state of mind should not have a role in generating make-believe truths about himself.

It is not so clear in the monster game what makes it make-believe that the child is afraid of a monster. The child *might* be performing for the benefit of an audience; he might be *showing* someone, an onlooker, or just his father, that make-believedly he is afraid. If so, perhaps he is like an on-stage actor. Perhaps we should regard his observable behavior as responsible for the fact that make-believedly he is afraid. But there is room for doubt here. The child experiences quasi-fear sensations as Charles does. And his audience probably has much surer access to his mental state than theater audiences have to those of actors. The audience may know him well, and the child does not try so hard or so skillfully to hide his actual mental state as actors do. It may be perfectly evident to the audience that the child has a case of quasi-fear, and also that this is a result of his realization that make-believedly a monster is after him. So it is not unreasonable to regard the child's mental state as helping to generate make-believe truths.

A more definite account of the situation is possible if the child is participating in the game solely for his own amusement, with no thought of an audience. In this case the child himself, at least, almost certainly understands his make-believe fear to depend on his mental state rather than (just) his behavior.[12] In fact, let us suppose that the child is an undemonstrative sort who does not scream or run or betray his "fear" in any other especially overt way. His participation in the game is purely passive. Nevertheless the child does experience quasi-fear when make-believedly the monster attacks him, and he still would describe himself as being "afraid" (although he knows that there is no danger and that his "fear" isn't real). Certainly in this case it is (partly) his quasi-fear that generates the make-believe truth he expresses when he says he is "afraid."

My proposal is to construe Charles on the model of this undemonstrative child. Charles may, of course, exhibit his "fear" in certain observable ways. But his observable behavior is not meant to show anyone else that make-believedly he is afraid. It is likely to go unnoticed by others, and even Charles himself may be unaware of it. No one, least of all Charles, regards his observable behavior as generating the truth that make-believedly he is afraid.

V

It is clear enough now what makes it make-believe that Charles fears the slime, assuming that make-believedly he does fear the slime. But more needs to be said in support of my claim that this is a make-believe truth. What needs to be established is that the relevant principle of make-believe is accepted or recognized by someone, that someone understands it to be in force. I contend that Charles, at least, does so understand it.

It is clear that Charles imagines himself to be afraid of the slime (though he knows he is not). He thinks of himself as being afraid of it; he readily describes his experience as one of "fear" – once he has a chance to catch his breath. So it is at least imaginary (and hence fictional) that he fears slime.

Charles's act of imagining himself afraid of the slime is hardly a deliberate or reflective act. It is triggered more or less automatically by his awareness of his quasi-fear sensations. He is simply disposed to think of himself as fearing the slime, without deciding to do so, when during the movie he feels his heart racing, his muscles tensed, and so forth. It is just such a disposition as this, we recall, that goes with implicit recognition of a principle of make-believe. If a child is disposed to imagine a pie to be six inches across when he discovers that that is the size of a glob of mud, this makes it reasonable to regard him as recognizing a principle whereby the glob's being that size makes it make-believe that the pie is also. Similarly, Charles's tendency to imagine himself afraid of the slime when he finds himself in the relevant mental state constitutes persuasive grounds for attributing to him acceptance of a principle whereby his experience makes it make-believe that he is afraid.[13]

Several further considerations will increase the plausibility of this conclusion. First, I have claimed only that Charles recognizes the principle of make-believe. There is no particular reason why anyone else should recognize it, since ordinarily only Charles is in a position to apply it and only he is interested in the make-believe truth that results. Others might know about it and realize how important it is to Charles. But even so the principle clearly is in important respects a personal one. It differs in this regard from the principles whereby an on-stage actor's behavior generates make-believe truths, and also from those whereby images on the movie screen generate make-believe truths about the activities of the green slime. *These* principles are fully public; they are clearly (even if implicitly) recognized by everyone watching the play or movie. Everyone in the audience applies them and is interested in the resulting make-believe truths.

This makes it reasonable to recognize two distinct games of make-believe connected with the horror movie – a public game and Charles's personal game – and two corresponding fictional worlds. The situation is analogous to that of an illustrated edition of a novel. Consider an edition of Dostoyevsky's *Crime and Punishment* which includes a drawing of Raskolnikov. The text of the novel, considered alone, establishes a fictional world comprising the make-believe truths that it generates, e.g., the truth that make-believedly a man named "Raskolnikov" killed an old lady. The illustration is normally understood not as establishing its own separate fictional world, but as combining with the novel to form a "larger" world. This larger world contains the make-believe truths generated by the text alone, plus those generated by the illustration (e.g., that make-believedly Raskolnikov has wavy hair and a receding chin), and also those generated by both

together (e.g., that make-believedly a man with wavy hair killed an old lady). So we have two fictional worlds, one included within the other: the world of the novel and the world of the novel-plus-illustration.

Charles's state of mind supplements the movie he is watching in the way an illustration supplements what it illustrates. The movie considered alone establishes a fictional world consisting only of the make-believe truths that it generates (e.g., that make-believedly there is a green slime on the loose). But Charles recognizes, in addition, a larger world in which these make-believe truths are joined by truths generated by Charles's experience as he watches the movie, and also by truths generated by the images on the screen and Charles's experience together. It is only in this more inclusive world that make-believedly Charles fears the slime. (And it is the larger world that occupies Charles's attention when he is caught up in the movie.)

The analogy between Charles's case and the illustrated novel is not perfect. The novel-plus-illustration world is publicly recognized, whereas the fictional world established by the movie plus Charles's experience of it probably is not. Dolls provide an analogy which is better in this respect. Anyone who sees a doll of a certain sort will recognize that it generates the truth that make-believedly there is a blonde baby girl. The doll, regarded simply as a sculpture to be observed from a distance, generates make-believe truths such as this. But a child playing with the doll is playing a more personal game of make-believe, one in which she herself is a self-portraying actor and the doll serves as a prop. What she does with the doll generates make-believe truths, e.g., the truth that make-believedly she is dressing the baby for a trip to town. Similarly, Charles uses the screen images as props in a personal game of make-believe in which he himself is a character. He plays his own game with the images. The screen images, of course, do not lend themselves to bring "dressed" or manipulated in all the ways that dolls do, and this limits the extent of Charles's participation in the game. But the relations and interactions between Charles and the images do generate a number of important make-believe truths: that make-believedly Charles notices the slime and stares apprehensively at it, that make-believedly it turns toward him and attacks, and that make-believedly he is scared out of his wits.[14]

One source of uneasiness about my claim that make-believedly Charles fears the slime may have been the impression that this can be so only if Charles belongs to the fictional world of the *movie*. (The movie itself doesn't depict Charles, nor does it make any reference to him, so he doesn't belong to the movie-world.) My two-worlds theory shows that this impression is mistaken and hence that the uneasiness based on it is out of place.

I have portrayed Charles so far as participating rather automatically in his game of make-believe. But he might easily slip into participating deliberately. The naturalness of his doing so gives added support to my claim that Charles does recognize a make-believe world that he and the slime share, even when his participation is not deliberate. Suppose that during the movie Charles exclaims, deliberately, to a companion or to himself, "Yikes, here it comes! Watch out!" How are we to understand this verbal action? Certainly Charles is not seriously asserting that a slime is coming and warning himself or his companion of it. Presumably he is asserting that it is *make-believe* that a slime is coming. But the indexical, 'here', carries an implicit reference to the speaker. So Charles's exclamation shows that he takes it to be make-believe that the slime is headed toward *him*; it shows that he regards himself as coexisting with the slime in a make-believe world.

But this does not take us to the bottom of the matter. "Yikes!" and "Watch out!" are not assertions, and so not assertions of what make-believedly is the case. Moreover, if in saying, "Here it comes," Charles were merely making an assertion about what make-believedly is the case, he could well have made this explicit and exclaimed instead, "Make-believedly the slime is coming!" or "The slime is coming, in the fictional world!" But these variants lack the flavor of the original. Charles's exclamatory tone is absurdly out of place when the make-believe status of the danger is made explicit. Compare how ridiculous it would be for an actor playing Horatio in a performance of *Hamlet* to exclaim, when the ghost appears, "Look, my lord, it comes, in the fictional world of the play!"

The comparison is apt. For Charles is doing just what actors do, *pretending* to make an assertion. He is pretending to assert (seriously) that the slime is headed his way. (Pretending to assert this is not incompatible with actually asserting that make-believedly the slime is coming. Charles might be doing both at once.) In my terms, Charles under-stands his utterance of 'Here it comes!' to generate the truth that make-believedly he asserts (seriously) that the slime is coming. He is playing along with the fiction of the movie, incorporating it into a game of make-believe of his own. This makes it obvious why it would not do to say, "Here it comes, in the fictional world!" Saying that is simply not (normally) how one would pretend to assert that a slime is (really) coming. The rest of Charles's verbal behavior is now easily explainable as well. In saying "Yikes!" and "Watch out!" he is pretending to express amazement or terror and pretending to issue a (serious) warning; make-believedly he is doing these things.

We have now arrived at the solution to a pair of puzzles. Why is it that in everyday conversation we regularly omit phrases like 'in the fictional world' and 'in the novel', whereas we rarely omit other intensional operators such as 'It is believed that', 'Jones wished that', 'Jones denies that'? Why do we so naturally say just "Tom and Becky were lost in a cave" rather than "In the novel Tom and Becky were lost in a cave," whereas it would be almost unheard of to shorten "Jones wishes that a golden mountain would appear on the horizon" to simply "A golden mountain will appear on the horizon" (even if the context makes it clear that Jones's wishes are the subject of conversation)?

The explanation lies in our habit of playing along with fictions, of make-believedly asserting, pretending to assert, what we know to be only make-believedly the case. We mustn't be too quick to assume that an utterance of '*p*' is merely an ellipsis for 'Make-believedly *p*' (or for 'In the novel *p*'). This assumption is wrong if the speaker make-believedly is asserting that *p*, rather than (or in addition to) asserting that make-believedly *p*. Charles's frantic, "Yikes, here it comes!" is an obvious case in point. A case only slightly less obvious is that of a person reading *The Adventures of Tom Sawyer* who remarks, gravely and with an expression of deep concern, that Tom and Becky are lost in a cave.

I do not suggest that the omission of 'in the novel' is *never* a mere ellipsis. "Tom and Becky were lost in a cave" uttered by a critic analyzing the novel could easily have been expanded to "In the novel Tom and Becky were lost in a cave" without altering the character of the remark. The critic probably is not pretending to assert that Tom and Becky were (actually) lost in a cave. But our habit of dropping fictional operators persists even in sober criticism, and testifies to the ease with which we can be induced to play along, deliberately, with a work of fiction.

In German the indicative mood is used ordinarily only when the speaker is committed to the truth of the sentence or clause in question. But fictional statements constitute a striking exception to this generalization; the indicative is used in fictional statements even though the speaker is *not* committed to their truth. (One says, for example, "*Robinson Crusoe hat einen Schiffbruch überlebt*," which is indicative, even though one is not claiming that there actually was a person named "Robinson Crusoe" who survived a shipwreck.) The explanation is that speakers are often pretending to express their commitment to the truth of sentences or clauses in fictional contexts. So naturally they use the indicative mood in these cases; they speak as they would if they were not pretending. And the habit of using the indicative persists even when there is little or no such pretense.

VI

The treatment of Charles's "fear of the slime" suggested above can serve as a model for understanding other psychological attitudes ostensibly directed toward fictional things. When it is said that someone pities Willy Loman, or worries about Tom and Becky, or detests Iago, or envies Superman, what is said is probably not literally true.[15] But the person is, actually, in a distinctive psychological (emotional?) state, even if that state is not pity or worry or hate or envy. And his being in this state is a result of his awareness of certain make-believe truths: that make-believedly Willy is an innocent victim of cruel circumstances, that make-believedly Tom and Becky might perish in the cave, that make-believedly Iago deceived Othello about Desdemona, that make-believedly Superman can do almost anything. The fact that the person's psychological state is as it is, and is caused by such beliefs, makes it make-believe that he pities Willy, worries about Tom and Becky, hates Iago, or envies Superman.

We have here a particularly intimate relation between the real world and fictional worlds. Insofar as make-believe truths are generated by a spectator's or reader's state of mind, he is no mere "external observer" of the fictional world. Ascertaining what make-believedly is true of himself is to a large extent a matter of introspection (or of whatever sort of "privileged access" one has to

one's own beliefs and sensations). In fact, when Charles watches the horror movie, for example, introspection is involved in ascertaining not merely that make-believedly he is afraid of the slime, but also make-believe truths about the nature and progress of his fear. If it is make-believe that his fear is overwhelming, or that it is only momentary, this is so because his quasi-fear sensations are overwhelming, or are only momentary. Make-believedly his fear grows more or less intense, or becomes almost unbearable, or finally subsides, etc., as his quasi-fear feelings change in these ways. So it is by attention to the nature of his own actual experience that Charles is aware of make-believe truths about the nature of his fear. He follows the progress of his make-believe fear by introspection, much as one who is literally afraid follows the progress of his actual fear.

It would not be too far wrong to say that Charles actually experiences his make-believe fear. I don't mean that there is a special kind of fear, make-believe fear, which Charles experiences. What he actually experiences, his quasi-fear feelings, are not feelings of fear. But it is true *of them* that *make-believedly* they are feelings of fear. They generate *de re* make-believe truths about themselves, and so belong to the fictional world just as Charles himself does. What Charles actually experiences is such that make-believedly it is (an experience of) fear.

Cases like that of Charles contrast strikingly with others in which an actual person belongs to a fictional world. Consider a performance of William Luce's play about Emily Dickinson, *The Belle of Amherst*, in which Julie Harris plays Emily Dickinson. Suppose that Emily Dickinson herself, with the help of a time machine or a fortuitous reincarnation, is in the audience. In order to discover make-believe truths about herself, including what make-believedly she thinks and feels, Dickinson must observe Julie Harris's actions, just as any spectator must. It is as though she is watching another person, despite the fact that that "person," the character, is herself. Dickinson has no special intimacy with make-believe truths about her own mental state.[16] The situation is basically the same if Dickinson should replace Julie Harris in the lead role and act the part herself. She still must judge from her external behavior, from what spectators could observe, whether or not it is make-believe that she is afraid or worried or whatever – and she might easily be mistaken about how she looks to spectators. It is still as though she considers herself "from the outside," from the perspective of another person.

This is clearly not true of Charles. It is not as though Charles were confronting another person, a fictional version of himself, but rather as though he himself actually fears the slime. (Nevertheless, he does not.) Make-believe facts about his fear, especially the fact that make-believedly it is his, are portrayed to Charles in an extraordinarily realistic manner. And make-believe facts about our pity for Willy, our dislike of Iago, and so forth, are similarly vivid to us. We and Charles feel ourselves to be part of fictional worlds, to be intimately involved with the slime, or Willy, or with whatever constituents of fictional worlds are, make-believedly, objects of our feelings and attitudes.

We see, now, how fictional worlds can seem to us almost as "real" as the real world is, even though we know perfectly well that they are not. We have begun to understand what happens when we get emotionally "involved" in a novel or play or film, when we are "caught up in the story."

The theory I have presented is designed to capture intuitions lying behind the traditional ideas that the normal or desired attitude toward fiction involves a *"suspension of disbelief,"* or a *"decrease of distance."* These phrases are unfortunate. They strongly suggest that people do not (completely) disbelieve what they read in novels and see on the stage or screen, that, e.g., we somehow accept it as fact that a boy named "Huckleberry Finn" floated down the Mississippi River – at least while we are engrossed in the novel. The normal reader does not accept this as fact, nor should he. Our disbelief is "suspended" only in the sense that it is, in some ways, set aside or ignored. We don't believe that there was a Huck Finn, but what interests us is the fact that *make-believedly* there was one, and that make-believedly he floated down the Mississippi and did various other things. But this hardly accounts for the sense of "decreased distance" between us and fictions. It still has us peering down on fictional worlds from reality above, however fascinated we might be, for some mysterious reason, by what we see.

On my theory we accomplish the "decrease of distance" not by promoting fictions to our level but by descending to theirs. (More accurately, we *extend* ourselves to their level, since we do not stop actually existing when it becomes fictional that we exist.) *Make-believedly* we do believe, we know, that Huck Finn floated down the Mississippi.

And make-believedly we have various feelings and attitudes about him and his adventures. Rather than somehow fooling ourselves into thinking fictions are real, we become fictional. So we end up "on the same level" with fictions. And our presence there is accomplished in the extraordinarily realistic manner that I described. This enables us to comprehend our sense of closeness to fictions, without attributing to ourselves patently false beliefs.

We are now in a position to expect progress on the fundamental question of why and how fiction is important. Why don't we dismiss novels, plays, and films as "mere fiction" and hence unworthy of serious attention?

Much has been said about the value and importance of dreams, fantasy, and children's games of make-believe.[17] It has been suggested, variously, that such activities serve to clarify one's feelings, help one to work out conflicts, provide an outlet for the expression of repressed or socially unacceptable feelings, prepare one emotionally for possible future crises by providing "practice" in facing imaginary crises. It is natural to presume that our experience of representational works of art is valuable for similar reasons. But this presumption is not very plausible, I think, unless something like the theory I have presented is correct.

It is my impression that people are usually, perhaps always, characters in their own dreams and daydreams. We dream and fantasize about ourselves. Sometimes one's role in one's dream-world or fantasy-world is limited to that of observing other goings-on. But to have even this role *is* to belong to the fictional world. (We must distinguish between being, in one's dream, an observer of certain events, and merely "observing," having, a dream about those events.) Similarly, children are nearly always characters in their games of make-believe. To play dolls or school, hobby horses or mud pies, is to be an actor portraying oneself.

I suggest that much of the value of dreaming, fantasizing, and making-believe depends crucially on one's thinking of oneself as belonging to a fictional world. It is chiefly by fictionally facing certain situations, engaging in certain activities, and having or expressing certain feelings, I think, that a dreamer, fantasizer, or game player comes to terms with his actual feelings – that he discovers them, learns to accept them, purges himself of them, or whatever exactly it is that he does.

If I am right about this, people can be expected to derive similar benefits from novels, plays, and films only if it is fictional that they themselves exist and participate (if only as observers) in the events portrayed in the works, i.e., only if my theory is on the right track.

I find encouragement for these speculations in the deliberate use of role-playing in educational simulation games, and as a therapeutic technique in certain kinds of psychotherapy (e.g., Gestalt therapy). A therapist may ask his patient to pretend that his mother is present, or that some inanimate object is his mother, and to "talk to her." He may then be asked to "be" the mother, and to say how he feels (when he "is" the mother), how he acts, what he looks like, etc. I will not venture an explanation of how such therapeutic techniques are effective, nor of why simulation games work. But whatever explanation is appropriate will, I suspect, go a long way toward explaining why we are as interested in works of fiction as we are, and clarifying what we get from them. The important place that novels, plays, and films have in our lives appears mysterious only on the supposition that we merely stand outside fictional worlds and look in, pressing our noses against an inviolable barrier. Once our presence within fictional worlds is recognized, suitable explanations seem within reach.

VII

A more immediate benefit of my theory is its capacity to handle puzzles. I conclude with the resolution of two more. First, consider a playgoer who finds happy endings asinine or dull, and hopes that the play he is watching will end tragically. He "wants the heroine to suffer a cruel fate," for only if she does, he thinks, will the play be worth watching. But at the same time he is caught up in the story and "sympathizes with the heroine"; he "wants her to escape." It is obvious that these two apparent desires may perfectly well coexist. Are we to say that the spectator is *torn* between opposite interests, that he wants the heroine to survive and also wants her not to? This does not ring true. Both of the playgoer's "conflicting desires" may be wholehearted. He may hope unreservedly that the work will end with disaster for the heroine, and he may, with equal singlemindedness, "want her to escape such an undeserved fate." Moreover, he may be entirely aware of both "desires," and yet feel no particular conflict between them.

My theory provides a neat explanation. It is merely make-believe that the spectator sympathizes with the heroine and wants her to escape. And he (really) wants it to be make-believe that she suffers a cruel end. He does not have conflicting desires. Nor, for that matter, is it make-believe that he does.

The second puzzle concerns why it is that works last as well as they do, how they can survive multiple readings or viewings without losing their effectiveness.[18]

Suspense of one kind or another is an important ingredient in our experience of most works: Will Jack, of *Jack and the Beanstalk*, succeed in ripping off the giant without being caught? Will Tom and Becky find their way out of the cave? Will Hamlet ever get around to avenging the murder of his father? What is in store for Julius Caesar on the Ides of March? Will Godot come?

But how can there be suspense if we already know how things will turn out? Why, for example, should Tom and Becky's plight concern or even interest a reader who knows, from reading the novel previously, that eventually they will escape from the cave? One might have supposed that, once we have experienced a work often enough to learn thoroughly the relevant features of the plot, it would lose its capacity to create suspense, and that future readings or viewings of it would lack the excitement of the first one. But this frequently is not what happens. *Some works*, to be sure, fade quickly from exposure, and familiarity does alter our experience in certain ways. But the power of many works is remarkably permanent, and the nature of their effectiveness remarkably consistent. In particular, suspense may remain a crucial element in our response to a work almost no matter how familiar we are with it. One may "worry" just as intensely about Tom and Becky while rereading *The Adventures of Tom Sawyer*, despite one's knowledge of the outcome, as would a person reading it for the first time. A child listening to *Jack and the Beanstalk* for the umpteenth time, long after she has memorized it word for word, may feel much the same excitement when the giant discovers Jack and goes after him, the same gripping suspense, that she felt when she first heard the story. Children, far from being bored by familiar stories, often beg to hear the same ones over and over again.

None of this is surprising on my theory. The child hearing *Jack and the Beanstalk* knows that make-believedly Jack will escape, but make-believedly she does *not* know that he will – until the reading of the passage describing his escape. She is engaged in her own game of make-believe during the reading, a game in which make-believedly she learns for the first time about Jack and the giant as she hears about them.[19] It is her make-believe uncertainty (the fact that make-believedly she is uncertain), not any actual uncertainty, that is responsible for the excitement and suspense that she feels. The point of hearing the story is not, or not merely, to learn about Jack's confrontation with the giant, but to play a game of make-believe. One cannot learn, each time one hears the story, what make-believedly Jack and the giant do, unless one always forgets in between times. But one can and does participate each time in a game of make-believe. The point of hearing *Jack and the Beanstalk* is to have the experience of being such that, *make-believedly*, one realizes with trepidation the danger Jack faces, waits breathlessly to see whether the giant will awake, feels sudden terror when he does awake, and finally learns with admiration and relief how Jack chops down the beanstalk, killing the giant.

Why play the same game over and over? In the first place, the game may not be exactly the same each time, even if the readings are the same. On one occasion it may be make-believe that the child is paralyzed by fear for Jack, overwhelmed by the gravity of the situation, and emotionally drained when Jack finally bests the giant. On another occasion it may be make-believe that the child is not very seriously concerned about Jack's safety and that her dominant feelings are admiration for Jack's exploits, the thrill of adventure, and a sense of exhilaration at the final outcome. But even if the game is much the same from reading to reading, one's emotional needs may require the therapy of several or many repetitions.

Notes

Work on this paper was supported by a grant from the American Council of Learned Societies. Earlier versions were read at a number of universities in the United States, Canada, and Australia. I am grateful for the many helpful suggestions made on these occasions. I am especially indebted to Holly S. Goldman, Robert Howell, and Brian Loar.

1   Chapter 14. Translated by Gerald F. Else (Ann Arbor: The University of Michigan Press, 1967).

2   I examine this barrier in a companion piece to the present paper, "How Remote Are Fictional Worlds from the Real World?" *Journal of Aesthetics and Art Criticism*, 37 (Fall 1978): 11–23.

3   By 'fear' I mean fear for oneself. Obviously a person can be afraid for someone else without believing that he himself is in danger. One must believe that the person for whom one fears is in danger.

4   Charles *might* scream *deliberately*. But insofar as he does, it is probably clear that he is only pretending to take the slime seriously. (See section v.)

5   Charles's responses are *caused* partly by a belief, though not the belief that he is in danger. (See section iv.) This belief is not a *reason* for responding as he does, and it doesn't make it "reasonable," in the relevant sense, to respond in those ways.

6   A "fictional truth" is the fact that a certain proposition is fictional.

7   I have developed the notion of make-believe truths and other ideas presented in this section more fully elsewhere, especially in "Pictures and Make-believe," *Philosophical Review*, LXXXI, 3 (July 1973): 283–319. Cf. also "Are Representations Symbols?," *The Monist*, LVIII, 2 (April 1974): 236–54. I should indicate that, in my view, there are no propositions "about" mere fictions, and hence none that are make-believe. It is make-believe not that Gulliver visited Lilliput, but that a man named "Gulliver" visited a place called "Lilliput." I shall occasionally ignore this point in the interest of simplicity, for example, when I write in section v as though the same slime resides in two different fictional worlds. Compare "How Remote Are Fictional Worlds from the Real World?," *op. cit.*, note 22.

8   From "Everything and Nothing," Borges, *Labyrinths: Selected Stories and Other Writings*, Donald A. Yates and James E. Irby, eds. (New York: New Directions, 1962), p. 248.

9   It is arguable that the purely physiological aspects of quasi-fear, such as the increase of adrenalin in the blood, which Charles could ascertain only by clinical tests, are not part of what makes it make-believe that he is afraid. Thus one might want to understand 'quasi-fear' as referring only to the more psychological aspects of Charles's condition: the feelings or sensations that go with increased adrenalin, faster pulse rate, muscular tension, etc.

10 One can't help wondering why Charles's realization that make-believedly he is in danger produces quasi-fear in him, why it brings about a state similar to real fear, even though he knows he is not really in danger. This question is important, but we need

not speculate about it here. For now we need only note that Charles's belief does result in quasi-fear, however this fact is to be explained.

11 This, I think, is at least approximately right. It is perhaps equally plausible, however, to say that the fact that Charles *believes* his quasi-fear to be caused by his realization that the slime endangers him is what makes it make-believe that his state is one of fear of the slime. There is no need to choose now between my suggestion and this variant.

12 Observers might, at the same time, understand his behavior alone to be responsible for his make-believe fear. The child and the observers might recognize somewhat different principles of make-believe.

13 These grounds are not conclusive. But the question of whether Charles accepts this principle is especially tricky, and there is reason to doubt that it can be settled conclusively. One would have to determine whether it is Charles's understanding that, if he were to have the quasi-fear sensations, etc., without realizing that he does and hence without imagining that he is afraid, it would still be fictional that he is afraid. If so, the fictional truth depends not on his imagining but on his quasi-fear, etc. It is hard to decide whether this is Charles's understanding, mainly because it is hard to conceive of his being ignorant of his quasi-fear sensations, etc. But insofar as I can get a grip on the question I think that the answer is affirmative.

14 One important difference between dolls and the screen images is that the dolls generate *de re* make-believe truths about themselves and the images do not. The doll is such that make-believedly *it* is a baby that is being dressed for a trip to town. But a screen image is not such that make-believedly it (the image itself) is a green slime.

15 Assuming of course that the person realizes that he is dealing with a work of fiction. Even so, arguments are needed to show that such statements are not literally true, and I shall not provide them here. But it is plausible that pity, worry about, hate, and envy are such that one cannot have them without believing that their objects exist, just as one cannot fear something without believing that it threatens one. Yet even if one can, and does, envy a character, for example, it may *also* be make-believe that one does so, and this make-believe truth may be generated by facts of the sort my theory indicates.

16 I have in mind those make-believe truths about her mental state which are generated by what happens on stage. Dickinson is not only a character in the play, but also a spectator. In the latter capacity she is like Charles; her actual mental state generates make-believe truths about herself. Dickinson is in a curiously ambiguous position. But it is not an uncommon one; people frequently have dreams in which they watch themselves ("from the outside") doing things.

17 A good source concerning make-believe games is Jerome L. Singer, et al., *The Child's World of Make-Believe* (New York: Academic Press, 1973).

18 David Lewis pointed out to me the relevance of my theory to this puzzle.

19 It is probably make-believe that someone (the narrator), whose word the child can trust, is giving her a serious report about a confrontation between a boy named "Jack" and a giant. Cf. my "Points of View in Narrative and Depictive Representation," *Noûs*, x, 1 (March 1976): 49–61.

16

Empathy and (Film) Fiction

Alex Neill

1

Ancient questions as to how and why it is that we can respond emotionally to characters and events which we know to be fictional, and whether it is rational to do so, have in recent years resurfaced and been at the heart of a debate as lively as any in contemporary aesthetics, a debate which continues to fill the pages of philosophical journals but which has so far resulted in little agreement even about the nature of the problems involved, let alone their solutions.[1] Part of the reason for this lack of resolution, I believe, is that our emotional responses to what we know to be fictional have typically been treated as monolithic; for example, since the very beginnings of the debate, the pity and the fear that works of fiction may evoke from us have been lumped together. But our emotional responses – whether to fictional or to actual persons and events – are not all of a kind. For example, we can distinguish (at least roughly) between emotional responses in which the focus of concern is *oneself* (as, for example, in fear for oneself), and those in which the focus of concern is *another*. And among "other-focused" emotional responses, we may distinguish between *sympathetic* responses (such as those in which I fear *for* you), and *empathetic* responses (for I may also feel fear *with* you). By looking closely at the variety of our emotional responses, and at the variety of the emotional responses that fiction can evoke in us, I suggest, we stand a better

chance of understanding those responses, the roles they play in our understanding and valuing of fiction, and their significance with respect to broader concerns in the philosophy of emotion and mind, than we do by treating them as if they constituted a homogeneous class.

With this broad strategy in mind, I wish to focus on empathy, with particular reference to the possibility of empathetic responses to fiction films. One (oversimple) way of getting at the difference between sympathetic and empathetic responses is as follows: with sympathetic response, in feeling *for* another, one's response need not reflect what the other is feeling, nor indeed does it depend on whether the other is feeling anything at all. Your happiness may make me happy for you, but it may also irritate me; and I may feel pity or fear for you irrespective of what *you* happen to be feeling. In contrast, in responding empathetically to another I come to *share* his feelings, to feel *with* him; if he is in an emotional state, to empathize with him is to experience the emotion(s) that he experiences.

It is interesting that empathy and empathetic responses have received short shrift in the contemporary debate on the nature and rationality of our emotional responses to fiction. In part, this is doubtless due to the tendency noted above to treat our emotional responses to fiction as homogeneous. But it has also been suggested that empathetic response simply does not play a significant role in our emotional engagement with fictional works in

Alex Neill, "Empathy and (Film) Fiction," *Post Theory*, eds. Noël Carroll and David Bordwell (Madison: University of Wisconsin Press, 1996): 175–94.

various genres. Richard Wollheim, for example, suggests that "the empathic audience does not provide the model for the understanding of the drama, and . . . any theory of the drama that puts him in the forefront is to that degree wrong."[2] Dolf Zillman notes that "It is a widely held belief that those exposed to drama featuring sympathetic, liked protagonists tend to 'identify' with those protagonists and to '*vicariously experience*' whatever those protagonists experience. In fact, this view is commonly treated as a secure and unquestionable key element of our understanding of the enlightenment that drama provides."[3] However, Zillman argues, this view – the view that empathetic responses are central to our experience of fiction – is far from "secure" and "unquestionable." He invites us to consider the responses to suspense films of children, who "tend to talk to their heroes, shouting out warnings of the dangers their heroes face (dangers about which the heroes, because of the very nature of suspense, are ignorant)" (142). If the child's response were empathetic, surely it should reflect or "be controlled by the hero's expression of calmness and self-confidence." But in fact the response is far from expressive of calm or confidence. Zillman argues that the hypothesis that our responses to suspense fictions are empathetic responses "thus not only fails to explain distress in response to most scenes of entrapment and peril" (where the hero/ine is calm and self-possessed), but also falsely predicts "an absence of distress unless (or until) the hero is seen in fear and agony" (142). At least with regard to suspense fictions, he concludes, our responses are better understood in terms of "feeling for" (in my terms, sympathy) than they are in terms of "feeling with" (in my terms, empathy).[4]

A similar point has been made by Noël Carroll, in the course of his argument to the effect that the notion of "character-identification" is unhelpful in attempting to understand our emotional engagement with the protagonists of fiction.[5] As we shall see, Carroll does leave room for an account of the place of empathy in our engagement with fiction. Indeed, he argues that in horror fictions the responses of the characters to monsters serve as "cues" for the responses of the audience, and that "our emotional responses as audience members are supposed to parallel those of characters in important respects" (18). However, Carroll's argument against "character-identification" is based in large part on his claim that "in a great many cases, the emotional state of the audience does not replicate the state of the characters": for example, "When the heroine is splashing about with abandon as, unbeknownst to her, a killer shark is zooming in for the kill, we feel concern for her. But that is not what she is feeling. She's feeling delighted" (90). Again, "if we feel pity at Oedipus' recognition that he has killed his father and bedded his mother, that is not what Oedipus is feeling. He is feeling guilt, remorse, and self-recrimination. And, needless to say, we are feeling none of these" (91). If empathy is construed as "feeling with," as the mirroring of a protagonist's emotional state by the audience, as I have construed it above, then Carroll's remarks suggest that empathetic responses do not play a large part in our emotional engagement with fiction.

2

Nonetheless, there are a number of factors which suggest that the possibility that empathetic response plays an important part in our engagement with works of fiction may merit further consideration. First, the idea that our emotional engagement with fiction, and in particular film fiction, is somehow rooted in something like "identification" with and empathetic response to the characters of fiction is, as Zillman notes, very widely held. For what it is worth, my own experience is that practically *all* those not "professionally" concerned with these issues with whom I have discussed them have made some sort of appeal to identification and empathy in explaining our emotional engagement with movies. Carroll is surely right to note that it is often unclear just what is meant by "identification" in discussion of our engagement with fiction, and that some of the meanings that are commonly attached to the notion render it at best of little explanatory value, at worst incoherent. However, the commonness of the claim that our affective responses to a work of fiction are somehow the result of identifying with its characters, and the equally common linking of "identification" with empathetic response, suggests that we should be very cautious before giving up the idea that empathetic responses may play an important role in our emotional engagement with fiction. In brief, a good many people claim that at the heart of their affective engagement with fiction is empathetic engagement. Such people may of course simply be confused about the meaning of "identification," or of "empathy," or indeed about the nature of their own responses. However, before drawing any conclusion of the latter sort, we ought to look closely at just what might be involved in responding empathetically to fiction.

The common tendency to talk of empathetic response and identification in the same breath suggests a further and related reason that such an investigation may be valuable. For the notion of identification has also attracted a good deal of attention from professional film theorists. In film theory, not surprisingly, reflection on identification has typically involved appeal to psychoanalysis. Anne Friedberg, for example, writes of identification as "that which conceals and defers the recognition of dissimilitude. *If fetishism is a relation incurred by the anxiety of sexual difference, identification is a relation incurred by the anxiety of pure difference.*... The process of identification is one of denying the difference between self and other. It is a drive that engages the pleasures of sameness. If the subject is constituted in a series of identifications which force similarity, identification is one long structural repetition of this denial of difference, a construction of identity based on sameness."[6] On this sort of analysis, identification is a pathological process, a process of "denial" incurred by "anxiety." And to the extent that empathetic responses depend on or involve identification, this sort of analysis suggests that our empathetic responses to others, be they fictional characters or actual persons, are at heart pathological responses, symptomatic of self-deception. Is this in fact the case? If so, and if the claims made by many people about the centrality of identification and empathy to our engagement with fiction are accurate, then we should be faced with a new version of one of the most ancient criticisms of storytelling: Plato's charge that poetry "waters the passions," to the detriment of reason. That possibility surely gives us good cause to take another look at the nature of empathetic engagement with fiction.

And this is not the only motivation that we have for doing so. The notion that empathetic engagement with others plays a central role in understanding and explanation has had and is gaining increasing support in contexts beyond that of discussion of our engagement with fiction. The idea that historical and social scientific explanation involves *verstehen*, that it depends on "seeing things from another's point of view," which I shall argue later is central to empathetic response, has a distinguished and influential history.[7] In moral philosophy and psychology, from the "moral sentiment" theories of Adam Smith and David Hume to recent and broadly speaking feminist work on "the ethics of care," our capacity for empathetic response has often been mooted as the source of morality.[8] And more recently, a growing number of philosophers and psychologists have been arguing that empathy is crucial to our "everyday" ability to understand, explain and predict the behavior of those around us: that our "folk psychological" attribution of mental states to others depends on empathetic understanding.[9] In short, there is an increasing acceptance, in a number of theoretical circles, of the importance of empathy in understanding and explanation. Of course, this does not in itself mean that empathy plays a large role in our engagement with and understanding of *fiction*. However, if empathy does play a crucial role in our understanding of history, of society, and of others, wouldn't it be at least somewhat *odd* to find that it is marginal or of little importance in our understanding of fiction? In sum, then, given the historical and growing emphasis on the role of empathetic thought and response in attempts by human beings to engage with, understand, and explain their worlds, it is surely worth our while to reflect further on the possible roles that empathy might play in our attempts to engage with, understand, and explain the worlds of works of fiction.

Finally, one of the arguments that is sometimes offered concerning the *value* that we attach to fiction suggests that empathetic responses have more than a marginal place in our affective engagement with fiction. It is often held that the value of fiction lies largely in what it can contribute to the education of emotion. For example, in the *Poetics*, Aristotle holds that the pleasure that we take in mimetic works is a pleasure that comes from learning. The source of the pleasure that we take in *tragedy*, he holds, lies in the arousal and subsequent *catharsis* of pity and fear. Thus Aristotle links "tragic pleasure" to both learning and to emotional response; which suggests that the *value* of tragedy lies (at least partly) in what it can contribute to our emotional education.[10] Similar positions about the value of art can be found in various versions of the expression theory of art. And George Eliot, describing herself as an "aesthetic" rather than a "doctrinal" teacher, linked the value of fiction with our affective engagement with it when she said that her aim was to arouse the "nobler emotions" in her readers, in order that

Alex Neill

they should be better able to experience pity and sympathy in their everyday lives.[11]

But just what contribution can fiction make to our emotional education? Part of the answer to this question, as Eliot hints, surely lies in the fact that fiction can make available to us new emotional experience. Now in many cases we can learn about the character of our emotions through reflection on the sympathetic responses which fiction may evoke from us; for example, reflection on the peculiarly ambivalent mixture of admiration and pity that the eponymous hero of Werner Herzog's *Fitzcarraldo* evokes from us may be a source of insight into the nature of both admiration and pity. In contrast to this sort of case, however, it seems reasonable to say that if we learn about any emotion through watching Nicholas Roeg's *Don't Look Now*, for example, it is grief. And yet we don't grieve *for* John and Laura Baxter (Donald Sutherland and Julie Christie). If what we learn about grief through watching the movie is based on the experience of emotion, then, it will be based on empathetic response: on grieving *with* them. Similarly, Abel Ferrara's *Bad Lieutenant* is in part a movie about loneliness; but loneliness is not something that we feel *for* others. Again, then, to the extent that what we learn about loneliness from the movie is based on emotional experience, our learning must be based on empathetic experience.

Indeed, and leaving fiction aside for a moment, one of the most important ways in which we can gain new emotional experience is through empathetic response. It is true that our sympathetic responses to others may be new to us; we may find ourselves surprised that we feel as we do, and we may be surprised at what we find ourselves feeling about. However, in feeling *with* another, empathetically rather than sympathetically, we may find ourselves feeling in ways that are not only new to us, but in ways that are in a sense *foreign* to us. In responding sympathetically to others, we may respond in ways that we did not know were "in us." But in responding empathetically, as I shall argue, we may respond in ways that are not in *us* at all: in ways that mirror the feelings and responses of others whose outlooks and experiences may be very different from our own. Hence empathetic engagement with others may play an important part in the education of emotion. If fiction makes available to us possibilities for empathetic as well as sympathetic emotional engagement, then, that will go a long way toward justifying (as well as

explaining) the claim that the value of fiction has a good deal to do with its contribution to education of emotion.

3

The considerations that I have outlined here suggest that our thinking about the ways in which we understand and value works of fiction may be illuminated by further exploration of the ways in which empathy might enter into our engagement with works of fiction. Thus far, I have said very little in particular about empathy and *film* fiction. In part, this is because I believe that the issues here are of quite general significance: I believe that further exploration of empathetic response may illuminate our engagement with fiction in all its forms. However, this is not to say that I regard the differences between the media of fiction as unimportant. Later, I shall have more to say about film fiction, in particular, and empathetic response. At this point, however, a couple of (necessarily brief) examples taken from fiction film may be useful in illustrating the ways in which empathetic response may be connected with understanding and valuing a work of fiction.

First, consider a well-known scene from Robert Wise's *The Haunting*. In the middle of the night, Eleanor (Julie Harris) and Theodora (Claire Bloom) are woken by a knocking or pounding sound coming from the corridor outside. For what seems an eternity, the sound continues, fading and rising (and as it fades other noises – a child's running footsteps, the sound of something being dragged across the floor, animal grunting – can be heard coming from the corridor) until it is deafeningly loud, and apparently directly outside the bedroom door. Finally, and suddenly, it stops, to be replaced by the sound of a woman's or girl's laughter. This is truly a terrifying scene; indeed, perhaps one of the most terrifying scenes in fiction film. (And all the more remarkable for its simplicity; apart from the sound effects, which are perfectly done and might justifiably be described as "special," the terror here depends on no technical wizardry.) And yet what sort of terror is it that the scene evokes in us? In watching it, we are not terrified for ourselves; we are under no illusion that *we* are in danger. We know that whatever it is that is outside that bedroom door "exists" only in the world of the film (if indeed it "exists" even there). Later, after the film is over, reflection may make us nervous – perhaps even terrified – about the ghosts who just might be outside *our* bedroom doors. But as we watch the scene, it is not for ourselves that we are terrified. It may be suggested that as we watch we are terrified *for* the two women in the film; that is, that our terror is sympathetic. And perhaps part of our terror here *is* sympathetic. But what this misses is the extent to which *our* terror is based on *their* terror; if *they* were not so terrified, neither should *we* be. In Carroll's terms, their responses (which we are shown in close-up shots of their faces) are the "cues" for our responses. But of course this does not mean that our responses are merely a matter of mimicry. Rather, and I shall have more to say about this later, we respond as we do because in this scene we see the situation that the two women are in *from their point of view*. We find it terrifying because *they* find it terrifying. In short, our terror here is at least largely empathetic terror; and without acknowledgment of the role of empathy in our experience of the scene, I suggest, our terror would hardly be intelligible.

Empathy also plays a critical role in our response to and understanding of Roeg's *Don't Look Now*. The film begins with the death by drowning of the Baxters' daughter, and it is this event, or rather its effects, which drives the film. The opening moments of the film, culminating in the child's death, are extremely powerful, and demand an emotional response from us. But what *sort* of response is demanded here? Well, given what happens to them, one might of course pity the Baxters. But such a response would, I suggest, be inadequate. And it would be so not simply for the reasons that pity is so often an inadequate response to the suffering of others, but rather, or also, because a different sort of response is necessary in order fully to *understand* the rest of the film. When they get to Venice, the Baxters meet two elderly English women, sisters, one of whom is blind and claims to have psychic powers. Indeed, she claims that she has "seen" the Baxters' daughter with them in Venice, and that the little girl is attempting to warn them to leave the city. Laura takes this very seriously. She is comforted by the thought that their child is somehow still with them; she pleads with John to meet and talk to the women; and she pleads with the women to try to "contact" the girl. More to the point for my purposes here, it is clear that we, the audience, are meant to take Laura seriously in all this. If we do not do so, if we regard her merely as pathetically

(and perhaps understandably) deluded, as we will if our governing or controlling response to her is one of pity, the rest of the movie will be lost to us; we simply will not understand the significance of the events that follow. The point here is that (at some level, anyway) Laura is *right* to take the psychic business seriously; and if we fail to do so, Roeg's extraordinarily powerful film turns into a second-rate suspense thriller. For example, consider John's lengthy search for Laura after he glimpses her riding on the funeral gondola with the two elderly women. If the psychic elements in the plot are regarded as mere charlatanry on the part of the English women, something that a confused and pathetic Laura has merely been taken in by, John's search for Laura itself becomes pathetic, a bizarre matter of illusion or mistaken identity. But of course it is not; and to understand that – and indeed the rest of the film – we, like Laura, have to take the psychic possibilities seriously. And that, at least for those of us who are not given to taking such things seriously, depends on our being prepared to see the events from her point of view, on our taking her perspective as our own; in short, on our responding empathetically. And as a result of seeing things from her perspective, we do not pity her, but come to feel something of her horror at the loss of her child. In short, I suggest, our controlling response to both John and Laura is not one of pity or sympathy, but rather one of shared horror at the events that have transformed their lives. And only by sharing their horror can we fully understand and be gripped by the events that follow.

4

Thus far, then, I have offered a number of reasons for thinking that there is good reason to take another look at the place of empathy in our engagement with fiction. The insistence of so many people that at least some of their responses to fiction are empathetic; the growing emphasis in other areas of philosophy and psychology on the role of empathy in understanding; the possible relationships between empathetic responses and the value that we attach to fiction – all these suggest that the subject merits further discussion. However, thus far I have said very little about what empathetic responses actually involve, beyond characterizing them as a matter of feeling with another, or sharing her feelings. It's time to say more. And first, it is important to notice that not all cases of shared response are cases of empathy. For example, if you and I both get letters informing us that we have not been short-listed for a lucrative and prestigious research fellowship, we may both feel disappointment, anger, a sense of futility, and so on. However, the fact that we share these feelings does not in itself make this an instance of empathy. For my feelings to be empathetic, the fact that I feel as I do must be related to the fact that you feel as you do; loosely speaking, empathy involves my feeling as I do *because* you feel as you do. Clearly, this "because" needs elaboration; just what sort of relationship must obtain between the psychological states of two people in order for the response of one to the other to be properly characterized in terms of empathy?

In a recent philosophical investigation of empathy, Susan Feagin argues that in empathetic responses the connection between my mental state and yours is made by way of *belief*. Empathy, she suggests, is a cognitive state; it is essentially a matter of my holding second-order beliefs about your beliefs. In empathizing with another, she argues: "a belief that something may happen to *him* affects me emotionally as if I were him. ... The beliefs involved in empathetic emotions will thus be slightly different from the beliefs involved in the emotions with which I empathize: if I am empathically afraid for (and with) my nephew that he will flunk out of school, it is because I believe that *he* believes that he is in danger..., or because I believe that *he* believes that if he doesn't pass the test he will flunk out...and I believe that he desires not to flunk out...."[12] "Empathetic emotions," Feagin argues, "always involve higher order beliefs than those involved in the emotion with which one empathizes: beliefs about someone else's beliefs."

Feagin's claim that empathy is founded on belief gives rise to a set of familiar-sounding problems with respect to the possibility of our empathizing with what we know to be fictional characters. For, Feagin says, fictional characters, inasmuch as they do not exist, do not *have* beliefs or feelings for us to form second-order beliefs about. Thus: "whether we are empathizing with the emotions of a real person depends on what our second order beliefs are. But whether we are empathizing with a fictional character does *not* depend on what our second order beliefs are. This is because there aren't any *first* order beliefs (or desires, or other psychological states) for them to

be about, since neither fictional characters, nor their psychological states, exist. The existence of the empathy [with a fictional character] therefore does *not* depend on whether we 'feel' the way the [character] feels, and for the right reasons" (493). However, Feagin thinks that we can nonetheless respond empathetically to fictional characters, and her suggestion is that in doing so, *imagination* rather than belief comes into play. On her view, in such cases "we don't form second order beliefs about an individual's first order beliefs, but rather *imagine* what these beliefs, desires, etc., might be" (494). On the one hand, then, empathizing with an actual person "involves the formation of second order beliefs about that person's beliefs"; in such cases empathy is "dependent on (or explained by) our beliefs about what is involved in the beliefs (desires, etc.) of the person with whom we empathize" (496). In contrast, empathizing with a fictional character depends on our *imagining* what her beliefs, desires, and so on, might be.

Feagin's account contains some valuable suggestions, which I hope to bring out and develop in what follows. However, her suggestion that in our empathetic responses to fiction imagination functions as an *alternative* to belief results in a distorted conception of empathy. We can begin to see this by noticing that forming second-order beliefs about another's beliefs is certainly not sufficient for empathy. On the one hand, my beliefs about what you believe may leave me utterly unmoved. On the other hand, such beliefs may move me to a sympathetic response; my belief that you believe that your roses have suffered terminal damage from greenfly, for example, may move me to pity (or, for that matter, to scorn or to glee): to feel something *for* or *about* you rather than *with* you.

What the account in terms of belief fails to capture is the sense in which empathizing with another is at least partly a matter of *understanding how things are with her*. (Empathy differs from sympathy in this regard; sympathizing with another doesn't depend on my getting her mental state, or for that matter anything else about her, right. If I don't, my sympathy may well be misplaced, but it will none the less be sympathy. In contrast, if I am wrong about the mental state and/ or situation of another, I won't be able to empathize with them at all. I shall return to this matter later.) And whatever this understanding of how things are with another amounts to, it is not simply a matter of holding (true) second-order beliefs about another's beliefs. We might more happily say that to empathize with another's depression (for example) involves having a sense of the *tone* of her beliefs, thoughts, desires and so on; or that it is partly a matter of coming to know *what it is like* to have certain beliefs, desires, hopes, and doubts.

5

These somewhat vague intuitions are explored and given substance by Milan Kundera in his novel *The Unbearable Lightness of Being*.[13] Kundera's central theme (or at any rate one of them) is compassion; he writes: "there is nothing heavier than compassion. Not even one's own pain weighs so heavy as the pain one feels with someone, for someone, a pain intensified by the imagination and prolonged by a hundred echoes" (31). Despite the conjunction of "with" and "for" here, Kundera's "compassion" is what I have been referring to as "empathy." He notes that while Latin-derived languages form the word "compassion" by combining the prefix "with" (*com-*) and the root "suffering" (*passio*), in other languages the word is translated by a noun formed of the prefix "with" combined with a word for "feeling." (Thus, he tells us, the Czech *soucit*, Polish *wspótczucie*, German *Mitgefühl*, Swedish *medkänsla*.) Compassion is in this sense "co-feeling," or "feeling-with"; to have compassion is "not only to be able to live with the other's misfortune but also to feel with him any emotion – joy, anxiety, happiness, pain. This kind of compassion ... therefore signifies the maximal capacity of affective imagination, the art of emotional telepathy" (20).

Kundera's discourse on compassion, which is woven into his fictional narrative, illuminates not only the possible scope of his readers' relationships to the characters, but also the relationships between the characters themselves. Early in the novel, Tomas's lover Tereza reveals to him that she has been through his desk and discovered love-letters written to him by his mistress, Sabina. Kundera writes: "Anyone who has failed to benefit from the Devil's gift of compassion (co-feeling) will condemn Tereza coldly for her deed, because privacy is sacred and drawers containing intimate correspondence are not to be opened. But because compassion was Tomas's fate (or curse), he felt that he himself had knelt before the open desk-drawer, unable to tear his eyes from Sabina's letter. He understood Tereza, and not only was he incapable

of being angry with her, he loved her all the more" (21). Instead of throwing Tereza out, Tomas feels her pain: "he seized her hand and kissed the tips of her fingers, because at that moment he himself felt the pain under her fingernails as surely as if the nerves of her hand led straight to his own brain." Kundera's extraordinarily powerful depiction of the relationship between Tomas and Tereza demonstrates the futility of any attempt to give an account of empathy solely in terms of belief; it is not simply Tomas's *beliefs* about Tereza's psychological state that enable him to understand her and share her pain. Empathizing with another, Kundera suggests, is above all an *imaginative* activity; it involves "the maximal capacity of affective imagination."

But appeals to imagination are all too often a signal that explanation has come to an end. Just what *sort* of imaginative activity is involved in empathy? Some remarks by Noël Carroll are suggestive with regard to this matter. Carroll argues that part of what underlies and makes possible our response to fictional characters is our "assimilation" of their situations. In part, he suggests, "this involves having a sense of the character's internal understanding of the situation; that is, having a sense of how the character assesses the situation." In other words, "I must have a conception of how the protagonist sees the situation; and I must have access to what makes her assessment intelligible." Carroll describes this as a matter of understanding a character's situation "internally" (95). Now in the case of horror, he suggests, this understanding is easily come by: since we and the protagonists of horror fictions "share the same culture, we can readily discern the features of the situation that make it horrifying to the protagonist"; given the similarities between the protagonists and us, "we easily catch on to why the character finds the monster unnatural" (96).

I believe that Carroll is right to mark the centrality of "internal" understanding in our engagement with fiction. And he is right that in (at least many) cases of horror fiction this understanding is not difficult to come by: we know how the protagonist feels when she is faced by a monster because we know how we would feel if we were faced by that monster. But in other cases, achieving "internal understanding" of a character's situation may demand rather more from us. Consider the case of Laura Baxter in *Don't Look Now*: we certainly "share the same culture" with her, but understanding her response to the claims made

Alex Neill

by the psychic woman requires more than merely reflecting on how we would feel when faced with such claims. If we are skeptical by nature, for example, or if we have never lost a child, our response is likely to be an extremely unreliable indicator of what her response is. In this sort of case, I suggest, achieving "internal understanding" of another, be she a fictional character or an actual person, requires that I imagine the world, or the situation that she is in, *from her point of view*. She becomes the "protagonist" of an imaginative project, a project in which I represent to myself her thoughts, beliefs, desires, feelings, and so on *as though they were my own*.[14]

To return to Kundera's novel: after Tereza returns to Prague leaving Tomas in Zurich, he at first feels "a beautiful melancholy." After a few days, his mood changes completely: "Tereza forced her way into his thoughts: he imagined her sitting there writing her farewell letter; he felt her hands trembling; he saw her lugging her heavy suitcase in one hand and leading Karenin on his leash with the other; he pictured her unlocking their Prague flat, and suffered the utter abandonment breathing her in the face as she opened the door" (30–1). Tomas's mood changes not because he comes to hold new *beliefs* about Tereza's beliefs, but because he comes to *imagine* her situation from her point of view rather than from his own. In doing so, he comes to see their world as Tereza must see it, to see how things are with and for *her*. And in doing so, his mood changes not to one of sympathy – he is not moved to *pity* Tereza – but rather to *match* hers; Tomas not only imagines but actually *suffers* her feeling of "utter abandonment." Kundera describes Tomas as "sick with compassion"; and an extreme example of the phenomenon that he describes so powerfully here is what is sometimes known as "sympathetic" or "phantom" pregnancy, where a man becomes so imaginatively involved in a woman's experience of pregnancy that he comes to experience some of the symptoms of pregnancy himself. As I have characterized the difference between sympathy and empathy, it would be more accurate to describe cases of this sort as "empathetic pregnancy," for what marks them out is the specificity of what the man involved feels: *he* feels what the *woman* feels; he feels *with* her rather than *for* her. In representing to himself in imagination the physical and psychological state of a pregnant woman, that is, a man may himself come *actually* to feel what the woman is *imagined* as feeling. This sort of case

serves to remind us how natural, indeed instinctive, is the sort of imaginative activity that lies at the heart of empathy. In many, perhaps most, cases, we do not have to set out to *try* to empathize with another; often, though not always, this sort of imaginative activity is something that happens *to* us, that we are passive to, rather than something that we actively have to *pursue*.

6

If empathy is essentially an imaginative activity, then, is there anything to be made of Feagin's proposal that empathizing with another "involves the formation of second order beliefs about that person's beliefs" (96)? I have argued that no account which attempts to construe empathy *solely* in terms of belief and judgment can possibly do justice to the concept; however, this is not to say that belief plays *no* role in empathizing with another. For one thing, holding beliefs of the sort that Feagin is concerned with is a *precondition* of empathy. I have suggested that the imaginative activity that is characteristic of empathy involves taking another's perspective on things, imaginatively representing to oneself the thoughts, beliefs, desires, and so on of another as though they were one's own. In order to do this, however, one has to know, or at least have some beliefs about, what the other's thoughts, beliefs, and desires *are*.[15] The less substantial the knowledge I have about another, the more difficult it will be to imagine things from his point of view; thus most of us will find it difficult to imagine the world from the point of view of a Hannibal Lecter, for example, and easiest to imagine in this way a state of affairs in which the protagonist is an imagined version of oneself. Furthermore, one's beliefs about another also act as a set of *constraints* on the imaginative activity that lies at the heart of empathizing with her. Consider the scenes in *Don't Look Now* where John Baxter catches glimpses of the small figure in the red mackintosh and hood. If I am imagining the events depicted from John's point of view, I cannot see the small figure "neutrally"; given what I know about John, I cannot help but see the figure as he does, as an unhappy child, a reminder (and perhaps more than that) of his daughter. The directions that a person's imaginings (in this sense), and so her empathizing, may take are *bound* by what she knows or believes about the protagonist of her imaginative project.

Recognition of the role played in empathy by one's knowledge of and beliefs about another allows us to see some of the ways in which an attempt to empathize with another may fail. First, it may be that the knowledge that I have about another is so slight that the kind of imaginative project that I have argued is central to empathy cannot get off the ground; if I know nothing about another's psychological state, I will be unable to represent it to myself as though it were my own, and empathizing with him will be impossible. Alternatively, I may fail to empathize with another if the beliefs that I have about him are largely false. In this case, some of the beliefs, desires, and so on that I represent to myself as though they were my own will not be *his* beliefs and desires, and so I will not come to see things as he sees them, nor – except perhaps by accident[16] – to feel as he feels. The more accurate my beliefs about another are, the more likely I am to be able to succeed in empathizing with him. Again, I may be unable to empathize with another if, although I have all the right beliefs about her mental state, for some reason I cannot represent that state to myself as though it were my own. In order for me to be able to imagine a state of affairs from the point of view of another, she must be to a certain extent *like myself*; and in some cases the beliefs, desires, and so on of another may be so alien to me that I will be unable to represent them to myself as though they were my own. As we have seen, empathy is essentially an imaginative activity, and failure to empathize with another may be essentially a (more or less understandable) failure of imagination.

The role of knowledge and belief in empathizing with others also goes a good way toward explaining the common tendency to regard film fiction as a medium which encourages – perhaps demands – empathetic response more than literary fiction does. As I said earlier, of the people with whom I have discussed these issues, almost all make some sort of appeal to identification and/or empathy in characterizing their responses to movies; far fewer do so in characterizing their engagement with literary fiction. And this tendency is mirrored in theoretical writing about our engagement with fiction, where discussion of character identification and audience identification is much more common in writing about film than it is in writing about literary fiction. Why is it that empathy is commonly regarded as more important in our experience of film fiction than it is in our experience of literary fiction? The answer, I suggest, lies

partly in the fact that in literary fiction, we are very often informed in great detail about the situation a character is in, and told precisely what her thoughts, desires, and so on are. This can mean that attempts to empathize with literary fictional characters have a great chance of success; as we have seen, the greater our knowledge of another's psychological state and situation, the more likely we are to succeed in empathizing with her. However, the detailed knowledge that we so often have about the psychological states of literary fictional characters may also be an *impediment* to empathizing with them. We may be told so much about such characters that we do not *need* to empathize with them in order to understand them. Our motive for empathizing with others, I suggest (and it may not be a conscious motive) is the desire to understand how things are with them. And, given sufficient information about another, we simply may not need to empathize with her in order to understand her.

Of course, this is not to say that we can never, or need never, empathize with literary fictional characters. But the considerations noted above suggest that when we do so, our empathy may well have a different character from our empathy with actual persons. The difference I have in mind here is not the difference that Feagin marks out, namely, the difference between empathizing on the basis of belief and empathizing on the basis of imagination. The difference is rather that in empathizing with actual persons, even persons very close to us, we rarely have the detailed knowledge of their psychological states and situations that we so often have about literary fictional characters. Empathy with actual persons is thus likely to be, and to feel like, a precarious business. But it may be the only way we have of understanding a fellow human being. And the same is true with regard to the characters of film fiction. We typically know much less about such characters than we do about literary fictional characters; empathy with them is thus likely to be more precarious than is empathy with literary fictional characters. But, as is the case with regard to actual persons, empathizing with a film fictional character may be the only way that we have of understanding her.

So in engaging with the characters of film fiction we are in a position much closer to the position we are in when we engage with actual persons than we are when we read about the characters of literary fiction. Of course, there is the obvious fact that in the former cases, sight and hearing play a critical role in our engagement as they do not in the latter case. But in addition to this, in the former cases empathy may be crucial to understanding in a way that it is often not in the latter case. And it is partly this, I suggest, that gives film fiction its value: it gives us practice, so to speak, in a mode of engagement and response that is often crucial in our attempts to engage with and understand our fellow human beings.

7

However, all this presupposes that empathetic response to fictional characters is possible in the first place. And it may be argued that on the account of empathy I have outlined here, any suggestion that certain of our affective or emotional responses to fictional characters may be empathetic responses is highly problematic. Indeed, it would seem that the problem we should be faced with in making this suggestion is just the problem with which, as I noted earlier, Feagin is largely concerned. For I have argued that although empathy cannot be construed *solely* in terms of belief or judgment, the imaginative activity which lies at the heart of empathetic response both presupposes and is constrained by one's knowledge of and beliefs about the other's psychological states. But as Feagin notes, neither fictional characters nor their psychological states exist. And if fictional characters do not *have* psychological states, how can we form beliefs about their beliefs, desires, hopes, and fears? Again, if fictional characters do not have feelings, what sense can be given to any suggestion that certain of our affective responses to fictional characters involve coming to *share* their feelings?

As we saw earlier, Feagin attempts to meet these difficulties by appealing to imagination; while empathizing with actual people involves forming second-order beliefs about their beliefs, she suggests, in empathizing with fictional characters we rather imagine what the beliefs, desires, and so on might be (494). It is clear, however, that the conception of imagination that Feagin has in mind here is not the conception I have sketched above. For while I have argued that the imaginative activity characteristic of empathy *involves* belief, for Feagin the very point of appealing to imagination here is as an *alternative* to belief. If Feagin is right, then, empathizing with a fictional character will be very different from empathizing with an actual person, both in her own terms and as I have characterized

the latter. More importantly, however, as it stands it is far from clear that Feagin's account of what it is to empathize with a fictional character is in fact an account of *empathy* at all. As we have seen, an attempt to empathize with another may *fail*. And I have argued above that failure to empathize is to be explained by reference to the knowledge or beliefs that the imaginer has about the psychological states of the person with whom he is attempting to empathize, from whose point of view he is imagining things. In Feagin's view, however, we do not *have* knowledge of or beliefs about the psychological states of a fictional character, since fictional characters – and hence their psychological states – do not exist. The question thus arises, What constrains or binds the imaginative activity that, on Feagin's account, constitutes empathizing with a fictional character, if that activity is not constrained by belief? Feagin is silent on this point, but some answer is needed. For if the imaginative project characteristic of empathizing with a fictional character is *un*constrained, there will be nothing by which to determine the success of such a project; there will be no way, that is, of deciding whether or not empathy has been achieved. Since empathy is based on a kind of imaginative activity that may fail, unconstrained imaginative activity cannot constitute empathy.

If empathy with fictional characters is to be explained in terms of imagination, then, we need some explanation of what constrains or binds imagination in this context. And in effect, I suggest, the explanation that is needed here will be provided by a successful account of the language of fiction. For a major criterion of adequacy that any such account must satisfy is that it be able to explicate the sense in which it is true, or at any rate "true," that (for example) the Baxters in Roeg's *Don't Look Now* had a pretty miserable time of things; and so that it be able to explain the sense in which we can *believe* that they had a miserable time. Following Kendall Walton, for example, it might be argued that it is fictional or "make-believe" that the Baxters existed, and fictionally or make-believedly the case that they had certain beliefs, desires, hopes, feelings, and so on; in which case, we can have *beliefs* about what is fictionally or make-believedly the case with respect to the Baxters and their psychological states.[17] I won't attempt to adjudicate here between the complex variety of accounts of the language and logic of fiction that have been offered to date; however, something *like* this must, I think, be right. And our beliefs about what is fictionally or make-believedly the case can, I suggest, ground and constrain the kind of imaginative project that I have argued is characteristic of empathizing with another. That is, beliefs of this sort can ground and constrain our imagining a situation or state of affairs from the point of view of a fictional character.[18]

A further difficulty that may be thought to arise with regard to the possibility of our responding empathetically to fiction is suggested by Richard Wollheim. As we saw earlier, Wollheim suggests that any account of our affective responses to fiction that puts empathetic responses to the fore must in that respect be wrong. For, Wollheim suggests, "the empathic member of the audience selects who it is whose deeds and inner states he will centrally imagine. [For example,] Watching *King Lear* he rewrites the text of Shakespeare so that it can be acted from the point of view of Gloucester."[19] The implication is that "rewriting" in this sense is an inappropriate way to engage with the text, and hence that inasmuch as empathy involves "rewriting," it is an inappropriate way of responding to the characters. In response to this suggestion, it might be argued that Wollheim's remarks have more than a whiff of aestheticism about them; a play – or a film – may be more enjoyable and more rewarding when "rewritten" in this sense. So why *not* "rewrite" it? But secondly, and more importantly, "rewriting" a work may not be necessary in order to respond empathetically to one or more of its characters. Certainly one does not have to "rewrite" *The Haunting* to see the events in the scene discussed earlier from the perspective of Eleanor and Theodora. And one does not distort Roeg's film by seeing the events from the point of view of Laura or John Baxter; indeed, I have argued that we may need to empathize with them, to see things from their point of view, if we are to understand the film. Nor does one have to "rewrite" or distort Shakespeare's text in order to imagine the world of *King Lear* from Gloucester's point of view; arguably *not* to respond in this way is to miss one of the central experiences that the play has to offer. Indeed, it might plausibly be argued that allowing the audience to see and to understand his or her fictional world from a variety of perspectives and characters' points of view – making a variety of empathetic responses to his or her work possible – is one criterion, among others, of a writer's or director's success.

8

I have argued, then, that in order to give anything like an adequate account of empathy we must recognize that empathy is *essentially* an imaginative matter, and that the imaginative activity characteristic of empathy both presupposes and is constrained by belief. Not only does empathizing with actual persons involve imagination as well as belief, but empathizing with fictional characters involves belief as well as imagination. So Feagin misconstrues the case when she claims that "unlike real life empathy, the art emotion of empathy [that is, empathy with fictional characters] is not dependent on (or explained by) our beliefs about what is involved in the beliefs (desires, etc.) of the person with whom we empathize" (496). It needs to be emphasized here that empathizing with a fictional character is not, pace Feagin, radically different from empathizing with an actual person. In empathizing with another, whether she be actual or fictional, one imagines the situation she is in from her point of view; one imaginatively represents to oneself her beliefs, desires, hopes, fears, and so on as though they were one's own. And in both cases, one may come *actually* to feel what the other in question, be she actual or fictional, is *imagined* as feeling. Imagination occupies center stage here not because it is needed specifically in order to explain certain of our affective responses to fictional characters, but rather because it is constitutive of empathy per se.

But given that we *can* empathize with fictional characters, *why* do we do so? The answer to this question, I believe, will be more or less the same as the answer to the question as to why we empathize with actual persons; the fact that we sometimes do one is no more and no less mysterious than the fact that we sometimes do the other. However, I am not at all confident about my ability to answer these questions adequately. For in large part, I think, they ask why it is that we *care* about each other and about fictions at all; and an adequate answer to that question is beyond me. However, we can say *something* about why it is that we sometimes respond empathetically to others. For in empathizing with others, we come to know how things are with them, by seeing the world from their point of view, as they see it, and feeling as they feel. In short, we come to understand them better; so that we are better placed to understand why they have reacted and behaved as they have done, and to predict how they will react and behave in the future.[20] And inasmuch as empathy contributes to our understanding of others, it has great practical value to us. Given that when we engage with fiction we want to understand its characters and events, then, and that empathizing with others (be they fictional or actual) contributes to our understanding of them, it is hardly surprising that in responding to works of fiction we sometimes respond empathetically to their characters. But the value of empathy does not lie solely in what it can contribute to our understanding of others and their worlds of experience. Empathizing with others also makes available to us possibilities for our *own* emotional education and development. In coming to see things as others see them and to feel as they do we gain a broader perspective on the world, an increased awareness and understanding of the possible modes of response to the world. In short, through responding empathetically to others we may come to see *our* world and *our* possibilities anew. That is valuable. And, as I suggested earlier, part of the value of fiction, and in particular film fiction, lies in the fact that by encouraging and sometimes demanding empathetic responses from us, it makes such broadening of perspective available to us.

Where then does this leave us with regard to the role of identification in our engagement with fiction? Earlier, I noted that on certain psychoanalytically inspired accounts, identification is construed as a pathological process, symptomatic of one or another form of anxiety and self-deception. And if empathetic responses are based on identification, as common parlance suggests, then on such accounts empathetic responses must themselves be regarded as pathological, as rooted in anxiety and self-deception. I do not believe that this is the case: one of the guiding thoughts in this essay has been that our empathetic responses to fiction can be invaluable in understanding and learning from works of fiction; so far from being symptomatic of self-deception, such responses may be the means to increased understanding of ourselves and of others. If this is accurate, then perhaps common parlance is misleading: perhaps empathetic responses to others do *not* depend on identification with them. On the other hand, perhaps empathetic responses *are* based on identification, and identification is not the pathological process that some theorists suggest that it is. I do not believe that it is worth trying to settle this issue. The fact is that the term "identification" can refer to so many different sorts of processes that as things stand it is simply not very helpful in attempts to get clear about our emotional engagement with fiction: as D. W. Harding writes, "We sacrifice little more with the term 'identification' than a bogus technicality."[21] I suggest that we need to reverse the approach so often taken in discussions of these matters: rather than beginning with a psychoanalytically inspired account of identification and then going on to consider its implications with regard to our experience of fiction, we need to *begin* with our experience of fiction. And in doing so, I believe, we will find ourselves needing and developing a wide variety of descriptive and explanatory resources more fine-grained than is the notion of identification. The concept of empathy, I suggest, is one such resource.

Notes

Thanks to David Bordwell, Curtis Brown, Noël Carroll, and Marianne Neill for helpful suggestions.

1 The first philosopher to address these questions, so far as I know, was the sophist Gorgias. See Jonathan Barnes, *The Presocratic Philosophers*, vol. 2, *Empedocles to Democritus* (London: Routledge, 1979), pp. 161–4. For a list of most of the important recent contributions to this debate, see the bibliography in B. H. Boruah's *Fiction and Emotion* (Oxford: Clarendon Press, 1988).
2 Richard Wollheim, "Imagination and Identification," in *On Art and the Mind* (Cambridge: Harvard University Press, 1973), p. 68.

3 Dolf Zillman, "Anatomy of Suspense," in *The Entertainment Functions of Television*, ed. Percy H. Tannenbaum (Hillsdale, NJ: Lawrence Erlsbaum, 1980), p. 141. Emphasis added.
4 Zillman himself uses "empathy" to cover "feeling for" as well as "feeling with."
5 Noël Carroll, *The Philosophy of Horror, or Paradoxes of the Heart* (New York: Routledge, 1990), pp. 88–96.
6 Anne Friedberg, "A Denial of Difference: Theories of Cinematic Identification," in *Psychoanalysis and Cinema*, ed. E. Ann Kaplan (New York: Routledge, 1990), p. 40.
7 For example, it is central in the work of Vico and Dilthey.

8 For examples, see Adam Smith's *The Theory of Moral Sentiments* (Oxford: Clarendon Press, 1976), David Hume's *A Treatise of Human Nature* (Oxford: Clarendon Press, 1978), and Carol Gilligan's *In a Different Voice* (Cambridge: Harvard University Press, 1982).

9 See Robert Gordon's much discussed paper "Folk Psychology as Simulation," *Mind and Language* 1 (1986): 158–71, and chapter 7 of his *The Structure of Emotions* (Cambridge: Cambridge University Press, 1987). *Mind and Language* 7, 1–2 (1992) is a special issue devoted to discussion of "simulation theory," which holds that empathetic understanding is central to our everyday, pretheoretical understanding of others. I am indebted here to Alvin Goldman's extremely helpful survey of some of the main issues involved, in his presidential address to the Pacific Division of the APA: "Empathy, Mind, and Morals," *Proceedings and Addresses of the American Philosophical Association* 66 (November 1992): 17–41.

10 Needless to say, just what Aristotle means by *catharsis* in the *Poetics* has been a subject of intense debate for centuries. The scholar who has done most to connect *catharsis* to learning, or "intellectual clarification," about the emotions is Leon Golden. See his *Aristotle on Tragic and Comic Mimesis* (Atlanta: Scholars, 1992). See also Martha Nussbaum, *The Fragility of Goodness* (Cambridge: Cambridge University Press, 1986).

11 Quoted by Peter Jones in his *Philosophy and the Novel* (Oxford: Clarendon Press, 1975), p. 66.

12 Susan L. Feagin, "Imagining Emotions and Appreciating Fiction," *Canadian Journal of Philosophy* 18 (1988): 485–500. The quotation is from pp. 489–90.

13 Milan Kundera, *The Unbearable Lightness of Being*, trans. Michael Henry Heim (New York: Harper and Row, 1984).

14 Here I am drawing on Alvin Goldman's "Empathy, Mind, and Morals," in *Proceedings and Addresses*, and especially on Richard Wollheim's discussions of empathy. See his "Imagination and Identification," in *On Art and the Mind*, and chapter 3 ("Iconicity, Imagination and Desire") of his *The Thread of Life* (Cambridge: Cambridge University Press, 1984). Wollheim makes a distinction between "central" and "acentral" imagining that in some respects parallels Carroll's distinction between "internal" and "external" understanding.

15 Thus Wollheim suggests that one of the restrictions on whom I can centrally imagine is that it must be "someone for whom I have, or have the capacity to form, a repertoire of substance" (*The Thread of Life*, p. 74). The "repertoire" that one has for a person with whom one empathizes consists of the beliefs that one has about his beliefs, desires, hopes, fears, and so on.

16 I have in mind here cases analogous to Gettier-type cases of true justified belief that is nonetheless not knowledge. See Edmund L. Gettier, "Is Justified True Belief Knowledge?" *Analysis* 23 (1965): 121–3.

17 See Kendall L. Walton, *Mimesis as Make-Believe* (Cambridge: Harvard University Press, 1990).

18 I discuss this and related issues concerning emotion, belief, and fiction in more detail in my "Fiction and the Emotions," *American Philosophical Quarterly* 30 (January 1993): 1–13.

19 Wollheim, "Imagination and Identification," p. 68.

20 Again, see Goldman's "Empathy, Mind, and Morals."

21 D. W. Harding, "Psychological Processes in the Reading of Fiction," in *Aesthetics in the Modern World*, ed. Harold Osborne (New York: Weybright and Talley, 1968), p. 309. See also Carroll's *The Philosophy of Horror*, pp. 88–96.

17

Identification and Emotion in Narrative Film

Berys Gaut

When film viewers are asked to describe their emotional reactions to films they often appeal to the notion of identification. They say things such as "I could really identify with that character," "the film was no good: there wasn't a single character I could identify with," or "I felt so badly about what happened to her, because I strongly identified with her." It is part of the folk wisdom of responding to films (and to literature) that audiences sometimes identify with characters, that the success or failure of a film partly depends on whether this identification occurs, and that the quality and strength of emotional responses depend on identification. It seems that any theorist interested in our emotional reactions to films must give an account of the nature of this process of identification and explain its importance in shaping responses. And there would appear to be no room for denying the existence and importance of spectatorial identification.

Yet film theory has exhibited a curious reaction to this folk wisdom. On the one hand psychoanalytically inspired theories have responded positively to these claims but treated them in hyperbolic fashion. Drawing on Lacan, such theories hold that the child is constituted as a subject through an act of identification with her own image in the mirror at the age of 6 to 18 months; the power of cinema in giving an impression of reality and as an ideological device lies in its ability to re-enact this basic process of identification.

Film identification according to Jean-Louis Baudry has a dual aspect:

> One can distinguish two levels of identification. The first, attached to the image itself, derives from the character portrayed as a center of secondary identifications, carrying an identity which constantly must be seized and re-established. The second level permits the appearance of the first and places it "in action" – this is the transcendental subject whose place is taken by the camera which constitutes and rules the objects in the "world."[1]

While they acknowledge the existence of character identification central to the folk theory, psychoanalytic theories thus demote it to a secondary status. The notion of the identification of the viewer with an invisible observer becomes central, an identification that constitutes the identity of the viewer as an illusorily unified, ideological subject. Besides this sidelining of the notion of character identification, the dominant trend in psychoanalytic theories also departs from the folk view in regarding the viewer as becoming a fetishist, sadist, and voyeur through his acts of identification.[2]

Those film theorists and philosophers who draw on analytical philosophy and cognitive science generally have little time for such psychoanalytic construals of spectators' responses. But rather than

Berys Gaut, "Identification and Emotion in Narrative Film," *Passionate Views*, eds. Carl Plantinga and Greg M. Smith (Baltimore: Johns Hopkins University Press, 1999): 200–16. Reprinted by permission of The Johns Hopkins University Press.

simply stripping out the psychoanalytic components from the notion of identification, they have in most cases rejected the claim that identification occurs at all. Noël Carroll writes that "identification...is not the correct model for describing the emotional responses of spectators";[3] Gregory Currie argues that identification does not occur in the point-of-view shot;[4] and even Murray Smith, who has some sympathy with the idea of identification, generally presents his own concept of engagement not as an analysis of identification but as an improved concept with which to replace it.[5]

This suspicion of the notion of identification by theorists of a cognitivist stripe is striking given the widespread use of it in ordinary viewers' reports of their interactions with films, and indeed of the use of the notion more generally in ordinary life, as when we talk of identifying with our friends. And it also fuels the accusation by psychoanalytic theorists that the cognitive paradigm is peculiarly unsuited to account for emotional responses to films. For if the cognitive view rejects appeal to a central notion required to explicate spectators' emotions, how can it give an adequate account of those emotions?

This, then, is the situation that confronts anyone interested in the notion of identification in film. The task of this chapter is to rehabilitate the notion of identification for cognitivist theories of film, to show that the notion does not suffer from the deep conceptual confusions alleged against it, and to demonstrate that it has explanatory power in accounting for spectators' emotional responses to films. The argument will require several new distinctions to be drawn, but these involve refining the notion of identification, not abandoning it.

The Concept of Identification

The notion of identification can seem deeply odd. Its etymological root is of "making identical." Thus it would seem that when I identify with a character I merge my identity with his, which would "require some sort of curious metaphysical process, like Mr. Spock's Vulcan mind-meld, between the audience member and the protagonist."[6] This is not just deeply odd but actually impossible: two people cannot be made (numerically) the same without ceasing to exist. But here, as quite generally, etymology is a bad guide to meaning. Any argument exploiting this etymology to show that identification does not exist would be like an argument that

noted that "television" has as its etymological root "seeing at a distance," argued that we do not literally see things at a distance when we look at a television screen, but only their images, and concluded that televisions do not exist. The question is not what the etymology of the term is but of what it means, and the meaning of a term is a matter of its use in the language.

So how do we use the term "identification" when we apply it to a character in a fiction? One use is simply to say that one cares for the character. To say that there is no one in a film with whom one can identify is simply in this usage to report that one does not care about what happens to any of the characters. But in such a use, the fact that I identify with a character cannot *explain* why I care for her, for such a purported explanation would be entirely vacuous. The natural thought here is that identification in the explanatory sense is a matter of putting oneself in the character's shoes, and because one does so one may come to care for her. But what is this notion of placing oneself in someone else's position?

Psychoanalytic and Brechtian theories, given their belief in mainstream cinema as a form of illusionism, might naturally hold that just as the viewer is somehow under the illusion that the cinematic events are real, so she is somehow under the illusion that she is the character with whom she identifies. But that would credit the viewer of a film with an extraordinary degree of irrationality; it would hold that she does not believe that she is sitting safely in the dark, as is clearly the case, but that she believes she is swinging from a rope on a mountaintop, or shooting at villains, or otherwise doing whatever the film represents the character as doing.

A more plausible version of this story would hold that a "suspension of disbelief" occurs in the cinema: the viewer believes that she is not the fictional character, but that belief is somehow bracketed from her motivational set. In such cases the viewer reacts *as if* she believes that she is the character depicted, even though she does not in fact believe this to be the case. But then many of the viewer's reactions to the film fail to make sense under this assumption: for instance, since characters in horror films rarely want to suffer the terrors that torment them, viewers who identify with these characters should storm out of the exits at the first appearance of these films, for on this construal of identification they should react as if they believed they were these characters.[7]

A better version of the identification view would hold, rather, that the viewer *imagines* herself to be the character with whom she identifies. This, then, is part of the explanation of why she comes to care for the character, if she indeed does. But this formulation raises new worries, for it may be objected that it makes no sense to talk about imagining oneself to be someone else. Arguably there are no possible worlds in which I am identical with some other person – they are simply worlds in which I possess that other person's properties without being him. So how can I imagine being another person? Similar worries apply if one holds that it makes no sense to think that I could be different in some radical way from the person I am (I could not have been a tenth-century female Eskimo, for instance). The reply is that even if one accepted claims of this kind, it would not follow that one could not imagine things that the claims hold are impossible. We can, in fact, imagine things that are not just metaphysically but even logically impossible – for instance, that Hobbes actually did square the circle (as at one time he thought he had done). And we do that not infrequently in responding to fiction – we may be asked to imagine people going back in time and conceiving themselves, we may be asked to imagine werewolves, or people turning into trees, or intelligent, talkative rats complaining about lordly, overbearing toads.

However, there is still a problem with holding that one imagines oneself to be another person when one identifies with him. As Richard Wollheim has noted, if I imagine myself to be a particular character (say, Jeeves), then since identity is a symmetrical relation, this is equivalent to the claim that I imagine Jeeves to be me. But the two imaginings are very different projects: in the former case I imagine myself in Jeeves's position, serving and manipulating Bertie Wooster; in the second case I imagine Jeeves surreptitiously taking over my life, and I become disconcertingly butler-like.[8]

What we should conclude from this is that the act of imaginative identification involves imagining – not, strictly speaking, being that other person, but rather imagining being in her situation, where the idea of her situation encompasses every property she possesses, including all her physical and psychological traits (so we imagine the world from her physical and psychological perspective). Hence what I do in imaginatively identifying myself with Jeeves is imagining being in his situation,

doing what he does, feeling what he does, and so on. And that is clearly different from imagining Jeeves being in my situation.

Wollheim has objected to this construal of identification: he holds that since I do not imagine myself to be identical to Jeeves, the account would allow me while imagining myself in his situation to imagine meeting him, which my imaginative project surely rules out.[9] And it is indeed true that my imaginative project rules this out, but that is in fact compatible with imagining myself to be in Jeeves's situation. For as we have understood the notion of a person's situation, it comprises all of his properties; these include not just his contingent properties but also his modal properties, such as necessarily not being a number, necessarily having the potential for self-consciousness, and necessarily not being able to meet himself. Thus Jeeves (fictionally) has the property of necessarily not being able to meet himself, that is, necessarily not being able to meet Jeeves. Hence, were the question raised of whether I could properly imagine myself meeting Jeeves when I am imagining myself in his situation, I ought to rule out imagining meeting him. For I ought to imagine possessing those of his properties which are relevant to this situation, in particular the modal property of being unable to meet Jeeves. Thus Wollheim's rejection of the account of identification in terms of imagining oneself in another's situation looks plausible only on an overly narrow understanding of someone's situation that excludes certain of his modal properties.

This account of identification also fits how we talk of imaginative acts. We frequently talk of understanding someone by imagining ourselves in her situation, of putting ourselves in her shoes. And we come to understand her by imaginatively projecting ourselves into her external situation, imaginarily altering those aspects of our personalities which differ from hers, and then relying on our dispositions to respond in various ways, so as to work out what other things she might reasonably be supposed to be feeling.[10]

Even on this construal of imaginative identification, however, the idea that identification occurs in films seems to encounter fundamental difficulties. It is often supposed that one of the central cases of cinematic identification is when we are shown a point-of-view shot; here surely we are asked to identify with a character: we literally take up her perspective. But this claim has met with a barrage of objections. Currie has urged that if identification occurred in the point-of-view shot; then the viewer would have to imagine that what happens to the character happens to her and that she possesses the most obvious and dramatically salient characteristics of the character, and it would have to be that she has or imagines she has some concern with and sympathy for the values and projects of the character. But none of these, says Currie, need be the case. I often do not imagine any of the events happening to the character happening to myself, nor do I imagine myself having any of his characteristics, nor need I have the least sympathy with him – consider, for instance, the frequent use of point-of-view shots in horror films, taken from the perspective of the killer.[11] Smith has also argued that the point-of-view shot need not give access to the character's subjectivity: indeed, the point-of-view shot in horror films often functions to disguise the killer's identity.[12]

These points about point-of-view shots are well taken, but they do not force us to abandon the claim that identification can occur in such cases. Once we construe identification as a matter of imagining oneself in a character's situation, the issue becomes pertinent of *which aspects* of the character's situation one imagines oneself in. As we have seen, we should construe the situation of the character in terms of what properties she possesses. Her physical properties include her size, physical position, the physical aspects of her actions, and so on. Her psychological properties can be thought of in terms of her perspective on the (fictional) world. But that perspective is not just a visual one (how things look to her); we can also think of the character as possessing an affective perspective on events (how she feels about them), a motivational perspective (what she is motivated to do in respect of them), an epistemic perspective (what she believes about them), and so forth. Thus the question to ask whenever someone talks of identifying with a character is *in what respects* does she identify with the character? The act of identification is aspectual. To identify perceptually with a character is to imagine seeing from his point of view; to identify affectively with him is to imagine feeling what he feels; to identify motivationally is to imagine wanting what he wants; to identify epistemically with him is to imagine believing what he believes, and so on. What the objections rehearsed above force us to see is that just because one is identifying perceptually with the character, it does not follow that one is identifying motivationally or affectively with him, nor

does it follow that one imagines that one has his physical characteristics.

This may seem to distort the concept of identification. Surely, it will be urged that the notion of identification is a global concept that is, we imagine, being in that person's situation in all respects, and in talking of aspectual identification we are in effect abandoning the notion of identification.

On the contrary, if identification were global, it could not in practice occur. Even a fictional character has an indeterminately large number of properties (most of which will be implicit, not explicitly stated by the text or film), and a real person has an infinite number of such properties. It would not be possible to imagine oneself as possessing all of these properties. And, of course, one does not do so: one picks on those characteristics that are relevant for the purpose of one's imagining. Nor should someone hold that even though one does not imagine all these properties holding of oneself, one ought to do so. For even if one held (which I earlier argued against) that identification with a character requires you to imagine being identical with that character, it is not in general true that one is required to imagine all of the consequences of one's imaginings. As Kendall Walton has pointed out, very often fiction requires you not to imagine such consequences; Othello speaks extraordinarily poetic verse, while saying that he is plain of speech, and yet no one notices this. Why is this so? To raise the question would be to ask a "silly question"; even though in the real world there would be an answer to this question, there is no answer in the world of the fiction.[13] What we are to imagine is shaped by the knowledge that we are looking at an artifact designed to prescribe certain imaginings, and our imaginings are shaped by the demands of the context.

It has sometimes been objected that the idea of identification is much too crude a notion, reducing the possibilities of our relations to characters to either being identified with a character or distanced from her, and thus we need to abandon the notion.[14] Once we recognize the existence of aspectual identification, we can see that recognition of these complexities is well within the grip of the notion of identification. Since we have distinguished different aspects of identification, we can hold that the fact that we are perceptually identified with a character does not entail that we are affectively identified with her – the fact that we are imagining seeing from her perspective does not *require* us to imagine wanting what she wants, or imagine feeling what she feels. It then becomes a matter of substantive theorizing to investigate under what conditions one form of identification fosters another. It would be surprising, given the complexity of film art in general, if one could find any invariant, law-like principles for linking different aspects of identification together. But that leaves plenty of space for investigating how one form of identification may tend (other things being equal) to promote another form, or for how certain film techniques may tend to enhance some kinds of identification.

So far we have been following out the implications of the thought that identification involves imagining oneself in another's situation. This idea of imaginative identification is, however, not exhaustive of all that people mean when they talk of identification. Consider the idea of empathy, which is naturally thought of as a kind of identification, and a very important one at that. If someone has a parent die, identifying with the bereaved person characteristically takes the form of taking on her feelings, sharing them ("I feel your pain," "I know what it's like to undergo that loss"). But note that this is different from the notion of affective identification as we have characterized it. That required the viewer to *imagine* feeling what a person (or a character fictionally) feels; empathy requires the viewer *actually* to feel what a person (or a character fictionally) feels.

Now it is plausible that empathy requires one imaginatively to enter into a character's mind and to feel with him because of one's imagining of his situation.[15] But that is to say that empathic identification requires some form of imaginative identification; it is not to conflate the two phenomena. It is possible to identify with a character affectively, imagining his sorrow, anger, or fear, yet not empathize with him, since one does not actually feel sorrowful, angry, or afraid with him. In fact, it is only those theorists who allow for the possibility of feeling real emotions toward merely imagined situations who can even allow for the existence of empathic identification with fictional characters (though they can, of course, allow for such identification with real people). The idea of empathic identification is that one feels toward the situation that confronts the character what the character (fictionally) feels toward it; and since that situation is merely fictional, the possibility of real emotions directed toward situations known merely to be fictional must be allowed.[16]

The final notion we need to discuss is that of sympathy. As earlier noted, sometimes to talk of identification with a character is simply to say that one sympathizes with him. But if we want to retain identification as an explanatory concept, we should mark this off as a distinct usage. And, in fact, sympathy and empathic identification are distinct notions. To sympathize with a character is in a broad sense to care for him, to be concerned for him. (We need not care for him merely because he is suffering sympathy in the narrow sense since one can talk, for instance, of having sympathy with the goals of a political party, even though that party is not suffering.) This care can be manifested in a variety of mental states: fearing for what may befall him, getting angry on his behalf, pitying him, feeling elated at his triumphs, and so forth. These states need have no relation to what he is feeling: I may pity him because he has been knocked into a coma in a road accident and is feeling nothing; I may be angry on his behalf for what has been done to him, even though he may be stoical about it; I may fear for what will befall him, even though he is sublimely unaware of the imminent danger in which he stands. Empathy, in contrast, requires one to share in the feelings one ascribes to him: I am empathically angry if and only if (I believe or imagine) that he is angry, and the thought of his anger controls and guides the formation of my anger.[17] So if he is in a coma and not feeling anything, nothing counts as empathizing with him. Since most people are concerned for themselves, empathizing with them will involve sharing this concern, and hence sympathizing with them. But the co-occurrence of sympathy and empathy is contingent on the psychology of the person with whom we are empathizing and sympathizing, rather than showing that these two kinds of dispositions to feel are the same.

These distinctions also allow us to answer an influential objection to the idea of identification advanced by Carroll. Carroll holds that identification with a character requires one to feel what she is feeling. But, he points out, the correspondence between what the viewer feels and what a character feels is normally at most a partial one. A woman is swimming in the sea, unaware that she is in imminent danger of attack by a shark: she is happy, we are tense and fearful. Oedipus feels guilt for what he has done: we do not feel guilt, but pity him. And Carroll holds that a partial correspondence of feelings is insufficient for identification.[18]

Insofar as Carroll is discussing the notion of identification here, it must be that of empathic identification, for he is discussing what the audience actually feels, not just what it imagines feeling. So, even if successful, his critique does not undermine the notion of imaginative identification. Moreover, because we have seen that the activity of identification is always aspectual (and therefore partial), it cannot be an objection to identification that the correspondences between what the audience is feeling and what the characters are fictionally feeling are only partial. For identification always is partial.[19] Further, what Carroll's examples show is that our responses to characters' situations are often sympathetic (we are concerned at the swimmer's situation, even though she does not recognize the danger and so feels no fear), rather than empathic. But this point hardly shows that empathy never occurs: when the swimmer does recognize the danger and panics, we then share her fear.

Carroll objects to this last move: he holds that we do not share the swimmer's fear because her fear is self-directed, whereas our fear is directed toward her. However, this objection fails to see the significance of the imaginative element involved in empathic identification. That is, we have to place ourselves imaginatively in the swimmer's situation in order to empathize with her. Thus when I imagine the shark's attack on the swimmer, I am imagining the shark's attack on me (since I am imaginarily in her situation), and hence I can share the swimmer's fear, since in both cases it is self-directed.[20]

Identification and Film Techniques

So far I have defended the concept of identification from the claim that it is mysterious or incoherent by distinguishing different kinds of identification: on the one hand, imaginative identification (imaginarily putting oneself in another's position), which is in turn subdivided into perceptual, affective, motivational, epistemic, and perhaps other forms of identification; and on the other hand, empathic identification, which requires one actually to share the character's (fictional) emotions because of one's imaginarily projecting oneself into the character's situation. On the basis of these different kinds of identification, one may come to sympathize with the character (this sympathy, as we have noted, is sometimes itself thought of as a kind of identification, but we shall treat it as one possible upshot of identification, since one can sympathize with someone without employing any sort of imaginative projection into his position). I have also deployed these distinctions to defend the claim that identification occurs in films against the sorts of objections that are often raised against it. Given these distinctions between different kinds of identification, we can now examine in more detail the role of identification in our relations to films.

As earlier remarked, the point-of-view shot is often thought of as the locus of character identification in film. In fact, it is the locus of perceptual identification (the viewer imagining seeing what the character fictionally sees), and it does not follow that the viewer identifies with the character in all other respects. The example of a shot in a horror film taken from the point of view of the killer shows that there is no necessary tendency to empathize with the character whose visual perspective we imaginarily occupy. However, since we now have the distinction between affective and empathic identification in place, we can see that there may be a tendency to affective identification resulting from this shot: that is, other things being equal this shot may get us to imagine what the character is feeling (though we need not actually feel it ourselves, i.e., we need not empathize with him). Consider the shot in *The Silence of the Lambs* taken from the point of view of Buffalo Bill, who is wearing green-tinted night-glasses, looking at Starling (Jodie Foster) while she flails around in the dark, desperately trying to defend herself from him. Certainly, we have no tendency here to empathize or sympathize with Bill – our sympathies lie entirely with Starling – but the shot does tend to foster our imagining of Bill's murderous feelings (partly because we can see their terrifying effect on Starling).[21]

The point-of-view shot, besides being an instance of perceptual identification and having a tendency to foster affective identification, also fosters a kind of epistemic identification. For the latter requires us to imagine believing what the characters fictionally believe; and some beliefs are perceptual. However, the idea of epistemic identification is broader than that of perceptual identification, since we may occupy the character's epistemic perspective by virtue of having our knowledge of what is happening restricted to her knowledge (this is characteristic of the detective film, for instance).[22]

Though the point-of-view shot is the characteristic form of perceptual identification in film, it is not the only type. This is demonstrated by another shot from *The Silence of the Lambs*. Consider the scene in which Starling and the other FBI agents are in the autopsy room with one of Buffalo Bill's victims, who has been partially flayed by him. It is only towards the end of the scene that we are finally shown the corpse itself; up to this point we are confined to watching the investigators' reactions, particularly Starling's. Watching Foster's finely nuanced performance, which registers barely controlled disgust and fear modulated by pity for the victim, we are invited to imagine what she sees without actually being shown it. The result is that what we imagine her seeing is very likely worse than what we are finally shown, since each viewer, watching the emotions registered on her face, is invited to imagine something that will justify these emotions, and so tends to imagine whatever would make these emotions appropriate to her: each imagines her own private nightmare scenario. Thus the expressive reaction shot, as well as the point-of-view shot, can cue the spectator to imagine seeing from the character's point of view.

Furthermore, as the example also shows, the reaction shot can be a more effective vehicle for affective and empathic identification with a character than is the point-of-view shot.[23] The reaction shot shows the human face or body, which we are expert at interpreting for signs of emotion, and through the art of a consummate actor like Foster we can obtain a very full sense of what the character is feeling. Hence we are provided with a large amount of information with which to engage accurately in affective identification.

Moreover, if we are confronted with visual evidence of an individual's suffering, we have a strong tendency to empathize and sympathize with her. Tales of mass disasters in distant countries also have the power to move us to empathy and sympathy, but generally more effective is a confrontation with the individual visage, with the particularities of an individual's plight etched in her expression. Recall the way, for instance, that aid agencies employ photographs of individuals in states of distress as a way more effectively to convey their message of mass suffering.

As noted earlier, the point-of-view shot also has some tendency to move us to affective identification. But it has the disadvantage of having less information to convey about what the character is feeling, and because of the absence of a shot of the face, has less power to move us to empathy and sympathy. The point-of-view shot has in fact fairly crude options available for the conveying of feelings. It may employ a shaking camera to convey unrest and uncertainty (think for instance of the hand-held, jiggling shots in Cassavetes' *A Woman Under the Influence* [1974], which convey something of the troubled minds of the married couple). It may employ low-angle shots to convey a sense of being dominated by other characters (think of some of the low-angle shots of Kane [Orson Welles] in *Citizen Kane* [1941]). Even more radically, the entire *mise en scène* may be set up so as to convey a character's troubled state of mind (think of the shot from the crazed artist Borg's perspective of the dinner guests in Bergman's *Hour of the Wolf* [1968]). If we contrast these fairly simple options with the subtleties of Foster's reaction shot in the autopsy scene, we can see that on the whole the reaction shot is more important than the point-of-view shot in mobilizing affective and empathic identification.

Epistemic identification also has a tendency to foster empathy, though in more indirect ways than does the expressive reaction shot. If our knowledge of what is fictional in the film corresponds to a high degree with that of a particular character, there is a tendency to identify affectively and to empathize with that character, even if we are antecedently not disposed to do so. Consider a scene in which we follow the movements of a group of criminals engaged on a job; we watch them being vigilant, stopping lest they be discovered, being alarmed at dangers, being hopeful about the success of the crime, and so on. In these cases where we have the same epistemic point of view on the events as they do, we can easily find ourselves empathizing with them and wanting their crime to succeed, even though normally we would not want this.

A more complex example of this phenomenon occurs in Harold Ramis's *Groundhog Day* (1993). Pete the weatherman (Bill Murray) is caught in a comic version of Nietzsche's eternal recurrence, condemned to live the same day over again and again until he gets it right. Our feelings for Pete are initially complex: his humor is hip and funny, but his cynicism is upfront, too, and our affections are divided between him and his colleagues. As the film progresses we increasingly empathize and sympathize with him. This is partly because he grows morally and becomes a more attractive figure. But it is also because we are stuck in the same epistemic situation as he is. No one apart from him and the viewer realizes that the scenes we are seeing have been played out many times before: we thus share the knowledge about what is happening with him and find it increasingly difficult to look at the world from any other point of view than his because we know that all the other characters do not appreciate what is going on. Here epistemic identification tends to foster our empathy and sympathy with the character.

In addition to these factors, there are others that tend to foster empathy and sympathy. First, empathy and sympathy are mutually self-reinforcing. To empathize with a character involves feeling what fictionally she is feeling; since most characters have a concern for their own welfare, by empathizing with them one will also be sympathetic to them, that is, one will be concerned for them. Conversely, if one is sympathetic to a character, one will tend to align one's emotions with his, feel what he feels, and so empathize with him.

Second, and more obviously, we tend to sympathize with characters who are represented as having various attractive traits. A wide range of traits can foster such responses: characters may be witty (as is Pete the weatherman), physically attractive, interestingly complex, and so forth. In Neil Jordan's *The Crying Game* (1992) our sympathies are mobilized toward Jody (the British soldier, played by Forest Whitaker), Fergus (the IRA member, played by Stephen Rea) and Dil (the transvestite, played by Jaye Davidson) by their vulnerability: Jody is vulnerable because he appears to be in imminent danger of being killed by the IRA yet is in Northern Ireland for no better reason than that he needed a job; Fergus is vulnerable because he does not believe in the credo of violence to which he is ostensibly committed and is himself then endangered by it (and his vulnerability is displayed in his remark to Jody that "I'm not good for much"); and Dil is vulnerable because of her marginal social and sexual situation. Besides these kinds of character traits that can promote empathy and sympathy, the knowledge of who is playing the character can also materially engage our feelings. Hitchcock, for instance, was master at deploying this technique. Considered in terms of his character traits, Scotty (James Stewart) in *Vertigo* (1958) is a fairly unsympathetic character; but we are encouraged to empathize with him partly because of our epistemic identification (up to the point of Madeleine/Judy's [Kim Novak] flashback we are unaware of the plot that

has been hatched against him, and are largely confined to his knowledge of events) and also because he is played by James Stewart, with his long history of playing folksy, sympathetic heroes.

So the notion of identification can be refined so as to avoid the objections frequently leveled against it, and this refinement allows us the creation of theories of some complexity by examining the relations between different kinds of identification. The refined notions still allow for an important connection between identification and emotion. This is displayed partly in the constitutive connection between empathic feelings and identification: empathy is feeling what a character feels because one imaginatively projects oneself into his situation. And the connection between identification and emotion is also displayed in some causal connections: as we have seen, epistemic identification tends to foster empathy, and affectively identifying with a character, particularly when her situation is vividly imagined, tends to produce empathy with him. Thus the common view that there is an important connection between identification and emotional response to films has received a partial defense, based on distinguishing different notions of identification. However, the theorist's claim that the point-of-view shot lies at the heart of cinematic identification has fared less well. It certainly constitutes a characteristic form of perceptual identification, but it is not the only form: the reaction shot, too, can invite us to imagine seeing from a character's perspective. And while the point-of-view shot may have some tendency to get us affectively to identify with the character concerned, it is not as effective in this respect as the reaction shot, and the latter is vastly more effective in engaging our empathy and sympathy.

Identification and Learning

Identification, then, plays an important role in our emotional responses to films. It also plays a significant part in teaching us how to respond emotionally to fictionally delineated situations. There are at least two basic forms that this kind of learning may take. The first is that through empathy our emotional reactions mirror those of a character, and that as she grows emotionally we do, too, learning to respond to situations in a way that we and she would previously have found inappropriate. The second basic type of learning results from identifying with a character, but coming to realize that her reactions are in some ways inappropriate to her situation, and discovering that there is a deeper perspective on her situation, different from her own. In the first case, both we and the character grow emotionally together; in the second only we may grow while the character remains much the same. The first possibility is illustrated by *The Crying Game*; the second by Max Ophuls's *Letter from an Unknown Woman* (1948).

In *The Crying Game* we are led after the traumatic death of Jody to identify (epistemically, affectively, and empathically) with Fergus, who is traumatized by Jody's death and eager to escape the IRA. Jody has asked Fergus to take care of his lover, Dil; Fergus has seen a picture of her and found her very attractive. He falls in love with her, she performs oral sex on him, and at the turning point of the film she appears naked before him: Dil is a man. Fergus is aghast, strikes Dil, throws up in the toilet, storms out. Since the audience has been epistemically closely identified with Fergus throughout, they are also likely to be astounded by the discovery (Jaye Davidson's impersonation of a woman is extraordinarily convincing). The rest of the film is the story of how Fergus comes to accept the fact that he loves Dil, even though Dil is male ("I preferred you as a girl"), and goes to prison for her sake.

The Crying Game is thematically very rich, engaging with issues of race, gender, and love. What is interesting for our purposes is how Fergus is represented as coming to accept that he loves Dil, even though his heterosexuality was not previously in doubt. Love transcends mere gender boundaries; not only is that a theme of the film, but the audience is also positioned to *want* Fergus and Dil to continue their erotic friendship, even after it is clear that Dil is a man. Because we are multiply identified with Fergus and because Fergus comes to accept his love for Dil, we too are encouraged to accept it. Here identification with a character whose attitudes toward homosexuality change fundamentally in the course of the film also encourages the audience through empathy to want the relationship to work out, and thus also encourages them to question their attitudes toward homosexuality.[24] This, then, is a particularly clear example of a film that deploys identification to get audiences to reconsider their emotional responses and to learn from a fictional situation.

Letter from an Unknown Woman is on the face of it a film that falls well within the conventions of the "woman's picture." Lisa (Joan Fontaine), the un-

known woman of the title, loves Stefan (Louis Jourdan) from a distance and is enamored of his musical prowess, the sense of culture and mystery that he brings to her cramped bourgeois life, when she first encounters him at puberty. Yet she talks to him only a handful of times and goes to bed with him only once, from which she conceives a son. For the sake of that son, she marries an honorable man, whom she respects but does not love, but throws it all away when she meets Stefan years later. Yet Stefan does not recognize her, and she leaves his apartment distraught, apparently having finally seen through his superficial charm and having grasped the fact that she was no more than another conquest to him. Yet the film is structured around the letter she writes to him while she is dying, a letter that reveals her still-hopeless infatuation with him, a letter that avers the great good that could have come out of their love – if only he could have remembered her, if only he could have recognized that she was his true muse, the woman who could have lent meaning to his life. Stefan, reading the letter, apparently accepts his responsibility and his failure, goes off to fight a duel with Lisa's husband, and thus departs to his certain death.

On the face of it, the film is a paradigm melodrama, a picture that intends not so much to jerk tears as to ladle them out in bucketfuls. And there is no doubt about the audience's multiple identification with Lisa. Here is the voiceover, and almost all the scenes in flashback are those in which she features; she is quiet and beautiful with a childlike charm and an impressive determination. The audience is thus epistemically, affectively, and empathically identified with her, and there is no doubt about the resulting sympathy that they are encouraged to feel for her. Yet in a real sense, Lisa never learns the significance of what has happened to her. Her dying letter is a testament to how if only Stefan had been able to love truly, to dedicate himself to her, their lives would have been immeasurably richer. So identification with Lisa on this interpretation of the film would lead to a reinforcement of the romantic attitudes that many of the original audience presumably brought with them when they came to see the film.

There is another way to interpret the film, however. Lisa is an obsessive person, unable to recognize that she is projecting her romantic fantasies onto a figure who does not in the least conform to them, and that she is pursuing these fantasies literally to the death, even though there is abundant evidence that she is deluding herself in a way guaranteed to lead to disaster. For this view there is much evidence in the film. Lisa says things in her letter that are contradicted by what we see: for instance, that "I've had no will but his [Stefan's] ever," whereas in fact it is transparently clear that Lisa has a very strong will of her own (she is willing to throw away her marriage on a chance of being with Stefan), while Stefan wanders through life with little sense of direction (he admits that he rarely actually reaches any place for which he sets out). These and other clues in the film give the audience evidence for a counter-perspective in the film, a point of view that is not Lisa's, which shows us that Lisa's views are partly fantasized distortions of her true situation.[25]

On this second (and I think better) way of interpreting the film, the audience is encouraged to identify with Lisa in several respects but is also provided with evidence that her actions are in certain respects foolish and self-deluded. If it grasps this counter-evidence, then what it has learned from the film is that certain of its romantic values are distorted, tending to encourage potentially disastrous self-delusions. Because the audience so much identifies with Lisa, it should take that lesson to heart; it cannot stand back and think that what has been shown about Lisa's values has nothing to do with its own, since it has seen those values enacted in a woman with whom it has closely identified. This, then, is the second way that identification with a character may teach an audience about correct emotional responses. On this model, the character does not grow emotion-

ally, but the audience does because of the way it has discovered that its values are flawed. Here identification plays a more indirect cognitive role than on the first model: to learn what it is appropriate to feel, the audience has to be prepared to detect the existence of a counter-perspective to that of the character. But identification functions to drive the lesson home, to show that the values and attitudes under attack are the audience's own, and thus to create the possibility of a real, lived change in their basic commitments. As this possibility illustrates, the Brechtian idea that identification must always function so as to render the audience uncritically receptive to conventional values is false. Identification may work in an appropriate context to drive home some hard lessons.

I have argued that philosophers and film theorists who reject the centrality of the psychoanalytic paradigm should not also reject, as they all too often do, the idea of identification. Despite the criticisms that have been laid against the coherence and the explanatory power of the concept, it does in fact have a valuable role of play in understanding our emotional responses toward films. As used by audiences to describe and explain their reactions to films, it is undoubtedly somewhat crude. But once we make necessary distinctions, the concept can be refined so that it plays a valuable part in film theory and in the analysis of individual films. Abandoning the idea of identification because of its deployment in psychoanalytic theory is worse than throwing the baby out with the bath water. It is a failure to identify with the baby.

Notes

A shorter version of the paper was read at the Society for Cinema Studies Conference at Ottawa in 1997, and I am grateful to the participants on that occasion for discussion of the paper.

1 Jean-Louis Baudry, "Ideological Effects of the Basic Cinematographic Apparatus," in *Film Theory and Criticism*, 4th edn., ed. Gerald Mast, Marshall Cohen, and Leo Braudy (New York: Oxford University Press, 1992), 311.
2 For a discussion and critique of these claims, see Noël Carroll, *Mystifying Movies: Fads and Fallacies in Contemporary Film Theory* (New York: Columbia University Press, 1988); and also see my "On Cinema and Perversion," *Film and Philosophy* 1 (1994): 3–17.
3 Noël Carroll, *The Philosophy of Horror, or Paradoxes of the Heart* (London: Routledge, 1990), 96.

4 Gregory Currie, *Image and Mind: Film, Philosophy and Cognitive Science* (Cambridge: Cambridge University Press, 1995), 174–6.
5 Murray Smith, *Engaging Characters: Fiction, Emotion and the Cinema* (Oxford: Oxford University Press, 1995). Sometimes, as on p. 73, he seems to think of the idea of engagement as an analysis of the notion of identification; more generally, as on p. 93, he presents it as a replacement for that identification.
6 Carroll, *Philosophy of Horror*, 89. I am not accusing Carroll of embracing the fallacious argument I attack in this paragraph.
7 See also ibid., 63–8, for a critique of illusionistic and suspension of disbelief theories of emotional responses to fictions.
8 Richard Wollheim, *The Thread of Life* (Cambridge: Harvard University Press, 1984), 75.
9 Ibid., 75–6.

10 This root idea of understanding another by imagining oneself in her place (the idea of *verstehen* as a mode of cognition of others) should be distinguished from the notion of simulation as employed in simulation theory. The latter construes the more basic notion of *verstehen* in computational terms. For an application of simulation theory to cinema, see Currie, *Image and Mind*. For some objections to this use of simulation theory, see my "Imagination, Interpretation, and Film," *Philosophical Studies* 89 (1998): 331–41.

11 Currie, *Image and Mind*, 174–6.

12 Smith, *Engaging Characters*, 157.

13 Kendall Walton, *Mimesis as Make-Believe: On the Foundations of the Representational Arts* (Cambridge: Harvard University Press, 1990), 174–83.

14 This has been urged by Smith in *Engaging Characters*, e.g., 222.

15 See Alex Neill, "Empathy and (Film) Fiction," in *Post-Theory: Reconstructing Film Studies*, ed. David Bordwell and Noël Carroll (Madison: University of Wisconsin Press, 1996).

16 For a convincing defense of the claim that such emotions are possible, see Richard Moran, "The Expression of Feeling in Imagination," *Philosophical Review* 103 (1994): 75–106.

17 See Neill, "Empathy and (Film) Fiction," for an illuminating discussion of the differences between empathy and sympathy.

18 Carroll, *Philosophy of Horror*, 90–2.

19 What Carroll says does not in any case support his position: "If the correspondences are only partial, why call the phenomenon identification at all? If two people are rooting for the same athlete at a sporting event, it would not appear appropriate to say that they are identifying with each other. They may be unaware of each other's existence" (Carroll, *Philoso-phy of Horror*, 92). But even if the spectators had exactly the same emotional states, they would still not be identifying with each other. Rather, empathic identification requires one to feel what another is feeling, *because* one recognizes that he is feeling it. This is why the spectators are not identifying with each other, not because of the fact that they are not sharing all their emotional states.

20 Carroll also objects that the swimmer's fear is based on a belief that she is in danger, whereas my empathic fear is based only on imagining that I am in danger. But this does not show that the fear is not shared, since as he has himself argued, the object of fear is a thought-content, whether or not it is asserted, and the thought content are the same in both cases. (For his "Thought Theory" of emotional response, see Carroll, *Philosophy of Horror*, 79–88.)

21 This shot also doubles as a reaction shot of Starling: for the significance of reactions, see below.

22 This is what Murray Smith terms allegiance with a character: see Smith, *Engaging Characters*, esp. chap. 5. He holds that the notion of identification cannot distinguish allegiance from other senses in which we are engaged with a character: but as we have seen, the notion of identification can in fact be refined so as to recognize this case.

23 For a fine discussion of this phenomenon, and of Truffaut's thoughts thereon, see Smith, 156–61.

24 For a discussion of *The Crying Game* to which I am indebted, see Matthew Kieran, "Art, Imagination, and the Cultivation of Morals," *Journal of Aesthetics and Art Criticism* 54 (1996): 337–51, at 338.

25 This construal of the film is argued by George Wilson in *his Narration in Light: Studies in Cinematic Point of View* (Baltimore: Johns Hopkins University Press, 1986), chap. 6.

18

In Fictional Shoes: Mental Simulation and Fiction

Deborah Knight

Though originally intended to deal with actual persons, mental simulation has recently been proposed as a model for our empathetic responses to fictional characters. What does mental simulation involve?[1] The standard answer is that we simulate how someone reasons if we want to predict their actions, and we simulate how they feel if we want a clear sense of how things are for them. The objective of simulation is to answer the question, "What is it like to be someone else?" Philosophers including Susan Feagin and Gregory Currie have argued that simulation can be applied to fictional characters. Perhaps the question here would be, "What is it like to be someone fictional?" What follows is an examination of mental simulation in both actual and fictional cases. My argument is that despite its attractions, mental simulation is less than wholly adequate to the task of accounting for our interest in, or our emotional involvement with, fictional characters.

I begin by considering the folk model of readerly and spectatorial engagement. Although I concede that, willy-nilly, many of us do talk as if characters are real people, doing so can miss important aspects of the fictionality of such characters as well as the formative role played by the narratives in which they appear. In the second section, I outline some of the problems with simulationism in its standard form, taking actual people as our interpretive targets. In the third and fourth sections, I turn to the application of mental simulation to fictional characters, dealing first with the idea that we are trying to simulate how characters reason in order to be able to predict their next actions, and then with the idea that we are trying to simulate their feelings. By this point, I hope to have shown reasons why we should at least be cautious about applying mental simulation either to people or to fictional characters. But there does seem to be something to the notion of simulation, so in the fifth section I turn to Susan Feagin's argument, in *Reading with Feeling*, that mental simulation can successfully be applied to fictions. Feagin's account of simulation is flawed, as I will argue, but her description of how we become emotionally involved with fictions is, I think, separable from those flaws and important in its own right. Considering her work will help us to regroup and see what it is about fiction that mental simulation models cannot adequately deal with, and why. But I suspect that the most deeply held presupposition for believing that mental simulation applies to fictions has not yet been identified. In my conclusion, I will offer a few Aristotelian remarks about narrative that suggest what is the matter with this presupposition.

The Folk Model

Empathy plays a central role in the role model of readerly or spectatorial engagement. Empathy is taken to be essential to the development of our moral imagination, and fiction (especially literary fiction, as opposed say to comic books and airport paperbacks) is considered a significant training ground for the practice of empathy. The idea is that our response to any fictional narrative is principally a response to its characters, and what we try to do is to understand what they are thinking and feeling.[2] Empathy rather than, say, sympathy is presumed to be key here because the sort of understanding we want to achieve involves us in the imaginative reduplication of how things are for someone else. To help see the difference between these attitudes, let us adopt Alex Neill's shorthand, which says that sympathy involves *feeling for*, whereas empathy involves *feeling with*.[3] Empathy is warranted in the context of fiction because we construe characters as people, and our interest in them is sustained by the same folk psychology we use to understand and interpret the actions of those around us. Granted, experiencing empathy does not mean that sympathy is precluded; nevertheless, it is empathy, in the sense of *feeling with*, that mental simulation aims at.

To apply mental simulation to fictional characters means that we treat characters as if they were people. This is no mere folk practice. It is nowhere so apparent as in the sort of ethical criticism of literature championed by Martha Nussbaum and Wayne C. Booth.[4] It is also evident in the self-described "cognitive" study of literature and film. Indeed, even in traditional sorts of literary discussions we might consider the beliefs and desires, the plans and hopes and fears of characters such as Macbeth, or Mrs Dalloway, or even Moon and Birdboot, those hapless theatre critics in Tom Stoppard's *The Real Inspector Hound*. But discussions of literature can also focus on things literary, not to mention things theoretical, so the tendency to talk solely as if characters are person-analogues is mitigated.

There is no point denying something so ubiquitous as the fact that one common way to discuss fictional characters is in the general idiom of folk psychology – in terms of beliefs and desires and so forth. But doing so exclusively means we neglect the formal, narratological, stylistic and thematic dimensions of fictional narratives. It means we underestimate the role of genres and of such modes as suspense, melodrama and comedy both in shaping our relationships with characters and in helping us understand their situations. To treat characters as if they were people means we will be much less inclined to consider them as textual elements in a fictional structure, or as focalizers of

metaphoric, symbolic, thematic or generic significance. In the meantime, it seems we are supposing that our understanding of characters is just like our understanding of actual persons, especially those we find ourselves in the midst of most of the time. But to discuss characters in the sorts of terms associated with folk psychology is not, as it turns out, identical to treating them as if they were people. I will be arguing that, common though this tendency might be, it gives a skewed view of how fictions work, and how they work on us. So let us look at mental simulation.

Mental Simulation

You know you have met a simulationist when they say they want to be in your shoes. For some simulationists, the objective is understanding. Alex Neill argues that understanding what someone else is going through involves our ability to "possess" their mental states: we imaginatively represent to ourselves "the thoughts, beliefs, desires, and so on of another as though they were one's own."[5] Other simulationists emphasize prediction. Jane Heal, who prefers the term "replication" to "simulation," writes: "What I endeavour to do is to replicate or recreate [the other's] thinking. I place myself in what I take to be his initial state by imagining the world as it would appear from his point of view and I then deliberate, reason and reflect to see what decision emerges."[6] Still other simulationists are concerned with explanation. Arthur Ripstein claims that to imagine "what it would be like to be in 'someone else's shoes' can serve to explain that person's actions."[7] What simulationists generally agree about is that by imagining you are in someone else's shoes, you can figure out what they believe or feel. What makes mental simulation attractive within the philosophy of mind is what Robert Gordon describes as the "very interesting possibility...of using *simulated* practical reasoning as a *predictive* device."[8] Because the usual vocabulary for explaining mental simulation includes terms such as make-believe, pretence, dramatic enactment, imaginative projection, and social role-playing, it is little wonder that it seems an apt model to apply to fictional literary and film narratives.[9]

The governing idea behind simulation is that understanding is possible because we share with others a similar way of processing beliefs, desires, and other attitudes. Alvin Goldman calls this our practical reasoning mechanism.[10] The mechanism is a black box. It computes "inputs" and generates "outputs." We don't know how it works, and don't need to know, but we assume it works pretty much like a practical syllogism.[11] What is involved when we simulate? We start by first blocking our own beliefs, desires, interests, fears, hopes and so forth, a process Goldman calls "quarantining."[12] We quarantine so that we do not contaminate the calculation with our own views. Then we imaginatively entertain the other's beliefs and desires. And we use *our* practical reasoning mechanism, the black box we all share – suitably adjusted for the specific beliefs and desires deemed to be held by the other – to predict the other's behaviour.

What makes mental simulation distinct from standard cases of practical reasoning is that the results of the simulation involve prediction rather than action.[13] This is why mental simulation is often described as an "off-line" activity, since – somewhat paradoxically – it is an activity that doesn't produce an action.[14] Simulationists say that the simulator manipulates or entertains *pretend* or *hypothetical* beliefs and desires without actually holding those beliefs to be true or wishing to have the desires in question satisfied. The calculation of inputs is supposed to generate a unique decision about what will be done, given our simulation of the other's circumstances and her relevant beliefs and desires. For many simulationists (Jane Heal and Susan Feagin are exceptions), it is our practical reasoning mechanism *itself* that does the calculating. So the prediction is not the result of what *I* think or even of *how* I think; it is what any of us would think, given the inputs which – by means of mental simulation – we share with the person whose action we want to predict or explain.

Let us turn to some problems that simulationism must confront. The first problem concerns the difficulties faced by our practical reasoning mechanism. Think what that black box has to contend with. Imagine its problems: the temptations of competing desires and the need to select one action from a range of options. Consider the complexities introduced by what we could do but for various reasons (ethical, prudential, and the like) would probably not do, things we would do but are unable to do, knowledge it should be taken for granted that we have but which we either don't have or don't realize is relevant. Tidy, discrete inputs are far from the norm. So our practical reasoning mechanism will have all the same problems we already experience in trying to understand

others. This means that no purpose is served by positing a practical reasoning mechanism to handle such processing: we are those black boxes already.

How *do* we arrive at the beliefs, desires, and so forth that we should attribute to the individual whose actions we want to predict? Saying that you imagine yourself to be in the other's shoes is surely not enough to account for how we specify whatever inputs seem appropriate. Recall Heal's claim that replication involves deciding on appropriate inputs based on imagining how the world appears from the other's perspective. Heal does not require the simulator to imagine the other's state of mind. To replicate her thoughts, you would only have to imagine how things are around her, and assume that how things are around her would cause her to have the same beliefs and desires you imagine. Granted, if the way the world is arranged around me involves seeing the bus coming, though I'm still a half block from the bus stop and I need to catch the bus, then how the world is arranged, relative to me and the approaching bus, might well lead someone to predict that I will sprint quickly to the corner. But even that prediction requires postulating stuff that is just not there, disposed in the world's arrangement, such as that it matters to me that I catch this bus, and that I am in good enough shape to think the run would be worth it. Or to take a simpler case, it is not obvious how the mere arrangement of the world could help anyone predict whether I will go to the kitchen to make a pot of tea.[15]

Simulation-based predictions face other problems. For example, one might imaginatively or empathetically but still quite arbitrarily hit upon a belief and a desire which combine to generate a prediction about another agent's action, and that prediction might turn out to be accurate, yet the agent may well have acted for an entirely different reason. Say you predict that someone will go to law school because she is smart, ambitious, and disciplined, because she wants a prestigious, professional career, and because she believes law would provide it. But the smart, ambitious, disciplined person in question who desires a prestigious, professional career and who does not doubt that law could provide it may go to law school to honour a promise to her family when actually she would rather be an architect: the right prediction (she goes to law school) but the wrong reasons. An accidentally correct prediction hardly amounts to understanding the other. Or one might make a prediction about another's action which turns out to be accurate without having engaged in anything like an activity of imaginative projection. I predict that, *ceteris paribus*, North Americans will drive on the right-hand side of the road in North America. Jerry Fodor often uses this as an example of successful folk psychological prediction. But clearly it does not require mental simulation, or even empathy. In fact, empathy by itself does not mean that our predictions stand a greater chance of being accurate than those that do not involve mental simulation, a point conceded by many simulationists.

A more damning problem for simulationism is that many, including sociopaths, are very good at figuring out how others think and react. They are good, in other words, at decision simulation. But such knowledge can easily be used *against* the person they are "simulating." Some psychologists believe that the skill such individuals have isn't truly empathy, and one can see why. Here we might usefully follow Martha Nussbaum, who notes that, while empathy seems to require compassion, mental simulation does not.[16]

Now I am prepared to concede that we all use folk psychology all the time, though seldom perfectly. We want to know why people behave as they do, and folk psychology is often the best tool at hand. To explain or predict other people's actions, we need to figure out their beliefs, opinions, ideas, preferences, and desires. We *do* need to know something about how things seem to them to be. Simulationists are surely on the right track about this. If we want to predict the behaviour of someone who is looking dangerously thin but who holds unshakably to the notion that she is overweight, we would be better advised to work with the false belief. But this raises a question. What allows us to discover just those beliefs, ideas and opinions, desires, fears, hopes and regrets that are salient to the other? The simulation theory doesn't explain this. In fact, mental simulation *just is* this ability to intuit or determine what is salient, but the theory doesn't give us any sense of how we do it, or what allows us to know when we've done it right. Recall that our prediction of another's action might be right even though the reasons we attribute are wrong. With these cautions in mind, let's look at what happens when mental simulation is applied to fictions.

Simulating Fictions

Simulationists always want to be in your shoes. Very well, let us imagine being in some fictional

character's shoes – which I guess amounts to imagining we are in fictional shoes. What are we doing when we try to imagine what it would be like to be someone fictional?

The problem is to be found, of course, in the difference between being real and being fictional. Peter Lamarque puts the problem this way: "What is fictional, to be sure, cannot be *real*, but characters, it seems, cannot be *nothing*. So what in the world are we talking about," he asks, when we talk about characters and their *fictional* mental states, actions, and so on? How can we be so intimate with fictional characters when part of what is involved in understanding their fictional status is to know that they are ontologically quite other than ourselves?[17] How is it rational to treat fictional characters as having mental states and attitudes? How do we find ourselves caring about them? Since fictional characters do not exist, there is no set of beliefs and desires which, if we were lucky, we could simulate. So it is quite opaque how an appeal to mental simulation can justify our predictions of fictional characters' actions, let alone our attribution of beliefs and desires to them. Indeed, an obvious criticism to raise against the ideal that we need mental simulation in order to understand characters depicted in most examples of prose fiction is that for the most part we are told directly what the beliefs and attitudes of at least the central characters are, making mental simulation quite unnecessary.

Lamarque solves the question about what on earth we are talking about when we talk about fictional characters by admitting that there are actually two perspectives we can adopt, the internal perspective and the external perspective. The internal perspective considers characters as if they were people, and the external perspective considers such literary matters as theme, style, and mode of representation. Fictional characters are "in some respects . . . just like you and me – they are persons – while in other respects they are radically unlike you and me – they are mere fictions."[18] To adopt the internal perspective is to treat fictional characters as being, at least in some respects, persons. Now Lamarque is no simulationist. Indeed, he argues that we need both external and internal perspectives to properly understand fictions. A clear limitation of simulationism is that it adopts only the internal perspective. If, in applying mental simulation to fictions, we cannot take into account anything falling under the external perspective, then much that matters to the understanding of fictional narratives drops out of sight. So it seems that fictional simulationism goes wrong on two counts. The first stems from the idea that we should treat characters as persons rather than as elements within a fiction. This is a misapplication of psychological explanation – not because it is inappropriate to apply psychological explanation to fictional cases, but because it is mistaken to ignore the fact that these cases are fictional. The second way it goes wrong is to assume that the reason readers and viewers would want to apply simulation to fictional cases is to be better able to predict the actions of characters.

What we need is to see why we aren't forced to conclude that characters are like us in the sense of being persons just because we talk about them in the idiom of folk psychology. What will help is a different way of thinking about folk psychology and the psychological explanations it undertakes to provide. As I have argued elsewhere, psychological explanation is an agent-centered, narrative-based interpretive practice.[19] As a practice, it is quite neutral as to whether the target of explanation is actual or fictional, real or made up: we use it for people as well as for Pooh-bears. It can be neutral in this way because it is focused on *agents* and thus not principally on people or fictional person-analogues. Now this would seem to play into the hands of the simulationists, since their view is that we can understand fictional characters in just the way we understand actual people. But here is the difference between my position and simulationism. While psychological explanation is neutral as between the actual and the fictional, whether something is actual or fictional will have a bearing on the sorts of explanations we produce.

Clearly, when we are dealing with specific cases – say, my aunt Barb on the one hand, or Emma Woodhouse on the other – whether someone is actual or fictional matters. Think of everything that becomes relevant if our target is a fictional character – things that have no conceivable role to play in our attempts to make sense of people. I am thinking, for example, of the genre or mode of the fiction; dominant themes, images, and motifs; the rhythm and/or pacing of the narrative; and in the case of film, mise-en-scène, sound, music, framing and camera movement, the contribution of the personae of the actors to the realization of characters, and so on. We have no access to any understanding of fictional characters in the absence of such features as these, because without these features, we have no access to fictional characters, period.

The second way simulationism goes wrong is to assume that the reason readers and viewers want to apply mental simulation to fictional cases is to be better able to predict the actions of characters. Is decision-simulation really the main motivation behind our attempts to understand fictional characters? It is not obvious that this is the primary means of engagement for readers and viewers, but even if it were, restricting themselves to what Lamarque calls the internal perspective means that they will miss a lot that could help them. Consider examples of genre fiction: say, Westerns, horror, or screwball comedy. Genre fictions rely on recognizable and systematic conventions, knowledge of which helps to orient us with respect to the particular work at hand. In such cases, the sorts of predictions that best sustain our interest are *generic predictions* – predictions keyed to things we can only recognize from the external perspective. Certain events are probable in horror fictions that are not probable in Westerns or in screwball comedies, or for that matter in real life.

In narrative fiction, as in life, what we tend to predict is the general outline of how a course of events might unfold. Or at least we anticipate certain possible ways the narrative might proceed, those that are most probable given what we already know. But we hardly restrict our predictions to what folk psychology would encourage us to presuppose. How often in horror films do women walk alone down deserted streets at night, or decide to explore further in a deserted house? You know you wouldn't do it if you were in her shoes, and you know she shouldn't, but she does it just the same. In the meantime, our interest in genre fictions (and in fictions generally) is often sustained because we can't always successfully predict just what characters will do next. And this is a good thing, for otherwise we would be bored and disappointed by always being able to foresee the twists and turns of the plot.

When we turn from genre fictions to such non-genre works that rely on the development of highly individuated characters (for example, *The Golden Bowl* or *Bad Timing: A Sensual Obsession*), we find that the successful prediction of action is less important to us than an understanding of the characters and their motivations. This is facilitated by the ways in which psychological information is made available (in the case of James's novel) or withheld (in the case of Roeg's film). When we have an abundance of psychological information, as for instance in works by Joyce or Proust, or in films such as Fellini's $8\frac{1}{2}$, predictions seem even less relevant. Then there is the question how to apply mental simulation to works which deliberately minimize our access to information about character psychology, as for example in such films as Michelangelo Antonioni's *L'Avventura*, Alain Resnais's *L'Année dernière à Marienbad*, or Jim Jarmusch's *Stranger than Paradise*.

But not all accounts of mental simulation assume that our primary goal is to predict the decisions of others based on our shared decision-making mechanism and our ability to replicate what others believe and desire. So mental simulation need not just be concerned with replicating another's *reasoning*; it can have something to do with imagining what the other *feels*. Indeed, it seems to involve something very much like feeling what the other feels. And this is no mere off-line ability.

Simulation and Feelings

When we move from an emphasis on reasoning to an emphasis on emotions, the account of simulation changes. When emotion is our primary focus, our responses are not necessarily off-line or pretend. The sorts of responses at issue here are not self-focused but rather other-focused.[20] Empathy and sympathy are both other-focused, as we saw Alex Neill suggesting when he said that empathy is *feeling with*, sympathy *feeling for*. What I feel for you when I sympathize with your disappointment may well have nothing to do with feeling disappointment myself, and need not necessarily involve my imaginatively feeling your disappointment. Or perhaps you feel humiliated. Although I am sympathetic, I probably don't necessarily feel humiliation. Even though I feel for you, my sympathy does not require that I feel what you feel. On the other hand, when I empathize with you, Neill suggests, what I feel "with you" is what you are feeling. If you are anxious, so am I. If you are joyous, so am I. If you are head over heels in love.... But wait a second. The emotion I experience empathetically when I am glad you are in love is very likely *not* what you are feeling, but rather a second-order response to the first-order response which is, properly, yours. It seems that empathetic responses are often second-order in this way, as sympathetic responses are also. Though I, too, feel

some emotion deeply, and though feeling it contributes to my ability to be concerned about you – and possibly even to understand how things are with you – it does not seem necessary that I replicate your emotions.[21]

A crucial difference between simulation thought about in terms of practical reasoning and simulation thought about in terms of empathetic emotional responses emerges here. Simulation conceived in terms of off-line practical reasoning casts the simulator as disinterested. The simulator imagines, but does not act, and thus is not engaged in any practical way with the other's situation – at least while simulating. This is perfectly captured in the quote from Heal, according to whom the simulator observes the world as if from the perspective of the other, and then reasons and reflects to see "what decision emerges." Nevertheless, emotional engagement does not at all seem to be limited to off-line experiences. When we are emotionally involved with fictions or with anything else, my guess is that we don't think of this involvement as in any sense disengaged or disinterested. Nor do we *imagine* ourselves to be emotionally involved. The emotions in question are not made up. Rather, they are evoked, aroused, experienced. So the evocation of emotion hardly fits the off-line view preferred by many simulationists.

It is trickier than one might initially suppose to sort out coincidentally shared emotional responses from ones that could properly be thought of as simulated. You are watching a medal presentation at the Olympics. The gold medalist is in tears. You are in tears. You are moved by the ceremony, and so is she. You are moved by the accomplishment, and so is she. Your feelings and hers seem to be shared, and you both appear to be moved by the same thing. But though your response is undoubtedly empathetic, it is unlikely you feel what she feels. There is an indexical asymmetry involved here, since what is at issue for her is that *she* has won the medal – a point you acknowledge, being quite aware that the target of your emotions is not that you have won the medal, but rather that she has. The asymmetry is compounded since you are aware of her, but in standard cases, she is unaware of you. This asymmetry is even more acute with fiction. You are aware of characters, but they are never aware of you, despite conventions such as direct address which affect such awareness.

It seems so obvious that the emotions we experience empathetically help us to understand how things are with others, and yet it is so hard to get the details right, especially this business about sharing the other's feelings. The problem extends from actual cases to fictional ones. If fictional characters can't be said to have beliefs and desires, they can't be said to experience emotions either, so there is no emotional fact of the matter that could ever allow us to know that the emotion we are experiencing is just the emotion a character is experiencing. But then, it can be a tricky matter to figure out just what emotion *we* are experiencing from the feeling alone. As Jenefer Robinson remarks, one "may have very similar feelings whether angrily despairing, tragically resolving, or suffering from the pangs of unrequited passion."[22] Part of what is needed to distinguish these feelings from one another is an object, that is, cognitive content. So even in our own cases, feelings can be pretty much alike but only coincidentally so, if they have different objects or cognitive contents. In the case of our empathetic concern for fictional characters, even treating them as if they had emotions, we might feel something very like what they "feel," yet our experiences could miss the cognitive content that is fictionally the object of the character's experiences. This difference in cognitive content might pose no problem for the general idea that empathy allows us to understand how things are with fictional characters, for instance if the cognitive content was second-order relative to the first-order cognitive content of the other's emotion. But it clearly suggests that we do not need to feel what the character would be feeling, if fictional characters had feelings.

Feagin on Simulation and Empathy

So far, I have offered reasons why we should be skeptical both about mental simulation and about its direct applicability to our understanding of fictional characters. But let us give it one more chance, by turning to Susan Feagin's account of mental simulation and the role of empathy in our attempts to understand and appreciate fictions. Feagin's account is important because it offers a defense of mental simulation with respect to fictional characters while stressing the disanalogies between persons and characters. Drawing on the work of Robert Gordon, Alvin Goldman and Arthur Ripstein, Feagin argues that, in the context of actual persons, mental simulation depends

upon the idea that there is some psychological fact of the matter which we can replicate. If there weren't, then whatever it was we were doing, it wouldn't be simulation. Yet Feagin is "reluctant to say there is some psychological fact of the matter with respect to fictional characters."[23] She argues that empathizing with an actual person "requires that one 'share' another's feelings, one 'feel' things as that person does or did," with the further condition that the simulator "engages in a simulation out of a desire to empathize with or understand . . . the person with whom one empathizes."[24] But whatever it means to empathize with a fictional character, what is happening "is not a relationship holding between two persons."[25] Rather, it is a relationship between an audience and a text. Here Feagin means the words on the page, in the literary case, and the complex amalgam of visual and aural cues in the cinematic case. What is at stake is the audience's relationship with characters as textual representations, rather than as person-analogues. In the context of fictions, whether or not one is empathizing is determined by the reader's (or viewer's) sensitivities to the text.[26] If we are sensitive to the text and respond empathetically to it, Feagin argues, then we can reasonably attribute the affect or emotion we are experiencing to a character if on reflection doing so "makes interpretive sense of the fictional work."[27]

But if we accept this point, it is no longer obvious what role mental simulation plays in fictional cases, since – contrary to the whole direction of Feagin's argument – what we are doing is simply projecting our own emotional responses, where they are evoked, to those characters to whom, on reflection, it makes interpretive sense to attribute them. This might count as interpretation, but it is not simulation. Moreover, it presupposes the reader's or viewer's ability to generate an interpretation of the work which such attributions would both shape and be the product of, and yet we are told little about what skills besides appreciation are involved in such interpretations.

I suggest that we must work harder to distinguish simulation from empathy in the two sorts of cases we have been considering, the case of emotional experience and the case of reasoning, since empathy seems to require indexical asymmetry and simulation tends to discount or overlook that asymmetry. Feagin's position is a curious one, since she holds that simulation just is empathy:

in simulating "what is going on in another person's mind...one empathizes with that other person."[28] According to Feagin, when simulation is working correctly, what we feel is what the other is feeling, what we think is the case is what the other thinks is the case, what we would do is what the other would do. For reasons I have already mentioned, this doesn't seem right, and seems even less right in fictional situations. We have as little clue how to know that we are correctly simulating an emotion in fictional situations as we have how to know whether we are correctly simulating how the world appears to the other in actual situations. These are problems for Feagin since she insists that simulation "is a success term" and that the "usefulness of simulation depends in part on one's ability to recognize what, if anything, one has successfully done."[29]

The most important thing Feagin contributes to our discussion of simulationism is the very sensible realization that empathy with respect to fictional characters is the product of our relationship to the text rather than to the character treated as a person. But Feagin also allows us to get a sense of why many readers and viewers do feel so closely connected to at least some fictional characters. In our imaginative engagement with fictions, there is much we have to do: we have to recognize a variety of narrational cues, sort information, assess probabilities, scan the horizon of action for possible developments, and occasionally we also have to reassess previous information which we only subsequently realize has a bearing on the events unfolding now. Not everything that we think about a fiction is explicitly stated (in the case of literature) or presented (in the case of film or drama). Often we must figure out what the character's plans are, or what her emotional response is, without having been told in so many words. To do so involves imaginative projection. Much of what we understand about fictional situations, and much of what we feel about fictional characters, follows from exactly this sort of imaginative engagement. But such engagement is not necessarily a result of empathy, nor is it necessarily connected to mental simulation. By conceding that in the case of fictional characters, there is nothing really there to simulate, Feagin has undercut her own attempt to apply mental simulation to characters. Nevertheless, she does cast light on the creative, constructive role that readers and viewers play in realizing fictional characters.

Concluding Aristotelian Remarks

Why apply mental simulation to fictional characters? One reason is to try to model the sort of cognitive and emotional involvement that we experience with fictional narratives. If we accept the idea that characters are best understood as if they were people, then the way is paved for doing just this.

However, to assume that characters can be assumed as if they were people is to import into the fictional domain two prerequisite ideas, both of which are dubious. One is that the themes and structure of any story are a by-product of characters and their interactions. Narratologists would see things as being the other way around. The second prerequisite idea is that the story world is analogous to the real world at least insofar as characters act freely, or no less freely than people do. Now it is true that fictional characters must regularly choose between options. Granted that, in narrative fictions, characters often have to deal with contingencies, accidents and other events that they could not reasonably have been expected to foresee. But in privileging characters at the expense of narrative structure, we mistake those contingencies as being actually contingent, when in fact they are determined parts of the final narrative. So it is my suspicion that the crucial motivating factor behind the idea that we can usefully apply mental simulation to the situations of fictional characters is the belief that in fiction, as in life, the narrative future is essentially open, and the central characters are able freely to determine their own course of events. This, of course, is an illusion.

Most fictional stories, and certainly the vast majority considered by people working in philosophy of literature or philosophy of film, are closed structures. They are the sorts of fictions that Aristotle spoke of as unities. What is a closed structure, on Aristotelian terms? It is a narrative in which the significant episodes are subordinated to an overarching plot that uses each one of them as a means of arriving at a particular conclusion. In short, it is a narrative with closure. A unified plot is quite a different animal from what Aristotle calls an episodic narrative, one that is built up out of a sequence of episodes which may not even have a single protagonist to provide the common thread. The elimination of any one sequence from an episodic narrative would perhaps cause the loss of an interesting anecdote. But it would not be a loss that affects the whole structure, since episodic narratives lack any overarching plot that links all their episodes teleologically to one another.

To be Aristotelian about narrative structure is to accept a particular sort of story causality, namely *entelechial* causality. The idea here is that most fictional narratives were conceived as, or are standardly read as, unified wholes. Where this sort of reading practice obtains, all sections of the unfolding narrative are understood as it were a priori to contribute to an overall structure, and to be meaningful precisely thanks to their part in that global structure. So, for example, events occurring seemingly by chance toward the beginning of the narrative should be expected to reveal their significance later on. Entelechial causality is a feature of much narrative fiction, but it is not a feature of life, unless you are a pretty single-minded determinist. Of course, if you were a single-minded determinist, mental simulation would not hold much attraction for you. Entelechial causality is sometimes described as backward causation: the conclusion of the narrative compels the previous events to have played out as they did. We may not be aware of the backwards causation until we get to the end of the story, but that doesn't mean that its force hasn't organized events throughout. Rick's decision to send Ilsa away with her husband at the conclusion of *Casablanca* is an excellent example. On the other hand, we may be more familiar with entelechial causality than we think. It is, after all, what assures us that Meg Ryan and Tom Hanks will meet on the observation deck of the Empire State Building at the conclusion of *Sleepless in Seattle*. But entelechial causality is not restricted to romantic melodramas and romantic comedies. It works just as relentlessly elsewhere, most obviously in tragedy – Aristotle's preferred genre.

Whether we are talking about Oedipus or Anna Karenina, the fate of these characters is determined by their tragic ends. The role of entelechial causality in so many fictional narratives ought to be an important reminder why it is not always particularly helpful to treat characters as if they were people, at least in the sense captured by Lamarque's "internal perspective." To adopt only the internal perspective is to be blind to the thematic and structural features of any plot that gives characters' actions their point.

On the other hand, if we acknowledge the disanalogies between fictional characters and persons, and admit that this has a formative influence on our understanding both of characters and the narratives in which they are featured, then we will need a different and dare I say a more formalist and narratological account of our appreciation and understanding of narrative fictions. The issues raised by the application of mental simulation to fiction have caused us to focus far too much on character, far too little on the stories in which characters assume whatever importance they have for us. Stories are structured things. Empathy and other sorts of imaginative activity will doubtless figure in such an account. But as I have tried to demonstrate, mental simulation seems not, in fact, to be what we are doing when we engage imaginatively with fictions. Certainly it is not what we are *primarily* doing. I believe that Susan Feagin makes exactly this point against herself when she argues that the empathetic reader projects her emotional responses onto characters, at least in situations where such projections contribute to the reader's overall interpretation of the story. So I conclude by suggesting that, whatever idea we might have about what is involved in being "in someone else's shoes," I don't think we have any idea at all what it would be like to be "in fictional shoes."[30]

Notes

1   The literature on mental simulation and its connection to folk psychology is well represented by the following anthologies: *Folk Psychology*, eds. Martin Davies and Tony Stone (Oxford: Blackwell, 1995); *Mental Simulation*, eds. Martin Davies and Tony Stone (Oxford: Blackwell, 1995); *Theories of Theories of Mind*, eds. Peter Carruthers and Peter K. Smith (Cambridge: Cambridge University Press, 1996).

2   Murray Smith, *Engaging Characters: Fiction, Emotion, and the Cinema* (Oxford: Oxford University Press, 1995).

3   Alex Neill, "Empathy and (Film) Fiction," in *Post-Theory: Reconstructing Film Studies*, eds. David Bordwell and Noël Carroll (Madison: University of Wisconsin Press, 1996), p. 182. [See also this volume, ch. 16.]

4 Martha Nussbaum, *Love's Knowledge: Essays on Philosophy and Literature* (New York: Oxford University Press, 1990); Wayne C. Booth, *The Company We Keep: An Ethics of Fiction* (Berkeley and Los Angeles: University of California Press, 1988).

5 Neill, "Empathy and (Film) Fiction," p. 186 and *passim*.

6 Jane Heal, "Replication and Functionalism," in *Folk Psychology*, eds. Davies and Stone, p. 47.

7 Arthur Ripstein, "Explanation and Empathy," *Review of Metaphysics* 40 (1987), p. 465.

8 Robert Gordon, "Folk Psychology as Simulation," in *Folk Psychology*, eds. Davies and Stone, p. 62. this point is defended by many others, notably Jerry Fodor and Daniel C. Dennett.

9 Gregory Currie, "Imagination and Simulation: Aesthetics Meets Cognitive Science," in *Mental Simulation* eds. Davies and Stone, pp. 151–69; Neill, "Empathy and (Film) Fiction"; Smith, *Engaging Characters*; Kendall Walton, *Mimesis as Make-Believe: On the Foundation of the Representational Arts* (Cambridge, MA: Harvard University Press, 1990).

10 Alvin Goldman, "Empathy, Mind, and Morals," in *Mental Simulation*, eds. Davies and Stone, p. 189.

11 Susan Feagin emphasizes this, writing that "simply generating the appropriate 'output' does not constitute a simulation; it must be done by sufficiently similar processes" (*Reading with Feeling* (Ithaca, NY: Cornell University Press, 1996), p. 87), adding that this is what makes simulation an instance of *modelling* rather than theorizing (p. 92).

12 Goldman, "Empathy, Mind, and Morals," p. 190.

13 Say that an agent A desires *x* and believes that *y* is a means to *x*. In an ordinary case of practical reasoning, the result would be the action that functions as the conclusion of the syllogism: therefore, agent A *y*s. Simulation effects the following variation. A unique desire (*x*) and a unique belief (that *y* is a means to *x*) are the inputs. The practical reasoning mechanism does whatever computation it does, and the output is the prediction (rather than the actual action): A will *y*. Or we could say, "If I were *A*, I would *y*." Jane Heal's version involves actually doing the deliberating oneself. For both cases, what results is the prediction of a unique action to be performed by the agent whose decision-making we have simulated.

14 A characterization of simulation as an "off-line" mental activity can be found in Stephen Stich and Shaun Nichols, "Folk Psychology: Simulation or Tacit Theory?" in *Folk Psychology*, eds. Davies and Stone, pp. 127–32.

15 This sketch of mental simulation is not far off what Jerry Fodor has called the Very Simple (Belief/Desire) Theory of Mind, in "A Theory of the Child's Theory of Mind," in *Mental Simulation*, eds. Davies and Stone, pp. 110–11. According to the VSTM, only beliefs and desires are recognized as acceptable inputs, and two generalizations cover the calculation: "1. *ceteris paribus* (i.e., in normal circumstances), people act in a way that will satisfy their desires if their beliefs are true" and "2. *ceteris paribus*, people's beliefs are true."

16 Martha C. Nussbaum, "Exactly and Responsibly: A Defense of Ethical Criticism," *Philosophy and Literature* 22, no. 2 (October 1998), p. 373.

17 Peter Lamarque, *Fictional Points of View* (Ithaca: Cornell University Press, 1996), p. 23.

18 Ibid., p. 34.

19 Deborah Knight, "A Poetics of Psychological Explanation," *Metaphilosophy* 28, nos 1–2 (January/April 1996), pp. 63–80.

20 Neill, "Empathy and (Film) Fiction," p. 175.

21 Ibid., p. 182.

22 Jenefer Robinson, "The Expression and Arousal of Emotion in Music," in *Aesthetics: A Reader in Philosophy of the Arts*, eds. David Goldblatt and Lee B. Brown (Upper Saddle River, NJ: Prentice Hall, 1997), p. 227.

23 Feagin, *Reading with Feeling*, p. 96.

24 Ibid., p. 95.

25 Ibid.

26 Ibid., p. 100.

27 Ibid., p. 98.

28 Ibid., p. 83.

29 Ibid., p. 93.

30 I gratefully acknowledge the assistance of the Social Sciences and Humanities Research Council of Canada. Thanks also to various audiences for their interest and responses: at the Society for Cinema Studies, the American Society for Aesthetics, Queen's University, Hull University, and the University of Reading. Special thanks to Peter Lamarque and Carlos Prado for commentaries.

PART VI

Topics in Film Criticism

Introduction

A central area of inquiry in the philosophy of art – and, therefore, in the philosophy of the moving image – is *metacriticism*. As the name "metacriticism" might suggest, its topic is criticism. The metacriticism of film is about film criticism. It concerns, among other things, the concepts film critics either presently employ or should employ in carrying out their activities. That is, in order to criticize (in the sense of analyze) a film, a critic will have to avail herself of various concepts. These include genre concepts, for example.

Crucial to analyzing, interpreting, or making sense of a film involves getting it in the right category. Part of what was going on in Noël Carroll's essay, "Film, Emotion, and Genre," in Part V was his attempt to clarify the concepts – in his case, the emotively grounded concepts – that we use to classify certain films as horror films, suspense films, and melodramas.

In addition to genre concepts, there are a wealth of others that are indispensable to the practice of film criticism. One thing that philosophers of film do is attempt to explicate clearly the criteria that govern the application of the relevant concepts. Authorship and national identity are two important categories that we frequently employ in order to understand films. So they are grist for the philosopher's mill.

Knowing a film is by Ozu alerts the film analyst to be on the lookout for certain recurring patterns and preoccupations. Similarly, being told that a film is by Tarkovsky informs the viewer about what to expect. We teach film connoisseurship, as we do the appreciation of any other artform, by introducing students to the master authors of cinema. That films have authors – or *auteurs*, as directors are often dubbed – has been a cornerstone of film criticism and film pedagogy for over five decades.[1] It is a central concept of film criticism and, therefore, since a primary task of the philosopher of film as metacritic is to illuminate the concepts that make the practice of filmmaking and film appreciation possible, the concept of cinematic authorship is a natural subject for investigation.

In "Cinematic Authorship," Paisley Livingston defines the notion of a cinematic author by means of the idea of an utterance. But Livingston does not only sketch the conditions in virtue of which we designate so-and-so as the author of a film (as opposed to merely the maker of a film). He also defends the concept of a film author against various objections that either (1) would deny that films have authors or (2) would regard anyone with any creative input whatsoever (all the actors, plus set designers, and so forth) as the authors of a film. That is, Livingston wants to show that there can be cinematic authors who are comparable to the authors of novels, despite the fact that films are far more complex to produce and almost always a more collaborative undertaking than a novel is.[2]

When a philosopher in his role as metacritic scrutinizes a concept, he not only analyzes (defines) it, but also addresses any problems that may beset the concept. Because film authorship appears to be so very different from literary authorship, some skeptics are tempted to say that the concept of cinematic authorship applies to nothing. Livingston, after limning the concept of cinematic authorship in terms of the idea of an intentional utterance, then shows that it applies to actual cases – for example, to the filmmaker Ingmar Bergman.[3]

Like authorship, the concept of national cinema is one that has been used perennially to organize thinking about film by critics, viewers, and even filmmakers. Probably even before films were catalogued in terms of their authors – Méliès, Porter, Griffith, Chaplin – they were categorized in terms of their national provenance. Learning that a film was American encouraged certain expectations about what one was going to see, whether one was a critic or a plain viewer. And some filmmakers also nurtured their national identity as a way of marketing their wares in terms of product differentiation.

The concept of national identity is a fundamental category for thinking and talking about film. And like authorship, it too has invited its fair share of skepticism. In a world allegedly going global, isn't the notion of national cinema obsolete? Indeed, even in the past, wasn't the idea somewhat suspect, since it seemed to rest upon the romantic conviction, popularized by Herder, that nations had spiritual essences that shaped the artworks, including films, that expressed them?

In her "National Cinema: The Very Idea," Jinhee Choi essays a careful reconstruction of the category of national cinema, acknowledging that some versions of it are severely flawed, but ultimately showing that it can survive dismissive criticism. She reviews a wide range of ways of understanding the concept and examines the pitfalls of each of them. However, finally, she defends the plausibility of a relational approach to the idea of national cinema.

Film interpretation is arguably a matter of explaining why a film has the elements that it does and why those elements are combined in the way they are.[4] Choi argues persuasively that the nation of origin of a film can play an explanatory role by connecting features of the film to the context of its creation. That is, the national origins of a film may play a causal role in its manner of construction. This may be so for myriad kinds of reasons, including cultural, institutional, and industrial ones. Identifying a film as Italian, or Indian, or Australian, then, can be informative; it can provide highly pertinent information about the way in which a film came to be as it is. This is not to claim that national identity is indispensable in every case of film analysis, or that it tells the whole story. But it may have a contribution to make as part of an overall interpretation of a film. And to the extent that film criticism is interpretive in this sense – committed to explaining

why a film takes the shape it does – classifying a film in terms of its nationality can be immensely informative. To jettison such a concept would be philosophically irresponsible.

Whereas Livingston and Choi might be characterized as refining basic concepts of film criticism that are already widely in use – as taking notions in common usage and distilling and defending their core elements – in his "Morals for Method" George Wilson is, among other things, involved in crafting or constructing certain concepts which, though not currently employed by critics and viewers, would, if adopted, greatly facilitate our understanding of film. The concepts that Wilson introduces are *epistemic distance, epistemic reliability*, and *epistemic alignment*. These concepts, Wilson maintains, will contribute to empowering viewers and critics to apprehend the subtle elaboration of narrative points of view in some of the most accomplished classics in the Hollywood canon.

Concepts enable us to comprehend more clearly the phenomena to which they apply. Thus, it is advantageous to have as sharp an understanding of the concepts we deploy as possible. But the philosopher's preoccupation with concepts is not confined solely to interrogating the concepts already at our disposal in the vocabulary of film criticism. The philosopher may also construct heretofore unvoiced or barely articulated concepts, which, if apposite, will facilitate our understanding of film. This is one way of understanding Wilson's article – as a call for enriching the repertoire of concepts we bring to bear in the criticism and interpretation of Hollywood films.

By saying that a philosopher *constructs* a concept, it is important to avoid the suggestion that the philosopher has *constructed* or invented or, in any other manner, brought into existence the phenomena to which the concept attaches. Articulating the relevant concept, if it is a legitimate one, *discovers* or, at least, highlights phenomena that already exist. A concept throws the spotlight on something that is already there; it does not create something out of nothing. The introduction of new critical concepts should enhance the accuracy of criticism with respect to its object. Such concepts make previously overlooked or ignored features of a film stand out in bold relief. Thus, the concepts Wilson proposes need to be tested against the movies they have been designed to illuminate. Do they pick out discernible features of the films in question and do they make better sense of them than competing conceptual frameworks? Do they, for example, make what might on alternative conceptualizations appear to be anomalies or incoherences explicable?

Just as some conceptual frameworks elucidate the phenomena to which they apply, others may obscure and distort. In "Morals for Method," Wilson argues that the dominant academic framework for the criticism and analysis of Hollywood cinema is conceptually unsuitable for tracking some of the greatest accomplishments of American cinema. Using Colin McCabe as his primary example of contemporary academic film analysis, Wilson especially challenges the prevailing dogma that mainstream movies are always best conceptualized as *transparent* – as effacing the fact that they are intentional constructions and leaving the impression that they are coherent renderings of "how things are." Wilson shows that this notion of transparency obscures what is actually going on in a number of Hollywood masterpieces, while, at the same time, illustrating that that achievement can be brought into focus by the sorts of concepts that Wilson advocates.

Wilson's article, like Livingston's and Choi's, is dialectical. It is involved in an argument with alternative viewpoints. Indeed, in all three cases, the authors of the articles in this section are engaged in disputing some of the leading doctrines of academic film analysis – that there are no cinematic authors, that the notion of national cinema is chimerical, and that Hollywood cinema is transparent. The authors hone the concepts they mean to defend in order to show the superiority of their categories over what is on offer from rival perspectives. In this, they all demonstrate that philosophical clarification does not occur in a vacuum, but through rigorously and critically contrasting one's own proposals with competing views.

Wilson not only contrasts his concepts with McCabe's. He also asks about what the methodology of the metacriticism of film should be. He begins, dialectically, by considering the conception of cinematic metacriticism developed by Brian Henderson in *A Critique of Film Theory*.[5] Wilson notes that Henderson's opinion of the program that cinematic metacriticism should implement is remarkably like the construction of a meta-language in linguistics. Henderson sees the task of the cinematic metacritic to be the isolation of the basic units of cinematic expression and of the combinatory rules that determine their formation into more complex constellations.

This should remind the reader of Gregory Currie's discussion of film as a language in Part II of this anthology. Like Currie, and for similar reasons, Wilson finds the suggestion that our understanding of film might be fruitfully approached by means of a linguistic model to involve grave misunderstandings of both cinema *and* language. Also, like Currie, Wilson believes that the best way to get at the significance of films is to attempt to locate the narrative intentions and purposes of the filmmaker, particularly in terms of the way in which the narrative point of the film is manipulated. This is, in fact, as Currie openly acknowledges, a view that Currie derives from Wilson, rather than vice versa.

Moreover, Wilson maintains that by attending to sophisticated elaborations of cinematic point of view in certain of the Hollywood classics, we will gain insight into our modes of perceiving film, which, in turn, may reveal "our search for closure and coherence in our long-term view of things." Thus, Wilson suggests a philosophical value available through film – a topic to which we will return in the last section of this book – at the same time that he intends to refute the position of McCabe and others that Hollywood filmmaking blinds us to our cognitive and perceptual prejudices.

Because Wilson's piece is the most general one, we have placed it first in this section. However, all three articles can be read as metacritical attempts to fashion and/or refine critical concepts for the purpose of facilitating greater accuracy in film analysis. At the same time, they can also be read as gestures of rehabilitation. Wilson wishes to recuperate some of the achievements of Hollywood cinema by introducing a set of conceptual distinctions that will enable us to follow intricate point-of-view structures where other contemporary film theorists find films posing as "reality narrating itself." Livingston means to rescue the cinematic author from Foucauldian dispersal or worse; and Choi defends the explanatory potential of national cinema. In each case, the conceptual clarification the philosophical metacritic offers functions to save the phenomena in question from neglect and to sustain an appreciation of film in all its diversity.

N.C.

Notes

1 For example, A. Astruc speaks of the *camera pen* in his "Naissance d'une nouvelle avant-garde: La caméra-stylo," in *Ecran Français* (1948), p. 144.

2 This debate originates, I think, because the concept of an author brings to mind the literary author who can, in principle, exert control over every dimension of her product. The poet, for example, is typically thought to be in complete control over her poem. This is not the case of the typical film director in the mainstream, commercial cinema. The creative contributions there flow from many sources – actors, writers, cameramen, and so forth. Thus, standardly neither the film director nor anyone else authors the film in the way that the literary author creates his story from top to bottom.

But perhaps the problem here is calling the filmmaker an author. Would it sound so strained if we said that many films have executive artists – persons (not necessarily the director) who have final say in what is being expressed and how it is being conveyed? After all, artforms other than film are as collaborative – theater, architecture, etc. We may feel that we do not wish to say they have authors, but we have no problem saying that they have executive or controlling artists. Maybe it is just the recent association we have with the word *author* and the notion of exclusive creation that causes the difficulty here. The real issue would appear to be whether films can have executive artists, and, of that, there seems little doubt.

On the other hand, in favor of those who think there is a genuine dispute here that cannot be as facilely dissolved as just suggested, it may be pointed out that the kind of creation under discussion in large part is the creation of meaning where, in turn, the notion of an author does have a just claim to being the concept we intend. What do you think?

3 Of course, there are filmmakers in the avant-garde tradition, like Stan Brakhage, who have utter and complete control of their films virtually in the way in which a poet has control of his poem. Brakhage is the sole creator in some of his films – the camera man, the editor, and even the only actor. Consequently, there is no questioning whether it is possible for there to be authors in film in the same – exclusive creator – sense that there can be in literature. However, the argument is not about cases like Brakhage, but about the more typical, collaborative film. That is why the case of someone like Bergman is more useful for Livingston than the case of a Brakhage would have been.

4 For an elucidation of this view of film interpretation, see the introduction to Noël Carroll's book *Interpreting the Moving Image* (Cambridge: Cambridge University Press, 2000).

5 Brian Henderson, *A Critique of Film Theory* (New York: Dutton, 1980).

19

Morals for Method

George M. Wilson

In a wide variety of classical narrative films, there are central characters whose perception and comprehension of their personal circumstances are shown to be dim, distorted, and severely restricted in relation to their need to see and understand the situations in which they act. The film viewer, from a position outside the relevant fictional world, sees how these characters' ways of apprehending the depicted action collide with the facts that their outlooks have failed to encompass. Thus, the audience is given object lessons in the faltering dynamics of perception over a period of time. However, it is equally the case, and equally important, that many films raise questions about the actual and potential illusions of spectatorship at the cinema. The morals that can be found about perceptual malfunction and misalignment *within* the boundaries of the film also effectively double back upon the viewers themselves. Naturally, the illusions of the film spectator tend to differ from those to which the various film characters succumb, but the revelations about viewer vulnerability are enough to undermine the apparent security of what has probably seemed to be a superior style of judiciously distanced observation. Object lessons about the "privileged" and "innocent" activity of film-mediated perception are therefore offered up as well.

I open with this observation in part because it contradicts a major motif in much structuralist and poststructuralist writing on film. It is often maintained, roughly, that the strategies, forms, and techniques of classical cinematic narrative lock members of an audience into an epistemic position that makes it impossible for them to criticize either their own habits of perception in film viewing or the modes of perceptual intelligence that the films themselves display. (We shall look more carefully at a version of this "prison house of movies" thesis in a moment.) Now, here is one site at which the more limited enterprise of understanding point of view in film can impinge forcefully upon what purports to be a much larger and more basic claim of a general theory of film. For it seems that the plausibility that has been attributed to the claim I have mentioned is almost wholly a function of the grand obscurity with which it is normally formulated combined with a wholesale failure to think through even the limited implications of a minimally adequate account of cinematic point of view. In any case, this is a thesis I wish to develop.[1]

Perhaps it will be helpful here to sketch out some components of narrational perspective which are of central importance to the present discussion. Certainly, it should be obvious from even the following brief outline how a sizeable variety of strategies of film narrative can arise under each of the headings that I will offer.

George M. Wilson, "Morals for Method," *Philosophy and Film*, eds. Cynthia A. Freeland, and Thomas E. Wartenberg (New York: Routledge, 1995): 49–67. This is a revised version of Chapter 10 in Wilson's *Narration in Light: Studies in Cinematic Point of View* (Baltimore: Johns Hopkins University Press, 1986): 191–207. Reprinted by permission of The Johns Hopkins University Press.

The proper viewing of a given film may require that members of its audience be situated at a certain *epistemic distance* from their usual habits of perception and common-sense beliefs. As noted, a spectator who is to achieve even a rudimentary understanding of a segment of film narrative must draw nonstop upon the incredible diversity of perceptual knowledge that we ordinarily and untendentiously assume we have about actual things and processes. This knowledge includes, of course, our more trustworthy beliefs about the nature and operation of the extra-cinematic world and about the ways they manifest themselves to us. It also includes, as a smaller but still important part, our prior knowledge of the techniques and conventions of film narrative and narration. In some films only part of this knowledge is meant to have application to the fictional world portrayed, while other strands of this knowledge are meant to be set in abeyance. It may be crucial to a correct viewing of such a film that our normal belief that things work in such-and-such a way is not fulfilled by *these things* appearing in *this* narrative. The result, when the strategy is successful, may be a view of our world as observed from a distanced metaphysical perspective. Therefore, assumptions about what features of our shared common-sense picture of the world are and are not projectable upon the world as pictured in a given film will help to constitute the viewer's epistemic base.

It is a different matter to inquire after the *epistemic reliability* of a film's narration. As a film proceeds, an audience's understanding of narrative developments depends not only upon its assimilation of the information with which it is directly presented but also upon its grasp of an imposing complex of inferences that it must make, consciously or unconsciously, from the visual manifolds that it is shown. It actually underscores the present point that it is probably impossible to lay down a definite boundary between what is strictly seen and what is merely inferred. A large and complicated part of the function of any film narration is to present immediately just enough material so that the desired inferences will reliably be drawn. But there is always an actual or potential gap between the inferences that will be made and the inferences that would, by some reasonable standard, be justified. Where a substantial disparity exists between the two classes, questions are implied either about the narration's power to construct a satisfactory fictional narrative or about the

audience's acceptance of that power. Any film narration, whether trivial or intricately problematic, is marked by implicit assumptions about the relations between actual and justifiable inferences made on its basis.

Finally, questions can also always be raised about the relations between the information that the audience progressively acquires concerning dramatic issues in the film and the information that one or several characters is shown to possess about the same topic. In other words, our *epistemic alignment* with the characters may vary from case to case. A number of different kinds of relation are possible here, and there are a number of different ways in which the narrative can set them up. As a rule, the audience enjoys an epistemic position superior to that of the fictional agents. The perception of these agents, after all, is confined within a line of narrative action which they cannot survey. However, this advantage may exist in limited respects only, and, in more extreme cases, no significant audience privilege may exist. Once again, the assumptions that underlie these relations of proximity to and distance from the characters help to shape the total way in which they enter the appraising spectator's consciousness. These are examples of questions about the epistemic authority of the film narration. We often can give a general characterization of the kinds of facts about the narrative which the narration is authorized to show, or we can specify certain significant overall constraints that exist upon the way in which that range of facts is shown. The remarks above concern themselves with the authority of the narration defined in relation to the situation of the characters, but, as we shall see, other poles of definition may be used as well.

The types of narrational assumption which are picked out within these three categories are not intended to exhaust the factors that pertain to cinematic point of view. Even allowing for a vagueness in that concept which leaves plenty of room for stipulation about what it is to include, this first, short taxonomy can and should be enlarged.

Let us return now to the view that classical film essentially restricts the epistemic situation of its viewer in a radical and deplorable fashion. Because it is impossible to examine all of the formulations of the view in question, I shall concentrate upon the version that figures centrally in a well-known and influential essay by Colin MacCabe.[2] MacCabe's argument turns upon his explication of a concept of a "classic realist text," a concept that he takes to be exemplified both in the standard nineteenth-century novel and in classical narrative films. The basic conventions of the latter are, according to MacCabe, the descendants of conventions of the former. He states that "a classic realist text may be defined as one in which there is a hierarchy among the discourses which compose the text, and this hierarchy is defined in terms of an empirical notion of truth." (153) Fortunately, this "definition" is partially amplified in connection with literary fiction as follows: "In the classical realist novel the narrative prose functions as a metalanguage that can state all of the truths in the object language – those words held in inverted commas [quotations of the characters' speech] – and can also explain the relation of this object language to the real. The metalanguage can thereby explain the relation of the object language to the world and the strange methods by which the object languages attempt to express truths which are straightforwardly conveyed in the metalanguage." (153)

The misuse of the "metalanguage/object language" distinction in this passage leaves the purported amplification murky, but MacCabe pretty clearly has in mind as "the metalanguage" the sentences of a novel which represent the speech acts of the narrator. (It will include everything except the quoted inner and outer speech of the characters.) Furthermore, what makes a literary text one that is "classic realist" is that its narrator has certain general characteristics. First, it seems that the narrator must be relatively omniscient, having the authority to bring together, reliably and without identification of a source of knowledge, the diverse kinds of material needed to explain the behavior, thoughts, and speech acts (the "discourses") of the characters. Second, because we are told that "the narrative discourse simply allows reality to appear and denies its own status as articulation," the classic realist narrator must be substantially undramatized and unselfconscious about the activity of narration. (154) In other words, when the pseudo-logical and pseudo-metaphysical jargon is cleared away, it turns out that MacCabe is traveling on the more familiar terrain of literary point of view.

Leaving aside all questions about the adequacy of MacCabe's conception of the traditions of the nineteenth-century novel, his presentation of this conception is used to set the conditions that a classic realist text in film must meet. He asks, "does this definition carry over into films where it is certainly less evident where to locate the dominant discourse?" Unsurprisingly, his answer is affirmative.

> It seems to me that it does. . . . The narrative prose achieves its position of dominance because it is in the position of knowledge and this function of knowledge is taken up in the cinema by the *narration* [italics mine] of events. Through the knowledge we gain from the narrative we can split the discourses of the various characters from their situations and compare what is said in these discourses with what has been revealed to us through narration. The camera shows us what happens – it tells the truth against which we can measure discourses. (155)

Consolidating his view, MacCabe adds that "the narrative of events – the knowledge which film provides of how things are – is the metalanguage in which we talk of the various characters in film." (156)

Therefore, the "dominant discourse" of classical film is supposed to be a form of visual narration such that:

1 it yields a form of epistemic access that is superior to the vantage points of the characters,

and

2 it fulfills expected standards of explanatory coherence (explains "how things are" in relation to the characters).

Further, the original stipulation that the dominant narration is defined by "an empirical notion of truth" hints at the idea that

3 it is meant to establish a level of objective truth about the characters and their situations which the viewer is able to discern through ordinary perception and commonsense forms of inference.

That MacCabe envisages something such as condition 3 is supported by the last part of the following remark: "The narrative discourse cannot be mistaken in its identifications because the narrative discourse is not present as discourse – as

289

George M. Wilson

articulation. The unquestioned nature of the narrative discourse entails that the only problem that reality poses is to go and look and see what *Things there are*." (157) Moreover, the earlier part of this quotation (and similar claims in MacCabe's essay) suggest that film narration is classic realist only if:

4   the film does not acknowledge its status as an intentional construction whose function is to depict a world of fiction,

and, related to this,

5   its image track is presented as overall transparent.

Finally, given the necessary existence of the properties described in 1. through 5. in the classic realist text, it follows for MacCabe that films with these properties "cannot deal with the real as contradictory"; and, in addition, they "ensure the position of the subject in a relation of dominant specularity." (157) What these charges amount to is not easy to make out, but the imputed consequences unquestionably sound pernicious.

Throughout his discussion, MacCabe presupposes that all classical narrative films are classic realist texts in the usage he wishes to establish. Indeed, the technical concept is introduced as a means of capturing the essential form and nature of traditional films. This presupposition, combined with his dark allegations about their putative limitations, is the basis of his demand for radically alternative, nonnarrative forms. Nevertheless, none of the five conditions listed above – with one possible exception – is uniformly exemplified even in Hollywood genre films. Let us briefly take up each of these conditions in the stated order.

About condition 1. It is true that most classical films adopt an essentially unrestricted narrational authority and do so in the service of an ideally objective overview of the narratives they portray. However, the predominance of this mode coexists with the option of film narration which operates, in a systematic and principled manner, under one or another global restriction upon what it is authorized to show and, through the editing, to juxtapose. I argue for the need for a theory of a point of view capable of accommodating everything from an extended, directly subjective rendering of a character's field of vision to a wholly unpsychologized schema of selection which mirrors some of the limitations governing human ob-

servation universally. Between these two extremes is a range of intermediate "nonomniscient" possibilities, each of which is notably distinct in its effects and implications from the others. Any framework of restricted narrational authority which has been consciously worked out determines the angle at which the viewer's experience of the film intersects the experience of the film's characters. It therefore helps to define the degree to which the viewer is entitled to assume that the film-mediated information is or is not mediated in turn by a reflected subjectivity or is otherwise conditioned by constraints on access which the other characters may or may not share. Whenever such issues of mediation or contraint occur, the epistemic superiority of the viewer's position is not assured. These issues can be subtle and complex, but MacCabe writes as if this kind of consideration can never seriously arise.

Most classical films satisfy the second condition of explanatory coherence. They have been designed to provide answers to the chief dramatic questions raised by the assorted dilemmas faced by the characters and to accomplish this in a manner that makes the resolutions of these questions definitive and clearly marked as such. And yet, a classically styled movie (such as *You Only Live Once*[3]) may appear on the surface to answer its highlighted questions fully and adequately while, at the same time, revealing in more muted ways that these surface answers ought to be suspect and that a more stable closure is difficult, if not impossible, to supply. When this acknowledgment of explanatory incompleteness is a key factor organizing the film's narration, I call that narration "rhetorically unreliable." The existence of this possibility already violates condition 2. But, alternatively, even when a film does contain the basis of a coherent resolution, it may be that the material that constitutes that basis has not been marked so as to signal overtly the explanatory force it bears. Usually, such a film will offer at least the outlines of a superficial closure, which the implicit explanatory counterstructure is intended to outweigh. In one good sense, this sort of narration is also unreliable, because its more overt gestures of resolution are likely to mislead; its true explanatory coherence will be opaque. It does not matter whether we count this explanatory opacity as violating condition 2 or not. It patently represents a sophisticated epistemic possibility that MacCabe's analysis certainly does not envisage.

The precise import of condition 3 is hard to pin down. MacCabe actually says that the classic realist text "fixes the subject in a point of view from which everything becomes obvious," but, taken literally, this is absurdly too strong. (161) I have supposed, in stating 3, that he means to maintain that whatever significance a classical film presents or expresses is knowable by "obvious" methods of observation and inference. This at least allows that the actual deployment of those methods may be indefinitely complicated. All that is required is that any such method is to be more or less familiar from commonsense practices of belief formation. It does not matter that this condition continues to be extremely vague, because any further specification will still be contravened by films that are epistemically distanced from any commonsense picture of the world that we hold. A film may force us to discover new patterns of perceptual intelligibility in the narrative action it depicts if we are to locate a unifying order and meaning in that action as it nonstandardly unfolds. When we have been distanced from our habitual styles of visual comprehension, it may take a deviant metaphysics or epistemology to yield a satisfactory configuration of sense within the film. Von Sternberg's *The Scarlet Empress* and *The Devil Is a Woman* are striking examples of this strategy.

We really do not need new grounds for rejecting the universal applicability of condition 4. It has already been noted that a film may tacitly acknowledge the inadequacy of some of its surface forms and structures. However, there are films that have characters who stand in some privileged relation to the film narration. Several possibilities of this kind may occur, but one among them is especially important for the topic of cinematic self-reference and self-acknowledgement. That is, a film may contain a character who embodies certain of the leading epistemic qualities of the narration and, thereby, of the implied film maker as well (for example, *Letter from an Unknown Woman*). Or, beyond this, such a character may assume a metacinematic power to which the narrative events appear to respond (*The Devil Is a Woman*). No doubt there are other, similar relationships of characters to film narration to be exploited, but it is difficult to survey the range in a perspicuous way. In any case, it is plain that the presence of a character who is seen as standing in for an implied film maker not only acknowledges the cinematic artifact but permits an elaborate articulation of the nature of that acknowledgment. Condition 4 can

seem an invariant of classical narrative film because the relatively effaced narrational styles of these films and the limitations upon theme and subject matter which they typically observe tend to force the self-consciousness of the narration to appear recessively behind the foregrounded mechanisms of plot. This concession, however, makes it no less a mistake to ignore the striking ways in which self-consciousness can and does occur.

A film whose narration is directly subjective throughout (such as *The Lady in the Lake*) is a counterexample to the last condition of overall transparency of the image track. Still, this sort of counterexample is of marginal interest; the transparency of the image comes closest of the five conditions to being a genuine norm of the traditional cinema. I understand "transparency" to mean that the individual shots of a film are designed to license viewers to take up the impression of having direct perceptual access to the visual appearance of items and events in the fictional world. Naturally, most films that exemplify overall transparency contain shots that do not meet this description, but then these departures from the norm will be suitably flagged and rationalized for what they are. For example, point of view shots from a character's perspective are fairly common, but, within a context of overall transparency, they are presented as direct *quotations*, provided by the narration, of a slice of a character's visual experience. Transparency assures the audience of an extensive base of information, guaranteed to be reliable, about the ways in which the fictional world and its constituents look and sound. Nevertheless, as extensive and important as this reliable foundation generally is, it is, in another way, a quite minimal base of information. Transparency, by itself, does not guarantee that the ambiguities, uncertainties, and outright contradictions that a manifold of appearances may generate over time will be resolved or otherwise explained away. For this reason, transparency potentially leaves open almost all of the issues about what kinds of consistency and intelligibility the appearances given in a film may have. Thus, if transparency is nearly an exceptionless condition of classical narrative film, it is largely because the condition is, in effect, so weak. It is, of course, a feature of many nonclassical, nonnarrative films as well. This relative weakness is often unintentionally obscured in film theory because "transparency" is also used to cover many or all of the first four conditions, but then its proper application is sizably reduced.

For instance, transparency seems thus inflated in MacCabe's essay where phrases such as "the empirical notion of truth" merely blot out the relevant distinctions.

I have tried to show, by this brief overview, how badly MacCabe's idea of a classic realist text distorts and impoverishes the possibilities available in traditional films. Like many other authors, he systematically supposes that the customary surface forms and strategies of these films define the limits of their possible concerns and accomplishments. Indeed, because of the variety of degrees of freedom which surface constraints permit, it is easy to deal rather briefly with the fundamental and supposedly congenital limitations that MacCabe imputes to the normal narrative structures. First, he asserts, as I mentioned in passing, that classical film "cannot deal with the real as contradictory." Once again, one is left to guess at the content of this complaint, but it seems to mean that, because he believes that a classical film always purports to establish an objective and intersubjectively available truth about its fictional history, this aim, he infers, precludes the possibility of exhibiting ways in which that very same history might be perceived from different, deeply conflicting perspectives – perspectives whose differences may be ultimately unresolvable. To this objection, my response is fairly simple: its falsity is demonstrated by a significant range of important films. In certain ways, *You Only Live Once* can be cited as an especially pure counterexample, but, in other instances as well there exists a standard, plot-oriented viewing that contradicts at many crucial points the richer and more challenging viewing that can be set forth.

At bottom, MacCabe and others of a similar persuasion are just confused about the nature and extent of the "objectivity" to which the classical forms are typically committed. Transparency, narrowly understood, is a weak commitment, and the superficial requirements of closure and effacement can be satisfied *only* superficially. Actually, I am tempted to assert the contrary of MacCabe's objection. It is in classical narrative film alone that a more or less determinate fictional history is portrayed by visual narration, which can simultaneously sustain both a salient, standard perspective and a distinct, oblique perspective, both of which may be equally and continuously coherent. Be this as it may, the range of possibilities which MacCabe mistakenly denies is central to what the narrative cinema can mean to us. Presumably, the lessons of alternative perspectives in these films are not un-related to the ways in which we see and comprehend ourselves when we attempt to make a connected narrative out of segments of our own lives and the lives of others.

MacCabe's associated indictment of traditional films is that they "ensure the position of the subject [that is, the viewer] in a relation of dominant specularity." When one first comes across this charge, one feels immediately that dominant specularity is not a position that one, as a sensitive filmgoer, would want to be in. The phrase evokes the picture of a brutish viewer who aggressively glares his films into submission. However, MacCabe's conception is rather the opposite. It is the conception of passive film spectators who, immersed in transparency, allow their perception and understanding of the screen events to be wholly the products of the narrative apparatus. It denotes the relation to film of viewers seduced from the critical use of their perception and understanding by the regimenting dictates of classical narrative and narration. This is the chief target of MacCabe's attack on the classic realist film text, and this passiveness is a phenomenon that merits his rightful, if somewhat overstated, concern. It is not to be denied that normal film viewing is too often intellectually passive and only superficially critical of its object. Far too often conventional films strongly encourage this stolidity and offer few rewards to alertness and analytical reflection. These complaints have over many years acquired the status of truisms, but they are, nonetheless, still true. What is distinctive about the position that MacCabe and other recent theorists occupy is the contention that the forms and strategies of classical film render this situation inevitable – render the practice of the cinema a prison house for the perceptually inert. It is supposed to be in the nature of the forms in question that they forego the possibility of eliciting a radical transformation of vision and a recognition of the vast contingency of the manner in which we ordinarily function as observers of the world. Once again, I can merely repeat that a detailed and rich reading of sample films testifies that these "essentialist" theses are false.

Much poststructuralist writing on film speculates on how it is that subjects are fixed in the position of dominant specularity and on the historical development and ideological consequences of this positioning. Setting aside reservations about how this speculation is usually conducted, I do not question that the specific seductions of the familiar dramatic cinema provide issues to be studied. What I do reject is any theory that makes these seductions a necessary consequence of the forms of classical film and ignores the scattered but triumphant instances that show that this is not the case. If we need a better account of the ideological suasion built into so much commercial film-making, we need just as badly a better account of the flexibility of those forms that make the classical triumphs into concrete, realized possibilities.

Late in his article, MacCabe proposes that "the method of representation (the language, verbal and cinematic) determines in its structural activity . . . both the places where the object 'appears' and the point from which the object is seen. It is this point which is exactly the place allotted to the reading subject." (160) Here, first of all, is yet another endorsement of the odd, unargued brand of formalist determinism to which I object. More important, however, is the explicitness with which it is maintained in this passage that a source of that determinism is the view that the fictional objects and events in a film and the ways in which they appear to a viewer are the results of the "*structural activity*" of the *languagelike elements* that are said to make up a film's narration. Of course, this is an established motif in much film theory of a vaguely structuralist orientation, but sheer repetition has hardly made its import less elusive.

This is not the place to examine the long and unhappy history of the notion of a language of film. Its manifestations are too numerous and too diverse; its confusions are too deeply entangled. Nevertheless, I think it is possible to say enough to shake the conviction that any sort of formalist determinism is supported by the methodological premise that representation in film is fundamentally a function of structural determinants of a quasi-linguistic kind. This conviction and its would-be basis set an agenda for theory of film which excludes the sorts of film criticism and approaches to theory which I have attempted to promote.

It will be helpful, in this context, to turn to a theorist who is more self-conscious about his assumptions and arguments and who is less tendentious in his aims than MacCabe. Brian Henderson, in his book *A Critique of Film Theory*, offers a revealing summary statement of what he counts as the domain of film theory. The reader is told that it encompasses questions about "the relations between film and reality, the relations between

film and narrative, and the question whether film is a language and, if so, what kind of language. Related to these questions is *the even more fundamental one of determining the basic units of film (and of film analysis) and the rules governing the combination of these units*" [italics mine].[4] Subsequently, long sections of *A Critique* are devoted to criticism of Christian Metz's attempts, in his early work, to identify "basic units of film" and their "rules of combination."[5] Throughout his book, Henderson's own seemingly a priori commitment to this type of implausible analytical atomism never wavers. His most extreme expression of this Democritean enthusiasm is found in the following passage: "Each [film theory] should provide a comprehensive model of cinematic units at all levels and of the modes of combination and interaction at each level. In short, a film theory should provide concepts, terms, and dynamic models of interaction for the analysis of cinematic parts and wholes of all kinds."[6] This reads, at first, like an invigoratingly ambitious prolegomena to a new, more objective, more scientific theory of film, until one pauses to wonder what scientific discipline could conceivably aim at such an enterprise. We would not even have the theory of the simple pendulum if physicists, in considering, for example, the grandfather clock, had demanded of themselves "dynamic models" of its various "components" at every "level" of (possible?) analysis. We probably would not have grandfather clocks. Finding fruitful and manageable questions in a given area of thought is usually at least as hard as finding answers to those questions. Symptomatically, one is hard-pressed to locate in Henderson's book a set of specific phenomena *derived from real films* which film theory is supposed to explain. Rather, it is flatly assumed from first to last that a general and largely unconstrained inquiry after "units," "rules," and "models" is well-conceived and valuable.

Naturally, the difficulty here is not that there is a lack of parts and wholes in film; everything in a film is a part and a whole of some kind for some analytical purpose. The difficulty, at least in the first instance, is that we are never informed what the cinematic units are units *of* or what general types of rules or laws of combination are supposedly at stake. Presumably, if these units and rules are to play a role within a systematic account of cinematic content (and, after all, this seems the goal), then the units are to be units of meaning (in some sense appropriate to film) and the rules are to be projective rules that determine the meaning of a "combination" from the meanings of its constituent units and the structural relations that the combination embodies. Admittedly, it is hard to be certain of even this much, because we are never given a single example of the hypothesized units or the associated rules, and we are never given any evidence that film narration comes in honest units that generate larger narrational complexes in accordance with determinate projective rules. Still, as noted, at least this construal of Henderson's remarks offers his conception a kind of theoretical role to play which he and MacCabe and a host of other kindred spirits so often deploy. Indeed, *if* the resulting conception had some substance, it might give a basis to that formalist determinism that MacCabe has been seen to favor. Limits to the expressive power of the putative film "language" – the "language" of classical film perhaps – would presumably set the limit to what such film can show. This, I think, is the idea that MacCabe has accepted.

With just this much set out, let us bypass the whole question of locating a conception of cinematic meaning which has promise of being subject to the type of theory envisaged, and let us not concern ourselves about the form that the projective laws or rules might have. (Needless to say, I believe that we are simply bypassing a hopeless morass in each case.) Rather, I want to focus upon a pair of more general assumptions which are engendered here and do their work in tandem. The first is that it *is* possible to segment a film (at least at a given "level") into visual and aural "units" whose "interaction" gives structure and content to the film as a whole. The second is that such a segmentation is epistemically prior to interpretation and forms the core of the evidential basis for whatever interpretation may ensue. It is this second assumption that provides the principal rationale for supposing that the truth of the first assumption would offer a useful foundation for film analysis and theory. Certainly from the two assumptions together, it follows that it is essential to an adequate theory of film that it provide an account of admissible modes of segmentation. Taken together, these assumptions define a kind of formalist foundationalism with respect to meaning in films. Other less "linguistic" versions are doubtlessly possible, but the present formulation encapsulates a conception that many, consciously or subliminally, have found compelling. It yields, in any case, an explicit statement of a methodo-

logical view with which I am at odds. The explicit statement permits a direct marshalling of the main grounds for repudiating this view and others of its ilk.

It is implausible to suppose that narrative, plot, or basic story line can be construed as a "level" where these assumptions fit. This point leaves open the possibility that films can be sliced along other dimensions that would yield a simple level more amenable to the project of segmentation. However, even this vague possibility seems foreclosed by suitable reflection on an example like the striking series of three shots from *The Lady from Shanghai*.[7] The shots are these: a truck pulls out in front of a car containing two men; a woman's hand presses a button; the car crashes into the truck. In viewing this segment, one has the impression that the pressing of the button causes the crash. We attribute, immediately and without conscious inference, a causal connection between the two events. If we think about segmenting this three-shot progression, two very broad possibilities arise:

(1) The onset and culmination of the accident constitute an independent segment crosscut with an unrelated segment showing the woman's action. The impression of causality is to be discounted as inadvertent and irrelevant to the content of the film.

(2) The whole series is a unified segment showing the button pressing to be a cause of the crash. If a shot of a cannon firing were followed by a shot of an explosion, we would view this pair of shots as showing cause and effect: the cannon's hitting a target would be an event in the film. In our present example, it is merely that the apparent causal connection is a good deal less familiar.

Now, how might one reach a decision between (1) and (2)? Surely, nothing in the three shots themselves – no interaction of units into which this series might be analyzed – will settle the matter. It is just this fact that initially makes (1) and (2) genuine alternatives. At the same time, this does not mean that there is no way in which the choice can be settled at all. I would contend that (2) is correct by showing how the attribution of strange causal powers to the woman is systematically integrated with her peculiar role in the surrealistic context of this unusual film. Obviously, this contention would depend upon a careful and detailed interpretation of *The Lady from Shanghai*, and it does not matter for present purposes whether the argument would be sound. The moral is that it is impossible to resolve a question of segmentation as elementary as the choice between (1) and (2) independently of a thorough analytical viewing of the total film. In this extreme but instructive case, we cannot even identify the *simpler fictional occurrences* in the film without an appeal to the widest framework that contains the problematic three shots. If this is so, then it must be a mistake to believe or hope that segmentation can be treated as prior to, and foundational for, interpretation. In general, the way in which we will be inclined to divide a stretch of film into "interacting levels and units" will rest on large problems about how narrative, narration, and associated aspects of structure are to be construed. The analytical atomism conveyed by the description of film theory given by Henderson ought to be replaced by a lively, reiterated sense of the holistic character of all interpretive work.

The considerations that underlie the general force of this example are these. In everyday perception, we often judge directly that one observed event has caused another, but the immediate perceptual data that elicit that judgment from us are substantially inadequate to give it conclusive grounds. Furthermore, we do not, upon reflection, believe otherwise: we readily grant that, in making the judgment, we have drawn upon a large and somewhat indeterminate mass of background belief about the world. The same is true when we judge that we have seen one and the same physical object at distinct times or that we have observed different stages of a single, continuous movement through space. In short, we do not imagine in any of these cases that such rudimentary and basic judgments are derived from our immediate visual experiences by means of projective rules that take features of that experience as their input. Indeed, it is implausible to suppose otherwise.

But then, why should the situation be essentially altered when what we have been "given" is a series of shots showing events that appear to be causally linked or a series that appears to show the same object or the same temporally extended movement photographed from different times and places? Here also, it is certain that the direct connections and re-identifications that we make are heavily conditioned by our preestablished beliefs about the film world, the actual world, and standing relations between the two. As in actual perception, these judgments about the content of the film will normally not be the rule-governed upshot of features depicted within the shots. Finally, if these considerations are correct – if even our rock-bottom judgments about the *identity of objects and events* within a film fail to satisfy the model of units and structural laws – then it is hard to grasp how more sophisticated judgments about filmic content and significance can reasonably be expected to satisfy the model either. The example from *The Lady from Shanghai* is useful because of the intuitive simplicity of the content in question. It thereby illustrates the hopelessness of finding some more fundamental "level" where the projective account might finally take purchase on the film. That is, the example demonstrates clearly and decisively that basic narrative events cannot, in general, be units *or* functions of units in the sense required, and once this is made salient no more simple level is to be found.

The objection that I have been sketching reflects the existence of a deep division about the relations between theory of film and film criticism, a division that is too deep, no doubt, to be settled by these brief remarks. In a passage that Henderson repeats twice in his book, he says, "film theory is, after all, a metacriticism or philosophy of criticism. It is pursued to improve film criticism through the determination of basic film categories and the identification of those assumptions about film on which any criticism is based...[F]ilm theory itself is the continued improvement and clarification of the principles and assumptions of film criticism."[8] It is instructive to set these assertions alongside a passage from Stanley Cavell's *The World Viewed*:

> The aesthetic properties of a medium are not givens. You can no more tell what will give significance to the unique and specific aesthetic possibilities of projecting photographic images by thinking about them or seeing some, than you can tell what will give significance to the possibilities of paint by thinking about paint or looking some over. You have to think about painting, and paintings; you have to think about motion pictures. What does this "thinking about them" consist in? Whatever the useful criticism of an art consists in.[9]

Clearly, I am sympathetic to much of what Cavell here suggests. In particular, I am inclined to see theory of film not as providing the foundations for criticism, but as more or less continuous with that which is most searching, articulate, explicit, and self-reflective *within* criticism. Moreover, these alternatives are not to be represented, as they often are, as a choice between rigorous methodology and impressionistic dabbling. Rigor, in any reasonable sense, and impressionism occur on both sides. For example, we have seen something in this paper of the speciousness of the claims to rigor made in the name of various structural hypotheses. The antifoundationalist sentiments I have expressed are not meant to be justified definitively by the present discussion, but I hope to have issued effective warning that the pretensions of first philosophy are as tempting and dangerous in the study of film as they have been in other fields of thought.

As indicated earlier, I believe that film theory needs to develop a minimally adequate account of point of view in the narrative cinema.[10] More specifically, I assume that point of view in film can be specified in terms of a set of assumptions about how the viewer is epistemically situated in relation to the narrative. Or, following Gerard Genette, we could just as well say that point of view is based upon the various ways in which information about the narrative is *systematically regulated* throughout all of or large segments of the narration.[11] Just as a theory of point of view in literature explores the broader systematic relationships that can hold between an activity of fictional telling and the fictional situations that are told, so a theory of point of view in film should study fictional activities of showing and their relations to the shown. Literary theory should be more than an inventory of strategies; it should explicate the ways in which the different strategies raise different problems about what the activity of narrative comprehension can and cannot achieve. Similarly, different narrational strategies in film differ in their implications for perceptual comprehension in any of a host of ways. Since verbal telling and cinematic showing are such very different narrational procedures, the issues that get raised in each case are not at all identical. Nevertheless, a network of substantial but limited analogies exists. The importance of point of view considerations in film and literature are much the same. The forms of narration in question substantially help to define the orientation of the viewer or reader in apprehending the fictional world of the work and thereby fix some of the most general attributes that diverse narrative elements are understood to have. Further, it is not only the apprehension of matters within the narrative that can be formed or altered in this way. One's perception of film or literature as mechanisms of narrative portrayal can also be reshaped at the same time. I assume that the power of techniques of point of view to transform the reading of a novel or short story are well-known, but the extent and depth of this power in films has not been adequately appreciated. There are reasonably determinate narrational structures that underlie the kind of global shift of prospect that I have stressed. These structures can be described and discussed in a style that makes plain their relevance to familiar issues about the quirky interplay of human perception and the world.

This approach has as its principal recommendation that such distinctions genuinely help to capture the rationale behind the works of film makers as diverse as Ford and von Sternberg, Lang and Ophuls, Renoir and Nicholas Ray. There may be other ways of stating the same or similar observations about the relevant films, but, at a minimum, these categories are not merely idling in the realm of the a priori: they accomplish straightforward and needed tasks. Also, even in their restricted generality, they serve to open up and enhance our sense of the epistemic possibilities of classical film. This can be a mixed blessing, because the implications that a broadened sense uncovers tends to lack theoretical tidiness and elegance and make the grander ambitions of theory more difficult to satisfy. Still, this situation is preferable to one in which an ambitious but too simple theory, such as MacCabe's, has swept the less predictable and more interesting possibilities out of sight from the beginning.

However, if assorted film theories have sinned in their treatment or lack of treatment of epistemic matters in film, more intuitive approaches have hardly fared better. A lot of film criticism and analysis whose theoretical concerns are negligible have been more than ready to make use of general epistemological concepts and dichotomies, impressing them in an ad hoc fashion on the films they scrutinize. It is, for instance, a cliché of film criticism to announce that a certain work deals with matters of "appearance and reality." No doubt this assessment is often enough correct, but the formula is simultaneously too weighty and too slight to characterize the questions about perception and knowledge which a reasonably sophisticated film propounds. The formula fails utterly to discriminate between the bleak investigations of cinematic manipulation in *You Only Live Once* and the more light-hearted self-consciousness about cinematic transparency in *North by Northwest*. It does nothing to help conceptualize the difference between Ophuls' delicate and distanced portrayal of Lisa's private world of fantasy in *Letter from an Unknown Woman* and von Sternberg's rendering of a public world in *The Devil Is a Woman*, whose very substance seems made of the most private fantasies of the film maker. The stereotyped characters and conclusion of *Rebel Without a Cause* are likely to be dismissed as the illusions of a simplifying social cinema unless it is noticed that the film's true closure is the expression of a cultural determinism that mocks our bland "reading" of stereotypes our social order presses upon us. The rhetorical strategies that inform these films and guide our experience of them are nuanced and complex, and an analysis of any one of them in terms of "appearance and reality" could only blunt an effort to describe the methods and issues at stake.

This stricture is or ought to be obvious, but it has apparently been less obvious that other very broad distinctions have been equally inflated and correspondingly impoverished. Talk of "first-person" and "third-person" film narration invites recurrent confusion, and the related pair, "subjective" and "objective," fares no better. It should also be clear that an opposition between "the transparency of classical narration" and "the reflexivity of modernist narration" is seriously misconceived, and that divisions of film narration into "omniscient" and "perspectival," "closed" and "open," "personal" and "impersonal," and so forth are bound to be grossly inadequate to the distinctions that fruitful film analysis requires. Admittedly, no taxonomy of point of view in film will yield a set of categories which cleanly carves up the domain of individual films, assigning to each its perfectly apt classification. Nevertheless, it is fair to expect that a minimally satisfactory

account will contain categories that are enlightening when we set out to think through a film of at least moderate intricacy. This requirement entails that any such taxonomy will have to be derived from an examination of the variety of epistemic factors which comes into play when film narration provides a determinate form of perceptual access to a connected series of narrational events. These factors, taken singly and in combination, can be realized in many ways, and it is the most central of these possibilities which the classifications of the point of view I have introduced are intended to designate. I am sure that these categories need to be extended and, in some cases, revised, but the objective has been to offer a perspicuous setting for the process of reconsideration to begin.

To my mind, the chief advantage of looking at the concept of cinematic point of view is that this approach places that concept in immediate conjunction with undeniably interesting questions about what we see and how we comprehend when we watch narratives in film. Many of these questions about how we operate in apprehending film stories have, quite naturally, interested most of the best film makers as well. Their work constitutes a heritage of reflection on film which has been registered in film, and it is important to retain that heritage and value it properly. There is, I believe, no art other than the cinema which has a comparable capacity to reconstruct analytically and thereby explicate the possible modes of perceiving a localized slice of human history as an evolving field of visible significance. Classical narrative film, in particular, engenders and investigates possible modes of seeing a pattern in the events of such a history – a pattern that yields, either genuinely or speciously, "the sense of an ending." It models, in this way, our search for closure and coherence in our long-term view of things. A theory of point of view in film, as I conceive it, is a theory of these reconstructed forms of being witness to the world.

Notes

1 This article is a revised version of chapter 10 of George Wilson's *Narration in Light* (Baltimore and London: The Johns Hopkins University Press, 1986); used by permission of the author and the publisher.

2 Colin MacCabe, "The Classic Realist Text," *Screen* 15, no. 2, 152–62, reprinted with omissions in *Realism and the Cinema*, ed. Christopher Williams (London: Routledge and Kegan Paul, 1980), 152–62. All page citations in the text are to this volume.

3 All of the films mentioned in this discussion are analyzed at length in *Narration in Light*.

4 Brian Henderson, *A Critique of Film Theory* (New York: E. P. Dutton, 1980), 3–4.

5   The relevant early work is found in Christian Metz, *Film Language: A Semiotics of the Cinema*, trans. Michael Taylor (New York: Oxford University Press, 1974).

6   Henderson, *A Critique of Film Theory*, p. 5.

7   I have deliberately simplified the description of this sequence from *Lady from Shanghai*. The three shots referred to constitute a part – the crucial part – of a somewhat longer series of shots. I have simplified in this way in order to avoid irrelevant complexity, and, I believe, the material that I have ignored does not affect the points that I am trying to establish. For a much longer and extremely interesting discussion of the issues raised by this specific sequence, see Edward Branigan, *Narrative Comprehension and Film* (London: Routledge, 1992), 39–56.

8   Henderson, *A Critique of Film Theory*, 49.

9   Stanley Cavell, *The World Viewed* (New York: Viking Press, 1971), 31.

10 The following paragraph is excerpted, with omissions, from chapter 5 of *Narration in Light*, 99–101.

11 Gerard Genette, *Narrative Discourse*, trans. Jane E. Lewin (Ithaca: Cornell University Press, 1980), 162.

20

Cinematic Authorship

Paisley Livingston

Authorship has long been a controversial topic in cinema studies. A central question is whether a 'traditional' conception of authorship should be applied to the cinema, or at least to some significant corpus of films. Although a positive response to that question helped to motivate the inclusion of film studies in the academic curriculum in the 1960s, current scholarly opinion tends to favour the idea that a traditional conception of authorship is not applicable to the cinema, either because this conception is simply false, or because authorship in film is fundamentally different from literary and other forms of authorship. Although author studies are still written and published, it is generally held that the work of an individual film-maker is best understood as figuring within a larger social process, system, or structure, be it a discursive, institutional, national, or international one. Some scholars allow that authorship obtains in instances of independent film production, but not in cases of studio-produced works. Yet even this thesis is controversial, and debate over the topic of authorship continues.

One shortcoming of many discussions of authorship is that insufficient attention is paid to the problem of analysing the 'traditional' conception of authorship that is supposed to be at stake in these debates. Often it seems to be wrongly taken on faith that we already have a strong, shared understanding of what this traditional conception of authorship entails. This shortcoming is apparent in the writings of both anti-individualists and individualists, for neither the champions of 'the great directors' nor the students of system and structure have provided detailed elucidations of the concept of authorship. The current chapter seeks to remedy this situation by doing some conceptual spadework. Section 1 looks at authorship in general and surveys some different strategies of definition. I describe and advocate one well-entrenched way of construing the term and point to some of the problems inherent in alternative approaches. Section 2 turns to the cinema and asks whether there are any good reasons why this notion of authorship is not applicable. I focus on the kinds of cases that are often thought to make authorship especially problematic in film, namely, those involving 'industrial' modes of production characteristic of commercial, mass-market cinema. Individual authorship, I claim, does obtain in some such cases, and I discuss the conditions under which this occurs. Section 3 provides a brief discussion of the contrast between anti-realist and realist conceptions of authorship, focusing on the common claim that the cinema is especially suited to the former.

In order to try to forestall some predictable misreadings, let me state at the outset that my goal in what follows is not to defend the idea that solitary artistic genius is the fundamental unit of all valuable cultural analysis. I do, however, maintain that an understanding of individual agency is crucial to the latter. I hold that many films emerge

Paisley Livingston, "Cinematic Authorship," *Film Theory and Philosophy*, eds. Richard Allen and Murray Smith (New York: Oxford University Press, 1997): 132–48. Reprinted by permission of Oxford University Press.

from a process of collective or individual authorship; others may have makers, but no author(s) – at least in the sense I elucidate.

1 What is an Author?

Ordinary usage of 'author' (and of cognate terms in other languages) is today extremely diverse. People are said to be the authors of such disparate items as letters, schemes, mischief, disasters, poems, philosophical treatises, cookbooks, someone's demise, instruction manuals, and so on, and the conditions under which one can become an author of such things are anything but simple. The diversity is even greater if we turn to earlier English usage, including those times when the 'traditional' conception of literary authorship supposedly got constructed and reigned supreme. According to the *Oxford English Dictionary*, both Alexander Pope and William Thackeray would have allowed that one's father could also be called one's author. 'Author' could refer not only to a writer, but to that person's writings. The editor of a periodical was its author. And in another now obsolete usage, 'author' designated the person on whose authority a statement was made, such as an informant.[1]

In light of such diverse usage, if the term 'author' is to serve as a helpful descriptive or explanatory tool in a context of systematic enquiry and scholarly debate, we need a consensus on a more limited and cogent usage. The absence of such a consensus, accompanied at times by a false belief that such a consensus in fact obtains, has fuelled confusion in the theoretical literature on authorship.

An example is the case of Michel Foucault's influential essay on authorship. Many readers of that essay have been surprised to be told that ordinary personal letters (i.e. not those of Madame de Sévigny) have writers, but not authors: 'Une lettre privée peut bien avoir un signataire, elle n'a pas d'auteur; un contrat peut bien avoir un garant, il n'a pas d'auteur. Un texte anonyme que l'on lit dans la rue sur un mur aura un rédacteur, il n'aura pas un auteur.'[2] Yet in everyday French and English, the writer of a letter or contract is its author. When a French schoolteacher finds an insulting slogan painted on the wall outside the schoolyard, 'Qui en est l'auteur?' is a question she may well ask, in spite of Monsieur Foucault's stipulation to the contrary. Yet it also seems clear that Foucault

did not think he was arbitrarily stipulating a new meaning for 'auteur'; on the contrary, he appears to claim that his technical usage corresponds to a real phenomenon, the 'author-function' as constructed in early modern Europe. Foucault hoped to focus attention on the historical emergence of some particular ways of treating texts, ways which are not, he claimed, either natural or necessary. He also wanted to promote some alternative ways of relating to texts. Although these motives may have been admirable, the flaw in Foucault's strategy is that the initial conceptual and verbal stipulation in fact vitiates the historical analysis (e.g. by wrongly stressing discontinuity where continuity is in fact more relevant). Given the many important counter-examples (ranging from Horace and Petrarch to Furetière, La Croix du Maine, and Du Verdier), we may conclude that authorship neither begins nor ends where Foucault says it does.[3]

Where, then, does authorship begin and end? Authorship may be a fuzzy concept, but it would be helpful to have a better sense of the spectrum on which it is to be located. What is wanted is a semi-technical notion of authorship that avoids at least some of the confusion and ambiguity of ordinary language without merely stipulating a usage that is theoretically self-serving or historically inaccurate. The failure to find such a notion makes theoretical debate over authorship in cinema a sterile game. Do we want to claim that films never have authors? Then let 'author' refer to the unmoved mover who is alone responsible for every property a film has, and it follows that no film has an author. Do we want to claim that films always have authors? Then let 'author' refer to anyone who plays any sort of causal role in endowing a film with any of its properties, and the authors of any given film become as numerous as the figures in a medieval master's picture of the Last Judgement.

As an attempted remedy to this situation, I shall sketch a provisional definition of 'author' as a term of art in critical enquiry. This definition is meant to occupy the middle ground between the two extremes just evoked, and should help set the stage for an exploration of authorship in the cinema. Consider, then, the following very broad (but not the broadest possible[4]) construction:

author = (def) the agent (or agents) who intentionally make(s) an utterance, where 'utterance' refers to any action, an intended function of which is expression or communication.

Such a definition is inscribed within, and relies upon, a very widespread and commonplace schema of agency and communication, the philosophical analysis of which is a well-developed yet ongoing project.[5] Some remarks on this definition's basic rationale are nonetheless in order. According to this broad definition, anything that is not an agent, that is, anything that is not capable of action, cannot be an author. For an action to occur, a system's (e.g. an organism's) behaviour must be oriented and proximally caused by that system's meaningful attitudes, such as its desires, beliefs, and intentions. Thus, if a computer is not capable of genuine action because it literally has no meaningful attitudes, then it cannot be an author, even though some of the configurations on its monitor are highly meaningful for some interpreter. The same would be true of the meaningful noises made by a parrot, as long as the bird does not intend to express or convey any attitudes by means of its sentence-like squawks. Expression, which is a matter of articulating or manifesting one's attitudes in some medium, need not be sincere, original, or even skilful for an instance of authorship to occur, but authorship does entail that the expressive utterance is an intentional action.[6] We are not, then, the authors of our dreams or of things muttered in our sleep, because these are not utterances.[7] Communication differs from simple expression in that the agent not only intends to make an attitude manifest, but tries to get this attitude, as well as the relevant intentions, recognized by some audience in the right sort of way. In saying that expression or communication is *an* intended function of an utterance, we allow that the author can act on other kinds of intentions when making an utterance. For example, a speaker can simultaneously intend to make his belief known while also hoping to impress his hearers with a display of eloquence. Note as well that the broad definition allows that more than one agent could be the maker of a single utterance: an utterance can have a collective author. For example, John and Mary jointly draft a letter, or make a video, to send holiday greetings and news to their parents. Finally, it should be pointed out that utterances need not be linguistic: 'utterance' is meant to designate any number of different expressive or communicative actions *or products thereof*, assuming that such products (e.g. objects or artefacts) are identified with reference to the relevant features of their context of production.[8] In the Daimonji Gozan Okuribi festival held in

August in Kyoto, huge fires outlining Kanji characters blaze on the slopes of five mountains surrounding the city. The intentional burning of these rather large, fiery words constitutes an utterance following the proposed definition. Fires of the same size and shape accidentally caused by a stroke of lightning would not.

The broad definition of 'author' just surveyed allows that most people are authors a lot of the time simply by virtue of performing unremarkable expressive and communicative actions. The intuitive basis of this approach is simple and, I think, provides good reasons for preferring this definition over other possible ones. We want to be in a position to say, for example, that some of our intentional doings are not a matter of authorship because there is no expressive intent behind them. Utterances, however, belong to a different category. And it makes sense to think that one is the author of one's utterances, even when they are a matter of the most ritualized morning greetings, because one exercises a significant degree of direct control over such behaviour and because one is, as the proximate causal source of that behaviour, in some sense responsible for it. Saying something at what one deems to be an appropriate moment, as opposed to saying some other phrase or nothing at all, is normally something one does on purpose, even if this action does not result directly from an episode of careful, conscious deliberation; to perform such an action intentionally, it is necessary to activate one's linguistic and social know-how. But to be the author of a particular utterance of 'Good morning' addressed to one's co-workers, one need not have invented the phrase or the social practice it fulfils. The broad usage of 'author' I have identified belongs, then, to a pragmatic framework in which the term is used to pick out the agent or agents who function as the proximate cause of utterances conceived of as intentional, expressive actions. Such a pragmatic framework can, of course, be the subject of sceptical doubts and eliminitivist counter-proposals, but it nonetheless remains a deeply entrenched, valuable, and arguably indispensable schema of interaction. It is, moreover, a schema that we frequently apply in discussions of the arts.[9]

In spite of such considerations in favour of a broad notion of authorship, some critics and theorists promote a narrower definition, such as one having nothing to do with utterances, or one restricted to some subset of utterances, such as literary (and other) works of art. The danger with this kind of approach, however, is that such stipulations appear implausible in the light of obvious counter-examples. It is arbitrary and purely stipulative to say that banal, non-artistic utterances have no authors, or to claim that great literary works have authors while pieces of pulp fiction do not. Another problem with such stipulations is that some strong version of aesthetic or hermeneutic intentionalism is built into the very definitions of 'utterance' and 'authorship'. Thus something's being an utterance is deemed equivalent to its having a meaning entirely determined by its author, and to be an author is held to be equivalent to the determination of an utterance's meaning.[10] Others, who oppose this sort of intentionalism, accept that this kind of strong or absolute intentionalism is entailed by authorship, and they deem it important to attack authorship as part of their opposition to that doctrine. It is crucial to see, however, that the cogency of such attacks depends entirely on the soundness of the prior assumption whereby authorship entails some form of overly strong intentionalist constraint on interpretation. If one recognizes that an utterance can be both intentionally produced by someone and have meanings that are not all and only those intended by that person, then it follows that strong intentionalism is not entailed by a broad conception of authorship. We can identify someone as the author of an utterance without having to say that that person has authored each and every meaning (or significance) that the utterance manifests.

Even if my objections to some of the alternatives are granted, it should be recognized that the broad definition just sketched hardly answers all of our questions about authorship. One may argue, for example, that while such a notion is cogent, it does not follow that literary and non-literary conceptions of authorship do not differ fundamentally. And it is the latter, and not the former, that provides the object of Foucauldian and other critiques. Do not the very conditions of *literary* authorship involve social factors that transcend the schemata of individualist pragmatics? An analogous argument focusing on the case of cinema will be taken up in the next section.

2 What is a Cinematic Author?

A first step in a straightforward approach to the definition of cinematic authorship is to adopt the broad notion of authorship proposed above while replacing 'utterance' with 'cinematic utterance'. One could add that, roughly speaking, an utterance is a cinematic one just in case the agent or agents who produce it employ photographic (and other) means in order to create an apparently moving image projected on a screen (or other surface).[11] Yet even if we assume that this is essentially the right approach to establishing the boundary between utterances in general and cinematic utterances, we must still address ourselves to a serious challenge, which runs as follows. Although the film medium is sometimes employed in ways covered by an everyday pragmatic notion of authorship, the cinema as a large-scale social phenomenon (e.g. the cinema *qua* institution or group of interrelated institutions and social systems) transcends that notion. It is one thing to speak of some individual being the author of the home movie he sent to his parents on the occasion of his father's birthday, but something else entirely to think of Fred Zinnemann or his collaborators as the author(s) of *High Noon* (a Stanley Kramer production that premiered in 1952). Not only does the actual nature of the process of production differ fundamentally in these two kinds of cases, but facts about the distribution and reception of the two utterances make it incorrect to apply the same conception of authorship to them. It is far from obvious how the idea of 'intentionally making an utterance' is to be applied in the case of a film to which many different people have made a number of significantly different contributions. Is Ned Washington, who wrote the lyrics for the ballad heard on the soundtrack, one of the authors of *High Noon*? Can or should an audience react to a Hollywood film the same way that the father responds to the home movie made by his son, that is, with many features of the author's context, character, aims, and activities in mind? The claim, then, is that the making and reception of commercially produced, feature-length films is complex in ways that are obscured by an everyday notion of expressive and communicative action, and thus a concept of authorship based on the latter is seriously misleading with regard to such works, which is what happens when one insists, for example, on thinking of the director as the author of the film.

In response to such an argument, it is important to note that the director is not always the author of an industrially produced motion picture. Only sometimes does a director's role in the productive process warrant the idea that he or she is the film's author. It may be useful to add that some industrially produced films are not accurately viewed as utterances having an author or authors because it is possible that no one person or group of persons intentionally produced the work as a whole by acting on any expressive or communicative intentions. The film may be the unintended result of disparate intentional and unintentional activities, in roughly the same way a traffic jam is the unintended and unwanted 'perverse effect' of many individual drivers' purposeful and accidental behaviour. The same, however, could be said of some small-scale, non-industrial cinematic artefacts, such as ill-begotten and accidental stretches of 'home movie'. The live issue, then, is not whether all films necessarily do or do not have authors in the broad sense introduced above, for it seems clear that they do not. The question, rather, is whether the kind of authorship we have in mind is absent in *all* (or even many) mass-produced commercial films.

As David Bordwell and Kristin Thompson put it, 'The question of authorship becomes difficult to answer only when asked about studio production', or more generally, about what they refer to as 'serial manufacture'.[12] Serial manufacture as they describe it is a process that resembles mass manufacture on an assembly line because it has a similar hierarchical division of labour. The difference, however, is that the final product is not a replica of a single prototype, but in some sense a unique film, even when it is a derivative instance of a familiar genre. In this mode of production, specialists with a striking variety of skills and tasks collaborate to create a unique final product. Amongst these specialists are figures who exercise control and provide guidance in function of a more or less schematic overall plan, which may or may not be known to the other contributors. Under what conditions does the product of serial manufacture have an author or authors, and what are the distinguishing features of authorship in such a context? In order to develop and illustrate my response, I shall sketch some 'ideal-typical' examples. I shall begin with a case of a serially manufactured film that has no author.

Case One: an authorless film

A rich and famous actor – we'll just call him KK – has a rather 'watery' idea for a film. Acting as both producer and star, KK invests his personal fortune and gets additional financial backing from various sources. It is agreed that KK will be entrusted with artistic control of the project. KK has no talent as a writer. Armed with his kernel idea for a story, he hires three scriptwriters and four script doctors in succession. The script that results from these writers' separate efforts is changed many times during an expensive and chaotic shoot in Hawaii. A first, very talented director who works on the film is fired and replaced when he and KK quarrel. While KK is away doing something else, another team of people start editing the resulting footage into a feature-length film. When the audience at a preview reacts negatively, KK panics and hires someone else to make a number of substantial cuts. KK does not say what those cuts should be, but merely enjoins the editor to 'fix it'. KK is unhappy with the rather incoherent and artistically flawed results, but the production has by now gone way over budget. KK meets with his backers and there is bitter disagreement about what to do. KK wants them to invest more money, but the other backers deem it best to cut their losses. A group of them finally team up to take control; they buy KK out and hire a new director to shoot some additional scenes and supervise the making of a final cut, which is what gets released commercially. A successful ad campaign attracts large audiences to see the result.

Although he had a lot to do with its production and appears throughout the film in the lead role, KK is not the work's author. After all, his contributions to the process of production ended long before the final cut was made. But the project's other financial backers are not the film's authors either. Nor are any of the different writers, directors, or technicians who have worked on the project. The film certainly has makers – lots of them – but no author. Why not? What aspect of authorship is missing from such a case? Bordwell and Thompson point out that authorship is often defined in terms of control and decision-making, and intuitively one wants to say that the project in Case One has got 'out of control'.[13] This seems right, but 'control' can mean many different things in such a context – from the ability to perform certain tasks in a skilled manner, to having and exercising some kind of social authority (such as legal ownership or some form of institutionally grounded power to get others to act on one's instructions). KK, who looks like the closest candidate for authorship in Case One, both has and lacks control in several senses of the word. KK, after all, has the initial idea for the film and acts on it, prompting and guiding other people's efforts to that end. Initially he controls the making of the film in the sense that he has the power to make such relevant decisions as the hiring, firing, and supervision of artists and technicians. When he accepts his partners' offer for a buyout, he agrees to abandon his involvement in, and rights over, the project in exchange for a part of his initial investment. Henceforth he enjoys no decision-making power or control.

Does the exercise of some sort of uninterrupted control, in the sense of the authority to make binding decisions, suffice to constitute cinematic authorship? Not at all, as the following example is designed to show.

Case Two: authority without authorship

Big John has made an immense amount of money trading in livestock and decides to invest some of it in the entertainment industry. He hires a producer and director and enjoins them to collaborate on the making of some sort of film, but because he wants to keep an eye on his investment, he stipulates that they must regularly submit their plans and results to him for his approval. This they do, and Big John soon realizes that he has a very poor understanding of this business. Again and again, he finds that he has no informed preferences concerning the decisions that need to be made, starting with the choice of genre and basic story idea. Yet his pride prevents him from admitting this to his employees, so he pretends to engage in careful deliberations before he tells them what to do. Often he simply approves the ideas they submit to him, but sometimes he has to choose between several proposed options, and on many occasions he must settle disagreements between his producer and director, who have strikingly different visions of the film they are making. Big John secretly makes all such decisions by flipping coins. So when the film has been made, Big John has effectively exercised an unchallenged decision-making authority throughout the project, and his random choices have had a significant impact on the work's nature. As luck would have it, the director and producer each get their way about half the time. Neither of them is the film's author, it would seem, but nor is Big John.

Why isn't Big John's decision-making constitutive of authorship? To answer this question, we must return to our basic pragmatic assumptions. Being an author, I have claimed, is intentionally

making an utterance, and an utterance is an expressive (and perhaps also a communicative) action, that is, one in which some agent (or agents) intends to make manifest some meaningful attitudes (such as beliefs and emotions). To make an attitude manifest is to do or make something, the cognition of which is likely, under the right conditions, to bring that attitude to mind. For example, Giacomo Leopardi arguably had a number of complex thoughts and feelings in mind when he wrote 'La ginestra', and he intended to fashion this poem so that at least some readers would experience similar emotions and ideas as a result of reading and thinking about it.[14] The attitudes that an author intends to make manifest in an utterance need not, of course, be ones that the agent sincerely holds or feels. In making an utterance, an author acts on an expressive intention, the content of which is a representation of some attitude(s) to be made manifest and of a means of so doing. The content of an intention can be referred to as a 'plan', and in this sense, following a plan – even a very schematic one that subsequently gets fleshed out and altered – is a necessary (but not a sufficient) condition of all intentional action, including the 'authoring' of any utterance.[15] This condition should not be misconstrued as requiring authors to have a perfect mental image of the final utterance in mind, prior to the beginning of the productive process. What the condition does require is that an author have at least a schematic idea of some of the attitudes he or she aims to make manifest in the utterance, as well as an idea of the processes by means of which this utterance is to be realized.

Returning now to the case of cinematic utterances, we may add that the expressive action constitutive of authorship must be performed through the making of an apparently moving image projected on a screen or other surface, which typically requires the production of what we can refer to as a cinematic text (roughly, the final cut or negative of which multiple positive, projectable prints can be made). This cinematic text is the principal means by which some agent intends to make some specific attitudes manifest. In straightforward cases of individual or independent cinematic production, cinematic authorship is a matter of an individual's making such a text as a means to realizing an expressive intention. In the case of serial manufacture, authorship involves not only making such a text oneself, but enlisting the aid of others in making one. A partial analysis of cinematic authorship, then runs as follows:

Cinematic author = the agent or agent(s) who intentionally make(s) a cinematic utterance; where cinematic utterance = an action the intended function of which is to make manifest or communicate some attitude(s) by means of the production of an apparently moving image projected on a screen or other surface.

Does Big John in Case Two satisfy these conditions? It is true that a cinematic text gets made, largely as a result of John's action, but it is far less clear that Big John has made an utterance. He does intend to pay to have a film made, and he also intends to exercise a high degree of control over the process of its making. He is the one who makes key decisions, accepting or rejecting the results of decisions made by others. At no point, however, does Big John have any specific attitudes in mind that he intends the cinematic text to make manifest, and when he makes decisions that are relevant to which attitudes the film is likely to make manifest, he acts at random. Big John may very well act on the intention that the film be expressive of attitudes – that is, of some attitudes as opposed to none at all – but he has no plans or aims concerning which attitudes these should be. He does not even act on the paradoxical modernist intention of having his film express his supreme indifference concerning the attitudes his work will make manifest. To make an utterance, one must act on one's plan concerning the attitudes being expressed, which is what Big John fails to do.

Big John is not the author; but what about his producer and director? Theirs is not a case of joint authorship because they have incompatible intentions with regard to the nature of the utterance they are involved in making, and only Big John's random edicts settle their struggle for control.[16] Nor is either of them, taken separately, the film's author. One cannot intentionally make a cinematic utterance unless one makes the cinematic text, and one is not the overall maker of a cinematic text unless one fulfils a particular kind of role in the productive process. What is that role? In cases of serial manufacture, a film's author does not do everything that has to be done for the text to be made, but when the author delegates tasks, he or she does have to have final say over which fruits of other people's labour do and do not get incorporated into the final work. When, during the editing of the film, Big John overrules one of his director's proposals and accepts the producer's idea, the director no longer functions as the film's author.

But with the next toss of the coin, the same holds for the producer. So Case Two is another instance where there are makers but no authors.[17]

It may be objected here that 'having final say' is somewhat vague, and that an author's authority is not exercised in a vacuum. An author's effective decisions are in many ways constrained by other agents' preferences and actions – or at least by what the author believes them to be. Thinking that the star will be furious and therefore impossible to work with if a certain scene is eliminated, the director decides to include it because he thinks this is the lesser evil. Anticipating the censor's action, the director cuts out an entire sequence. Imagining (quite wrongly) that the audience will require comic relief, the director includes such a sequence. In spite of the external constraints – real or imagined – all such decisions are authorial decisions.

There are, however, cases involving situations where the interpersonal influence is of a different sort. I have in mind cases where a decision relative to an utterance's expressive content is ordained by someone who wields the requisite power (e.g. legal or institutional power) to issue a well-founded ultimatum to the text's maker(s): either you do it, or you are fired and someone else will. 'Well-founded' in this context means simply that the person who makes this threat both has the power to act on it successfully and fully intends to do so if the antecedent condition is not satisfied. Whence another case to be considered.

Case Three: taking orders

Jeanne, a talented young film student who has written an ambitious script, meets an encouraging and generous producer. He helps her get the backing she needs for a pet project and appears to offer her the opportunity to make the film she wants to make. With the help of a cooperative and talented crew, she gets all the footage she thinks she needs. But the trouble starts when the producer gets a look at a rough cut. 'This will never sell', he tells her, and he issues an ultimatum: either she cuts out a long, central sequence he finds too difficult for a popular audience, or she will be fired and someone else will finish the film following his plan. A talk with the lawyers convinces her that these are in fact her only two options, and after due reflection, she capitulates. By giving in, she keeps her name in the credits and appears as the film's director. But is she the work's author?

One's judgement concerning such a case is likely to vary in function of the expressive significance of the changes that Jeanne has made in compliance with the producer's ultimatum. Jeanne has chosen to go ahead and make the film under these coercive conditions, so the expressive action of making the film is still hers, but aspects of the film's content are not of her choosing. Whether the global fact of authorship is vitiated as a result depends on the extent to which Jeanne's expressive intentions have been realized. One can readily imagine cases at either end of the spectrum, as well as difficult, borderline examples. It may be best, then, to think of global authorship of a work as a matter of degree. To the extent that the decision the producer imposes on Jeanne is not destructive of her plan for the film, she remains the work's author, even though she has complied to someone else's orders. In a case where her key ideas are sacrificed, Jeanne is hardly, or just barely, the work's author. But a director who has no choice but to accept relatively minor cuts thought of by a producer remains the work's author to a large degree.[18]

Authorship in a context of serial manufacture may usually be a matter of degree, but it need not always be so. I shall now evoke a case of successful individual authorship in such a context.

Case Four: authorship in the studio

Many aspects of the making of Ingmar Bergman's 1962 film *Winter Light* are vividly described by Vilgot Sjöman in his book on the subject.[19] Although this was not a Hollywood mega-production, it was not an instance of independent film-making either, for Bergman was working squarely within the Swedish Film Industry's studio system. Yet the division of labour in that context was influenced by Bergman's very special talents and powers. Bergman wrote his own script, did some of the casting, directed the actors, supervised the editing and the sound-mixing, and worked closely with his cinematographer. Bergman also exercised a high degree of control over the choice of locations, props, make-up, and many other technical matters. At no point during the production process did any producer or other figure coercively require him to reverse an artistic decision he had made (although he did often accept other people's advice about possible changes). We are wholly warranted, then, in characterizing him as the author of the work, even though we know that he did not personally create or think up everything that can be seen in the film. For example, when we hear bits of J. S. Bach's music in a Bergman film, we know that Bergman did not compose or perform this music, but we can still recognize him as the author of the film as a whole, as well as of this particular utilization of music in film. He has made the decision about whether to use music at all, and where to put it in the film. He has chosen a particular part of a musical composition, as well as a particular performance of this music, and such decisions function as a significant instance of artistic expression in the overall film (e.g. by conveying Bergman's romantic ideas about the ethical status of some pieces of music).

Bergman, then, is the author of *Winter Light*. He initiated and guided its making, skilfully engaging in many of the diverse tasks involved, while supervising and exercising control over the activities of his collaborators. It is important to add that although Bergman enjoyed a huge measure of authority while making the film, he worked very hard to solicit a collaborative dialogue with his co-workers. For example, part of Bergman's special talent as a cinematic author derives from his ability to help his actors and actresses give remarkable performances. Unlike many film directors, Bergman read through the script together with the performers, analysing and discussing every line in an effort to arrive at a shared understanding of the story and characterizations. In Sjöman's image, Bergman resembled a foreman who showed the building plans to his co-workers, asking for suggestions for changes, and hoping to make sure they grasped the overall plan. The foreman image is apt because it underscores both Bergman's high degree of involvement in the making of the work as well as the help he got from others, but it also depicts him as the ultimate author of the work as a whole.

3 Real and Unreal Authors

So far I have considered authorship as an activity of actual agents. In so far as an interpretation makes claims about authorship, it can be false. There is, however, a rival conception (or family of conceptions) regarding the relation between interpretation and authorship. Following this anti-realist line, interpreters of a film should construct an image of the work's author without being guided by evidence concerning actual processes of production. The interpreter still frames ideas about the attitudes expressed in the work, but does so without asking whether those attitudes were in fact intentionally made manifest by anyone. Instead, the interpreter simply pretends or makes believe that the attitudes expressed in the text were expressed by someone. The make-believe persona that emerges from this sort of interpretative process is referred to variously as the 'real', 'fictional', 'implied', or 'postulated' author.

I find this model of interpretation unattractive, but cannot review here the complex debate between realist and anti-realist approaches to authorship. Instead I shall focus primarily on issues pertaining specifically to the cinema.[20] Two reasons are often given why the cinema is supposed to be especially suited to an anti-realist notion of authorship: (1) an ontological one having to do with the complex nature of cinematic production; and (2) an epistemological one having to do with the difficulty or impossibility of acquiring sufficient evidence about a film's making.

Is it the very nature of film-making that helps warrant the adoption of authorial anti-realism? I think not. Film production is not always qualitatively more complex – or less authorial – than work in other media, so the interpreter must decide, on a case-by-case basis, whether a film has or has not been made in a way that involves individual or collective authorship or some other sort of process. Such a decision requires reference to the evidence concerning real authorship. In cases where it is discovered that individual authorship obtains, why should the interpreter pretend or make believe that the attitudes expressed are those of an author? If I genuinely believe, for example, that Bergman was the author of *Winter Light*, why should I pretend to attribute the film's expressive qualities to the activity of a non-existent, but all-too-Bergmanian, author-surrogate? If, on the other hand, the interpreter discovers that neither collective nor individual authorship obtained, why should we continue to think of the text's expressive qualities as the intended results of an author's activities? An unauthored film can, like a traffic jam or a randomly generated computer message, display various properties that I can dislike or enjoy without having to attribute them to an imaginary maker. So in neither the case of an authored nor an unauthored film does the adoption of a fictional idea of authorship find any special warrant in the specific nature of cinematic authorship.

With regard to the epistemological claim, it is again misleading to suppose that the cinematic medium, or any specific mode of cinematic production, is especially suited to an anti-realist approach to authorship. The evidentiary difficulties surrounding our access to cinematic authorship are not always insurmountable; sometimes the evidence supports reasonable – but of course fallible – inferences about events involved in a work's making. It is true that often we cannot get all of the evidence we would like to have, and it is logically possible that all of the evidence we do have is misleading. But that is, unfortunately, a familiar truth about all historical knowledge.

A more plausible anti-realist line runs as follows. For various practical reasons, most film spectators simply do not know what went on during the making of the film they are viewing, yet the interpretative process requires them to attribute attitudes and implicit meanings to someone's expressive activity. It would in many cases be a factual error for such viewers to assume that the expressed attitudes were those of the text's real maker(s), so it is best for them simply to make believe that the attitudes expressed are those of a fictional author. Such make-believe cannot be wrong, because it is just a fiction that enhances the viewer's appreciation of the film.

In response, one may argue that knowing about a work of art's production tends to enhance insight and appreciation. To hold that such knowledge is unnecessary or undesirable because it is often unattainable looks like a case of 'sour grapes'. Why not recognize that such knowledge is always desirable, but sometimes out of reach? What is more, we may wonder how the spectator can form an adequate make-believe image of authorship in the absence of evidence about the real author's situation, skills, and activities. Under what conditions would such a spectator be able to make believe that a film had no author, but emerged from a chaotic process involving various people's activities? Textual appearances, which are the anti-realist's sole basis, can be deceptive: a cinematic text that emerges from a chaotic and uncoordinated production could look as though it has been made by a single author, and a work crafted by a single (or collective) author could look like something emerging from an uncontrolled or highly conflictual process. The spectator who fashions a make-believe author on the basis of textual evidence alone is blind to the difference, and can only work with a default assumption favouring authorial control.

I contend, on the contrary, that spectators and scholars alike ought to be attuned to such differences in histories of production. In short, critical insight, appreciation, and explanation are better served by an interpretative principle according to which it is the viewer's and critic's goal to arrive at interpretations which match, as opposed to diverge from, the work's features, including those involving its causal history.

Notes

I would like to acknowledge financial support for this research provided by both the SSHRC and FCAR. Thanks as well to Murray Smith for comments on a draft of this chapter.

1 Cognate terms in other languages (e.g. the French *auteur*) are also used in such disparate ways, but I shall not document this claim here.

2 Michel Foucault, 'Qu'est-ce qu'un auteur?' in *Dits et écrits 1954–1988*, ed. Daniel Defert and François Ewald (Paris: Gallimard, 1994), 789–821; citation, p. 798. The published English translations of this essay are unreliable (e.g. one of Foucault's own footnotes is presented as a translator's comment), and were based on a talk given in the United States, which diverged in interesting ways from the initial French lecture of 1969. I translate the cited passage as follows: 'A personal letter may well be signed by someone, but it still has no author; a contract may have a guarantor, but it has no author. An anonymous text that one reads on a wall when walking down the street will have a writer, but it will not have an author.'

3 The literature on Foucault's historical inaccuracies is quite large. With specific reference to his claims about the author-function, it is instructive to consult the following: Roger Chartier, *L'Ordre des livres: lecteurs, auteurs, bibliothèques en Europe entre le XIVe et XVIIIe siècle* (Paris: Alinéa, 1992), 35–67; Denis Dutton, 'Why Intentionalism Won't Go Away', in Anthony J. Cascardi (ed.), *Literature and the Question of Philosophy* (Baltimore: Johns Hopkins University Press, 1987), 194–209; M. H. Abrams, 'What is a Humanistic Criticism?', in Dwight Eddins (ed.), *The Emperor Redressed: Critiquing Critical Theory* (Tuscaloosa: University of Alabama Press, 1995), 13–44.

4 For a broader notion of authorship of cinematic works, see Berys Gaut's contribution to this volume.

5 I survey a range of topics related to agency and literature in *Literature and Rationality: Ideas of Agency in Theory and Fiction* (Cambridge: Cambridge University Press, 1991). For some background on pragmatic and action-theoretical assumptions, see Paul Grice, *Studies in the Way of Words* (Cambridge, Mass.: Harvard University Press, 1989); Stephen C. Levinson, *Pragmatics* (Cambridge: Cambridge University Press, 1983); François Recanati, *Meaning and Force: The Pragmatics of Performative Utterances* (Cambridge: Cambridge University Press, 1987); Dan Sperber and Deirdre Wilson, *Relevance: Communication and Cognition*, 2nd edn. (Oxford: Blackwell, 1995); Alfred R. Mele, *Springs of Action: Understanding Intentional Behaviour* (New York: Oxford University Press, 1992), and *Autonomous Agents: From Self-Control to Autonomy* (New York: Oxford University Press, 1995).

6 For an analysis of intentional action, see Alfred R. Mele and Paul K. Moser, 'Intentional Action', *Noûs*, 28 (1994), 39–68.

7 Freudians are likely to disagree with this move, but I shall not enter into the tired debate surrounding the soundness of this or that psychoanalytic doctrine. Suffice it to say that dreaming and talking in one's sleep are behaviours devoid of the kinds of planning, deliberation, choice, and effort that accompany successful authorship of even the most banal sort, such as writing a legible and cogent letter to a friend. It is perhaps significant that psychoanalytic discussions of the arts have largely abandoned Freud's interest in creativity and authorship in favour of a one-sided emphasis on the consumer's more passive activity. One reason for this shift in emphasis may be that watching a movie seems analogous to dreaming in ways that using cinematic technology does not.

8 In this regard, utterances are like works. For background, see Jerrold Levinson, *Music, Art, and Metaphysics: Essays in Philosophical Aesthetics* (Ithaca, NY: Cornell University Press, 1990); Gregory Currie, *An Ontology of Art* (New York: St Martin's, 1989); and Levinson's review of the latter in *Philosophy and Phenomenological Research*, 52 (1992), 215–22.

9 For arguments supporting this thesis, see Noël Carroll, 'Art, Intention, and Conversation', in Gary Iseminger (ed.), *Intention and Interpretation* (Philadelphia: Temple University Press, 1992), 97–131.

10 For a straightforward example of this sort of view, see Stanley Fish, 'Biography and Intention', in William H. Epstein (ed.), *Contesting the Subject: Essays in the Postmodern Theory and Practice of Biography and Biographical Criticism* (West Lafayette, Ind.: Purdue University Press, 1991), 9–16. For criticisms of Fish, see Alfred R. Mele and Paisley Livingston, 'Intentions and Interpretations', *Modern*

Language Notes, 107 (1992), 931–49, and George M. Wilson, 'Again Theory: On Speaker's Meaning, Linguistic Meaning, and the Meaning of a Text', in Mette Hjort (ed.), *Rules and Conventions: Literature, Philosophy, Social Theory* (Baltimore: Johns Hopkins University Press, 1992), 1–31.

11 Here I follow Gregory Currie, who similarly declines to deal with verbal (and other) issues related to filmic utterances' relation to television and other possible, related media. See his *Image and Mind: Film, Philosophy, and Cognitive Science* (Cambridge: Cambridge University Press, 1995), 1–16.

12 David Bordwell and Kristin Thompson, *Film Art: An Introduction*, 4th edn. (New York: McGraw-Hill, 1993), 30.

13 Ibid.

14 My argument does not depend on this specific example. For background, however, see John Alcorn and Dario Del Puppo, 'Giacomo Leopardi's "La Ginestra" as Social Art', *Modern Language Review*, 89 (1994), 865–88.

15 For background, see Mele and Moser, 'Intentional Action'. Requiring that an agent's A-ing can only be an instance of intentionally A-ing if the agent follows a plan rules out cases of causal deviance and specifies that the content of the relevant attitudes (such as the agent's intention) plays the right sort of role in generating the action. Mele and Moser's thorough analysis also includes clauses ruling out cases where an action is not intentional because its successful realization of the intended state of affairs involves too large an element of luck, or an overly inaccurate understanding of the processes involved.

16 The director and producer do share some intentions, but not the ones necessary for an intentional production of a joint utterance, i.e. those relative to the work's expressive content. For background on shared intention, see Michael E. Bratman, 'Shared Intention', *Ethics*, 104 (1993), 97–113.

17 Nor would I speak of 'multiple authorship' here, unless we follow Jack Stillinger in using that term to refer to cases where more than one agent fashions a text in the absence of any agreement or shared plan. See his *Multiple Authorship and the Myth of Solitary Genius* (New York: Oxford University Press, 1991). For his discussion of cinema, see pp. 174–81. Stillinger rightly suggests that authorship is often dispersed in the industrial process of production, but I cannot agree with his empirically dubious conclusion that 'the idea of director as sole author will not hold up under scrutiny; it is simply not possible for one person, however brilliant, to provide the entire creative force behind so complex a work as a motion picture', p. 179.

18 And as Murray Smith usefully suggests, there is a spectrum of external constraints, at one end of which we find the strongest forms of coercion.

19 Vilgot Sjöman, *Dagbok med Ingmar Bergman* (Stockholm: Norstedts, 1963).

20 For excellent treatments of the topic, see Berys Gaut (this volume) and Robert Stecker, 'Apparent, Implied, and Postulated Authors', *Philosophy and Literature*, 11 (1987), 258–71. I discuss a number of relevant anti-intentionalist arguments in my 'Characterization and Fictional Truth in the Cinema', in David Bordwell and Noël Carroll (eds.), *Post-Theory: Reconstructing Film Studies* (Madison: University of Wisconsin Press, 1996), 149–74.

21

National Cinema, the Very Idea

Jinhee Choi

A glance at recent literature on national cinema gives the impression that the notion of national cinema is a dated term, no longer a useful category for analyzing films. Globalization, among many other things, seems to be the major reason to reconsider the concept of national cinema. Through the process of globalization, networks that connect different parts of the world become faster and more dense. Economic and cultural commodities as well as information travel the world more rapidly than ever before. But what seems to be at stake is not merely the fast circulation and distribution of goods and information around the world, but also the fact that such cultural and economic exchanges blur what we used to think of as national boundaries and identities.

National cinema, either as an art form or as entertainment, is often considered to be a cultural product that forms and exemplifies a certain national identity or nationhood. However, if what's been said about globalization is correct, the link between national cinema and nationhood is loosening. This concern over – or salute to – the dissolution of national boundaries calls for a serious reconceptualization of national cinema. A seemingly popular solution to this problem is to replace the notion of national cinema with something more in concert with the globalization process: world cinema should be approached as "transnational" cinema instead of as national cinema. However, there seems to be some conceptual confusion that

needs to be disentangled before we can determine whether the notion of national cinema should be disregarded altogether.

Many arguments that surround national cinema – such as concerns about cultural imperialism due to the domination of Hollywood cinema in the world, or arguments against or in favor of governmental controls that would protect domestic films – are based on different notions of national cinema. I suggest that there are three ways to approach national cinema: "a territorial account," "a functional account," and "a relational account." In this paper, I will argue that approaching a national cinema according to its national origin or in light of its function within a nation-state will fall short of capturing the idea and role of national cinema, and I will argue for the need to assess national cinema relationally.

1 National Cinema, the Very Idea

One of the simplest ways to identify a national cinema is by virtue of its nation of origin. That is, "national cinema" refers to a body of films produced within a certain nation-state. For example, French cinema is cinema that is produced in France. Determining a national cinema according to its national origin seems to require at the very least one minimum condition: "territorial" boundaries. A national cinema is the product of activities and institutions *within* a nation-state. "National cinema" construed in this way is used as an indexical term, referring to the totality of films that are produced within a nation-state. I call this approach the "territorial account."

It is interesting to note that this notion of national cinema can often be found in arguments in favor of governmental regulations to protect domestic film industries from Hollywood cinema. The main concern underlying such claims is an economic one: the domestic film industry in a given nation-state is affected by forces that exist largely outside of national boundaries. Obviously the major threat is Hollywood cinema which has dominated the world market since the early 1910s. One of the consequences of this domination has been the uneven distribution of resources and the capital, which, in turn, results in imbalances between the proportion of imported and locally produced films. Hollywood cinema keeps the domestic film industry of other nation-states from sustaining or developing the infrastructure that is necessary to compete with Hollywood cinema.

A territorial account of national cinema, even in its simplest form, faces a conceptual difficulty. The collective processes and practices of film production make it difficult to maintain even the minimum requirement, i.e., territorial boundaries. Consider run-away productions: either to get around the import quota set by a country or to take advantage of cheaper production costs, production companies often shoot films in other parts of the world. For example, Italian Westerns were often shot in Spain. So, perhaps, a film should be classified as an instance of a national cinema based not on its shooting location, but rather according to the ownership of and the right to its product: that is, to whom does the film belong? In the film industry, the copyright to a film is owned by the production company or a studio. Hence, the relation between a film and its national origin is an indirect, transitive one: the nationality of a cinema is determined by and transferred from the nationality of a production company or a studio. With this in mind, we can modify the territorial definition of national cinema as follows: A film is an instance of a national cinema based on the nationality of its production company or studio.

A territorial account of national cinema, even in this modified form, faces another conceptual difficulty. Co-production strategies in film productions – both treaty based co-productions among different nation-states or equity based co-productions among corporations – raise a question

as to how to determine the ownership of a film and how to single out the nationality of a film. Co-production is not a recent phenomenon. Films have been co-produced since the 1920s, bringing together resources and experience from different nation-states. Recently, co-production within regional film industries has become one of the popular options in the effort to compete with Hollywood. For example, the Pacific Rim Consortium for Public Broadcasting (PACRIM) was formed to facilitate transpacific co-productions. European countries created pan-European co-production funds called Eurimages in 1989, with an aim to form a pan-European market and to produce films that would secure pan-European cultural identity.[1] The European blockbuster *Astérix and Obélix vs. Caesar* (1999), was co-produced by France, Germany, and Italy. Is this French, or German, or Italian cinema?

Furthermore, multinational media conglomerates operate and invest across national borders, such that any specific nationality is difficult to assign.[2] For example, Rupert Murdoch, the head of News Corp., which is an Australian-based publishing conglomerate, acquired a controlling interest in 20th Century Fox in the US, in British Sky Broadcasting in the UK, and in Star TV in Hong Kong.[3] Janet Staiger claims, "anyone attempting to figure out what 'nation' any major film conglomerate 'belongs' to is really attempting the impossible – and *the unnecessary*" (her italics).[4]

If a territorial approach to national cinema is a more production- and industry-based approach, a functional approach identifies instances of national cinema based on what a film embodies at the level of text and how it functions within a nation-state. National cinema has often been examined in light of both what it purports to reinforce and what it reacts to: national identity and Hollywood, respectively. If an attempt to define national cinema in connection with national identity can be called a "functional" account, an attempt to define national cinema in terms of product differentiation – i.e. how it differs from Hollywood cinema and other national cinemas – can be called a "relational" account.[5] Although many approaches to national cinema combine these two, I will distinguish the two for the sake of conceptual clarity. For the underlying assumptions of each approach give rise to different problems and thus demand different solutions with regard to the status of national cinema in this age of globalization. I will first examine the functional approach.

Due to its long domination of film markets around the world, Hollywood cinema has presented itself as a cultural and economic threat to most countries around the world. Other film communities, either through conscious governmental effort to protect domestic film industries and/or through local film movements, have developed means to compete with Hollywood cinema. But national cinema cannot be defined solely negatively. To do so would leave us with only two big categories: Hollywood cinema and the rest. If so in order to differentiate between various national cinemas, we need an additional criterion. National identities become handy when we come to an impasse in sorting out the differences among national cinemas.

In explaining the national identity that a national cinema attempts to reinforce, film scholars often appeal to Benedict Anderson's notion of a nation as an *imagined community*.[6] Anderson claims that a nation is an imagined community that provides its members with a sense of identity and belonging. Such an identity, according to Anderson, is achieved through the consumption of the products of modern print culture, including newspapers and novels. As national history unfolds in newspapers, literature, and the media against the backdrop of familiar settings and locales, readers acquire a sense of community marked by national boundaries as well as a sense of shared history and destiny. Although Anderson does not include film as a means of constructing nationhood, given the fact that a film narrative, like novels and other forms of literature, unfolds within space and time with a national specificity, film would also seem to be able to evoke a sense of national identity within the viewer.

The Andersonian idea of nation often figures in many film scholars' explanations of national cinema. Susan Hayward, for instance, relies heavily on Anderson's notion of nation to articulate the relation between national identity and national cinema. Following Anderson, Hayward postulates a nation as an entity that provides imagined continuity and collectivity that enables its members to form their identities. For Hayward, French national cinema, explicitly or implicitly, either reinforces or reconstructs the dominant ideology of the nation.[7] Hayward tries to avoid the pitfall of postulating national identity as monolithic by emphasizing the fact that the articulation of nationhood is mediated at various levels and thus national cinema is not "pure and simple re-flections of history, but rather a transformation of history."[8]

However, Hayward's characterization of national cinema as a reflection or (re)construction of national ideologies trivializes the notion of national cinema in that, according to her definition, every French film is directly or indirectly about France. Mette Hjort, adopting Michael Billig's notion of banal nationalism, reminds us of the need to distinguish "banal aboutness" from "thematization."[9] She further questions the usefulness of national cinema in the former sense. That is, even if a film is set in a specific location in a nation and uses its mother language, those elements often pass unnoticed by the viewer unless they are focalized. For instance, New York City can function as a generic setting, as in the TV show *Friends*, or it can be thematized as a specific location, as in Woody Allen's *Manhattan* or *Annie Hall*. Hjort argues, correctly in my view, that unless elements that are specific to a nation play significant narrative functions, the film would not fulfill the purpose of leading the viewer to assume a national identity.

Arguments for the protection of a national film industry from American cultural imperialism are often based on a version of the functionalist conception of national cinema. A typical argument goes like this: National cinemas invite the viewer to imagine herself or himself as a member of a national community and culture; the popularity of Hollywood cinema prevents domestic film industries from providing such opportunities; thus Hollywood cinema homogenizes national cultures. But is it obvious that such an argument is sound? For one of the underlying assumptions is that the presence of a production sector in the domestic film industry is a necessary and sufficient condition for the cultural expression of a nation-state. This naturally leads to the question of whether a functionalist approach to national cinema (upon which the argument is based) is feasible. I will argue that it is not.

There are various criticisms of a functionalist approach to national cinema: for one, national identities are said to be constructed, and thus it is questionable whether such identities are distinctive of particular national culture. For another, if a national cinema requires homogeneous responses from the audience of a nation-state or a sense of unity among its citizens, few films would fall under the category of national cinema, given the diverse reception of national cinema at home or abroad. I will call the former the "anti-essentialist" challenge, and the latter the "reception" problem. I will deal with the anti-essentialist challenge first.

To understand the implications of the anti-essentialist argument, we need to be cautious. An anti-essentialist can take an extreme position by arguing that there is no national culture whatsoever independent of texts; it is all constructed and there exist only competing representations. Or, one can argue that there is no pure, authentic culture unique to a given nation.[10] These two are separate arguments. For the former denies ontologically the existence of national culture altogether, while the latter denies only the privileging of any specific national, cultural traditions.

But however it is construed, the anti-essentialist argument is not fatal to the functionalist approach. It is important to note that the functionalist definition of national cinema has two parts: (i) what it represents at the level of text and (ii) how it functions for members of a national community. The anti-essentialist argument aims mainly to refute the first part. If so, a functionalist can defend his or her position by pointing out that even if national identity as represented in a film is fictional in the sense that it is constructed, it can still have causal influence on the viewer. If the function of a national cinema is to mobilize its citizens and to build a sense of nationhood and identity, the fictional status of so-called "national culture" would not necessarily deter it from functioning as such. What is at stake here is not necessarily the constructed nature of national culture per se, but the viewer's acceptance of some putative national culture as authentic. In a similar vein, the apparent authenticity of a culture represented on film may lead the viewer to imagine, however unwarrantedly, that he or she has been participating in unique cultural practices.

Both types of arguments draw our attention to the epistemological issue of whether national cinema properly conveys national culture. It is a legitimate concern in so far as we should not hastily ascribe an essence to a national culture, based merely on textual grounds. For example, Noël Burch and Geneviève Sellier inform us of an interesting datum about plot structure of French cinema in the 1930s – that is, an incestuous father/daughter relationship may be found in 30 percent of French films made during that period![11] However, we cannot infer directly from this datum any truths about the sexuality of the French and culture. For films are not direct reflections of

society; there is always a mediation between the two. But a distinction should still be made between whether or not a national cinema reliably and accurately represents national culture vs. whether or not a national cinema fulfills its purported function within a nation-state.

I will now turn to the second challenge to the functionalist approach; this challenge raises a question with regard to how national cinema is consumed and received. For example, Andrew Higson is skeptical about the capacity of a national cinema to evoke a sense of community or belonging among its audience members. His skepticism lies in the diverse reception of British films in the domestic market. British films such as *Four Weddings and a Funeral* (1994) and *The Full Monty* (1997), which were shot and produced in Britain, did not appear to evoke Britishness for the British audience.[12] Higson's concern regarding the heterogeneous reception of films is legitimate in that we cannot predict how individual films will be received nationwide or abroad, nor can we know if responses to film are convergent nationally and/or internationally. If a functionalist approach to national cinema does indeed require a homogenized experience among its viewers, Higson's objection is right on target.

Higson argues instead that national cinema should be conceived mainly as a brand name or a selling point to secure the domestic and the international market.[13] By "national cinema," Higson seems to mean a certain national "flavor" or "tone" rendered by the narrative, setting, or the nationality of the cast and crew.[14] For example, the award-winning *Shakespeare in Love* aims to be British even though the film was a UK–US co-production of The Bedford Falls, Warner Brothers, and Miramax.

However, "national cinema" in the above sense seems to be rather superficial. For it does not do justice to how "national cinema" has been treated as a substantial category within film history; nor does it explain how the concept of national cinema functions as a frame of reference for viewers and critics. Even if, as Higson claims, national cinema matters as a brand name to viewers or to award judges, in order for national cinema to function as such, the viewer, both domestic and abroad, should be able to form, presumably based on discernible textual properties, certain conceptions about that brand.

A relational account of "national cinema," like Higson's account, underscores the fact that a national cinema is often aimed at product differentiation in a film market. However, "national cinema" as a filmic category is more than a mere brand name. In order for a body of films to form a category of "national cinema," they should manifest common characteristics – narratively and/or stylistically – that significantly depart from those of Hollywood and other national cinemas. For example, Korean action films would not constitute a fruitful category unless they can substantially differentiate themselves from both Hollywood and Hong Kong action cinema. In addition, a relational approach to national cinema does not conceive of national cinema as a means to an end: i.e., a vehicle to embody national identity or cultural heritage. A national cinema's association with its national history or heritage is only one of the many ways in which a national cinema can assert itself. As Thomas Elsaesser nicely puts it, "national cinema makes sense only as a relation, not as an essence, being dependent on other kinds of filmmaking."[15] Thus, the significance of the emergence of a national cinema can be properly situated within a historical context only in comparison to Hollywood and/or other national cinemas.

A relational account of "national cinema" leads us to reconsider the false dichotomy between "national" and "transnational" cinema. Current debates on national vs. transnational cinema treat these two categories as if they corresponded to two different "modes" of film practice. A "national cinema" is produced by a domestic film industry, is circulated within a nation-state, and appeals to a national audience; whereas "transnational cinema" is financed internationally, is distributed more widely than simply within the country of production, and is able to appeal to an audience across national boundaries.[16] However, national cinema in my view weaves in and out of these two sets of industrial modes. For example, in the case of art cinema, even though it is circulated through international film festivals – and in that sense it is transnational – it will still sustain a strong affiliation with its nation of origin: art cinema very often functions as if it were a representative of a nation-state.

A better way to approach difference usages of "national cinema" in filmic discourse is not in terms of its "distribution mode," but in terms of its "scope" of the term. National cinema as a category often oscillates between a supra-category – which encompasses both the nation-bound and

the transnational film practices which filmmakers in a nation-stage engage – and a sub-category – which is formed when combined with other filmic categories such as genre or filmic mode. When a national cinema is viewed as a supra-category, it not only includes films that are aimed for a domestic audience but also films that are more internationally circulated. In such a case, national cinema is often associated with a handful of *auteurs* or their oeuvres. Ingmar Bergman is one of the directors who represents the Swedish cinema of the 1950s and '60s. Similarly, Satyajit Ray, a Bengali director, represents India. The relation between *auteur* and national cinema is quite complex in that non-Hollywood *auteur* directors are often recognized as such at venues such as international film festivals, which form a market distinct from mass-oriented markets. Furthermore, and quite ironically, their films, sometimes tailored for festival tastes, tend not to attract large domestic audiences. Despite the pitfall of attributing the originality and creativity of the styles of these directors to something culturally specific – i.e., attempting to locate the origins of their styles in traditional art forms unique to their respective cultures – films directed by *auteurs* do elicit in the viewer some conception of a national cinema. In the next section, I will touch upon how works of *auteur* directors function as *exemplars* of national cinema.

On the other hand, when national cinema functions as a sub-category, it provides us with a fine-grained way to assess a sub-genera of a filmic category. There are three ways to think of national cinema as a sub-category, although they certainly do not exhaust all the cases. First, national cinema, in its adjectival form, can be used as a national label that differentiates itself from Hollywood and other national cinemas within a genre. The "national" label often piggy-backs on genre, as in the Italian Western, Hong Kong Gangster-Noir, and Japanese Anime. Such a label is in fact designed to designate characteristics distinctive to films branded as such. For example, Sergio Leone's Spaghetti Westerns, such as *For a Fistful of Dollars* (1964), *For a Few Dollars More* (1965), and *The Good, The Bad and The Ugly* (1966), adopt and rework the classic formula for the American Western of the 1940s and '50s. In Leone's Westerns, the threshold of good and bad becomes more blurred than in the American Western. Unlike American Westerns, where the hero and the villain represent (respectively) opposite moral values, in

Leone's films the protagonists are morally ambivalent. They often act out of selfish motivation (usually financial gain), which they share with the villains. Character psychology is also more complex than that of characters in American Westerns, who possess only a few recognizable character traits. Leone's visual style is also distinct from Hollywood style, in his insistence on using extreme close-ups of characters' faces.[17] In this case, the nationality of a group of films does function as a sub-category, with which viewers associate distinctive features.

Second, national cinema as a sub-category can designate a corpus of films directed by a group of filmmakers who share an aesthetic framework and/or ideology at specific historical moments. Examples of this include French Impressionism, Soviet Montage, German Expressionism, and Italian Neorealism. The rise of these film movements cannot be summed up in a few sentences taking note of the historical contexts in which they emerged, but one of the motivations behind each of these film movements can be found in their respective attempts at product differentiation. When Erich Pommer, the producer of the majority of German Expressionist films, was asked why the German film industry made expressionist films, he answered: "The German film industry made 'stylized films' to make money.... Germany was defeated; how could she make films that would compete with the others? It would have been impossible to try to imitate Hollywood or the French. So we tried something new: the expressionist or stylized films."[18] Pommer's interview suggests that German expressionist films were not mere reflections of German society after World War I, but aimed to provide unique themes and aesthetics that would provide German films with the capacity to compete with other national cinemas, including Hollywood cinema, in an international film market.

Third, national cinema, when associated with a "new wave," refers to the elevated status of films produced within a nation-state, due to the changes within the film industry and film culture, which are often propelled by a generational shift. Initiated by the French New Wave in the late 1950s and '60s, "new wave" cinemas, like tides, ebb and flow across countries: the Japanese New Wave, the Hong Kong New Wave, Fifth Generation directors in China, New Taiwanese Cinema, New Iranian Cinema, and the Korean New Wave. New Wave phenomena are different from film movements, in that the former lack the stylistic consistency which is often found in the latter, but national cinema characterized as "new wave" provides the viewer with recognizable characteristics – such as common themes, the emergence of new genres, or shifts in the mode of production – that bear relevance to the viewer's understanding of films.

So far I have examined three accounts of national cinema: territorial, functional, and relational. The territorial and functional accounts of national cinema foreground economic and ideological aspects of national cinema, respectively. However, neither of these approaches is satisfying. The former is unable to capture adequately the mode of film production that becomes more prevalent in the international film market; whereas the latter limits the function of national cinema to a vehicle to promote national identity, neglecting other capacities that national cinema possesses as a filmic category. On the contrary, I have suggested that national cinema should be viewed relationally. We can properly understand the significance of a national cinema as a cinematic category only within a historical context in comparison with other national cinemas. In the next section, I will examine how we acquire the concept of a national cinema and how the concept of "nationality" may figure in our understanding and appreciation of national cinema.

2 National Cinema and National Identity

A relational approach to national cinema underlines the fact that national cinema is not a given, but is classified as such only when there exists a set of identifiable characteristics that mark itself from other national cinemas. How, then, do we as viewers acquire the concept of national cinema? What is the relation between national cinema and national identity? I wish to argue that we form the concept of national cinema via *prototypes* or *exemplars*. Although I adopt terminology such as "prototype" and "exemplar," from philosophical theories of concepts in general, I do not presuppose that either the prototype or the exemplar theory of concept formation is a proper model for concepts in general. That inquiry is beyond the scope of this project. Nevertheless, these frameworks are pertinent to the case of national cinemas, and illuminate the contingent relation between national cinemas and national identities.

A prototype is a set of *typical* features that characterize a category. For example, instead of thinking of "bachelor" as "an unmarried man," we often think of "bachelor" in terms of typical features we associate with bachelors: they are "afraid of commitment," "love to party," and "are into sports." Typical features associated with a category are ones that are diagnostic, statistically frequent, or salient among members of the category. In that sense, typical features, unlike defining features, can be contingent, i.e. not necessarily essential, for category membership.[19] That is, among bachelors, we can find someone who is eager to commit to a relationship, or does not party often, or hates sports. Such a bachelor, then, would be a less typical bachelor than the ones who show all three features mentioned above. It is also important to note that the features constituting a prototype have relative value and weights corresponding to their importance. For example, bachelors' attitudes toward relationships – i.e. that bachelors are afraid of commitment – is a more salient feature associated with bachelors than are elements of their lifestyle – such as partying and a preference for sports.

Given this, what are the features that characterize national cinemas? They vary from national cinema to national cinema, but they can include the mode of production (including distribution and exhibition), film style, narrative structure or theme, and film genre. For example, Indian cinema stands out due to its massive quantity of film production, which exceeds the number of films produced in Hollywood, and its reliance on musical numbers. The mode of exhibition in Japanese silent cinema distinguishes itself from that in Western cinema, based on the role and popularity of a commentator benshi.

Films of the New Iranian Cinema, which were applauded at film festivals in the late 1980s and 1990s, share certain characteristics at the level of narrative: (i) a minimalist plot structure that revolves around children pursuing trivial goals – (*Where is the Friend's House?* (1987), *The Mirror* (1997) – or disaster-stricken villagers and people on the outskirts of urban settings – e.g., *Through the Olive Trees* (1994), *The Taste of Cherry* (1997), *The Wind Will Carry Us* (1999) – and (ii) a reflexive narrative structure set against the making of a movie within the movie – *The Mirror, Through the Olive Trees, Moment of Innocence* (1996).

Hong Kong cinema is often associated with specific film genres such as the martial arts film and its typical narrative structure. Viewers who are acquainted with Hong Kong martial arts films are aware of some of the recurring plot structures: the revenge plot, the quest plot, and the contest plot, to name but a few. These plot structures are not mutually exclusive, and can be combined within a single film. There are usually competing martial arts schools, and fights are triggered because (i) the protagonist is eager to avenge the death of a loved one (e.g., family member, friend, master), (ii) competing schools try to find a secret document or weapon that is necessary to perfect their martial arts skills, and (iii) the protagonist enters a fighting contest. However, this does not mean that these features are common to every instance of Hong Kong martial arts film. These are typical features – prototypes – that characterize the category, but are not essential to it.

If prototypes are sets of features that are exhibited by many category members, exemplars are individual instances of a category.[20] For example, instead of thinking of "vehicles" as a means of carrying or transporting something, one can think of "vehicles" via exemplars, such as bicycles, cars, buses, and trucks. Exemplars are often used to decide the membership of a target object by comparing the target with sets of examples stored in memory.[21] When we are asked whether a skateboard is a vehicle, we will answer the question based on similarities between skateboards and other examples of vehicles stored in our memory. According to Jesse Prinz, exemplars work better than prototypes when it comes to supra-categories.[22] If the basic category is one that maximizes both intra-categorical similarities and inter-categorical differences, supra-categories are a higher level of categories under which several basic categories can be subsumed. Concepts such as vehicles, clothing, and furniture belong to supra-categories and instances of such supra-categories differ significantly from one another.

Adopting terminology such as "prototype" and "exemplar" enables us to explain how the concept of "national cinema" functions both as a supra-category that designates the totality of cinema *loosely* associated with a nation-state and as a sub-category, when combined with a genre, a film movement, or a phenomenon. When "national cinema" is used as a supra-category, viewers tend to characterize a national cinema in light of a limited number of films they have encountered or a few works directed by directors that the viewer is familiar with. The important point here is that we cannot form a concept of national cinema unless we have experiences of films associated with a conception of a nation-state. The more one encounters instances of a national cinema, the more one will be in a position to characterize the national cinema in a more fine-grained way. However, when one has only had limited experience of a national cinema, the few instances one has experienced will function as exemplars. When the non-scholar thinks of Japanese cinema, Godzilla is likely to come to mind.

One of the advantages of thinking of national cinema in terms of prototypes or exemplars is that we can avoid the pitfall of restricting the value of national cinema to a vehicle for exemplifying national identity. It is because prototypes or exemplars are defined in terms of typicality and frequency, not in terms of essence. Even though we find traces or elements of national history or identity in prototypical instances or exemplars of a national cinema, the relationship between the two should be construed as contingent, not as necessary.

One might object to my categorical approach to national cinema by questioning the benefit of calling a cinema "national" if nationality does not figure at all in our understanding of national cinema. What is "Iranian" about Iranian cinema? What is the purpose of calling them "Hong Kong" martial art films, if they do not manifest anything specific to Hong Kong culture? In my view, nationality and local identity figure in our understanding of cinema, but in a more or less indirect and, sometimes, abstract way. I will examine how national identity may seep into a film text in light of Kristin Thompson's notion of "motivation."

Thompson suggests that we understand the function of filmic devices – both narrative and stylistic – using the concept of "motivation." Filmic devices perform functions within a work, but the work must provide some reasons why those devices are employed. The reason that the work suggests for the presence of any given device can be called a "motivation."[23] According to Thompson, there are four types of motivations: realistic, compositional, transtextual, and artistic. I will argue that nationality – or our conception of a nation – *can* figure into our understanding of these motivations.

Realistic motivation justifies the presence of a device by recourse to plausibility or verisimilitude. To understand films, we bring in our real-life schemata. For example, in *When Harry Met Sally*, the fact that Sally (played by Meg Ryan) lives in a small apartment seems plausible given the salary of a writer for a magazine: she cannot afford a big apartment in New York City. Compositional motivation offers a reason for planting an event or a device so as to advance the narrative. In swordplay films, parents or family members of the protagonist are often murdered in the beginning of the film, which then causes the protagonist to avenge their deaths. Sometimes, a reason to include certain devices can be found outside the text. In Jacques Demy's musical *Umbrellas of Cherbourg*, people sing, instead of talking, throughout the entire film. The reason for that can be found in the generic norms of musicals. Last, artistic motivation, which Thompson finds the most difficult to define, can be thought of as a reason to employ certain devices so as to enhance the aesthetic qualities of a film. The presence of a device can be artistically motivated in conjunction with the other three functions – realistic, composition, and transtextual – or can become salient on its own while the other three functions are withheld.[24] For example, the graphic match used in the montage sequence of breakfast scenes in *Citizen Kane*, which signifies the deterioration of the marriage between Kane and Emily over time, not only makes the characters look visually distanced from each other, but also makes the scene more visually coherent and unified.

How, then, does the nationality of a filmmaker, or of a film, matter in explaining these types of motivations? Viewers can appeal to the idea of realism in order to make sense of a setting or of narrative devices. When I taught Godard's *Breathless* for an introductory film course, upon being asked why the pregnancy of Patricia is treated so casually and is never brought up later in the film, one of my students answered, "it's French," and followed that with an anecdotal experience she had in France. I don't think it was the right answer and she confused what is "real" in life with aesthetic "realism," but for her, her conception of French people seemed to explain Michel's blunt response to Patricia's pregnancy.

That response notwithstanding, I do believe that knowledge of the cultural or the political history of a country could help the viewer to understand the realistic motivations of certain films. For example, I was struck by the favorable portrayal of the Japanese in Hou Hsiao-hsien's *A City of Sadness* (1989), one of Hou's Taiwan

Jinhee Choi

Trilogy. In the beginning of the film, for instance, Shisuko visits Hinomi at the hospital to give a sword and a poem to Hinoe – who is Hinomi's brother – and a Kimono to Hinomi. Shisuko is saddened by the thought that she will soon leave Taiwan and thanks Hinomi and her brother for their hospitality. My response can be partly explained by the fact that I was unaware of Japanese colonial policies on Taiwan, which were significantly different from their policies on China or on Korea. I learned only later that Hou's rendering of Japanese colonialism in his film is not implausible. Unlike China or Korea, Taiwan's relationship with Japan during the occupation was arguably more one of co-dependence, rather than one of coercion.[25] Until the outbreak of World War II in the Pacific, Taiwan's economy actually grew. Japanese authorities did not see any compelling reason to use Taiwan as a military base.

Our knowledge of the cultural heritage of a nation-state can also help us understand the compositional/transtextual motivations of a film. For example, the norms and conventions found in martial arts films have their roots in other art forms: martial arts novels and theater. Audiences who are acquainted with such norms would not find it hard to accept that protagonists in martial arts films often fly from tree to tree or from rooftop to rooftop. Moreover, one can find an affinity between martial art films and martial arts serials in terms of narrative structure; their plots are constructed rather loosely and episodically instead of following a tighter causal logic, which is typical in Hollywood films.

It is true that the traditional arts or other art forms of a country can have an influence on the formation of a certain genre in a national cinema, but we need to be cautious when weighing such influences and judging whether the norms or conventions found in traditional arts are unique to the culture in question. Often, the origin of the episodic structure of martial arts films and novels can be too hastily attributed to a difference in worldview of various ethnic groups: i.e., while Westerners comprehend a phenomenon in terms of cause-effect, Asians apprehend a phenomenon in a holistic manner.[26] Such an approach neglects a certain common ground between different cultures: the additive structure – adding one episode to the next, or presenting one fight after another – is not unique to martial arts films or novels. Westerns and sports dramas contain narrative structures quite similar to that of martial arts films –

e.g., Sam Raimi's contemporary Western, *The Quick and the Dead.*

A better way to understand the differences in narrative structure between Hollywood cinema and that of other national cinemas is to view them in terms of their common function. A narrative must last for a certain amount of time in order for the viewer to be aligned with the protagonist or to maximize emotive effects in the viewer. Furthermore, if a protagonist achieves his or her goal immediately, the story must end soon after. One of the convenient ways to prolong a narrative is to insert a series of obstacles that the protagonist needs to overcome. These events can be causally linked, as in typical Hollywood films, or can be connected in a more episodic manner, as in martial arts films. If so, various ways to advance and prolong the narrative in different national cinemas, while coated with cultural ingredients, in fact perform a similar function.

Last, how does the cultural heritage of a nation-state influence artistic motivation? There is a tendency in film studies for critics and film scholars to appeal to the indigenous art forms of a country in order to explain the distinctive visual style of an *auteur*. For example, Mizoguchi's use of long takes is often compared to Japanese scroll paintings, and it is pointed out how both explore the temporal duration of the viewing experience.[27] Or Ozu's use of shots of an object or of a landscape as a transition to the next scene is taken to be indebted to Japanese cultural heritage, and is compared to pillow words in Japanese poems, which are located at the end of a five-syllable line, but modify the first word in the next line.[28]

Whether such analogies are drawn for heuristic purposes (i.e., we can understand better the functions of such stylistic devices by comparing them with similar devices in other art forms), or whether their claims are much stronger (i.e., there are causal relations between such distinctive styles and the presence of other art forms in their culture) is unclear and needs to be further investigated in light of the directors' intentions and the production circumstances ("influence" is a much weaker notion than "causality"). However, it is also an undeniable truth that some directors are aware of the standards and norms of film festivals and consciously explore stylistic devices that appear distinctive to their cultures in order to be recognized. "Art cinema" nowadays, becomes "art" in cinema. If so, the relation between national cinema and its heritage should not necessar-

318

ily be viewed in terms of influence or cause, but rather in terms of the materials or options that filmmakers explore and develop in their works. In that sense, there is still a connection to be made between the nationality of a filmmaker and the artistic motivation of his or her film.

I have examined whether the nationality of a filmmaker or of a cinema has any bearing on the way we understand functions or motivations – realistic, compositional, transtextual, and artistic – of films: I have argued that it can, but it does so in a rather contingent way. Exactly how the political or cultural history of a nation-state to which a filmmaker belongs has an impact on film itself should be examined in light of the norms of the filmic field.

Before I conclude this section, there is one further connection to be made. National history or heritage may seep into filmmakers' choices of narrative or stylistic devices. But what kind of impact does it have on our concept of a national cinema? The more frequently filmmakers of a given nation-state adopt and rely on elements specific to their nation, the greater chance for such elements to be associated as prototypical features of that national cinema. However, one of the benefits of adopting the prototype theory of national cinema is that the connection between national cinema and nationality is one of probability, not of essence. National cinema does not reflect or reveal an "essence" of nationality or its culture. Rather, the latter provides the former with ingredients to explore.

Notes

1 Toby Miller et al., *Global Hollywood* (London: BFI Publishing, 2001), p. 89.
2 Ibid., p. 101.
3 Tino Balio, "Adjusting to the New Global Economy: Hollywood in the 1990s," in *Film Policy: International, National and Regional Perspectives*, ed. Albert Moran (London and New York: Routledge, 1996), p. 34.
4 Janet Staiger, "A Neo-Marxist Approach," in *Film and Nationalism*, ed. Alan Williams (New Brunswick: Rutgers University Press, 2002), p. 234.
5 Philip Schlesinger, "Sociological Scope of 'National Cinema,' " in *Cinema and Nation*, eds. Mette Hjort and Scott Mackenzie (London: Routledge, 2000), p. 22.
6 Benedict Anderson, *Imagined Communities: Reflections on the Origin and Spread of Nationalism*, revised edn. (London: Verso, 1992).
7 Susan Hayward, *French National Cinema* (London: Routledge, 1996), pp. 14–15.
8 Ibid.
9 Mette Hjort, "Themes of Nation," in *Cinema and Nation*, eds. Hjort and Mackenzie, pp. 108–9.
10 Stuart Hall seems to endorse this line of argument, although he combines the two. See Hall, "The Question of Cultural Identity," in *Modernity and its Futures*, eds. Stuart Hall, David Held, and Tony McGrew (Cambridge: The Open University Press, 1992), pp. 296–9.
11 Burch and Sellier, "The 'Funny War' of the Sexes in French Cinema," in *Film and Nationalism*, ed. Williams, p. 153.
12 Andrew Higson, "The Limiting Imagination of National Cinema," in *Cinema and Nation*, eds. Hjort and Mackenzie, p. 65.
13 Ibid., pp. 69–70.
14 Ibid.
15 Thomas Elsaesser, "Putting on a Show: The European Art Movie," *Sight and Sound* 4 (April 1994), pp. 25–6.
16 Higson, "Limiting Imagination of National Cinema," pp. 67–8.
17 Peter Bondanella, "A Fistful of Pasta: Sergio Leone and the Spaghetti Western," in *Italian Cinema: From Neorealism to The Present*, 3rd edn. (New York: Continuum, 2001), pp. 255–6.
18 George A. Huaco, *The Sociology of Film Art* (New York: Basic Books, Inc., 1965) pp. 35–6.
19 Jesse Prinz, *Furnishing the Mind* (Cambridge: MIT Press, 2002), p. 52.
20 Ibid., p. 63.
21 Ibid., p. 65.
22 Prinz uses the term "superordinate" categories instead.
23 Kristen Thompson, *Breaking the Glass Armor: Neoformalist Film Analysis* (Princeton: Princeton University Press, 1988), p. 16.
24 Ibid., p. 19–20.
25 Hayman Kublin, "Taiwan's Japanese Interlude, 1895–1945," in *Taiwan in Modern Times*, ed. K. T. Sih, Asia in the Modern World Series, no. 13. St. John's University, pp. 344–6.
26 Richard E. Nisbett et al., "Culture and Systems of Thought: Holistic Versus Analytic Cognition," *Psychological Review* 108, no. 2 (2001), pp. 291–310.
27 Noël Burch, *To the Distant Observer: Form and Meaning in the Japanese Cinema* (Berkeley: University of California Press, 1979), pp. 228–9.
28 Ibid., pp. 160–1.

PART VII

Film and Ethics

Introduction

Though some of the discussions encountered thus far in this anthology may have struck readers new to the field as strange – such as the question of whether fiction films have fictional narrators – the topic of this section, film and ethics, explores the relation of two items that have long been associated in everyday thinking. The idea that certain movies might undermine common decency or morality is usually revived several times a year by this or that pundit warning of the imminent collapse of social values; while, on the other hand, different films are often commended for improving moral understanding or advancing superior moral standards. If only because of their close connection to the emotions, films are apt to call forth an ethical response, since the emotions themselves frequently involve an ethical dimension – generally they are either moral themselves (as is the emotion of indignation), or they give rise to morally significant behavior. But, in any event, the conjunction of ethics and motion pictures is unlikely to perplex most as peculiar.

Although we are all familiar with the common tendency of labeling this film as evil and that one as morally ennobling, the question of the grounds upon which we do so is more obscure. Indeed, it is a philosophical question. As we shall see, some commentators, generally called formalists, do not think that it is appropriate to enlist moral criteria when evaluating any artwork, including motion picture artworks. But even where the philosopher believes that the moral evaluation of a film is apposite, the issue of how it is possible needs to be elucidated.

In the first essay in this section, "Film Criticism and Virtue Theory," Joseph H. Kupfer supplies the grounds for praising certain films for their positive moral contributions. Specifically, Kupfer argues that popular films can enhance our comprehension of the virtues and the vices, and, thereby, enlarge our moral understanding.

When we encounter a film, we try to make sense of it; we interpret it; we attempt to grasp its significance. In the process of interpreting a film, we bring our ideas about the actual world and our standing concepts, including our moral ones, to bear on the persons and actions that comprise the film. Because the cognitive stock that we deploy in order to interpret a film makes reference to the world in which we live, Kupfer contends that we can learn about reality, including moral reality, in the course of making sense of a film. For interpreting a motion picture may enjoin reorganizing and modifying our cognitive stock, if we are to assimilate the film rationally. In order to construe a certain motion picture satisfactorily, that is, we may, as Kupfer notes, have to deepen, expand, narrow, shift, or otherwise recalibrate our moral concepts and, in the process, thus clarify and refine our command of them. Film interpretation in this way may hone our moral understanding and increase our sensitivity in applying moral concepts in everyday affairs.

Many important popular films, Kupfer maintains, are about framing or showcasing various virtues and/or vices – embedding them in concrete narrative contexts where their essential features and their relation to other character traits become more readily accessible for reflection than they are in the hurly-burly commerce of daily life. Interpreting such films – which is the enterprise of the book from which Kupfer's article is excerpted[1] – is a matter of getting clear about what the film in question implies is essentially at stake with respect to the pertinent virtue (or virtues) at issue in the drama, and also how that virtue or vice is related, conceptually, to other character traits. Moreover, once that interpretation is completed, the net result may involve the enrichment of our relevant concepts of virtue and vice, and the sophistication of the subtlety and finesse we exercise in our use of said concepts. A film, in other words, can be a case study in certain species of virtue and vice, and by working through the case study – in interpreting the film – we can improve the cognitive, perceptual, and moral skills we need to process comparable phenomena day in and day out.

An example of what Kupfer is getting at is the film *Parenthood*, to which he devotes a chapter of his book.[2] As its title indicates, *Parenthood* is about parenting – notably about the virtues and vices thereof. That is, the film initiates an investigation into the personal qualities and character traits that make for good and bad parents. The dramatic personae cross four generations and include a great-grandmother, grandparents, parents, and a pair of expecting newlyweds. This diverse cast inevitably puts in motion a play of comparison and contrast in the viewer's mind as various styles of fathering and mothering are paraded before us. The film invites – even prompts – us to measure this graduated display of parents against each other, to ask who is successful, to what extent, and why, as well as who is remiss and what is the nature of their defects. The parental virtues of this character stand out against the insufficiencies and failings of that character, and vice versa. The film illuminates the virtues and vices of parenthood by laying before us a studied array of mutually informing contrasts such that as we come to interpret the significance of these juxtapositions, we simultaneously gain a sharpened appreciation of what constitutes virtuous parenting versus flawed and even vicious parenting.

Parenthood functions as an elaborate thought experiment – like Kant's contrast between the moral and the prudent change-maker – only with many more terms of comparison. Moreover, this thought experiment puts the viewer in a position to gather a wealth of information concerning the criteria we employ to recognize cases of what we shall count as virtuous and vicious parenting. As Kupfer points out, *Parenthood* encourages us to apprehend as the cardinal excellences of parenting

a kind of interpersonal adaptability and attentiveness – an ability to see one's children as autonomous and independent individuals with their own desires, and a willingness to adjust to and accommodate their legitimate projects of self-realization. Contrariwise, through salient examples, the film illustrates that vicarious projection and inattention to the autonomous child are definitive of defective parenting. The film coaxes from us these insights into the virtues and vices of parenting as we size up and interpret the behavior of the characters. We are led to these conclusions maieutically in a way analogous to Socrates' elicitation of mathematical truths from the slave boy in the *Meno*.

Kupfer's approach to film provides us with one way to go about commending a film morally. We may applaud it, if it abets moral understanding, including insight into or facility in applying moral concepts, such as various categories of virtue and vice. But though this may provide grounds for praising a film morally, how does our moral evaluation of a film combine with our evaluation of the film as a work of art? For surely it would appear that the moral evaluation of a film and the artistic evaluation of it are different, since they can go in utterly opposite directions. An artistically accomplished film can be simultaneously evil, and a morally efficacious one may be artistically challenged. How do we make an all-things-considered judgment in cases like that?

This is the problem that Mary Devereaux addresses in her article "Beauty and Evil: The Case of Leni Riefenstahl's *Triumph of the Will*." This particular film forces attention to the issue of the relation of moral value to artistic value because, though allegedly one of the most cinematically beautiful films ever made, it is also exceedingly immoral, endorsing, as it does, Nazism wholeheartedly and without qualification. *Triumph of the Will* is ostensibly artistically masterful but it is at the same time repugnant morally. Inasmuch as we are predisposed to think of beauty and goodness as a couplet, we find *Triumph of the Will* disturbing. Shouldn't its evil commitments count against its artistry? But if so, what philosophical grounds are available for doing so?

Of course some commentators, called formalists, reject this task outright. They deny that the moral deficiencies of a film should ever count against it in our assessment of the artistic value of the motion picture in question. The filmmaker *qua* artist is an expert in making and combining images – in composing shots and editing them together and in orchestrating onscreen movement, gesture, and behavior. That is what a filmmaker as a film artist does. She is not a philosopher, a political scientist, or a polemicist. She knows about cameras, angles, rhythms, the movement of bodies in space, and so forth. One judges her as a film artist in terms of the grace, beauty, and fluidity of her imagery. The filmmaker is a creator of moving images, not ideas. She is an artist, not a theorist.

One admires Bernini for the appearance of St. Theresa that he sculpts from stone and not for his theological acumen. Similarly, the formalist insinuates, Leni Riefenstahl is responsible for the look of *Triumph of the Will* and not its ideology (Hitler was responsible for that). Moreover, by most accounts, it is a very good-looking film – its mobile cameras and carefully calculated editing are said to forge a cinematic rhythm that many find breathtaking. In terms of the art of the film, Riefenstahl deserves high marks. That the film is evil does not detract from its artistic value. Do her camera movements become any less awesome for tracking Hitler? Would they be more beautiful if Gandhi were her subject? Thus, the formalist argues, the artistic value of a film is separate from its moral value and, consequently, the moral status of a film is irrelevant to a determination of its artistic caliber.

One objection to this sort of formalism is that it is too simplistic. Certainly, it may be objected, the work of a film artist involves more than moving cameras. That cannot be all we attend to when we evaluate her accomplishment. The film artist cannot be judged completely irrespective of the content of the film she is making. For whether or not her camera movement, editing, and so on are artistically effective will depend in large measure on their appropriateness to the subject matter the filmmaker is presenting. Olympian camera movements – no matter how eye-fetching – are not the correct formal choice for projecting the humility of a character, since the rhetorical "volume" of the device will be, unsuitably, too "loud" for the content. Formalism that is oblivious to content altogether is inadequate, since it ignores an obvious aspect of artistic invention – the discovery of the forms that will work best with the content of the film. Considerations of content, then, *may* play a role in the evaluation of a film.

However, a sophisticated formalist can take this observation in his stride. He can concede that content is relevant to artistic evaluation. One must know what the content of the film is in order

to gauge whether the formal strategies chosen to convey it are brilliant ones, suitable ones, barely acceptable or ridiculous ones. But admitting this much does not involve including a moral evaluation of the content in our estimate of the artistic value of the work. With respect to *Triumph of the Will*, knowing that it is an endorsement of the Nazi self-image enables us to adjudge the consistently large-scale proportions of the film to be fitting stylistic choices. But the endorsing of Nazism itself is not something that Riefenstahl *qua* artist did. Let us say that it was what Riefenstahl as a citizen did. As an artist, she discovered the cinematic forms that made that endorsement gripping. That the cinematic forms work perfectly with the subject at hand merits artistic accolades. What the subject is stands outside the process of artistic evaluation. Just as the inhumanity of the religious beliefs it represents does not count against regarding the Assyrian statue to be magnificently crafted artistically, neither does the savagery of National Socialism weigh against the artistic accomplishment of *Triumph of the Will*. For it may be said to capture Hitler's self-conception exquisitely.

Nevertheless, Devereaux rejects this version of sophisticated formalism. She introduces her article by noting that most people find the co-existence of beauty and evil in *Triumph of the Will* disturbing. Sophisticated formalism, Devereaux notes, cannot account for why viewers find this feature of *Triumph of the Will* so unsettling. From this she surmises that sophisticated formalism is not an adequate model of our appreciative response to *Triumph of the Will*. Furthermore, Devereaux argues that the very fact that we are disturbed by the co-presence of beauty and evil in *Triumph of the Will* indicates that fundamentally we do not believe that the artistic value of an artwork is utterly disjunct from its moral value nor that artistic evaluation should be insulated from moral evaluation.

But there still remains the question of how it is possible to factor the morality of a film into its artistry. With respect to *Triumph of the Will*, Devereaux points out that Riefenstahl not only created an ensemble of cinematic devices; she also created a vision or point-of-view regarding Nazism. Through composition, camera movement and editing, Riefenstahl projects an idealized and ebullient conception or portrait of National Socialism – that of a highly unified and powerful movement with a virtually endless stream of selfless followers. This vision of Nazism is as much an artifact of

Riefenstahl's artistry as the fluidity of her camera movements. Thus, it is an appropriate consideration to raise when assessing the film artistically. If the vision that Riefenstahl confected is deficient, the artistry of the film is compromised to that degree.

Another way to put Devereaux's point is this: the vision of Nazism in *Triumph of the Will* is an essential feature of the artwork that *Triumph of the Will* precisely is. *Sans* that vision of Nazism, a film would not be *Triumph of the Will*. Moreover, evaluating a film *qua* artwork requires engaging and assessing all the features of the work that make it essentially what it is. With reference to *Triumph of the Will*, this entails engaging and assessing its vision of Nazism. That is something for which Riefenstahl is artistically responsible. But pondering the vision of Nazism that *Triumph of the Will* broadcasts will involve acknowledging the moral issues that it provokes. And since the moral vision of Nazism conjured up by Riefenstahl is morally flawed, to that extent *Triumph of the Will* is flawed. For that vision of Nazism is an essential feature of the artwork *Triumph of the Will*. And if an essential feature of an artwork is defective, then the artwork is defective to the same degree. For if what makes the film exactly the artwork it is is blemished, then the artwork as such must be marred.

Though Devereaux's argument is one that many will find compelling, it is not likely that it will sway many sophisticated formalists. Devereaux accuses these formalists of making it impossible for moral repugnance to play a role while we are doing aesthetics, and for being unable to account for why we find the conjunction of beauty and evil in *Triumph of the Will* so troubling. But might not the formalist respond that these charges are merely question-begging? The formalist may agree that many people find the nexus of beauty and evil in *Triumph of the Will* troubling, but then go on to add that they should get over it. Once one sees things as the formalist recommends, all discomfiture will evaporate. The disturbance Devereaux says people feel is really a function of their commitment to a bad theory – the ancient Platonic view that truth, beauty, and goodness are of a piece. As soon as people let go of this prejudice and embrace the right theory (formalism), all their upsetment will dissipate. Similarly, when they appreciate the truth of formalism, they will relinquish the expectation that moral repugnance should have a role to play in aesthetics. Simply to

presuppose that it does have a role stacks the deck against formalism. Can Devereaux dodge the charge that she is merely begging the question against formalism? Inquiring minds want to know.

On the other hand, even if Devereaux's objections against the sophisticated formalist fail, might she not still have a point when she contends that Riefenstahl's vision of Nazism is an essential element in the artistic construction of *Triumph of the Will* and that, therefore, that vision must figure in any estimate of the artistic value of the film? What do you think?

Mary Devereaux is concerned with establishing the grounds upon which we may criticize as an artistic failing the immorality of a film. But many are eager to go beyond criticizing immoral films. They want to censor them. In American society, this is often the case with pornographic and markedly violent films. In "A First Look at the Pornography/Civil Rights Ordinance: Could Pornography Be the Subordination of Women?" Melinda Vadas attempts to articulate an intelligible basis, informed by feminism, for banning pornographic films.

Vadas's argument is offered in the context of certain longstanding debates in the philosophy of law, and these debates, in turn, shape the kinds of points Vadas needs to make in order to motivate the case for censoring pornography. Since censorship involves the mobilization of state power for the purpose of regulating pornography, the would-be censor must operate with some criterion of when it is legitimate for the state to intervene in the sexual choices of its citizenry. The censor cannot assume that censorship is warranted whenever a film is immoral. The censor must invoke some principle – shared by people who are socially liberal about sexual mores as well as by those who are more conservative – if the prohibitions at issue are to garner public acceptance.

Perhaps the most influential statement of such a principle in the Anglo-American tradition was propounded in *On Liberty* by John Stuart Mill, who maintained that "the only purpose for which power may be exercised over any member of a civilized community, against his will, is harm to others." For obvious reasons, this is called the Harm Principle; its animating idea is that in matters pertaining to relations between consenting adults, state interference is permissible only if the aforesaid relations result or are apt to result in harm to third parties. For example, certain kinds of sexual relations, like oral sex, between consenting adults cannot be prohibited according to the Harm Principle inasmuch as these activities pose no threat to third parties. However, since an activity such as public gun fighting on the streets of Laredo endangers innocent bystanders, it may be banned, even if the participants engage in it of their own free will.

The Harm Principle represents the liberal consensus in the English-speaking world regarding the grounds for state intervention in what might otherwise appear to be the private lives of citizens. Adherence to the Harm Principle, indeed, is one of the factors that inclines us to call a society liberal. The Harm Principle is a hurdle that any censor must clear if she hopes to establish prohibitions that will be acceptable to puritans and liberals alike.

Vadas, and the feminists who have inspired her, know this. That is why they are at pains to identify pornography as a form of subordination. For if pornography is a matter of subordination – specifically a matter of violating the equality rights of women and of treating them as of a lesser moral importance than men – then pornography is implicated in compromising or setting back the interests of women and, therefore, counts as a harm. For to harm someone is to set back their interests, and compromising a person's rights is a way of setting back their interests. Thus, if it can be shown that pornography is involved in the subordination of women, then the censor may appeal to the Harm Principle in order to ban the dissemination of pornography.

One way in which censors often attempt to invoke the Harm Principle is to maintain that the behavioral consequences of the consumption of pornography by men poses an imminent threat to innocent third parties, namely women. That is, it is hypothesized that men who read or view pornography are prone to harass, rape, or otherwise abuse women. Pornography is said to be the theory; rape the practice. If this correlation could be confirmed as possessing a high degree of probability, the Harm Principle could be leveled against pornography.

However, as is well known, it is very, very difficult to substantiate causal hypotheses of this sort. About the most that can be defended in this domain is that the consumption of pornography *may* play a role in acts of violence against women where the perpetrators in question are already predisposed toward violence against women. But this hardly justifies a blanket prohibition of pornography with regard to all men, since arguably not all – and perhaps not most or even a great many – men are predisposed toward violence against women.[3]

Yet the invocation of the Harm Principle that Vadas makes ingeniously eludes the problem of establishing the behavioral consequences of pornography that are alleged to be caused by its consumption. For Vadas, and the feminists whose suggestions she is developing, have not posited a claim about the behavioral consequences of viewing pornography. They have not made any predictions about the harms to women that are likely to ensue if men are allowed to consume pornography. Vadas et al. are asserting that pornography in and of itself *is* or constitutes a harm to women – specifically, it *is* the harm of subordination.

Vadas's case does not rest upon proving that pornography will probably bring about harm to women in its wake. She is not claiming that once men view pornography a substantial number of them will predictably go out and do violence to women. That is an empirical hypothesis – one that requires the sort of scientific confirmation that no one so far has been able to deliver to the satisfaction of all the parties to this debate. Instead, the claim that Vadas propounds is a conceptual one, a claim that *by definition* pornography falls under the category of harm, insofar as it is an instance of the subordination of women. That is, pornography may be judged to be harmful to women whether or not it has the additional causal propensity to incite rape or other forms of violence against women, since pornography *is*, in the first instance, the harm of subordination, independent of whatever further causal tendencies it may possess.

The background of Vadas's argument, as she explains in her article, is the prototype of an ordinance, designed by the feminist writer Andrea Dworkin and the lawyer Catharine MacKinnon, which prototype various communities in the United States and Canada have striven to turn into law. Among its many interesting innovations, the Dworkin/MacKinnon ordinance defines pornography as "the graphic, sexually explicit subordination of women." Some may charge that this is not an accurate definition of pornography, since in common parlance graphic sexual displays where the participants are portrayed as equals, playfully engaged in mutually rewarding sex, rather than the women being subordinated demeaningly, also usually count as pornography so long as the sex is explicit enough. However, identifying pornography with subordination, whether or not that accurately accords with ordinary usage, dialectically engineers an end-run around defenders of pornography who argue that the censors have failed to meet the requirements of the Harm Principle insofar as no one has yet conclusively demonstrated that the consumption of pornography leads, with statistically significant regularity, to violence toward women. But, as we have seen, the subordination-of-women maneuver outflanks this reservation. If nothing else, Dworkin and MacKinnon have found an intriguing opening in the discussion of pornography and the Harm Principle, and exploited it.

Nevertheless, there has been resistance to their proposal. One leading source of anxiety is that it violates customary linguistic meaning – the notion that pornography itself subordinates anything, it is said, is literally nonsense. How could pornography literally *be* the subordination of women? Pornography may lead to the subordination of women. But how can it – in and of itself – subordinate women? That sounds like what philosophers call a category mistake – the impossible or conceptually inappropriate attribution of a feature of one category to a member of an alien category, as in the assertion that pigs fly. "Pornography subordinates" sounds just as oxymoronic. But can it be rejected as quickly? Vadas thinks not, and it is the purpose of her essay to show that sense may be made out of the notion that pornography subordinates women.

The idea *may* be intelligible which, then, implies that the Dworkin/MacKinnon ordinance need not be dismissed out of hand as absurd. This is a very modest claim. But even so, it requires a great deal of philosophical skill and imagination to get it off the ground

So the crux of the issue for Vadas is the intelligibility or coherence of the notion that pornography subordinates women – that pornography as such is an instrument of the subordination of women. Of course, a reasonable person would agree that pornography may depict or show the subordination of women – think of bondage films. But to say that a film depicts subordination is quite different than saying that it is doing or performing the subordination itself. Showing a film clip of the assassination of John Kennedy is a far cry from assassinating Kennedy. To suppose otherwise is to court conceptual confusion. Thus, by parallel

thinking, a reasonable person might claim that to equate the depiction of the subordination of women in pornographic films with the literal subordination of women is equally absurd – a violation of logical thinking, an offense to the depth grammar of our concepts. But if that is so, then the Dworkin/MacKinnon ordinance rests on a conceptual error and is a non-starter from the get-go.

What Vadas wants to do is to show that the ordinance is not necessarily absurd and thus should not be discounted as a category mistake. Vadas intends to convince us that it is at least intelligible to allege that pornography subordinates women – that the charge is conceptually kosher – even if it sounds like a weird way of talking. Vadas does not commit herself to the truth of the allegation, but only to the proposition that it is a live possibility from a logical and grammatical viewpoint. It is not a non-starter, in other words.

By subordination, Vadas means: "To subordinate an individual or a group of individuals . . . is to place that person or group of persons socially in a class of those whose intrinsic or inherent moral worth or standing is not of the first rank, and whose rights are thereby of lesser scope, importance or weight than others." This itself is an impediment to those so treated and thus patently a harm. Furthermore, the social establishment of a group's inferiority can lead to political oppression, which is morally harmful to both the oppressed and the oppressor. Vadas does not suppose that her article conclusively proves either of these claims, but only demonstrates that there is nothing necessarily confused conceptually about advancing these charges. Though these assertions may be false, they nevertheless are coherent.

In the philosophy of language, there is an area of inquiry called Speech Act Theory. Speech Act Theory is based on the insight that we not only report how the world is by way of words; we also *do* things with words – that is, we change the way the world is by means of what we say. When the minister of the peace intones "I now pronounce you man and wife," a new fact dawns – another couple is now married. Vadas wants to argue that we may not only perform actions with words, perhaps our paradigmatic symbolic instruments. We may also perform actions by way of another sort of symbols, namely pictures – specifically, Vadas wants to argue that by means of graphic pornographic pictures, women are subordinated.

In order to explain how this is possible, Vadas introduces us to a series of subtle concepts. The first of these is the *direct transfer of predicates*. In the sentence "The grass is green," the phrase "is green" is the predicate. When I look out the window and I say "The grass is green," "is green" is the predicate of my sentence. Now suppose that I take a color photograph of the lawn. It shows that the relevant color-property of the lawn is *greenness*. Let us say that the photo conveys the predicate "…is green" to the viewer. Because the predicate that I would apply to the lawn in my sentence and the predicate applicable to the lawn in the color photo is applicable in the same sense, Vadas says that the predicate "…is green" in this case transfers directly to the photo – greenness is equally and in the same way a property of the pertinent swath of grass and of its representation in the photograph.[4]

That is, according to Vadas, predicates attributable to an object, action, person, or event may transfer to a depiction of said object, action, person, or event. For example, a given rose is red. If I take a snapshot of it and my picture portrays a red rose describable by the predicate "…is red" – which predicate is also attributable in the same way to the referent of the snapshot in nature – then the predicate has "transferred" from the rose in nature to the snapshot. The transfer is direct, moreover, since the predicate "…is red" applies equally and in the same sense to the rose in nature and also to the depiction of the rose. Obviously, this notion of the direct transfer of predicates will be strategic in making the case that pornographic pictures subordinate women, since "…subordinates women" is a predicate.

Ostensibly, the direct transfer of predicates contrasts with *prepositional predicate transfer*. The latter occurs when the predicate in question transfers not to the depiction as a whole but only to what is depicted. The preceding rose is sweet-smelling. The redness of the rose transfers directly to its depiction. But its fragrance does not. The rose smells sweet, but the photo does not. Yet the photo still is *of* a sweet-smelling rose. In this case, the predicate "…is sweet-smelling" applies (or is transferred) to the photo only prepositionally inasmuch as it is not itself sweet-smelling but only *of* something that is sweet-smelling. It will be Vadas's contention that the predicate "…subordinates women," with respect to pornographic films, transfers directly and not merely prepositionally from pornographic stagings to pornographic films.

If Vadas's distinctions thus far show anything substantial, it is only that there are some direct predicate transfers from the referents of pictures to the pictures themselves. Next, she argues that value predicates can be so transferred. Let us return to the example of the rose. Suppose that it not only can be said to be red (a descriptive predicate) but also to be beautiful. A competent photo of this rose will capture that feature of it. The predicate in the true assertion "That is a beautiful rose" transfers directly to a competent photo of the rose. It will be a beautiful photo. Furthermore, among the value predicates that can transfer directly to films are moral predicates.

If the Iraqi prisoners in Abu Graib *were humiliated* by being stripped and shackled in dog collars, then a photo of them in that condition equally humiliates them in virtue of the direct transfer of predicates. Moreover, this is putatively what their captors believed; this seems to be one of the reasons they took the photos. Similarly, if Juanita is honored by receiving a gold medal for first prize in the spelling contest, then a photograph of her in the school paper equally honors her. Thus, it is the case that at least some morally charged predicates transfer directly from their referents to pictures thereof. "…subordinates women" is a morally charged predicate. Is it not possible that it transfers directly from the pro-filmic event to the pornographic film that pictures it?

Before making this last move, Vadas needs one final distinction – between what she calls the *material* scene and the *depictionary* scene. Recall that most pornographic films nowadays are fictional. The handyman comes to the back door and, before you know it, he is in bed with the lady of the house. Of course, this is not an actual handyman; he is an actor, as is the housewife. The "material scene" is the label Vadas assigns to what is actually going on in front of the camera – two actors sexually engaged; the "depictionary" scene is the name that Vadas assigns to what is going on in the fictional world where a handyman and a housewife are locked in sexual congress.

For the purpose of the case for censorship, Vadas wants us to focus on the depictionary scene and the moral predicates that attach to it. Why? Because in the real world, the actress playing the housewife might not be someone we could uncontroversially describe as being subordinated – she could be the producer of the film who voluntarily "submits" to the caresses of the male actor for profit. She might even be an exhibitionist who uses the opportunity of being a sex worker to gratify not only her bank account but her sexual impulses, In short, there is no guarantee that the actress is being subordinated in the material scene that gives rise to the fiction.[5] On the other hand, the character she is playing is being portrayed as subordinated – ostensibly subordinated to male desire, an instrument of male pleasure, the meaning of whose existence is solely to satisfy masculine desire, and, therefore, of lesser moral worth than the handyman.

In sum, then, Vadas is arguing that, with respect to picturing, there is a phenomenon called the *direct transfer of predicates* in which the predicates applicable to an object, person, action, and/or an event apply equally to a depiction of the aforesaid objects, persons, actions, and/or events. Sometimes value predicates transfer directly. The depictionary scenes of pornographic films – the fictional scenes played out in front of the camera – show women by nature to be the mere tools of male lust, subordinated, and rightfully so, to masculine desire. That women are *subordinated* in these fictional portrayals is a moral predicate applicable to the relevant depictionary scenes and it transfers directly to the pornographic movies that show them. It is not (or, at least, it may not be) a matter of prepositional transfer, but of direct predicate transfer and, therefore, warrants the assertion that "pornography subordinates women." The injustice or harm of subordination represented in the fictional or depictionary scenes transfers directly to the pertinent pornographic films which may, in consequence, be censored under the authority of the Harm Principle.

Sketching the argument formulaically, it goes like this:

1 If pornography harms anyone, then it is subject to state action, including censorship. (This invokes the Harm Principle.)
2 If pornography contributes to injustice, then it harms women. (Being subjected to injustice is one form of harm.)
3 If pornography subordinates women, then it contributes to injustice. (Subordination involves the violation of one's right to equal treatment, and, therefore, is an injustice.)
4 In virtue of the direct transfer of value predicates, if pornography portrays women as subordinated (in the depictionary scene), then it is a subordinating depiction of women – i.e., it subordinates women. (This relationship is what Vadas's article was designed to motivate.)

5 Pornography portrays women as subordinated (in the depictionary scene). (Hypothesis.)
6 Therefore, pornography subordinates women (from 4,5).
7 Therefore, pornography is subject to state action (from 6, 1, 2, 3). (NB: state action here might involve censorship or the enforcement of law suits against pornographers or some form of regulation; basically the argument establishes that state intervention with respect to pornography is permissible.)

Admittedly, this argument is a bit stronger than what Vadas is out to prove. Her aim is only to establish that an argument like this one is not conceptually confused. However, for heuristic purposes, let us suppose that Vadas wants us to take this argument at face value, since that will make it easier to probe, among other things, whether its claims to conceptual sobriety are plausible.

Presumably everyone will agree with the first three premises. The first merely appeals to the Harm Principle, the second to a putatively unobjectionable conception of injustice, and the third to a standard notion of subordination. The fourth and the fifth premises are where the action is in this argument.

The fourth premise is the key to Vadas's case for the intelligibility of the claim that pornography subordinates women. The prospects for such an assertion depend upon the feasibility of the notion of the direct transfer of predicates. This idea relies upon the persuasiveness of certain paradigmatic examples – putatively the notion of the direct transfer of predicates is acceptable, since these examples appear clear-cut. But in fact the examples do not show exactly what Vadas needs them to show.

Take the case of the red rose. The rose may be described by the predicate "…is red," but the *photograph* of the red rose is not accurately described as red, unless it is red throughout, as it would be if the photographer employed the right kind of filter. That is, there are likely to be colors other than red in the photo as well, thereby precluding calling the photo, as such, red. Usually a color photo of a red rose will not be describable as a red photo. Similarly, even if the rose is describable as beautiful, a photograph of a beautiful rose is not necessarily a beautiful photograph. Imagine taking a picture of a beautiful rose with a grotesquely distorting lens on the camera. The result need not be a beautiful picture and, in all probability, it would not be. Or imagine a snapshot of a beautiful rose being taken by an unpracticed cameraman like myself. It could turn out to be a god-awful ugly photo, though nevertheless, it would still be a photo *of* a beautiful rose.

The point here is that Vadas's examples do not really support the idea that there is such a thing as the direct transfer of predicates. It is not the case that a depiction of a red rose gives rise to a red depiction or that the photograph of the beautiful rose gives rise to a beautiful photograph. At best the transfer pertains to parts of the depiction and not to the whole of the depiction. It is an equivocation to maintain that there is invariably a direct predicate transfer from the red, beautiful rose to its depiction as such, since the depiction itself (as opposed to its referents) need not be either beautiful or red. Only parts thereof are.

Therefore, it will not be plausible, on the basis of these examples, to conjecture analogously that it is possible to move from a depictionary scene of subordination to the allegation that a motion picture representation of said scene subordinates. Rather, part of the image shows that a man is subordinating women, much as the reasonable person imagined before we began speculating about the existence of direct predicate transfer; it is not the case that the image as such – as the sum of all of its parts – subordinates women. Or, at least, given her examples, it is hard to see how Vadas could maintain this without equivocation.

A photo of a beautiful house shows a beautiful house. But there is no reason to expect that the photograph of the beautiful house will be a beautiful photograph. Think of all those nondescript real estate advertisements that show palatial mansions with well-appointed landscapes. The beauty of those homes will never get those photographs into the Museum of Modern Art's photography collection. Why? Because beauty, *pace* Vadas, does not directly transfer to the very photographs of beautiful things. If she wants us to think that the direct transfer of predicates is an intelligible notion, then she will have to find more compelling examples in order to establish the credentials of this concept.

Even the direct transfer of the predicate *red* in her case of the red rose does not pass muster, since if the red rose appears in the photograph on a green lawn, it would surely be a mistake to call the photograph as a whole red. Why is this important? Because for Vadas to claim that a film of a woman being subordinated itself subordinates women, she, Vadas, needs the predicate transfer to go from part of the depictionary scene to the entire depiction as such. However, the examples she has used to establish that there is something identifiable as direct predicate transfer that works in the way she requires do not support the hypothesis that such a phenomenon exists. So it looks as though the fourth premise is false and that the required notion of direct predicate transfer is not a reliable one.

But maybe we are looking at the wrong examples. Perhaps the notion of direct predicate transfer would be more convincing if we considered moral predicates. The prisoners *were humiliated* by being stripped and manacled, and, *ex hypothesi*, they *were humiliated* by the photograph that recorded this. Likewise Juanita *was honored* by receiving the medal, and the photo in the school newspaper documenting this event *honored* her as well. Do these examples support Vadas's case?

Consider a news clip of a terrorist leader being cheered by his followers after the success of an attack on civilians in a foreign country which killed thousands. Imagine that this newsreel is shown on network television in the nation that has suffered this attack. Do the networks honor the terrorist leader by airing the news clip? That seems unlikely. The networks might be showing it to underscore how callous the terrorists are – how they smile and laugh while thousands suffer and grieve. Or the networks might simply be reporting that the terrorist leader was honored. It does not follow from simply showing the news clip that the network is also honoring the terrorist leader.

Of course, one might use the clip to honor the terrorist leader. Perhaps that is how his followers use the clip to recruit more volunteers to the cause. But the honoring here depends on the purposes to which the footage is put. The footage itself does not necessarily honor the terrorist. It may be used simply to report that such and such happened or it may even be used to disgrace the terrorist – to expose him as a hardhearted monster.

So "... honors x" does not seem to be a compelling example of the kind of direct predicate transfer Vadas needs. Nor does "... humiliates x" work either and for the same reasons. When Amnesty International displays the photos of American soldiers humiliating Iraqi prisoners, it does not thereby humiliate the Iraqi prisoners, but rather excoriates the American prison guards. Similarly, the photos may be reproduced in a newspaper in order to document that these things happened in Abu Graib. That is probably how the *New York Times* would explain their publication of some of the photos. Again, everything hinges on the use to which the depiction is put and that, in turn, depends on the intention of those who are exhibiting it. We have not yet encountered any compelling evidence that there is something like automatic direct transfer of moral predicates of the sort required by Vadas's argument.

Moreover, if the use to which a film is put is connected to the intentions of its exhibitors, then isn't it highly unlikely that the producers and distributors of pornographic films intend to subordinate women? Their intentions are to arouse, to make money, and to entertain. Some of them, like Larry Flynt and Hugh Heffner, might even claim that they want to liberate their sexually repressed fellow citizens. But, in any event, it is unlikely that most pornographers intend their depictions to subordinate women. And without the relevant intentions, the mere filming of a depictionary scene in which the woman's sole purpose is to provide male pleasure does not amount to subordinating women. It could even be part of a feminist exposé of the vileness of pornography. Moreover, Vadas has failed to explain, with respect to the supposed mechanics of direct predicate transfer, how we get from the putative subordination of one woman in the depictionary scene to the film, as such, allegedly subordinating *women* (all women?).[6] Again, the fourth premise would appear to be in dire trouble.

The fifth premise hypothesizes that pornography does depict women as subordinated. Undoubtedly, this is true of some pornography. Some pornography, for example, is sadistic. But is it the case that all pornography is of this sort? As noted earlier, might there not be pornography that shows a couple, respectful of each other's autonomy, relishing sex – the man and the woman each

devoted equally to pleasuring the other? Vadas, Dworkin, and MacKinnon seem to deny the existence of such pornography by definition. But do you think that this is an acceptable way to proceed?

In general, it seems difficult to get one's mind around the idea that a pornographic film could subordinate women (in general?). In what palpable way do dirty pictures projected on Skid Row set back or compromise the rights of the wealthy society women uptown? Moreover, even if it were the aim of pornography to subordinate women, as a matter of empirical observation, it does not seem very effective. For, at least in the United States, it would appear that the period that coincides with the greatest expansion of the pornography industry (beginning in the 1970s) also correlates with the most momentous expansion of women's empowerment in American history.

Though serious problems may be raised with Vadas's treatment of the pornography issue, she has thoughtfully addressed a question that is wider than pornography – viz., how is it that we may regard films as doing something immoral? She has proposed the mechanism of direct predicate transfer. Though a tantalizing concept, it is fraught with problems. But a concept like it, only without its shortcomings, would surely be a welcome addition to the moral philosophy of motion pictures. We do often speak of some films as though they were literally immoral, where we do not mean simply that they will have immoral consequences. But on what basis is this possible? What structures enable films to constitute immoral acts? The notion of the direct transfer of predicates is an attempt to explain this. It is probably an unsuccessful attempt. But the need for an explanation is still pressing. Do you have any ideas about what such an explanation might look like?

N.C.

Notes

1 Joseph H. Kupfer, *Visions of Virtue in Popular Film* (Boulder, Colorado: Westview Press, 1999).
2 We highly recommend that interested readers take a look at this chapter. It is an excellent piece of criticism and a model of Kupfer's philosophical-ethical method of interpretation. See Kupfer, *Visions of Virtue in Popular Film*, pp. 91–122.
3 It should be noted that the Harm Principle is not the only grounds upon which state regulation of

pornography might be warranted. There is also the Offense Principle. This principle presupposes that people have a right not to be offended by being accosted unexpectedly in public by things that are likely to outrage their sensibilities. Thus, there are laws against public nudity. However, the Offense Principle will not justify the prohibition of pornography, since people can be shielded from being surprised and upset by pornographic material by means short of censorship. For example, the dissemination of pornography may be restricted by zoning in such a way that as long as people steer clear of those precincts of town they will not be accosted by what they regard as offensive pornographic imagery. Likewise, the government might require that pornography be labeled in such a way that anyone who opens this magazine or attends that film showing knows ahead of time that they are risking an encounter with graphic sexual material. The Offense Principle warrants state regulation, but state regulation less coercive than censorship. Thus, if feminists are committed to banning pornography, the Offense Principle is not the legal tool they need. The Harm Principle is. And that is why Dworkin, MacKinnon, and Vadas are interested in the proposition that pornography subordinates.

4 Unfortunately, Vadas sometimes tends to blur the distinction between properties and predicates in her article.

5 Of course, it may in fact be the case that the actress is being subordinated in the material scene. In her memoir, the porn star Linda Lovelace claims that her sexual performances were involuntarily compelled.

6 Against the notion of the direct transfer of predicates, gay activists may argue that it makes no sense to say that the domination depicted in certain genres of gay films made by gay artists for gay audiences subordinates gay people. Such films are made to satisfy various sexual fantasies. They are, at the very least, a form of entertainment. It would be absurd to imagine that they are a matter of gay people subordinating gay people. They are a form of sexual play designed to arouse certain sensibilities and are obviously not an attempt by one segment of the gay population to subordinate another segment. Moreover, for similar reasons, many gay people are opposed to the Dworkin/MacKinnon ordinance. They maintain that it interferes with their sexual freedom. They think that it is silly to think that pornography that plays to gay s-m fantasies contributes to the subordination of heterosexual women. And they find the prospect of bans on their pornography itself to be a form of oppression.

22

Film Criticism and Virtue Theory

Joseph H. Kupfer

Film Criticism

We had the experience but missed the meaning,
And approach to the meaning restores the
experience . . .
                                    T. S. Eliot, Four Quartets

Interpretive levels and assumptions

I am concerned with fiction films, films that tell stories in the colloquial sense that novels, theater plays, and raconteurs tell stories. The stories told in these films, then, are film fictions or movie stories. Fiction films are distinguished from other films such as documentaries, advertisements, travelogues, instructional or educational films, and artistic (non-narrative) explorations of the medium. The term director or filmmaker is used when referring to the team of people responsible for making the film, which is typically headed by the director.

I approach interpretations of movie fictions as a layered structure or edifice. At the base of the interpretive structure are the first-order descriptive claims that refer directly to perceptual images and sounds. These descriptions tend to pick out discrete, discriminable images and scenes in a relatively uncontroversial way. Topping off the structure are comprehensive claims about the story's meaning that encompass the lower-level statements. The comprehensive assertions are supported by the lower-level statements but, in turn, organize and

make sense of them. In between the top and bottom levels are numerous strata of inferences and construals of meaning. Let's start at the foundation.

Interpretations are grounded in more or less indisputable descriptions of what happens in the story. As these statements refer directly to what is observable, they are basic, or first-order, descriptions. The first-order account of *Psycho*, for example, includes the claims that Norman Bates runs a hotel and that he watches a hotel patron, Marion, through a peephole. We take the cinematic depiction of character and events as providing uncontestable story data. The cinematic depiction is like reading that Captain Ahab had lost a leg pursuing a great white whale.

The assumption of narrative facticity is a basic convention for reading novels and viewing fiction movies. Imagine the oddness of someone challenging basic descriptive claims, saying: "Yes, we see Norman apparently running the Bates motel and spying on Marion, but how can we be sure? Maybe we are mistaken." Such a challenge to basic, first-order descriptive claims is to miss how the convention of facticity is necessary for readers or viewers to make sense of a story. It would be like thinking that evidence exists outside the fictional presentation that might change our minds about what we see. The basic content of what we see or are told just does constitute the narrative facts.

However, conventions do exist for exceptions to the assumption of facticity. There may be cine-

Joseph H. Kupfer, "Film Criticism and Virtue Theory," *Visions of Virtue in Popular Film* (Boulder: Westview, 1999): 13–34.

Joseph H. Kupfer

matic or narrative clues that an unreliable narrator is telling a story, such as the storyteller in Ford Maddox Ford's novel *The Good Soldier*. A classic way for films to generate uncertainty about what actually takes place in the story, one that is self-reflective about storytelling, is to present multiple, incompatible versions of the tale, as in Akira Kurosawa's *Rashomon*. Films that are open-textured, or open-texted, in this way usually trade on this feature. Ambiguity or uncertainty about what really occurs is essential to interpreting the film. The films I consider, however, are of the prosaic variety – straightforward narratives for which numerous uncontestable descriptions can be asserted. For instance, the statement "Carter Burke tries to kill Ripley" is a first-order description of the story told by *Aliens*.

As we leave the foundational descriptions of the story, we initially make inferences, which can be considered immediate because they are made directly from first-order descriptions and because they, too, tend to be unproblematic. In *The African Queen*, Rose Sayer manages a weak smile and offers more tea and bread in response to Charlie Allnut calling attention to his loud gastric rumblings. We immediately infer that she wishes to change the subject to something more pleasant. When the boy Kevin grimaces as he maneuvers to catch a fly ball during a baseball game in the film *Parenthood*, we are justified in making the immediate inference that he is tense and unsure of himself.

We do not always make inferences from first-order descriptions and subsequent immediate inferences in a one-to-one, atomistic fashion. Instead, we often derive implications from clusters of scenes, collages of images, and counterpoints of dialogue. Thus, we combine our immediate inference about Kevin's nervousness with the inference that his father, Gil, suffers an excessive sense of parental responsibility for Kevin's welfare. Together, these inferences imply that Gil's attitude and the behavior it produces are probably contributing to Kevin's insecurity.

When we make a case for our interpretations of movies to other people, we typically marshal evidence and inferences so as to ground higher-level claims in lower-order inferences and, finally, in descriptive statements about the movie text. Although we may begin a piece of criticism with summary generalizations stating what the film is about, a hierarchical structure of argument is usually discernible within the discussion. As with scientific hypotheses, however, the order of

discovery or creativity tends to be quite different from the format we use to present or justify our interpretation of a film.

Our intermediate and higher-order meaning statements frequently dawn on us as a result of unexpected concatenations: Disparate scenes appear to fit together; seemingly unrelated intermediate inferences suggest an overarching theme; a striking image draws diverse moments in the film to itself and to each other like a magnet. Even when our exposition proceeds neatly from description to immediate inference to intermediate inference, stage by stage, it is a reconstruction for clarity of communication from a more rough-and-tumble process of discovery and ordering, and reordering upon yet further discovery.

Moreover, as we offer intermediate-level conjectures about such aspects of the story as character motivation and symbolic weightiness, we must necessarily tie together different portions and dimensions of the film. It is as if we are backing away from the film, trying to see a variety of images and scenes in relationship to one another. In the movement away from basic description and immediate inference, we see connections between and among them and higher-level interpretive claims. In this movement also lie the most creative and interesting features of interpretation.

As we well know, the same movie fiction is subject to different and diverging interpretations; nevertheless, ordinary moviegoers and critics alike assume a common referent for these interpretations. For our purposes, the common referent of interpretation is that which is picked out by first-order descriptions and immediate inferences. I use the term text to mean an object available for public inspection. Interpretive claims find their eventual support in textual referents. However, citing the text rarely resolves interesting interpretive disagreements or indicates which interpretations are better than others.

We assume movie fictions are purposive, that the cinematically rendered tale has a point, without necessarily assuming that the filmmaker actually had these particular (or any) purposes in mind. The point or meaning of a film is indeterminate because the text is amenable to different construals of meaning. Consequently, viewers of movie fictions have a degree of freedom in interpreting them. The overall meaning of the film is captured in comprehensive, summary generalizations that are supported by the interpretive edifice. Exercising interpretive freedom responsibly and convincingly involves tethering the contestable intermediate and summary ascriptions to the text by means of first-order descriptions and immediate inferences. How well the contestable or summary ascriptions are textually grounded depends on the number of such foundational supports and the plausibility of the inferences drawn.

No movement beyond the basic descriptions and the immediate inferences from them would be possible without a backdrop of other conventional assumptions for making sense of movie fictions. Of course, most of these conventions are taken for granted in viewing and interpreting films. Only in such self-conscious reflection as this do we make them explicit. For example, we typically take the sequence of events as they are presented in the film to be identical with the temporal sequence of events in the story being shown. Conventions and contexts, such as those suggesting flashbacks, indicate the movie's departure from the linear directionality of time, which we habitually transfer from the real world.

In fact, we naturally assume a rough resemblance between the world portrayed in the fiction movie and the real world. Assumptions of reality resemblance include temporal and spatial uniformity, object individuation and continuity, and causal linkage among events. We operate with these assumptions unless we are cinematically cued to see the world of the movie fiction as different from our own. Similarly, familiar conventions let us know when we are seeing the world through a character's eyes (in contrast to an objective camera point of view), when time has elapsed, or when place has changed.

In *Groundhog Day*, for example, we are given ample evidence that the people in Punxsutawney, Pennsylvania, are reliving the same day and that only Phil Connors remembers what occurs from one "same" day to the next. But aside from this big exception to the laws of spatio-temporal uniformity and temporal directionality, everything else in the world of this movie fiction resembles the real world.

No matter how bizarre the tale of fantasy or science fiction, a good deal of resemblance is necessary for viewers to find the fictional world intelligible. The requirements of intelligibility always constrain the extent to which the fictional world can deviate from reality as we conceive it. If the fictional world departs too much from the actual one, viewers simply cannot make sense of it. Of course, that can be the point of a film. In such cases, the meaning of the film is not going to be found primarily within its story but will be discovered in how the unintelligibility of the events portrayed is cinematically constructed.

Critical perspectives

Interpretations are appropriations of movie texts, and all are from a perspective or viewpoint. No interest-free, or nonperspectival interpretations are possible. As John Dewey points out, "Critic and artist alike have their predilections."[1] Because criticism is judgment, Dewey tells us, critics reveal themselves in their criticisms.[2] The particular approach a critic takes may tell us as much about the critic's tastes or concerns as it does about the film being examined.

Films can be interpreted from many viewpoints, reflecting various values and interests. As noted in the Introduction, the dominant trend in recent academic film studies has been to interpret films from a linguistic, Marxist, or psychoanalytic perspective or some combination of those perspectives. Interpretation in this vein tends to underplay the importance of the story for the sake of placing the film in a social or psychological context of creation and reception. Critics who are concerned with the significance of the story, as I am, are hardly of one mind. Their interests can range over narrative style, social commentary, religious symbolism, metaphysical or psychological outlook, and historical placement.

The point of a story is not always obvious, and where obvious, further meanings or complexities may be enfolded within the central idea that require creative viewing and reflection. Critical creativity includes resourcefulness and decision-making because the movie fiction is indeterminate. Not only is it open to the panorama of interpretations resulting from the many perspectives from which a film can be approached, but within a given perspective, a film is amenable to different interpretations. Different interpretations can be justified by reference to the text because, as noted earlier, film fictions underdetermine their interpretations, allowing for indefinitely many implications to be drawn from a movie text. As Peter Jones writes of the texts of novels: "There are no formal limits to the ways in which texts may be taken."[3]

Because the movie fiction is open to competing interpretations, critics view films and think about them creatively. Creative freedom is necessitated

Joseph H. Kupfer

by textual indeterminacy of meaning and significance. Critics vary in their powers to discriminate
parts and nuance, as well as in their abilities to
discern thematic threads with which to weave
these elements into a meaningful whole. According
to Dewey, "This unifying phase, even more than
the analytic, is a function of the creative response
of the individual who judges. It is insight . . . It is at
this point that criticism becomes itself an art."[4]

The danger lurking in critical creativity is that
critics can make more of the text than is warranted
and ground too little of their interpretation in it.
They then use the movie fiction as a springboard
for their own flights of fancy instead of fitting their
inventiveness more faithfully to the story. Dewey
again astutely observes how "sometimes critics of
the better type substitute a work of their own for
that they are professedly dealing with. The result
may be art but it is not criticism."[5] For Dewey, the
more creative the critics, the more susceptible they
are to this temptation. Critics cannot overreach
unless they are blessed with ingenuity and aesthetic acuity.

The diversity in viewpoints from which movies
are interpreted probably accounts for the most
striking differences among interpretations. Interpreters naturally emphasize those components of
the story and propose organizational schemes
that are consonant with their specific backgrounds
and interests. From various interpretations, we
infer diverse meanings about life. For example,
my interpretation of *Rob Roy* stresses features of
the film that coalesce around themes of moral
language use.

In contrast, a Marxist perspective would produce an interpretation whose unifying thrust
and points of accent would be very different.
The meaning of the story would tend to be cast
in terms of control over the means of production
and the economic stratification that limits Rob
Roy's options, including his inability to see natural
allies in the impoverished tinkers. A more historically minded critic would probably emphasize the
decline of the Scottish clans as a consequence of
the centralization of politico–military power or as
the product of changes in the political economy,
such as those due to technological innovation.

The interpretations of film offered in this book,
of course, are framed by the theme of virtue and
my interest in virtue theory. In contemporary critical language, I "thematize" the films, although
the thematization is typically ascribed directly to
the films, not to my thought processes. Thus,

I speak of Patty's lack of autonomy as represented
in the film *Parenthood*, even though I am the one
seeing it there. This locution is typical of interpretations for two reasons. For critics to qualify all
of their comments as the result of their interpretive efforts is distracting. More importantly perhaps, interpreters are trying to get readers and
viewers to see their interpretations fleshed out in
the features of the text. To call attention to one's
own thematic agenda easily interferes with bringing the reader into that thematic perspective.

I do not mean to suggest that interpretations are
exclusively the result of a perspective that viewers
bring to the film. This may be more prevalent in
academic film studies, and it certainly describes
the way my interpretations are presented here.
However, there are times when the film itself
draws us to particular features of the narrative
and orients us in one way rather than another in
its viewing. Whether we subsequently fit those
features or that orientation into a previously existing framework of significance or are led to an
unanticipated vantage point is an open question.
For example, I was struck by the role played by
Chief Brody's virtuous character in his triumph
over the shark in *Jaws*. The movie seemed to
direct my attention to this feature, but I may
have been prepared to fasten on the contrast between moral and technical excellence by my background and interests.

We can learn from movie fictions because the
construals we make of them have reference to the
world in which we live. Indeed, the viewpoint
from which we fashion an understanding of the
film already reflects our everyday interests, beliefs,
and values. We do not perform our interpretive
activity in a vacuum and then happily discover that
the interpretation speaks so incisively to our life!
Our life's interests filter our movie perception,
especially when we seriously scrutinize the movie
for purposes of systematic interpretation.

In addition, the interpretive viewpoint we bring
to the text can be modified by it. In the course of
interpreting the film, our views about real life can
deepen, expand, narrow, shift, or even do an about-
face. Before viewing the film *Fresh*, for example,
I had some ideas about the nature of practical wisdom. Watching the film's protagonist apply advice
about playing chess to the people who wield power
over him prompted me to rethink an aspect of this
rare and stunning virtue. In particular, I thought
about a particular agility of mind, which I now
believe is inherent in practical wisdom.

Movie fictions can be a basis for a new understanding of the world. Even when we look at them from an established viewpoint or ideology, the resulting interpretation can apply to actual experience in promising ways. The interplay between my prior understanding of virtue and my experience of the film *Rob Roy* yielded an interpretation that revolves around the theme of moral standards of language use. In leading me to connect virtue with language and moral community, the emergent theme also enabled me to explain the particular virulence of the evil characters in *Rob Roy*. Generalizations about moral communities and the evil that opposes them seem to me now to apply to everyday life, although not usually with the clarity with which they inform this film.

Were the interests or perspectives we bring to the interpretation of film inviolate or static, moviegoing would soon become monotonous. One of the pleasant surprises of watching and discussing films is the way an interpretive angle favored at one viewing of a film can be modified or supplanted by a different approach at a later time. The change in interpretation may be caused by alterations in ourselves that occurred between the two movie experiences, but it can be wrought by the film itself – by relationships and meanings in the film that we now happen to notice but missed on earlier viewing. What critics find important depends on their interpretive outlooks, but what strikes critics as salient in the movie can also determine the interpretive strategy.

Successful interpretations

When I say that interpreting movie fictions assumes that they have a purpose or point, I do not imply that the purpose is the filmmaker's. Even where ascertainable, the filmmaker's intentions or goals are not authoritative in constructing or assessing interpretations of films. As with all art, once a film is made, it is a public object open to interpretation according to conventions of intelligibility and the interpreter's creative response.

What a filmmaker tries or intends to accomplish in making a film is distinct from what interpreters take the film to mean. For one thing, not all intentions of filmmakers are realized in the film. For another, some unintended cinematic effects are indeed realized in the finished product. Problems of intentionality in art have been well articulated, and I do not wish to unreel the arguments here.[6] I mention a few of the more glaring

difficulties with intentionality in interpretation to allay any concerns that my talk of a film's purposes may arouse.

Among the more blatant problems with deferring to the artist's intentions as definitive of interpretation is the consequence that artists could not discover new things in their work nor could they change their interpretation of their work once they were finished. Some artists explain that they do not know what they intend until they actually make their art, and this is incompatible with giving authority to intentions of the artist that exist prior to the creative process. As if these difficulties were not enough to undermine the attractiveness of intentionality in criticism, consider the problem of deciding the intention, or even a consistent set of intentions, operating in works of collective creativity such as we find in film. How is a critic to ascertain which are the relevant or authoritative intentions among the writers, producers, editors, actors, cinematographer, and director?

It is precisely to avoid such monumental detective work and subsequent adjudication that some film critics turn to the plans and intentions of directors alone. But recourse to only the director's state of mind seems ad hoc, and it still leaves open the slew of other difficulties, even if otherwise acceptable. Of course, rejecting intentionality as a procedure for assessing or deriving interpretations does not preclude looking to the director, or others involved in making the film, for suggestive lines of interpretation. What a director had in mind, like a writer's drafts or a producer's projected goals, may or may not prove helpful in a critical construal of a movie fiction. But this is an altogether different tack to take, one that gives no special privilege to the director's purposes.

My approach to film interpretation clearly works better for some films than for others. For instance, some films seem to cry out for historical or social interpretations. The film *Matewan* (1987), by John Sayles, is about the first coal miners' strike in the United States, which took place early in the twentieth century. Situating the movie fiction within the country's nascent labor movement and European emigration to the United States is probably a more fruitful approach than looking at the film after my fashion, as a self-contained moral fable. Other films lend themselves to psychoanalytic exploration, such as Hitchcock's *Vertigo* (1958). As mentioned, films whose form undermines narrative continuity are perhaps best interpreted on a metanarrative level. When films depart radically from the storytelling structures characteristic of most movies, we should think first of interpreting them as commenting on film-making or the film medium rather than primarily as telling stories whose significance is paramount.

Different kinds of criticism reflect different questions asked and different aims. No one interpretive approach can respond to the spectrum of questions or tangle of interests that movie-goers and critics may have. As I understand it, interpretation stands in between the movie text and the viewer's experience. The text and the experience determine an interpretation's value, but in different ways. As I have been arguing, the text supports or justifies the interpretation, from intermediate inferences through subsequent building of meaning, to summary statements of the film's overall themes and views.

On the other hand, the experience of viewers vindicates the creative work of interpretation. Interpretations are vindicated when they help viewers see more in the film – more details, more significance in those details for the overall work, more connections among the parts and aspects of the film, more meaning altogether in the story. Sometimes an interpretation gives viewers a complete perspective for viewing the film more rewardingly. But perhaps more edifying are interpretations that stimulate viewers to think about films more vigorously for themselves, using the remarks of the critic as a guide to create their own interpretations.

On a smaller scale, movie-goers may simply find a view that a critic claims is implied in a movie is indeed in it. Such corroboration is not the same thing as agreeing with the view that is implied. Consider the conclusion of the film *An Officer and a Gentleman* (1982). Dressed in Navy whites, Zack Mayo (Richard Gere) marches into the factory where Paula Pokrifki (Debra Winger) toils and sweeps her up into his arms. Zack carries Paula out of the factory life, and out of the film, amid the cheers of her former coworkers. It seems reasonable to construe this finale as expressing the view that a woman's salvation is to be found in a close relationship with a successful man. Finding that construal plausible, and therefore helpful in appreciating the meaning of the movie, does not commit us to agreeing with it.

The difference between finding interpretive claims borne out by movie fictions and finding them true of our actual world leads me to comment further on the interpretations I make in this book. I have chosen films whose visions of virtue seem to me to be right. Interpreting these movie fictions has amplified my understanding of virtue and vice, as well as the place of various virtues in our social lives. The moral generalizations that I propose, therefore, have a double reference – to the film fiction and to the real world. Taken as referring to the movie fiction, the generalizations purport to enhance movie appreciation. Taken as referring to reality, the general claims are supposed to capture truths about human life.

The correctness or plausibility of the general moral claims taken in one sense is independent of the claims taken in the other. Readers need not agree with me that the claims implied by a movie are true of the real world in order to find them fruitful in their experience of the movie. The reverse could also be the case, that readers find the generalizations true or plausible of the real world but not very satisfying when it comes to interpreting a film. In either event, I hope readers will take up the gauntlet and think of a more accurate understanding of moral life or develop more illuminating interpretations of the movies.

Unlike much very good, instructive criticism, I have chosen to examine only films I find worthwhile. Consequently, readers will find little in the way of evaluative judgments in my commentaries. My capsule evaluation of the films is that they are all very good. They have their flaws, but I hope I will be forgiven for not paying much attention to them. As an acid test of my judgment, I suggest the reader compare the films I discuss with other popular movies in their respective genres. Compare *The African Queen*, for instance, to other romantic adventure films such as *Romancing the Stone* (1984) or the Indiana Jones series of movies.[7] These more recent films are filled with attractive characters, well-paced plots, and settings replete with ambience and invention. But do they explore anything comparable to the transformative power of romantic friendship with the subtlety or depth found in *The African Queen*?

As with all interpretation, the crucial question is whether the interpretations I offer lead viewers to a richer appreciation of the films than they would have had otherwise. In Dewey's terms, the value of criticism lies in furthering the "reeducation of perception of works of art."[8] My movie interpretations are guided by Dewey's conception of the value of criticism, yet another topic worthy of full-scale discussion in its own right. He maintains that criticism fulfills its educational office by directing "the perception of others to a fuller and more ordered appreciation of the objective content of works of art."[9]

Because the emphasis of this book is on moral views I find implied in the films, I have focused on the larger meanings and themes of movie fictions. But good interpretation also leads to an appreciation of detail, in the service of the larger meaning to be sure, but also for its own sake. In constructing an interpretation, critics are occasionally struck by a moment that at first seemed unimportant but that on subsequent viewing appears laden with meaning. Sometimes the first glimmer of significance is the result of nothing more than the fact of the detail catching our eye. Charlie Allnut kicking the boiler aboard the African Queen is one such detail for me. He says, "I kinda like kicking her. She's all I've got." Just because the incident snagged my attention, I lingered over it and wondered how it fit into the bigger picture.

No claims are made here about the possible or likely effects on audiences of the visions of virtue I find portrayed in the films. Exposure to images of virtue alone is not likely to alter people much, although such exposure could inspire us to reexamine our lives. The popularity of the films examined here, however, might indicate the concern of audiences for moral character or their attraction to the struggle between virtue and vice. I now turn to the concept of virtue with which I approach the films.

Virtue Theory

Give me that man / That is not passion's slave, and I will wear him / In my heart's core, ay, in my heart of heart.

Shakespeare, Hamlet

Types of virtue

Thanks to Alasdair MacIntyre's lucid and provocative *After Virtue* and the impetus supplied by several other prominent philosophers, the virtues have returned to center stage as a lively topic among academic philosophers, educators, and people of letters. But interest in the virtues has never really been far from the thoughts of mass audiences whenever they read novels, watched plays, or viewed movies.[10] Narrative arts have always emphasized the character of their characters, whether the protagonist be a Scrooge or a Ulysses, an Othello or a Huck Finn. Audiences,

elite and popular, are drawn to questions of virtue and vice perhaps because so much of our welfare depends on our own character and because we prosper and suffer at the hands of other people on account of their moral traits.

Virtues are excellent qualities of individuals that make them valuable to themselves and to other people. They are relatively settled dispositions to act, feel, desire, and think in specifiable patterns. These dispositions can be manifested in indefinitely many ways.[11] Thus, the same behavior can indicate different virtues (or vices), and a particular virtue (or vice) can be expressed in very different, even opposite, behaviors. For example, waiting for someone to give us a gift might exhibit friendship, patience, generosity, or forgiveness. On the other hand, the virtue of kindness can be shown by refraining from commenting on another person's behavior, as well as by offering constructive criticism of someone's behavior.

As excellent traits, virtues naturally make those individuals who possess them more attractive and desirable than people who do not have them. Virtues can be classified according to the different sorts of strengths people have. Intellectual virtues, for example, are responsible for success in problem solving or theorizing, especially in mathematics or science. Moral virtues can also be distinguished from aesthetic virtues, such as nobility and wit, and the meliorating virtues, such as gentleness and unpretentiousness.[12] Meliorating traits make life more pleasant, cooperation more likely, and difficult situations more tolerable. James Wallace finds in the distinctively moral virtues the qualities that enable individuals to flourish.[13] Just as biological abilities, such as a hound's olfactory sense, enable animals to flourish, moral virtues are crucial to human thriving.

Some moral virtues are "executive," enabling the execution of actions, strategies, and projects. Executive virtues are instrumental to our carrying out plans and realizing our ends.[14] Not only do these virtues enable us to perform successfully in general, but they are often critical to moral action. Because doing what we believe is right may be difficult for us, they can also be described as virtues of willpower or self-mastery.[15] Virtues such as determination, patience, and resourcefulness enable us to overcome obstacles to acting on our moral beliefs and values, and so have a distinctive bearing on moral life.

Courage seems to be an especially important and dramatic virtue of execution or willpower.

Joseph H. Kupfer

We must be courageous when moral conduct is risky, and courage can be essential to the expression of other virtues. Individuals may need courage to keep their integrity, to be patient, or to maintain their loyalty. In the film *Rob Roy*, Rob most obviously displays courage in risking his life for the sake of his clan and his honor. But he is also courageous in remaining steadfast to his good friend McDonald when all his kinsmen believe the worst of McDonald. In maintaining McDonald's innocence, Rob not only risks the lives of his family and the clan's survival, but he risks looking like a fool.

In contrast to the executive virtues of self-mastery are the substantive virtues that motivate our action. They supply our ends, including particular ethical patterns of behavior, emotion, or judgment.[16] The substantive virtues include compassion, generosity, loyalty, justice, and humility. For example, generosity prompts us to look for occasions to give what we value to others, for their own sake. Loyalty motivates us to believe the best of our friends and to stand by them when they are in trouble. Justice also supplies us with action-guiding ends. When the reconnaissance expedition learns that Burke has tried to kill Ripley and Newt, in the movie *Aliens*, Ripley's sense of justice moves her to urge returning Burke to stand trial rather than be executed on the spot.

Executive and substantive virtues complement one another. Executive virtues are the means by which we perform the actions motivated by the substantive virtues. We do not act out of courage or patience, for instance, but by means of these virtues. But we do act out of loyalty or compassion and not by means of them. Executive virtues without the substantive are morally directionless; substantive virtues without the executive are without efficacy. Although nonmoral virtues, such as wit and friendliness, are interesting, keeping to the moral virtues in the analyses of the films in this book is work enough. When nonmoral virtues are discussed, their relevance to moral virtue is the purpose.

Edmund Pincoffs argues that what makes (substantive) virtues moral is that "they are forms of regard ... for the interests of others."[17] The substantive virtues mentioned do seem to motivate individuals to pay attention to, and act for, the welfare of other people. Therefore, the egoism exhibited by Phil Connors in *Groundhog Day* is not just one vice among many. Rather, it is a wholesale renunciation of the moral enterprise, which sometimes requires sacrificing one's personal interests for the sake of other people.

Pincoffs appears to be at odds with James Wallace in what he sees as the definitive dimension of moral virtue. Whereas Pincoffs takes regard for other people as individuating the moral virtues, Wallace understands virtue in terms of human flourishing. However, the two views can be seen as different emphases, which dovetail in the social nature of human wellbeing. Strong social relations are needed for human flourishing, and the virtues promote social life through their regard for the welfare of others. The substantive virtues supply a regard for other people's needs and interests, and the executive virtues increase the likelihood that those needs will be met and their interests satisfied. Speaking of the conventions that inescapably govern social life, Wallace points out the importance of the virtues: "Whatever variations this [conventional] form of life admits of, such things as ... conscientiousness, benevolence, restraint, and courage tend in their ways to foster it."[18]

The best societies are conspicuous by what the virtues free their members from worrying about concerning other individuals – deception, violence, corruption, indifference, and capricious or stifling governance. The virtues are the necessary attributes for happy common life because we need to be able to rely on others, as well as to count on ourselves, in order to flourish. For Alasdair MacIntyre, the best communities are built on a shared concept of the good. The members of such a community are held together not merely by mutual advantage. Rather, they agree on an ideal of living.[19]

The virtues that members of a healthy community esteem facilitate achieving the ideal way of life, but they are also ingredient to it. For example, the character traits of peacefulness and cooperativeness, which the Amish hold in high regard, not only promote the ideal of living shared by the Amish people, but these virtues are also part of that ideal. We see a community governed by a shared concept of the good in the film *Rob Roy*. The bonds of good character, and mutual awareness of it, sustain the MacGregor clan. In sharp contrast are the social organizations depicted in *Jaws* and *Aliens*, in which people are connected almost exclusively by economic interest rather than by a moral ideal of communal life.

342

Aristotle's heritage

Because the virtues, of whichever stripe and in whatever combination, are necessary to social life and individual flourishing in society, every culture has some conception of valuable character traits. However vague their definition or boundaries, some traits are promoted in a society's members, while others are discouraged. It seems plausible that all cultures subscribe to some version of courage, justice, honesty, and wisdom, as it is difficult to imagine how a culture could survive, let alone prosper, without these particular virtues. As Alasdair MacIntyre argues, courage is a virtue because "the care and concern for individuals, communities and causes . . . requires the existence of such a virtue."[20] Care and concern for one's community are necessary for social success. Since threats to a community and its members inevitably arise in the course of events, the willingness of individuals to risk harm to themselves for the greater good seems to be necessary and valuable to all societies.

Cultural differences in how particular virtues are defined or ordered exist, but such variations are compatible with the broad claim that virtues exist in all societies and that particular virtues likely cross cultural borders. Regardless of how truthfulness, justice, or kindness are precisely understood, or what their scope of application includes, versions of these attributes of character seem to be prized universally.

Although I believe the virtues possess some form of cultural universality, the purposes of this book hardly require it. The films examined here are popular Hollywood movies and so are heavily influenced by, if not firmly embedded in, the Western tradition of the virtues. According to MacIntyre, the Western tradition, which includes the Judeo-Christian heritage, is deeply ingrained with appropriation of and response to "Aristotle, whose account of the virtues decisively constitutes the classical tradition as a tradition of moral thought."[21]

Without necessarily subscribing to Aristotle's biology, metaphysics, or view of the ideal political state, we in the West operate within Aristotle's conception of virtue. We do so in part because he writes so extensively and insightfully about virtue itself, as well as about the particular virtues. We are also influenced by Aristotle's understanding because of the widespread impact of classical thinking on Western culture and because of the Aristotelian philosophy passed down by Aquinas.

According to Aristotle, virtues are necessary for personal and social goods, but they are not merely a means for attaining them. The virtues help constitute these valuable aspects of life. For example, both social cooperation within a community and trust in friendship demand truthfulness. But truthfulness is not simply a means to cooperation or trust; rather, it is constitutive of communal harmony and the bonds of friendship. Similarly, within friendship, openness is not just an instrument for the attainment of intimacy. Self-disclosure is part of the fabric of intimacy.

Thus, although it is true to say that virtues enable people to live well, we cannot think of good life as specifiable independent of the virtues. Acting on the virtues is what we mean by a good life. We describe the action itself as acting virtuously. The entwinement of virtue, activity, and well-being can be seen within the narrower confines of specific activities. The virtues are necessary for technical success, such as Phil Connors's piano playing and ice sculpting in *Groundhog Day*. However, "the enjoyment of the activity and the enjoyment of the achievement are not the ends at which the agent aims, but the enjoyment supervenes upon the successful activity in such a way that the activity achieved and the activity enjoyed are one and the same state."[22]

Virtues are qualities that promote attainment of those goods that are internal to activities. When values are internal to an activity, we delight in the activity itself, and the goods of which we partake cannot be described, understood, or experienced apart from the activity. The goods internal to playing a team sport are found in the playing – the exertion of muscle, the competition, the way different individuals jell as a team, and the freedom (and need) to improvise. On the other hand, goods external to such an activity might be praise, fame, status, or payment, valued and achievable apart from the playing of the sport.

MacIntyre goes into detail in explaining the structure of a practice, how values are internal to it, and why the virtues are necessary to participating in the practice so as to realize those internal values. We need only note here the integral role of the virtues in engaging in the panoply of practices that make up the domains and disciplines of life: technical and theoretical work, family and community, arts and games, hobbies and avocations. Virtues enable us to locate ourselves in the reigning traditions and to subject ourselves to the standards that govern the relevant practices. As a result of such virtues as honesty and justice, we are able to communicate with people who are similarly engaged as well as gauge our relative progress. By means of traits such as diligence, discipline, and even courage, we can develop the capacities and skills germane to the practices.

What MacIntyre seems to overlook is that virtues are also needed when we perform activities simply for their instrumental benefits. When we treat a social or technical practice merely as a means to an end, we must nevertheless exhibit certain excellences of character. Should we play baseball for money, perform surgery for glory, or work with a political party in order to be elected, success is likely to require tenacity, self-confidence, moderation, or resourcefulness. Most of these virtues are executive. To realize the values internal to a practice, however, substantive virtues seem additionally required. Put simply, then, a web of virtues is needed to derive the values that are both external and internal to practices. The virtues are essential to living well, in all its aspects.

Even though the virtues promote practical success, we should act virtuously irrespective of anticipating it in specific situations. In discussing *Groundhog Day*, I argue that the goods internal to a practice can be had only when ignored, or looked past, for the sake of engaging in the activity itself. The irony for Phil Connors is that he receives the adulation of the townspeople of Punxsutawney, for both his good deeds and his piano playing, only when he undertakes the ethical and musical endeavors for their own sakes.

Internal to exercising the virtues is a vital value. Whether we are engaged in technical or ethical pursuits, we find value in the virtuous activity itself. This is because the virtues are the forms by which people realize their human potential. Inherent in developing our distinctively human potential is the most fundamental of internal goods. The good is vital because it defines a life truly and fully human. In Aristotelian terms, we are most alive when realizing our human natures, and this is one and the same thing as acting virtuously. Success in achieving moral and technical ends also flows naturally from putting the virtues into practice. Consequently, Aristotle finds the virtues central in a human life that, taken as a whole, can be called good. Our lives are deficient and therefore incomplete insofar as they are lacking the virtues – in number and degree.

The virtues themselves, moreover, are incomplete without judgment. Judgment is essential because concrete circumstances enter into the requirements and constituents of virtuous (and vicious) conduct. The same action that would be courageous in one situation may be rash in another. Whereas compassion in one circumstance may commend leaving someone alone, in another context providing consolation or diversion may be the compassionate thing to do.

People with practical wisdom, phronesis, exercise good judgment in particular situations. In the midst of people's diverse interests and purposes, mingled and merged, individuals with practical wisdom are able to estimate how much to do and when to do it. Moral matters necessarily are concerned with "more or less," hence, Aristotle's claim that the virtue lies in the mean between the extremes of more and less – the vices. Knowledge about ethics, including the virtues, consists in imprecise generalizations, which cannot cover all contingencies. Moral knowledge therefore has a large empirical component, and practical wisdom involves being able to learn from one's own experience, as well as the successes and setbacks of other people.

The virtue of narrative

In MacIntyre's view, in order to make sense of human action we have to situate the behavior within a historical understanding of the individual. The meaningful construal of behavior as having this rather than that intention, or as pursuing one goal rather than another, requires a temporally extended account of a subject capable of responsible choice. A relatively unified conception of self is needed to find human conduct intelligible, and such unity is supplied by a narrative account of the life of an individual. To make sense of action by reference to the purposes of an agent with enduring character traits, we require "a concept of a self whose unity resides in the unity of a narrative which links birth to life to death as narrative beginning to middle to end."[23] Obviously, I cannot do justice here to questions of personhood or the intelligibility of human behavior, but I hope that sketching MacIntyre's response to them points to a potential value of movies.

The argument made by MacIntyre is that if we wish our descriptions of human conduct to be more than a list of disconnected, discontinuous behaviors, we must provide some form of biographical account. Since the concept of personhood, or responsible agency, demands a narrative of a human life, ascribing virtue and vice to individuals also presupposes constructing the appropriate stories for them. Discussions of moral character make sense only if we conceive of people as having histories.

Because of the presuppositions of intelligibility, MacIntyre claims that narrative history of a certain kind turns out to be the basic and essential genre for the characterisation of human actions."[24] If MacIntyre's approach is roughly correct, either by itself or as an integral component of a larger theory, then looking to stories such as movie fictions is most appropriate in the exploration of the virtues. The narrative arts are not merely ancillary to understanding human nature and the many ways it can go right or wrong. Rather, stories uniquely capture formal aspects of the lives of individuals, real and imagined, needed for us to make sense of them.

Martha Nussbaum further specifies a MacIntyrean position by stressing the importance of narratives to the moral imagination and the virtues that especially depend upon it. The forgiveness or mercy we show wrongdoers, for example, depends on inquiry into and appreciation for the details of their individual histories. Nussbaum notes how the merciful attitude "entails regarding each particular case as a complex narrative of human effort in a world full of obstacles."[25]

As with entering into the lives of fictional characters, the merciful attitude toward actual people requires putting ourselves in their place, with their histories of misfortunes and mistakes. A supple, energetic imagination vivifies for us a wrongdoer's social milieu, distorted experience, and destructive options. Nussbaum's description of how imagination and feeling are wed by the structure of the novel applies to the form of film as well: "It is a form of imaginative and emotional receptivity," in which the life of another penetrates "into one's own imagination and heart."[26] Because the trajectory of narrative underlies the appreciation of the lives of both fictional characters and actual people, our experience of movie fictions can inform our understanding of real individuals – in general outline or in particular situations.

In providing detailed, complex pseudo-biographies, movies augment more abstract philosophical analysis. Film fictions are like case studies in law, filled with the subtlety and messiness that

naturally elicit attention to those loose ends of life so easily lost on the clean edges of academic theory. As mentioned above, practical judgment deals with particular situations, and when it is effective, judgment alights on what is morally important in the particular. The concrete particular "must be seized in a confrontation with the situation itself."[27] Movies present simulacra or representations of actual and possible particular situations and can thereby clarify what exactly practical judgment is supposed to grasp.

In contrast to the particularity of narrative, philosophers must generalize, even when championing the irreducible significance of particularity in moral judgment. Thus, Martha Nussbaum generalizes about the limits of generalization. She points out that practical wisdom is the capacity to deal with novelty and contextual variety with a "responsiveness and yielding flexibility . . . that could not be adequately captured in any general description."[28] The film *Fresh*, however, is able to depict concretely how extrapolating from one particular situation to another takes a nimble imagination, abetted by insight into the vagaries of human desire and fear. The cinematic rendering not only illustrates Nussbaum's necessarily general observation but also elaborates on it.

The films I examine extend and modify the Aristotelian moral tradition – in general and in its particulars. We in the West take our bearings from this tradition in part because we have been shaped by it, yet our lives interrogate and redefine its perspective. Our culture and the Aristotelian heritage that it reflects are as narratively figured as the lives of actual individuals or the characters in movie fictions. Changes in family and social conditions, for example, narratively reshape the development and exercise of virtuous character.

The conception of virtue with which I work, therefore, should be understood as situated within "a tradition which always sets itself in a relationship of dialogue with Aristotle, rather than in any relationship of simple assent."[29] This book is an effort to participate in that dialogue by reinterpreting the Aristotelian perspective in light of popular American movies, which confront it with a contemporary sensibility. The wisdom and resiliency of the Aristotelian view of virtue are confirmed in its practical relevance to modern life.

Notes

1 John Dewey, *Art as Experience* (New York: Minton, Balch, 1934), p. 313.

2 Ibid., p. 308.

3 Peter Jones, *Philosophy and the Novel* (Oxford: Oxford University Press, 1975), p. 191.

4 Dewey, *Art as Experience*, p. 313.

5 Ibid., p. 314.

6 A locus classicus of trenchant criticism of intentionalism is the essay by W. K. Wimsatt and Monroe Beardsley, "The Intentional Fallacy," *Sewanee Review* 54 (1946): 468–88.

7 This series, starring Harrison Ford in the title role, begins with *Raiders of the Lost Ark* (1981), continues with *Indiana Jones and the Temple of Doom* (1984), and concludes with *Indiana Jones and the Last Crusade* (1989). *Jewel of the Nile* (1985), the sequel to *Romancing the Stone*, again pairs Michael Douglas with Kathleen Turner, providing a romantic continuity missing from the Indiana Jones series.

8 Dewey, *Art as Experience*, p. 324.

9 Ibid.

10 Hence the recent success of William Bennett's anthology *The Book of Virtues*, as well as the children's cartoon show based on it.

11 For strong reasons to think of virtues and vices as dispositions rather than as habits, see Edmund Pincoffs' *Quandaries and Virtues* (Lawrence: University Press of Kansas, 1986), pp. 79–80.

12 Ibid., p. 85.

13 James Wallace, *Virtues and Vices* (Ithaca: Cornell University Press, 1978), p. 19.

14 See David Pears, "Aristotle's Analysis of Courage," *Midwest Studies in Philosophy* 3 (1980): 274–85.

15 See Andreas Eshete, "Character, Virtue, and Freedom," *Philosophy* 57 (October 1982): 495–513; and Robert C. Roberts, "Will Power and the Virtues," *Philosophical Review* 93 (April 1984): 224–47.

16 Roberts, "Will Power and the Virtues," p. 228.

17 Pincoffs, *Quandaries and Virtues*, p. 89.

18 Wallace, *Virtues and Vices*, p. 36.

19 Alasdair MacIntyre, *After Virtue* (Notre Dame, Ind.: Univ. of Notre Dame Press, 1981), pp. 146–7.

20 Ibid., p. 179.

21 Ibid., p. 138.

22 Ibid., p. 184.

23 Ibid., p. 191.

24 Ibid., p. 194.

25 Martha Nussbaum, "Equity and Mercy," *Philosophy and Public Affairs* 22 (Spring 1993): 83–125, 103.

26 Ibid., p. 108.

27 Martha Nussbaum, *The Fragility of Goodness* (Cambridge: Cambridge University Press, 1986), p. 301.

28 Ibid., p. 304.

29 MacIntyre, *After Virtue*, p. 154.

23

Beauty and Evil: The Case of Leni Riefenstahl's *Triumph of the Will*

Mary Devereaux

I

Leni Riefenstahl's documentary of the 1934 Nuremberg rally of the National Socialist German Workers' Party, *Triumph of the Will*, is perhaps the most controversial film ever made. At once masterful and morally repugnant, this deeply troubling film epitomizes a general problem that arises with art. It is both beautiful and evil. I shall argue that it is this conjunction of beauty and evil that explains why the film is so disturbing. My aim in this essay is to explore the relationship of beauty and evil in *Triumph of the Will* and to use this examination of a particular case as a way of investigating the more general problem of beauty and evil in art. Having looked at this case in detail, I want to draw some broader conclusions about the inadequacy of the usual solution to the problem of beauty and evil in art and to suggest the direction we should move in to develop an account of aesthetic value rich enough to handle cases as difficult as *Triumph of the Will*.

My main aim is philosophical, but I shall have to turn to more concrete matters before taking up the philosophical issues. I will briefly describe the historical background of the film and the circumstances in which it was produced (Section II). I will also provide some sense of *Triumph of the Will* itself, that is, of its artistic strategy and how it contributes to the film's overall effect (Section III). I will then be in a position to turn to the

problem of beauty and evil in the film and to the more general problem of beauty and evil in art that is my central concern (Sections IV–VI).

II

The 1934 Nuremberg party rally was one of several mammoth political rallies sponsored by the Nazi Party between 1923 and 1939. It lasted seven days, involved tens of thousands of participants, and was estimated to have drawn as many as 500,000 spectators.[1]

The film of these events was made at Hitler's personal request and with his support. Hitler himself gave the film its title, *Triumph des Willens*. He also went to Nuremberg to help with the preproduction planning, carefully orchestrating the spectacle that would involve thousands of troops, marching bands, and ordinary citizens.

Like the rally, the film's production was a large, well-organized event. Riefenstahl's crew consisted of 172 persons: 36 cameramen and assistants, 9 aerial photographers, 17 newsreel men, 17 lighting technicians, and so on.[2] The crew, uniformed as SA (Sturmabteilung der NSDAP) men so that they would not be noticeable in the crowd,[3] used thirty cameras and worked nonstop for a week. Riefenstahl held daily directorial meetings at which each member of the camera crew received instructions for the next day. Scenes were

Mary Devereaux, "Beauty and Evil: The Case of Leni Riefenstahl's *Triumph of the Will*," *Aesthetics and Ethics: Essays at the Intersection*, ed. Jerrold Levinson (Cambridge: Cambridge University Press, 1998): 227–56.

rehearsed beforehand, and the front ranks of the Labor Service men were trained to speak in unison.[4]

Concerned that the long parades, endless speeches, and days of nearly identical events would bore her audience, Riefenstahl rejected the static format and voice-over commentary of the conventional newsreel. Instead, she adopted and expanded methods of mobile photography developed by Abel Gance and others for the (fictional) feature film. Wherever possible she had rails and tracks laid throughout the rally site, including a circular track built around the speakers' podium[5] and a lift installed on a 140-foot flagpole. The crew was even instructed to practice roller skating.[6] These devices enabled Riefenstahl to infuse shots of her frequently stationary subjects with action and motion.

Distilled from sixty-one hours of footage, in a process of editing that Riefenstahl worked twelve to eighteen hours a day for five months to complete, the final version of the film ran just over two hours. Its intensely dynamic visual material was set to a score of Wagnerian music, German folk songs, military marches, and party anthems (including the official party anthem, "Das Horst Wessel Lied") intercut with the sound of cheering crowds and party speeches. The result, in both style and effect, was a radical departure from the standard newsreel. An innovation in documentary filmmaking, *Triumph of the Will* was also, as is generally recognized, a major contribution to the history of film.

The film premiered at the Ufa Palast in Berlin in March 1935 before an audience of foreign diplomats, army generals, and top party officials, including Hitler.[7] None of the Nazi officials, not even Hitler, had seen the film in advance[8] – an extremely unusual circumstance at the time, since no film could be screened in private or public until it was passed by the censorship board.[9] Some party members thought the film "too artistic," though whether the objection was to artistic technique itself or to the film's suitability for political use isn't clear. Others, especially members of the army, were angry at Riefenstahl's omission of most of the military exercises (the footage had been shot in bad weather). Hitler, however, was delighted with the film.[10] Although it is difficult to know exactly how widely *Triumph of the Will* was shown or how it was received,[11] it apparently enjoyed some popular success, despite the German public's preference for entertainment films.

In any case, artistically, *Triumph of the Will* immediately established itself, winning recognition not only in Germany (where it was awarded the 1935 National Film Prize), but also abroad, where it won the Gold Medal at the Venice Film Festival. Two years later, it won the Grand Prix at the 1937 Paris Film Festival, where, to their credit, French workers protested Riefenstahl's appearance when she came in person to accept her award.

III

In turning to the film itself, there are three things to note: its structure, its vision, and its narrative strategy. Each of these features contributes to the film's notable effect.

Structurally, *Triumph of the Will* has twelve sections or scenes, each focused on a particular party rally event: Hitler's arrival in Nuremberg, the Hitler Youth rally, the folk parade, Hitler's address to the SA, and so on. The film *appears* to present these events as they unfold. In fact, Riefenstahl ignores chronological order almost entirely, working instead to create a rhythmic structure for the film.[12] Her aim, she states, was "to bring certain elements into the foreground and put others into the background," to create a dramatic succession of highlights and retreats, peaks and valleys.[13] This musical structure was created largely in the editing room, where, working without a script, Riefenstahl used a variety of means – alternating scenes of day and night, moving from solemnity to exuberance, and generally altering the pace of the film from sequence to sequence and within the individual scenes themselves – to give the film a determinate rhythmic structure.

This rhythmic structure is manifest in sequences such as the film's third section, "The City Awakening." The portrait of early-morning Nuremberg begins slowly and lyrically as the camera travels high above the quiet, mist-covered rooftops of the old city. Church bells toll and the film dissolves to a lively shot of morning activity in the tented city used to house rally participants. Here, drums beat and bugles announce the start of day for residents, who emerge jauntily from their tents to wash, shave, and eat breakfast. The tempo and pace of this montage of daily activity increase, climaxing in brightly lit shots of healthy, bare-chested youths, working and singing old German folk songs as they polish shoes, haul wood for the camp stoves, and prepare for the more serious activities of the rally itself.

By building these scenes to a crescendo of dramatic intensity, Riefenstahl means to hold the spectator's attention and generate some of the same enthusiasm and excitement felt by rally participants. These same techniques are used throughout the film, in scenes of Hitler's speeches, troop reviews, and the like. Even the most prosaic subjects, such as the repetitive passages of military marching, are made visually interesting and dramatic by these techniques. Not surprisingly, these tightly organized rhythmic sequences are quite effective.

Much has been written on the formal features of Riefenstahl's art.[14] What has not been generally appreciated is that the film's artistic achievement is not merely structural or formal. Equally important is Riefenstahl's masterful command of traditional narrative means: theme and characterization, the use of symbolism, and the handling of point of view. It is the use of these devices to tell a *story* – the story of the New Germany – that, combined with the structural techniques already surveyed, creates the vision of Hitler and National Socialism that makes *Triumph of the Will* so powerful.

That vision is one in which the military values of loyalty and courage, unity, discipline, and obedience are wedded to a heroic conception of life and elements of German *völkisch* mythology. In Riefenstahl's hands, an annual political rally is transformed into a larger historical and symbolic event. *Triumph of the Will* presents the Nazi world as a kind of Valhalla, "a place apart, surrounded by clouds and mist, peopled by heroes and ruled from above by the gods."[15] Seen from the perspective of the film, Hitler is the hero of a grand narrative. He is both leader and savior, a new Siegfried come to restore a defeated Germany to its ancient splendor.

In establishing this heroic vision, Riefenstahl works with several striking motifs: the swastika, the German eagle, flags, Albert Speer's towering architecture, torches and burning pyres, moon and clouds, the roar of the crowds, Hitler's voice. Her strategy is to use these aural and visual motifs to establish three key ideas, encapsulated in the National Socialist slogan *Ein Volk. Ein Führer. Ein Reich* (One People. One Leader. One Empire). These three ideas, introduced by Riefenstahl in slightly different order, are the *Führerprinzip*, leader principle or cult of the leader (the *Führer*), the unity of the people or national community (the

Volk), and the strength and power of the German nation (the *Reich*). Each has a central role both in the film's vision of Hitler and in its story of the New Germany.[16]

The first and most important idea, the *Führerprinzip*, has obvious roots in messianic Christianity.[17] The idea of a great historical figure or great man who has the will and power to actualize the true will of the German people was frequently dramatized in Nazi cinema. But *Triumph of the Will* is the only Nazi film that directly identifies this mystical leader with Hitler himself. From its very first frames, Riefenstahl's film presents Hitler as the leader long sought by the German people and as "the bearer of the people's will."[18] He is a god-like, mystical figure who descends – literally – from the clouds, his plane flying in over the mist-enshrouded towers and spires of medieval Nuremberg. These shots of the advancing plane are intercut with striking aerial footage of Nuremberg – a city representative of the old Germany and of the glorious Teutonic past, its castle a bulwark against foreign intruders. The shadow of the approaching plane falls over the columns and columns of marching troops who fill the streets below. All this takes place as themes from Wagner's *Die Meistersinger* slowly give way to the Nazi Party anthem, much as the old Germany slowly gives way to the new. The climax of this scene comes several minutes into the film when the plane lands, its door opens, and Hitler appears to a roar of approval from the waiting crowds. By such means, Riefenstahl makes Hitler's arrival at the rally – as well as his every subsequent appearance – resonate with deep historical and national significance for the German people.[19]

In the early sequences of the film, Riefenstahl stresses not only Hitler's messianic leadership, but his humanity. This is a leader who moves among the people, who shakes hands and smiles. Shots of Hitler are intercut with shots not only of enormous crowds but of individuals, especially children, laughing and smiling. Even small details, like Hitler stopping his motorcade to accept flowers from a mother and child along the road, are designed to support the film's vision of Hitler as the much-beloved father of the German people.

The second key idea of *Triumph of the Will* is the unity of the support for Hitler among the German people (*ein Volk*). Within the universe of the film, *everyone* supports Hitler. The crowds that fill scene after scene are staggering in number, their enthusiasm unending. Nowhere do we see anyone

– a postman, a traffic cop, or a pedestrian – engaged in ordinary business. Day after day, the narrow Nuremberg streets are filled to overflowing with old and young. People hang from the windows; they throng the stadium. All yearn to catch a glimpse of the *Führer*.

The beauty and sheer exuberance of these scenes celebrate these pro-Nazi sentiments. Indeed, several scenes appear to have been explicitly constructed to demonstrate that Hitler's support knows no class or regional barriers. For example, in the fifth sequence of the film, the presentation of the Labor Services, 52,000 corpsmen appear in review before Hitler at an enormous outdoor rally. Riefenstahl begins with the usual documentary-like shots of the men as they stand in formation, shouldering their shovels like guns and reciting patriotic slogans. But then she does something unusual. She constructs a montage of individual faces calling out the names of their *Heimat*, or regional homeland. "Where do you come from, comrade?" asks their leader. "From Friesland." "And you, comrade?" "From Bavaria." "And you?" "From Kaiserstuhl." "And you?" "From Pomerania . . . from Königsberg, Silesia, the Baltic, the Black Forest, Dresden, Danube, from the Rhine, and from the Saar. . . ."

This carefully crafted passage makes the idea of a national community visually (and aurally) concrete. Hitler's supporters, the film shows us, are a unity – one people – despite their differences; it is Hitler – one leader – who brings them together. The stirring music, the marshaling of flags, and the great German eagle towering over the stadium underscore the importance of the contribution of even the most ordinary laborers to the New Germany – planting forests, building roads "from village to village, from town to town." In the words of the workers themselves: "*Ein Volk. Ein Führer. Ein Reich – Deutschland.*" The effect is one of order and national purpose, a national purpose made manifest in the final shot of the sequence: the Labor Services men marching toward the camera, their image superimposed over Hitler's raised fist.[20]

The third and final idea central to *Triumph of the Will*, one *Reich*, is most prominent in the film's final sequences. Here Riefenstahl's strategy is the visual display of power (*Macht*).[21] Her aim is to show the enormous military forces that stand behind the *Führer* and the solidity of their support.[22] In demonstrating power, the ritual of the mass meeting itself had a central role: the waving swas-

tikas, the uniforms, the legions of marching, chanting followers, the torches against the night sky – all contributed to the spectacle designed to display Hitler's personal and political power.[23]

Triumph of the Will does more than present a set of ideas; it weaves them into a story, makes them part of a grand narrative. The 1934 party Congress had two titles: the Party Day of Unity and the Party Day of Power. Riefenstahl works with the themes of both unity and power, manipulating artistic form not only to create enthusiasm for Hitler and the National Socialists but to evoke fear. As noted, the opening of the film focuses on cheerful scenes emphasizing the spontaneous loyalty of ordinary people. Party and military forces are little in evidence. In contrast, the two final sequences – the military parade with which the Nazis leave Nuremberg and the somewhat anticlimactic final congress – center on Hitler, high-ranking party officials, and regiment after regiment of tightly disciplined troops. There are no smiles or laughing children, no young boys, no women with flowers. These are men – ready to go to war.

Running nearly twenty minutes, the final parade sequence is the longest of the film. Riefenstahl presents a seemingly inexhaustible stream of massed forces. We see the straight-legged, stiff-kneed marching troops from every angle, constantly moving, in a dazzling display of dynamic editing. Riefenstahl cuts back and forth between shots of the men in uniform, party officials, and Hitler. In contrast to the opening scenes, Hitler stands alone, apart from the people: watching, saluting, receiving ovations. The mood is somber. The power of the Nazis is presented as daunting and unquestionable.

To summarize, then, Riefenstahl weaves the narrative and thematic elements of her film around the central National Socialist slogan *Ein Führer. Ein Volk. Ein Reich* as tightly as she weaves the visual elements of eagle and swastika. As she tells it, the tale of Hitler – stalwart and alone, heroic – is the tale of the German people. His will is their will. His power their future. It is all this and more that makes *Triumph of the Will* the powerful film it is.

IV

Clearly, *Triumph of the Will* is a troubling film. My claim is that it is so because of its conjunction of beauty and evil, because it presents as beautiful a vision of Hitler and the New Germany that is morally repugnant. But might not there be a simpler, more straightforward explanation of the film's disturbing nature? Can't it be wholly explained by the fact that the film is a documentary?

As a *documentary* film, *Triumph of the Will* is disquieting because the events it portrays are themselves disquieting. As a documentary *film*, *Triumph of the Will* conveys the sheer immediacy of these events. We view Hitler's speeches, the flag ceremonies, the spot-lighted evening assemblies as if they were happening *now*. And our knowledge that what we are seeing stands in a causal chain of events that led to the Second World War and the Holocaust makes this immediacy chilling. It is as if we were watching the buds of these horrors unfold before our eyes.

But Riefenstahl's film does more than document historical events. And it is more than an ordinary documentary. *Triumph of the Will* is also troubling because it is a work of Nazi propaganda. The word 'propaganda' originated in the celebrated papal society for "propagating the faith" established in 1622. In modern contexts, the term has taken on more specifically political connotations. In claiming that *Triumph of the Will* is a work of propaganda, I mean that it is designed to propagate the Nazi faith – and mobilize the German people. *Triumph of the Will* thus unites the older religious connotations of 'propaganda' with the modern political connotations, presenting National Socialism as a political religion. Its images, ideas, and narrative all aim at establishing the tenets of that religion: Hitler is a messianic leader, Germany is one *Volk*, and the Third Reich will endure for a thousand years.

It may come as some surprise, then, to learn that the film's status as propaganda is controversial. Amazingly, Riefenstahl and her supporters deny that *Triumph of the Will* is a work of propaganda. And because there is a controversy – in fact, a rather heated one – we need to pause briefly to take up this issue. Riefenstahl and her supporters contend that her concerns in *Triumph of the Will* – as in all her films – were aesthetic, not political: that it was the cult of beauty, not the cult of the *Führer*, that Riefenstahl worshiped. The claim is that stylistic devices like the cloud motif in the film's opening sequence, the rhythmic montage of faces in the Labor Services sequence, and so on were *just* that: stylistic devices meant to avoid

newsreel reportage, enrich the film artistically, and nothing more.[24]

Certainly Riefenstahl *was* preoccupied with beauty in *Triumph of the Will*. Her films of the 1936 Berlin Olympics, her photographs of the Nuba, indeed the whole of her artistic corpus, make clear that visual beauty was one of her central artistic preoccupations. But the claim that a concern for beauty and stylistic innovation is the only thing going on in *Triumph of the Will* is undermined by the film itself. As we have seen, the film is aimed not simply at stylistic innovation and formally beautiful images, but at using these means to create a particular vision of Hitler and National Socialism.

The pure-aestheticism defense is also belied by the historical record. Riefenstahl was, as she willingly admits, a great admirer of Hitler. Attending a political rally for the first time in her life in February 1932, she was "paralyzed," "fascinated," "deeply affected" by the appearance of Hitler and the crowd's "bondage to this man."[25] Even at the end of the war, by which point she, like many Nazi sympathizers, claims to have harbored doubts about Hitler's plans for Germany, Riefenstahl, by her own admission, "wept all night" at the news of his suicide.[26] To this day, Riefenstahl has never distanced herself from the political content of *Triumph of the Will* or any of the other films she made for Hitler.[27] Nor, despite years of ostracism and public controversy, has she shown – or even feigned – remorse for her artistic and personal association with many members of the Nazi Party.

It might be added that Riefenstahl agreed to film the 1934 Nuremberg rally only on condition that she be given complete artistic control over the project, a condition to which Hitler apparently agreed. She demanded, and got, final cut. Thus, we can assume that the film Riefenstahl made – the film organized around the ideas of *Ein Führer. Ein Volk. Ein Reich* that presents Hitler as savior to the German people, and that describes the Nazi future as full of promise – is the film she chose to make.

The film's history also supports its status as propaganda. Goebbels, who as minister for People's Enlightenment and Propaganda, was largely responsible for the creation of the *Führer* myth, thought the film a great achievement, unprecedented in its representation of Hitler as father of the German people and leader of the New Germany. In recommending that *Triumph of the Will* be awarded the National Film Prize, Goebbels proclaimed:

The film marks a very great achievement.... It is a magnificent cinematic vision of the Führer, *seen here for the first time with a power that has not been revealed before*. The film has successfully avoided the danger of being merely a politically slanted film. It has translated the powerful rhythm of this great epoch into something outstandingly artistic; it is an epic, forging the tempo of marching formations, steel-like in its conviction and fired by a passionate artistry.[28]

Indeed, so successful was *Triumph of the Will* in articulating the *Führerprinzip* that, as one historian of German propaganda put it, "there was no need to make another film about Hitler ..."[29] *Triumph of the Will* was the definitive Nazi documentary about the *Führer*. Although a series of later films associated Hitler with other great men of Germany's past (e.g., Bismarck and Schiller), no other documentary about the *Führer* was, in fact, ever commissioned.

Riefenstahl also maintains that *Triumph of the Will* was what might be called "a pure documentary," that it merely records the reality of the loyalty and hope Hitler once inspired. In her words, the film "is purely historical.... It is *film-verité*. It reflects the truth that was then, in 1934, history. It is therefore a documentary. Not a propaganda film."[30]

This second line of defense is clearly at odds with the first: her claim that the film's concerns are purely aesthetic. She wants, on the one hand, to tout her considerable artistic accomplishments in giving life to the boring speeches and endless marching and, on the other hand, to maintain that she did little but record events as they unfolded, that her film is *cinema verité*. Can she really have it both ways? But let us bracket the issue of consistency and good faith and simply note that the claim of pure documentation, like the claim of pure aestheticism, is refuted by the film's structure. As we have seen, *Triumph of the Will* is a carefully crafted, artfully constructed film. Its principles of organization are governed not by the chronological sequence of the events depicted in the film, but by the demands of the film's narrative vision: the highly selective (and distorted) story about Hitler of which Riefenstahl is the author.

Of course, documentaries are never just transcriptions of events. Documentary filmmakers always edit and construct. They always take a point of view. But even allowing for this general point, it remains true that *Triumph of the Will* is an extreme case of a documentary film whose organization is governed by political aims.

The pure-documentary defense also conveniently overlooks certain crucial features of the relation between the film and its subject matter. One of the most remarkable facts about *Triumph of the Will* is that the reality it records is a reality it helped to create. This is what Siegfried Kracauer was getting at when he made his famous "faked reality" charge:

...from the real life of the people was built up a faked reality that was passed off as the genuine one; but this bastard reality, instead of being an end in itself, merely served as the set dressing for a film that was then to assume the character of an authentic documentary.[31]

Riefenstahl, in other words, helped to set up the spectacle her film was designed to document. As she herself acknowledged in a now-famous remark, "[T]he preparations for the Party Convention were made in concert with the preparations for the camera work."[32]

One can of course argue that, unlike the staged scenes of Nazi events made in Hollywood, this "faked event" was part of Nazi history: a real event, not just the set of a movie. But this real event did not just "unfold"; it was constructed in part *to be* the subject of her film. By "faked reality," Kracauer can be understood to mean something like what we would now call a "media event." Furthermore, in filming this event, Riefenstahl gave form to Hitler's vision of Germany's future. To cite her own words, she took "nothing but speeches, marches, and mobs" and brought this material alive, creating a stirring film spectacle that could be replayed again and again. Riefenstahl used her considerable talent and her art to create an image that helped further and sustain the vision of National Socialism shared by Hitler, Goebbels, and Speer. Surely much of the infamy of the 1934 rally is due to Riefenstahl's film.

We can close this discussion of the controversy over the film's status as propaganda by noting that both lines of defense (the aesthetic and the documentary) are framed in terms of Riefenstahl's intentions. Each of these arguments is of the form: "*Triumph of the Will* is not a work of propaganda, because Leni Riefenstahl did not intend to make a work of propaganda." Did Leni Riefenstahl *intend* to make a work of propaganda? If the question is

"Did she think to herself, 'I'm going to make a work of Nazi propaganda'?" the answer is probably no. But this is the wrong question. The right question is: "Did she think something to the effect that 'I'm going to show Hitler in a way that will mobilize the German people in his support'?" And the answer to this question, presumably, is yes. Had Hitler won the war, Riefenstahl wouldn't be defending herself by disavowing the intention to make a work of propaganda.

In any case, the debate about Leni Riefenstahl's intentions (what was going on "in her head") is largely beside the point.[33] For the question whether *Triumph of the Will* is a work of propaganda is a question about the *film*, not a question about (the historical person) Leni Riefenstahl. And as we have seen, the answer to this question is plainly yes.[34]

So *Triumph of the Will* is a work of Nazi propaganda. And that is clearly part of what makes the film so troubling. But Riefenstahl is not the first or last artist to make fascist art. Hundreds of propaganda films were made in German between 1933 and 1945. Many, like the feature film *Jud Süss*, had much wider popular success. And some, like the virulently anti-Semitic "documentary" *Der ewige Jude* (The Eternal Jew, 1940), had arguably as harmful an effect on German thought and behavior.

Triumph of the Will is distinguished from these and other Nazi propaganda films in two ways. First, it is extremely well made. (And the fact that it is an excellent work of propaganda is part of what makes it so disturbing.) But the film is more than first-class propaganda. It is also a work of art. A work of creative imagination, stylistically and formally innovative, its every detail contributes to its central vision and overall effect. The film is also very, very beautiful. *Triumph of the Will* can be properly called a work of art because it offers a beautiful, sensuous presentation – a vision – of the German people, leader, and empire in a recognized artistic genre (documentary) of a recognized artistic medium (film). It is the fact that *Triumph of the Will* is an excellent work of propaganda *and* a work of art that explains why Riefenstahl's film has more than historical interest and why it has a place in film and not just history classes.

V

As art, *Triumph of the Will* is problematic for reasons other than those associated with its excellence as a work of propaganda (e.g., its capacity to mobilize the German people in the 1930s), and it is as art that *Triumph of the Will* is most disturbing. What makes *Triumph of the Will* problematic and disturbing as art is its artistic vision: its vision of the German people, leader, and empire. Riefenstahl's film portrays National Socialism (something morally evil) as beautiful. To view the film in the way in which it was intended to be seen is to see and be moved by (what Riefenstahl presents as) the beauty of National Socialism.

If this is right, it raises a question about how we are to respond to this film. Its every detail is designed to advance a morally repugnant vision of Hitler, a vision that, as history was to prove, falsified the true character of Hitler and National Socialism. Enjoying *this film* – recognizing that we may be caught up, if only slightly, in its pomp and pageantry or be stirred by its beauty – is likely to make us ask, "What kind of person am I to enjoy or be moved by this film?"[35] Isn't there something wrong with responding in this way to a Nazi film?

This worry arises because *Triumph of the Will* presents National Socialism as attractive and, in so doing, aims to make us think of National Socialism as good. Hitler and what he stood for are commended. This is different from a case like Klaus Mann's novel about Nazism, *Mephisto*, where the evil described is clearly not presented as attractive or as meant to win our allegiance. Riefenstahl doesn't just ask us to imagine finding the *Führer* and his message appealing, but actually to find them so.[36]

The concern is not only that if I enjoy such a film, I may be led to act badly (e.g., to support neo-Nazi movements), but also that certain kinds of enjoyment, regardless of their effects, may themselves be problematic. Pleasure in this work of art (like pleasure in a work of art that celebrates sadism or pedophilia) might lead one to ask not just about what one may *become*, but about who one is *now*. The point is an Aristotelian one. If virtue consists (in part) in taking pleasure in the right things and not in the wrong things, then what is my character now such that I can take pleasure in these things?

Triumph of the Will also raises pressing questions about the attitude we should adopt toward the film as art. Should we praise it for its widely acclaimed aesthetic qualities despite its celebration of National Socialism? We recognize D. W. Griffith's *Birth of a Nation* as an important film despite its racism, and we admire the Pyramids despite the great human cost paid for their production. Should we similarly bracket questions of good and evil in looking at *Triumph of the Will?* Alternatively, should we insist that the moral implications of Riefenstahl's work undermine its aesthetic value? Or is this formulation of the problem too simple?

These questions merely highlight the long-standing general problem of beauty and evil: that aesthetic and moral considerations may pull in different directions. The problem emerges not only with *Triumph of the Will* and the other cases mentioned earlier but with, for example, the literary works of the Marquis de Sade and T. S. Eliot. The problem posed by the conflict between the demands of art and the demands of morality is familiar. What are we to make of it?

For much of the twentieth century, the standard solution to this conflict has been to recommend that we look at art from an "aesthetic distance." As originally described by Edward Bullough in 1912, an attitude of aesthetic distance allows us to set aside the practical concerns of everyday life, including questions of a work's origins, its moral effects, and so on, and concentrate exclusively on the work of art itself. By "the work itself" Bullough means, of course, the work's "formal" (i.e., its structural and stylistic) features. Bracketing all non-formal features frees us, at least temporarily, "to elaborate experience on a new basis,"[37] much as we do in appreciating the beauty of a fog at sea despite its danger.

The basic strategy here is simple: when approaching a work of art that raises moral issues, sever aesthetic evaluation from moral evaluation and evaluate the work in aesthetic (i.e., formal) terms alone. This is the formalist response to the problem of beauty and evil. Formalism treats the aesthetic and the moral as wholly independent domains. It allows us to say that, evaluated morally, *Triumph of the Will* is bad but, evaluated aesthetically, it is good.

In recent decades, formalism has become rather unfashionable, having been subjected to serious criticism by feminists, philosophers of art, and others. Formalism nevertheless plays a dominant role in discussions of *Triumph of the Will.* One explanation for this is that the formalist strategy may seem especially well suited to cases such as *Triumph of the Will.* Like Bullough's fog at sea, the Nazi content of Riefenstahl's film *is* threatening. And it is certainly true that without some measure of distance, we risk being too overcome with emo-

tion or too caught up in what is morally objectionable to attend to what makes the work aesthetically good. Viewing the film from a disinterested (what Bullough calls an "objective") point of view gives us a way of setting aside the components that make it morally objectionable. This enables us to appreciate at least some of the features that make it aesthetically good. If the strategy works, there *is* no problem of beauty and evil. Indeed, one of the aims of formalism is to show that there is really no such problem – to show that it is illusory.

But in the case of *Triumph of the Will,* the formalist strategy fails. It won't work here, not because we're too obsessed by the moral issues to assume a properly distanced standpoint, or because when we assume a posture of aesthetic distance we forget about the historical realities associated with the film, or because adopting an attitude of aesthetic distance toward a film like *Triumph of the Will* is itself an immoral position (though some may wish to argue that it is).[38] Nor does adopting an attitude of aesthetic distance require that we literally forget about the historical realities. Aesthetic distance is, after all, only a shift in perspective, and a temporary one at that.

The reason the formalist strategy fails in the case of *Triumph of the Will* is that distancing ourselves from the morally objectionable elements of the film – its deification of Hitler, the story it tells about him, the party, and the German people, and so on – means distancing ourselves from the features that make it the work of art it is. If we distance ourselves from these features of the film, we will not be in a position to understand its artistic value – that is, why this lengthy film of political speeches and endless marching is correctly regarded as a cinematic masterpiece. We will also miss the beauty (horrifying though it is) of its vision of Hitler.

Like all religious and political works of art (e.g., Dante's *The Divine Comedy,* Orwell's *1984,* Wright's *Native Son*), *Triumph of the Will* has a message.[39] We can bracket that message – that is, the political elements and aims of the film – in favor of its strictly formal elements, just as we can read *The Inferno* while ignoring its Christianity. But in doing so we omit an essential dimension of the film, and an essential dimension of its beauty. To see *Triumph of the Will* for the work of art it is and to fully grasp its beauty, we need to pay attention to its content – to just those elements of the film that formalism directs us to set aside.

In emphasizing the importance of the film's content, I don't mean to underplay the significance of its formal elements. Unquestionably, a large part of what the film is, and of what makes it artistically valuable, consists in its striking images and beautiful patterns of movement. Moreover, the purely formal features of *Triumph of the Will*, considered in abstraction from their contribution to the film's message, are (as formalism teaches us) unproblematically beautiful.

But *Triumph of the Will* is a work of artistic mastery – perhaps, I dare say, of genius – not merely because of the film's purely formal features (the beauty of Riefenstahl's cinematography, her skillful editing techniques, etc.) but, perhaps most important, because of its artistic vision, its particular, utterly horrifying vision of Hitler and National Socialism. That vision is the essence of the film.

If taking an attitude of aesthetic distance means paying attention only to the formal aspects of the work (to the image and not to what it means), then aesthetic distance fails in the case of *Triumph of the Will* because it requires us to ignore the essence of the film.

Now, defenders of formalism can opt for a more complex understanding of aesthetic distance, one that does not require us to bracket an artwork's content. According to this view (call it "sophisticated formalism"), understanding a work of art consists in grasping and appreciating the relationship between its form and content, that is, the connection between the message and the means used to convey it. Artistic success consists in expressing a particular message in an effective way. Sophisticated formalism thus allows – indeed requires – us to pay attention to the particular content of the work. On this subtler view, we can't just ignore the content of art or its message. We must attend to the relation between a work's form and content, if we are to appreciate the work itself.

Sophisticated formalism introduces a new conception of the aesthetic. The simpler version of formalism defined the aesthetic narrowly, in terms of a work's formal elements, considered by themselves. The new, more complex conception tracks the *relation* between form and content. A work's aesthetic achievement consists in the skill with which it expresses its content. Understood in this way, the aesthetic value of *Triumph of the Will* involves not just its formal accomplishments, but also how these stylistic means are used to convey feelings of awe, admiration, and oneness with Hitler.

Note that sophisticated formalism doesn't require abandoning the distinction between aesthetic and moral evaluation. As with the simpler version, with sophisticated formalism, aesthetic evaluation belongs to one domain, moral evaluation to another. Sophisticated formalism tells us to judge not the message but its expression. In this respect, the approach we are meant to take toward the National Socialist elements of Riefenstahl's documentary is no different from the approach we are meant to take toward the Christianity of *The Divine Comedy* or *Paradise Lost*. Our finding the message conveyed by *Triumph of the Will* repulsive (or attractive) should not therefore affect our aesthetic judgment. Nor should it affect our aesthetic response to the film.

Indeed, according to sophisticated formalism, *Triumph of the Will* and works of art like it shouldn't (from an aesthetic point of view) cause any problem at all. We can distance ourselves from – that is, set aside – the moral dimension of the work's content while still *paying attention to* that content – that is, the way in which the film's content figures in its expressive task.

Is this broader, more inclusive understanding of aesthetic distance satisfactory? The answer, I think, is no. Even sophisticated formalism, with its richer concept of the aesthetic, makes it impossible to talk about the political meaning of *Triumph of the Will*, the truth or falsity of its picture of Hitler, whether it is good or evil, right or wrong – *while doing aesthetics*. These cognitive and moral matters are ones we are meant to distance ourselves from when engaged in the business of aesthetic evaluation. Sophisticated formalism doesn't ignore content, but it does *aestheticize* it. When we follow its recommendations, we adopt an aesthetic attitude toward the Christianity of *The Divine Comedy* and an aesthetic attitude toward the National Socialism of *Triumph of the Will*. Sophisticated formalism is, after all, a kind of formalism. It focuses on the (formal) relation between form and content. From its perspective, the content of the film (its vision) is relevant to evaluation only insofar as it is expressed well or badly. Thus, even on sophisticated varieties of formalism, essential elements of *Triumph of the Will* remain irrelevant to its aesthetic evaluation. Hence, here too, formalism fails to respond fully to the work of art that *Triumph of the Will* is.

Content is not always as important as it is in the case of *Triumph of the Will*, but here, as in the case of much political and religious art, the formalist response makes it difficult or impossible to explain why works like *Triumph of the Will* should be considered problematic in the first place.

At this point there are two ways to go. We can say that there is more to art than aesthetics or that there is more to aesthetics than beauty and form. The first option allows us to keep the historically important, eighteenth-century conception of the aesthetic intact. (It is in effect the conception of the aesthetic introduced by sophisticated formalism.) This conception has the advantage of keeping the boundaries of the aesthetic relatively narrow and clearly defined. And it keeps aesthetic evaluation relatively simple. Questions of political meaning, of truth and falsity, good and evil, right and wrong fall outside the category of the aesthetic. One implication of adopting this option is that, since there are works of art that raise these issues, the category of the artistic outstrips the category of the aesthetic.

The second option broadens the concept of the aesthetic beyond its traditional boundaries. It says that we are responding to a work of art "aesthetically" not only when we respond to its formal elements or to the relationship between its formal elements and its content, but also whenever we respond to a feature that makes a work the work of art it is. (These features may include substantive as well as formal features.) On this second option, the aesthetic is understood in such a way as to track the artistic, however broadly or narrowly that is to be understood.[40]

It is this second route that I recommend. Let me at least briefly say why. The first option remains wedded to a conception of the aesthetic that preserves the eighteenth-century preoccupation with beauty. This is a rich and important tradition, but it focuses – and keeps us focused – on a feature of art that is no longer so important to us. Indeed, one of the significant and widely noted facts about the development of modern art is that beauty is no longer central to art. The price of regarding this conception of the aesthetic as the only legitimate one is to marginalize aesthetics – isolating it from much of the philosophy of art – and, indeed, from much of our experience of art.

Opting for this broader conception of the aesthetic gives us a more inclusive category, one more adequate to what art is in all of its historical and cultural manifestations and to the full range of its values. It sets much of what we humanly care about back into the aesthetic arena and offers a much more complete view of the value of art.[41]

My claim, which employs this richer conception of the aesthetic, is, then, that in order to get things aesthetically right about *Triumph of the Will*, we have to engage with its vision. And this means that we have to engage with the moral issues it raises. This nonformalist notion of the aesthetic rides piggyback on a nonformalist conception of art. It doesn't require wholesale abandonment of the distinction between aesthetic and moral value. We can, for example, still distinguish between the formal beauty of *Triumph of the Will's* stylistic devices and its moral status as a work of National Socialist propaganda. Nor does it require denying that art and morality belong to different domains. But it does require recognizing that there are areas where these domains overlap and that certain works of art, especially works of religious and political art, fall within this overlapping area.

VI

In Section IV, we began by canvassing different explanations for the troubling nature of *Triumph of the Will:* that it is disturbing because of the horrible events it documents, because it is a work of propaganda, because it propagates a highly selective and distorted picture of Hitler and National Socialism. Each of these factors helps to explain why the film is troubling, but none of them gets at what is, I have argued, the most unsettling feature of the film: its conjunction of beauty and evil.

We then, in Section V, considered the standard solution for dealing with the problem of beauty and evil, namely, formalism, which holds that aesthetic evaluation can be severed from moral evaluation and that art *qua* art must be evaluated in formal terms alone. Each of the two versions of formalism we considered, simple and sophisticated, maintained that the problem posed by the juncture of beauty and evil in *Triumph of the Will* (and works like it) is illusory. The simple version attempted to dissolve the problem of the juncture of beauty and evil by focusing on the formal features of the film and relegating the film's content to a domain outside the boundaries of aesthetic evaluation. The sophisticated version attempted to dissolve the problem by focusing on the relation of form and content in the film. It, too, held consideration of the film's morally objectionable content (its vision) to fall outside the domain of aesthetic evaluation. But, as we have seen, formalism fails in the case of *Triumph of the Will* because in bracketing the very components that make the film morally objectionable (i.e., its content), it also brackets the film's essence as a work of art – its vision of National Socialism.

The failure of formalism shows that the problem of beauty and evil is real. Indeed, each of the candidate explanations for the threatening nature of the film can be recast as accepting and giving different interpretations to this problem. As a documentary, *Triumph of the Will* conjoins beautifully rendered footage and the celebration of horrible historical events; as propaganda, the film conjoins a masterfully constructed political narrative and a distorted picture of Hitler's character and aims; as formal expression, it conjoins masterful cinematography and morally repugnant content. But the most trenchant account of the relation of beauty and evil in *Triumph of the Will* focuses on the fact that the film renders something that is evil, namely National Socialism, beautiful and, in so doing, tempts us to find attractive what is morally repugnant.

The upshot of these reflections is that the question we considered before – How are we to respond to *Triumph of the Will*? – can't be evaded. As we have seen, there are really two questions here, one about us, one about how we are to evaluate the film as art.

First, the question about us. What does it mean about us if we find this film beautiful? Does it show that there is something wrong with our character? That we really approve of or endorse fascism or the doctrines of National Socialism? That we approve of the Final Solution? The answer to the question about us depends on what, in finding the film beautiful, we are responding *to*. As the simple version of formalism showed, some elements of the film are unproblematically beautiful: the film's fine camera work, its rhythmic editing, and so on. Responding to these elements of the film isn't the same as endorsing its National Socialism. One can respond to the formal elements of the film without supporting the work's message. Nor is there anything problematic about responding to the relation between form and content in the film. If we are responding not to the film's content *per se*, but only to how that content is *presented*, then, here too, we are not endorsing the film's message.

My analysis, however, shows that there is another feature of the film that is not so innocuous: its vision. In order to respond fully to the film as a work of art, we must respond to this vision. In-deed, my analysis implies that appreciating the film as a work of art requires responding to the beauty of this vision of National Socialism. But this means that the proper formulation of the question about us is, What kind of people are we if we find this vision beautiful? It is not immediately obvious that we *can* find this vision beautiful without endorsing fascism or the doctrines of National Socialism.

Here it is important to be very clear about what is meant by the film's vision. When I speak of the film's vision, I do not mean something that might be meant by the word 'vision', namely the abstract doctrines or ideals of National Socialism, but rather the film's deifying portrait of Hitler as the beloved father of a happy, smiling people and of a national community unified by its desire to labor for the New Germany.

Appreciating the beauty of this vision (seeing the possible appeal of the idea of a benevolent leader, of a unified community, of a sense of national purpose) is not the same thing as finding the doctrines or ideals of National Socialism appealing. I can consistently see this concrete vision as beautiful (or attractive) and reject the doctrines and ideals of the National Socialists, be utterly horrified by what they did, and so on.

There is a step between finding the film's concrete artistic vision beautiful and endorsing the doctrines and ideals of National Socialism. The step is a moral one, a step we need not (and, of course, should not) take. So it is possible to appreciate the beauty of the film's vision without compromising ourselves morally. But, it is important to note, one of the central aims of *Triumph of the Will* is to move its audience to take this step, to find the historical realities and doctrines of National Socialism appealing. Part of the evil of the film consists in the fact that it is designed to move us in this way – in the direction of evil.

That the film aims to move us to find National Socialism appealing is also one of the things that makes responding to it so problematic. The film *is* potentially corrupting. To appreciate the beauty of its vision – or to acknowledge our appreciation – is to open ourselves to a work that presents us with the temptations of fascism. One reason that the sense that there is something troubling about *Triumph of the Will* will not – and should not – go away is that there *is* something morally dangerous about the film.

I want now to turn to the second question: How should the fact that the film is evil figure in our evaluation of it as a work of art? Having gotten clearer about the real insidiousness of the film, we may be tempted to claim that it is of little or no artistic value. But this response won't do. *Triumph of the Will* clearly is of artistic value. As we have seen, it is an extremely powerful film, perhaps even a work of genius.

Should we then say that *Triumph of the Will* is a terrific work of art, despite its insidiousness? Here I think we should hesitate. For all its accomplishments, *Triumph of the Will* is flawed. It is flawed because its vision is flawed. Its vision is flawed because it misrepresents the character of Hitler and National Socialism and because it presents as beautiful and good things that are evil, namely Hitler and National Socialism. These flaws are relevant to the evaluation of *Triumph of the Will* as art because, as our examination makes clear, the film's vision of National Socialism is part of the work of art that it is. If that vision is flawed, then so is the work of art.

One explanation of our enduring reservations about the film is that many of us have certain intuitions about the relation of beauty and goodness. One place those intuitions get articulated is in Plato. Even those of us who are not Platonists are heirs to a Platonic tradition that identifies beauty and goodness, a tradition that conceives of the beautiful as consisting not only in giving pleasure to the senses but also in engaging and satisfying the mind and spirit. (For example, in the *Phaedrus*, beauty is thought to awaken the longing and passion for what is higher, for the Good.)[42] It is this ancient, strongly entrenched strand of thinking which, I suggest, accounts for the sense that there is something paradoxical about a work of art that so tightly weaves the beautiful and the morally evil. Indeed, one of the most shocking things about *Triumph of the Will* is that it so clearly demonstrates that beauty and goodness can come apart, not just in the relatively simple sense that moral and aesthetic evaluation may diverge, but in the more frightening sense that it is possible for art to render evil beautiful.[43]

If *Triumph of the Will* shows that the Platonic tradition is wrong to identify beauty and goodness, it also provides support for the idea that the *unity* of beauty and goodness is a standard by which art should be measured. If good art must not only please the senses, but also engage and satisfy us intellectually and emotionally, then we are, I suggest, justified in criticizing *Triumph of the Will* for rendering something evil beautiful.

We are justified in doing so not just as moralists but as critics of art. This is not to say that works of art should only show good people doing good things, or that they are meant to endorse only conventional conceptions of goodness. Nor is it meant to deny that a work of art – even one as morally flawed as *Triumph of the Will* – may nevertheless be of artistic value. But there is reason, I am claiming, to withhold the highest aesthetic praise from works of art that present as beautiful, attractive, and good what, on reflection, can be seen to be evil.[44]

One question remains. If Riefenstahl's film is flawed in the ways I have described, why watch it? Well, we obviously don't sit down to watch *Triumph of the Will* for fun. But it is an important film. It is worth watching because of its historical value as a chronicle of the rise of fascism in Germany and of events leading to the Second World War and as a case study in how propaganda works. It is also worth watching for its formal beauty and expressive power. In addition, we may watch *Triumph of the Will* for much the same reason some feminists examine works of pornography: so that in confronting these works we may learn something about a way of seeing the world we reject.

There are at least two further reasons for watching the film. The more obvious one is that part of preventing a recurrence of fascism involves understanding how fascism came to be thought attractive, how parties like the National Socialist German Worker's Party called upon and met certain underlying human wishes of many Germans in the 1930s (e.g., for a strong leader, for community, for a sense of national purpose). Deciding not to ban (or avoid) materials like *Triumph of the Will* means learning not to deny, but to live with, the historical reality of the Third Reich. The second, related reason is that confronting the film's vision of National Socialism may allow us to understand more fully ourselves as human beings. Imagining seeing the world as Riefenstahl represents it, however disturbing, may enable us to confront, and come a little closer to comprehending, both the real and potential tendencies that have come to define human evil.

The most important reason, though, for watching *Triumph of the Will* is that it provides the very conjunction of beauty and evil we find so unsettling. It allows us to see that beauty and evil can, and have been, conjoined. And it allows us to see that one of the disturbing things about art is that it can make evil appear beautiful and good. Thus, what we might think is a reason for *not* watching the film is, upon reflection, the very reason we should watch it.

A methodological coda. In the course of our examination of the problem of beauty and evil, we have spent a great deal of time focusing on the historical and artistic details of one particular case. It is worth considering why. We had to look at the historical specificities of the film because, as a documentary and as a work whose subject is a particular historical event, *Triumph of the Will* is a historically specific work. We had also to look at the artistic details of the film in order to see how *Triumph of the Will* poses issues that give rise to the more general philosophical problem of beauty and evil. This detailed historical and artistic examination was part of a larger strategy of looking at a particular case as a means of exploring the more general problem of beauty and evil in art. But why start with a particular case? Why not begin with the more general issue and work to the particular case? The reason, which I can state here in only an abbreviated way, is that the problem of beauty and evil in art is real, but it becomes real only insofar as it arises in particular cases. We go to the particular cases because that is where the issue comes to life. The historical and analytic work of this essay is not mere propaedeutic to the philosophical inquiry but is inextricably bound up with the philosophical inquiry itself. This is not a new approach, but one whose locus classicus is Plato's discussion of Homer in Books 2 and 3 of the *Republic*.

Notes

For comments on earlier drafts of this essay, I thank Ted Cohen, Michael Hardimon, Deborah Lefkowitz, Jerry Levinson, and Claudine Verheggen.

1 Estimates of the number of people who came to the Nuremberg rally vary. The city already had a population of 350,000. For a detailed discussion of the 1934 rally and its attendants, see Hamilton T. Burden's *The Nuremberg Party Rallies: 1923–1939* (New York: Praeger, 1967), esp. 79, 85–7, 90.
2 Renata Berg-Pan, *Leni Riefenstahl* (Boston: Twayne, 1980), 99.
3 Ibid.
4 Siegfried Kracauer, *From Caligari to Hitler: A Psychological History of the German Film* (New York: Noon Day Press, 1960), 301.
5 Leni Riefenstahl, *Leni Riefenstahl: A Memoir* (New York: Picador, 1987), 160.
6 Ibid., 159. Erik Barnouw offers one of the most interesting and detailed descriptions of the film coverage of the Nuremberg rally and the lengths to which Riefenstahl went to get it. See his *Documentary: A History of the Non-Fiction Film* (Oxford: Oxford University Press, 1983), 101–3.
7 David Welsh, *Propaganda and the German Cinema, 1933–1945* (Oxford: Clarendon Press, 1983), 149.
8 Riefenstahl, *A Memoir*, 165–6.
9 The Reich Cinema Law, which went into effect in February 1934, stipulated that all kinds of films, even film advertising and film stills, were to be submitted to the censorship board. Both private and public screenings were covered by this law, and each film print was required to carry an embossed stamp of the German eagle. That *Triumph of the Will* by-passed this considerable legal machinery suggests that Hitler had complete faith in Riefenstahl's political "soundness." See Welsh, *Propaganda*, 17–22.

10 Berg-Pan, *Leni Riefenstahl*, 131.
11 Some reports indicate that the film ran in all the major German cities but only for a short time, others that it continued to be shown throughout the Nazi era. In the absence of historical evidence, it is also unclear to what extent the film was used for purposes of propaganda or with what effect. Again, historians and critics disagree. Some credit the film with winning many to Hitler's cause; others maintain that the film was little seen outside the largest cities and not widely used by the Nazis.
12 See David B. Hinton, *The Films of Leni Riefenstahl* (Metuchen, N.J.: Scarecrow Press, 1978), 36–7.
13 Andrew Sarris (ed.), *Interviews with Film Directors* (New York: Avon Books, 1967), 461.
14 See, e.g., Welsh, *Propaganda*, and Berg-Pan, *Leni Riefenstahl*.
15 Richard Meran Barsam, *Filmguide to "Triumph of the Will"* (Bloomington: Indiana University Press, 1975), 27–8.
16 Unlike most commentary on *Triumph of the Will*, which stresses the film's idolization of Hitler (e.g., Riefenstahl's use of low-angle shots and backlighting), the interpretation I offer here, to my knowledge, stands alone in stressing the use Riefenstahl makes of the three interlocking ideas of *Ein Führer, Ein Volk*, and *Ein Reich*.
17 It also has roots in the Nazi's distorted reading of Nietzsche. For this history of the concept of the *Führerprinzip*, I follow Welsh's illuminating discussion in *Propaganda*, 145–7.
18 For more on this notion of Hitler as "the bearer of the people's will," see ibid.
19 On the symbolic importance of Nuremberg for the Nazi rallies, see Burden, *Nuremberg Party Rallies*, 3–9.
20 The extent of the staging of this sequence has been much discussed. Certainly this closing shot could

not have been filmed without considerable advance planning and cooperation from the troops, none of whom look at the camera.

21 The idea that power must not only be held but visibly displayed is something that Riefenstahl takes from Hitler and the Nazis. As Eugen Hamadovsky, who later became the Third Reich's national broadcasting director, wrote in 1933: "All the power one has, even more than one has, must be demonstrated. One hundred speeches, five hundred newspaper articles, radio talks, films, and plays are unable to produce the same effect as a procession of gigantic masses of people taking place with discipline and active participation" (cited in Welsh, *Propaganda*, 149).

22 The solidity of Hitler's support was important to emphasize in light of the Roehm purge. In what came to be known as the Night of the Long Knives (June 30, 1934), Ernst Roehm and other SA leaders suspected of treachery against Hitler were roused from their beds and shot without hearings of any kind.

23 For a discussion of the importance of mass meetings in the projection of the *Führer* cult, see Welsh, *Propaganda*, 148.

24 See, e.g., Hinton, *The Films of Leni Riefenstahl*, 58.

25 Riefenstahl, *A Memoir*, 101.

26 Ibid., 304–5.

27 In addition to *Triumph of the Will*, Riefenstahl made an earlier documentary for Hitler, a short, hastily organized film on the 1933 Nuremberg rally. This film, *Victory of Faith*, introduced Riefenstahl to the documentary film form. Following *Triumph of the Will*, she made a third party rally film, *Day of Freedom*. This last film was made to appease the Wehrmacht generals she had angered by their underrepresentation in *Triumph of the Will*.

28 *Volkischer Beobachter*, May 1, 1935. Cited in Welsh, *Propaganda*, 158. Emphasis added.

29 Welsh, *Propaganda*, 159.

30 Riefenstahl quoted in Sarris (ed.), *Interview*, 460.

31 Kracauer, *From Caligari to Hitler*, 301.

32 This remark is widely cited. Its source is Riefenstahl's book on *Triumph of the Will*, *Hinter den Kulissen des Reichsparteitag Films* (Munich: Franz Eher, 1935).

33 For a good introduction to the standard debates over authorial intention, see Gary Iseminger's collection, *Intention and Interpretation* (Philadelphia: Temple University Press, 1992).

34 As it is, the film cannot be legally shown in Germany because it is a work of National Socialist propaganda.

35 Ted Cohen raises similar questions about laughing at jokes in bad taste. See his "Jokes," in *Pleasure, Preference and Value: Studies in Philosophical Aesthetics*, ed. Eva Schaper (Cambridge University Press, 1983), 120–36.

36 The distinction between a work that asks us to *imagine* a certain response (e.g., being amused, being attracted to) and one that asks us really *to be* amused, attracted, and so on is discussed by Berys Gaut in "The Ethical Criticism of Art," in *Aesthetics and Ethics: Essays at the Intersection*, ed. Jerrold Levinson (Cambridge University Press, 1998).

37 Edward Bullough, " 'Psychical Distance' as a Factor in Art and as an Aesthetic Principle," *British Journal of Psychology* 5 (1912): 87–98, 108–17.

38 Some have argued that by adopting an attitude of aesthetic distance toward certain kinds of artistic representations we risk hardening ourselves to real human suffering. Being willing to run that risk for mere aesthetic pleasure may be thought morally insensitive and a kind of moral fault.

39 What it is for a work of art to have a message is, of course, a matter of great complexity. On the general question of what an artwork's saying something amounts to and how we determine what, among various possibilities, it says, see, e.g., Jerrold Levinson's "Messages in Art," *Australian Journal of Philosophy* 73, no. 2 (June 1995): 184–98. While not addressing these issues directly here, I am assuming that works of art are capable of communicating attitudes and beliefs toward what they describe or otherwise present. What those attitudes and beliefs are is something a work itself manifests when read against the background of its cultural and historical context.

40 An example of this general approach can be found in Wayne Booth's *The Company We Keep: An Ethics of Fiction* (Berkeley: University of California Press, 1988).

41 I am not, of course, suggesting that we abandon the older conception of the aesthetic completely; as I have acknowledged, it is a useful, although not exhaustive, conception.

42 In the *Phaedrus*, Plato also argues that the sight of beauty may arouse an appetite or lust unconnected with deeper feeling (the appetite of "a four-footed beast" [250c]). But, he maintains, in people of reasonable nature and training, the sight of beauty arouses complicated feelings of awe, reverence, and fear, which in turn warm and nourish the soul, motivating it to pursue the good. My concern in this essay, however, is with the broad outlines of a tradition inherited from Plato and not with the considerable subtleties of the Platonic texts themselves.

43 Making this move – allowing that the attitudes a work endorses may compromise its artistic value – is likely to meet with the objection that adopting such a (nonformal) standard of evaluation compromises art's autonomy. The worry here is that a standard that evaluates art in ethical or political terms will expose it – perhaps unwittingly – to various forms of

interference, e.g., the whims of political fashion or religious intolerance. This is a serious worry, but it rests on a misunderstanding. The suggestion that moral or political considerations may be relevant to the evaluation of art does not entail that such considerations be the only factors relevant to their evaluation, nor does it imply that these considerations must invariably take priority.

Most important, such an evaluative standard does not entail the abandonment of the idea of artistic autonomy. The principle of art's autonomy, properly understood, is the idea that works of art deserve a "protected space," a special normative standing. The idea that art deserves this protection is traditionally defended by appealing to a formalist theory of art, but it can also be defended on straightforward political grounds. The basic idea here is that works of art are a political good. They deserve protection because, as forms of expression, they often play an important social and political role: articulating exist-

ing ways of seeing and thinking or challenging and pushing beyond them.

Thus, the suggestion that *Triumph of the Will* is of less artistic value because of its celebration of National Socialism is a rejection of formalist standards of artistic evaluation; it is not a rejection of artistic autonomy. This analysis of the idea of artistic autonomy is based on my "Aesthetic Autonomy and Its Feminist Critics," forthcoming in *The Encyclopedia of Aesthetics*, ed. Michael Kelly (Oxford: Oxford University Press). For a more developed response to worries about censorship, see my "Protected Space: Politics, Censorship and the Arts," in *Aesthetics: Past and Present*, ed. Lydia Goehr, *Journal of Aesthetics and Art Criticism*, 50th Anniversary Issue (Spring 1993): 207–15.

44 The view that the endorsement of ethically bad attitudes can be an aesthetic failure of a work is defended by Berys Gaut in "The Ethical Criticism of Art."

24

A First Look at the Pornography/Civil Rights Ordinance: Could Pornography Be the Subordination of Women?

Melinda Vadas

For a philosopher immersed in the analytic tradition, the "pornography issue" may be puzzling.
This issue has been subjected, as the years of its
tenure *as* an issue have increased, to a more and
more complex analysis. The very definition of
pornography has expanded, almost geometrically,
from a few words to a few paragraphs to a few
pages.[1] Early in the literature – a literature which
now seems as quaint as the cosmological visions of
the pre-Socratics – the general motivation for discussion and analysis seemed to be to explain why
"dirty pictures," though perhaps not everyone's
cup of tea, were not particularly harmful,[2] and
were certainly nothing that a sane, liberal-minded
society would restrict *by law*[3] (Lord Devlin's
model society not being sane in its reliance on
subjectivism and certainly not liberal-minded in
its legislation of the good[4]).

In those dear dead days of simplicity, to have
suggested that pornography itself (and not its censorship or actionability) had a direct relation not to
questions of mere value or virtue but to questions
of *justice* – and justice in the strictest deontological
sense, not some utilitarian simulacrum – would
have been seen as confused, irrational, or duplicitous.[5]

Then feminists began looking at pornography,
most of them writing outside the analytic tradition
and many writing outside of any (academic) philosophical tradition whatever.[6] Articles were written, definitions abounded, these were criticized

and (usually) expanded; pornography was examined from every (as it were) angle. On some accounts, pornography started to look pretty bad.[7]
(Of course, in the intervening years, pornography
itself had got worse, more violent, more "sick,"
and so on.) Still, the question of what all this –
'this' representing perhaps a state of extreme disvalue – had to do with *justice* was not made clear.

The Analysis of Pornography: A History that Ends in a Category Mistake?

Now we have, as I see it, the conceptual culmination of this newer feminist investigation into
pornography encoded in what is most often referred to as the Dworkin/MacKinnon ordinance.[8]
The ordinance was written by Andrea Dworkin, a
feminist writer, and Catharine MacKinnon, a
feminist lawyer. Dworkin and MacKinnon had
been hired by the city of Minneapolis to develop
an ordinance that would help the city control the
problems related to "adult" material. The ordinance they wrote was passed by the city council, but
vetoed by the mayor. It has since gone through
various court battles at various levels of the American legal system, being most recently summarily
dismissed by the Supreme Court. No doubt some
form of it will surface again. In any case, it is
not the ordinance's legal status that interests me
here. I am interested rather in its status as contain-

Melinda Vadas, "A First Look at the Pornography/Civil Rights Ordinance: Could Pornography Be the Subordination of Women?" *The Journal of Philosophy* 84(9), 1987: 487–511.

ing a possibly meaningful philosophical claim. "Pornography," the ordinance states, "is the graphic sexually explicit subordination of women...." This definition of pornography should make any English speaker sit bolt upright. Note the use of the 'is' of identity between 'pornography' and '...subordination'. Now that is peculiar. And the peculiarity is not, as is usually the case in law, a function of mere legal jargonizing – the party-of-the-first-part sort of talk – but is *conceptual*.[9] And because the peculiarity is conceptual, it is, I think, philosophically interesting.

A befuddled reader might sensibly react to the Dworkin/MacKinnon definition of pornography as she would, say, to the claim, "Green is where the post office can be found." This statement (or "statement") is also conceptually "off," but not *horribly* so. In fumbling with its near-sense, the mind, being the mind, tries to revive the claim, as in, "Well, the remark must here refer to a board game, like Monopoly, and it is upon the green square that the game's post office is situated." Now the mind can rest, having made complete sense of the remark. In the Dworkin/MacKinnon case, the reader striving for sense might translate the given definition by mentally adding a few words, as in "Pornography is the graphic sexually explicit *depiction of the* subordination of women." Now the definition makes perfect sense. But this amended definition is not what the ordinance provides. The ordinance says that pornography is the subordination of women. Has the analysis of pornography ended, thanks to these feminists, with something like what Gilbert Ryle[10] called a category mistake or, to use A. C. Baier's term, a "semi-sentence"?[11] Surely, according to what I call the "reasonable view" of pornography, it would seem so.

Pornography: The Reasonable View

The reasonable view of pornography remains straight and strong, the bones beneath the pile of paper flesh generated on this issue. The reasonable view has an incredibly deep and tenacious hold on our common sense and its near relative, our common moral consciousness. This may be because the reasonable view is true or because, though it is not true, it is conceptually welded to something else which is, and we cannot see the point of separation between this coin's true head and its false tail.

Like all moral views, the reasonable view is not unrelated to an epistemology and a metaphysic,[12]

though these are not (as they usually are not) directly stated. The reasonable view is simply this: "Pornography is sexually explicit material – pictures on paper or film, or words on a page. Some people enjoy looking at this material; others do not. To forbid by law the production and dissemination of this material[13] is an act of moralistic piety gone unconscionably governmental – or outright tyranny. If you don't like the words, citizen, just don't read the words. If you don't like the pictures, friend, just don't look at the pictures." With some minor adjustments for principles of public offense[14] and property devaluation,[15] pornography on the reasonable view is rather quickly found to be something outside the area of deontological note.[16] The *ease* with which this conclusion is reached might itself give us pause. We might reflect on this ease and we might recall one of Ludwig Wittgenstein's many suggestive remarks: "The decisive moment in the conjuring trick has been made, and it was the very one that we thought quite innocent."[17] So, on the one hand, we have the simple and reasonable view of pornography and, on the other hand, what looks to be a conceptually bizarre view, the Dworkin/MacKinnon view – something coming, almost, from another form of life. And here we may recall another dark saying of Wittgenstein's: "If a lion spoke, we could not understand him" (§7). If Dworkin/MacKinnon is any indication of the radical feminist form of life, some might be tempted to ascribe the same leonine inscrutability to its opaque practitioners.

The Law of Noncontradiction Applied to our Case

Now I assume that, unless we adopt some kind of fashionable relativism,[18] if one of these views of pornography is correct – the reasonable view or the Dworkin/MacKinnon view – the other is not. Either pornography is, at worst, a bad thing[19] which we would rather not have about but which justice requires us to tolerate, or it is, in addition to being a bad thing, something whose production or dissemination is an actual injustice of some particular sort in that it violates the rights of (usually) women.

Although I am, like, I imagine, almost everyone else, strongly attracted to the reasonable view (because it *is* reasonable), the bizarre view expressed by Dworkin/MacKinnon is to me of greater philosophical interest, because and not in spite of its conceptual peculiarity. This peculiarity suggests an entirely new paradigm, a virtually different world – or extreme mental confusion. Leaving open the possibility that it might be the former, I have begun an investigation. Naturally, one cannot examine this "different world" and its plausibility as a conceptual map all at once. In what follows below, I begin, in a typical, analytic, immoderately small-potatoes way, to begin to try to determine the answer to what seems to me to be a precedential question, viz., Under what conditions, if any, can a representation (here, a pornographic representation) *literally do*[20] what Dworkin/MacKinnon claims pornography does, that is, subordinate women? Whether or not these conditions of subordination do or could hold in this or any other possible world is, naturally, a subject for another time.

An Equivalence

If, as Dworkin/MacKinnon claims, "Pornography is the … subordination of women," then I do believe it follows that pornography subordinates women. (If x is the subordination of y, then x subordinates y.) And the reverse entailment is also true; that is, if pornography subordinates women, it follows that pornography is the subordination of women. (If x subordinates y, then x is the subordination of y.) Thus, pornography subordinates women if and only if pornography is the subordination of women. (x subordinates y if and only if x is the subordination of y.) My reason for pointing out this equivalence is heuristic, since it seems that the "shallow" or ordinary grammatical structure of English makes the 'x subordinates y' formulation more linguistically ordinary, more idiomatic, than the 'x is the subordination of y' formulation.

An Unwelcome Guest

Much to my dismay as an analytic lover of the circumscribed, I found that, in order even to wave at or gesture toward an explanation of either of the above equivalent claims, I was required to turn my attention to the examination of some seemingly unrelated and fairly ragged notions. So now I turn to what I was disgusted[21] to find climbing aboard my conceptual boat – viz., to the notion of a *practice*.

Practices and Their Constituents

A practice is a socially established, socially orchestrated human activity that aims at certain goals or internal goods.[22] Ideologies[23] provide the conceptual support for practices, and institutions are the arenas in which practices are manifested and which materially support those practices. Although not every human activity is part of a practice, very many, perhaps most, are.[24] Practices may have more or less explicit sets of rules and procedures, be more or less generally recognized as practices, have a more or less direct tie to "natural" needs and desires, and cover a more or less broad area of human endeavor. Examples of practices are baseball, medicine, poetry, filmmaking, still photography, racism, militarism,[25] and sexuality.[26]

Within every practice, just as within the world at large, there are those things which occur (e.g., events and actions) and those things which exist (e.g., individual persons or objects, states of affairs). To say this is just to say that the world of the practice is categorized by the same ontological cookie cutter as the rest of the world – whatever that cookie cutter is. This is to be expected, since of course the practice *is* just part of that larger world. The difference, however, between, say, an event that is part of a practice (e.g., striking out in the practice of baseball) and an event that is not part of a practice (e.g., a tree falling on an uninhabited island) is that the former event gains its identity, not as an event, but as the event it is – gains, that is, its meaning, significance, and characterization – in virtue of its being a part of and informed by its practice. All the constituents of a practice – its events, objects, actions, and so on – are what I call *practice informed*. That is, their identity – their meaning, significance, and characterization – is a function of their practice. In order to stress the practice-based nature of that identity, I refer to these constituents, generally, as *practice constituents* and, specifically, as *practice actions, practice objects*, and so on.[27]

The identity of a practice constituent can be traced backward to its generation by the practice's ideology and forward to a manifestation in the practice's supporting institution(s). For example, in the practice of medicine, the identity of the practice action of surgery – what surgery means within the practice, what counts as surgery, what characterizes surgery as surgery – is generated by an ideology that includes beliefs about the causes of disease, the proper and improper techniques of cure, the paradigm of human health, and so on, and the supporting institutions (e.g., hospitals, doctors' out-patient facilities) display or manifest this practice-identified surgery. Although the practice posits benign intentions on the part of the surgeon, as well as some degree of skill, that the individual surgeon may have neither benign intentions (he intends to make money by performing an unnecessary procedure) nor great skill (he's a bumbler) does not make his action any less surgery. The identity of his action is given by the practice, not by the individual practitioner. Even if he directly intends to kill you, he kills you *by performing surgery*, for that is the practice identity of his action.[28]

The practice-informed identity of practice constituents is nonsubjective and determinate. For example, in the practice of baseball, the third futile swing at a good pitch is the practice action of *striking out*. That the third futile swing at a good pitch is that action of striking out is not a matter of individual opinion. (Of course, it may be an open question whether or not the pitch was good.) It is also not a matter of opinion whether the batter who struck out has been bested by the pitcher or not. If he struck out, he has been bested by the pitcher. The practice identity of the action is such that one can say with certainty that the third futile swing at a good pitch is striking out, and that the unfortunate batter who performs this action is in fact bested by the pitcher. The batter on his third futile swing cannot change the identity of his action by closing his eyes and repeating to himself, "I am not striking out, I am not striking out," or by any other change in attitude or behavior.

The nonsubjective identity of practice objects follows this same pattern. In the practice of baseball, a certain type of wooden or metal object is a *bat*. That is the identity of that practice object. To claim, as some might be tempted to do, that the material substratum "beneath" a practice object (or action or event) is its *real* identity – to claim, for example, that a bat is *really* just a piece of wood – is a confusion and sometimes perhaps a lie. There is no more proper, basic, or real identity than practice identity. To provide an extreme example, someone who used an oven from Auschwitz as a punch bowl, claiming it was *really* only a waterproof container, would be someone caught up in this confusion about "real" versus practice identity. Logically speaking, there cannot be many

identities for a single practice constituent, and, given that we cannot opt out of human practices by fiat, practice identity *is* identity. A bat is, nonsubjectively, a bat, not "really" a piece of wood. And the qualities needed in order to be a good bat, or a good batter, are also and similarly nonsubjective practice-functions. In those cases in which it might be said that "the same" object or event is part of two conflicting practices – e.g., a raised arm might be a salute or a request for a teacher's recognition – the practices themselves will generally have procedures for establishing the legitimacy or precedence of their own informing power. (This stamp of the practice may or may not be governed by explicit rules.) At the mass political rally, the raised arm is a salute;[29] in the classroom it is a request for recognition.

It is possible for two conflicting practices to lay simultaneous claim to an event or object, but, in this conflict of meaning or identity, the victory of the one practice over the other is never complete. The cloud of the lost meaning threatens reidentification at every moment. Survival of an unwelcome practice might actually depend on this very instability and confusion. At the moment the malevolent identity of the practice constituent becomes nearly evident, the unwelcome practice can hide the actual identity of its constituent behind the more palatable identity generated by the conflicting practice. ("No, they are not saluting the Führer, they are merely asking for permission to speak.") And the wolf in sheep's clothing looks very like a sheep.

The indications of this dissimulation – of one practice hiding an identity behind another – are various. One clue is the effect of the use of "really" locutions, this effect being the production of an incoherence in a practice-informed explanation. ("If they are *really* just requesting recognition, then why is no one being called upon?") Another can be found in a break or gap in what is ordinarily a discernible, solid line connecting the practice's ideology and the alleged identity of the action or object, a break which may itself be recognized by the bizarre effects of the practice constituent (e.g., claims for teacher recognition should not induce mass chanting). Practices that rely on this type of dissimulation are properly suspect. We are led to wonder what practice identities they are hiding, and why.

A point related to the above is this: since the identity of a practice constituent is practice informed, it follows that this identity is a function

365

Melinda Vadas

of the given, extant practice, whatever it is, and not of some other ideal but nonextant practice, *even if that unrealized practice is objectively preferable*. For example, even if four-strikes-and-then-out baseball might be preferable (morally or rationally) to our present game, the third futile swing at a good pitch is still, nonsubjectively, the action of striking out. To say of a batter on his third futile swing, "He is not *really* striking out because it would be ever so much better if four strikes, not three, were out," is, at best, an extremely misleading way of saying that the present practice of baseball should be altered. And, similarly, to say of this unfortunate batter that he has not *really* been bested by the pitcher because baseball as we play it is a terrible game, or should be abolished, or only placates the workers, or whatever, is just false. The value predicates and characterizations that modify practice constituents are, just like the factual predicates and characterizations, functions of the given practice. A claimed reversion to an *ideal* practice identity for some constituent is the most common form of the type of dissimulation discussed above. But it is foolish and sometimes dangerous to forget that it is the real practice that makes the reality.

Depictions of Practice Constituents

A depiction of a practice constituent, like the practice constituent itself, gains its nonsubjective identity from whatever practice or practices inform it. The fact that the various kinds of depiction making are *themselves* practices entails that the identity of a depiction may be *doubly* practice informed because it exists in an area, if not of *conflict*, then of *overlap* between two practices. The depiction-making practice may add something to the identity of the depicted constituent, or it may function like a blank tablet or mirror on which the depicted practice merely makes its identifying mark. A photo *of a baseball bat*[30] is a photo of a baseball bat because the practice of baseball informs the identity of that photograph. Because the practice of baseball informs the identity of that photograph, the picture is really a picture of a baseball bat, and not "really" a picture of a piece of wood, just as the bat itself is really a bat, and not "really" a piece of wood. Similarly, a film of a batter on his third futile swing is really a depiction of a batter striking out, and not "really" a depiction of certain body movements of a man in funny

pants. Just as, given an extant nondepictionary practice, the practice constituents of that practice are nonsubjectively identifiable and characterizable, so too are depictions of these practice constituents. Just as to hold a depictionary mirror up to a pig is to reveal a pig, so too to hold a depictionary mirror up to a batter striking out is to reveal a batter striking out.

Whether the depictionary practice adds to the identity of the depicted practice constituent or not, there is no room for reasonable debate on the identity of these doubly or singly informed depictions. Is the depiction of a batter on his third futile swing at a good pitch a depiction of a batter striking out, or not? is an absurd question. (Again, just as one can question whether or not the pitch is good, one can also question whether or not the depiction is of a good pitch – it might be shown a hair off the plate. *This* indeterminacy does not affect my point.) And, again, even if one can offer good and compelling reasons why four-strikes-and-then-out baseball would be morally or rationally preferable to our present game, the depiction's identity as a depiction of striking out and as a depiction of the batter being bested by the pitcher is a function of the extant, not the ideal, practice. Again, one *cannot* say, "That is not *really* a depiction of a batter striking out or being bested by the pitcher because it would be ever so much better if four strikes, not three, were out." Again, that would be at best an extremely misleading way of saying that the present practice of baseball should be altered. The predicates, including value predicates, that properly and accurately characterize depictions of doubly or singly informed practice constituents are, like those predicates which characterize the nondepictionary practice constituents, functions of the extant, informing practice or practices, not of a material "practice-free" reality, and not of some other ideal or imaginary practice.

Predicates,[31] like 'is striking out', may apply to both practice constituents and depictions of practice constituents. However, what I call the *transfer* of these predicates from constituent to depiction may occur in one of two ways, which I call *direct* and *prepositional*.

Direct and Prepositional Transfer of Predicates

A predicate may be said to *transfer directly* from a practice (or, for that matter, from a nonpractice) object, event, or action to a depiction of that object, event, or action, just in case the given predicate applies both to the action, object, or event and its depiction without equivocation or other change in meaning, and the predicate applies to the depiction because it applies to the object, action, or event. For example, the predicate 'is red' applies to a real rose and may also apply, in the same sense of 'is red' to a depiction of the rose, and it applies to the depiction because it applies to the rose. In other words, the picture of the rose is red because the rose itself is. Thus, 'is red' is a predicate that transfers directly from the object to the depiction of the object. Or, alternatively, we can say 'is red' is a directly transferring predicate.[32]

On the other hand, there are predicates that transfer from the object, event, or action to a depiction of one of these only with the aid of a preposition such as 'of' or 'about'. A predicate transfers only *prepositionally* if, though it does transfer, a direct transfer of the predicate produces a change in the meaning of the predicate, or the predicate does not apply to the depiction because it applies to that which is depicted. For example, the predicate 'is sweet-smelling' applies to a real rose. But this predicate does not transfer directly to a depiction of the rose. The photograph of the rose is not sweet-smelling. Rather, it is a photograph *of* a sweet-smelling flower. Thus, 'is sweet-smelling' transfers from the rose to the photograph of the rose only prepositionally, or, we can say, 'is sweet-smelling' is a prepositionally transferring predicate. (Of course, any predicate that transfers directly will also transfer prepositionally.)

There are also predicates that might be said not to transfer directly *or* prepositionally from objects, events, or actions, to the depictions of these. (I say "might be said" because one can explain the phenomenon of alleged nontransfer by claiming that the predicate in question fails to transfer because it does not in fact apply to the original object or event either). Our understanding of this mechanism of nontransfer is made easier if we recognize the practice-informed nature of the constituents of the various representational practices (film-making, photography, etc.), a nature neither more nor less practice informed than that of other constituents of other practices. In order to emphasize this practice-informed nature and to explain what seems to be a total lack of predicate transfer in some instances, I distinguish below between what I call "material" and "depictionary" scenes.

Material and Depictionary Scenes

In one sense of 'of', the question, What is that a depiction of? can mean (using the practice of film-making as the clearest paradigm): What fakery (e.g., ketchup "blood," styrofoam "snow") was used to produce the desired representational effect? What *materially speaking* was before the camera? In this sense of 'of', film footage from a Western may be a picture *of* an actor named John Wayne riding a mechanical horse across a hot, klieg-lit soundstage in southern California. That characterization or identity can be called *the material scene*. In another sense of 'of', the question, What is that a depiction of? means What is the depiction supposed to depict? (What, in my argot, is the practice identity of this constituent?) In this sense of 'of', the answer to that question is: It's a picture of Tex Walker (the character) riding across the snowy plains of Montana on his trusty horse Spike. This is the *depictionary scene*. Clearly, if the material 'of' were what we used in the question, What is that a depiction of? all movies would be movies of actors making movies, which clearly they are not.

This ambiguity creates a problem, or at least a pseudo problem, because predicates that apply to material scenes often do not transfer in any way to depictions of those scenes. For example, if the soundstage in the above-noted scene is very hot because of the klieg lights, the predicate 'is hot' does not transfer, even prepositionally, to the depiction. It is not a depiction of a hot day. It is a depiction of a cold, snowy day.

This ambiguity of 'of' and the choice between providing a material or depictionary description of such scenes is, however, just another (fairly well hidden) example of the same confusion reflected in the Is it really a bat or really a piece of wood? question. The representational arts are *also* practices, and their practice constituents have real identities that are practice informed. The film scene with John Wayne is not "really" a scene of an actor named John Wayne on a mechanical horse any more than a bat is "really" just a wooden stick or a baseball player is "really" just a man in funny pants. The identity of the practice constituent (the scene on film) just *is* its practice identity. There is none more basic or more real. Of course it is a shot of a snowy day. Of course it is a picture of Montana. (Cf. "Of course he is striking out – that's his third swing.") Naturally, *in another practice*, the identity of these constituents changes. But that we already knew. Not that this changed constituent would *look* any different, any more than a bat looks different from a (bat-shaped) piece of wood. It is the practice that produces the identity of the constituent. Change the practice, and you change the identity.

A complication arises in identifying the practice constituent in those cases in which the representational practice depicts a constituent of another (additional) practice. For example, in a movie about baseball, the identity of a given depiction is a *twin* function of *both* informing practices – here, baseball and film-making. So what might we have a depiction *of*? An overweight actor pretending to hit a home run with a papier-mâché bat? No, that is the material scene. The practice identity of the depiction (which is to say, its identity) is that it is a depiction of a famous baseball player hitting a home run. What gives the depictionary scene this identity is *both* the practice of film-making and the practice of baseball. That is, the practice of film-making informs the identity of the depiction no less than the practice of baseball. In this practice, a depiction of something made, materially, of papier-mâché is a depiction of a wooden baseball bat, not a depiction of a papier-mâché movie prop.[33] That practice constituents (baseball bats, surgeons' scalpels, KKK crosses) have a practice identity (regardless of their material identity as plaster of paris, tin foil, or cardboard) in fictive settings is no more remarkable than that the English language, spoken in a novel or on film, retains its standard meaning. The sentence, 'He has arrived', spoken on a stage, still means what it does in life, even though no one has arrived and an actor speaks the words without the usual intention. Similarly, a film's practice object, e.g., a cardboard bat, is a baseball bat, not a cardboard movie prop. Like the English language, the bat's identity is its practice identity – and here that identity is a twin function of the practices of baseball and film-making.

Direct and Prepositional Transfer of Value Predicates

A *value* predicate is a predicate that ascribes moral or nonmoral goodness or badness itself (where goodness and badness are inclusive of rightness and wrongness) or ascribes that which is morally or nonmorally good or bad to some practice (or nonpractice) object, event, or action. Some value predicates transfer directly from "original" to depiction, and some transfer only prepositionally. An example of a direct transfer of a value predicate from an object to its depiction would be the predicate 'is beautiful' as applied to a rose. This value predicate transfers directly from the rose to a photograph of the rose, since the predicate may apply to the depiction in the same sense in which it applies to the rose, and may apply to the depiction because it applies to the rose. On the other hand, the predicate 'is a valuable floral specimen', transfers only prepositionally to the depiction of the rose. The depiction is not a valuable floral specimen, rather, it is a depiction *of* a valuable floral specimen.

This direct transfer of value predicates may take place between many practice constituents and their depictions. For example, consider the practice of social etiquette. Within this practice, certain actions shame or disgrace the agent of those actions, whereas others bring the agent social approval or even honor. Mistakenly drinking the water in one's fingerbowl, for example (especially if one slurps it loudly and exclaims, "Great soup!") is an action that would surely disgrace the foolish dinner guest. In describing this incident, we might say, e.g., "Clara was disgraced by this action," or, alternatively and equivalently, "This action disgraces Clara." Does the predicate 'disgraces Clara' transfer, though, to a depiction of this unfortunate event? (Let us say that the host's nephew, Elwood, was videotaping the party.) And, if the predicate, 'disgraces Clara', does transfer, does it transfer directly or prepositionally? Is Elwood's videotape footage of Clara slurping the water in her fingerbowl a depiction that disgraces Clara? Or is it merely a depiction *of* an action that disgraces Clara? (Again, if the predicate transfers directly, it also transfers prepositionally.) It goes without saying that drinking water in one's fingerbowl is a practice action; its meaning and significance are a function of its practice membership. In another practice, it might represent the height of sophistication and good manners, a point irrelevant here. I believe that critical reflection reveals that the predicate in the above instance transfers directly from the practice action to the depiction of it. Elwood's videotape footage disgraces Clara. The predicate 'disgraces Clara' is used with the same meaning when applied to both action and depiction, and it applies to the depiction because it applies to the action. It is not the case that

Clara is literally disgraced by the actual drinking and only metaphorically disgraced by Elwood's videotape.

The same direct predicate transfer would occur if the fingerbowl-slurping episode were part of a movie, and Clara a character in that movie. The character would be shamed or disgraced by her actions as revealed in the movie. Here the predicate transfers from this constituent of the practice of social etiquette as an extant material and conceptual construct, rather than from a particular, real-life finger-bowl slurping. (Transfers, we might say, from slurping as a type, rather than a token, to a token.) There may be no value-predicate transfer from the material scene of actress Jane Smith pretending to drink water in a fake fingerbowl to the depiction on the screen.

Let us consider another example of direct predicate transfer of a value predicate. A baseball player has the fans standing in the bleachers, applauding his record-breaking home run. Given the conventions of the practice of baseball – given this ovation's practice identity – this group applause is an action that honors this player. A photograph, taken by a local newspaper reporter, which depicts the standing ovation, also honors this player. The predicate 'honors this player' transfers directly from the practice constituent (the ovation) to a depiction of it. Again, there is no change in the meaning of the predicate, and the photograph honors the player because the original action honored him.

The following final example of direct predicate transfer of a value predicate is instructive because it illuminates the relationship between the performative power of certain utterances within certain practices (here, "I award you this medal") and the process of predicate transfer.

In an honor-awarding ceremony in the military, the utterances made are performative; that is, the utterances themselves accomplish the task of bestowing honor. The medal wearer is then honored, or continues to be honored, by wearing the medal bestowed in this ceremony. We might say that the "power" of the bestowal of honor moves, in this practice, from the performative utterance to the related object, the medal itself. The soldier so honored now continues to be honored by wearing his medal. A depiction of the soldier wearing his medal also honors the soldier. 'Honors this soldier' is here a directly transferring

value predicate. The picture honors the soldier in precisely the same sense in which the medal does, and it honors him because the medal does. However, both the medal itself and the photograph honor the soldier in virtue of their relationship to the honor-awarding ceremony of this practice and to the performative utterances of that ceremony.

Generally, as the above examples bear out, the value predicates that directly transfer from practice constituents to depictions are those which have a strong notional component – *not* that we can mentally assign the predicates or not, as we might with equal facility think of a red or of a green triangle – but that the practice's assignment of the predicate to the practice constituent is locked within and constrained by the real and interrelated meanings of practice experience rather than, say, constrained by physical laws or logical impossibilities. Put another way, we can say that these directly transferring value predicates are more closely related to the real social meanings that create our experience than to the material edges of reality, though it *should not be forgotten* that these material edges do have a bearing on this predicate assignment as well (and that the meaning/material distinction is ultimately specious). Reflection and example might reveal these directly transferring value predicates to include 'shames', 'honors', 'degrades', 'defames', 'exalts', 'elevates', and – significantly for the case under examination – 'subordinates'.

The Irrational Assignment of Value Predicates to Practice Constituents

Suppose that, as may in fact sometimes be the case, those who receive medals in the military – and that is to say those who are honored – are men who should not, ideally speaking, be honored. (Suppose that they are Nazi soldiers being honored for killing Jewish civilians.) Can we then say, The photo of this Nazi soldier with his medals is not a photo that *really* honors the soldier, because those medals are *really* a sign of dishonor? This claim, like the claim that the baseball player on his third strike is not really striking out, because it would be objectively better if four strikes were out, is a confusion. It is a misleading way of saying that the practice that awards medals for killing Jews should be abolished. We *can* say that the practice, through its constituent (the medal), presents what is evil as good, and that a depiction of the practice constituent also presents what is evil as good. Indeed, it is this axiological transposition that makes a morally unacceptable practice morally unacceptable.[34] In presenting the dishonorable as honorable, the Nazi practice condemns itself. A photo of a Nazi wearing all his medals for killing Jews is a photo that honors what is evil and dishonorable. The photo honors what it should not because the medals honor what they should not. To say this is not to say that the photo does not *really* honor the soldier, because it does. We could say that those who are honored by practices that honor the dishonorable are thereby and in fact dishonored by being honored in this way, but the locution 'not *really* being honored' remains misleading, and it in fact *makes inexplicable* our proper value judgment of the depiction. If the Nazi is not really being honored by this photo, then why is this picture contemptible? In looking at the photo of the Nazi with all his medals, we do *not* say, "Ah, finally this swine has received his just deserts," but rather, "How terrible that anyone would choose to honor such a man."

In sum, when a practice makes this type of axiological transposition (viz., presenting evil as good or good as evil), to say that the given practice constituent is not *really* good or not *really* evil is a confused way of saying that the practice has performed an axiological transposition, and that no practice should perform such a transposition. We cannot go on to suggest either that *this* abhorrent practice should not have performed the given axiological transposition or to suggest that the transposition be undone. We cannot suggest that *this* practice should not have performed the transposition because such a statement implies that the transposition is inessential to the practice's identity, when that is not in fact the case. Axiological assignments, transposed or not, are part of what sketch out a practice's identity; e.g., part of what gave Nazism its practice identity just was its axiological perversity. And neither can this transposition be undone. The practice's presentation of evil as good or good as evil presents us with a compound meaning for the given constituent which, like all meanings, can never be erased, though, if the transposition is noted within the context of a morally perspicacious society, we may hope that the presentation of this constituent's perverse meaning will fall into disuse.[35]

The Meaning of 'Subordination' as this Term is Used in the Pornography/Civil Rights Ordinance

Not every action that harms women subordinates women, and not all representations that portray women in a negative light – e.g., representations that make women look foolish or stupid or vain – subordinate women. To subordinate an individual or group of individuals – using the term 'subordinate' as I believe it is used within the context of the Pornography/Civil Rights Ordinance[36] – is to place that person or group of persons socially in the class of those whose intrinsic or inherent moral worth or standing is not of the first rank, and whose rights are thereby of lesser scope, importance, or weight than the rights of others. Such a social placement of women into the class of intrinsic moral inferiors would indeed, as the ordinance also says, represent "a substantial threat to . . . the equality of citizens in the community."[37] The social establishment of a group's intrinsic moral inferiority quite naturally leads to their political oppression, and so close is this relationship between the social stamp of intrinsic moral inferiority and political oppression that it is more illuminating to see these disvalues as twin aspects of a single social coin, rather than as held together by a cause-and-effect relationship.

The social assignment of intrinsic moral inferiority to a group of persons – and, that is to say, their subordination – is quite other than a mere assertion of such inferiority, as would be made by the statement, 'Women are morally inferior to men', or as might be entailed or implied by the assertion, 'Women should be sexually abused by men'.[38] The social assignment of intrinsic moral inferiority to women, the placement of women in the class of intrinsic moral inferiors, the subordination of women, is an actual, empirical, and not merely or essentially linguistic placement, though it is not of course a *physical* placing or moving. One may be assigned a social place without one's body being moved. One may, for example, actually, empirically place or be placed at the bottom of one's graduating class without thereby changing one's spatial-temporal location. One can be subordinated without leaving the house. This fact does not make one's subordination "symbolic" or "metaphorical" any more than the above-mentioned scholastic placement is symbolic or metaphorical.

Although the social assignment of intrinsic moral inferiority to women cannot, by its very nature, be father to the *fact* of women's intrinsic or inherent moral inferiority (that would require some effort of patriarchal genetic engineering in which women were, say, turned into tobacco plants), the assignment to the class of intrinsic moral inferiors is nevertheless a real assignment to a real social category. Such a claim for the existence of an actual social category of intrinsic moral inferiority raises many questions beyond the scope of this article. One question would be that of the ontological or metaphysical status of the entity (society) that allegedly has these categories. We might ask whether or not it would be illuminating to attempt a reduction from the paradigm that speaks of a metaphysically real society to one that speaks only of individuals and their beliefs and attitudes. Briefly, I do not believe that this notion of society and the social can be illuminatingly explained by reference only to individuals and their mental states even if, as is surely the case, society is in some sense made up of individuals. Reductionistic schemes or paradigms are unwelcome if we lose predictive and explanatory power through the reduction – which is to say, if the adoption of the reductive scheme causes us to lose the *desired* epistemic access to the phenomenon under examination, the reductionistic scheme cannot be recommended.[39]

Whether or not a paradigm that has no room for a metaphysically real notion of society does in fact cause us to lose desired epistemic access to some phenomenon (here, the phenomenon of subordination) cannot be decided, one way or the other, by pointing to the odd falls from validity which occur if we reason across paradigms. From 'It is certain that the social placement of some group into the class of moral inferiors is unjust' we cannot infer 'It is certain that x-x_n's false belief in y-y_n's intrinsic moral inferiority is unjust'. The inference will not hold even if we drop the modal operator, 'it is certain that', since to believe falsely in another's moral inferiority is not unjust, but only bad. This fall from validity only illustrates the problem of choosing a paradigm, but does not decide the outcome of that choice.[40]

Could Pornography be the Subordination of Women?

If to subordinate someone, in the sense explained, is to place that person socially into the class of intrinsic moral inferiors, then 'subordinate' is a value predicate. It is among those predicates which may transfer directly from a practice constituent to a depiction of such a constituent, provided of course that the conditions for such direct transfer are met. Thus, pornographic depictions could subordinate women, if the predicate 'subordinates' transfers without change of meaning from constituent to depiction and if the predicate applies to the depiction because it applies to the practice constituent.[41] As argued above, a predicate may apply to a practice constituent or to a depiction of a practice constituent, even though the assignment of the predicate is a function of an irrationality that has infected the practice. Just as the Nazi's medals honor what are in fact a despicable man's despicable actions – but honor him nonetheless – so constituents in our practice of sexuality and their pornographic depictions may subordinate, in the sense of placing the subordinated into the class of moral inferiors, those who are in fact moral equals – but subordinate them nonetheless. Of course, it is as irrational to subordinate moral equals as it is to honor despicable actions, but we cannot, on the grounds of this irrationality, say either "the medals do not honor" or "the depictions do not subordinate."[42]

So it seems that we have an affirmative answer to the precedential question of our investigation into the conceptual structure of the Dworkin/MacKinnon Ordinance, i.e., an affirmative answer to the question, Could pornography be the subordination of women? The seeming conceptual oddity of the ordinance's definition of pornography as "the graphic sexually explicit subordination of women" is revealed as neither odd nor uniquely generated, given the fairly common phenomenon of direct predicate transfer from practice constituents to their depictions.

A Brief Outline of Some Normative Entailments of the Above Analysis

What is wrong with the reasonable view quoted above is that it fails to allow for direct predicate transfer from practice constituents to their depictions, a failure which is compounded by the reasonable view's implicit adoption of a reductionistic paradigm which destroys epistemic access to the phenomenon of subordination, as such subordination is referred to within the context of the ordinance. Thus, the reasonable view does not have conceptual room for naming the production or dissemination of pornography as an injustice, but can at most see such actions as producing a state of mere disvalue. Since there is a morally relevant difference between producing a state of mere disvalue and bringing about an injustice, as well as a morally relevant difference between the additional and further harm engendered by producing a state of mere disvalue and the harm engendered by bringing about an injustice, the reasonable view will have different normative entailments from the civil-rights view.

On the civil-rights view, the additional harm related to producing or disseminating pornography (such as the harm represented by sex crimes) is directly and relevantly related to the producer's or disseminator's contribution toward the creation of women as a subordinated class, a contribution and creation which is itself an injustice. On the reasonable view, any further harm that is causally related to producing or disseminating pornography is related to the permissible, if devalued, action of producing or disseminating this merely depictionary material. On the civil-rights view, the additional harm is akin to that harm caused by a bank robber's pistol waving, which causes a frightened customer to die of a heart attack. The robber may be held responsible for this death, even though he did not intend it, because it is a causal consequence of a certain faulty and risk-creating aspect of his action. On the reasonable view, the harm caused by pornography is akin to that harm caused by my rude rebuff of a fellow bank customer's friendly greeting, which rebuff causes him to die of a heart attack. I cannot be held responsible for this death because, even though it is causally related to my faulty action, the faulty aspect of my action (its rudeness) did not create the risk of death or the realization of that risk. Rude actions do not ordinarily create such risks; and, if we find them faulty, that is not *why* we find them faulty. In the case of the bank robber, however, we can say that his pistol-waving action violated the rights of the bank customers to (among other things) personal safety in a public place, and it was just this faulty aspect of his action which created the risk and the realization of that risk.[43] Unjust actions often, though not always, create such additional risks. On the civil-rights view, it is the sexual subordination of women that is pornography which grounds and explains the faulty aspect of producing or disseminating it, and this faulty aspect creates an additional and further risk, the risk that members of this subordinated class will become the victims of sex crimes. *Why* the initial act of production or dissemination is faulty (because of its contribution to the creation of a subordinated class of persons) and *how* the additional harm (produced by sex crimes) comes about are linked by the faulty aspect of the original act. Actually to contribute to the creation of a class of subordinated people is concomitantly to create the foreseeable risk that they will be victimized by those who are acting in response and relation to this actual subordination. Contributing to the actual creation of such a subordinated class of people is relevantly different from suggesting or recommending that others engage in certain illicit behavior – although the latter may be within the bounds of just action, the former is not.

On the reasonable view, pornography is merely depictionary material, and, though it may be bad or faulty to produce or disseminate such material, in that the material depicts or recommends the subordination of women, the material does not literally or actually subordinate women, and therefore the producers and disseminators of this material are not bringing about a state of affairs in which women are actually subordinated, but are only bringing about a state of affairs in which women are depicted as subordinated. Therefore, these parties are not responsible, on the reasonable view, for what might happen if they *were* to bring about such a state of affairs of actual subordination, for they have not brought about such a state of affairs. On the reasonable view, mere depictions, as such, do not contribute to the creation of the practice identity of women as a subordinated class; thus, in producing or disseminating such depictions one is not engendering either a state of injustice or even a direct risk for others. Of course, those who hold the reasonable view recognize that agents acting upon the information or recommendations provided by pornographic depictions might harm others. If this occurs, however, the agents of harm are themselves responsible for the harm, not the creators or disseminators of the depictions. One who holds the reasonable view will naturally say that the agents simply should not have acted on the information or recommendations imparted. On the civil-rights view, pornography not only provides information and recommendations, but contributes to the actual and literal creation of women as a subordinated class, a class whose members may then be additionally victimized by those acting in response to this preestablished subordination.

Notes

1 An example of a fairly standard (medium-length, too) definition of pornography would be Longino's: "Pornography ... is verbal or pictorial material which represents or describes sexual behavior that is degrading or abusive to one or more of the participants *in such a way as to endorse the degradation*." Helen Longino, "What Is Pornography," in Laura Lederer, ed., *Take Back the Night* (New York: William Morrow, 1980), p. 43. Some problems with this idea of "endorsement" – problems tangential to my inquiry – are noted by Alan Soble in "Pornography: Defamation and the Endorsement of Degradation," *Social Theory and Practice*, XI, 1 (Spring 1985): 61–87.

2 And of course some claim these representations are socially and personally helpful, sexually liberating, and so on. See, for example, G. L. Simon's "Is Pornography Beneficial?" in Thomas A. Mappes and Jane S. Zembaty, eds., *Social Ethics* (New York: McGraw Hill, 1977), pp. 243–8.

3 This is not to say that otherwise sane and liberal-minded societies have not restricted pornography by law, for of course they have. The arguments of liberal theorists – see, for example, Ronald Dworkin's *Taking Rights Seriously* (Cambridge, Mass.: Harvard, 1977), especially ch. 10, "Liberty and Moralism" – stress that restrictions against such material, under the aegis of legislating the good, are inconsistent with liberal political theory.

4 See his *The Enforcement of Morals* (New York: Oxford, 1965), ch. 1.

5 Again see Dworkin, especially ch. 11, "Liberty and Liberalism," p. 262, on which page Dworkin states that showing the movie *Deep Throat* is not a threat to any principle of justice.

6 See, for example, Susan Griffin's fairly high-flying *Pornography and Silence* (New York: Harper and Row, 1982).

7 The by-now classic investigation and analysis of pornography is Andrea Dworkin's *Pornography: Men Possessing Women* (New York: Perigee, 1981). See also the chapter "Anti-Feminism," in her *Right-wing Women* (New York: Perigee, 1982). *Take Back the Night, op. cit.*, is an anthology of women, all self-identified as feminists, writing about and criticizing pornography.

8 The title "Pornography/Civil Rights Ordinance" is preferred by the ordinance's supporters, whereas the title "Dworkin/MacKinnon Ordinance" is preferred by its detractors. I use the two titles interchangeably.

This ordinance implies that there is a connection between pornography and justice, in that producing and selling pornography (as well as other pornographically related activities) is seen as a violation of the rights of (usually) women. I will touch only tangentially upon this question of justice in this essay, since I believe other questions having to do with the possible conceptual status of pornographic representations come first.

The ordinance defines pornography as follows (This is taken from the version – the ordinance has several versions – reprinted in *Ms. Magazine* (April 1985): 46):

1 Pornography is the graphic sexually explicit subordination of women through pictures and/or words that also includes one or more of the following: (i) women are presented dehumanized as sexual objects, things, or commodities; or (ii) women are presented as sexual objects who enjoy pain or humiliation; or (iii) women are presented as sexual objects who experience sexual pleasure in being raped; or (iv) women are presented as sexual objects tied up or cut up or mutilated or bruised or physically hurt; or (v) women are presented in postures or positions of sexual submission, servility, or display; or (vi) women's body parts – including but not limited to vaginas, breasts, or buttocks – are exhibited such that women are reduced to those parts; or (vii) women are presented as whores by nature; or (viii) women are presented being penetrated by objects or animals; or (ix) women are presented in scenarios of degradation, injury, torture, shown as filthy or inferior, bleeding, bruised or hurt in a context that makes these conditions sexual.

2 The use of men, children, or transsexuals in the place of women in (1) above is pornography for the purposes of this law.

9 As evidence of the ordinance's conceptual difficulty, one can look to the sympathetic, but adverse, opinion of Judge Frank Easterbrook [quoted in *Off Our Backs* (April 1986): 6]: "Depictions of subordination tend to perpetuate subordination. The subordinate status of women in turn leads to affront and lower pay at work, insult and injury at home, battery and rape on the streets ... (but) this simply demonstrates the power of pornography as speech." Clearly, Easterbrook mentally translated the ordinance's definition of pornography into a more sensible form, ignoring the copula of identity between 'pornography' and 'subordination'. The ordinance does not merely say that, in depicting subordination, pornography causes subordination. The ordinance says that pornography *is* subordination.

10 *The Concept of Mind* (New York: Barnes & Noble, 1949).

11 "To make a new point it may be necessary for the philosopher, as much as for the poet or the scientist, to speak in a new form of words not simply trans-

Melinda Vadas

latable into any of the old forms. But the philosopher who speaks too often in semisentences runs the risk of semiunderstanding from only a semiaudience." See "Nonsense," in Paul Edwards, ed., *Encyclopedia of Philosophy* (New York: MacMillan, 1967).

12 In both "Feminism, Marxism, Method, and the State," in *The Signs Reader* (Chicago: University Press, 1983), pp. 227–56, and "Not a Moral Issue," *Yale Law and Policy Review*, II, 321 (1984): 321–45, Catharine MacKinnon maintains that objectivity, in the sense of aperspectivity, is the way in which gender males both create and describe the world. From the point of view of such "aperspectivity" only direct, John-hits-Mary causal harm is recognized as the harm that creates injustice. Thus, if no such harm is connected with producing pornography, such production cannot be unjust.

13 Or – which is different – to make it actionable in the manner of the Pornography/Civil Rights Ordinance.

14 See Joel Feinberg's "The Offense Principle," in Mappes and Zembaty, *op. cit.*, pp. 252–7.

15 See the case of *Young v. American Mini Theaters, Inc.* described in Archibald Cox's *Freedom of Expression* (Cambridge, Mass.: Harvard, 1981), p. 34.

16 Again, I think that obscenity law, in legislating matters related to the good, is a deontological aberration. The just act/good act distinction is severely sketched by Charles Fried in *Right and Wrong* (Cambridge, Mass.: Harvard, 1979): "But while the demands of justice are implacable within their proper domain, it is . . . inappropriate and unnecessary to extend them outside of that domain. [There] the scale of judgment is marked, if at all, in degrees of praise only" (173 and 176). In other words, as long as what we do is within the bounds of just action, it is no one else's business adversely to judge, much less to prohibit or restrict, what we do. The production of pornography – as pornography is ordinarily defined by obscenity laws – falls into this realm of personal discretion.

17 *Philosophical Investigations*, G. E. M. Anscombe, ed. (New York: MacMillan, 3rd ed., 1958), §308.

18 A sensible non-Platonic defense of normative realism is given by Thomas Nagel in *The View from Nowhere* (New York: Oxford, 1986), especially in the section "Realism and Objectivity," pp. 138–43.

19 Again, some claim it is a positively good thing.

20 Of course, the notions of the literal and the metaphoric are problematic. I am working here with our intuitive and imperfect understanding of these concepts. Unless one wants to stack one's philosophical deck, it is important not suddenly to move the line between what counts as literally subordinating someone (versus metaphorically subordinating her) when examining the case of pornography. Cf. Nan Hunter's comment on the metaphoric nature of

pornographic subordination in "Is One Woman's Sexuality Another Woman's Pornography?" *Ms.* (April 1985): 123.

21 Disgust is, of course, the proper analytic response to this ragged world's failure to be amenable to the strengths of one's taxonomic tools.

22 My notion of a practice draws from that of Alasdair MacIntyre [See his *After Virtue* (Notre Dame, Ind.: University Press, 2d ed., 1984), p. 187], but MacIntyre seems to regard practices as functionally related to the human virtues, and I do not.

23 My (fairly stipulative) notion of an ideology is such that it includes *all* of a practice's conceptual support, such as its rules, principles, value judgments, and purposes. These may or may not be known by the practitioners. Thus, nothing in my notion of an ideology requires that it be either covert or oppressive. This somewhat extended notion of an ideology allows us to see the structural similarity between social units like baseball and social units like racism. It also allows us to see how ideologies partially overlap to link practices together to form a single social reality – e.g., baseball and racism may share some conceptual support in their ideological inclusion of value judgments about the desirability of hierarchy or competition. A concise introduction to both the Marxist and the non-Marxist concepts of ideology can be found in David McLellan's *Ideology* (Minneapolis: Minnesota UP, 1986).

24 I do not believe that this near ubiquity extends the concept of a practice into meaninglessness. It is not that the concept is either overbroad or empty, but rather that practices are as common as societies themselves are.

25 Not everything that is a practice has a convenient, unambiguous English word to refer to it. 'Racism' and 'militarism' for example, might be taken by some to refer to ideologies, rather than practices.

26 Michel Foucault's writings on sexuality make this point clearly. See his *The History of Sexuality* (New York: Vintage Books, 1980) and *The Use of Pleasure* (New York: Pantheon, 1985).

To say that an activity is a practice is not, of course, to deny that it incorporates certain "natural" needs and desires. Baseball, though a practice, certainly incorporates certain "natural" needs and desires (e.g., for physical exercise). It is in fact hard to imagine a practice that did not, in some way, incorporate human needs and desires. This incorporation is at least part of the reason the practice exists. If we keep this fact of incorporation in mind, the seeming peculiarity of calling sexuality a practice disappears.

27 To characterize this identity partially in terms of meaning and significance is already to indicate that I am applying a notion of identity which internalizes social context. (In which case, to call it "context" is rather misleading.) In finding the identity of prac-

374

tice constituents to be a function of their practices, I am denying the meaningfulness of a concept of identity free of social context, such as that said to characterize what have been called "basic actions." [For a discussion of the problems associated with basic actions see Michael Simon's "The Social Nature of Action" in his *Understanding Human Action* (Albany: SUNY Press, 1982 pp. 24–40).] I am further extending the concept of an identity which internalizes social context to objects and individuals as well. Though I do not do so here, this same application of a context-internalized identity may also be successfully extended to feelings and other mental states – see, for example, Robert Kraut's "Feelings in Context," *Journal of Philosophy*, LXXXIII, 11 (November 1986): 642–52; or Naomi Scheman's "Individualism and the Objects of Psychology," in Sandra Harding and Merrill Hintikka, eds., *Discovering Reality* (Boston: D. Reidel, 1983).

My account of a context-internalized identity differs from that of Simon and Kraut only in that I stress a smaller social unit, a practice, as being the generator of that identity, rather than society or social reality at large.

28 A surgical tool is an example of a practice object whose identity, though certainly practice informed, has a connection to the practice's ideology which is both weaker and more indirect than the connection between that ideology and the practice action of surgery. Generally, the connection between an ideology and the identity of practice actions is both more direct and stronger, while the connection between ideology and the identity of practice objects is more indirect and weaker. Put in a linguistic mode, the move from some ideological statement or statements, e.g., 'The purpose of surgery is to cure disease' and 'This is a scalpel' is more roundabout and attenuated than the move from 'The purpose of surgery is to cure disease' and 'This action is surgery'.

The differing degrees of the tightness and strength of these ideological connections is, I believe, revealed in our intuitive, commonsense judgments that, for example, what the surgeon does can only be identified as surgery, while his tools, put to a different use in a different practice, might easily and properly be thought of as having metamorphosed into entirely different things (like garden clippers). Because of what is *in general* this stronger connection between a practice's ideology and practice actions, practice actions (as opposed to practice objects) are not good candidates for an attempted re-identification/metamorphosis through a new practice – for as long as the old practice and its ideology are extant (or even remembered), the metamorphosis to a new identity will be unlikely to occur.

29 This may be so even if the agent does not intend to salute. "[T]he fact that an action must be subjectively or intersubjectively meaningful need not be taken to imply that its meaning has to be what the agent thinks it is" (Simon, p. 37).

30 The ambiguity of 'of' in the phrase 'picture *of* a baseball bat' is discussed in the section below, "Material and Depictionary Scenes."

31 I use the term 'predicate' to refer to the entire expression that attaches to the subject term. 'Predicate', in this sense, includes the copula.

32 What will count as a predicate applying to the depiction *because* it applies to the "original" is itself practice mediated. For example, a photo could be taken of a bitter-tasting rose and, in developing the photo, the photographer might take a bite of the rose and its bitter taste might cause her to spill a bitter-tasting fluid on the photograph. It would then be true to say that the photo of the rose was bitter tasting because the rose itself was bitter tasting; that is, the rose's bitterness was part of the causal and explanatory link that produced the bitter-tasting photo of the rose. Nevertheless, 'is bitter tasting' is not here a directly transferring predicate since the practice of photography has no ideological room for this transfer. (That is, the rules and procedures of photography – which are part of its ideology – do not incorporate the concept of taste, though they might come to do so, at which time 'is bitter tasting' might become a directly transferring predicate.) Thus, part of what determines the existence or absence of direct predicate transfer are the (perhaps changing) ideologies of the involved practices.

33 This distinction between material and depictionary scenes is of direct importance in the moral and juridical evaluation of the pornography issue, since it is often said that pornographic portrayals are *really* only of actresses and actors playing scripted parts (tomorrow the porn queen will play Lady Macbeth) and not, say, photos of real rapes or other real crimes against women. But this opinion is the product of a double confusion. It is a confusion because, first, there is a failure to understand the doubly practice-informed nature of these pornographic depictions. A pornographic depiction of a rape is a depiction of a rape, not of an actress pretending to be raped, just as the depiction in the Western film is of Tex riding across Montana on a horse, not of John Wayne on a soundstage in California. A depiction of an actress pretending to be raped is a different scene, though it might not look any different (recall again the bat and the bat-shaped piece of wood). Secondly, those who attempt to ameliorate the possibly severe moral judgment of pornographic depictions also fail to note that, if the stories of the survivors are true, pornographic depictions often have material and depictionary identities that are one and the same. [See for example

Melinda Vadas

Linda Marchiano's *Ordeal*, written under her better known name, Linda Lovelace, with Mike McGrady (Seacaucus, NJ: Citadel Press, 1980)] That is, depictionary scenes of a woman being raped may be produced by filming material scenes of a woman being raped. In some cases, this collapse between material and depictionary scenes is highly contingent (one can easily produce a depictionary scene of a woman being raped without an identical material scene), but, in other cases, the collapse may be all but necessary (How can one produce a photographic depiction of a woman's exposed genitals without an identical material scene?).

34 The words from Isaiah (5:20–3) are apposite here: "Woe unto you who call evil good, and good evil, who turn darkness into light and light into darkness, who make bitter sweet and sweet bitter. Woe unto you!"

35 It seems to be possible for some practice constituents, especially practice objects, to be claimed and re-identified by new practices. For example, the naturally "kinky" hair of Black Americans, along with their very skin color, was seized from its racist presentation as shameful and made into a sign of pride and honor. This change in meaning was made possible, however, not by a mere collective mental act, but by the (partial) abolition of the practice of racism and the birth of the social practice of anti-racism. It is significant that other practice constituents of racism, such as lynching and insulting forms of address, could not be transformed or re-identified. There is probably no hard and fast rule determining which practice constituents can be re-identified and which not (Could the Nazi swastika ever become a symbol of Jewish self-affirmation?), and the impossibility of re-identifying most practice constituents is certainly not a logical one.

36 See Andrea Dworkin's "A Word People Don't Understand," in *Ms.* (April 1985): 46. Also Catharine MacKinnon in "Coming Apart," *Off Our Backs* (June 1985): 6.

37 The Pornography/Civil Rights Ordinance, Section One, reprinted in *Ms.* (April 1985): 46.

38 In "The Minneapolis Ordinance and the FACT Brief," *Women's Review of Books* (May 1986): 8, Rosemary Tong indirectly reveals the irreducibility of such social placement to perlocutionary effect. This particular irreducibility is just a specific instance of the difficulties that follow from the sort of paradigm shifts discussed below.

39 Of course, whether or not the access is desired is the question. It is axiomatic that change of one's paradigm destroys a certain type of explanatory power, viz., that of the old paradigm. We cannot, for example, explain the moves of a chess player *as chess moves* by describing the movement of the molecules of her body, even though, as is surely the case, the chess player is made up of molecules. The switch

from the "Chess Game Paradigm" to the "Physics Paradigm" destroys the possibility of that old explanation being given. In the new paradigm, chess players assume the status of the metaphoric, and to speak of them as real is a reification. Similarly, we cannot explain the phenomenon of the social placement of women into the class of intrinsic moral inferiors *as subordination* by describing the mental states of individuals, even though society is as surely composed of individuals as the chess player is composed of molecules. The switch from the "Social Paradigm" to the "Individual Paradigm" destroys the possibility of the social subordination explanation being given. In the new, reductionistic paradigm, society assumes the status of the metaphoric, and to speak of it as real is a reification.

A good account of the general debate between methodological individualists and holists is given in Simon, pp. 41–55. For a discussion of the relationship between feminism and various forms of individualism, see "The Critique of Individualism" in Jean Grimshaw's *Philosophy and Feminist Thinking* (Minneapolis: Minnesota UP, 1986), pp. 162–87.

40 This paradigm-related fall from validity is, *qua* fall from validity, like that generated by our inability to substitute in extentionally equivalent expressions in certain contexts. (E.g., John believes that Mark Twain wrote *Tom Sawyer*, but it does not follow that he believes that Samuel Clemens wrote *Tom Sawyer*.) But the opacity of beliefs does not place any object of knowledge beyond our reach (John could come to know that Samuel Clemens wrote *Tom Sawyer*), whereas a change of paradigms does do so. Paradigm changes destroy (and create) epistemic objects: "[T]hough the world does not change with a change of paradigm, the scientist afterward works in a different world" [Thomas Kuhn, *The Structure of Scientific Revolutions* (Chicago: University Press, 2d ed., 1970), p. 121.] In the case under discussion, the phenomenon of subordination, and its attendant and obvious injustice, can be lost in a paradigm change.

41 Since, as I have noted above, the representational arts are themselves practices, it can be the case that the identity of one of their practice constituents (e.g., a picture of a chess game) is doubly practice informed, and thus that identity is not entirely a function of the nonrepresentational practice (here, chess). Although it is clear that some value predicates of *non*practice objects can be generated by the representational practice alone (e.g., a beautiful picture of rotting fruit), it is not clear that nonaesthetic value predicates relating to a nonrepresentational practice constituent (e.g., a home run) can be so generated, much less gainsaid, by the representational practice, especially if one posits the existence of an overlapping ideology that both the represen-

tational and nonrepresentational practice share. Specifically, we might ask if it would be possible for pornographic representations to subordinate women even though the identity of the nonrepresentational practice constituents so represented contributed not at all to women's subordination. [If I follow her correctly, Susanne Kappeler's point in *The Pornography of Representation* (Minneapolis: Minnesota UP, 1986) is that the subordination of women may occur through the mechanism of the representational practice alone, regardless of the nonrepresentational practice identity of that which is represented.]

It is certainly the case that the identity of a *depiction* of someone performing practice action *x* is other than the identity of someone performing practice action *x*, the depiction and the doing being informed by two different practices. It seems to me, however, empirically unlikely, if not impossible, that these identities would not influence each other, though the influence of the nonrepresentational practice is not necessarily the greater. [For an account of general representational to nonrepresentational influence on identity, see Robert Schwartz's "The Power of Pictures," *Journal of Philosophy*, 12 (December 1985): 711–20.]

42 And we could not truthfully make these negating statements about the medals that honor or the depictions that subordinate until such time as these practices have been abandoned as socially real, ac-

tive practices *and* have either been entirely forgotten, obliterated from human memory, with such total erasure giving their constituents less social meaning than a blade of grass, *or* until they have been entirely replaced by new practices that would generate radically new social meanings. But this entire replacement of one practice by another is problematic. It would require the death of the institutions and ideology of the old practice as well as the complete abandonment of its illegitimate but nevertheless familiar and rewarding (to some) elements. The difficulties here are that, as long as human beings exist, the destruction of practice-generated meaning through social amnesia is a practical impossibility, and the replacement of one practice by another, in that it requires giving up what is perceived by some as familiar and good, is unlikely to occur except through a massive social cataclysm – and the degree of the massiveness of this required cataclysm would be a function of the degree and importance of that perceived good. Given these difficulties, it is more often the case that the "new" practice is not so new after all.

43 I draw this distinction between that which may and may not be imputed to the agents of faulty actions from Joel Feinberg's "Sua Culpa" in his *Doing and Deserving: Essays in the Theory of Responsibility* (Princeton, NJ: University Press, 1970), pp. 187–221.

PART VIII

Film and Knowledge

Introduction

Not only documentary films but fiction films are sometimes praised for the knowledge they allegedly impart, although, perhaps more often, they are taken to task for the false beliefs they are suspected of fostering. Upon the release of *Signs*, a commentator in the *New York Times* upbraided the film for perpetuating silly ideas about the origin of the phenomenon of crop circles upon which M. Night Shyamalan's thriller is based; while the editors of *The Skeptical Inquirer* have launched a crusade against fantasy cinema across the board for reinforcing the superstitious false beliefs to which they maintain too many of the public still cling. Moreover, the conviction, discussed in Part VII, that movies may add to or subtract from our fund of moral understanding likewise belies the assumption that the relation of film – or, at least, some films – and claims to knowledge is not odd in any way.

Indeed, some filmmakers are even said to broker philosophical insight. In the 1960s, directors like Bergman and Antonioni were treated as celluloid existentialists, discoursing on the plight of humanity in a meaningless universe, while Bresson was regarded as a theologian of sorts, just as, earlier, Dreyer had been. Soviet montagists such as Eisenstein and Vertov were said to advance Marxist philosophy by means of cinema, while in – as it was called in those days – the "First World," Lang was associated with the philosophy of determinism and Ozu with Zen. The commonplace connection between film and knowledge in general and even philosophical knowledge in particular is readily documented. However, it may be more difficult to defend than is usually imagined.

In "The Philosophical Limits of Film," Bruce Russell stresses the ways in which typical films differ from our standard expectations for knowledge claims, especially philosophical ones. If I say that humans are taller than monkeys, you expect me to support that with some evidence. If I show you one human who is taller than one monkey, that will not be enough. Moreover, if I show you a picture of one human from a fictional movie who is taller than a monkey, that will not suffice in the least. After all, the movie could be *The Amazing Colossal Man*. That is, fictional men need not provide evidence about the height of actual men, since they are made-up men – they can be as tall as Gulliver is to the citizens of Lilliput. And yet when it is alleged that a fictional movie gives us knowledge about the world – that, for instance, prison wardens are all sadists – isn't it the case that this putatively general knowledge is based on no more than a single example, and an imaginary one at that?

Thus, Bruce Russell maintains that a fiction film is an insufficient vessel for delivering general knowledge, either of the necessary or the probable variety. Even if such a film were to succeed in conveying a true belief to its audience, it would not provide knowledge, since knowledge requires justification and a belief delivered without sufficient evidential warrant is not justified. Moreover, to count as genuine philosophical knowledge, a putatively true belief, such as "every human action is determined," must be accompanied by an argument. But how many films contain the requisite argumentation, and, even if they do, is the argumentation achieved by cinematic means or merely downloaded onto the soundtrack? Without the adequate forms of evidential support, can fiction films really make any general, epistemically acceptable knowledge claims and, without explicit argumentation, can they really amount to philosophy?

Russell concedes that a film might function as a counterexample to some general claim, such as "Crime does not pay." He believes that Woody Allen's *Crimes and Misdemeanors* works this way. For a general philosophical claim, one that is held to be necessarily true – as in "Necessarily, crime does not pay" – *can* be defeated by a single *possible* (a.k.a. logically conceivable) case, and such a fictional example, like the case of Judah Rosenthal in *Crimes and Misdemeanors*, may be conceived with no taint of incoherence or self-contradiction about it. On the other hand, the same claim cannot be validated by a single fiction film, such as *A Simple Plan*, that endorses the aforesaid generalization, since the evidence available from *A Simple Plan* is too slight, and is made up anyway, and is not accompanied by argument. *A Simple Plan* does not afford knowledge (*justified* true belief), let alone philosophical knowledge.

Russell's argument is a philosophical one. But what is striking about it may be that if we accept the criteria that Russell demands for knowledge claims, especially philosophical ones, much philosophy, let alone many films, will fail to be sources of knowledge. Recall that part of Russell's attack is based on the observation that many films provide only one example, or, at best, only a handful of examples, to motivate their generalizations, and, to make matters worse, the example(s) is (are) fictional. But isn't that also often the case with philosophy? We are offered made-up examples (i.e., fictional narratives) – of people in the Original Position behind the Veil of Ignorance, or locked in a Chinese Room, or transported to Twin Earth, or immersed in a vat with electrodes attached to only part of them, their brains – and then asked to contemplate the general truths these situations appear to entail about justice, about understanding a language, about reference, and so forth. If fictional narratives functioning as examples – or, as they are called in philosophy, thought experiments – are legitimate tools for reaching generalizations in the hands of philosophers, why, we may ask Russell, can't filmmakers use them to the same end?

To this, Russell is apt to reply that when philosophers, properly so-called, use examples, they accompany them with explicit argumentation. Literally speaking, this is not really true. Many of Wittgenstein's thought experiments in his *Philosophical Investigations* are not followed by arguments in the sense Russell has in mind. Moreover, in a philosophical conversation, disputants often sketch examples without spelling out their relevance to the discussion and their implications. They expect their fellow-conversationalists to work that out on their own and, as can be easily observed at any philosophy conference, listeners do so with regularity, and often remarkable alacrity. In the flow of ordinary philosophical discourse, an example or thought experiment, often in the form of a fictional narrative, unaccompanied by formal argumentation, is itself generally accepted as a form of argumentation. Yet, if that passes for argument at the American Philosophical Association, then there should be no reservations about certain fiction filmmakers laying claim to philosophy.

Russell is unlikely to sit back idly and swallow this reasoning. He is prone to demand that for something to merit the mantle of philosophy, it must involve explicit argumentation. An example or thought experiment that leaves it to the listener to fill in its relevant, unstated implications will not be an argument in his book. Thus, the issue of whether a fiction film can produce philosophical knowledge revolves importantly about what we are willing to allow to pass as living up to the standards of philosophical argumentation. Russell appears to believe that it must be something rather formal and explicit that concludes with deductive necessity – like the schematic we offered of Vadas's argument in our introduction to Part VII. But is that too narrow and austere a view?

In "Motion Pictures as a Philosophical Resource" Lester H. Hunt advocates a more expansive notion of philosophical argumentation than the draconian version Russell appears to prefer. Hunt agrees that narrative fictions can function argumentatively as counterexamples to philosophical views. That may be one interpretation of the *Twilight Zone* episode "A Quality of Mercy" which Hunt analyzes at length. But Hunt maintains that there may also be other ways in which fictional-narrative examples may operate argumentatively in philosophical debate. A narrative example may raise a question that calls for an explanation. For instance, when Socrates tells the very plausible story of the way in which he got Meno to reach certain mathematical conclusions – which Meno had not been taught as far as anyone remembered – by asking the slave boy a series of pointed questions in a certain order, the story itself asks for an explanation. How did the young slave manage to produce this recondite knowledge without prior tutelage? Socrates suggests that Meno was able to do so because he had learned these truths in an earlier life. Anamnesis or reincarnation, that is, explains the mysterious but nevertheless possible phenomenon that Socrates recounts in his fictional example.

To the extent that Socrates' hypothesis can explain the possible state of affairs the fiction encapsulates, his hypothesis wins plausibility. If Socrates' explanation is the best explanation of the case – if it is better than any competing explanation – it becomes more and more appealing. Alas, reincarnation is not the best explanation of Meno's performance, but were it so, most philosophers would admit that it would start to shift the burden of proof to those skeptical of the idea of reincarnation.

Hunt is certainly correct in observing that philosophers typically credit the preceding style of argumentation to be legitimate. To advance a hypothesis – reincarnation or whatever – one argumentative strategy is to introduce a plausible story of which it is the best explanation. This type of argument is based on the use of fictional narrative examples that dispose the listener to arrive on his own at a certain explanation or hypothesis in order to make sense of the story – much as a joke leads a listener to a certain interpretation of its punch line. The hypothesis so educed, of course, is the one the philosopher wishes to support.

The reasoning in response to such fictional-narrative examples, like the interpretation of the punch line of the joke, is elaborated in the mind of the listener and not necessarily laid out formally and explicitly in the way Russell would seem to desire. Furthermore, the conclusion does not come with deductive necessity or apodicticity. The conclusion is an hypothesis to the best explanation – an inductive, or, perhaps better, abductive inference and, therefore, only a probable one.

As Hunt puts it, there are cases in which "the story resonates with our pre-existing notions of what the world is like or should be like. This assumption, applied to the example, indicates that the story calls for an explanation. The story is perceived as a tale of something that could happen, or be right or wrong, and so forth. The ideas that would explain it thereby gain plausibility and, if they are not already believed, are shown to be worth a closer look."

This, *pace* Russell, is a standard piece of dialectical operating procedure in philosophy: the fictional-narrative thought experiment that gathers credibility for certain hypotheses by eliciting them as the best explanation of the story at hand.[1] Moreover, there is no reason to think that fictional film narratives cannot function in a way comparable to yarns that philosophers spin.

In the introduction to the previous section of this anthology, we discussed the way in which the film *Parenthood* could be interpreted to convey moral knowledge of the virtues and vices of parenting. Various styles of parenting, associated with different fictional characters, are juxtaposed in the film in ways that make it difficult to resist comparing and contrasting them. Most viewers, relying on their ordinary beliefs about the world, will be hard pressed to avoid the conclusion that Helen – though she initially strikes us as a hapless, nervous wreck – is a far better parent than the much more self-confident Nathan and his father-in-law Frank. This then places the viewer in the position where he is encouraged to explain to himself why this conclusion should be so. And the most persuasive answer, given the structure of the narrative, is that Helen is open to recognizing her daughter as an autonomous individual with her own desires and that Helen is prepared to adjust to this; whereas Nathan and Frank are blind to their offspring, treating them as little more than pretexts for the vicarious projection of their own wishes and fantasies. This hypothesis – that acknowledging the autonomy of one's children is an excellence of parenthood, whereas projection is a deadly vice – is the best explanation of the differential assessments that we make of Helen, Nathan, and Frank. Furthermore, inasmuch as this hypothesis would appear to apply with equal force to the evaluation of real-life parenting, the idea is a serious contender as an essential feature of virtuous parenthood, no matter that it is proffered on the back of a fictional narrative. For that is also the argumentative vehicle of so many successful philosophical arguments, driven by thought experiments articulated as fictional narratives. Why should the rules of argument change when we move from the philosophy seminar room to the movie auditorium?

Although Hunt defends an expanded range for filmic philosophy beyond the confines stipulated by Russell, Hunt believes that the possibility of philosophizing by way of film is far less open than that of philosophizing in literature. His primary reason for this is that putatively philosophy, like literature, but unlike the motion picture, is primarily an affair of words. So literature, like philosophy, can say more than film.

But how relevant is this, if it is relevant at all? Like *Parenthood*, the literary masterpiece *Great Expectations* by Charles Dickens explores the excellences of parenthood by means of juxtaposing a series of parental figures – Pip's sister, her husband Joe, Magwitch, and Miss Haversham – who we compare and contrast for the purpose of isolating what constitutes virtuous parenting and its opposite.[2] But, I submit, the motion picture *Parenthood* probes the essence of virtuous parenting more deeply than *Great Expectations* because it has a larger, more variegated, and more sharply delineated selection of characters. It cuts no difference that *Great Expectations* has a lot more words than *Parenthood*. That is, there is no reason to presume that a literary narrative will give us deeper philosophy than a film just because it is more exclusively verbal. For the variables that may make for more supple philosophy may be a matter of narrative complexity of a sort that may not be dependent upon verbal expression as such.

In addition, one worries that Hunt may be guilty of identifying one style of motion picture-making with its essence. Though Hollywood-type motion picture production favors action, dramatic and otherwise, over words, especially in comparison with literature, not all cinema is like this. Many of the motion picture videos of Jean-Luc Godard and Steven Fagin are as garrulous as any novel by Thomas Mann and their voice-over commentaries are probably even more so when it comes to theoretical jargon. Why imagine that fiction film narratives done in this more loquacious manner cannot match novels and treatises word-for-word? It will not do to say that these are not motion pictures, properly so-called, since that is apt, as we saw in the second section of this volume, to beg the question.

If Lester Hunt maintains that Russell's conception of philosophical argument is unrealistically restricted, Karen Hanson – in "Minerva in the Movies: Relations Between Philosophy and Film" – might be understood as finding someone like Russell's vision of philosophy to be too hidebound and blinkered. Russell apparently construes philosophy in terms of deductive arguments that conclude with generalizations. Hanson has a more commodious vision of philosophy. It can include the careful description and delineation of paradox-

ical human behaviors which, however rare or obscure, nevertheless command attention, if we are to give a comprehensive account of human experience.[3] Hanson gives as an example of philosophy of this sort Sartre's fictional depiction of a case of self-deception in which a woman in the throes of being seduced is apparently oblivious to what is going on, while, nevertheless, she is to some degree complicit with it. For Hanson, it is also the task of philosophy to isolate these anomalous though, at the same time, exemplary moments of human contrariness and self-deception, while simultaneously articulating and thereby illuminating, as best one can, the mechanics that underpin these behaviors by disclosing, often descriptively, the various interacting layers of intentionality in play. In the case from Sartre, he displays perspicuously the forces in motion in this particular instance of self-deception in a way that begins to render it intelligible.

But if this counts as philosophy – as a species of existential phenomenology, let us say – might not motion pictures provide an equally revealing optic on the secrets of the soul?[4] Film too can exemplify in telling ways phenomena like denial, self-deception, and other pathologies in a fashion that can lend explanatory insight into the structure of the psychic knots in question and, in addition, into the conditions that incline us to dub them aberrant.

Alfred Hitchcock's *Vertigo* not only illustrates the point that love involves a dimension of fantasy – sometimes euphemistically called idealization – but also indicates how the projective processes engaged in this fantasy can get desperately out of control once denial takes over. A film like *Vertigo* exemplifies a pathology of romantic love – of male projection and female enabling – not in the sense that it is a statistically representative case study, but in the sense that it provides an existential phenomenology of the dynamics of romantic love by locating its inherent tendencies through a foregrounding of its potential excesses. If such a demonstration-through-exemplary-depiction is philosophy, as Hanson believes it is, then a film's lack of evidence and argument is not, contra Russell, disqualifying, since even without evidence and argument, a fictional case may capture and exemplify, in an elucidating way, the tangles of the human heart and psyche, thereby enabling us to apply the fictional exemplar in a way that limns actual cases.

Russell maintains that films lack sufficient evidence to support generalizations – they do not provide us with enough cases and the cases are made up anyway. This might be dragooned as an objection not only to the assertion that film imparts philosophical knowledge, but also to the suggestion that it imparts knowledge of any sort. But surely this sets the requirements for communicating knowledge too high. A newspaper think-piece may introduce its thesis with little more to motivate it than an anecdote or even a parable. The author will leave it up to the reader to fill out the proof on her own, using what she believes about the world to put flesh on the proposal.

That is, it is understood in most of the journalism we read and the lectures we hear that the audience needs to test the hypothesis at issue in the laboratory of her own mind, using her own knowledge of how things are as her mortar and pestle. We do not, however, say that the journalist or the lecturer has failed to communicate knowledge to us just because it has been left up to the audience to find the supporting evidence on her own. But then why should it stand differently with film? If a thesis is clearly communicated and we are either implicitly or explicitly invited to ascertain whether or not it obtains in our own experience of the world, why deny that the film is in the business of conveying knowledge, since we would not refrain from saying that of a comparable think-piece on the op-ed page of a newspaper? Most of what we regard as communicating knowledge does not wear on its sleeve all the evidence that it requires.

Films can certainly alert us to facts about the world of which we were hitherto either unaware or only dimly aware. When I was very young, I saw John Ford's *How Green Was My Valley* for the first time. Early on in the film, there is a scene in which there is an argument at the dinner table of the Morgan family over unionizing. The *pater-familias* is dead set against the idea. Those of his sons who work in the coal mine are for it. He forbids them to speak of the matter in the name of good table manners. In response, they leave home in protest. Only the youngest son, the pre-pubescent Hugh, remains, alone at the table with his father.

The old man stares down at his plate, his eyes narrowly focused on his food. Hugh deliberately clanks his knife against his plate once or twice.

When that attracts no response, Hugh forces a cough. Finally the father says, "Yes, my son, I know you are there," thus acknowledging – as Hugh wishes him to – his obedience, his loyalty, and his respect for the traditional rules that govern table behavior in the Morgan household.

That day I got a lesson in human psychology. I learnt that what seemed to be inadvertent acts – like a knife glancing off a plate – could be an intentional signal, a request for acknowledgment, at the same time that it could be a statement of fealty. I learnt that there was a realm of communication of which I had only been barely aware, if at all. Surely what *How Green Was My Valley* offered me was knowledge.[5] But it was knowledge in the form of a clear example – indeed, perhaps one more legible than the ones that surrounded me on a daily basis – which I could then transfer to the world outside the cinema in order to recognize similar real-life cases. The film was not an enumerative catalogue of mounting evidence. It was a single, particular, invented case. But it seems wrong to say that I did not derive knowledge of the existence and operation of nonverbal communication from it just because I was only exposed to one case and a made-up one at that. For I was given what I needed to confirm the observation on my own steam. Films may bequeath empirical discoveries to us without supplying the evidence themselves. They may leave it up to us to find the pertinent substantiating data on our own, as do most of the nonfiction articles we read and lectures that we attend.[6]

Films are indubitably well-suited to give us empirical insight into recurring patterns of human behavior – including some that may be more arcane than others – by means of clear examples whose actual analogues we may go on to find in our own encounters with life. And where that cinematic depiction of the pertinent recurring patterns involves a revealing glimpse into some or another paradox of the human heart, we might, like Karen Hanson, be willing to call it philosophy – philosophy construed as something beyond mere argument and rather more of the nature of the discovery of the deepest and most difficult truths of human experience.

N.C.

Notes

1 Though above, emphasis is being put on the use of the fictional-narrative example or thought experiment as a device for eliciting abductive inferences, it should not be thought that Hunt thinks that this is the only way in which fictional examples can figure in philosophical arguments. He also thinks they may function as counterexamples, in what he calls generalization arguments, as illustrations that clarify philosophical claims, and so forth. A useful exercise might be to try to list all of the ways in which Hunt thinks that fictional examples can perform a service in philosophical arguments. Indeed, there are probably also functions that Hunt has not itemized, such as the use of fictional examples to set up philosophical puzzles, as in the famous case of the Myth of Gyges' Ring that Russell alludes to. Thus, another useful exercise is to try to chart all the roles in philosophical argumentation that you can enumerate for fictional examples. The important thing to remember is that when it comes to the connection between fiction and knowledge, including the relation of fictional narrative examples to argumentation, there are more relationships here than one. There are many – and many of different shapes and sizes. The way for the discussion to go wrong without fail is to presume that there is one and only one (legitimate) relationship in this domain.

2 See Noël Carroll, "The Wheel of Virtue," *The Journal of Aesthetics and Art Criticism* 60, no. 1 (Winter, 2002). See also, Noël Carroll, "Art and the Moral Realm," in *The Blackwell Guide to Aesthetics*, ed. Peter Kivy (Oxford: Blackwell, 2004).

3 Indeed, when, at the Museum of the Moving Image, Hanson gave the talk that became the essay anthologized in this volume, she spoke of philosophy as the most comprehensive picture of what is; as if *philo sophia*, the love of knowledge, was the love (and the discovery) of all knowledge – whether general or particular, descriptive or deductive (with the knowledge pertaining to human experience, nevertheless being first among equals).

4 In John Huston's *The Maltese Falcon*, Sam Spade's speech at the end of the film, in which he explains why he is going to turn in the woman he loves to the police, displays in bold relief the psychic tactics the mind seeks to deploy to defend its integrity (Spade's obligation to the deceased Archer), its reputation, and its security from the irrational blandishments of love. Spade knows that he can't trust her because she will betray him, so he intends to put himself out of harm's way by having her locked up. He also knows it will be bad for business if he does not avenge Archer's death. As Spade rehearses his reasons for "sending her over," we are granted a microscopic view of the soul wrestling with contradictory impulses in search of a resting point. Though the case is a particular one, it discloses a pattern of thought which is no less revelatory of psychic needs and resources for being rare. It is exemplary both in the sense that it has a kind of salient singularity that, at the same time, sheds light on other cases by clearly articulating what is psychologically at stake in this situation and others like it.

5 Perhaps needless to say, I do not mean to suggest that this account of my experience with *How Green Is My Valley* represents the only way in which knowledge may be acquired from films. There are a great many ways that this may occur. A useful exercise might be to try to inventory as many different ways of deriving knowledge from films that you can think of. What is important to remember is that the list will be long and varied. It is probably only an occupational hazard of philosophers that they expect one and only one way for knowledge to be related to film/fiction. But the world is rarely as neat as some philosophers expect it to be.

6 Indeed, this sentence is an example of what I have in mind. I have not offered you lists and lists of articles that advance knowledge claims without ticking off the evidence. I have proposed the thesis that this is very frequently the case and invited you to assess that claim against your own experience of, for example, reading newspaper think-pieces. If you think that I've actually called your attention to something you never knew before but think, reflecting upon your experience, that I've hit the mark, then I've conveyed to you a bit of knowledge without enumerating the evidence myself but rather leaving the work up to you.

25

The Philosophical Limits of Film

Bruce Russell

In this discussion I will argue that film can vividly introduce philosophical problems and can solve some problems by showing us what is possible. But it cannot show us what is probable and sometimes not even what is possible.

I Why be Moral?

Ever since Plato philosophers have been concerned with the relationship between morality and practical reason. Is it possible for there to be an action that is prohibited by morality but permitted, or even required, by practical reason? Surely, if you have a ring that will make you invisible, like the one Socrates describes in the Republic, and so will allow you to get away with all sorts of wrongdoing, at least sometimes it will be in your interest to act wrongly. Insofar as practical reason requires us to act in our self-interest, or as we would most want to act if we were fully informed, uncoerced and thinking clearly, then practical reason could require us to do what is morally prohibited.

Plato, of course, argued that it is always better to be just than unjust, that is, to be a just than an unjust person. His argument is that there is disharmony in the soul of an unjust person and that will ultimately make life worse for him, regardless of how much worldly success he enjoys.

There are two obvious responses to this argument. First, it does not address the question of whether it is ever practically rational to *act* immorally since it focuses on the difference between just and unjust persons, or lives, rather than actions. If Plato is right in thinking it is better to be a just than an unjust person, why not be a just person and on rare occasions perform unjust acts when it is particularly beneficial to you and it is very unlikely that you'll be caught? Second, it seems that an unjust person need not have disharmony in his soul, which suggests that Plato's definition of justice as harmony in the soul is mistaken. So why couldn't it be better to be a clever thief whose life is controlled by reason than a persecuted saint with harmony in his soul?

II Happiness and Immorality in Two Films

Arguments for acting morally fall into two general types. The first type says that your internal life will be so horrible if you do what is wrong that it will not pay in the long run to act immorally. You will be so plagued by guilt and remorse, or fear of being caught, that the wrongdoing will not pay. The other says that if you act wrongly the probability that you will be discovered and punished is so great that it does not pay to take the risk. Woody Allen's *Crimes and Misdemeanors* (Orion, 1989) focuses on the first answer; *A Simple Plan* (Paramount, 1998; based on a novel and

Bruce Russell, "The Philosophical Limits of Film," *Film and Philosophy* (Special Edition, 2000): 163–7. Reprinted by permission of the Society for the Philosophic Study of the Contemporary Visual Arts.

screenplay by Scott B. Smith) focuses on the second answer but ultimately sides with the first.

In *Crimes and Misdemeanors* Judah Rosenthal (Martin Landau) is a wealthy and successful opthamologist who wants to end a two-year affair with Dolores Paley (Angelica Huston). But Dolores claims she has sacrificed business and romantic opportunities to be with Judah and does not want to give him up. She writes Judah's wife Miriam (Claire Bloom), telling her of the affair and requesting a meeting with her to "clear things" between the three of them. Luckily for Judah, he intercepts the letter before his wife opens it. Judah tries to talk Dolores into ending the affair quietly, but when he fails, he contacts his brother Jack (Jerry Orbach) who suggests hiring a hit man to solve the problem. Fearing that his life and family will be destroyed, and that Miriam will be humiliated if she finds out, Judah pays Jack to handle the problem, knowing that he intends to have Dolores killed.

After Dolores is killed, Judah imagines a conversation involving his father Sol and his aunt May at a seder dinner where he is present as a child. His father says that if a man kills, one way or another he will be punished. When a friend interjects, "If he's caught, Sol," Sol responds, "that which originates from a black deed will blossom in a foul manner." On the other hand, Judah's aunt May thinks that if a man kills someone then, "If he can do it and get away with it and he chooses not to be bothered by the ethics, then he is home free."

For a time it looks as if his father is right for soon after the murder we see a nervous, anxious, guilt-ridden, unhappy Judah Rosenthal. However, in a few months things change radically. We see Judah and Clifford Stern (Woody Allen) alone in a back room at the wedding of the niece of Cliff's wife. Judah tells Cliff his story which he passes off as a fictional account of a murder with "a very strange twist." We know Judah is talking about himself when he tells Cliff that the murderer in his story was plagued by deep-rooted guilt, panic stricken, on the verge of a mental collapse and an inch away from turning himself in when one morning, after a long vacation, he awakens and "the sun is shining, his family is around him and mysteriously the crisis is lifted." After that his life returns completely to normal, and he finds that he is not punished but prospers. He is no longer plagued by guilt and is genuinely happy.

Earlier in the film Judah had said he was a man of science and had always been skeptical of religion, even as a child. When talking with Cliff, Judah says that after the murder "little sparks of his religious background which he had rejected are suddenly stirred up." But he is able to reject that background again and find peace of mind. Clearly, Woody Allen's message in this film is that crime can pay if you are not caught. The internal sanctions need not be strong enough, or their effects last long enough, to make wrongdoing the worse choice. It helps if you are not religious because then you won't worry that "God's eyes are always on you," a claim made by Judah's father that has stuck in Judah's mind but whose grip on Judah fades along with the failing eyesight of rabbi Ben, Judah's patient and confidant who by film's end is completely blind.

Until the end of the movie, the main focus of *A Simple Plan* is on whether three people will be caught for the crimes they have committed. Hank Mitchell (Bill Paxton), his brother Jacob (Billy Bob Thornton) and Jacob's friend Lou Chambers (Brent Briscoe) discover a crashed, private plane covered with snow and containing 4.4 million in cash. They surmise the money is drug money and propose to keep it until people discover the plane in the spring once the snow melts. The original plan is for Hank to keep it and if no one comes looking for it once the plane is found, the three will split it up and move away. If they do come looking for the money, Hank will burn it all.

When Hank brings home the money, there is a discussion between Hank and his wife Sarah (Bridget Fonda) about whether keeping it would be stealing and so, wrong. Hank argues that it is not if it is "dirty" drug money, though Sarah thinks it would be stealing in any case. Eventually Sarah finds a newspaper article telling about a 4.4 million dollar ransom that was paid to some kidnappers for the return of someone's daughter. So eventually it becomes clear that keeping the money is stealing even if it would not be if it were drug money.

Of course, lots of things go wrong before spring arrives. When Hank and Jacob return to the plane to put a half million dollars back in it to make it look like nothing was taken, a farmer on a snowmobile runs across Jacob who is serving as a lookout while pretending to fix a flat tire. Jacob and the farmer know each other and have a brief conversation. When the farmer starts off in the direction of the plane and Hank, Jacob hits him in the back of the head with a tire iron and thinks he has killed him. Hank returns and puts the farmer on the snowmobile, planning to run it off the road and make his death look like an accident. However, along the way the farmer regains consciousness, and Hank then smothers him to death and proceeds to carry out his original plan.

Hank and Jacob get in deeper when Jacob later ends up killing Lou to save Hank, and Hank kills Lou's wife Nancy to make it look like a domestic fight was the cause of the deaths. They are able to convince the sheriff that Lou shot his wife when she tried to shoot him (she actually tried to shoot Hank after Jacob killed Lou) and that Jacob shot Lou when he threatened Hank.

The last unexpected turn takes place when one of the kidnappers shows up pretending to be an FBI agent. The kidnapper, the sheriff and Hank go out to the downed plane with Hank having just learned from his wife Sarah that the supposed FBI agent is really one of the kidnappers whose money and dead brother are in the plane. At the plane, the kidnapper kills the sheriff, and Hank kills the kidnapper. Jacob, who shows up late after talking with Sarah, says that he "doesn't want to sit around the rest of his life and think about this" and asks his brother to shoot him with the kidnapper's gun. Jacob threatens to kill himself with the sheriff's gun if Hank does not shoot him and that death would be difficult for Hank to explain to the authorities. So reluctantly Hank kills his brother.

In the end, this means that Hank has killed four people: the farmer, Lou's wife, the kidnapper and his brother. And he ends up burning the money when he learns that the FBI copied down ten percent of the serial numbers on the bills. He is made unhappy by recalling his evil deeds, especially the shooting of his brother. The moral of this story is that crime does not pay even if you do not get caught. Unlike Judah Rosenthal, Hank cannot forget his foul deeds. The point of *Crimes and Misdemeanors* seems to be that crime can pay; of *A Simple Plan* that it does not. However, these conclusions are compatible if the one is a statement about what is possible and the other about what is probable.

III Film and Philosophy

Certainly film can raise philosophical questions in a vivid and interesting way. The question of what makes an action wrong is raised at two points in

A Simple Plan. The first is when Hank and Sarah argue over whether taking the money would be stealing if it were drug money and so money to which the owners had no *legitimate* claim. This film does not raise the issue of whether stealing is always wrong, and so whether taking the money is wrong even if it is stealing. And it does not raise the question of whether it is wrong even if it is not stealing. A strong case can be made that Hank, Jacob and Lou should turn the money into the authorities, whose job it is to determine who should get the money, even if it is "dirty" money and even if keeping it is not stealing.

The second case comes at the end of the film. Is it wrong of Hank to kill his brother, at his brother's request, knowing that the consequences for everyone will be better if he does? Perhaps it would not be wrong if Jacob's suicide were rational. And why would it be wrong even if the suicide is irrational since we are to assume that Hank cannot prevent it? Of course, it can be argued that what Hank should do is not kill his brother, regardless of whether the threatened suicide is rational or not, and then turn himself and the money in. Clearly, this is an interesting case for consequentialists and non-consequentialists alike to consider.

A Simple Plan also raises the question of what makes people happy. Early in the film Hank relates that his father told him when he was a kid that what it takes to be a happy man is "a wife that loves you, a decent job, and friends and neighbors who like and respect you." However, the question of what *makes*, or causes, someone to be happy is not itself a philosophical question. The philosophical question is about what features make a certain state of the person a state of happiness rather than something else, that is, what the essential nature of happiness is. The question of how people are made happy is a psychological one.

Of course, the main question these two films raise is not about wrongdoing and happiness themselves but about the relationship between wrongdoing and happiness. *A Simple Plan* shows that wrongdoing can lead to unhappiness, even when it is not discovered. *Crimes and Misdemeanors* shows that the opposite is also possible, that immorality sometimes pays. So a film can refute a philosophical thesis, say, that necessarily, wrongdoing will make you unhappy or will be contrary to your self-interest.

But film cannot establish a philosophical thesis. This will obviously be true if all philosophical theses are claims that something is necessarily true, say, that necessarily, happiness is an intrinsic good or that necessarily, if you know something you are justified in believing it. No one can establish that something holds in all possible worlds by presenting an example or two from a possible world depicted in film.

But it will also be true if philosophical claims are only about the actual world. No one can establish on the basis of, for instance, *A Simple Plan* that people will probably get caught or their lives will be made miserable if they commit a heinous deed. It is the actual rate of being caught, and the actual percentage of people who are made unhappy after committing a horrible act, that determines whether it is reasonable to believe that "crime doesn't pay." A film might remind us of the evidence we know of already, but it cannot supply the relevant evidence itself. Imaginary situations cannot supply real data.

And while films can present counterexamples to some claims to necessary truths, they cannot do that for all such claims. Suppose one grants that *Crimes and Misdemeanors* shows that it is possible for wrongdoing to be in a person's self-interest, to be what he most wants to do on reflection and to be what makes the person the happiest in the situation. Still, one can legitimately ask whether it shows that wrongdoing can ever be practically rational. In part, this is because what is practically rational is a function of what it is *reasonable for a person to think* about an action's impact on his self-interest, happiness and fulfillment of desires. And, as I have argued, this is a function of the actual evidence about the impact of a person's action, evidence which is not given in a fictional film. But, in addition, it is an open question whether practical rationality is *solely* a function of self-interest, happiness and desire fulfillment. To defeat the view that it is, a film would have to portray a situation where it is practically irrational for someone to do something even though it is clearly in his self-interest, will make him happy and is what on reflection he most wants to do. However, I think our views of practical rationality are not clear enough to allow us, or a film, to present what amounts to a counterexample to the view that practical reason is solely a function of a person's own self-interest, happiness and/or desire-fulfillment. *Crimes and Misdemeanors* offers a case where it is morally wrong to do what is in a person's self-interest, etc., but it is not obvious that performing the morally wrong action is practically irrational and practically irrational because it is morally wrong. Philosophical argument might establish that it is, but a film that does not itself contain philosophical argument cannot.

So I conclude that the philosophical contribution of films is limited to raising philosophical questions and offering counterexamples to proposed necessary truths, where the concepts involved in their statements are clear enough to allow counterexamples to be constructed. Of course, films can remind us of things we already know, such as the likelihood that something will go awry or that we will be plagued by guilt if we do wrong, and these reminders can have great practical value. Films can also motivate us to find out what we do not already know or to double-check what we think we know. And obviously films can be enjoyed! But these last three benefits are not contributions to philosophy, anymore than advice on what will make us happy is.

26

Minerva in the Movies: Relations Between Philosophy and Film

Karen Hanson

A famous declaration that film might supplant philosophy is made by Alexandre Astruc in his 1948 article, "The Birth of a New Avant-Garde: *La Caméra-Stylo*." His own footing for this claim is grounded on the now familiar assimilation of film to language. This connection is, however, to his mind, only lately established:

> The cinema is quite simply becoming a means of expression, just as all the other arts have been before it, and in particular painting and the novel. After having been successively a fairground attraction, an amusement analogous to boulevard theatre, or a means of preserving the images of an era, it is gradually becoming a language. By language, I mean a form in which and by which an artist can express his thoughts, however abstract they may be, or translate his obsessions exactly as he does in the contemporary essay or novel. That is why I would like to call this new age of cinema the age of *caméra-stylo* [camera-pen].[1]

Why is it so attractive to assert that film is a language? If we want to call language anything that we can imbue with significance, anything from which we can derive meaning, then of course we will want to call film "language." (But how much, exactly what, is then claimed? Compare "the language of flowers," "the language of dress.") Or, if we

think that all art is best understood as language, all media as kinds of language, and we see that film is a medium of art, then again the conclusion is plain.

But this cannot be a fair measure of Astruc's position. This thinking would leave unmotivated his evident desire to assimilate film to specifically verbal media. Why is he not inclined to pursue his own comparison of film and painting? Why is it for him "the camerapen" and not, say, "the camera-brush"?

The answer in this case seems to involve a shade of Leo Tolstoy: Astruc says that "the fundamental problem of the cinema is how to express thought," and he implies that he is distinguishing thought and feeling. (Cf. "All thought, like all feeling, is a relationship between one human and another....")[2] This distinction might, then, be a device to delineate the species of art, and it might be held to substantiate the insistence that film is a language, that the camera is the equivalent of the pen, not the brush: Painting, like cinema, may be a means of expression and a vehicle of communication, but paintings communicate *feelings*, not thoughts. The vehicle of *thought* is language.

This may have some plausibility. We do not expect a painting to embody a syllogism. (A painting can show us "The Death of Socrates," but can it give us the most familiar syllogism, "All men are mortal. Socrates is a man. Therefore, Socrates is mortal."?) We do not expect a painting to present a theorem

Karen Hanson, "Minerva in the Movies: Relations Between Philosophy and Film," *Persistence of Vision* 5, 1987: 5–11. Reprinted by permission of Karen Hanson.

and its proof (consider: "the sum of the square of the hypotenuse of a right-angled triangle is equal to the sum of the square of its sides"). Nor do we expect a painting to inform us of a detailed theory (consider, say, the special theory of relativity) and of the evidence and arguments which support that theory.

But do we expect or think film can do these things? Astruc does; and he doesn't take the tasks lightly. He includes among the problems that must be solved if the communicative capacities of film are to be fully realized the development of the cinematic equivalents of "verbal tenses and logical relationships."[3] (When these problems are solved, will there be the film versions of, say, standard material implication? How will it differ from the different logical relations of implication in, say, modal and relevance and tense logics? How will some of these differ from the cinematic assertion of, say, causal implication? If Astruc's film linguists begin problem-solving at the point where Aristotle began logical theory, what will they do, then, for the categorical syllogism? What, e.g., will they use for a universal proposition ["All men are mortal," "No man is brave"]?)

If we have difficulty envisioning some of these developments, it might occur to us that sheer possibilities are not in fact the central requisites for productive and satisfying action. Does film itself *need* the characteristics, the possibilities, of spoken and written language? "Everything is permitted" may well be a cry of despair, not joy; and a vision of film in which *everything* is possible may be oppressive, not energizing, an obstacle to an appreciation and development of the array of distinctive capacities which are not future possibilities but present actualities. Nietzsche may be right: "The essential thing 'in heaven and upon earth' seems . . . to be, [he suggests], a protracted *obedience* in *one* direction: from out of that there always emerges and has always emerged in the long run something for the sake of which it is worthwhile to live on earth. . . ."[4]

But, of course, the question here remains: What *is* the direction of film? Where do *its* calls come from and where do they lead if one practices obedience? This is Astruc's answer:

> [Cinema] can tackle any subject. . . . The most philosophical meditations on human production, psychology, metaphysics, ideas, and passions lie well within its province: I will even go so far as to say that contemporary ideas and philosophies of life are such that only cinema can do justice to

them. [He quotes the claim – made by Maurice Nadeau, in the newspaper, *Combat* – that "if Descartes lived today, he would write novels."] With all due respect . . ., a Descartes of today would already have shut himself up in his bedroom with a sixteen millimeter camera and some film, and would be writing his philosophy on film: for his *Discours de la Méthode* would today be of such a kind that only the cinema could express it satisfactorily.[5]

Descartes' *Discourse*, we must remember, contains vivid and compelling pieces of intellectual autobiography. We may also recollect that it was written in French, the language of the people, not Latin, the language of the academy, so that it might reach and be understood by a public outside the confines of college and church. It is true that the motivation to autobiography and the urge to communicate one's views might well find expression today in filmmaking. (Whether this expression would be *adequate*, if one's film were made "shut up" in one's bedroom, would seem to depend on the life one wants to record, what one wants to communicate, and, perhaps, whether one has shut others up *with* one. The seventeenth-century Descartes does present the picture of a solitary writer, and he could of course produce such a picture alone. His thoughts, though, range over conversations, travels, social architecture, and city planning, as well as fixing on his indubitable soul, the Divine Existence, and some problems of biology and cosmology. The Cartesian filmmaker, shut up in his bedroom, will presumably have to have that room well stocked with props; he will probably not be able to work utterly alone; or he will have to portray a vastly different set of preoccupations.)

In any case, autobiographical and audience concerns aside, what most philosophers probably remember first about the original *Discourse* is that it is a description and justification of a method we might employ, Descartes says, to discover "all things knowable to men."[6] Synthesized out of Descartes' qualified admiration for the "arts or sciences" of logic, geometrical analysis, and algebra, the method is usually called "geometrical," for it recommends proceeding, in any inquiry, from limited axioms, by small deductive steps constrained by clear rules. Thus we might, the seventeenth-century Descartes says, produce "long chains of reasoning, so simple and easy," which will yet enable us, in every sphere, "to reach the most difficult demonstrations."

The thought of this Cartesian method should remind us of an important difference between written language and film. As has been noted by Stanley Cavell, "writing can be read at any tempo, at any length, re-read at will."[7] Inquiries and demonstrations structured by the geometrical method absolutely depend upon this fact about writing, about our relation to writing and to all written notations. Astruc anticipates the idea of home projectors and cassettes, and it might be thought that the proliferation of such technology would allow film the deployment of the geometrical method, allow us to grasp cinematic "chains of reasoning" of any length, by allowing us to *view* at our own intellectual tempo, studying *again* each element in a difficult cinematic lemma, as we feel the need.

But looking at a film frame by frame isn't seeing the movie, whereas going at one's own pace through a geometrical proof, taking the time one happens to need to grasp each individual step, is exactly what *is* required to see, to get, the proof. The proof has *no* pace of its own; but the film does. We may of course see a movie again, and repeated viewings may indeed enhance understanding; but the cinema has what Cavell calls a "*natural* evanescence" – "its events exist only in motion."[8] Geometrical proofs are *still*; they have, if anything has, Platonic *permanence*.

All this suggests, however, is a set of problems with writing the old *Discourse* on film. Astruc's counterfactual is in fact more radical than the suggestion that if Descartes were alive today he would write the *Discourse* on film: Astruc claims a Descartes *of* today would write a *new Discourse*. And *its* thought would "be of such a kind that only the cinema could express it satisfactorily." What is it about our "contemporary ideas and philosophies of life ... that only the cinema can do justice to them"? Astruc does not say; but he does say that to do them justice, to express contemporary thoughts, proffer contemporary philosophical meditations, to realize the age of the *caméra-stylo*, "the cinema [must] break free from the tyranny of what is visual."[9]

But *can* it thus break free? And why should it want to? Does "the visual" rule cinema in a way which deserves to be called tyrannical? Rousseau says in *The Social Contract* (Book I, Ch. 8) that "obedience to a law one prescribes to one's self is freedom." Astruc seems to have an appetite for the most abstract logic and metaphysics; but to be driven by "the impulse of mere appetite is slavery," to be bound by, bound to assert, and to try to satisfy this sort of master, no matter the conditions or context, might be degrading.

The service of pure metaphysics can certainly be divine, as it is in Plato; the development of abstract logic and logical theory, sublime, as in Frege. But philosophical projects, which are detached from epistemological concerns, or which are aimed specifically at a realm unconditioned by the peculiarities of this world, seem inappropriate models for the movies. In philosophical and mathematical logic, in some constructive metaphysics, *perspectives* disappear. The fact that human beings are *placed* in the world, each, that is, always at some *particular* place, drops out as irrelevant. The visual does not rule despotically here, nor does sound, nor do, for that matter, the interests of any of the senses. But is this quiet, invisible heaven a good setting for a film?

There are, I think, other spheres for the filmmaker, more promising subjects for the motion picture camera. And film may find in these regions, in these topics, some companionship with philosophy after all. We need not seek to break film's necessary tie to the visual, nor need we countenance the suggestion that philosophy has suddenly changed its nature, solved or outgrown all the preoccupations and the forms through which it lived prior to 1948. There are branches of philosophy which never shed but always flower with a concern for perspectives and points of view. Epistemology and moral theory, philosophy of perception, philosophy of mind in the dominant Western traditions of the modern age, i.e., since Descartes – all these either take such a concern as a basic requirement for their distinctive inquiries or, more self-consciously, take the objects of this concern as suitable objects for specific investigation.

Film, too, both presupposes and explores these particular concerns; so it is here that we may just find a kind of natural affinity between philosophy and film. This affinity can ground mutual support and illumination; it needn't destroy independence, one partner in the relationship fully assimilating, incorporating, like a vampire, the other, or, like a shallow cad, merely using the other. Astruc's call for film to become or to supersede philosophy betrays insufficient attention to, or respect for, the possibility of some objectively interesting differences. This call might not have come at all, and Astruc would have expressed more faith in the achievements and the prospects of film, had he recognized and admitted a simple fact: not all thought is expressed in language.

Karen Hanson

Philosophical thought often grows from the consideration of examples; it also uses examples to
enhance or make plain the plausibility of general
contentions or claims of particular necessities, and
it uses counterexamples to refute or dispute those
generalizations or alleged necessities. Films, too,
can mount arguments, and they certainly proceed
by a form of what might be called exemplification.
But film and philosophy bear different relations to
their examples, and must treat them differently.
This is nowhere more evident than on the common ground of the interest each has in the character, the nature, and the characteristic problems
of persons.

Let me barely note – for example – just one
problem of persons, the problem of self-deception,
and use this brief notation simply as a hint at the
kinds of differences – of relation and treatment –
which might deserve a fuller account. A classic
philosophic treatment of self-deception is found in
Sartre's *Being and Nothingness*, where he asks us to

> Take the example of a woman who has con-
> sented to go out with a particular man for the
> first time. She knows very well the intentions
> which the man...cherishes regarding her. She
> knows also that it will be necessary sooner or
> later for her to make a decision. But she does
> not want to realize the urgency; she concerns
> herself only with what is respectful and discreet
> in the attitude of her companion....If he says
> to her, "I find you so attractive!," she disarms
> this phrase of its sexual background; she at-
> taches to the conversation and to the behavior
> of the speaker, the immediate meanings, which
> she imagines as objective qualities. The man
> who is speaking to her appears to her sincere
> and respectful as the table is round or square,
> as the wall coloring is blue or gray. The qual-
> ities thus attached to the person she is listening
> to are in this way fixed in a permanence like
> that of things....Suppose he takes her hand.
> This act of her companion risks changing the
> situation by calling for an immediate decision.
> To leave the hand there is to consent in herself
> to flirt, to engage herself. To withdraw it is to
> break the troubled and unstable harmony
> which gives the hour its charm....We know
> what happens next; the young woman leaves
> her hand there, but she *does not notice* that she
> is leaving it. She does not notice because it
> happens by chance that she is at this moment
> all intellect....And during this time the di-

vorce of body and soul is accomplished [self-
deceptively]; the hand rests inert between the
warm hands of her companion – neither consenting nor resisting – a thing.[10]

How would this scene play in the movies?

I have deliberately, by choosing Sartre's prose,
made more difficult the case for the intuition of a
difference here between film and philosophy.
Sartre's examples are always exceptionally suggestive and detailed. If we had turned instead to
some American analytical philosophers' papers on
this topic, we could have encountered a severe
strain of reduction, much less respect for imaginative development and narrative precision. We
could have been asked to "consider the woman
who knows she is dying of cancer but refuses to
admit it, even to herself," to "take the example of
the athlete who refuses to recognize the manifest
diminution of his physical prowess," to "discuss
the case of the man who refuses to accept his
knowledge that his wife no longer loves him." I
want to suggest that there is an inevitably schematic quality to the examples of philosophic writing; and the flat, emaciated analytic specimens
might seem initially better to display the bones of
this suggestion.

But even *with* the Sartrean example, if we try to
imagine the cinematic transcription of what the
philosopher there represents, we face immediate
problems. What does this woman look like? How is
she dressed? What about her companion? – And
what is his manner? Where are they? Is it a
crowded cafeteria in the sunny noon hours? –
A smokey bar at midnight? – or a private apartment in the early evening? Sartre in fact acknowledges that he is *not* depending on a complete
specification of circumstances in order to make
his case ("the table is round or square"; the walls
may be "blue or gray," any color); but *just* some of
these features *can* be crucial to the film's *showing*
self-deception *or not*. To turn only to the woman's
appearance, to see that appearance in film is *not* a
superficial matter, can we imagine Mae West as
Sartre's self-deceived protagonist? Could *any* cinematic equivalent of this sort of self-deception be
achieved if we tried to cast, say, Greta Garbo as
the woman of bad faith? Could *she* appear thus
opaque to herself?[11]

Yet film can certainly portray self-deception
superbly. (Cf., e.g., some of Eric Rohmer's films,
for instance *La Collectionneuse*.) Movies can describe this problem *fully*, give us non-paradoxical

accounts of the phenomenon – and it is just this that is usually seen as the philosophic task. (Descriptions of the phenomenon as involving "lying to oneself," "knowing the truth and yet hiding or suppressing it from oneself," "believing what one knows to be false," and so on, are *not*, as they stand, philosophically acceptable precisely because of their paradoxical nature. The philosophic task is to capture this real phenomenon, but in terms which dissolve the paradox, or dispel the puzzle of apparent impossibility. And film can evidently take on and discharge this task.)

My own favored prose account of the philosophic puzzle of self-deception is one that might have been suggested by film's depictions of cases or might be thought supported by the fact of those clear depictions. Regarding as central to a concern with this problem cases which present the appearance of deception not merely by, but also about the self (or its aspects), I want to claim that attributions of self-deception or bad faith are made when an individual's self-interpretation is thought to disagree with a standard, with an interpretation not necessarily correct, but derived from and functioning in the conduct of a community.[12] The locus of the incoherency of self-deception would not, then, be found wholly within an individual. We would instead look at points of conflict between the individual's perspective, the individual's interpretation of himself or herself, and the community's view of that individual (or at points of conflict, typically diachronic, that mark self-estrangement. A person can charge him- or herself with self-deception, but this would seem to involve changing perspectives, moving to what is lately taken to be the, or a new, community perspective, and standing to survey earlier behavior, attitudes, etc., and to assess earlier self-interpretations.)

But notice that if this idea of disagreement or conflict is to account for attributions of self-deception, then the fact of self-reflection, and the tendency and shape of particular self-interpretations, cannot be inherently hidden from, intrinsically inaccessible to others. It would only be when it seems clear that there has been self-reflection, and this self-reflection has yielded an interpretation we take to be clearly at odds with what we expect would be seen through the community's perspective, that we would make a charge of self-deception. There must be something overt, something in the conduct of the individual we call self-deceived, that is not in harmony with what we feel

are socially justified expectations or judgments of him or her. And this overt conduct surely is not limited to the linguistic. Self-interpretation, as a kind of thought, may be found in and throughout behavior, understood as disclosed, expressed, asserted in gesture, posture, mien.

Now if something like this account is philosophically tenable, we can also begin to grasp some of the reasons cinematic accounts of self-deception can be so persuasive: we view the subjects of film but are not viewed by them, and thus we are empowered in judgment. Persons with whom we live will openly contest our interpretations of them, but we have no social interaction with the persons we see on the screen. Those screened individuals do, though, with every gesture show self-reflection, offer self-interpretation; and yet nonetheless, the perspective *we* have in viewing them is, as it were, the *only* perspective on them and on the events in which they are implicated. It is no wonder we feel assured in our judgments about them.

Our ability to discern one human liability as against another may also be enhanced – we might, that is, more confidently separate self-deception from, say, social deception, or wishful thinking, or irrational faith, or plain denseness, or whatever, because the context and facts required for disambiguation of this sort seem to be wholly present.[13] The film bestows an apparently full circumscription of context, relevant events and occasions; and, as Cavell claims, the reality presented is a world *past*.[14] That can make the moral point of hesitancy in the judgment of others seem to lose its standing, can make the worries about our own immersion in partialities and in certain problems of vision and insight seem to lose their force. The way can then seem remarkably clear for the presentation of a case of self-deception, a case where we, feeling secure in the occupation of a kind of *standard* perspective, seeing all there is to see, take the object of our sight to assert or be bound by a *mistaken* self-interpretation. Film can, that is, completely realize the occasions on which we will take ourselves to see self-deception; it can present not only compelling cases, but cases which, remarkably, in their *evident* quality, tender at the same time their own accounts.

Thus a *filmed* example of self-deception will be anything but schematic. The congruence I have tried to suggest between two kinds of approach to the problem of an *account* of the puzzle of self-deception, a congruence which might serve for

Karen Hanson

mutual reinforcement, *is* just congruence, a matter of agreement, correspondence, harmony. Coincident *results* may be produced by very different *means*.

In the traditional activities of philosophy, examples *are* schematic – sometimes bare outlines. But even when they are more than outlines, even when they are lush and suggestive, they are and they are meant to be, meant to be seen as, tendentious. They are *used* – sometimes to make, sometimes to support, sometimes to destroy a point. In film, exemplification can *be* the point. Now of course a film, a filmmaker, may have other aims as well; but if the filmmaker does not respect exemplification *as* an end in itself, she or he will probably not be able, with those examples, to make other points, to communicate additional thoughts.

Film can offer philosophy instruction on this issue. The philosophical employment of examples involves a constant liability to, a standing danger of, reductive assertion. Film can teach against, and so help guard against, the philosophical tendency to deaden or to lose the life in examples. And philosophy can return a favor in kind, by making more of the thought of films. These reciprocal gifts would not help realize Astruc's vision of the proper relation between film and philosophy, the former supplanting the latter. But such reciprocity would allow for a kind of mutual re-placement, each enterprise sometimes repositioning the other, film and philosophy sometimes moving one another to more satisfying ground.

Notes

1 Alexandre Astruc, "The Birth of a New Avant-Garde: La Caméra-Stylo," *Ecran Français* 144, 1948; reprinted in *The New Wave*, ed. Peter Graham (New York: Doubleday, 1968), 17. Subsequent references to this article are also to the Graham edition.
2 Astruc, 20.
3 Ibid., 22.
4 Friedrich Nietzsche, *Beyond Good and Evil*, trans. R. J. Hollingdale (Baltimore: Penguin Books, 1972), p. 93.
5 Astruc, 19.
6 René Descartes, *Discourse on Method*, trans. Laurence Lafleur (Indianapolis: Bobbs-Merrill, Liberal Arts Press, 1960), Part Two, p. 15.
7 Stanley Cavell, "On Makavejev on Bergman," in *Themes Out of School* (San Francisco: North Point Press, 1984), 110.
8 Cavell, "The Thought of Movies," in *Themes Out of School*, 11.
9 Astruc, 18.
10 Jean-Paul Sartre, *Being and Nothingness*, pt. 1, chap. 2, sec. 2, trans. Hazel Barnes (New York: Philosophical Library, 1956).
11 In conversation after I read this paper at a symposium on film and philosophy sponsored by Queens College, at the American Museum of the Moving Image, William Rothman suggested we might test "Tippi" Hedren for the Sartrean scene – a plausible proposal.
12 I develop and argue for this claim in more detail in *The Self Imagined* (London: Routledge & Kegan Paul, 1986).
13 This does not mean that all our judgments about the character of a particular film character will be derived from what is shown in just this one film. As William Rothman reminded me, a star's special and specific aura, e.g., may seem to shine, no matter the setting in which the star appears. (On this point, see Stanley Cavell's argument in *The World Viewed* [New York: Viking, 1971] that "the individuality of stars was defined by their self-identity through repeated incarnations" [p. 75].) But here again, our distance from the stars, our unseen viewing of them, can make them the perfect objects for clear and distinct, unambiguous, labels.
14 Cavell, *The World Viewed*, 23.

27

Motion Pictures as a Philosophical Resource

Lester H. Hunt

I

What sort of contribution can fictional motion-picture narratives make to the sort of understanding that philosophy seeks? At first hearing, this question might seem almost absurd. Philosophy, after all, is like science in that it possesses various resources for getting closer to the truth, including traditions and conventions that require participants to make their ideas about the world and our place in it as clear and explicit as possible, and to subject them to ruthless criticism. Although motion pictures often (perhaps always) express ideas about such matters, the activity of making motion pictures utterly lacks these sorts of traditions and conventions. It is a completely different sort of activity from those that produce new science and new philosophy, and it has a completely different function.

Though everything I have just said is true, it would be fallacious to jump to the conclusion that the motion picture has no contribution to make to philosophical inquiry. I will argue for the claim that the motion picture is an instance of a wider category of things that not only can but already *do* make substantial contributions to the philosophical search for truth: namely, narrative. Along the way, I will also offer a few comments on the difference between motion-picture narratives and other sorts of narratives.

II

I will begin by focusing my attention on a fairly simple case of something that, at least in a sufficiently broad conception of the matter, can count as an example of film: namely, an episode of a dramatic television show. The episode I have in mind is "A Quality of Mercy," from the third season of *The Twilight Zone*.[1] The script, written by series creator Rod Serling, was inspired by his experiences in the airborne infantry during the "mopping up" activities that came at the end of Allied operations in the Philippines during World War II. The episode begins with the date, "August 6, 1945," superimposed over a downward pan through dense foliage, into a camp of American infantry, somewhere in what we later learn is the Philippine Islands. The soldiers in the camp are "observing" for a mortar company: calling them by radio with reports on where their shells are actually landing and trying to guide their aim onto the target. The target is a cave on the other side of a clearing, where a small company of Japanese soldiers, many of them sick, wounded, or starving, is holed up. The shelling is not going well. Though the Japanese in the cave are not positioned to do much damage, they seem to be immune to an artillery assault. For the moment, the men persist with the shelling, since the most obvious alternative – a direct ground assault – would most likely be quite deadly to both sides. The man currently in charge is

Lester H. Hunt, "Motion Pictures as a Philosophical Resource," first published in this volume. © 2006 by Blackwell Publishing Ltd.

Lester H. Hunt

Sgt. Causarano (Albert Salmi), the Lieutenant having recently been killed. When one of the men asks him what they are likely to do next, he says "Well, they're going to fire for effect until late this afternoon and if we can't smoke 'em out, maybe we'll bypass 'em." The men are very relieved to hear this. They are mortally weary of fighting and, now that it is obvious that the Japanese are beaten, they have little desire to do something that will have a heavy cost in human lives and cannot be expected to do much good. Obviously, they are concerned that the lives spent may be their own, but they also seem to be feeling some compassion for the enemy. Staring thoughtfully into the mouth of the cave, Sgt. Causarano says, "There's no one to tell them the war's over for them. Those poor guys."

Suddenly, a Jeep rolls into camp. It brings Lt. Katell (Dean Stockwell), the replacement for the officer who was killed. Katell brusquely demands an account of their current situation, and is told of the fruitless shelling of the cave. His immediate reaction, as he examines the cave through binoculars, is: "[I] think we're going to have to do it frontally. Just move right in there and wipe 'em out." The men are very unhappy with this idea. Sgt. Causarano suggests that, at least, they wait until the end of the day before making any decisions. He points out that, since Lt. Katell has never been in combat before, he should take very seriously the advice of those who have more experience. Katell is suspicious of the motives behind this advice. He suspects that their brutal combat experience has caused a general failure of nerve: "Are you tired of killing Japs, is that it? Or you've just got no stomach for it?" He berates the men for various infractions of military discipline and courtesy.

At nightfall, the men are gearing up for a frontal assault. Sgt. Causarano makes one last attempt to dissuade Katell: "Look, we *could* bypass them. There aren't 20 Japs in there and they're sick and half starved."

"But they're Japs."

"They're men, Lieutenant."

"When you're ordered to fight a war, you fight a war. And you kill until you are ordered to stop killing."

"What's your pleasure Lieutenant? How many have to die before you're satisfied?"

"Offhand, I'd say all of 'em. No matter who they are or where they are. If they are the enemy, they get it!"

At that moment, as he reaches for an ammunition pouch, Lt. Katell knocks over the binoculars. They

fall to the ground, broken. But the man who picks up the binoculars and hands them to him is a Japanese soldier, who addresses him as Lt. Yamuri. Katell – actually, he is apparently now Yamuri – simply stares at him, too stunned at first for words.[2] All the men around him appear to be Japanese. A few baffled questions reveal that the date is May 4, 1942. They are on Corregidor Island, and he is a Lieutenant in the all-but-victorious *Japanese* army. The men in the cave across the clearing are 20 or 30 Americans who have failed to escape from the Philippines with their lives. Artillery having failed to destroy the American position, the men are about to launch a frontal assault, which Yamuri is ordered to lead. He is of course not inclined to do so. Realizing that it would be very foolish to try to convince these men that he is somehow in the wrong army, he tries to play the hand that fate has dealt him. Dazed and awkward, he points out to the Captain in charge (Jerry Fujikawa) that the Americans are wounded and can do little harm. "Perhaps we can leave them there," he suggests, "bypass them" – offering the same advice he rejected when offered by Causarano. The Captain is appalled by the suggestion:

A reminder Lieutenant, the identity of the men in the cave: They are Americans. They are enemy. Healthy, wounded, walking or lying, they are the enemy.... The comparative health and well-being of the enemy, his comfort or discomfort, the degree of his anguish or incapacities, have no more bearing on a tactical move or decisions of command than the fortunes of an anthill that you step on as we move out to attack! They are enemy! They are American!

When Yamuri feebly protests "But they are *men*!" the Captain yells, "They are enemy and this is war! And in war you kill! You kill until you are ordered to stop killing!" When Yamuri yells "No!" the Captain strikes him to the ground.

As the Japanese soldiers move out to destroy the American position, Yamuri stops the Captain long enough to ask him, "May I ask the Captain, what is his pleasure? How many must die before he is satisfied?"

"Offhand, Lt. Yamuri, I would say, all of them. I don't care where they are or who they are, if they are the enemy, they are to be destroyed."

Lt. Yamuri stoops again to pick up the broken binoculars and finds that he is facing Sgt. Causarano. He is Lt. Katell again. As he gropes for the

398

words to tell Causarano what has just happened to him, a message arrives over the radio announcing that Hiroshima has been bombed and all units are ordered to pull back and wait to see if the Japanese surrender. Causarano misinterprets Katell's look as he stares silently at the cave. "Well, I wouldn't fret," Causarano says, "there'll be other caves, other wars, other human beings you can knock off." "God help us," Katell mutters, "I hope not."

III

There are several things I would like to say about this narrative, things that seem important for our present purposes and also seem close to being obviously true.

First, as I hope my retelling has made clear, it seems to have the character of *an argument*. That is, it seems to be, and to be presented as, a collection of considerations tending to either increase or diminish – in this case, probably the latter – the plausibility of a certain possible belief, and these considerations moreover are presented as *reasons* for having either more or less confidence that this belief is true. It appears to be an argument against a certain belief.

Second, the belief against which it argues seems to be a philosophical idea. The fundamental idea that both Katell (in his first incarnation) and the unnamed Japanese Captain advocate seems to be this: none of the normal moral strictures against killing applies to enemy personnel in the conduct of war. This is just the sort of idea that is discussed in a branch of ethics that is often called "just war theory." In particular, it seems to be an application or a version of a familiar doctrine, called "realism," which maintains that moral judgments (at least in anything like the usual sense of that term) do not apply to the conduct of war.[3]

Third, though the episode consists of dialogue with little action, and depicts mostly heated debates, it does not function as a philosophical dialogue.[4] Though its words state positions and they are delivered in tones of voice that would be appropriate to attempts to persuade, its author does not try to persuade us by means of verbal arguments. In fact, the most eloquent statement of Katell's initial realist claim comes *after* the course of narrated events have placed both Katell and the audience in a position that sets them *against* the idea. The Japanese Captain's impressive peroration produces not enhanced belief

but mounting horror, culminating in the moment that Yamuri shouts "No!"

The fourth almost-obvious point I wish to make is that the author of this narrative seeks to operate on our beliefs by means of the narrative itself. The course of events itself is crucial to the argument he presents. When Lt. Katell expresses his realist notions of warfare, there is probably a significant part of the audience (the audience at which the narrative was originally aimed, at least) that would not find the idea at all unreasonable. The way in which he applies it to the present case may be too extreme, but the idea in itself has something to be said for it. When Katell becomes Yamuri, and is asked to apply it to Americans, the same idea seems less reasonable.[5] Yet no character says this in so many words, nor does Serling's voice-over narration. It is effected by the narrative itself.

IV

It is almost obvious that the narrative here constitutes an argument against a philosophical position. Nonetheless, it is not entirely obvious how to put this argument into words, partly because there are different ways in which the narrative and dialogue might be interpreted. One fairly straightforward formulation of the argument would be to say that it presents a *counterexample* to Katellian realism. This would involve interpreting Katell's words – "If they are the enemy, they get it!" – as an expression of a universal principle: people who are at war (whoever they might be) may blamelessly kill their enemies without limit (whoever *they* might be). The narrative then presents Katell, and through him the audience, with a case in which this universal principle yields results that are unacceptable.

On the other hand, the same narrative might be interpreted as a sort of generalization argument. In that case, Katell's words would be interpreted as meant to apply only to his country and its enemies: Whoever is our enemy, just because they are the enemy, may be destroyed without limit. The course of events in which he becomes Yamuri, together with the fact that the Japanese Captain is giving the same reason for exterminating Americans that he himself gave for exterminating Japanese, indicate to him (and therefore to the audience) that the characteristic that allegedly qualifies the Japanese for potential extermination was also possessed by the Americans when they were hopelessly besieged on Corregidor. If it is what gives us the right to destroy them completely, then it would also have given them the same right to destroy us in like circumstances.

My point here, of course, is not that these arguments are sound and ought to convince the viewer that some version of realism is wrong. That would be a curious claim to make for any brief treatment of the issue, even one that takes place in the medium of overtly philosophical prose. What is relevant to my point, and I think obviously true, is that this narrative raises considerations that should be taken seriously in any philosophical discussion of realism. More exactly, it raises difficulties that, were they presented to the proponents of the relevant sort of doctrine, would deserve a thoughtful attempt at a response. If this is representative of the sort of thing that a motion picture can do, then such works clearly have a non-negligible capacity to contribute to philosophical enlightenment.

Here, some would object that there is an obvious way in which "A Quality of Mercy" is not at all representative of what motion pictures in general are like. The particular way in which it reduces the credibility of the ideas that it subjects to criticism relies on a feature of its plot that is very peculiar and not at all like those of most motion pictures (and indeed most narratives in general): namely, the fact that the unfortunate Katell is transformed into Yamuri while retaining the beliefs, values, and the inner "self" of Katell. He is then asked to apply one of his own ideas in this new context, where it turns out this same self, using these same beliefs and values, finds it unacceptable. The objection would be that my comments on this narrative would only apply to a very narrow genre of fiction: namely, "fantasy" narratives, in which obviously impossible events (such as this one) are essential plot elements. Nothing relevantly similar happens in other sorts of fiction.

My answer to this objection is, quite simply, that relevantly similar things do happen in other sorts of fiction, including motion pictures. First, notice what is actually going on in Serling's narrative. As I just suggested, it isn't quite accurate to say that Katell becomes a different person. What, for the sake of brevity, I have spoken of as "becoming Yamuri" could be more accurately described as finding himself in different circumstances (something like: having the body, name, and physical location of a Japanese officer), circumstances in which he has to consider factors that

he has not foreseen or considered before. Finally, he does not remain in this circumstance, but "becomes Katell" again (if I may put it that way) and, moreover, retains the new thoughts that he acquired while he (so to speak) was Yamuri. That is, these thoughts are not ones that he had just because he was Yamuri and had Yamuri's options and interests. Though having to entertain Yamuri's circumstances are what brought him to these thoughts, their truth and importance does not seem to him to depend on his actually being Yamuri. As he stares silently into the mouth of the cave at the end of the drama, the cave looks different to him than it did the last time he was Katell. The fact that he once contemplated Yamuri's circumstances continues to make a difference.

As odd as this may sound, I submit that, in all these respects, Katell is like the motion-picture audience. Viewers of motion pictures, as they view them, must consider circumstances – those of the fictional characters – which are distinct from their own and which it may be they have not foreseen or considered before. Of course, they do not become the characters who inhabit these circumstances, nor do they think that they do so, and they judge them using their own beliefs and values. The fictional world that for the moment they must consider presents them with a wealth of concrete particulars to which these ideas and beliefs can be applied.[6] Since these particulars may differ widely from those in which the viewer first acquired these beliefs and values, this process might produce surprising results. These results can affect the beliefs they hold when they are no longer viewing the motion picture and actively contemplating this fictional world, because that world might well be logically relevant to what their beliefs ought to be.

In addition, Serling's little narrative suggests an interesting truth about the way in which motion pictures – and narrative in general – make their contribution. In both the interpretations I have given, the argument I have found in it works mainly by use of example. In fact, the narrative itself, or part of it, *is* the example that drives the argument.[7] Katell changes his mind as a result of a process of reasoning, but this process is not prompted by any previously unfamiliar ideas or principles that someone has expressed to him. The Japanese Captain expresses certain ideas, to be sure, but they are ones with which Katell is already familiar. Crucial to his changing his mind is the fact that for the moment these ideas are applied to a concrete situation in which they yield results that he finds unacceptable. Given this, Katell finds that he must change his ideas. The details of the process by which this happens depends, as I have said, on how one interprets the argument in the narrative. We may suppose that his realism is a universal claim and that Yamuri's circumstances constitute a counterexample to it, or we may suppose that he had never thought of universalizing it and events in Yamuri's circumstances invite him to universalize it and test it against these unforseen conditions. Further, insofar as the viewer has entertained the possibility that Katellian realism is correct, the narrative has, from a logical point of view, precisely the same significance for the viewer that it has for the fictional Katell. What the narrative contributes to the viewer's cognition is not so much the abstract and universal as the concrete and particular. To the extent that it works on the viewer's mind in an argument-like way, it works as an argument-by-example.

V

This, finally, suggests a fairly definite answer to the question with which I began: namely, the question of the contribution that motion pictures can make to the sort of understanding that philosophy seeks. The answer, however, is only available if one has shed a common preconception concerning what philosophical discourse is like. It is natural to think of philosophical argumentation as if it were a process that moves from one putative universal truth to another. This sort of reasoning is of course typical of philosophical discourse, but it is by no means the only sort there is. Philosophers often argue by means of example. One familiar case of this is the passage in Plato's *Meno* in which he enhances the plausibility of his notion of the innateness of knowledge by narrating an episode in which Socrates elicits a mathematical truth from the untutored slave boy simply by asking him questions. I think the logic that underlies Plato's narrative is basically the same as the one at work in, to cite another example, a little scenario that I sometimes present to students in order to show them the inherent plausibility of utilitarianism. Suppose, I say, that you are about to dial the phone and order a pizza for yourself and some friends. You have asked for everyone's pref-

erences as to what toppings they want and found that their preferences are all quite different. You can't afford to have everyone get exactly what they want. In addition, some people find other's preferences offensive (e.g., anchovies). What do you do? And why? Of course, there are various answers to the first of these two questions, but they tend to have certain things in common, such as giving everyone part of what they want, and avoiding making anyone too unhappy. Again, there are many ways of formulating an answer to the second question as well, but they tend to have a lot to do with making the people affected by your decision, in general and all around, as happy, or as little unhappy, as you can. And that appears to amount to some sort of utilitarianism.

As I have said, I think the logic of this bit of argumentative discourse is fundamentally the same as that of the dialogue with the slave boy in the *Meno*. Plato's narrative carries with it the unstated but crucial premise that this is just the sort of thing that *could* happen: it is possible to elicit knowledge just by asking questions, provided that they are asked in the right order. The issue that Socrates addresses is, how do we explain this? He points out that it could be explained on the basis of the supposition that the knowledge actually came from within the boy himself, so that it lends some plausibility to his doctrine of *anamnesis*. My own argument for utilitarianism works in essentially the same way. The students construct their own narrative of how they would solve the pizza problem. Each thinks that the solution he or she arrives at is a reasonably good one. The challenge is to explain why it is a good one. The answer is something that looks like some form of utilitarianism. In both cases, the example that serves as the basis of the argument does so by way of an additional unstated premise – that some event in it could happen or would be right or good if it did. An idea that can satisfactorily explain the putative truth of this additional premise, to the extent that it can do so, gains plausibility by virtue of the fact.

Clearly, there are philosophical ways of arguing that proceed primarily by giving examples. Further, such examples are commonly, as in both these cases, narratives. This, then, is an important contribution that motion pictures can make to the sort of understanding that philosophy seeks: motion-picture narratives can serve as philosophical examples, in many cases as vivid and gripping ones. In addition, though a full discussion of the various ways in which philosophical argument can advance by presenting examples is obviously more than I can attempt here, we already have reason to think that there is a variety of ways in which narrated examples can advance philosophical argument. First, and rather obviously, they can be used as counterexamples to one theory or another. In addition, even when functioning as a counterexample, a narrative can play a distinct sort of role as part of a more complex argumentative framework, such as a generalization argument. Beyond that, there are the cases in which a narrative becomes a basis for new insights by providing the occasion for an explanation.[8] In these cases, the story resonates with our pre-existing notions of what the world is like, or should be like. This assumption, applied to the example, indicates that the story calls for an explanation. The story is perceived as a tale of something that happens, or can happen, or of something that would be right or wrong, or good or bad if it were to happen. How can one best explain the (assumed) fact that the events in the story could happen, or be right or wrong, and so forth?[9] The ideas that would best explain it thereby gain plausibility and, if they are not already believed, are shown to be worth a closer look.[10]

VI

As I have suggested repeatedly, everything I have said so far about motion pictures as a philosophical resource also applies to narrative in general. This leaves us with the important question: What difference is there in this respect between motion pictures and other sorts of narrative? In particular, to focus on what is probably the most important contrasting sort of narrative: What is the difference between motion picture narrative and literary narrative? I think the answer to this question is that, unfortunately, motion pictures are less philosophical than literary narrative insofar as they are less suited to the task of embodying arguments. To explain why, I must make a few more comments – obvious ones, I hope – on the nature of motion pictures and on the sort of argument I have said they can convey.

In my comments so far about "argument by example," I have at times spoken for economy's sake as if examples can be arguments. Strictly speaking, though, this is not true. A narrative, insofar as it is serving as an example, is simply a

representation of a concrete series of events. It can only be presented as a reason for believing something if that something, the conclusion, is either expressed or implied. There must also be ideas involved that imply a relevant connection between the concrete narrated events and the conclusion. Some of these connecting ideas must be general in nature, and not simply about the concrete series of events. This, I think, is more or less obvious, once one thinks of it.

The point I wish to make about the nature of motion-picture narrative is, I hope, at least as obviously true. Such narratives resemble literature in that one of the expressive resources that they use is language: they can contain dialogue between the characters, voice-over narration, inter-titles projected on the screen, documents (such as letters and telegrams) directly represented on the screen, and so forth. However, they differ from literature in that words are a less prominent expressive resource. The sheer difference in quantity of words is impressive. In a novel, the words of the author are the medium through which the events in the narrative reach the novel's audience. In motion pictures, the medium is the image track and sound track. The sound track, of course, conveys words (usually), but also conveys music and sound effects: non-verbal sounds. As a novel is adapted to film, it is transferred to a medium that has means of representation not available to the novel, and in the process the medium that is the sole resource of the novel, words, slips considerably in importance. There are far fewer words in a film than there are in a novel.

Finally, and once again obviously, consider the simple fact that if a narrative is to either express or imply a conclusion or a general truth that connects in the relevant way the events in the narrative with the ideas in the conclusion, there is no medium that can do this as effectively as words. Though visual images or music could perhaps suggest what general truth the artist has in mind, nothing can do so as lucidly as stating that truth in so many words.

If we consider these three rather obvious comments together, we can see something which is not quite so obvious: that the capacity of the motion picture to present us with an argument, or even with an implicit argument (an argument with some premises implied and not expressed) is more limited than that of literature. In Walter van Tilberg Clark's novel, *The Oxbow Incident*, the author presents a narrative that is plainly meant as an argument against lynching, and against the sort of impatient, let's-get-it-over-with view of justice that (in his view) lynching represents.[11] The narrative, which superficially resembles a conventional Western, tells of a posse hastily formed to pursue some men who have stolen some cattle and reportedly killed a ranch hand in the process. They find some men with cattle from the ranch that has been robbed. The men claim that they bought the cattle but have no receipt to prove it. Relying on circumstantial evidence and driven by impatience with recent failures on the part of the courts to do justice to thieves and murderers, the group decides to hang the culprits on the spot, rather than turning them over the sheriff and the judge. It turns out that the men are innocent, and that the ranch hand, though slightly injured by the real rustlers, has not been killed. This narrative in a sense speaks for itself. It is rather obvious what the implicit conclusion and general premise are. The author wishes to conclude that mob justice is always a bad idea, on the grounds that it goes wrong in this case because of faults and limitations that it shares with any attempt at summary judgment. But in the course of the narrative, dialogue between some of the more philosophically inclined characters offers a variety of possible ways to interpret the bare narrative events of which they are a part. The liberal-minded merchant Mr. Davies, obviously the author's mouthpiece, goes to considerable lengths to explain why decision-making through legal and democratic frameworks is superior to decision-making by individuals, including a herd of individuals, such as a lynch-mob. In addition, Mr. Sparks, an itinerant African-American preacher, criticizes the actions of the posse as an attempt on the part of mortals to usurp the position of God, and the bitter, quasi-Nietzschean Gerald Tetley explains the same actions in terms of a cowardly submission to a herd instinct. In Lamar Trotti's excellent script for the William Wellman film based on the book (1943), most of these philosophical dialogues disappear. A simple version of the core of Davies's argument is presented, but it is expressed in a letter from the hanged man to his wife, which the Henry Fonda character reads aloud after it has been proven that the author of the letter is in fact innocent. The effect is powerful and memorable, but conceptually it is a stripped-down version of what the book conveys. In the comparative absence of philosophical comment, the speaks-for-itself meaning of the narrative becomes much more prominent: the film reminds us that quick "justice" can easily get the wrong person.

VII

So far, my argument can be summarized very briefly as follows. Motion pictures can make a contribution to philosophical inquiry because they can offer arguments on subjects of philosophical interest. What they offer are narratives, and narratives can function as philosophical examples. Insofar as philosophical inquiry can proceed by means of argument by example, there is clearly a potential for motion pictures to make a contribution. However, an example by itself is no argument. Some observations about the example must be added. To the extent that the capacity of motion pictures to make such observations is limited, compared with that of literature, their capacity to contribute to philosophy by means of argument is similarly limited.[12]

Having said this much, I should quickly add that perhaps the most important way in which a motion picture can lead to philosophical enlightenment is by means of arguments in which an interpreter *uses* the concrete narrative to make a point, one that may or may not have been part of the filmmaker's intentions, by supplying connecting ideas which may or may not have been in the narrator's mind.[13] The interpreters who do this may be philosophical writers who are trying to convince others of their theories, but they may also be the audience members themselves, as they reflect on the implications of the tales they see projected on the screen.

Further, it is possible that the most important way in which motion-picture narratives contribute to philosophical insight is not by functioning as part of an argument at all. In philosophy, examples serve not merely as the basis for arguments for ideas, they also serve as illustrations of ideas. As such, they play a role that is quite different from convincing us that some proposition is true or not. Rather, they help us to decide what a given idea is, or should be. They can help us to distinguish, among other things, between what is truly part of a concept and what is merely associated with it by habitual associations. This function is in particular one of the benefits of the sort of film that has genuine value as a work of art, inasmuch as such films have a marked tendency to avoid clichés. The chubby little homunculus played by Peter Lorre in *M* deviates sharply from our standard notions of what a serial killer is like. The deceived and abandoned lover in Max Ophuls's and Howard Koch's *Letter from an Unknown Woman* begins her relationship with her seducer by stalking him, and ends by writing a letter that causes his death, jarring against the standard conception of woman as victim. If we insist that love is, by definition, a morally elevating force, then a careful consideration of Scotty's obsessive manipulation of Madeleine/Judy in *Vertigo* should challenge us to either revise our definition of love or change our ideas of what it is to be morally elevated. Ultimately, though, motion pictures may resemble the humble laboratory rat in that its cognitive value may be found in what we do with it, rather than in what it tells us.

Notes

1 It aired for the first time on December 29, 1961.
2 In the modernist spirit of *The Twilight Zone*, this sudden change is, of course, never explained. Is Katell momentarily insane and imaging what he is experiencing? Is God teaching him a lesson? We are never given a clue.
3 For a classic discussion of realism, see Michael Walzer's *Just and Unjust Wars* (New York: Basic Books, 1977).
4 I should emphasize the predominance of dialogue in this drama, as it is one of several ways in which it manages to deviate from cliché. Though it is about the "horrors of war" and is set in the midst of combat, it depicts no act more violent than a slap in the face.
5 This brings up another way in which this episode deviates from the clichéd treatment of these issues: the usual way in which to make this sort of case against realism would be to ask: How would you like to have the enemy apply this idea against you? Instead, what Serling does is ask: How would you like to have to apply this idea against your own people? I suspect the reason he did it this way was more or less practical. He wanted to have someone express the idea in a circumstance that would speak against it. If Katell had been transformed into one of the Americans in the cave in Corregidor, he would not have been interacting with anyone who would be interested in defending realism. The Americans in the cave would all be against it. If the author is to explore the issue in dialogue, Katell must find himself on the Japanese side.
6 Martha Nussbaum, in her *Poetic Justice* (Boston: Beacon Press, 1995), rightly makes much of this idea, the notion that fictional narrative can invite us to contemplate the worlds of people who are differently circumstanced from ourselves. However, she stresses the contribution this makes to the education of our moral sentiments, while I am stressing the cognitive effects.
7 For further discussion of the ways in which narratives can function as philosophical examples, see Noël Carroll's "The Wheel of Virtue," *The Journal of Aesthetics and Art Criticism* 60, no. 1 (Winter 2002).
8 Bruce Russell, in "The Philosophical Limits of Film," chapter 25 in this volume, claims that the only philosophical role of film (other than introducing philosophical problems) is to provide counter-examples to theories that allege necessary truth, by showing that the things the theory claims to be impossible are in fact possible. I think this assumes an excessively narrow conception of what examples can accomplish.
9 The judgments we make, to the effect that events in the story are probable, or would be right or wrong (and so forth), are important, and if they are suggested by the way the story is narrated, they may be said to be part of the argument that the narrative presents. Bruce Russell (p. 390) cautions us that: "A film might remind us of the evidence that we know of already, but it cannot supply the relevant evidence itself. Imaginary situations cannot supply real data." This is true, but the implications of this truth depend on whether it is applied to an idea that functions as a premise or as the conclusion of the argument presented. If a story reminds us of something we already know in order to build on this knowledge by drawing conclusion from it, it is not doing anything any more illicit than any other argument that contains premises that are not justified by the argument itself.
10 I should emphasize that this sort of argument only increases the plausibility of the conclusion, merely gives it some evidentiary support, and does not apodeictically prove it. Bruce Russell (see notes 8 and 9 above) appears to frame his discussion of film as a philosophical resource in terms of whether a narrative "establishes that" a conclusion is true. This is a practice that would tend to bar from consideration the sort of explanation-based reasoning that I have been discussing here, which lacks such logically overwhelming force. In fact, it would tend to rule out all types of argument that aim at credibility-enhancement in the absence of apodeictic pretensions, a category that probably includes many valuable philosophical arguments.
11 The novel, which was written in 1937 and 1938, was inspired by Clark's horror at the rise of Nazism, which he saw as a product of this conception of justice. See "Afterward," by Walter Prescott Webb, in Walter van Tilburg Clark, *The Oxbow Incident* (New York: Signet, 1960), pp. 223–4.

12 I confess that, as I write this, I suffer a pang of philosophical shame. I am associating myself too closely for comfort with the common, and in my opinion bogus, observation that motion pictures are really a visual medium. *Painting* is a visual medium. The novel is a verbal medium. And modern motion pictures as we know them in the post-silent era, the "talkies," are obviously both. If film were purely visual, it would have virtually no value as a source of philosophical insight. It would be hard to imagine an argument to the effect that paintings can easily be the vehicles of philosophical arguments. Novels on the other hand, can be very obviously and even obtrusively philosophical. I am saying that film lies somewhere between these extremes.

13 Two interesting books that use films in this way to explore issue of philosophical interest are: Thomas E. Warberg, *Unlikely Couples: Movie Romance as Social Criticism* (Boulder, Colorado: Westview Press, 1999), and Joseph Kupfer, *Visions of Virtue in Popular Film* (Boulder, Colorado: Westview Press, 1999).

Select Bibliography, by Jinhee Choi

Joseph Agassi, "Movies Seen Many Times." *Philosophy of the Social Sciences* 8 (1978): 398–405.

Richard Allen, "Cognitive Film Theory." In Richard Allen and Malcolm Turvey (eds.), *Wittgenstein, Theory and the Arts*. New York: Routledge, 2001.

——, "Looking at Motion Pictures." In Richard Allen and Murray Smith (eds.), *Film Theory and Philosophy*. Oxford: Oxford University Press, 1997.

——, *Projecting Illusion: Film Spectatorship and the Impression of Reality*. New York: Cambridge University Press, 1995.

——, "Psychoanalytic Film Theory." In Toby Miller and Robert Stam (eds.), *A Companion to Film Theory*. Oxford: Blackwell, 1999.

—— and Murray Smith (eds.), *Film Theory and Philosophy*. Oxford: Oxford University Press, 1997.

Joseph Anderson, *The Reality of Illusion: An Ecological Approach to Cognitive Film Theory*. Carbondale: Southern Illinois University Press, 1996.

—— and Barbara Anderson, "Motion Perception in Motion Pictures." In Teresa de Lauretis and Stephen Heath (eds.), *The Cinematic Apparatus*. New York: Palgrave Macmillan, 1985.

Dudley Andrew, *The Major Film Theories*. New York: Oxford University Press, 1976.

——, "The Unauthorized Auteur Today." In Min Collins, Hilary Radner, and Ava Preacher Collins (eds.), *Film Theory Goes to the Movies: Cultural Analysis of Contemporary Film*. New York: Routledge, 1992.

Amédée Ayffre, "A World of Images." *Philosophy Today* 3 (1959): 12–34.

Roland Barthes, *Camera Lucida, Reflections on Photography*. New York: Farrar, Straus & Giroux Inc., 1981.

André Bazin, "The Ontology of the Photographic Image." *What is Cinema?*, vol 1. Berkeley: University of California Press, 1967.

Monroe C. Beardsley, "The Authority of the Text." In Gary Iseminger (ed.), *Intention and Interpretation*. Philadelphia: Temple University Press, 1992.

Chris Belcher, "Can Film Be the Most Realistic Art?" *Southwestern Philosophical Studies* 2 (1977): 90–4.

Gunter Bentele, "The Functions of a Semiotic of Film." *Kodikas/Code* 1 (1979): 78–93.

Max Black, "Metaphor." *Proceedings of the Aristotelian Society* 55 (1954–5): 273–94.

H. Gene Blocker, "Pictures and Photographs." *Journal of Aesthetics and Art Criticism* 36 (1977): 155–62.

George Bluestone, "Time in Film and Fiction." *Journal of Aesthetics and Art Criticism* 19 (1961): 311–16.

Raymond D. Boisvert, "Philosophical Themes in Bertolucci's Conformist." *Teaching Philosophy* 7 (1984): 49–52.

David Bordwell, "Contemporary Film Studies and the Vicissitudes of Grand Theory." In David Bordwell and Noël Carroll (eds.), *Post-Theory: Reconstructing Film Studies*. Madison: University of Wisconsin Press, 1996.

——, *Making Meaning: Inference and Rhetoric in the Interpretation of Cinema*. Cambridge: Harvard University Press, 1989.

——, *Narration in the Fiction Film*. Madison: University of Wisconsin Press, 1985.

Peggy Z. Brand, "Complex vs. Hybrid Media." *Persistence of Vision* 5 (1987): 12–16.

Edward Branigan, *Narrative Comprehension and Film*. New York: Routledge, 1992.

Leo Braudy, "The Rise of the Auteur." In *Narrative Informant*. New York: Oxford University Press, 1995.

Alan B. Brinkley, "Toward a Phenomenological Aesthetics of Cinema." *Tulane Studies in Philosophy* 20 (1978): 1–17.

Carol Brownson, "Objectivity and Nonfiction." *Philosophic Exchange* 14 (1983): 47–54.

Warren Buckland, *The Film Spectator: From Sign to Mind*. Amsterdam: Amsterdam University Press, 1995.

William Bywater, "Major Film Theories." *Film Criticism* 1 (1977).

Steven M. Cahn, "A Clockwork Orange Is Not About Violence." *Metaphilosophy* 5 (1974): 155–7.

Noël Carroll, "Art, Intention and Conversation." In Gary Iseminger (ed.), *Intention and Interpretation*. Philadelphia: Temple University Press, 1992.

——, "Art and Mood." *Monist* 84/4 (2004): 521–55.

——, "Art, Narrative and Emotion." In Mette Hjort and Sue Laver (eds.), *Emotion and the Arts*. New York: Oxford University Press, 1997.

——, "Art, Narrative and Moral Understanding." In Jerrold Levinson (ed.), *Aesthetics and Ethics: Essay at the Intersection*. New York: Cambridge University Press, 1998.

——, "Art, Practice and Narrative." *Monist* 71 (1988): 140–56.

——, *Beyond Aesthetics: Philosophical Essays*. Cambridge: Cambridge University Press, 2001.

——, "Defending Theorizing: Responses to Casebier and Goldman." *Film and Philosophy* 5–6 (2002): 100–5.

——, *Engaging the Moving Image*. New Haven: Yale University Press, 2003.

——, "Essence of Cinema?" *Philosophical Studies*. 89/2–3 (1998): 323–330.

——, "Fiction, Nonfiction and the Film of Presumptive Assertion: A Conceptual Analysis." In Richard Allen and Murray Smith (eds.), *Film Theory and Philosophy*. Oxford: Oxford University Press, 1997.

——, "Film, Emotion and Genre." In Carl Plantinga and Greg M. Smith (eds.), *Passionate Views*. Baltimore: Johns Hopkins University Press, 1999. (Ch. 14 in this volume.)

——, "Horror and Humor." *Journal of Aesthetics and Art Criticism* 57/2 (1999): 145–60.

——, "Humor." In Jerrold Levinson (ed.), *The Oxford Handbook of Aesthetics*. Oxford: Oxford University Press, 2003.

——, "Interpreting the Moving Image: Replies to Commentators." *Film and Philosophy* 5–6 (2002): 172–9.

——, "On Jokes." *Midwest Studies in Philosophy* 16 (1997): 280–301.

——, "On Kendall Walton's Mimesis as Make-Believe." *Philosophy and Phenomenological Research* (1991): 383–7.

——, "Margolis, Mechanical Reproduction and Cinematic Humanism." *Film and Philosophy* 5–6 (2002): 138–42.

——, "Moderate Moralism." *British Journal of Aesthetics* 36/3 (1996): 223–8.

——, *Mystifying Movies: Fads and Fallacies in Contemporary Film Theory*. New York: Columbia University Press, 1988.

——, "Non-fiction Film and Postmodernist Skepticism." In David Bordwell and Noël Carroll (eds.), *Post-Theory: Reconstructing Film Studies*. Madison: University of Wisconsin Press, 1996.

——, "The Paradox of Junk Fiction." *Philosophy and Literature* 18/2 (1994): 225–41.

——, *Philosophical Problems of Classical Film Theory*. Princeton: Princeton University, 1988.

——, *Philosophy of Art: A Contemporary Introduction*. New York: Routledge, 1999.

——, *Philosophy of Horror: Paradoxes of the Heart*. New York: Routledge, 1990.

——, *A Philosophy of Mass Art*. New York: Oxford University Press, 1998.

——, "Prospects for Film Theory: A Personal Assessment." In David Bordwell and Noël Carroll (eds.), *Post-Theory: Reconstructing Film Studies*. Madison: University of Wisconsin Press, 1996.

——, *Theorizing the Moving Image*. New York: Cambridge University Press, 1996.

——, "The Wheel of Virtue: Art, Life and Moral Knowledge." *Journal of Aesthetics and Art Criticism*. 60:1 (2002): 3–26.

Allan Casebier, "Bibliography on Film and Dreams." In Vlada Petric (ed.), *Film and Dreams: An Approach to Bergman*. South Salem: Redgrave Publishing Co., 1981.

——, "The Concept of Aesthetic Distance." *Personalist* 52 (1971): 70–91.

——, *Film Appreciation*. New York: Harcourt Brace Jovanovich, 1976.

——, *Film and Phenomenology: Towards a Realist Theory of Cinematic Representation*. New York: Cambridge University Press, 1991.

——, "Noël Carroll's Theorizing the Moving Image." *Film and Philosophy* 5–6 (2002): 86–92.

——, "Reductionism without Discontent: The Case of Wild Strawberries and Persona." *Film/Psychology Review* 4 (1980): 15–25.

——, "Representation of Reality and Reality of Representation in Contemporary Film Theory." *Persistence of Vision* 5 (1987): 36–43.

——, "Violence in Mass Media Drama: Assessment in Terms of Context." *Etc.: A Review of General Semantics* 38 (1981): 312–18.

—— and Janet Jenks Casebier, *Social Responsibilities of Mass Media*. Lanham: University Press of America, 1978.

Stanley Cavell, *Cities of Words: Pedagogical Letters on a Register of the Moral Life*. Cambridge: Belknap Press, 2004.

——, *Contesting Tears: The Hollywood Melodrama and the Unknown Woman*. Chicago: University of Chicago Press, 1996.

——, "The Fact of Television." *Daedalus* 111 (1981): 75–96.

——, "North by Northwest." *Critical Inquiry* 7 (1980–1): 761–76.

——, *Pursuits of Happiness*. Cambridge: Harvard University Press, 1981.

——, *Themes Out of School: Effects and Causes*. Chicago: University of Chicago Press, 1988.

——, "The Thought of Movies." *Yale Review* 72 (1983): 181–200.

——, "Ugly Duckling, Funny Butterfly: Bette Davis and Now, Voyager." *Critical Inquiry* 16/2 (1989): 213–47.

——, "What Becomes Things on Film?" *Philosophy and Literature* 2 (1978): 249–57.

——, *The World Viewed: Reflections on the Ontology of Film*. Enlarged Edition. Cambridge: Harvard University Press, 1979.

Seymour Chatman, *Coming To Terms: The Rhetoric of Narrative in Fiction and Film*. Ithaca: Cornell University Press, 1990.

——, *Story and Discourse: Narrative Structure in Fiction and Film*. Ithaca: Cornell University Press, 1978.

Jinhee Choi, "A Reply to Gregory Currie on Documentary." *Journal of Aesthetics and Art Criticism* 59/3 (2001): 317–19.

——, "All the Right Responses: Fiction and Warranted Emotions." *British Journal of Aesthetics* 43/1 (2003): 308–21.

——, "Fits and Startles: Cognitivism Revisited." *Journal of Aesthetics and Art Criticism* 61/2 (2003): 149–57.

——, "Leaving It Up to the Imagination: POV Shots and Imagining From Inside." *Journal of Aesthetics and Art Criticism* 63/1 (2005): 17–25.

Frank Cioffi, "Intention and Interpretation in Criticism." In Joseph Margolis (ed.), *Philosophy Looks at the Arts: Contemporary Readings in Aesthetics*. Revised Edition. Philadelphia: Temple University Press, 1978.

Terry Comito, "Notes on Panofsky, Cassirer and the 'Medium of the Movies'." *Philosophy and Literature* 4 (1980): 226–41.

Amy Coplan, "Empathic Engagement with Narrative Fictions." *Journal of Aesthetics and Art Criticism* 62/2 (2004): 141–52.

Donald M. Crawford, "The Uniqueness of the Medium." *Personalist* 51 (1970): 447–69.

Philip Crick, "Toward an Aesthetic of Film Narrative." *British Journal of Aesthetics* 17 (1977): 185–8.

Bryan Crow, "Talking about Films: A Phenomenological Study of Film Significance." In Stanley Deetz (ed.), *Phenomenology in Rhetoric and Communication*. Center for Advanced Research in Phenomenology/University Press of America, Washington DC, 1981.

Gregory Currie, *Arts and Minds*. Cambridge: Oxford University Press, 2005.

——, "Cognitivism." In Toby Miller and Robert Stam (eds.), *A Companion to Film Theory*. Oxford: Blackwell, 1999.

——, "The Film Theory that Never Was: A Nervous Manifesto." In Richard Allen and Murray Smith (eds.), *Film Theory and Philosophy*. Oxford: Oxford University Press, 1997.

——, *Image and Mind*. New York: Cambridge University Press, 1995.

——, "Imagination and Make-Believe." In Berys Gaut and Dominic Lopes (eds.), *The Routledge Companion to Aesthetics*. New York: Routledge, 2001.

——, "Imagination and Simulation: Aesthetics Meets Cognitive Science." In Martin Davies and Tony Stone (eds.), *Mental Simulation*. Oxford: Blackwell, 1995.

——, "The Long Goodbye: The Imaginary Language of Film." *British Journal of Aesthetics* 33/3 (1993): 207–19. (Ch. 7 in this volume.)

——, "Mental Simulation and Motor Imagery." *Philosophy of Science*. 61/1 (1997): 161–80.

——, "The Moral Psychology of Fiction." *Australasian Journal of Philosophy* 73/2 (1995): 250–9.

——, "Narrative Desire." In Carl Plantinga and Greg M. Smith (eds.), *Passionate Views*. Baltimore: Johns Hopkins University Press, 1999.

——, "The Paradox of Caring: Fiction and the Philosophy of Mind." In Mette Hjort and Sue Laver (eds.), *Emotion and the Arts*. New York: Oxford University Press, 1997.

——, "Photography, Painting and Perception." *Journal of Aesthetics and Art Criticism* 49/1 (1991): 23–9.

——, "Realism of Characters and the Value of Fiction." In Jerrold Levinson (ed.), *Aesthetics and Ethics: Essays at the Intersection*. New York: Cambridge University Press, 1998.

——, "The Structure of Stories." In *The Nature of Fiction*. New York: Cambridge University Press, 1990.

——, "Visible Traces: Documentary and the Contents of Photographs." *Journal of Aesthetics and Art Criticism* 57/3 (1999): 285–97. (Ch. 10 in this volume.)

——, "Visual Fictions." *Philosophical Quarterly* 41/163 (1991): 129–43.

——, "Visual Imagery as the Simulation of Vision." *Mind and Language* 10/1–2 (1995): 25–44.

—— and Ian Ravencroft, *Recreative Minds: Imagination in Philosophy and Psychology*. New York: Oxford University Press, 2003.

Robert Curry, "Films and Dreams." *Journal of Aesthetics and Art Criticism* 33 (1974): 83–9.

E. M. Dadlez, "Quasi-Fearing Fictions." *Film and Philosophy* 5–6 (2002): 1–13.

——, *What's Hecuba to Him? Fictional Event and Actual Emotions*. University Park: Pennsylvania State University Press, 1997.

Arthur Danto, "Art, Evolution and the Consciousness of History." *Journal of Aesthetics and Art Criticism*. 44 (1986): 223–34.

——, "The Artworld." In Joseph Margolis (ed.), *Philosophy Looks at the Arts: Contemporary Readings in Aesthetics*. Revised Edition. Philadelphia: Temple University Press, 1978.

——, "Depiction and Description." *Philosophy and Phenomenological Research* 43 (1982): 1–19.

——, "Moving Pictures." *Quarterly Review of Film Studies* (Winter, 1979): 1–21. (Ch. 8 in this volume.)

——, "Narration and Knowledge." *Philosophy and Literature* 6 (1982): 17–32.

——, "Narrative and Style." *Journal of Aesthetics and Art Criticism* 49/3 (1991): 201–9.

——, "Philosophy As/And/Of Literature." *Proceedings and Addresses of the American Philosophical Association* 58 (1984): 5–20.

Arthur Danto, "Seeing and Showing." *Journal of Aesthetics and Art Criticism* 59/1 (2001): 1–9.

Stephen Davies, *Definitions of Art*. Ithaca: Cornell University Press, 1991.

Gilles Deleuze, *Cinema 1: the Movement-Image*. Minneapolis: University of Minnesota Press, 1986.

——, *Cinema 2: the Time-Image*. Minneapolis: University of Minnesota Press, 1989.

Mary Devereaux, "Beauty and Evil: The Case of Leni Riefenstahl's *Triumph of the Will*." In Jerrold Levinson (ed.), *Aesthetics and Ethics: Essays at the Intersection*. New York: Cambridge University Press, 1998. (Ch. 23 in this volume.)

——, "In Defense of Talking Film." *Persistence of Vision* 5 (1987): 17–27.

George Dickie, "Defining Art." *American Philosophical Quarterly* 6 (1969): 253–6.

Dina Dreyfus, "Cinema and Language." *Diogenes* 35 (1961): 23–33.

Joffre Dumazedier, "The Cinema and Popular Culture." *Diogenes* 31 (1960): 103–13.

William Earle, "Revolt Against Realism In the Films." *Journal of Aesthetics and Art Criticism* 27 (1968).

Dirk Eitzen, "Comedy and Classicism." In Richard Allen and Murray Smith (eds.), *Film Theory and Philosophy*. Oxford: Oxford University Press, 1997.

——, "When is a Documentary?" *Cinema Journal* 35/1 (1995): 81–102.

Jon Elster, *Sour Grapes: Studies in the Subversion of Rationality*. Cambridge: Cambridge University Press, 1983.

Dan Flory, "Aesthetic Cognition and Visible Intelligibility." *Film and Philosophy* 5–6 (2000–1): 143–50.

Milton S. Fox, "The Art of the Movies in American Life." *Journal of Aesthetics and Art Criticism* 3 (1944): 39–52.

Cynthia A. Freeland, "Explaining the Uncanny in the Double Life of Veronique." *Film and Philosophy*, Special Edition (2001): 34–50.

——, "Feminist Film Theory As Ideology Critique." In Kevin Stoehr (ed.), *Film and Knowledge: Essays on the Integration of Images and Ideas*: Jefferson, NC: McFarland, 2002.

——, "Feminist Frameworks for Horror Films." In David Bordwell and Noël Carroll (eds.), *Post-Theory: Reconstructing Film Studies*. Madison: University of Wisconsin Press, 1996.

——, "Film Theory." In Alison M. Jaggar and Iris Marion Young (eds.), *A Companion to Feminist Philosophy*. Oxford: Blackwell, 1998.

——, *The Naked and The Undead: Evil and the Appeal of Horror*. Boulder: Westview Press, 2002.

——, "Penetrating Keanu: New Holes, but the Same Old Shit." In William Irwin (ed.), *The Matrix and Philosophy: Welcome to the Desert of the Real*. Chicago: Open Court, 2002.

——, "Revealing Gendered Texts." *Philosophy and Literature* (1991): 40–58.

—— and Thomas Wartenberg, *Philosophy and Film*. New York: Routledge, 1995.

Jonathan Friday, "Transparency and the Photographic Image." *British Journal of Aesthetics* 36/1 (1996): 30–42.

E. I. Gabrilovich, "The Image of the Scientist in the Art of the Film." *Soviet Studies in Philosophy* 16 (1977): 26–32.

Gaggi, Silvio 1978. "Semiology, Marxism and the Movies." *Journal of Aesthetics and Art Criticism* 36: 461–69.

W. B. Gallie, "Art as an Essentially Contested Concept." *Philosophical Quarterly* 6 (1956): 97–116.

Berys Gaut, "Art and Knowledge." In Jerrold Levinson (ed.), *The Oxford Handbook of Aesthetics*. Oxford: Oxford University Press, 2003.

——, "On Cinema and Perversion." *Film and Philosophy* 1 (1994): 3–17.

——, "Cinematic Art." *Journal of Aesthetics and Art Criticism* 60/4 (2002): 299–312.

——, "The Enjoyment Theory of Horror: A Response to Carroll." *British Journal of Aesthetics* 35/3 (1995): 284–9.

——, "The Ethical Criticism of Art." In Jerrold Levinson (ed.), *Aesthetics and Ethics: Essays at the Intersection*. New York: Cambridge University Press, 1998.

——, "Film Authorship and Collaboration." In Richard Allen and Murray Smith (eds.), *Film Theory and Philosophy*. Oxford: Oxford University Press, 1997.

——, "Identification and Emotion in Narrative Film." In Carl Plantinga and Greg M. Smith (eds.), *Passionate Views*. Baltimore: Johns Hopkins University Press, 1999.

——, "Imagination, Interpretation, and Film." *Philosophical Studies* 89/2–3 (1998): 331–41.

——, "Interpreting the Arts: The Patchwork Theory." *Journal of Aesthetics and Art Criticism* 51/4 (1993): 597–609.

——, "Just Joking: The Ethics and Aesthetics of Humor." *Philosophy and Literature* 22/1 (1998): 51–68.

——, "Making Sense of Films: Neoformalism and its Limits." *Forum for Modern Language Studies*. 31/1 (1995): 8–23.

——, "Metaphor and the Understanding of Art." *Proceedings of the Aristotelian Society* 97 (1997): 223–41.

——, "The Paradox of Horror." *British Journal of Aesthetics* 33/4 (1993): 333–45.

——, "The Philosophy of the Movies: Cinematic Narration." In Peter Kivy (ed.), *The Blackwell Guide to Aesthetics*. Maldon, MA: Blackwell, 2004.

Elena Gheorghe, "The Interpretation between the Aesthetic and the Extra-Aesthetic in the Art of the Film," *Philosophie et Logique* 24 (1980): 169–78.

Jack Glickman, "On Sparshott's 'Vision and Dream in the Cinema.' " *Philosophic Exchange* 1 (1971): 131–6.

Alan Goldman, "Specificity, Popularity and Engagement in the Moving Image." *Film and Philosophy* 5–6 (2002): 93–9.

Nelson Goodman, *Languages of Art: An Approach to the Theory of Symbols*. Indianapolis: Hackett, 1976.

Jennifer Hammett, "The Ideological Impediment: Epistemology, Feminism and Film Theory." In Richard Allen and Murray Smith (eds.), *Film Theory and Philosophy*. Oxford: Oxford University Press, 1997.

Oswald Hanfling, "Fact, Fiction, Feeling." *British Journal of Aesthetics* 36/4 (1996): 356–66.

Karen Hanson, "Minerva in the Movies: Relations Between Philosophy and Film." *Persistence of Vision* 5 (1987): 5–11.

Gilbert Harman, "Semiotics and the Cinema: Metz and Wollen." *Quarterly Review of Film Studies* 2 (1977): 15–24.

David Harrah, "Aesthetics of the Film: The Pudovkin-Arnheim-Eisenstein Theory." *Journal of Aesthetics and Art Criticism* 13 (1956): 163–74.

Jean C. Harrell, "Phenomenology of Film Music." *Journal of Value Inquiry* 14 (1980): 23–34.

Brian Henderson, *A Critique of Film Theory*. New York: Dutton, 1980.

E. D. Hirsch Jr., "In Defense of the Author." In Gary Iseminger (ed.), *Intention and Interpretation*. Philadelphia: Temple University Press, 1992.

Mette Hjort and Sue Laver (eds.), *Emotion and the Arts*. New York: Oxford University Press, 1997.

Edward W. Hudlin, "Understanding the Realist Tendency in the Cinema." *Journal of Aesthetic Education* 14 (1981): 81–91.

John Hyman, "Words and Pictures." In John Preston (ed.), *Thought and Language*. New York: Cambridge University Press, 1997.

——, "Vision and Power." *Journal of Philosophy* 91/5 (1994): 236–52.

——, "Causal Theory of Perception." *Philosophical Quarterly* 42 (1992): 277–96.

Ian Jarvie, "Is Analytic Philosophy the Cure for Film Theory?" *Philosophy of the Social Sciences* 29/3 (1999): 416–40.

——, "Bazin's Ontology." *Film Quarterly* 14 (1960): 60–1.

——, "Sir Karl Popper (1902–94): Essentialism and Historicism in Film Methodology." *Historical Journal of Film, Radio and Television* 15/2 (1995): 301–5.

——, *Movies and Society*. New York: Basic Book, 1970.

——, "Philosophers at the Movies: Metaphysics, Aesthetics, and Popularization." *Persistence of Vision* 5 (1987): 74–106.

——, " 'Philosophic Dialogue on Film': a Screen Treatment." *Post Script* 6/1 (1986): 5–31.

——, *Philosophy of Film: Epistemology, Ontology, Aesthetics*. London: Routledge & Kegan Paul, 1987.

——, "The Problem of the Real in Ethnographic Film." *Current Anthropology* 24 (1983): 313–25.

——, "Seeing Through Movies." *Philosophy of the Social Sciences* 8 (1978): 374–97.

——, "Toward an Objective Film Criticism." *Film Quarterly* 14 (1961): 19–23.

Peter Jasa, "The Film: Reflection or Communication?" *Magyar Filosofiai Szemle* (1974.): 791–807.

William C. Johnson, Jr., "Literature, Film and the Evolution of Consciousness." *Journal of Aesthetics and Art Criticism* 38 (1979): 27–38.

Jesse Kalin, "Ingmar Bergman's Contribution to Moral Philosophy." *International Philosophical Quarterly* 17 (1977): 83–100.

Andrew Kania, "The Illusion of Realism in Film." *British Journal of Aesthetics* 42/3 (2002): 243–58.

Abraham Kaplan, "Realism in the Film: A Philosopher's Viewpoint." *Quarterly of Film, Radio and Television* 7 (1953): 370–84.

Haig Khatchadourian, "Film as Art." *Journal of Aesthetics and Art Criticism* 33 (1975): 271–84.

——, "Movement and Action in Film." *British Journal of Aesthetics* 20 (1980): 349–55.

——, "Remarks on the Cinematic/Uncinematic Distinction in the Film Art." *Quarterly Review of Film Studies* 3 (1978): 193–98.

Peter Kivy, "Music In the Movies: A Philosophical Enquiry." In Richard Allen and Murray Smith (eds.), *Film Theory and Philosophy*. Oxford: Oxford University Press, 1997.

Steven Knapp and Walter Benn Michaels, "The Impossibility of Intentionless Meaning." In Gary Iseminger (ed.), *Intention and Interpretation*. Philadelphia: Temple University Press, 1992.

Deborah Knight, "Aristotelians on Speed: Paradoxes of Genre in the Context of Cinema." In Richard Allen and Murray Smith (eds.), *Film Theory and Philosophy*. Oxford: Oxford University Press, 1997.

——, "Back to Basics: Film/Theory/Aesthetics." *Journal of Aesthetic Education* 31/2 (1997): 37–44.

——, "Making Sense of Genre." *Film and Philosophy* 2 (1994): 58–73.

——, "Selves, Interpreters, Narrators." *Philosophy and Literature* 18/2 (1994): 274–86.

——, "Whose Genre Is It, Anyway? Thomas Wartenberg on the Unlikely Couple Film." *Journal of Social Philosophy* 32/3 (2002): 330–8.

——, "Why We Enjoy Condemning Sentimentality: A Meta-Aesthetic Perspective." *Journal of Aesthetics and Art Criticism* 57/4 (1999): 411–20.

——, "Women Subjectivity and the Rhetoric of Anti-Humanism in Feminist Film Theory." *New Literary History* 26/1 (1995): 39–56.

Jiri Kolaja and Arnold W. Faster, "Berlin, the Symphony of a City as a Theme of Visual Rhythm." *Journal of Aesthetics and Art Criticism* 23 (1965): 353–8.

Francis J. Kovach, "Metaphysical Analysis of Film." *South Western Journal of Philosophy* 1 (1970): 152–61.

Joseph Kupfer, *Visions of Virtue in Popular Film*. Boulder: Westview, 1999.

——, "The Work of Love – At Work on Board the African Queen." *Film and Philosophy* 5/6 (2002): 60–76.

Douglas P. Lackey, "Reflection on Cavell's Ontology of Film." *Journal of Aesthetics and Art Criticism.* 32 (1973): 271–3.

Flo Leibowitz, "Apt Feelings, or Why 'Women's Films' Aren't Trivial." In David Bordwell and Noël Carroll (eds.), *Post-Theory: Reconstructing Film Studies.* Madison: University of Wisconsin Press, 1996.

——, "The Incredible Shrinking: Mystifying the Woman Spectator." *Persistence of Vision* 5 (1987): 62–7.

——, "Marxist Film Theory." *Socialist Review* 15/2 (1985): 127–39.

——, "Why Interpretation Matters: On Carroll and Film Interpretation." *Film and Philosophy* 5–6 (2002): 151–5.

Steve Z. Levine, "Monet, Lumière and Cinematic Time." *Journal of Aesthetics and Art Criticism* 36 (1978): 441–7.

Jerrold Levinson (ed.), *Aesthetics and Ethics: Essays at the Intersection.* New York: Cambridge University Press, 1998.

——, "Defining Art Historically." *British Journal of Aesthetics* 19 (1979): 232–50.

——, "Film Music and Narrative Agency." In David Bordwell and Noël Carroll (eds.), *Post-Theory: Reconstructing Film Studies.* Madison: University of Wisconsin Press, 1996.

Andrew Light, "Does the Audience Matter? On Carroll and Visual Argument." *Film and Philosophy* 5–6 (2002): 156–63.

——, *Reel Arguments: Film, Philosophy and Social Criticism.* Boulder: Westview, 2003.

George W. Linden, "Film, Fantasy and the Extension of Reality." *Journal of Aesthetics and Art Criticism* 18 (1984): 37–54.

——, "Film and a Novel Future." *Journal of Aesthetic Education* 8 (1974): 55–64.

——, *Reflections on the Screen.* San Francisco: Wadsworth Publishing Co., 1970.

——, "Ten Questions about Film Form." *Journal of Aesthetic Education* 5 (1971): 61–74.

Paisley Livingston, 1997. "Cinematic Authorship." In Richard Allen and Murray Smith (eds.), *Film Theory and Philosophy.* Oxford: Oxford University Press, 1997.

——, *Literary Knowledge: Humanistic Inquiry and the Philosophy of Science.* Ithaca: Cornell University Press, 1988.

——, *Literature and Rationality: Ideas of Agency in Theory and Fiction.* Cambridge: Cambridge University Press, 1991.

Dominic McIver Lopes, "The Aesthetics of Photographic Transparency." *Mind* 112/447 (2003): 433–48. (Ch. 2 in this volume.)

——, "Art Media and the Sense Modalities: Tactile Pictures." *Philosophical Quarterly* 47/189 (1997): 425–40.

——, "Imagination, Illusion and Experience of Film." *Philosophical Studies* 89/2–3 (1998): 343–53.

Dominic McIver Lopes, "From Languages of Art to Art in Mind." *Journal of Aesthetics and Art Criticism* 58/3 (2000): 227–31.

——, "Pictorial Color: Aesthetics and Cognitive Science." *Philosophical Psychology* 12/1 (1999): 415–28.

——, *Understanding Pictures.* New York: Clarendon/Oxford University Press, 1996.

——, "Vision, Touch and the Value of Pictures." *British Journal of Aesthetics* 42/2 (2002): 191–201.

Wolfgang A. Luchting, "Hiroshima, Mon Amour, Time and Proust." *Journal of Aesthetics and Art Criticism* 21 (1963): 299–314.

James Manley, "A Profound Banality in the Film." *Journal of Aesthetics and Art Criticism* 17 (1958): 20–3.

——, "Artist and Audience, Vampire and Victim: The Oral Matrix of Imagery in Bergman's Persona." *Psychocultural Review* 3 (1979): 117–39.

Joseph Margolis, "Film as a Fine Art." *Millennium Film Journal* 14/15 (1984–5): 89–104.

——, "Mechanical Reproduction and Cinematic Humanism." *Film and Philosophy* 5–6 (2002): 114–30.

——, "Le Significant Imaginaire, malgré lui." *Persistence of Vision* 5 (1987): 28–36.

Sally Markowitz, "Romance as Rebellion." *Persistence of Vision* 5 (Spring 1987): 68–73.

Patrick Maynard, "Drawing and Shooting: Causality in Depiction." *Journal of Aesthetics and Arts Criticism* 44 (1985–6): 115–29.

Peter McCormick, "Moral Knowledge and Fiction." In *Fiction, Philosophies and the Problems of Poetics.* Ithaca: Cornell University Press, 1988.

Paul McGlynn, "Point of View and the Craft of Cinema: Notes on Some Devices." *Journal of Aesthetics and Art Criticism* 32 (1973): 187–95.

Aaron Meskin and Jonathan M. Weinberg, "Emotion, Fiction, and Cognitive Architecture." *British Journal of Aesthetics* 43/1 (2003): 18–34.

Paul Milano, "Music in the Film: Notes for a Morphology." *Journal of Aesthetics and Art Criticism* 1 (1941): 89–94.

Richard Moran, "The Expression of Feeling in Imagination." *The Philosophical Review* 103/1 (1994): 75–106.

Roger Munier, "The Fascinating Image." *Diogenes* 38 (1962): 85–94.

Hugo Münsterberg, *The Film: A Psychological Study.* New York: Dover Publications, 1970 (originally published as *The Photoplay: A Psychological Study*, New York: D. Appleton and Co., 1916).

——, "Why We Go To the Movies." *Cosmopolitan,* December 15, 1915: 22–32.

James Naremore, "Authorship and the Cultural Politics of Film Criticism." *Film Quarterly* 44/1 (1990): 14–23.

Alex Neill, "Empathy and (Film) Fiction." In David Bordwell and Noël Carroll (eds.), *Post-Theory: Reconstructing Film Studies.* Madison: University of Wisconsin Press, 1996.

——, "Fear, Fiction and Make Believe." *Journal of Aesthetics and Art Criticism* 49/1 (1991): 47–56.

James W. Newcomb, "Eisenstein's Aesthetics." *Journal of Aesthetics and Art Criticism* 32 (1974): 471–6.

David Novitz, *Knowledge, Fiction and Imagination*. Philadelphia: Temple University Press, 1987.

Douglas J. Ousley and R. P. Kolker "A Phenomenology of Cinematic Time and Space." *British Journal of Aesthetics* 13 (1972): 388–96.

V. F. Perkins, *Film As Film: Understanding and Judging Movies*. Middlesex: Penguin Books, 1972.

Carl Plantinga, "Defining Documentary: Fiction, Nonfiction and Projected Worlds." *Persistence of Vision* 5 (1987): 44–54.

——, "Movie Pleasures and the Spectator's Experience: Toward a Cognitive Approach." *Film and Philosophy* 2 (1995): 3–19.

——, "Moving Pictures and the Rhetoric of Nonfiction: Two Approaches." In David Bordwell and Noël Carroll (eds.), *Post-Theory: Reconstructing Film Studies*. Madison: University of Wisconsin Press, 1996.

——, "Notes on Spectator Emotion and Ideological Film Criticism." In Richard Allen and Murray Smith (eds.), *Film Theory and Philosophy*. Oxford: Oxford University Press, 1997.

——, *Rhetoric and Representation in Fiction Film*. Cambridge: Cambridge University Press, 1997.

Leland A. Poague, "Literature vs. Cinema: The Politics of Aesthetic Definition." *Journal of Aesthetic Education* 10 (1976): 75–91.

Renalto Poggioli, "Aesthetics of Stage and Screen." *Journal of Aesthetics and Art Criticism* 1 (1941): 63–9.

Trevor Ponech, "Complexity and Literary Aesthetics." *Eidos* 9/2 (1990): 243–55.

——, "Visual Perception and Motion Picture Spectatorship." *Cinema Journal* 37/1 (1997): 85–100.

——, "What is Non-Fiction Cinema?" In Richard Allen and Murray Smith (eds.), *Film Theory and Philosophy*. Oxford: Oxford University Press, 1997.

——, *What is Non-Fiction Cinema? On the Very Idea of Motion Picture Communication*. Boulder: Westview, 1999.

Stephen Prince, "Psychoanalytic Film Theory and the Problem of the Missing Spectator." In David Bordwell and Noël Carroll (eds.), *Post-Theory: Reconstructing Film Studies*. Madison: University of Wisconsin Press, 1996.

Gerald Rabkin, "The Conventions of Film: A Response to Professor Sparshott." *Philosophical Exchange* 1 (1971): 125–30.

Colin Radford, "How can we be moved by the fate of Anna Karenina?" *Proceedings of the Aristotelian Society*, Suppl. 49 (1975): 67–81.

Henry P. Raleigh, "Film: The Ambiguous Art." *Journal of Aesthetic Education* 16 (1982): 69–76.

——, "Film: The Revival of Aesthetic Symbolism." *Journal of Aesthetics and Art Criticism* 32 (1973): 219–27.

Hector Rodriguez, "Ideology and Film Culture." In Richard Allen and Murray Smith (eds.), *Film Theory and Philosophy*. Oxford: Oxford University Press, 1997.

William Rothman and Marian Keane, "Cavell's Philosophy and What Film Studies Calls 'Theory': Must the Field of Film Studies Speak in One Voice?" *Film and Philosophy* 2 (1994): 105–10.

——, *Reading Cavell's The World Viewed: A Philosophical Perspective on Film*. Detroit: Wayne State University Press, 2000.

Pierre Rouve, "Aesthetics of the Cinema" *British Journal of Aesthetics* 12 (1972): 148–57.

Elliot Rubinstein, "Bunuel's World or The World of Bunuel." *Philosophy and Literature* 2 (1978): 237–48.

Bruce Russell, "The Philosophical Limits of Film." *Film and Philosophy* (2000): 162–7. (Ch. 25 in this volume.)

Robert A. Schultz, "Diagnosing Disputes in Film Criticism." *Journal of Aesthetic Education* 13 (1979): 57–72.

Roger Scruton, "Photography and Representation." In *The Aesthetic Understanding: Essays in the Philosophy of Art and Culture*. South Bend: St. Augustine's Press, 1983. (Ch. 1 in this volume.)

Alexander Sesonske, "Aesthetics of Film." *Journal of Aesthetics and Art Criticism* 33 (1974): 51–7.

——, "Cinema Space." In David Carr and Edward S. Casey (eds.), *Society for Phenomenology and Existential Philosophy. Explorations in Phenomenology*. The Hague: Martinus Nijhoff, 1973.

——, "Time and Tense in Cinema." *Journal of Aesthetics and Art Criticism* 38 (1980): 419–26.

——, "Vision via Film Form." *Journal of Aesthetic Education* 5 (1971): 53–60.

Roger A. Shiner, "Getting to Know You." *Philosophy and Literature* 19 (1985): 80–94.

Carol Siegal, "When No Means No and Yes Means Power: Locating Masochistic Pleasure in Film Narratives." In Nancy Easterlin and Barbra Riebling (eds.), *After PostStructuralism*. Evanston: Northwestern University Press, 1993.

Gregory M. Smith, *Film Structure and the Emotion System*. Cambridge: Cambridge University Press, 2003.

Murray Smith, *Engaging Characters: Fiction, Emotion and the Cinema*. Oxford: Clarendon Press, 1995.

——, "Film Spectatorship and the Institution of Fiction." *Journal of Aesthetics and Art Criticism* 53/2 (1995): 113–29.

——, "Gangsters, Cannibals, Aesthetes, or Apparently Perverse Allegiances." In Carl Plantinga and Greg M. Smith (eds.), *Passionate Views*. Baltimore: Johns Hopkins University Press, 1999.

——, "Imagining from The Inside: POV, Imagining Seeing, and Empathy." In Richard Allen and Murray Smith (eds.), *Film Theory and Philosophy*. Oxford: Oxford University Press, 1997.

Joel Snyder, "Photography and Ontology." *Grazer Phisophische Studien* 19 (1983): 21–46.

—— and Neil Walsh Allen, "Photography, Vision and Representation." *Critical Inquiry* 2/1 (1975): 143–69.

F. E. Sparshott, "Medium and Convention in Film and Video." *Millennium Film Journal* 14/15 (1984–5): 72–88. (Ch. 6 in this volume.)

——, "Vision and Dream in the Cinema." *Philosophical Exchange* 1 (1971): 111–22.

Ralph Stephenson, "Space, Time and Montage." *British Journal of Aesthetics* 2 (1962): 249–58.

Jerome Stolnitz, "Balazs: The Dilemma of Humanism in the Movies." *Journal of Aesthetic Education* 10 (1976): 25–43.

——, "The Boatman of Kaizu: A Study in Movie Fantasy." *Philosophy and Literature* 1 (1977): 222–37.

——, "Kracauer: Thing, Word, and Interiority in the Movies." *British Journal of Aesthetics* 14 (1974): 351–64.

Kevin W. Sweeney, "Constructivism in Cognitive Film Theory." *Film and Philosophy* 2 (1995): 33–44.

Jerzy Toepliz, "On the Cinema and the Disruption of the Arts System." *Diogenes* 72 (1970): 112–33.

Andrew Tudor, *Theories of Film*. New York: Viking Press, 1974.

Malcolm Turvey, "Seeing Theory: On Perception and Emotional Response in Current Film." In Richard Allen and Murray Smith (eds.), *Film Theory and Philosophy*. Oxford: Oxford University Press, 1997.

Melinda Vadas, "A First Look at the Pornography/Civil Rights Ordinance: Could Pornography be the Subordination of Women?" *The Journal of Philosophy* 84/9 (1987): 487–511. (Ch. 24 in this volume.)

Rudolph Von Abele, "Film as Interpretation: A Case Study of *Ulysses*." *Journal of Aesthetics and Art Criticism* 31 (1973): 487–500.

Kendall Walton, "Fearing Fictions." *Journal of Philosophy* 75/1 (1978): 5–27. (Ch. 15 in this volume.)

——, *Mimesis as Make Believe: On the Foundations of the Representational Arts*. Cambridge: Harvard University Press, 1990.

——, "On Pictures and Photographs: Objections Answered." In Richard Allen and Murray Smith (eds.), *Film Theory and Philosophy*. Oxford: Oxford University Press, 1997.

——, "Transparent Pictures: On the Nature of Photographic Realism." *Critical Inquiry* 11/2 (1984): 246–77.

Nigel Warburton, "Seeing through 'seeing through' photographs." *Ratio* (1988): 64–77.

Thomas E. Wartenberg, "Cinematic Humanism or Grand Theory: A Critique of Margolis." *Film and Philosophy* 5/6 (2002): 131–7.

——, "Interpreting Films Philosophically". *Film and Philosophy* 5/6 (2002): 164–71.

——, *Unlikely Couples: Movie Romance as Social Criticism*. Boulder: Westview, 1999.

Allen Weiss, "Cartesian Simulacra." *Persistence of Vision* 5 (1987): 55–61.

Morris Weitz, "The Role of Theory in Aesthetics." In Joseph Margolis (ed.), *Philosophy Looks at the Arts: Contemporary Readings in Aesthetics*. Third Edition. Philadelphia: Temple University Press, 1987.

Trevor Whittock, *Metaphor and Film*. Cambridge: Cambridge University Press, 1990.

Mark R. Wicclair, "Film Theory and Hugo Münsterberg's *The Film: A Psychological Study*." *Journal of Aesthetic Education* 12 (1978): 33–50.

Robert Wicks, "Photography as a Representational Art." *British Journal of Aesthetics* 29/1 (1988): 1–9.

T. E. Wilkerson, "Pictorial Representation: A Defense of the Aspect Theory." *Midwest Studies in Philosophy* 16 (1991): 152–66.

George Wilson, "Again, Theory, On Speaker's Meaning, Linguistic Meaning, and the Meaning of a Text." In Mette Hjort (ed.), *Rules and Conventions: Literature, Philosophy, Social Theory (Parallax: Re-Visions of Culture and Society)*. Baltimore: Johns Hopkins University Press, 1992.

——, "On Film Narrative and Narrative Meaning." In Richard Allen and Murray Smith (eds.), *Film Theory and Philosophy*. Oxford: Oxford University Press, 1997.

——, "Le Grand Imagier Steps Out: The Primitive Basis of Film Narration." *Philosophical Topics* 25/1 (1997): 295–318. (Ch. 12 in this volume.)

——, "Morals for Method." In Cynthia A. Freeland and Thomas Wartenberg, *Philosophy and Film*. New York: Routledge, 1995. (Ch. 19 in this volume.)

——, *Narration in Light: Studies in Cinematic Point of View*. Baltimore: Johns Hopkins University Press, 1986.

Jack C. Wolf, "Carroll's 'From Real to Reel.'" *Philosophic Exchange* 14 (1983): 55–8.

Richard Wollheim, "Iconicity, Imagination and Desire." *The Thread of Life*. Cambridge: Cambridge University Press, 1984.

Sol Worth, "Pictures Can't Say Ain't." *Vegas* 12 (1975): 85–108.

Index

Index

Index

seeing
  directly 120
  fictional from a perspective 190–3
  imaginarily 177–9, 181
  through 38, 39–43, 120–4
  ways of 35, 38, 41–2, 54, 111–12, 297
segmentation 294–5
Seilman, Heinz 167
selection in filmmaking 137, 168, 197
self-deception 384, 394–5
self-deconstruction 16, 47
self-reference, cinematic 291
Sellier, Geneviève 313
semantic theory of art 21–2
semiotic systems 92, 197
sense-data 69
sentences
  and images 97
  truth-value of 104
seriousness of art 33
Serling, Rod 397–9, 400
Shakespeare, William 341
shot–reverse–shot editing 97
shots
  ambiguity in content 194
  as documentary 148, 149, 151
  as naturally iconic images 197
showing the fictional, and fictional showing 187–90
Shyamalan, M. Night 381
sights, and sounds 67–70
silent films 47, 60, 74, 79
simulacrum 28, 29
simulation 3, 122
  decision 274, 275
  educational games 244
  and empathy 277–8
  and feelings 276–7
  and fiction-directed emotion 216
  mental and fiction 271–80
Sjöman, Vilgot 306
skepticism 3, 7, 15, 35–8, 39
slide shows 125–6
slow fade out 98
Smith, Adam 249
Smith, Harry 129
Smith, Murray 261, 263
Smith, Scott B. 388
Socrates 324, 382–3, 401
solipsism, film relieves anxiety of 54–5, 65
sounds
  diegetic 197
  and sights 67–70
Soviet Montage 8, 32, 52, 315, 381
Sowers, Robert W. 79, 80
space
  disconnection from 58–9, 123–4
  dynamization of 73
Sparshott, Francis 53, 58–60, 61, 63, 82–90, 123

spatial relations 84–5
spatio-temporal discontinuities 86–9, 337
spectacle 100–1, 127
spectators see audience
Speech Act Theory 328
Spielberg, Steven 46
"stabile" 108–9
Staiger, Janet 311
Stanford, Leland 110
stars 71–2, 75
  film 55–6, 79, 107, 127
  personae 216
  theatre 55–6
stasis, as a stylistic choice 125–6
state intervention 326–32
statues, moving 108–9
still photography 63, 85, 125
stop–motion 84
Stoppard, Tom 272
story meaning 94–5
structuralism 293, 296
structure
  closed 16, 278–9, 290, 292
  open 16, 206
  rhythmic 348–9
style 13, 28, 53
  development of 114, 117
  realist compared with creationist 52–3
style argument 9–10, 37–8
  see also control argument
stylistics, fiction and non-fiction 157, 158
subjectivity
  escape from 69–70
  overcome by photography 54–5, 69–70
  time as the form of 86
subordination of women, pornography as 327–32, 362–77
surrealism 28, 59, 78
suspense films 3, 214, 225, 229–32, 244–5, 272
  children's responses 248
suspension of disbelief 214, 235, 243, 261
Sweden 314
syllogism 391, 392
symbolism 32, 59, 61, 276, 349
symbols 328
sympathy 215, 247–8, 264, 265, 267, 272

tableau vivant 102
Taiwan 315, 318
Tan, Ed S. 219
Tarkovsky, Andrei 47, 283
"tearjerkers" see melodrama
technological innovations 15–17
teleology 114, 116
telephoto shots 85
television 2, 47
  commercials 88
  drama 397–9